PRENTICE HALL

WORLD STUDIES

Don't miss these powerful teacher timesavers!

Teacher's Edition Step-by-step guide for teachers ensures that objectives are met, provides reading strategies, makes point-of-use suggestions for using resources, and offers differentiated instruction.

Teaching Resources

All-in-One Teaching Resources Everything you need to teach in one location—including lesson plans, worksheets, tests, and transparency planner—making it easy to find materials, prep for class, and teach exciting lessons.

PRENTICE HALL
TeacherEXPRESS™
Plan • Teach • Assess

TeacherExpress CD-ROM Powerful lesson planning, resource management, testing, and an interactive Teacher's Edition, all in one place, make class preparation quick and easy!

Teacher's Edition

PRENTICE HALL
WORLD STUDIES
LATIN AMERICA

Geography • History • Culture

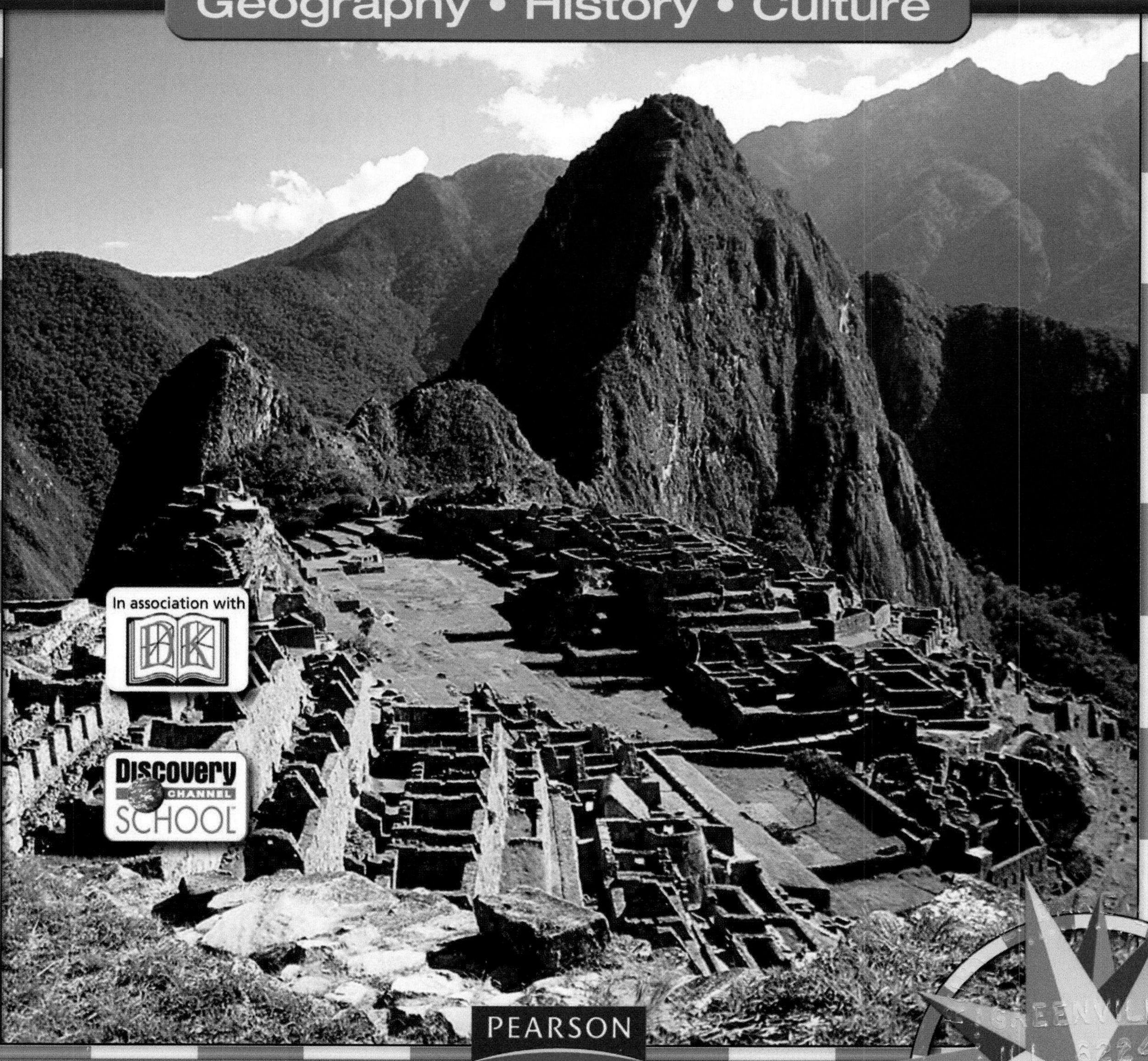

In association with

Discovery
CHANNEL
SCHOOL

PEARSON
Prentice
Hall

Needham, Massachusetts
Upper Saddle River, New Jersey

Program Consultants

Heidi Hayes Jacobs

Heidi Hayes Jacobs has served as an education consultant to more than 1,000 schools across the nation and abroad. Dr. Jacobs serves as an adjunct professor in the Department of Curriculum on Teaching at Teachers College, Columbia University. She has written two best-selling books and numerous articles on curriculum reform. She received an M.A. from the University of Massachusetts, Amherst, and completed her doctoral work at Columbia University's Teachers College in 1981. The core of Dr. Jacobs's experience comes from her years teaching high school, middle school, and elementary school students. As an educational consultant, she works with K–12 schools and districts on curriculum reform and strategic planning.

Michal L. LeVasseur

Michal LeVasseur is the Executive Director of the National Council for Geography Education. She is an instructor in the College of Education at Jacksonville State University and works with the Alabama Geographic Alliance. Her undergraduate and graduate work were in the fields of anthropology (B.A.), geography (M.A.), and science education (Ph.D.). Dr. LeVasseur's specialization has moved increasingly into the area of geography education. Since 1996 she has served as the Director of the National Geographic Society's Summer Geography Workshops. As an educational consultant, she has worked with the National Geographic Society as well as with schools and organizations to develop programs and curricula for geography.

Senior Reading Consultants

Kate Kinsella

Kate Kinsella, Ed.D., is a faculty member in the Department of Secondary Education at San Francisco State University. A specialist in second-language acquisition and adolescent literacy, she teaches coursework addressing language and literacy development across the secondary curricula. Dr. Kinsella earned her M.A. in TESOL from San Francisco State University, and her Ed.D. in Second Language Acquisition from the University of San Francisco.

Kevin Feldman

Kevin Feldman, Ed.D., is the Director of Reading and Early Intervention with the Sonoma County Office of Education (SCOE) and an independent educational consultant. At the SCOE, he develops, organizes, and monitors programs related to K–12 literacy. Dr. Feldman has an M.A. from the University of California, Riverside in Special Education, Learning Disabilities and Instructional Design. He earned his Ed.D. in Curriculum and Instruction from the University of San Francisco.

Acknowledgments appear on page 232, which constitutes an extension of this copyright page.

Prentice Hall World Studies is published in collaboration with DK Designs, Dorling Kindersley Limited, 80 Strand, London WC2R ORL. A Penguin Company.

Cartography Consultant

DK Andrew Heritage

Andrew Heritage has been publishing atlases and maps for some 25 years. In 1991, he joined the leading illustrated nonfiction publisher Dorling Kindersley (DK) with the task of building an international atlas list from scratch. The DK atlas list now includes some 10 titles, which are constantly updated and appear in new editions either annually or every other year.

ISBN 0-13-128031-7
45678910   08 07 06

Table of Contents

LATIN AMERICA

NCLB and Social Studies T12
Reading Support T14
Differentiated Instruction T18
Geographic Literacy T20
Assessment T22
Skills Scope and Sequence T24
Pacing Options T25
Correlation to the National Geography Standards T26
Correlation to the NCSS Curriculum Standards T28
Instructional Strategies T32

Develop Skills

Use these pages to develop students' reading, writing,
and geography skills.

Reading and Writing Handbook RW1

MAP◆MASTER™ Skills Handbook M1

How to Read Social Studies: Target Reading Skills. .M18

Introduction to Latin America 1

📖 **Regional Overview** 2

Build a Regional Background

Introduce students to the geography, history, and culture of the region.

CHAPTER 1 Latin America: Physical Geography . . . 8

1 Land and Water 10
   Video: *The Geography of Latin America*

2 Climate and Vegetation 15

3 Resources and Land Use .24

   Chapter 1 Review and Assessment 31

CHAPTER 2 Latin America: Shaped by Its History . 38

1 Early Civilizations of Middle America 40

2 The Incas: People of the Sun 45

3 European Conquest 50
   Video: *Pizarro and the Empire of Gold*

4 Independence 57

5 From Past to Present 64

   Chapter 2 Review and Assessment 69

CHAPTER 3 Cultures of Latin America 72

1 The Cultures of Mexico and Central America 74

2 The Cultures of the Caribbean 82
   Video: *Caribbean Music: It's All in the Mix*

3 The Cultures of South America 87

   Chapter 3 Review and Assessment 93

Focus on Countries

Create an understanding of the region by focusing on specific countries.

CHAPTER 4 Mexico and Central America 96

Country Databank 98
> Video: *Mexico and Central America:*
> *Navigating the Highs and Lows*

1 Mexico: Moving to the City .102
> Video: *Living in Mexico: Natural Hazards*

2 Guatemala: Descendants of an Ancient People 109
> Video: *Guatemala's Coffee Economy*

3 Panama: An Important Crossroads 116
> Video: *Panama: Deforestation*

Chapter 4 Review and Assessment 123

CHAPTER 5 The Caribbean **126**

Country Databank 128
> Video: *The Caribbean: Dynamic Lands*
> *and Cultures*

1 Cuba: Clinging to Communism 134
> Video: *Baseball and Cuba Go Hand in Glove*

2 Haiti: A Democracy in Progress 142
> Video: *Haiti: A Striving Nation*

3 Puerto Rico: An American Commonwealth 148
> Video: *Puerto Rico: Past and Present*

Chapter 5 Review and Assessment 155

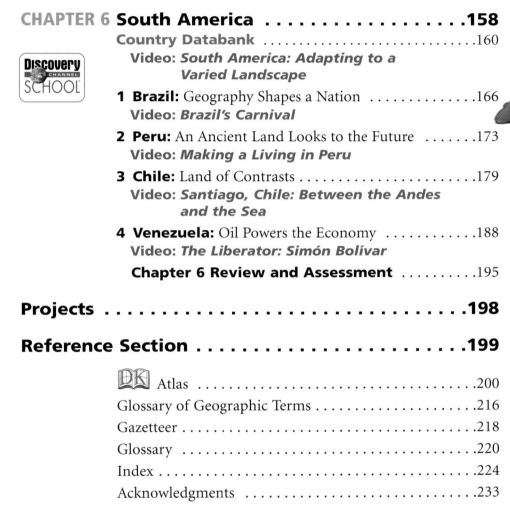

CHAPTER 6 South America **158**

Country Databank 160
  Video: *South America: Adapting to a*
        Varied Landscape

1 Brazil: Geography Shapes a Nation 166
  Video: *Brazil's Carnival*

2 Peru: An Ancient Land Looks to the Future 173
  Video: *Making a Living in Peru*

3 Chile: Land of Contrasts 179
  Video: *Santiago, Chile: Between the Andes*
        and the Sea

4 Venezuela: Oil Powers the Economy 188
  Video: *The Liberator: Simón Bolívar*

Chapter 6 Review and Assessment 195

Projects **198**

Reference Section **199**

Atlas 200
Glossary of Geographic Terms 216
Gazetteer 218
Glossary 220
Index 224
Acknowledgments 233

- Learn map skills with the MapMaster Skills Handbook.
- Practice your skills with every map in this book.
- Interact with every map online and on CD-ROM.

Maps and illustrations created by DK help build your understanding of the world. The DK World Desk Reference Online keeps you up to date.

The World Studies Video Program takes you on field trips to study countries around the world.

The *World Studies* Interactive Textbook online and on CD-ROM uses interactive maps and other activities to help you learn.

COUNTRY DATABANK

Read about all the countries that make up Latin America.

Antigua and Barbuda 128
Argentina 160
Bahamas 129
Barbados 129
Belize 98
Bolivia 161
Brazil 161
Chile 161
Colombia 162
Costa Rica 99
Cuba 129
Dominica 130
Dominican Republic 130
Ecuador 162
El Salvador 99
Grenada 130
Guatemala 99
Guyana 163
Haiti 131
Honduras 100
Jamaica 131
Mexico 100
Nicaragua 101
Panama 101
Paraguay 163
Peru 163
Puerto Rico 131
Saint Kitts and Nevis 132
Saint Lucia 132
Saint Vincent and the Grenadines 132
Suriname 164
Trinidad and Tobago 133
Uruguay 164
Venezuela 165

Literature

A selection by a Latin American author brings social studies to life.

The Surveyor by Alma Flor Ada 34

COUNTRY PROFILES

Theme-based maps and charts provide a closer look at countries, regions, and provinces.

Mexico (Economics) 104
Guatemala (Culture) 111
Panama (Geography) 118
Cuba (Government) 137
Haiti (History) 144
Puerto Rico (Government) 151
Brazil (Culture) 170
Peru (Geography) 174
Chile (Economics) 180
Venezuela (Economics) 190

Links

See the fascinating links between social studies and other disciplines.

Links Across Time
    Why "Latin" America? 12
Links Across the World
    The Baseball Connection .138
Links to Language Arts
    V. S. Naipaul: Trinidad and Beyond 84
    The "Real" Robinson Crusoe 183
Links to Math
    The Concept of Zero 41
Links to Science
    What Is a Hurricane? 17
    Earthquake-Proof Buildings 48
    The Photosynthesis "Factory" 167

Skills for Life

Teach skills that students will use all of their lives.

Analyzing and Interpreting Climate Maps 22

Making a Timeline 62

Distinguishing Fact and Opinion 80

Drawing Inferences and Conclusions 114

Comparing and Contrasting 140

Synthesizing Information 186

Citizen Heroes

Introduce people who have made a difference in their country.

To Be a Leader: José Martí 60

Mothers of the "Disappeared" 90

Justina Tzoc: A Voice for Change 112

Loune Viaud: Winner of Human Rights Award 145

Target Reading Skills

Chapter-by-chapter reading skills help students read and understand social studies concepts.

Using the Reading Process 8

Clarifying Meaning 38

Using Cause and Effect 72

Using Context 96

Identifying the Main Idea 126

Comparing and Contrasting .158

DK Eyewitness Technology

Detailed drawings show how technology shapes places and societies.

Aztec Farming 43

The Panama Canal 121

Discovery Channel School Video/DVD

Explore the geography, history, and cultures of the countries of Latin America.

The Geography of Latin America 11

Pizarro and the Empire of Gold 55

Caribbean Music: It's All in the Mix 85

Mexico and Central America: Navigating
    the Highs and Lows 98

Living in Mexico: Natural Hazards 106

Guatemala's Coffee Economy 111

Panama: Deforestation 119

The Caribbean: Dynamic Lands and Cultures 128

Baseball and Cuba Go Hand in Glove 135

Haiti: A Striving Nation 143

Puerto Rico: Past and Present 151

South America: Adapting to a Varied Landscape 160

Brazil's Carnival 168

Making a Living in Peru 176

Santiago, Chile: Between the Andes and the Sea 184

The Liberator: Simón Bolívar 193

Same-Shape Maps	M6
Equal-Area Maps	M7
Robinson Maps	M7
Western Europe	M8
London	M9
Political Africa	M10
Physical Africa	M11
India: Climate Regions	M12
India: Official Languages	M13
Migration to Latin America, 1500–1800	M14
World Land Use	M16
Latin America: Relative Location	2
Latin America: Relative Size	2
Political Latin America	3
Physical Latin America	4
Latin America: Major Hydroelectric Plants	5
Focus on Countries in Latin America	6
Latin America: Physical	9
Regions of Latin America	11
Latin America: Climate Regions	16
Latin America: Vegetation Regions	20
Latin America: Natural Resources	25
Latin America: Place Location	32
Latin America: Early Civilizations	39
European Conquest of the Americas	54
South American Independence	59
Latin America: Place Location	70
Latin America: Languages	73
Latin America: Place Location	94
Mexico and Central America: Political	97
Mexico: Resources and Manufacturing	104
The Growth of Mexico City	106
Guatemala: Languages	111
Shipping Routes and the Panama Canal	117
Panama: Vegetation	118
Mexico and Central America: Place Location	124
The Caribbean: Political	127
Cuba: Political	137
Haiti: Political	144
Puerto Rico: Population Density	151
The Caribbean: Place Location	156
South America: Political	159
Brazil: Population Density	170
Peru: Three Regions	174
Chile: Products and Resources	180
Venezuela: Products and Resources	190
South America: Place Location	196

MAP✦MASTER™ Interactive

Go online to find an interactive version of every MapMaster™ map in this book. Use the Web Code provided to gain direct access to these maps.

How to Use Web Codes:

1. Go to **www.PHSchool.com**.

2. Enter the Web Code.

3. Click Go!

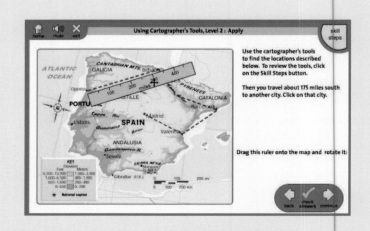

Atlas 200
   The World: Political 200
   The World: Physical 202
   North and South America: Political 204
   North and South America: Physical 205
   United States: Political .206
   Europe: Political 208
   Europe: Physical 209
   Africa: Political 210
   Africa: Physical 211
   Asia: Political 212
   Asia: Physical 213
   Oceania 214
   The Arctic 215
   Antarctica 215

Charts, Graphs, and Tables

Latin America: Sources of Energy 5
Vertical Climate Zones 18
World Coffee Prices, 1960–2000 28
Timeline: Mayan, Aztec, and Incan Civilizations,
   A.D. 300–1600 46
The Columbian Exchange .55
Foreign Debt of Latin American Nations, 2001 66
The World's Five Largest Cities, 2000 77
Mexico's Exports 104
Mexico's Trading Partners 104
Guatemala: Ethnic Groups 111
Mayan Towns 111
Panama: Main Products and Activities 118
Panama: Economic Activities 118
Cuba: Control of Productive Land, 1980 and 1997 137
Party Representation in Cuba and
   the United States, 2002 137
Timeline: Haiti's History of Foreign Influence 144
One in Seven Haitians Has Emigrated 144
Haiti Today 144
Puerto Ricans in the Mainland United States, 2000 . . .149
Citizen Status in Iowa versus Puerto Rico 151
2000 Puerto Rico Election Results 151
Two Cities, Two Climates 168
Cultural Regions of Brazil 170
Brazil's Ethnic Groups 170
Peru: Characteristics of Three Regions 174
Peru's Population 174
Chile: Average Annual Income per Citizen 180
Chile's Exports 180
U.S. Petroleum Imports From Venezuela, 1975–2000 . .189
World Crude Oil Prices, 1970–2001 190
Leading World Oil Exporters, 2001 190
Venezuela: Earnings From Exports, 2002 190

NCLB Implications for Social Studies

The No Child Left Behind (NCLB) legislation was a landmark in educational reform designed to improve student achievement and create a fundamental shift in American education. In the essay that follows, we will explore the implications of NCLB on social studies curriculum, instruction, assessment, and instructional programs.

Facts about NCLB

The No Child Left Behind Act of 2001 (NCLB) calls for sweeping educational reform, requiring all students to perform proficiently on standardized tests in reading, mathematics, and (soon to be added) science by the year 2014. Under NCLB, schools will be held accountable for students' academic progress. In exchange for this accountability, the law offers more flexibility to individual states and school districts to decide how best to use federal education funds. NCLB places an emphasis on implementing scientifically proven methods in teaching reading and mathematics, and promotes teacher quality. It also offers parental choice for students in failing schools.

Effects on Curriculum, Instruction, and Assessment

Since the primary focus of NCLB is on raising the achievement of students in reading and mathematics, some educators have wondered how it relates to social studies. Some teachers have expressed concerns that since NCLB does not require yearly testing of social studies, state and school districts may decide to shift resources and class time away from teaching social studies. However, NCLB considers the social studies areas of history, geography, economics, and government and civics to be core academic subjects. Many states are requiring middle grades social studies teachers to be highly qualified in history and geography in order to comply with the principle of improving teacher quality in NCLB.

NCLB sets the goal of having every child meet state-defined education standards. Since social studies educators have been leaders in the development of standards-based education and accountability through student testing over the past decade, many state and local districts have their own standards and assessments for social studies already in place. Assessment, including screening, diagnostic, progress-monitoring—including end-of-year, end-of-schooling, grade level, district, and state testing—and large-scale assessments, will continue to play a significant role in shaping social studies curriculum and instruction in the near future.

Integrating Reading into Social Studies Instruction

Due to the increased emphasis on reading and mathematics required by NCLB, social studies teachers may be called on to help improve their students' reading and math skills. For example, a teacher might use a graph about exports and imports to reinforce math skills, or a primary source about a historical event to improve reading skills. The connection between reading and social studies is especially important. Since many state and local assessments of reading require students to read and interpret informational texts, social studies passages are often used in the exams. Therefore, social studies teachers may assist in raising reading scores by integrating reading instruction into their teaching of social studies content.

Implications for Instructional Programs

The environment created by the NCLB legislation has implications for instructional programs. In keeping with the spirit of NCLB, social studies programs should clearly tie their content to state and local standards. Programs should also provide support so that all students can master these standards, ensuring that no child is left behind. An ideal instructional program is rooted in research, embeds reading instruction into the instructional design, and provides assessment tools that inform instruction—helping teachers focus on improving student performance.

Prentice Hall Response

We realize that raising the achievement level of all students is the number one challenge facing teachers today. To assist you in meeting this challenge, Prentice Hall enlisted a team of respected consultants who specialize in middle grades issues, reading in the content areas, and geographic education. This team created a middle grades world studies program that breaks new ground and meets the changing needs of you and your students.

With Prentice Hall, you can be confident that your students will not only be motivated, inspired, and excited to learn world studies, but they will also achieve the success needed in today's environment of the No Child Left Behind (NCLB) legislation and testing reform.

In the following pages, you will find the key elements woven throughout this World Studies program that truly set it apart and assure success for you and your students.

Teacher's Edition Contents in Brief

Reading Support T14

Differentiated Instruction T18

Geographic Literacy T20

Assessment T22

Skills Scope and Sequence T24

Pacing Options T25

National Geography Standards Correlation T26

NCSS Curriculum Standards Correlation T28

Instructional Strategies for Improving Student Comprehension T32

Research on Effective Reading Instruction

Why do many students have difficulty reading textbooks? How can we help students read to learn social studies? In the pages that follow, we examine the research on the challenge of reading textbooks; explain the direct, systematic, and explicit instruction needed to help students; and then show how Prentice Hall has responded to this research.

What is skilled reading?

Recent research (Snow et al., 2002) suggests that skillful and strategic reading is a long-term developmental process in which "readers learn how to simultaneously extract and construct meaning through interaction with written language." In other words, successful readers know how to decode all kinds of words, read with fluency and expression, have well-developed vocabularies, and possess various comprehension strategies such as note-taking and summarizing to employ as the academic reading task demands.

Many students lack reading skills

Sadly, many secondary students do not have solid reading skills. In the early years, students read mainly engaging and accessible narratives, such as stories, poems, and biographies. But in the upper elementary years, they shift toward conceptually dense and challenging nonfiction, or expository texts. It is no accident that the infamous "Fourth-Grade Slump" (Chall and Jacobs, 2003; Hirsch 2003)—a well-documented national trend of declining literacy after grade four—occurs during this time. The recent National Assessment of Educational Progress (NAEP, 2002) found that only 33 percent of eighth-grade students scored at or above the proficient level in reading.

Even students quite skilled in reading novels, short stories, and adolescent magazines typically come to middle school ill-equipped for the rigors of informational texts or reading to learn. They tend to dive right into a social studies chapter as if reading a recreational story. They don't first preview the material to create a mental outline and establish a reading purpose. They have not yet learned other basic strategies, including reading a section more than once, taking notes as they read, and reading to answer specific questions.

Dr. Kate Kinsella
Reading Consultant for *World Studies*
Department of Secondary Education
San Francisco State University, CA

Dr. Kevin Feldman
Reading Consultant for *World Studies*
Director of Reading and Early Intervention
Sonoma County, CA

"Even students quite skilled in reading novels, short stories, and adolescent magazines typically come to middle school ill-equipped for the rigors of informational texts or reading to learn."

The unique demands of textbooks

The differences between textbooks and the narratives students are used to reading are dramatic. The most distinctive challenges include dense conceptual content, heavy vocabulary load, unfamiliar paragraph and organizational patterns, and complex sentence structures. Academic texts present such a significant challenge to most students that linguists and language researchers liken them to learning a foreign language (Schleppegrell, 2002). In other words, most secondary students are second language learners: they are learning the academic language of informational texts!

Effective reading instruction

Research illustrates that virtually all students benefit from direct, systematic, and explicit instruction in reading informational texts (Baker & Gersten, 2000). There are three stages to the instructional process for content-area reading:

(1) **before reading:** instructional frontloading;

(2) **during reading:** guided instruction;

(3) **after reading:** reflection and study.

Before reading

Placing a major emphasis on preteaching, or "front-loading" your instruction—building vocabulary, setting a purpose for reading, and explicitly teaching students strategies for actively engaging with the text—helps you structure learning to ensure student success (see Strategies 1 and 2 on pages T32-T33). Frontloading strategies are especially critical in mixed-ability classrooms with English language learners, students with special needs, and other students performing below grade level in terms of literacy.

During reading

In guided instruction, the teacher models approaches for actively engaging with text to gain meaning. The teacher guides students through the first reading of the text using passage reading strategies (see Strategies 3-7 on pages T33-T35), and then guides discussion about the content using participation strategies (see Strategies 8-11 on pages T35-T37). Finally, students record key information in a graphic organizer.

After reading

During the reflection and study phase, the teacher formally checks for student understanding, offers remediation if necessary, and provides activities that challenge students to apply content in a new way. To review the chapter, students recall content, analyze the reading as a whole, and study key vocabulary and information likely to be tested.

References

Baker, Scott and Russell Gersten. "What We Know About Effective Instructional Practices for English Language Learners." *Exceptional Children*, 66 (2000):454–470.

Chall, Jeanne S. and Vicki A. Jacobs. "Poor Children's Fourth-Grade Slump." *American Educator* (Spring 2003):14.

Donahue, P.L., et al. *The 1998 NAEP Reading Report Card for the Nation and the States* (NCES 1999-500). Washington, D.C.: U.S. Department of Education, Office of Education Research and Improvement, National Center for Education Statistics, 1999.

Griggs, W.S., et al. *The Nation's Report Card: Reading 2002* (NCES 2003-521). Washington D.C.: U.S. Department of Education, Institute of Education Sciences, National Center for Education Statistics, 2003.

Hirsch, E.D., Jr. "Reading Comprehension Requires Knowledge—of Words and the World." *American Educator* (Spring 2003):10-29.

Kinsella, Kate, et al. *Teaching Guidebook for Universal Access*. Upper Saddle River, NJ: Prentice Hall, 2002.

Schleppegrell, M. "Linguistic Features of the Language of Schooling." *Linguistics and Education*, 12, no. 4 (2002): 431–459.

Snow, C., et al. *Reading for Understanding: Toward an R&D Program in Reading Comprehension*. Santa Monica, California: The Rand Corporation, 2002.

Reading Support

Putting Research Into Practice

Prentice Hall enlisted the assistance of Dr. Kate Kinsella and Dr. Kevin Feldman to ensure that the new middle grades world studies program would provide the direct, systematic, and explicit instruction needed to foster student success in reading informational texts. To help students rise to the challenge of reading an informational text, *World Studies* embedded reading support right into the student text.

Embedded Reading Support in the Student Text

Before students read

- **Objectives** set the purpose for what students will read.
- **Target Reading Skill** for the section is explained.
- **Key Terms** are defined up front with pronunciation and part of speech.

During the section

- **Target Reading Skill** is applied to help students read and understand the narrative.
- **Key Terms** are defined in context, with terms and definitions called out in blue type.
- **Reading Checks** reinforce students' understanding by slowing them down to review after every concept is discussed.
- **Caption Questions** draw students into the art and photos, helping them to connect the content to the images.

After students read

- **Section Assessment** revisits the **Key Terms**, provides an opportunity to master the **Target Reading Skill**, allows student to rehearse their understanding of the text through the **Writing Activity**.

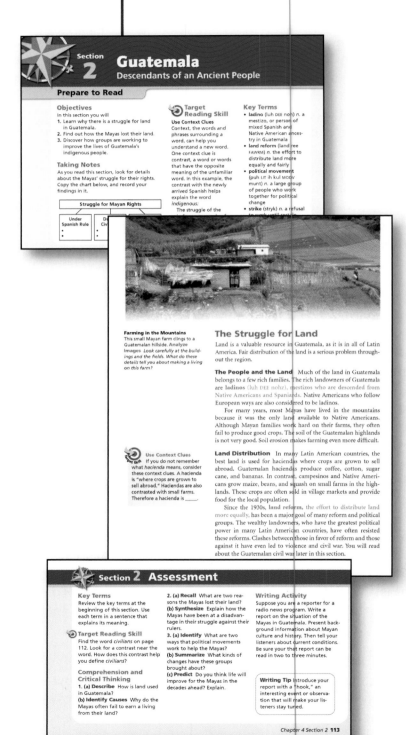

Putting Research Into Practice

World Studies offers teachers guidance in direct, systematic, and explicit reading instruction. The instructional sequence in the Teacher's Edition explicitly guides you in the use of effective strategies at each stage of the instructional process.

Reading Instruction in *World Studies* Teacher's Edition

Before Reading

Every lesson plan begins with suggestions that help you integrate frontloading strategies into your teaching. Build Background Knowledge activates and builds prior knowledge. Set a Purpose for Reading prompts students to predict and anticipate content and motivates students to engage with the text. Preview Key Terms helps students learn Key Terms to understand the text. Target Reading Skill models a reading strategy to help students gain meaning from the text. Vocabulary Builder gives teachers definitions and sample sentences to help teach high-use words.

During Reading

In the "Instruct" part of the lesson plan, you can use suggestions for getting students actively engaged in the text. Guided Instruction clarifies high-use words, applies a passage-reading strategy to promote text comprehension, and guides discussion to construct meaning. Independent Practice prompts students to reread and take notes in the graphic organizer provided to rehearse understanding.

After Reading

The lesson plan closes with specific strategies for the reflection and study phase after reading is completed. Monitor Progress checks students' note taking, and verifies students' prereading predictions. Assess and Reteach measures students' recall of content and provides additional instruction if needed. Review Chapter Content promotes retention of key concepts and vocabulary.

Integrated Reading Resources

The *World Studies* program provides instructional materials to support the reading instruction in the Teacher's Edition.

The **All-in-One Teaching Resources** provides reading instruction support worksheets, such as a Reading Readiness Guide, Word Knowledge, and Vocabulary Development.

Students can use the **Reading and Vocabulary Study Guide** (English and Spanish) to reinforce reading instruction and vocabulary development, and to review section summaries of every section of the student text.

Research on Differentiated Instruction

It's basic, but it's true—not all our students learn in the same manner and not all our students have the same academic background or abilities. As educators, we need to respond to this challenge through the development and utilization of instructional strategies that address the needs of diverse learners, or the number of children who "fall through the cracks" will continue to rise (Kame'enui & Carnine, 1998).

Providing universal access

Universal access happens when curriculum and instruction are provided in ways that allow all learners to participate and to achieve (Kinsella, et al., 2002). Teachers who teach in heterogeneous, inclusive classrooms can provide universal access by modifying their teaching to respond to the needs of typical learners, gifted learners, less proficient readers, English language learners, and special needs students. Many of these learner populations benefit from extensive reading support (see pages T14-T17).

It is also critical to properly match the difficulty level of tasks with the ability level of students. Giving students tasks that they perceive as too hard lowers their expectations of success. However, giving students assignments that they think are too easy, undermines their feelings of competence (Stipek, 1996). Therefore, it is important for a program to give teachers leveled activities that allow them to match tasks with the abilities of their individual students.

When students connect to and are engaged with the content, comprehension and understanding increase. Technology, such as online activities, can provide an ideal opportunity for such engagement. It also can be used to provide additional opportunities to access content. For example, a less proficient reader may reinforce understanding of a key concept through watching a video. A complete social studies program makes content available in a variety of formats, including text, audio, visuals, and interactivities.

"Universal access happens when curriculum and instruction are provided in ways that allow all learners to participate and to achieve (Kinsella, et al., 2002)."

Kame'enui, Edward and Douglas Carnine. *Effective Teaching Strategies that Accommodate Diverse Learners.* Upper Saddle River, NJ: Prentice Hall, 1998.

Kinsella, Kate, et al. *Teaching Guidebook for Universal Access.* Upper Saddle River, NJ: Prentice Hall, 2002.

Stipek, D.J. "Motivation and Instruction," in R.C. Clafee and D.C. Berlinger (Eds.), *Handbook of Educational Psychology.* New York: Macmillan, 1996.

Putting Research Into Practice

Prentice Hall recognizes that today's classrooms include students with diverse backgrounds and ability levels. Accordingly, the *World Studies* program was designed to provide access to the content for all students. The program provides both the instructional materials to meet the learning needs of all students and the guidance you need to accommodate these needs.

Differentiated Instruction in the Teacher's Edition

The Teacher's Edition was designed to make it easy for teachers to modify instruction for diverse learners. Teaching strategies, provided by Dr. Kate Kinsella and Dr. Kevin Feldman, to help you modify your teaching are incorporated into every lesson plan. Specific activities help you differentiate instruction for individual students in five categories—less proficient readers, advanced readers, special needs students, gifted and talented, and English language learners. Resources are identified as being appropriate for use by each of these categories. All resources are also assigned a level—basic, average, and above average—so you know exactly how to assign tasks of appropriate difficulty level.

All-in-One Teaching Resources

Everything you need to provide differentiated instruction for each lesson, including reading support, activities and projects, enrichment, and assessment—in one convenient location.

World Studies Video Program

Students will benefit from our custom-built video program—the result of an exclusive partnership with Discovery Channel School—making content accessible through dynamic footage and high-impact stories.

Student Edition on Audio CD

The complete narrative is read aloud, section by section, providing extra support for auditory learners, English language learners, and reluctant readers. Also available is the Guided Reading Audio CD (English/Spanish), containing section summaries read aloud.

Interactive Textbook—The Student Edition Online and on CD-ROM

The Interactive Textbook allows students to interact with the content and includes reading aids, visual and interactive learning tools, and instant feedback assessments.

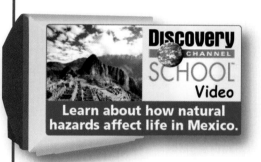

Learn about how natural hazards affect life in Mexico.

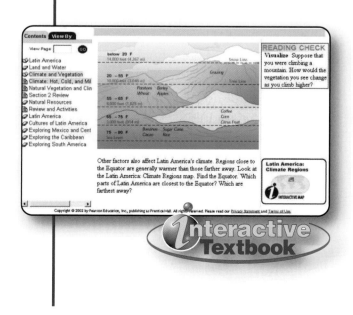

Research on Geographic Literacy

As the *Geography for Life: National Geography Standards* (1994) state, "There is now a widespread acceptance among the people of the United States that being literate in geography is essential if students are to leave school equipped to earn a decent living, enjoy the richness of life, and participate responsibly in local, national, and international affairs." A middle grades social studies program needs to help teachers produce students who are literate in geography.

Geographic literacy defined

Results for the 2001 National Assessment of Educational Progress (NAEP) Geography assessment show that the average scores of fourth- and eighth-grade students have improved since 1994. The average score of twelfth-grade students, however, has not changed significantly. In order to make the critical leap from basic geography skills to the kind of geographic literacy needed by the twelfth grade and beyond, a program must teach both geography content and geography skills, and then help students think critically. Geography content is made up of the essential knowledge that students need to know about the world. Geography skills are the ability to ask geographic questions, acquire and analyze geographic information, and answer these questions. To be truly literate in geography, students must be able to apply their knowledge and skills to understand the world.

Elements for success in middle grades

Students in the elementary grades don't always get enough training in geography. In order to help all students gain a base upon which to build middle grades geographic literacy, a program should introduce basic geography skills at the beginning of the school year.

The quality of maps is also vital to the success of a middle grades world studies program. Maps must be developmentally appropriate for middle grades students. They should be clean, clear, and accurate. Maps should be attractive and present subject matter in appealing ways, so that students *want* to use them to learn.

Another element that can lead to success is the incorporation of technology into the teaching and learning of geography, specifically the Internet. Research has shown that 8th grade students with high Internet usage scored higher in geography (NAEP, 2001).

U.S. Department of Education, Office of Educational Research and Improvement, National Center for Education Statistics, National Assessment of Educational Progress (NAEP), 2001 Geography Assessment.

Andrew Heritage
Head of Cartography
Dorling Kindersley (DK)

"Maps should be attractive and present subject matter in appealing ways, so that students *want* to use them to learn."

Putting Research Into Practice

Prentice Hall partnered with DK—internationally known for their dynamic atlases—to develop the *World Studies* program. DK's Andrew Heritage and his world-renowned cartography team designed all maps, resulting in stunning, high quality maps that are middle grades appropriate.

The MapMaster™ System

World Studies offers the first interactive geography instruction system available with a world studies textbook.

Introduce Basic Map Skills

The MapMaster Skills Handbook, a DK-designed introduction to the basics, brings students up to speed with a complete overview at the beginning of every book.

Build Geographic Literacy with Every Map

Scaffolded questions start with questions that require basic geography content and skills, and then ask students to demonstrate geographic literacy by thinking critically about the map.

Activate Learning Online

MapMaster Interactive—online and on CD-ROM—allows students to put their knowledge of geography skills and content into practice through interactivities.

Extend Learning with DK

- **DK World Desk Reference Online** is filled with up-to-date data, maps, and visuals that connect students to a wealth of information about the world's countries.

- **DK Compact Atlas of the World** with Map Master Teacher's Companion provides activities to introduce, develop, and master geography and map skills.

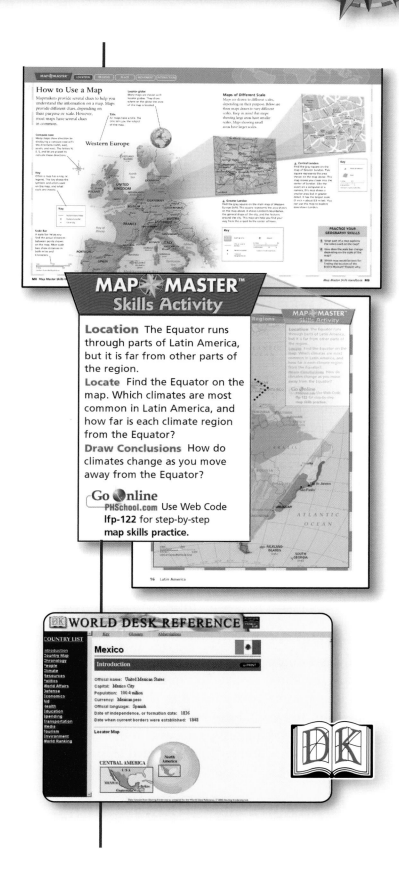

Research on Assessment

Meeting the NCLB challenge will necessitate an integrated approach to assessment with a variety of assessment tools. With the spotlight now on *improving* student performance, it is essential to use assessment results to inform instruction.

Assessments Tools for Informing Instruction

The key to success is using a variety of assessment tools coupled with data analysis and decision making. Teachers work with information coming from four kinds of assessment.

Screening assessments are brief procedures used to identify at-risk students who are not ready to work at grade level.

Diagnostic assessments provide a more in-depth analysis of strengths and weaknesses that can help teachers make instructional decisions and plan intervention strategies.

Progress-monitoring assessments (sometimes referred to as benchmark tests) provide an ongoing, longitudinal record of student achievement detailing individual student progress toward meeting end-of-year and end-of-schooling, grade level, district, or state standards.

Large-scale assessments, such as state tests and standardized tests, are used to determine whether individual students have met the expected standards and whether a school system has made adequate progress in improving its performance.

Ongoing Assessment

Daily assessment should be embedded in the program before, during, and after instruction in the core lessons. Legitimate test preparation experiences also should be embedded in the program. Test preparation involves teaching students strategies for taking tests, such as eliminating answers, reading comprehension, and writing extended response answers.

Eileen Depka
Supervisor of Standards and Assessment
Waukesha, WI

"Meeting the NCLB challenge will necessitate an integrated approach to assessment with a variety of assessment tools."

Putting Research Into Practice

Prentice Hall developed the *World Studies* program with a variety of assessment tools, including ongoing assessment in the student text.

Assessments for Informing Instruction

World Studies was designed to provide you with all four kinds of assessment.

- **Screening test** identifies students who are reading 2-3 years below grade level.

- **Diagnostic tests** focus on skills needed for success in social studies, including subtests in geographic literacy, visual analysis, critical thinking and reading, and communications skills, as well as vocabulary and writing.

- **Benchmark tests**, to be given six times throughout the year, monitor student progress in the course.

- **Outcome test**, to be administered at the end of the year, evaluates student mastery of social studies content standards.

Ongoing Assessment

- **Student Edition** offers section and chapter assessments with questions building from basic comprehension to critical thinking and writing.

- **Test Prep Workbook** and **Test-taking Strategies with Transparencies** develop students' test-taking skills and improve their scores on standardized tests.

- **ExamView® Test Bank CD-ROM** allows you to quickly and easily develop customized tests from a bank of thousands of questions.

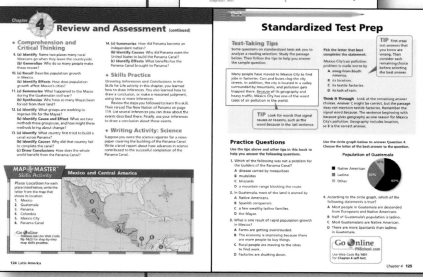

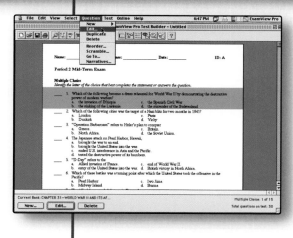

Latin America Skills Scope and Sequence

Prentice Hall *World Studies* contains a comprehensive program of core skills. Each skill is taught in every book of the series. A Target Reading Skill is located at the beginning of each chapter and expanded upon in each section within the chapter. Core skills are also taught either in the "Skills for Life Activity" in the Student Edition, or in a "Skills Mini Lesson" in the Teacher's Edition. In addition, worksheets for the students' use in completing each skill are located in the All-in-One Teaching Resources. The chart below lists the skills covered in *Prentice Hall World Studies Latin America* and the page where each skill is taught.

Latin America Analysis Skills	SE	TE
Analyzing Graphic Data		p. 66
Analyzing Images		p. 18
Analyzing Primary Sources		p. 52
Clarifying Meaning	pp. 38, 40, 42, 44, 45, 46, 49, 50, 54, 56, 57, 59, 61, 64, 66, 68	pp. 38B, 40, 45, 50, 57, 64
Comparing and Contrasting	pp. 140–141, 158, 166, 169, 172, 173, 177, 178, 179, 181, 185, 188, 191, 194	pp. 140–141, 158B, 166, 173, 179, 188
Decision Making		p. 137
Distinguishing Fact and Opinion	pp. 80–91	pp. 80–81
Drawing Inferences and Conclusions	pp. 114–115	pp. 114–115
Identifying Cause and Effect/Making Predictions	pp. 72, 74, 77, 79, 82, 83, 86, 87, 88, 92	pp. 72B, 74, 78, 82, 87
Identifying Frame of Reference and Point of View		p. 117
Identifying Main Ideas/Summarizing	pp. 57, 59, 61, 126, 134, 136, 139, 142, 146, 147, 148, 153, 154	pp. 57, 84, 126B, 134, 142, 148 p. 12
Making Valid Generalizations		p. 111
Problem Solving		p. 54
Recognizing Bias and Propaganda		pp. 62–63
Sequencing	pp. 62–63	p. 146
Supporting a Position		pp. 186–187
Synthesizing Information	pp. 186–187	p. 170
Transferring Information From One Medium to Another		p. 104
Using the Cartographer's Tools		pp. 96B, 102, 109, 116
Using Context	pp. 96, 102, 107, 108, 109, 110, 113, 116, 120, 122	
Using the Reading Process	pp. 8, 10, 13, 14, 15, 19, 21, 24, 29, 30	pp. 8B, 10, 15, 24
Using Reliable Information		p. 118
Using Special-Purpose Maps	pp. 22–23	pp. 22–23

Pacing Options

World Studies offers many aids to help you plan your instruction time, whether regular class periods or block scheduling. Section-by-section lesson plans for each chapter include suggested times, based on the 18-week course configuration below. Teacher Express CD-ROM will help you manage your time electronically.

Latin America Pacing Options			9-week unit	12-week unit
Chapter 1	Section 1 Section 2 Section 3	Land and Water Climate and Vegetation Resources and Land Use	3 2 3	5.5 2.5 4
Chapter 2	Section 1 Section 2 Section 3 Section 4 Section 5	Early Civilizations of Middle America The Incas: People of the Sun European Conquest Independence From Past to Present	1 1 1 2 2.5	1.5 1.5 1.5 3 3.5
Chapter 3	Section 1 Section 2 Section 3	The Cultures of Mexico and Central America The Cultures of the Caribbean The Cultures of South America	2 1 2.5	3 1.5 3.5
Chapter 4	Section 1 Section 2 Section 3	Mexico: Moving to the City Guatemala: Descendants of an Ancient People Panama: An Important Crossroads	2 2.5 3	2.5 3 3.5
Chapter 5	Section 1 Section 2 Section 3	Cuba: Clinging to Communism Haiti: A Democracy in Progress Puerto Rico: An American Commonwealth	3 1.5 3	3.5 1.5 4
Chapter 6	Section 1 Section 2 Section 3 Section 4	Brazil: Geography Shapes a Nation Peru: An Ancient Land Looks to the Future Chile: Land of Contrasts Venezuela: Oil Powers the Economy	2 1.5 2.5 3	3 1.5 3 3.5
		Total Number of Days	**45**	**60**

Correlation to *Geography for Life,* the National Geography Standards

On the following pages, *Prentice Hall World Studies Latin America* is correlated with *Geography for Life*, the National Geography Standards. These standards were prepared in response to the Goals 2000, Educate America Act, by the Geography Education Standards Project. Participating in the project were the American Geographical Society, the Association of American Geographers, the National Council for Geographic Education, and the National Geographic Society. Concepts and skills contained in the Geography Standards are incorporated throughout the program. This correlation displays places where the standards are directly addressed.

Standard	Latin America	
The World in Spatial Terms		
Standard 1 Use maps and other geographic representations, tools, and technologies to acquire, process, and report information from a spatial perspective.	MapMaster Skills Handbook, Regional Overview Chapter 1; Sections 1, 2, 3 Chapter 2, Sections 1, 2, 3, 4 Chapter 4; Section 1, 2, 3 Chapter 5; Sections 1, 2, 3 Chapter 6; Sections 1, 2, 3, 4	
Standard 2 Use mental maps to organize information about people, places, and environments in a spatial context.	MapMaster Skills Handbook Chapter 1; Section 3 Chapter 4; Section 1	
Standard 3 Analyze the spatial organization of people, places, and environments on Earth's surface.	MapMaster Skills Handbook Chapter 1; Sections 1, 2, 3 Chapter 4; Sections 1, 2 Chapter 5; Section 3 Chapter 6; Section 1	
Places and Regions		
Standard 4 Understand the physical and human characteristics of places.	Regional Overview Chapter 1; Sections 1, 2 Chapter 4; Sections 1, 2 Chapter 6; Sections 1, 2, 3, 4 Country Databanks	
Standard 5 Understand that people create regions to interpret Earth's complexity.	MapMaster Skills Handbook Chapter 1; Sections 1, 2 Chapter 4; Section 1 Chapter 5; Section 3 Chapter 6; Section 2	
Standard 6 Understand how culture and experience influence people's perception of places and regions.	Chapter 3; Sections 1, 2, 3 Chapter 4; Sections 1, 2, 3 Chapter 5; Sections 1, 2, 3 Chapter 6; Sections 1, 2, 3, 4	
Physical Systems		
Standard 7 Understand the physical processes that shape the patterns of Earth's surface.	MapMaster Skills Handbook Chapter 1; Sections 1, 2, 3 Chapter 2; Section 5 Chapter 6; Sections 1, 2	
Standard 8 Understand the characteristics and spatial distribution of ecosystems on Earth's surface.	MapMaster Skills Handbook Chapter 1; Sections 1, 2, 3 Chapter 4; Secrtion 3 Chapter 6; Sections 1, 2, 3	

Correlation to *Geography for Life*, the National Geography Standards *(continued)*

Standard	Latin America
Human Systems	
Standard 9 Understand the characteristics, distribution, and migration of human populations on Earth's surface.	Chapter 2; Sections 1, 2, 3, 5 Chapter 3; Sections 1, 2, 3 Chapter 4; Section 1 Chapter 5; Sections 1, 2, 3 Chapter 6; Sections 1, 2, 3, 4
Standard 10 Understand the characteristics, distribution, and complexity of Earth's cultural mosaics.	Chapter 2; Sections 1, 2, 3 Chapter 3; Sections 1, 2, 3 Chapter 4; Sections 1, 2 Chapter 5; Sections 1, 2, 3 Chapter 6; Sections 1, 2, 3, 4
Standard 11 Understand the patterns and networks of economic interdependence on Earth's surface.	Chapter 1; Section 3 Chapter 2; Section 5 Chapter 3; Sections 1, 3 Chapter 4; Sections 1, 3 Chapter 5; Sections 1, 3 Chapter 6; Sections 1, 3, 4
Standard 12 Understand the processes, patterns, and functions of human settlement.	Chapter 2; Sections 1, 2, 3, 5 Chapter 3; Sections 1, 2, 3 Chapter 4; Section 1 Chapter 5; Section 3 Chapter 6; Sections 1, 2, 3, 4
Standard 13 Understand how the forces of cooperation and conflict among people influence division and control of Earth's surface.	Chapter 2; Sections 1, 2, 3, 4, 5 Chapter 4; Sections 2, 3 Chapter 5; Sections 1, 2, 3 Chapter 6; Section 1
Environment and Society	
Standard 14 Understand how human actions modify the physical environment.	Chapter 2; Section 5 Chapter 4; Sections 1, 3 Chapter 6; Sections 1, 3
Standard 15 Understand how physical systems affect human systems.	Chapter 1; Sections 1, 2, 3 Chapter 3; Section 3 Chapter 6; Sections 2, 3
Standard 16 Understand the changes that occur in the meaning, use, distribution, and importance of resources.	Chapter 1; Sections 1, 3 Chapter 2; Section 5 Chapter 6; Sections 3, 4
The Uses of Geography	
Standard 17 Understand how to apply geography to interpret the past.	Chapter 2; Sections 1, 2, 3 Chapter 3; Section 2 Chapter 5; Section 3 Chapter 6; Sections 2, 3, 4
Standard 18 Understand how to apply geography to interpret the present and plan for the future.	Chapter 1; Section 3 Chapter 3; Section 1 Chapter 4; Section 1 Chapter 5; Sections 1, 2, 3 Chapter 6; Sections 1, 3, 4

Correlation to the NCSS Curriculum Standards

On the following pages *Prentice Hall World Studies Latin America* is correlated with *Expectations of Excellence*, the Curriculum Standards for Social Studies. These standards were developed by the National Council for the Social Studies to address overall curriculum design and comprehensive student performance expectations.

Standard	Latin America
Performance Expectations 1: Culture	
• compare similarities and differences in the ways groups, societies, and cultures meet human needs and concerns • explain how information and experiences may be interpreted by people from diverse cultural perspectives and frames of reference • explain and give examples of how language, literature, the arts, architecture, other artifacts, traditions, beliefs, values, and behaviors contribute to the development and transmission of culture • explain why individuals and groups respond differently to their physical and social environments and/or changes to them on the basis of shared assumptions, values, and beliefs • articulate the implications of cultural diversity, as well as cohesion, within and across groups	Chapter 2; Sections 1–3 Chapter 3; Sections 1–3 Chapter 4; Section 2 Chapter 5; Sections 1, 3 Chapter 6; Section 2
Performance Expectations 2: Time, Continuity, and Change	
• demonstrate an understanding that different scholars may describe the same event or situation in different ways but must provide reasons or evidence for their view • identify and use key concepts such as chronology, causality, change, conflict, and complexity to explain, analyze, and show connections among patterns of historical change and continuity • identify and describe selected historical periods and patterns of change within and across cultures • identify and use processes important to reconstructing and reinterpreting the past • develop critical sensitivities regarding attitudes, values, and behaviors of people in different historical contexts • use knowledge of facts and concepts drawn from history, along with methods of historical inquiry, to inform decision-making about and action-taking on public issues	Chapter 2; Sections 1–5 Chapter 4; Section 2
Performance Expectations 3: People, Places, and Environment	
• elaborate mental maps of locales, regions, and the world that demonstrate understanding of relative location, direction, size, and shape • create, interpret, use, and distinguish various representations of the earth • use appropriate resources, data sources, and geographic tools to generate, manipulate, and interpret information • estimate distance, calculate scale, and distinguish geographic relationships • locate and describe varying landforms and geographic features and explain their relationship with the ecosystem • describe physical system changes and identify geographic patterns associated with them • describe how people create places that reflect cultural values and ideals • examine, interpret, and analyze physical and cultural patterns and their interactions • describe ways that historical events have been influenced by, and have influenced, physical and human geographic factors in local, regional, national, and global settings • observe and speculate about social and economic effects of environmental changes and crises resulting from natural phenomena • propose, compare, and evaluate alternative uses of land and resources in communities, regions, nations, and the world	Chapter 1; Sections 1–3 Chapter 2; Section 5 Chapter 3; Sections 1, 3 Chapter 4; Sections 1, 3 Chapter 5; Sections 1–3 Chapter 6; Sections 1–3 MapMaster Regional Overview

Correlation to the NCSS Curriculum Standards *(continued)*

Standard	Latin America
Performance Expectations 4: Individual Development and Identity	
• relate personal changes to social, cultural, and historical contexts • describe personal connections to place—as associated with community, nation, and world • describe the ways family, gender, ethnicity, nationality, and institutional affiliations contribute to personal identity • relate such factors as physical endowment and capabilities, learning, motivation, personality, perception, and behavior to individual development • identify and describe ways regional, ethnic, and national cultures influence individuals' daily lives • identify and describe the influence of perception, attitudes, values, and beliefs on personal identity • identify and interpret examples of stereotyping, conformity, and altruism • work independently and cooperatively to accomplish goals	Chapter 2; Sections 1–2 Chapter 3; Sections 1–3 Chapter 4; Section 1 Chapter 5; Sections 1–3 Chapter 6; Section 2
Performance Expectations 5: Individuals, Groups, & Institutions	
• demonstrate an understanding of concepts such as role, status, and social class in describing interactions of individuals and social groups • analyze group and institutional influences on people, events, and elements of culture • describe the various forms institutions take and the interactions of people with institutions • identify and analyze examples of tensions between expressions of individuality and group or institutional efforts to promote social conformity • identify and describe examples of tensions between belief systems and government policies and laws • describe the role of institutions in furthering both continuity and change • apply knowledge of how groups and institutions work to meet individual needs and promote the common good	Chapter 2; Sections 3, 5 Chapter 4; Sections 2–3 Chapter 5; Sections 1–2 Chapter 6; Section 1
Performance Expectations 6: Power, Authority, and Governance	
• examine persistent issues involving the rights, roles, and status of the individual in relation to general welfare • describe the purpose of government and how its powers are acquired, used, and justified • analyze and explain ideas and governmental mechanisms to meet needs and wants of citizens, regulate territory, manage conflict, and establish order and security • describe the ways nations and organizations respond to forces of unity and diversity affecting order and security • identify and describe the basic features of the political system in the United States, and identify representative leaders from various levels and branches of government • explain conditions, actions, and motivations that contribute to conflict and cooperation within and among nations • describe and analyze the role of technology as it contributes to or helps resolve conflicts • explain how power, role, status, and justice influence the examination of persistent issues and social problems • give examples and explain how governments attempt to achieve their stated ideals at home and abroad	Chapter 2; Sections 1–5 Chapter 4; Sections 1, 2, 3 Chapter 5; Sections 1, 2, 3 Chapter 6; Sections 1, 2, 3, 4

Correlation to the NCSS Curriculum Standards *(continued)*

Standard	Latin America
Performance Expectations 7: Production, Distribution, and Consumption	
• give examples of ways that economic systems structure choices about how goods and services are to be produced and distributed • describe the role that supply and demand, prices, incentives, and profits play in determining what is produced and distributed in a competitive market system • explain differences between private and public goods and services • describe a range of examples of the various institutions that make up economic systems • describe the role of specialization and exchange in the economic process • explain and illustrate how values and beliefs influence different economic decisions • differentiate among various forms of exchange and money • compare basic economic systems according to who determines what is produced, distributed, and consumed • use economic concepts to help explain historical and current events in local, national, or global concepts • use economic reasoning to compare different proposals for dealing with contemporary social issues	Chapter 1; Section 3 Chapter 2; Section 5 Chapter 6; Sections 1–4
Performance Expectations 8: Science, Technology, and Society	
• examine and describe the influence of culture on scientific and technological choices and advancement • show through specific examples how science and technology have changed peoples' perceptions of their social and natural world • describe examples in which values, beliefs, and attitudes have been influenced by new scientific and technological knowledge • explain the need for laws and policies to govern scientific and technological applications • seek reasonable and ethical solutions to problems that arise when scientific advancements and social norms or values come into conflict	Chapter 2; Section 5 Chapter 3; Sections 1–3 Chapter 4; Sections 1,3 Chapter 6; Sections 1,4
Performance Expectations 9: Global Connections	
• describe instances in which language, art, music, and belief systems, and other cultural elements can facilitate global understanding or cause misunderstanding • analyze examples of conflict, cooperation, and interdependence among groups, societies, and nations • describe and analyze the effects of changing technologies on the global community • explore the causes, consequences, and possible solutions to persistent contemporary and emerging global interests • describe and explain the relationships and tensions between national sovereignty and global interests • demonstrate understanding of concerns, standards, issues, and conflicts related to universal human rights • identify and describe the roles of international and multinational organizations	Chapter 2; Sections 3, 5 Chapter 3; Sections 1–3 Chapter 4; Sections 1–3 Chapter 5; Sections 1–3 Chapter 6; Sections 1, 3, 4

Correlation to the NCSS Curriculum Standards *(continued)*

Standard	Latin America
Performance Expectations 10: Civic Ideals and Practices	
• examine the origins and continuing influence of key ideals of the democratic republican form of government, such as individual human dignity, liberty, justice, equality, and rule of law • identify and interpret sources and examples of the rights and responsibilities of citizens • locate, access, analyze, organize, and apply information about selected public issues—recognizing and explaining multiple points of view • practice forms of civic discussion and participation consistent with the ideals of citizens in a democratic republic • explain and analyze various forms of citizen action that influence public policy decisions • identify and explain the roles of formal and informal political actors in influencing and shaping public policy and decision-making • analyze the influence of diverse forms of public opinion on the development of public policy and decision-making • analyze the effectiveness of selected public policies and citizen behaviors in realizing the stated ideals of a democratic republican form of government • explain the relationship between policy statements and action plans used to address issues of public concern • examine strategies designed to strengthen the "common good," which consider a range of options for citizen action	Chapter 2; Sections 3–5 Chapter 4; Sections 2–3 Chapter 5; Sections 1–3

Instructional Strategies for Improving Student Comprehension

In response to today's environment of the NCLB legislation and testing reform, Prentice Hall asked Dr. Kate Kinsella and Dr. Kevin Feldman to provide specific instructional strategies you can use to improve student comprehension. Their guidance informed the development of the *World Studies* Teacher's Edition. The lesson plans in this Teacher's Edition incorporate the following instructional strategies to enhance students' comprehension.

There is no single magical strategy that will solve all of the difficulties students encounter in reading challenging content area texts. Secondary students in mixed-ability classrooms depend on teachers to use a consistent set of research-informed and classroom-tested strategies in a patient and recursive manner—not the occasional or random use of different strategies. Students will not become skillful readers of content area texts in a week or two of instruction. However, when teachers engage students in the consistent use of a well-chosen set of content reading strategies appropriately matched to the demands of the text and the students' level of knowledge, their ability to comprehend difficult grade level texts will be dramatically enhanced.

Strategy 1: Set a Purpose for Reading

This program has two types of activities designed to help students set a purpose for reading: an Anticipation Guide and a KWL chart. The two types rotate by section.

A. Anticipation Guide

Purpose: To focus students' attention on key concepts, and guide them to interact with ideas in the text

1. Distribute the *Reading Readiness Guide*. Read each statement aloud, and then ask students to react to the statements individually and in groups, marking their responses in the Before Reading column.

2. Use the worksheet as a springboard for discussing the section's key concepts as a unified class. Refrain from revealing the correct responses at this time, to avoid taking away the need for them to read the text.

3. Have students read the section with the purpose of finding evidence that confirms, disproves, or elaborates each statement in the *Reading Readiness Guide*.

4. After students finish reading, have them return to the statements and mark the After Reading column on their worksheets. Have them locate information from the text that supports or disproves each statement.

5. Discuss what the class has learned and probe for any lingering confusion about key concepts.

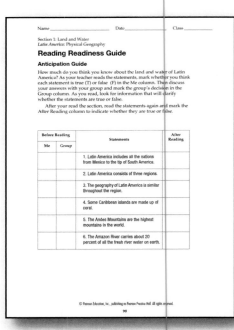

B. KWL

Purpose: To engage students before, during, and after reading

The KWL worksheet guides students to recall what they **K**now, determine what they **W**ant to learn, and identify what they **L**earn as they read.

1. Distribute the *Reading Readiness Guide.* Brainstorm with the group about what they already know about the topic. List students' ideas on the board. Encourage students to generate questions at points of ambiguity.

2. Students then list pieces of information they already know and questions they want to answer in the first two columns of their worksheets.

3. As students read the section, ask them to note information that answers their questions or adds to what they know.

4. After reading, facilitate a class discussion about what the students have learned. Clarify any lingering confusion about key concepts.

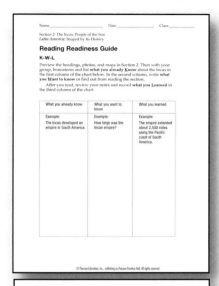

Strategy 2: Teach High-Use Academic Words

Purpose: To teach students words used often in academic texts, beyond the content-specific Key Terms

How to Do It

1. Have students rate how well they know each word on their *Word Knowledge* worksheets. Tell them there is no penalty for a low rating.

2. Survey students' ratings to decide which words need the most instruction.

3. Provide a brief definition or sample sentence for each word. (See Vocabulary Builder at the beginning of each section for definitions and sample sentences.) Rephrase your explanation, leaving out the word and asking students to substitute it aloud.

4. Work with students as they fill in the "Definition or Example" column of their *Word Knowledge* worksheets.

5. Point out each word in context as you read the chapters. Consider allowing students to earn extra credit if they use a word correctly in class discussion or assignments.

Strategy 3: Oral Cloze

Purpose: To help students read actively while the teacher reads aloud

How to Do It

1. Choose a passage and direct students to "read aloud silently using their inner voices." Be sure students understand reading is an active process, not simply a listening activity, and their job is to follow along—eyes riveted to each word, saying the words to themselves as you read aloud.

2. Tell students to be on their "reading toes," for you will be leaving out an occasional word and their task is to chorally supply the word.

3. The first few times you use the Oral Cloze, demonstrate by telling the students in advance what word you will be leaving out, directing them to read the word at the right time. Practice this a few times until they have the feel for the procedure. Leave out fewer words as students become more familiar with the Oral Cloze and require less direction to remain focused during teacher read alouds.

Instructional Strategies

Strategies for Improving Student Comprehension *(continued)*

Strategy 4: Choral Reading

Purpose: To have students attend to the text in a non-threatening atmosphere

How to Do It

1. Choose a relatively short passage.

2. Tell students that you will all read the text aloud at once. Direct students to "keep your voice with mine" as they read.

3. Read the passage slowly and clearly.

4. Have students read the text again silently.

Strategy 5: Structured Silent Reading

Purpose: To give students a task as they read silently to increase their attentiveness and accountability

How to Do It

1. Assign a section to read silently. Pose a question for the whole class to answer from their silent reading, such as the Reading Check question at the end of each subsection. Model how one thinks while reading to find answers to a question.

2. When students get used to reading to answer the Reading Check question, pose more in-depth questions, progressing from factual recall to questions that stimulate interpretive or applied thinking.

3. Teach students to ask and answer their own questions as they read. Model this process by reading a section aloud and asking and answering your own questions as you read.

4. After the students have finished reading, engage the class in a brief discussion to clarify questions, vocabulary, and key concepts.

Strategy 6: Paragraph Shrinking

Purpose: To increase comprehension during reading

How to Do It

1. Partner struggling students with more proficient students and assign a manageable portion of the text.

2. Ask one member of each pair to identify the "who or what" the paragraph is about and tell the other.

3. Have the other member of the pair identify important details about the "who or what" and tell the other.

4. Ask the first member to summarize the paragraph in fifteen to twenty words or less using the most important details. The second member of the pair monitors the number of words and says "Shrink it!" if the summary goes over twenty words.

5. Have the partners reverse roles and continue reading.

6. Discuss the reading as a class to make sure students' paragraphs have correctly hit upon the main ideas of the passage.

Strategy 7: ReQuest (Reciprocal Questioning)

Purpose: To ask and answer questions during reading to establish a purpose for reading and monitor one's own comprehension

How to Do It

1. Prepare students to read by doing the section's Build Background Knowledge, Set a Purpose for Reading, and Preview Key Terms activities.

2. Begin reading a brief portion of the text aloud. Ask and answer your own questions about the text, progressing from recall to critical thinking questions.

3. After modeling this question and response pattern with a brief passage, ask students to read the next section of the text. Tell students that they will be taking turns asking you questions about what they read, and you will answer their questions, just like you modeled for them.

4. Ask students to read the next section. Inform them that you will be asking them questions about the section and they will be answering your questions.

5. Continue to alternate between student-generated questions and teacher-generated questions until the entire designated passage has been read. As students become used to the strategy, they gradually assume more responsibility in the process.

6. When the students have read enough information to make predictions about the remainder of the assignment, stop the exchange of comprehension questions. Instead, ask prediction questions, such as, "What do you think will be discussed in the next section? Why do you think so?"

7. Assign the remaining portion for students to read silently. Then lead a wrap-up discussion of the material.

Strategy 8: Idea Wave

Purpose: To engage students in active class discussions

How to Do It

1. Pose a question or task.

2. Give students quiet time to consider what they know about the topic and record a number of responses.

3. Whip around the class in a fast-paced and structured manner (e.g. down rows, around tables), allowing as many students as possible to share an idea in 15 seconds or less.

4. After several contributions, if there tends to be repetition, ask students to point out similarities in responses rather than simply stating that their idea has already been mentioned.

Strategies for Improving Student Comprehension *(continued)*

Strategy 9: Numbered Heads

Purpose: To engage students in active class discussions

How to Do It

1. Seat students in groups of four and number off one through four (if possible, combine established partners to form groups of four).

2. After giving the discussion prompt, allow students to discuss possible responses for an established amount of time.

3. Remind students to pay close attention to the comments of each group member because you will be randomly selecting one student to represent the best thinking of the entire group.

4. Call a number (one through four), and ask all students with that number to raise their hands, ready to respond to the topic at hand in a teacher-directed, whole-class discussion.

5. Add comments, extend key ideas, ask follow-up questions, and make connections between individual student's comments to create a lively whole-class discussion.

6. Provide any summary comments required to ensure that all students understand critical points.

Strategy 10: Think-Write-Pair–Share

Purpose: To engage students in responding to instruction

How to Do It

1. **Think**—Students listen while the teacher poses a question or a task related to the reading or classroom discussion. The level of questions should vary from lower level literal to higher order inferential or analytical.

2. **Write**—Provide quiet thinking or writing time for students to deal with the question, and go back to the text or review notes. Have students record their ideas in their notebooks.

3. **Pair/Share**—Cue students to find a partner and discuss their responses, noting similarities and differences. Teach students to encourage one another to clarify and justify responses.

4. Randomly call on students to share during a unified class discussion after they have all rehearsed answers with their partners.

5. Invite any volunteers to contribute additional ideas and points of view to the discussion after calling on a reasonable number of students randomly.

6. Direct students to go back to notes and add any important information garnered during the partner and class discussions.

Strategy 11: Give One, Get One

Purpose: To foster independent reflection and peer interaction prior to a unified class discussion

How to Do It

1. Pose a thought-provoking question or a concrete task to the class.

2. Allow three to five minutes of quiet time for students to consider what they may already know about the topic and jot down a number of potential responses.

3. Ask students to place a check mark next to the two or three ideas that they perceive as their strongest and then draw a line after their final idea to separate their ideas from those that they will gather from classmates.

4. Give students a set amount of time (about eight to ten minutes) to get up from their seats and share ideas with classmates. After finding a partner, the two students exchange papers and first quietly read each other's ideas. They discuss the ideas briefly, then select one idea from their partner's list and add it to their own, making sure to accurately copy the idea alongside the partner's name.

5. When one exchange is completed, students move on to interact with a new partner.

6. At the end of the exchange period, facilitate a unified class discussion. Call on a volunteer to share one new idea acquired from a conversation partner. The student whose idea has just been reported then shares the next idea, gleaned from a different conversation partner.

Professional Development

For more information about these strategies, see the end of each chapter's Interleaf.

Objective

- Learn how to read nonfiction critically by analyzing an author's purpose, distinguishing between facts and opinions, identifying evidence, and evaluating credibility.

Prepare to Read

Build Background Knowledge   L2

Write the phrase "Don't believe everything you read" on the board. Ask students to brainstorm examples that illustrate the saying. Provide a few simple examples to get them started. (*tall tales, advertisements*)

Instruct

Reading Informational Texts   L2

Guided Instruction

- Tell students that they must actively evaluate the information in most of the nonfiction they read.

- Read the sample editorial on this page aloud. Tell students that an editorial usually expresses a person's opinion. Ask students to consider why the author wrote this editorial. (*The author expresses the opinion that the proposal to build the new shopping center should have been approved.*) Ask **How might this purpose affect what the editorial says?** (*The author may present information in the best possible light to prove his or her belief.*)

- Another important step in evaluating nonfiction is distinguishing between facts and opinions. Ask each student to write one fact and one opinion, on any subject, in their notebooks. Use the Idea Wave strategy (TE, p. 35) to get students to share their facts and opinion. If students have incorrectly categorized examples, help them to see why.

Reading Informational Texts

Reading a magazine, an Internet page, or a textbook is not the same as reading a novel. The purpose of reading nonfiction texts is to acquire new information. On page M18 you'll read about some 🔄 **Target Reading Skills** that you'll have a chance to practice as you read this textbook. Here we'll focus on a few skills that will help you read nonfiction with a more critical eye.

Analyze the Author's Purpose

Different types of materials are written with different purposes in mind. For example, a textbook is written to teach students information about a subject. The purpose of a technical manual is to teach someone how to use something, such as a computer. A newspaper editorial might be written to persuade the reader to accept a particular point of view. A writer's purpose influences how the material is presented. Sometimes an author states his or her purpose directly. More often, the purpose is only suggested, and you must use clues to identify the author's purpose.

Distinguish Between Facts and Opinions

It's important when reading informational texts to read actively and to distinguish between fact and opinion. A fact can be proven or disproven. An opinion cannot—it is someone's personal viewpoint or evaluation.

For example, the editorial pages in a newspaper offer opinions on topics that are currently in the news. You need to read newspaper editorials with an eye for bias and faulty logic. For example, the newspaper editorial at the right shows factual statements in blue and opinion statements in red. The underlined words are examples of highly charged words. They reveal bias on the part of the writer.

> More than 5,000 people voted last week in favor of building a new shopping center, but the opposition won out. The margin of victory is irrelevant. Those radical voters who opposed the center are obviously self-serving elitists who do not care about anyone but themselves.
>
> This month's unemployment figure for our area is 10 percent, which represents an increase of about 5 percent over the figure for this time last year. These figures mean unemployment is getting worse. But the people who voted against the mall probably do not care about creating new jobs.

- Tell students that identifying evidence is another way to read nonfiction critically. Ask students to look again at the facts highlighted in the sample editorial. **Does the evidence presented in these facts convince you that building a new shopping center is a good idea?** (*The evidence is incomplete—the author has not shown that the new shopping center would solve the unemployment problem.*)

- Tell students that analyzing an author's purpose, distinguishing between fact and opinions, and identifying evidence are all ways to evaluate the credibility of the author. Tell students to look at the checklist for evaluating Web sites. Ask students to think about Web sites they have visited. Do those Web sites pass the checklist's test? Why or why not?

Identify Evidence

Before you accept an author's conclusion, you need to make sure that the author has based the conclusion on enough evidence and on the right kind of evidence. An author may present a series of facts to support a claim, but the facts may not tell the whole story. For example, what evidence does the author of the newspaper editorial on the previous page provide to support his claim that the new shopping center would create more jobs? Is it possible that the shopping center might have put many small local businesses out of business, thus increasing unemployment rather than decreasing it?

Evaluate Credibility

Whenever you read informational texts, you need to assess the credibility of the author. This is especially true of sites you may visit on the Internet. All Internet sources are not equally reliable. Here are some questions to ask yourself when evaluating the credibility of a Web site.

- ☐ Is the Web site created by a respected organization, a discussion group, or an individual?
- ☐ Does the Web site creator include his or her name as well as credentials and the sources he or she used to write the material?
- ☐ Is the information on the site balanced or biased?
- ☐ Can you verify the information using two other sources?
- ☐ Is there a date telling when the Web site was created or last updated?

Reading and Writing Handbook **RW1**

Independent Practice

Ask students to bring in an editorial from the local newspaper, or distribute copies of an appropriate editorial. Ask students to critically assess their editorial by analyzing the author's purpose; underlining facts and circling opinions in the text of the editorial; summarizing the evidence presented in the editorial; and finally drawing a conclusion about the credibility of the editorial.

Monitor Progress

Pair students and have them share their editorial assessments. Ask them to explain the reasoning behind the conclusions they drew about the editorial's credibility. Circulate and offer assistance as needed.

Assess and Reteach

Assess Progress ▉L2
Collect students' papers and review their assessments.

Reteach ▉L1
If students are struggling, tell them to approach the task by asking themselves the following questions as they read a piece of nonfiction: **Why** did the author write this? **How** has the author made his or her points, using facts or opinions? **What** evidence has the author used to support the main idea? **Who** is the author, and what sources has he or she used?

Extend ▉L3
To extend this lesson, tell students to turn to the Table of Contents in the Student Edition and pick a chapter name that intrigues. Then, ask them to search the internet and find two Web sites about the chapter's topic. Finally, ask them to use the checklist on this page to evaluate each Web site and compare the two in terms of credibility.

Differentiated Instruction

For Advanced Readers ▉L3
Draw students' attention to the checklist under the heading "Evaluate Credibility." Ask students to create a similar checklist for analyzing an author's purpose, distinguishing between fact and opinion, and identifying evidence.

For Special Needs Students ▉L1
If special needs students are having trouble making the distinction between facts and opinions, partner them with more proficient students to do the *Distinguishing Fact and Opinion* lesson on the Social Studies Skill Tutor CD-ROM.

⊙ *Distinguishing Fact and Opinion,* **Social Studies Skill Tutor CD-ROM**

Objective

- Use a systematic approach to write narrative, persuasive, expository, and research essays.

Prepare to Read

Build Background Knowledge　L2

As a group, brainstorm all the ways that people use writing to communicate. Start them with these examples: labeling a folder, writing an email. Conduct an Idea Wave (TE, p. T35) and write students' responses on the board. Tell them that people often write to express ideas or information. Give them *Four Purposes for Writing* and tell them to keep it in their notebooks for future reference.

All in One Latin America Teaching Resources, *Four Purposes for Writing,* p. 6

Instruct

Narrative Essays　L2

Guided Instruction

- Tell students that narrative essays tell a story about their own experiences. Discuss the steps listed in the Student Edition.

- Choose an event in your own life (or invent one) such as visiting friends in another city. Write your topic on the board and model how to list details *(what the trip was like, what you did while you were there, what your friends are like.)* Cross out the least interesting details.

- Think aloud as your form your topic into a sentence that conveys the main idea of your essay.

- Tell students that you will go on to flesh out the details into a colorful story.

Independent Practice

- Tell students to write a narrative essay about a recent positive experience. Have student pairs brainstorm topics.

Writing for Social Studies

Writing is one of the most powerful communication tools you will ever use. You will use it to share your thoughts and ideas with others. Research shows that writing about what you read actually helps you learn new information and ideas. A systematic approach to writing—including prewriting, drafting, revising, and proofing—can help you write better, whether you're writing an essay or a research report.

Narrative Essays

Writing that tells a story about a personal experience

1 Select and Narrow Your Topic

A narrative is a story. In social studies, it might be a narrative essay about how an event affected you or your family.

2 Gather Details

Brainstorm a list of details you'd like to include in your narrative.

3 Write a First Draft

Start by writing a simple opening sentence that conveys the main idea of your essay. Continue by writing a colorful story that has interesting details. Write a conclusion that sums up the significance of the event or situation described in your essay.

4 Revise and Proofread

Check to make sure you have not begun too many sentences with the word *I.* Replace general words with more colorful ones.

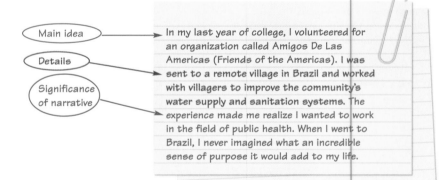

Main idea
Details
Significance of narrative

In my last year of college, I volunteered for an organization called Amigos De Las Americas (Friends of the Americas). I was sent to a remote village in Brazil and worked with villagers to improve the community's water supply and sanitation systems. The experience made me realize I wanted to work in the field of public health. When I went to Brazil, I never imagined what an incredible sense of purpose it would add to my life.

- Give students *Writing to Describe* to help them write their essays. After they have written the body of their essay, give them *Writing the Conclusion* to help them complete it.

All in One Latin America Teaching Resources, *Writing to Describe,* p. 8; *Writing the Conclusion,* p. 9

Monitor Progress

Have students share their drafts with their partners. Give them *Using the Revision Checklist* and ask them to review their partners' papers. Urge them to provide constructive criticism and suggestions for improvement.

All in One Latin America Teaching Resources, *Using the Revision Checklist,* p. 9

Persuasive Essays

Writing that supports an opinion or position

① Select and Narrow Your Topic
Choose a topic that provokes an argument and has at least two sides. Choose a side. Decide which argument will appeal most to your audience and persuade them to understand your point of view.

② Gather Evidence
Create a chart that states your position at the top and then lists the pros and cons for your position below, in two columns. Predict and address the strongest arguments against your stand.

③ Write a First Draft
Write a strong thesis statement that clearly states your position. Continue by presenting the strongest arguments in favor of your position and acknowledging and refuting opposing arguments.

④ Revise and Proofread
Check to make sure you have made a logical argument and that you have not oversimplified the argument.

Main Idea

Supporting (pro) argument

Opposing (con) argument

Transition words

> It is vital to vote in elections. When people vote, they tell public officials how to run the government. Not every proposal is carried out; however, politicians do their best to listen to what the majority of people want. Therefore, every vote is important.

Reading and Writing Handbook **RW3**

Persuasive Essays   L2

Guided Instruction
- Tell students that the purpose of writing a persuasive essay is to convince other people to believe your point of view. However, you must use solid, reliable evidence and arguments to make your points.
- Model the thought process by pointing out how the writer presents his or her argument in the paragraph on this page.

Independent Practice
- Tell students to write a persuasive essay about a topic that is important to them. Have students form pairs. One student in each pair should state his or her position. The other student then shares opposing arguments, which the first student should refute in his or her essay. Then the pairs switch roles.
- Give students *Writing to Persuade* to help them write their essays.

  All in One **Latin America Teaching Resources,** *Writing to Persuade,* p. 11

Monitor Progress
If students are having trouble structuring their paragraphs, give them *Structuring Paragraphs* and *Creating Paragraph Outlines* to provide a framework.

  All in One **Latin America Teaching Resources,** *Structuring Paragraphs,* p. 12; *Creating Paragraph Outlines,* p. 127

Differentiated Instruction

For Less Proficient Readers   L1

Tell students to use looping to help them focus on a topic. Have them follow these steps: Write freely on your topic for about five minutes. Read what you have written and circle the most important idea. Write for five minutes on the circled idea. Repeat the process until you isolate a topic narrow enough to cover well in a short essay.

Expository Essays ▣L2

Guided Instruction
- Read the steps for writing expository essays with students.
- Tell students that the graphic organizer example given on the Student Edition page is for a cause and effect expository essay. They might use a Venn diagram for a compare and contrast essay and a flow-chart for a problem and solution essay.
- Model how to create a topic sentence from the information in the cause and effect graphic organizer. *(Sample topic sentence: In Mexico, several factors are causing rural families to move from the countryside to the city.)*
- Create a brief outline showing how you will organize the paragraphs in your essay.

Independent Practice
Tell students to write an expository essay based on a recent current event. Have them brainstorm ideas with a partner, then choose which type of essay best suits their topic (cause and effect, compare and contrast, or problem and solution.) Give them *Writing to Inform and Explain* and *Gathering Details* to help them start drafting their essays.

> **Latin America Teaching Resources,** *Writing to Inform and Explain,* p. 13; *Gathering Detail,* p. 14

Monitor Progress
If students are struggling with their essays, give them *Writing a Cause-and-Effect Essay* or *Writing a Problem-and-Solution Essay.*

> **Latin America Teaching Resources,** *Writing a Cause-and-Effect Essay,* p. 15; *Writing a Problem-and-Solution Essay,* p. 16

Research Papers ▣L2

Guided Instruction
Go over the steps for writing a research paper carefully. Ask students to share questions about the process, using the Idea Wave structured engagement strategy (p. T35). Answer any questions they might have.

Expository Essays
Writing that explains a process, compares and contrasts, explains causes and effects, or explores solutions to a problem

❶ Identify and Narrow Your Topic
Expository writing is writing that explains something in detail. It might explain the similarities and differences between two or more subjects (compare and contrast). It might explain how one event causes another (cause and effect). Or it might explain a problem and describe a solution.

❷ Gather Evidence
Create a graphic organizer that identifies details to include in your essay.

Cause 1	Cause 2	Cause 3
Most people in the Mexican countryside work on farms.	The population in Mexico is growing at one of the highest rates in the world.	There is not enough farm work for so many people.

Effect
As a result, many rural families are moving from the countryside to live in Mexico City.

❸ Write Your First Draft
Write a topic sentence and then organize the essay around your similarities and differences, causes and effects, or problem and solutions. Be sure to include convincing details, facts, and examples.

❹ Revise and Proofread

Research Papers
Writing that presents research about a topic

❶ Narrow Your Topic
Choose a topic you're interested in and make sure that it is not too broad. For example, instead of writing a report on Panama, write about the construction of the Panama Canal.

❷ Acquire Information
Locate several sources of information about the topic from the library or the Internet. For each resource, create a source index card like the one at the right. Then take notes using an index card for each detail or subtopic. On the card, note which source the information was taken from. Use quotation marks when you copy the exact words from a source.

> Source #1
> McCullough, David. *The Path Between the Seas: The Creation of the Panama Canal, 1870-1914.* N.Y., Simon and Schuster, 1977.

❸ Make an Outline
Use an outline to decide how to organize your report. Sort your index cards into the same order.

> Outline
> I. Introduction
> II. Why the canal was built
> III. How the canal was built
>   A. Physical challenges
>   B. Medical challenges
> IV. Conclusion

RW4 Reading and Writing Handbook

Differentiated Instruction

For Gifted and Talented ▣L3
Tell students that a verb is in active voice when the subject performs the action named by the verb. A verb is in passive voice when the subject undergoes the action named by the verb.

Give these examples:

Passive voice: The house is being painted by my sister and me.

Active voice: My sister and I are painting the house.

Tell students that using the active voice whenever possible will make their writing more dynamic and concise.

Introduction

Building the Panama Canal

Ever since Christopher Columbus first explored the Isthmus of Panama, the Spanish had been looking for a water route through it. They wanted to be able to sail west from Spain to Asia without sailing around South America. However, it was not until 1914 that the dream became a reality.

Conclusion

It took eight years and more than 70,000 workers to build the Panama Canal. It remains one of the greatest engineering feats of modern times.

4 Write a First Draft

Write an introduction, a body, and a conclusion. Leave plenty of space between lines so you can go back and add details that you may have left out.

5 Revise and Proofread

Be sure to include transition words between sentences and paragraphs. Here are some examples:

To show a contrast—*however, although, despite.*

To point out a reason—*since, because, if.*

To signal a conclusion—*therefore, consequently, so, then.*

Evaluating Your Writing

Use this table to help you evaluate your writing.

	Excellent	Good	Acceptable	Unacceptable
Purpose	Achieves purpose—to inform, persuade, or provide historical interpretation—very well	Informs, persuades, or provides historical interpretation reasonably well	Reader cannot easily tell if the purpose is to inform, persuade, or provide historical interpretation	Purpose is not clear
Organization	Develops ideas in a very clear and logical way	Presents ideas in a reasonably well-organized way	Reader has difficulty following the organization	Lacks organization
Elaboration	Explains all ideas with facts and details	Explains most ideas with facts and details	Includes some supporting facts and details	Lacks supporting details
Use of Language	Uses excellent vocabulary and sentence structure with no errors in spelling, grammar, or punctuation	Uses good vocabulary and sentence structure with very few errors in spelling, grammar, or punctuation	Includes some errors in grammar, punctuation, and spelling	Includes many errors in grammar, punctuation, and spelling

Reading and Writing Handbook **RW5**

Independent Practice

- Have students consider topics for a research paper. Give them *Choosing a Topic* to help them learn how to evaluate potential topics.

  All in One **Latin America Teaching Resources,** *Choosing a Topic,* p. 17

- Once students have selected a topic, tell them they will need facts to support their ideas. Give them *Using the Library, Summarizing and Taking Notes,* and *Preparing Note Cards* to help them start their research.

  All in One **Latin America Teaching Resources,** *Using the Library,* p.18; *Summarizing and Taking Notes,* p. 19; *Preparing Note Cards,* p. 20

Monitor Progress

Give students *Writing an Introduction* and *Writing the Body of an Essay* to help them write their essays.

All in One **Teaching Resources,** *Writing an Introduction,* p. 21; *Writing the Body of an Essay,* p. 22

Assess and Reteach

Assess Progress L2

Ask student to pick the best essay they have written so far and evaluate it using the rubric on this page.

Reteach L1

Collect students' essays and self-evaluations. Meet with students to go over good points and areas for improvement. Revisit each type of essay as needed with the whole class.

Extend L3

To extend this lesson, tell students there are many other different types of writing. Have them complete *Writing for Assessment* and *Writing a Letter* to learn about two more types of writing.

All in One **Teaching Resources,** *Writing for Assessment,* p. 23; *Writing a Letter,* p. 24

MapMaster Skills Handbook
Step-by-Step Instruction

Objective
- Identify and define the five themes of geography.

Prepare to Read

Build Background Knowledge `L2`

Assign students to small groups and give them five minutes to write a definition of geography. Then write the five themes of geography on the board. Remind students that a theme is an important underlying idea. As a class, decide which parts of their definitions go under each of the geography themes. For example, "landforms" would fall under the theme of place.

Instruct

Five Themes of Geography `L2`

Guided Instruction
- Divide the text using the headings and ask students to read the pages using the Structured Silent Reading technique (TE, p. T34). Clarify the meanings of any unfamiliar words.

- Ask students to give the relative locations of their home.

- Mention the popularity of different kinds of ethnic foods in the United States. Ask **What theme of geography are these foods a good example of?** *(movement)* Encourage students to name other examples of the movement of cultural traditions from one region to another.

- Discuss the climate in your area. Ask **How does the environment affect how we live?** *(affects dress, travel, sports and other recreational activities, the way homes are built)*

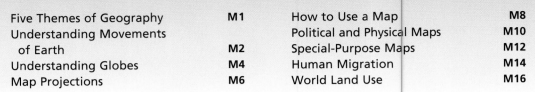

CONTENTS

Five Themes of Geography M1
Understanding Movements of Earth M2
Understanding Globes M4
Map Projections M6
How to Use a Map M8
Political and Physical Maps M10
Special-Purpose Maps M12
Human Migration M14
World Land Use M16

Go Online **PHSchool.com** Use Web Code **lap-0000** for all of the maps in this handbook.

Five Themes of Geography

Studying the geography of the entire world is a huge task. You can make that task easier by using the five themes of geography: location, regions, place, movement, and human-environment interaction. The themes are tools you can use to organize information and to answer the where, why, and how of geography.

LOCATION

1 Location answers the question, "Where is it?" You can think of the location of a continent or a country as its address. You might give an absolute location such as 22 South Lake Street or 40° N and 80° W. You might also use a relative address, telling where one place is by referring to another place. *Between school and the mall* and *eight miles east of Pleasant City* are examples of relative locations.

▲ **Location**
This museum in England has a line running through it. The line marks its location at 0° longitude.

MapMaster Skills Handbook

Differentiated Instruction

For English Language Learners `L1`

Students may find it difficult to pronounce some of the multisyllable words in this section such as *relative, environment, interaction, government, signature,* and *communicate.* Show students how to break down these words into smaller parts to help them sound out the pronunciation.

For Advanced Readers `L3`

Have students find articles in newspapers or magazines that illustrate the five themes of geography. Have students underline the relevant sections and identify the theme or themes they illustrate. Suggest that students create a bulletin board to share their examples with the class.

REGIONS

2 Regions are areas that share at least one common feature. Geographers divide the world into many types of regions. For example, countries, states, and cities are political regions. The people in any one of these places live under the same government. Other features, such as climate and culture, can be used to define regions. Therefore the same place can be found in more than one region. For example, the state of Hawaii is in the political region of the United States. Because it has a tropical climate, Hawaii is also part of a tropical climate region.

MOVEMENT

4 Movement answers the question, "How do people, goods, and ideas move from place to place?" Remember that what happens in one place often affects what happens in another. Use the theme of movement to help you trace the spread of goods, people, and ideas from one location to another.

PLACE

3 Place identifies the natural and human features that make one place different from every other place. You can identify a specific place by its landforms, climate, plants, animals, people, language, or culture. You might even think of place as a geographic signature. Use the signature to help you understand the natural and human features that make one place different from every other place.

INTERACTION

5 Human-environment interaction focuses on the relationship between people and the environment. As people live in an area, they often begin to make changes to it, usually to make their lives easier. For example, they might build a dam to control flooding during rainy seasons. Also, the environment can affect how people live, work, dress, travel, and communicate.

◀ **Interaction**
These Congolese women interact with their environment by gathering wood for cooking.

PRACTICE YOUR GEOGRAPHY SKILLS

1 Describe your town or city, using each of the five themes of geography.

2 Name at least one thing that comes into your town or city and one that goes out. How is each moved? Where does it come from? Where does it go?

MapMaster Skills Handbook **M1**

Independent Practice

Partner students and have them complete *The Five Themes of Geography*.

All in One **Teaching Resources,** *The Five Themes of Geography,* p. 27

Monitor Progress

As students complete the worksheet, circulate to make sure that individuals comprehend the material. Provide assistance as needed.

Assess and Reteach

Assess Progress   L2

Have students complete the questions under Practice Your Geography Skills.

Reteach   L1

Help students create a concept web that identifies the five themes of geography. Start filling in blank *Transparency B17: Concept Web* to model how to identify information to clarify each theme. For example, under Regions students might write "share common feature such as government, climate, culture." Encourage students to refer to their webs to review the themes.

Latin America Transparencies, *Transparency B17: Concept Web*

Extend   L3

To extend the lesson, ask students to find out about any plans for new buildings, highways, or other types of construction in your area. Ask students to predict how these changes will affect the community's environment.

Answers

PRACTICE YOUR GEOGRAPHY SKILLS

1. Answers should include an example of each of the five themes that relates to your community.

2. Students' answers should provide examples of goods, ideas, or things that move into and out of your community.

MapMaster Skills Handbook   **M1**

Objective

- Explain how the movements of the Earth cause night and day, as well as the seasons.

Prepare to Read

Build Background Knowledge

Remind students that while the Earth revolves around the sun, it also rotates on its own axis. Review the meanings of "revolve" and "rotate" in this context. Ask students to brainstorm ways that the Earth's revolving and rotating might affect their lives. Conduct an Idea Wave (TE, p. T35) to generate a list of ideas.

Instruct

Understanding Movements of Earth L2

Guided Instruction

- Read the text as a class using the Oral Cloze technique (TE, p. T33). Explain that the illustration on pages M2 and M3 show the information in the text visually. Clarify the meanings of any unfamiliar words.

- Ask students **How does Earth rotating on its axis cause day and night?** *(It is daytime on the side of Earth facing the sun, while the side facing away from the sun is dark.)*

- Ask **How does the tilt of Earth affect the seasons?** *(The farther away a part of Earth is from the sun's rays, the colder it is.)*

Independent Practice

Partner students and have them complete *Understanding the Movements of the Earth.*

> **All in One Latin America Teaching Resources,** *Understanding Movements of the Earth,* p. 28

Understanding Movements of Earth

The planet Earth is part of our solar system. Earth revolves around the sun in a nearly circular path called an orbit. A revolution, or one complete orbit around the sun, takes 365 ¼ days, or one year. As Earth orbits the sun, it also spins on its axis, an invisible line through the center of Earth from the North Pole to the South Pole. This movement is called a rotation.

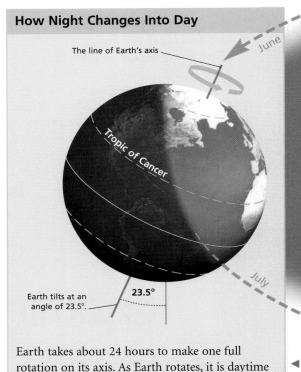

How Night Changes Into Day

The line of Earth's axis

Tropic of Cancer

Earth tilts at an angle of 23.5°.   23.5°

Earth takes about 24 hours to make one full rotation on its axis. As Earth rotates, it is daytime on the side facing the sun. It is night on the side away from the sun.

▼ **Spring begins**
On March 20 or 21, the sun is directly overhead at the Equator. The Northern and Southern Hemispheres receive almost equal hours of sunlight and darkness.

Equator

June May April

July August September

◄ **Summer begins**
On June 21 or 22, the sun is directly overhead at the Tropic of Cancer. The Northern Hemisphere receives the greatest number of sunlight hours.

M2 MapMaster Skills Handbook

Background: Links Across Place

Sunrise and Sunset Most people have heard the saying "The sun rises in the east and sets in the west." However, the sun does not ever actually change position. Every day, Earth rotates on its axis so that as each region faces the sun, it experiences day. The rotation continues so that as a region turns away from the sun, it experiences night. The sun stays in the same place. A person viewing sunrise or sunset is really seeing Earth's slow turn on its axis, not the sun rising or setting.

The Seasons

Earth's axis is tilted at an angle. Because of this tilt, sunlight strikes different parts of Earth at different times in the year, creating seasons. The illustration below shows how the seasons are created in the Northern Hemisphere. In the Southern Hemisphere, the seasons are reversed.

Earth orbits the sun at 66,600 miles per hour (107,244 kilometers per hour).

March
February
January

Tropic of Capricorn

December
November
October

Diagram not to scale

Arctic Circle
Tropic of Cancer
Equator
Tropic of Capricorn

▲ **Winter begins**
Around December 21, the sun is directly overhead at the Tropic of Capricorn in the Southern Hemisphere. The Northern Hemisphere is tilted away from the sun.

◄ **Autumn begins**
On September 22 or 23, the sun is directly overhead at the Equator. Again, the hemispheres receive almost equal hours of sunlight and darkness.

MapMaster Skills Handbook **M3**

PRACTICE YOUR GEOGRAPHY SKILLS

1. What causes the seasons in the Northern Hemisphere to be the opposite of those in the Southern Hemisphere?

2. During which two days of the year do the Northern Hemisphere and Southern Hemisphere have equal hours of daylight and darkness?

Monitor Progress

As students do the worksheet, circulate to make sure individuals comprehend the key concepts. Provide assistance as needed.

Assess and Reteach

Assess Progress L2
Have students complete the Practice Your Geography Skills questions.

Reteach L1
If students are having trouble understanding these concepts, create a model to demonstrate Earth's revolution. Use a foam ball to represent Earth. Insert a pencil through the ball to represent Earth's axis, labeling the ends "North Pole" and "South Pole." Draw the Equator perpendicular to the axis. Place a light source in the center of a table to represent the sun. Then tilt the ball at a slight angle and move it around the light to mimic Earth's revolution. Have students notice the point at which each pole is nearest the sun and identify what season it would be in each hemisphere.

Extend L3
To extend the lesson, ask students to consider Earth's relationship to its satellite, the Moon. Ask them to research on the Internet to answer these questions: "Does the Moon rotate like Earth? Does the Moon revolve around Earth as Earth revolves around the sun?" To help students start their research, give them *Doing Searches on the Internet*.

 Latin America Teaching Resources, *Doing Searches on the Internet,* p. 29

Differentiated Instruction

For Special Needs Students L1

Have students act out the revolution of Earth around the sun. Assign one student the role of "the sun," and other students the roles of Earth at four different times of the year. Have them walk through a year's cycle. Show *Color Transparency LA 1: The Earth's Revolution and the* *Seasons* to guide them. Ask them to simulate the tilt of Earth's axis as shown in the illustrations on pp. M2–M3.

📖 **Latin America Transparencies,** *Color Transparency LA 1: The Earth's Revolution and the Seasons*

Answers

PRACTICE YOUR GEOGRAPHY SKILLS

1. The seasons are reversed in the Northern Hemisphere and Southern Hemisphere because Earth is tilted. When one hemisphere is tilted towards the sun, the other hemisphere is tilted away from the sun.

2. September 22–23 and March 20–21

Objectives

- Understand how a globe is marked with a grid to measure features on Earth.

- Learn how to use longitude and latitude to locate a place.

Prepare to Read

Build Background Knowledge L2

Tell students that in this lesson, they will learn how to use globes. Ask students what it would be like to see Earth from a spacecraft. Discuss the shape that students would see. Then discuss why a globe is a more accurate rendering of Earth than a flat map. Point out that a globe is like a model car in that it is a small version of something larger. If a globe is available, have students examine it.

Instruct

Understanding Globes L2

Guided Instruction

- Read the text as a class using the Oral Cloze technique (TE, p. T33). Have students study the illustrations carefully.

- Ask **What line of latitude divides the Northern and Southern Hemispheres?** *(the Equator)* **At what degrees latitude is this line?** *(0º)*

- Ask **Where do the lines of longitude come together?** *(at the North and South poles)* **What is the name of the meridian at 0 degrees?** *(Prime Meridian)*

- Have students look at the global grid on *Color Transparency LA 3: The Global Grid.* Ask **What is the global grid?** *(a pattern of lines formed where the parallels of latitude and meridians of longitude cross)* **What continent in the Eastern Hemisphere does the 100E° meridian pass through?** *(Asia)*

  📖 **Latin America Transparencies,** *Color Transparency LA 3: The Global Grid.*

Understanding Globes

A globe is a scale model of Earth. It shows the actual shapes, sizes, and locations of all Earth's landmasses and bodies of water. Features on the surface of Earth are drawn to scale on a globe. This means that a small unit of measure on the globe stands for a large unit of measure on Earth.

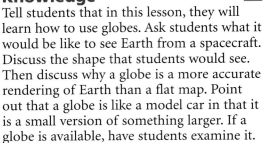

Northern Hemisphere
Equator (0° latitude)
Southern Hemisphere

Parallels of Latitude

Geographers divide the globe along imaginary horizontal lines called parallels of latitude. One of these latitude lines is the Equator, located halfway between the North and South Poles. Parallels of latitude are measured in degrees (°). One degree of latitude represents a distance of about 69 miles (111 kilometers).

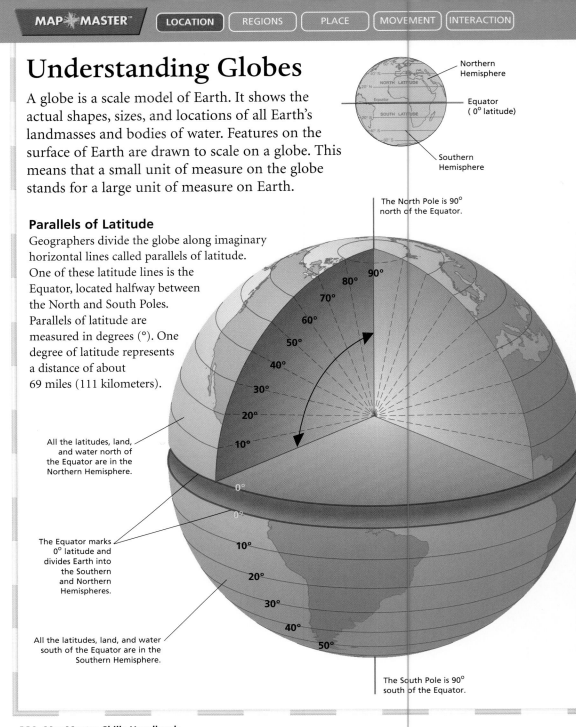

The North Pole is 90° north of the Equator.

All the latitudes, land, and water north of the Equator are in the Northern Hemisphere.

The Equator marks 0° latitude and divides Earth into the Southern and Northern Hemispheres.

All the latitudes, land, and water south of the Equator are in the Southern Hemisphere.

The South Pole is 90° south of the Equator.

M4 MapMaster Skills Handbook

Background: Links Across Time

The First Globes Historians believe that the first globe may have been made in the second century B.C. by a Greek geographer known as Crates of Mallus. The mathematician Ptolemy represented Earth as a globe in his written works in the second century A.D. In late 1492 Martin Behaim made a terrestrial globe that although inaccurate by today's knowledge, reflected the best geographical knowledge of the time. This globe still exists and is on display in Behaim's hometown of Nuremberg, Germany.

Meridians of Longitude

Geographers also divide the globe along imaginary vertical lines called meridians of longitude, which are measured in degrees (°). The longitude line called the Prime Meridian runs from pole to pole through Greenwich, England. All meridians of longitude come together at the North and South Poles.

PRACTICE YOUR GEOGRAPHY SKILLS

1 Which continents lie completely in the Northern Hemisphere? In the Western Hemisphere?

2 Is there land or water at 20° S latitude and the Prime Meridian? At the Equator and 60° W longitude?

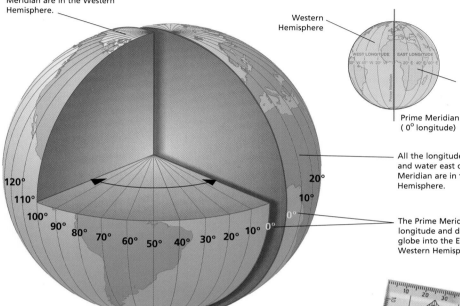

All the longitudes, land, and water west of the Prime Meridian are in the Western Hemisphere.

Western Hemisphere

Eastern Hemisphere

Prime Meridian (0° longitude)

All the longitudes, land, and water east of the Prime Meridian are in the Eastern Hemisphere.

The Prime Meridian marks 0° longitude and divides the globe into the Eastern and Western Hemispheres.

120° 110° 100° 90° 80° 70° 60° 50° 40° 30° 20° 10° 0°

20° 10° 0°

The Global Grid

Together, the pattern of parallels of latitude and meridians of longitude is called the global grid. Using the lines of latitude and longitude, you can locate any place on Earth. For example, the location of 30° north latitude and 90° west longitude is usually written as 30° N, 90° W. Only one place on Earth has these coordinates—the city of New Orleans, in the state of Louisiana.

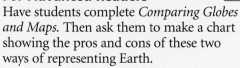

▲ **Compass**
Wherever you are on Earth, a compass can be used to show direction.

MapMaster Skills Handbook **M5**

Independent Practice

Have students work in pairs to complete *Understanding Hemispheres* and *Understanding Latitude and Longitude.*

All in One Latin America Teaching Resources, *Understanding Hemispheres,* p. 30; *Understanding Latitude and Longitude,* p. 31

Monitor Progress

As students do the worksheets, circulate to make sure pairs understand the key concepts. Show *Color Transparency LA 2: The Hemispheres* to help students.

Latin America Transparencies, *Color Transparency LA 2: The Hemispheres*

Assess and Reteach

Assess Progress

Have students answer the questions under Practice Your Geography Skills.

Reteach

Use the DK Atlas activity *Understanding Latitude and Longitude* to review these skills with students. Have students complete the activity in pairs.

All in One Latin America Teaching Resources, *DK Compact Atlas of the World Activity: Understanding Latitude and Longitude,* p. 32

Extend

To extend the lesson, have students complete *Using Latitude and Longitude.* Then have students use the map and with a partner, play a game of Can You Find …? Each partner takes a turn giving the coordinates for a place on the map and the other partner must name the place.

All in One Latin America Teaching Resources, *Using Latitude and Longitude,* p. 33

Differentiated Instruction

For Less Proficient Readers L1

For students having difficulty understanding the concept of a global grid, give them *Understanding Grids* and help them complete it. Then follow up with *Using a Grid.*

All in One Latin America Teaching Resources, *Understanding Grids,* p. 34; *Using a Grid,* p. 35

For Advanced Readers L3

Have students complete *Comparing Globes and Maps.* Then ask them to make a chart showing the pros and cons of these two ways of representing Earth.

All in One Latin America Teaching Resources, *Comparing Globes and Maps,* p. 36

Answers

PRACTICE YOUR GEOGRAPHY SKILLS

1. Northern Hemisphere: North America; Europe; Western Hemisphere: North America; South America

2. water; land

Objectives

- Compare maps of different projections.
- Describe distortions in map projections.

Prepare to Read

Build Background Knowledge **L1**

In this lesson, students will learn how cartographers depict Earth on a two-dimensional map. Remind students that if they were traveling in a spaceship, they would see Earth as a globe. Ask if they could ever see the entire Earth at one time from space. Help students recognize that a flat map is the only way to see all of Earth at one time.

Instruct

Map Projections **L2**

Guided Instruction

- Read the text as a class using the Choral Reading technique (TE, p. T34). Direct students to look at the relevant maps after you read each section together. Follow up by having students do a second silent reading.

- Help students locate Greenland on the Mercator and Robinson maps. Ask **What difference do you notice in the way Greenland is shown?** *(It appears much larger on the Mercator Map.)* **How would you explain this?** *(The Mercator is a same-shape map and the shapes toward the poles are enlarged.)*

- Ask **Where does the distortion usually occur on an equal-shape map?** *(at the edges of the map)*

- Have students compare Antarctica on the three projections. *(It is largest and most distorted on the Mercator map; smallest on the equal-area map; covers the entire bottom edge of the Robinson map.)*

Map Projections

Maps are drawings that show regions on flat surfaces. Maps are easier to use and carry than globes, but they cannot show the correct size and shape of every feature on Earth's curved surface. They must shrink some places and stretch others. To make up for this distortion, mapmakers use different map projections. No one projection can accurately show the correct area, shape, distance, and direction for all of Earth's surface. Mapmakers use the projection that has the least distortion for the information they are presenting.

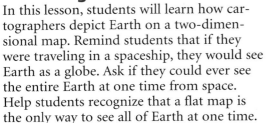

▲ **Global gores**
Flattening a globe creates a string of shapes called gores.

Same-Shape Maps

Map projections that accurately show the shapes of landmasses are called same-shape maps. However, these projections often greatly distort, or make less accurate, the size of landmasses as well as the distance between them. In the projection below, the northern and southern areas of the globe appear more stretched than the areas near the Equator.

To turn Earth into a same-shape map, mapmakers must stretch the gores into rectangles.

Equator

Stretching the gores makes parts of Earth larger. This enlargement becomes greater toward the North and South Poles.

Equator

Mercator projection ▶
One of the most common same-shape maps is the Mercator projection, named for the mapmaker who invented it. The Mercator projection accurately shows shape and direction, but it distorts distance and size. Because the projection shows true directions, ships' navigators use it to chart a straight-line course between two ports.

M6 MapMaster Skills Handbook

Differentiated Instruction

For Special Needs Students **L1**

If students have difficulty understanding why distortion occurs, draw a simple picture on an orange. Then have students try to peel the orange in one piece. Challenge students to place the peel flat on a piece of paper without any tears and spaces. Talk about what happens to the drawing. Explain that mapmakers face this same challenge when drawing Earth on a flat paper.

For Gifted and Talented **L3**

Have students complete *Great Circles and Straight Lines*. Then ask them to use their completed page and a globe to explain the concept of great circles to the class.

All in One Latin America Teaching Resources, *Great Circles and Straight Lines,* p. 38

Equal-Area Maps

Map projections that show the correct size of landmasses are called equal-area maps. In order to show the correct size of landmasses, these maps usually distort shapes. The distortion is usually greater at the edges of the map and less at the center.

PRACTICE YOUR GEOGRAPHY SKILLS

1 What feature is distorted on an equal-area map?

2 Would you use a Mercator projection to find the exact distance between two locations? Tell why or why not.

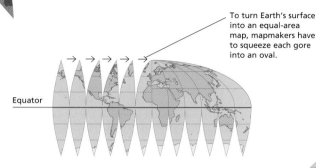

To turn Earth's surface into an equal-area map, mapmakers have to squeeze each gore into an oval.

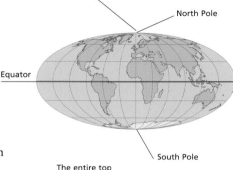

The tips of all the gores are then joined together. The points at which they join form the North and South Poles. The line of the Equator stays the same.

North Pole

Equator

South Pole

Robinson Maps

Many of the maps in this book use the Robinson projection, which is a compromise between the Mercator and equal-area projections. The Robinson projection gives a useful overall picture of the world. It keeps the size and shape relationships of most continents and oceans, but distorts the size of the polar regions.

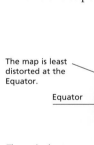

The entire top edge of the map is the North Pole.

The map is least distorted at the Equator.

Equator

The entire bottom edge of the map is the South Pole.

MapMaster Skills Handbook **M7**

Independent Practice

Have students work with partners to complete *Understanding Projection*.

All in One Latin America Teaching Resources, *Understanding Projection,* p. 37

Monitor Progress

As students do the worksheet, circulate to make sure individuals comprehend the key concepts. Provide assistance as needed.

Assess and Reteach

Assess Progress   L2

Have students complete the Practice Your Geography Skills questions.

Reteach   L1

Use *Maps with Accurate Shapes: Conformal Maps* and *Maps with Accurate Areas: Equal-Area Maps* to help students go over the information in the lesson. Model thinking for each question and partner students to complete each page together. Circulate to provide explanations and help as students work.

All in One Latin America Teaching Resources, *Maps with Accurate Shapes: Conformal Maps,* p. 39; *Maps with Accurate Areas: Equal-Area Maps,* p. 40

Extend   L3

To extend the lesson, ask students to complete *Maps with Accurate Direction: Azimuthal Maps.* Then have students write a sentence or two describing the different projections they have learned about.

All in One Latin America Teaching Resources, *Maps with Accurate Directions: Azimuthal Maps,* p. 41

Background: Biography

Gerardus Mercator The Mercator projection takes its name from a Flemish geographer, Gerhard Kremer (1512–1594). Kremer, who used the Latin form of his name, Gerardus Mercator, wrote books on ancient geography and cartography. He made his first world map in 1538. In 1554 he made a map of Europe. In 1568, the first map using the Mercator projection bearing his name appeared. Mercator also began an atlas of his maps, which was finished by his son and published in 1594.

Answers

PRACTICE YOUR GEOGRAPHY SKILLS

1. shapes
2. No; the Mercator projection distorts distances.

Objective

- Identify and use the parts of a map.

Prepare to Read

Build Background Knowledge　L1

In this lesson, students will learn about the practical aspects of maps. Ask students to name reasons that they might use a map; for example, to find directions, boundaries, distances. Conduct an Idea Wave (TE, p. T35) to generate a list of ideas. List the ideas on the board.

Instruct

How to Use a Map　L2

Guided Instruction

- Divide the text and captions in the lesson using the headings and ask students to read the pages using the Structured Silent Reading strategy (TE, p. T34). Remind students to use the illustrations to acquire additional understanding. Refer to the list on the board, then ask students which map part (key, compass rose, scale, symbol, title) would be helpful in using a map for a specific purpose.

- Ask **What is the purpose of a compass rose?** (to show directions)

- Talk about how the three maps show different amounts of Earth's surface. Ask **Which map shows the largest area?** (Western Europe) **Which map shows the smallest area?** (Central London)

- Ask **What are some symbols that you might find on a map key?** (border, national capital, city, airport, park, point of interest)

Independent Practice

Partner students and have them complete *Using the Map Key* and *Using the Compass Rose*.

All in One Latin America Teaching Resources, *Using the Map Key,* p. 42; *Using the Compass Rose,* p. 43

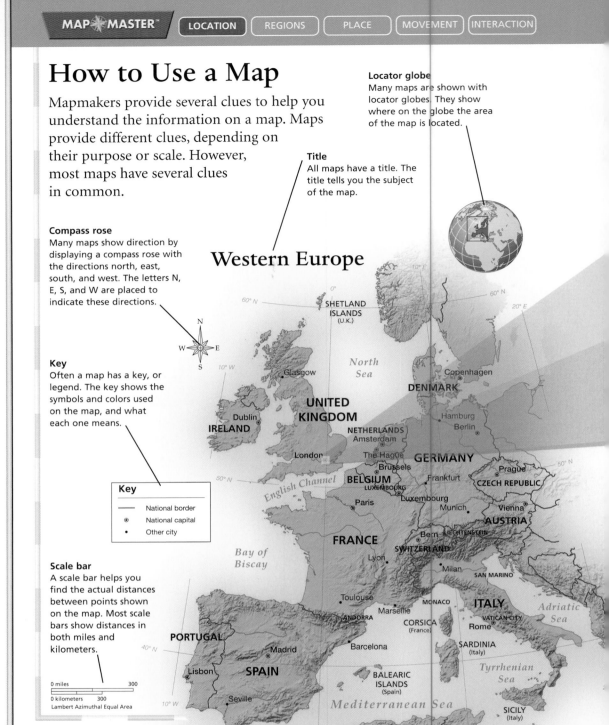

MAP MASTER™　LOCATION　REGIONS　PLACE　MOVEMENT　INTERACTION

How to Use a Map

Mapmakers provide several clues to help you understand the information on a map. Maps provide different clues, depending on their purpose or scale. However, most maps have several clues in common.

Locator globe
Many maps are shown with locator globes. They show where on the globe the area of the map is located.

Title
All maps have a title. The title tells you the subject of the map.

Compass rose
Many maps show direction by displaying a compass rose with the directions north, east, south, and west. The letters N, E, S, and W are placed to indicate these directions.

Key
Often a map has a key, or legend. The key shows the symbols and colors used on the map, and what each one means.

Key
— National border
⊛ National capital
• Other city

Scale bar
A scale bar helps you find the actual distances between points shown on the map. Most scale bars show distances in both miles and kilometers.

Western Europe

0 miles 300
0 kilometers 300
Lambert Azimuthal Equal Area

M8 MapMaster Skills Handbook

Differentiated Instruction

For Less Proficient Readers　L2

If students have difficulty recalling the purposes of different parts of a map, have them make a table using each map part as a heading. Under each heading, help students list the important function or functions of that map part. Suggest that students refer to their table when they are working with maps.

For English Language Learners　L1

Some of the words in the lesson, such as *symbol* and *scale,* may be unfamiliar to students acquiring English. Have students identify difficult words, look them up in the dictionary, and write sentences explaining what the terms mean.

Maps of Different Scales

Maps are drawn to different scales, depending on their purpose. Here are three maps drawn to very different scales. Keep in mind that maps showing large areas have smaller scales. Maps showing small areas have larger scales.

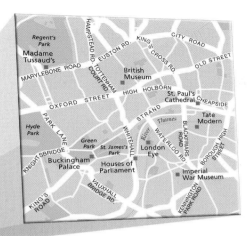

▲ **Central London**
Find the gray square on the map of Greater London. This square represents the area shown on the map above. This map moves you closer into the center of London. Like the zoom on a computer or a camera, this map shows a smaller area but in greater detail. It has the largest scale (1 inch represents about 0.9 mile). You can use this map to explore downtown London.

Key

■ Point of interest

   Park

0 miles   0.5   1

0 kilometers   1

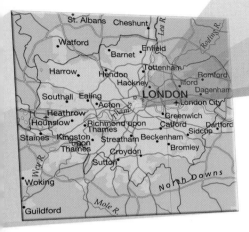

▲ **Greater London**
Find the gray square on the main map of Western Europe (left). This square represents the area shown on the map above. It shows London's boundaries, the general shape of the city, and the features around the city. This map can help you find your way from the airport to the center of town.

Key

▢ Built-up area   ✈ Airport

── City or county border

⊙ National capital

• Town or neighborhood

0 miles   10   20

0 kilometers   20

Lambert Conformal Conic

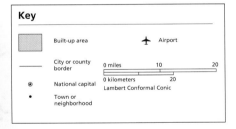

PRACTICE YOUR GEOGRAPHY SKILLS

1 What part of a map explains the colors used on the map?

2 How does the scale bar change depending on the scale of the map?

3 Which map would be best for finding the location of the British Museum? Explain why.

MapMaster Skills Handbook **M9**

Assess and Reteach

Assess Progress   L2
Have students complete the questions under Practice Your Geography Skills.

Reteach
Some DK Atlas Activities will be helpful in reteaching the lesson. Give students more practice using these concepts by doing the activities for *Using the Map Key; Using the Compass Rose;* and *Using the Map Scale.*

All in One Latin America Teaching Resources, *DK Compact Atlas of the World Activity: Using the Map Key,* p. 44; *DK Compact Atlas of the World Activity: Using the Compass Rose,* p. 45; *DK Compact Atlas of the World Activity: Using the Map Scale,* p. 46

Extend   L3
To extend the lesson, have students complete *Comparing Maps of Different Scale* and *Maps with Accurate Distances: Equidistant Maps.*

All in One Latin America Teaching Resources, *Comparing Maps of Different Scale,* p. 47; *Maps with Accurate Distances: Equidistant Maps,* p. 48

Answers
PRACTICE YOUR GEOGRAPHY SKILLS

1. key

2. Maps showing large areas have smaller scales. Maps showing small areas have larger scales.

3. the map of Central London; it shows the streets in more detail and includes the British Museum as a point of interest

Objectives

- Understand and use political maps.
- Understand and use physical maps.

Prepare to Read

Build Background Knowledge L1

Tell students that they will learn about political maps and physical maps in this lesson. Explain that a political map is one that shows the boundaries and cities of an area as established by its people. Physical maps show information about the physical features of the area. These physical features would exist whether people lived in a place or not.

Instruct

Political Maps L2
Physical Maps L2

Guided Instruction

- Read the text as a class using the Choral Reading technique (TE, p. T34) and ask students to study the map.

- Ask students to identify what river forms the boundary between Zimbabwe and South Africa. (*Limpopo River*). Then ask them to name at least two capitals on the Mediterranean Sea. (*Tripoli, Algiers, Tunis*)

- Read the text with the class and draw students' attention to the map and its key.

- Explain that sea level is the average height of the ocean's surface; sea level is at zero elevation. Ask students what color represents sea level on the map key. (*dark green*)

- Have students find the Qattara Depression. Ask **What is its elevation?** (*from 0 to 650 feet*)

- Ask **What is the difference between elevation and relief?** (*Elevation is the height of land above sea level while relief shows how quickly the land rises or falls.*)

Answers

PRACTICE YOUR GEOGRAPHY SKILLS

1. solid line, star in a circle, dot
2. Luanda

Political Maps

Political maps show political borders: continents, countries, and divisions within countries, such as states or provinces. The colors on political maps do not have any special meaning, but they make the map easier to read. Political maps also include symbols and labels for capitals, cities, and towns.

PRACTICE YOUR GEOGRAPHY SKILLS

1 What symbols show a national border, a national capital, and a city?

2 What is Angola's capital city?

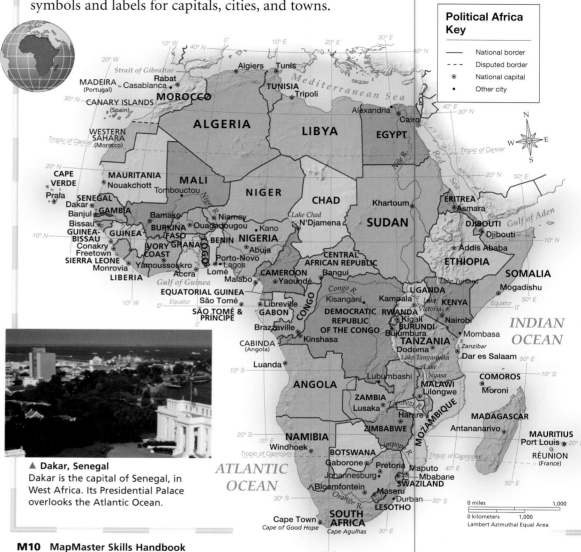

Political Africa Key

- ――――― National border
- – – – – Disputed border
- ⊛ National capital
- • Other city

▲ **Dakar, Senegal**
Dakar is the capital of Senegal, in West Africa. Its Presidential Palace overlooks the Atlantic Ocean.

0 miles 1,000
0 kilometers 1,000
Lambert Azimuthal Equal Area

M10 MapMaster Skills Handbook

Background: Global Perspectives

Africa's Highest Peaks Africa's two highest mountains are both extinct volcanoes that rise near the equator on the eastern part of the continent. The tallest mountain, Kilimanjaro in Tanzania, reaches 19,340 feet (5,895 m) at its highest point. Although snow covers its peaks, farmers raise coffee and plantains on the lower southern slopes of Kilimanjaro. Africa's second highest mountain is Mt. Kenya at 17,058 feet (5,199 m) located in central Kenya. Like Kilimanjaro, it is snowcapped in its highest regions. Both Kilimanjaro and Mt. Kenya are attractions for mountain climbers from all over the world.

Physical Maps

Physical maps represent what a region looks like by showing its major physical features, such as hills and plains. Physical maps also often show elevation and relief. Elevation, indicated by colors, is the height of the land above sea level. Relief, indicated by shading, shows how sharply the land rises or falls.

PRACTICE YOUR GEOGRAPHY SKILLS

1 Which areas of Africa have the highest elevation?

2 How can you use relief to plan a hiking trip?

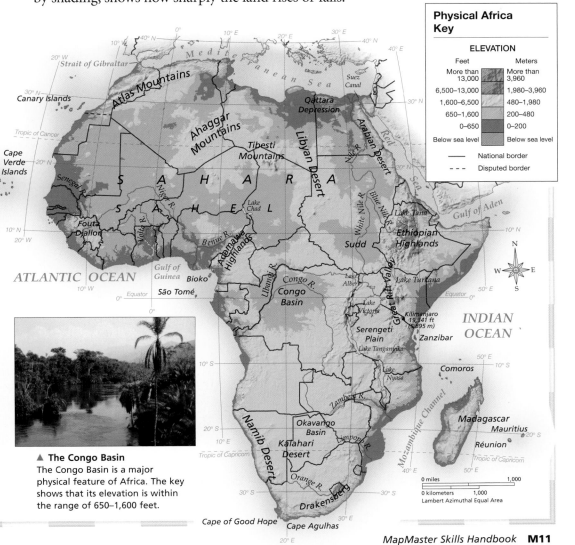

Physical Africa Key

ELEVATION

Feet	Meters
More than 13,000	More than 3,960
6,500–13,000	1,980–3,960
1,600–6,500	480–1,980
650–1,600	200–480
0–650	0–200
Below sea level	Below sea level

——— National border

- - - Disputed border

0 miles 1,000
0 kilometers 1,000
Lambert Azimuthal Equal Area

▲ **The Congo Basin**
The Congo Basin is a major physical feature of Africa. The key shows that its elevation is within the range of 650–1,600 feet.

MapMaster Skills Handbook **M11**

Independent Practice

Have students complete *Reading a Political Map, Reading a Physical Map* and *Elevation on a Map* working with partners.

All in One Latin America Teaching Resources, *Reading a Political Map,* p. 49; *Reading a Physical Map,* p. 54; *Elevation on a Map,* p. 55

Monitor Progress

As students complete the worksheets, circulate around the room to make sure individuals understand the key concepts. Provide assistance as needed.

Assess and Reteach

Assess Progress L2

Have students answer the questions under Practice Your Geography Skills on pages M10 and M11.

Reteach L1

Use the DK Atlas Activities *Reading a Political Map* and *Reading a Physical Map* to review the concepts in this lesson.

All in One Latin America Teaching Resources, *DK Compact Atlas of the World Activity: Reading a Political Map,* p. 50; *DK Compact Atlas of the World Activity: Reading a Physical Map,* p. 56

Extend L3

To extend the lesson, have students fill in the name of each country and its capital on the outline maps *North Africa, West and Central Africa,* and *East and Southern Africa.* Also, ask them to use colors and shading to indicate the Atlas Mountains, the Ethiopian Highlands, the Congo Basin, and the Namib Desert.

All in One Latin America Teaching Resources, *Outline Map 22: North Africa,* p. 51; *Outline Map 23: West and Central Africa,* p. 52; *Outline Map 24: East and Southern Africa,* p. 53

Differentiated Instruction

For Special Needs Students L1
Reuse *Reading a Political Map* to help students understand the features of a political map. Point to the symbol for a national border in the key, then trace the borders of several countries. Invite students to trace others.

All in One Latin America Teaching Resources, *Reading a Political Map,* p. 49

For Advanced Readers L3
Challenge students to explore the concepts of relief and elevation further by completing *Relief on a Map* and *Maps of the Ocean Floor.*

All in One Latin America Teaching Resources, *Relief on a Map,* p. 57; *Maps of the Ocean Floor,* p. 58

Answers

PRACTICE YOUR GEOGRAPHY SKILLS

1. mountains; the areas with the purple or brown coloring

2. It can help you find out how the land rises and falls.

Objectives

- Understand and use climate maps.
- Understand and use language maps.

Prepare to Read

Build Background Knowledge **L1**

Ask students to think of as many meanings for the word *special* as they can. Tell them that maps can be special too. Ask **What do you think a special-purpose map might show?** List suggestions on the board.

Instruct

Special-Purpose Maps: Climate **L1**

Guided Instruction

- Ask students to read the text using the Structured Silent Reading strategy (TE, p. T34). Point out that the map shows Bangladesh, Bhutan, Nepal, and parts of Myanmar and Pakistan as well as India.

- Point out the map and key. Ask **What areas have a tropical wet climate?** *(area along the southern western coast; eastern part of Bangladesh)*

- Ask **What color represents an arid climate?** *(brown)*

Independent Practice

Partner students and have them complete *Reading a Climate Map*.

All in One Latin America Teaching Resources, *Reading a Climate Map*, p. 59

Monitor Progress

As students complete the worksheet, circulate around the room to make sure individuals comprehend the key concepts. Provide assistance as needed.

Answers

PRACTICE YOUR GEOGRAPHY SKILLS

1. the key
2. No cities are shown in the arid or semi-arid regions.

M12 *MapMaster Skills Handbook*

Special-Purpose Maps: Climate

Unlike the boundary lines on a political map, the boundary lines on climate maps do not separate the land into exact divisions. For example, in this climate map of India, a tropical wet climate gradually changes to a tropical wet and dry climate.

PRACTICE YOUR GEOGRAPHY SKILLS

1 What part of a special-purpose map tells you what the colors on the map mean?

2 Where are arid regions located in India? Are there major cities in those regions?

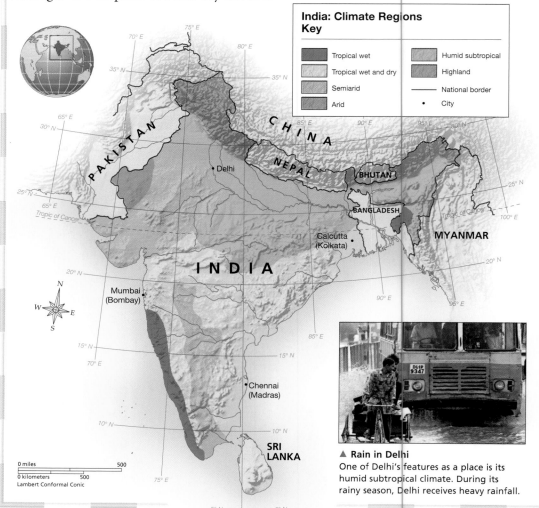

India: Climate Regions Key

- Tropical wet
- Tropical wet and dry
- Semiarid
- Arid
- Humid subtropical
- Highland
- National border
- • City

▲ **Rain in Delhi**
One of Delhi's features as a place is its humid subtropical climate. During its rainy season, Delhi receives heavy rainfall.

M12 MapMaster Skills Handbook

Differentiated Instruction

For English Language Learners **L1**

If students are unfamiliar with words in the lesson, help them identify and look up those words in the dictionary. For example: *arid*—adj. having little or no rainfall; dry *humid*—adj. having a lot of water; damp *semi*—adj. part or partially

Follow up by having students determine the meaning of *semiarid*.

For Gifted and Talented Students **L3**

Give students *Reading a Climate Graph*. Ask students to compare the information in the graph with the information on the map above. Ask them to write a sentence synthesizing about the climate of Mumbai.

All in One Latin America Teaching Resources, *Reading A Climate Graph*, p. 60

Special-Purpose Maps: Language

This map shows the official languages of India. An official language is the language used by the government. Even though a region has an official language, the people there may speak other languages as well. As in other special-purpose maps, the key explains how the different languages appear on the map.

PRACTICE YOUR GEOGRAPHY SKILLS

1 What color represents the Malayalam language on this map?

2 Where in India is Tamil the official language?

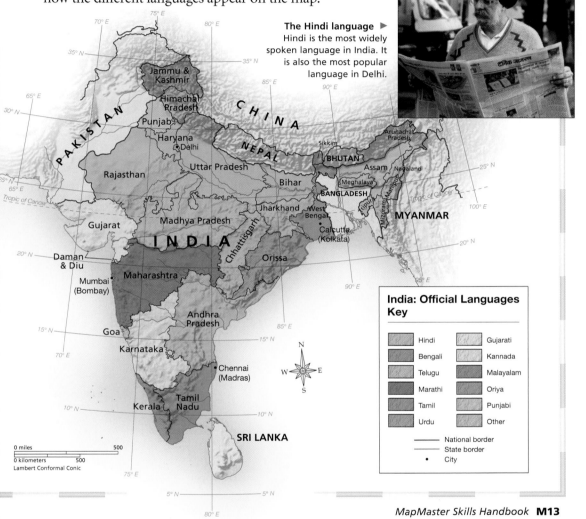

The Hindi language ▶ Hindi is the most widely spoken language in India. It is also the most popular language in Delhi.

India: Official Languages Key

Hindi	Gujarati
Bengali	Kannada
Telugu	Malayalam
Marathi	Oriya
Tamil	Punjabi
Urdu	Other

—— National border
—— State border
• City

0 miles 500
0 kilometers 500
Lambert Conformal Conic

MapMaster Skills Handbook **M13**

Background: Daily Life

The Hindi Language Hindi is the official language of India and is the primary language for about 300 million people. Hindi is the written form of Hindustani that is used by Hindus. English is also spoken by many Indians and is considered the language of politics and commerce. However, the diversity of the country is reflected in the enormous number of languages spoken there, more than 1,500 in all. Ten of India's major states are organized along linguistic lines, and the Indian constitution recognizes 15 regional languages.

Special-Purpose Maps: Language L2

Guided Instruction

- Read the text as a class. Draw students' attention to the map and its key.

- Have students consider the diversity of official languages. Ask **Why might it be important for a country to have a common language in addition to regional ones?** *(Communication is easier with a common language.)*

Independent Practice

Have students work with partners to read another special purpose map, *Reading a Natural Vegetation Map*.

> **All in One Latin America Teaching Resources,** *Reading a Natural Vegetation Map*, p. 61

Monitor Progress

As students complete the worksheet, circulate around the room and make sure individuals understand key concepts. Provide assistance as needed.

Assess and Reteach

Assess Progress L2

Have students answer the questions under Practice Your Geography Skills on pages M12 and M13.

Reteach L1

To help students understand how to use a special purpose map, have them practice the skill using *Analyzing and Interpreting Special Purpose Maps.*

> ◉ *Analyzing and Interpreting Special-Purpose Maps,* Social Studies Skills Tutor CD-ROM

Extend L3

Have students learn about another type of special-purpose map by completing *Reading a Time Zone Map.* Then ask students to find out the time zones in India and create their own time zone map, using *Outline Map 26: South Asia.*

> **All in One Latin America Teaching Resources,** *Reading a Time Zone Map.* p. 63; *Outline Map 26: South Asia,* p. 62

Answers

PRACTICE YOUR GEOGRAPHY SKILLS

1. dark pink
2. southeast India

Objectives
- Learn why people migrate.
- Understand how migration affects environments.

Prepare to Read

Build Background Knowledge L1
Remind students that they studied the theme of movement earlier in this unit. Brainstorm with students why people move from place to place, particularly those who move from one country to another. Use Numbered Heads (TE, p. T36) to generate ideas.

Instruct

Human Migration L2

Guided Instruction
- Divide the text using the headings and ask students to read the pages using the Partner Paragraph Shrinking technique (TE, p. T34). Clarify the meanings of any unfamiliar words.

- Have students look at the map. Ask **From what European countries did people migrate to the Americas in the years between 1500-1800?** *(Portugal, Spain, France, Netherlands, England)*

- Ask **Where did the French settle in Latin America?** *(French Guiana and Haiti)* **Which European country had the most possessions in the Americas?** *(Spain)*

- Ask **Why were some Africans forced to migrate?** *(They were imported as slaves from their homeland. Europeans wanted them to work on the land they claimed in the Americas.)*

Human Migration

Migration is an important part of the study of geography. Since the beginning of history, people have been on the move. As people move, they both shape and are shaped by their environments. Wherever people go, the culture they bring with them mixes with the cultures of the place in which they have settled.

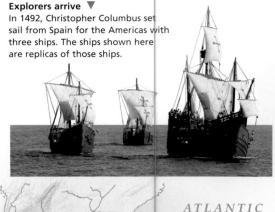

Explorers arrive ▼
In 1492, Christopher Columbus set sail from Spain for the Americas with three ships. The ships shown here are replicas of those ships.

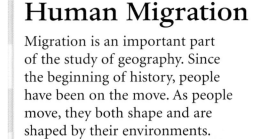

▲ **Native American pyramid**
When Europeans arrived in the Americas, the lands they found were not empty. Diverse groups of people with distinct cultures already lived there. The temple-topped pyramid shown above was built by Mayan Indians in Mexico, long before Columbus sailed.

Migration to the Americas, 1500–1800
A huge wave of migration from the Eastern Hemisphere began in the 1500s. European explorers in the Americas paved the way for hundreds of years of European settlement there. Forced migration from Africa started soon afterward, as Europeans began to import African slaves to work in the Americas. The map to the right shows these migrations.

M14 MapMaster Skills Handbook

Differentiated Instruction

For Less Proficient Readers L1
Review with students the meaning of "push" and "pull" factors in terms of human migration. Model for students how to make a table with the headings Push and Pull. Then work with students to list as many factors as they can under each heading.

For Advanced Readers L3
Have students complete *Analyzing Statistics*. When they have finished, have them write a paragraph explaining how economic and social statistics are related to "push" and "pull" factors.

All in One Latin America Teaching Resources, *Analyzing Statistics,* p. 65

PRACTICE YOUR GEOGRAPHY SKILLS

1 Where did the Portuguese settle in the Americas?

2 Would you describe African migration at this time as a result of both push factors and pull factors? Explain why or why not.

"Push" and "Pull" Factors

Geographers describe a people's choice to migrate in terms of "push" factors and "pull" factors. Push factors are things in people's lives that push them to leave, such as poverty and political unrest. Pull factors are things in another country that pull people to move there, including better living conditions and hopes of better jobs.

Migration to Latin America, 1500–1800 Key

→ European migration
→ African migration
— National or colonial border
········ Traditional African border
▦ African State

▦ Spain and possessions
▦ Portugal and possessions
▦ Netherlands and possessions
▦ France and possessions
▦ England and possessions

▲ **Elmina, Ghana**
Elmina, in Ghana, is one of the many ports from which slaves were transported from Africa. Because slaves and gold were traded here, stretches of the western African coast were known as the Slave Coast and the Gold Coast.

Independent Practice

Have students work with partners to complete *Reading a Historical Map.* Have students be ready to explain how the movement of European groups changed the map of Africa. *(Much of Africa was colonized by Europeans.)*

All in One Latin America Teaching Resources, *Reading a Historical Map,* p. 64

Monitor Progress

As students complete the worksheet, circulate around the room and make sure individuals understand key concepts. Provide assistance as needed.

Assess and Reteach

Assess Progress L2

Have students complete the questions under Practice Your Geography Skills.

Reteach L1

Help students make an outline of the lesson. Show *Transparency B15: Outline* as a model. Then work with students to identify the main points. Encourage students to refer to their outlines to review the material.

Latin America Transparencies, *Transparency B15: Outline*

Extend L3

To extend the lesson, have students complete *The Global Refugee Crisis.* Then ask them to choose a specific region on the graph and find out more about refugees from one country in that region.

Go Online
PHSchool.com For: Environmental and Global Issues: *The Global Refugee Crisis*
Visit: PHSchool.com
Web Code: lhd-4001

Answers

PRACTICE YOUR GEOGRAPHY SKILLS

1. Brazil

2. most likely push factors because people were forced to leave; the need for workers in the Americas was a pull factor although it was the Europeans who responded to it by importing Africans as slaves

Objectives

- Understand and use a land use map.
- Learn how land use and economic structures are linked.

Prepare to Read

Build Background Knowledge **L1**

Discuss with the class the ways that people in your community are using land. For example, is all the land used for homes? How much is used for commercial purposes? What kinds? Are there farms or manufacturing facilities? Point out that communities in all parts of the world use land in different ways.

Instruct

World Land Use **L2**

Guided Instruction

- Read the text as a class using the Oral Cloze strategy (TE, p. T33). Follow up by having students do a second silent reading. Encourage students to study the map and photographs.

- Talk about the difference between commercial and subsistence farming. Have them look closely at the photographs on pages M16 and M17. Ask **How do the tools and equipment people use differ in these types of farming?** (*Large power machines are used in commercial farming; hand tools are used in subsistence farming*) **Why might people use more land in commercial farming?** (*Machines make it possible to cultivate more land: the more land cultivated, the more sales possible.*)

- Ask **What color represents nomadic herding on this map?** (*light purple*) **In what parts of the world is this an economic activity?** (*Africa, Asia*)

- Ask **Why might some parts of the world have little or no land use activity?** (*Land and/or climate might not be suitable for farming or other activity.*)

World Land Use

People around the world have many different economic structures, or ways of making a living. Land-use maps are one way to learn about these structures. The ways that people use the land in each region tell us about the main ways that people in that region make a living.

World Land Use Key

	Nomadic herding
	Hunting and gathering
	Forestry
	Livestock raising
	Commercial farming
	Subsistence farming
	Manufacturing and trade
	Little or no activity
——	National border
- - - -	Disputed border

▲ **Wheat farming in the United States**
Developed countries practice commercial farming rather than subsistence farming. Commercial farming is the production of food mainly for sale, either within the country or for export to other countries. Commercial farmers like these in Oregon often use heavy equipment to farm.

Levels of Development

Notice on the map key the term *subsistence farming*. This term means the production of food mainly for use by the farmer's own family. In less-developed countries, subsistence farming is often one of the main economic activities. In contrast, in developed countries there is little subsistence farming.

▲ **Growing barley in Ecuador**
These farmers in Ecuador use hand tools to harvest barley. They will use most of the crop they grow to feed themselves or their farm animals.

NORTH AMERICA

SOUTH AMERICA

0 miles   2,000
0 kilometers   2,000
Robinson

M16   MapMaster Skills Handbook

Background: Global Perspectives

Agriculture Almost 50 percent of the world's population is occupied in agriculture. A much higher proportion of this is in developing countries where dense populations, small land holdings, and traditional techniques predominate. In areas where there is intense cultivation using people and animals but few machines, the yield is low in relation to the output of energy. In leading food producing countries such as the United States, industrial farms make use of new technology and crop specialization to increase output.

▲ **Growing rice in Vietnam**
Women in Vietnam plant rice in wet rice paddies, using the same planting methods their ancestors did.

PRACTICE YOUR GEOGRAPHY SKILLS

1 In what parts of the world is subsistence farming the main land use?

2 Locate where manufacturing and trade are the main land use. Are they found more often near areas of subsistence farming or areas of commercial farming? Why might this be so?

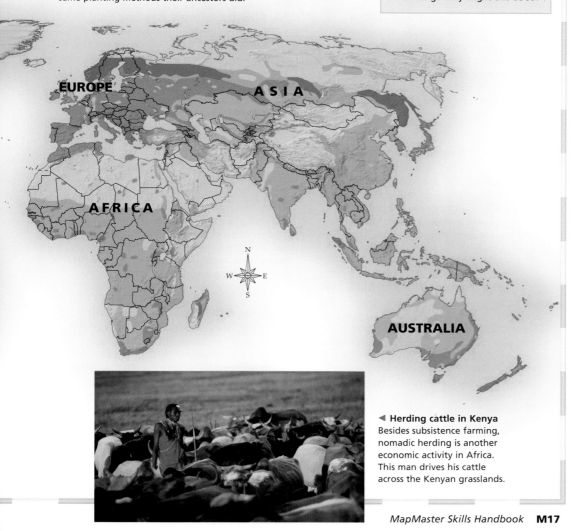

EUROPE

ASIA

AFRICA

AUSTRALIA

◄ **Herding cattle in Kenya**
Besides subsistence farming, nomadic herding is another economic activity in Africa. This man drives his cattle across the Kenyan grasslands.

MapMaster Skills Handbook **M17**

Independent Practice

Partner students and have them complete *Reading an Economic Activity Map.* Have students be ready to offer explanations for how the economic activity in Somalia might affect the lives of people there.

All in One **Latin America Teaching Resources,** *Reading an Economic Activity Map,* p. 66

Monitor Progress

Circulate around the room as students complete the worksheet to make sure individuals comprehend the key concepts. Provide assistance as needed.

Assess and Reteach

Assess Progress   L2

Have students complete the questions under Practice Your Geography Skills.

Reteach   L1

Help students make a table to identify the main kinds of land use. Draw a model on the board for students to follow. Use these headings: Nomadic Herding, Forestry, Livestock Raising, Commercial Farming, Subsistence Farming, Manufacturing and Trade. Under each heading, help students write a short explanation. Then have students find one or two places on the map in their books where that activity takes place.

Extend   L3

To extend the lesson, have students complete *Reading a Natural Resources Map.* Point out that this map shows mineral resources. Then ask students to write a paragraph relating mineral resources to land use.

All in One **Latin America Teaching Resources,** *Reading a Natural Resources Map,* p. 67

Answers

PRACTICE YOUR GEOGRAPHY SKILLS

1. Africa, Asia, South America

2. areas of commercial farming; both manufacturing and trade and commercial farming require technology which is found in developed countries

---

Differentiated Instruction

For English Language Learners   L3

Students may find it difficult to pronounce some of the multisyllable words in this section such as *nomadic, subsistence, commercial,* and *forestry.* Model how to break down these words into smaller parts to help students sound out the pronunciation.

Teaching the Target Reading Skills

The Prentice Hall *World Studies* program has interwoven essential reading skills instruction throughout the Student Edition, Teacher's Edition, and ancillary resources. In Latin America, students will learn six reading skills.

Student Edition The *World Studies* Student Edition provides students with reading skills instruction, practice, and application opportunities in each chapter within the program.

Teacher's Edition The *World Studies* Teacher Edition supports your teaching of each skill by providing full modeling in each chapter's interleaf and modeling of the specific sub-skills in each section lesson.

All in One Teaching Resources The *World Studies* All-in-One Teaching Resources provides a worksheet explaining and supporting the elements of each Target Reading Skill. Use these to help struggling students master skills, or as more practice for every student.

Target Reading Skills

The Target Reading Skills introduced on this page will help you understand the words and ideas in this book and in other social studies reading you do. Each chapter focuses on one of these reading skills. Good readers develop a bank of reading strategies, or skills. Then they draw on the particular strategies that will help them understand the text they are reading.

Chapter 1 Target Reading Skill

Using the Reading Process Previewing can help you understand and remember what you read. In this chapter you will practice using these previewing skills: setting a purpose for reading, predicting what the text will be about, and asking questions before you read.

Chapter 2 Target Reading Skill

Clarifying Meaning If you do not understand something you are reading right away, you can use several skills to clarify the meaning of the word or idea. In this chapter you will practice these strategies for clarifying meaning: rereading, reading ahead, paraphrasing, and summarizing.

Chapter 3 Target Reading Skill

Using Cause and Effect Recognizing cause and effect will help you understand relationships among the situations and events you are reading about. In this chapter you will practice these skills: identifying cause and effect, recognizing multiple causes, and understanding effects.

Chapter 4 Target Reading Skill

Using Context Using the context of an unfamiliar word can help you understand its meaning. Context includes the words, phrases, and sentences surrounding a word. In this chapter you will practice using these context clues: definitions, contrast, and your own general knowledge.

Chapter 5 Target Reading Skill

Identifying the Main Idea Since you cannot remember every detail of what you read, it is important to identify the main ideas. The main idea of a section or paragraph is the most important point, the one you want to remember. In this chapter you will practice these skills: identifying both stated and implied main ideas, and identifying supporting details.

Chapter 6 Target Reading Skill

Comparing and Contrasting You can use comparison and contrast to sort out and analyze the information you are reading. Comparing means examining the similarities between things. Contrasting is looking at differences. In this chapter you will practice these skills: comparing and contrasting, identifying contrasts, and making comparisons.

Assessment Resources

Use the diagnosing readiness tests from **AYP Monitoring Assessments** to help you identify problems before students begin to study Latin America.

Determine students' reading level and identify challenges:

📄 *Screening Tests*, pp. 1–10

Evaluate students' verbal skills:

📄 *Critical Thinking and Reading Tests*, pp. 25–34

📄 *Vocabulary Tests*, pp. 45–52

📄 *Writing Tests*, pp. 53–60

LATIN AMERICA

The ancient peoples of Latin America created great civilizations from the riches of their land and their own ideas and skills. Their descendants have mixed with newcomers from around the world to create modern societies that blend the old and the new into vibrant and distinctive cultures.

Guiding Questions

The text, photographs, maps, and charts in this book will help you discover answers to these Guiding Questions.

1. **Geography** What are the main physical features of Latin America?

2. **History** How has Latin America been shaped by its history?

3. **Culture** What factors have affected cultures in Latin America?

4. **Government** What types of government have existed in Latin America?

5. **Economics** How has geography influenced the ways in which Latin Americans make a living?

Project Preview

You can also discover answers to the Guiding Questions by working on projects. Several project possibilities are listed on page 198 of this book.

Assess students' social studies skills:

- 📄 *Geographic Literacy Tests*, pp. 13–20
- 📄 *Visual Analysis Tests*, pp. 21–24
- 📄 *Communications Tests*, pp. 35–44

The *World Studies* program provides instruction and practice for all of these skills. Use students' test results to pinpoint the skills your students have mastered and the skills they need to practice. Then use *Correlation to Program Resources* to prescribe skills practice and reinforcement.

- 📄 *Correlation to Program Resources*, pp. 64–77

Guiding Questions

- This book was developed around five Guiding Questions about Latin America. They appear on the reduced Student Edition page to the left. The Guiding Questions are intended as an organizational focus for the book. The Guiding Questions act as a kind of umbrella under which all of the material falls.

- You may wish to add your own Guiding Questions to the list in order to tailor them to your particular course.

- Draw students' attention to the Guiding Questions. Ask them to write the questions in their notebooks for future reference.

- In the Teacher's Edition, each section's themes are linked to a specific Guiding Question at the beginning of each chapter. Then, an activity at the end of the chapter returns to the Guiding Questions to review key concepts.

Project Preview

- The projects for this book are designed to provide students with hands-on involvement in the content area. Students are introduced to some projects on page 198.

- *Book Projects* give students directions on how to complete these projects, and more.

  All in One **Latin America Teaching Resources,** *Book Project: Visions of Latin America*, pp. 73–75; *Book Project: Latin America in the News*, pp. 76–78; *Book Project: A Latin American Concert*, pp. 79–81; *Book Project: Explorer's Dictionary*, pp. 82–84

- Assign projects as small group activities, whole-class projects, or individual projects. Consider assigning a project at the beginning of the course.

Objectives

- Describe the relative location and size of Latin America.
- Investigate the major languages of Latin America.
- Examine the physical features of Latin America.
- Explain why Latin America is ideal for hydroelectricity plants.

Prepare to Read

Build Background Knowledge L2

Have students brainstorm a list of words or impressions related to Latin America and write them on the board. Tell students that they will either confirm or revise these impressions during their study of the region.

Instruct

Investigate Latin America L2

Guided Instruction

- Read the introductory, Location, and Regions paragraphs as a class. Divide the class into small groups of three or four.
- Hand out the *Regional Overview* worksheet. Direct students to fill in the worksheet as they study the Regional Overview.

  All in One Latin America Teaching Resources, *Regional Overview*, pp. 89–91

Independent Practice

Ask the groups to write a statement describing Latin America's location and size in comparison to the United States.

Monitor Progress

Circulate and make sure the groups are communicating effectively.

Answers

LOCATION Santiago and Brasília–opposite seasons; Mexico City–same seasons

REGIONS Latin America's Pacific Coast is almost four times longer.

Investigate Latin America

Latin America is a vibrant region in the midst of change. The region's northern edge is marked by the boundary between the United States and Mexico. To the south, it extends to the tip of South America. Latin America covers about 14 percent of Earth's surface.

▲ San Cristóbal de las Casas, Mexico

LOCATION
1 Explore Latin America's Location

Recall from the MapMaster Skills Handbook that when it's winter north of the Equator it's summer south of the Equator, and vice versa. Trace the line of the Equator on the map above with your finger. Next, break into small groups. Tell each other in what season your birthdays fall. Work together to figure out in what season your birthdays would be if you all lived in Santiago, Chile. What would the seasons be if you lived in Brasília, Brazil? If you lived in Mexico City, Mexico?

REGIONS
2 Compare the Size of Latin America and the United States

How does Latin America's length compare to the length of the continental United States? Take a piece of string and curve it along the west coast of the United States from the border with Canada to the border with Mexico. Cut the string the same length as the coast. Now see how many string lengths fit along the west coast of Latin America. Start at northern Mexico. Finish at the southern tip of South America. How many times longer is Latin America's Pacific Coast than the coast of the United States?

Mental Mapping

Everything in Its Place List the names of some Middle American, South American, and Caribbean countries on the board. Include Mexico, Panama, Haiti, Brazil, Puerto Rico, Peru, Guatemala, Cuba, Chile, and Venezuela.

Distribute *Outline Map 4: Latin America: Physical*. Ask students to locate as many countries on the maps as they can from memory, without looking in their textbooks. Tell them to write the names of the countries they cannot locate on the water area of the map near the correct landmass. They can update their outline maps as they study the region.

All in One Latin America Teaching Resources, *Outline Map 4: Latin America: Physical*, p. 92

Political Latin America

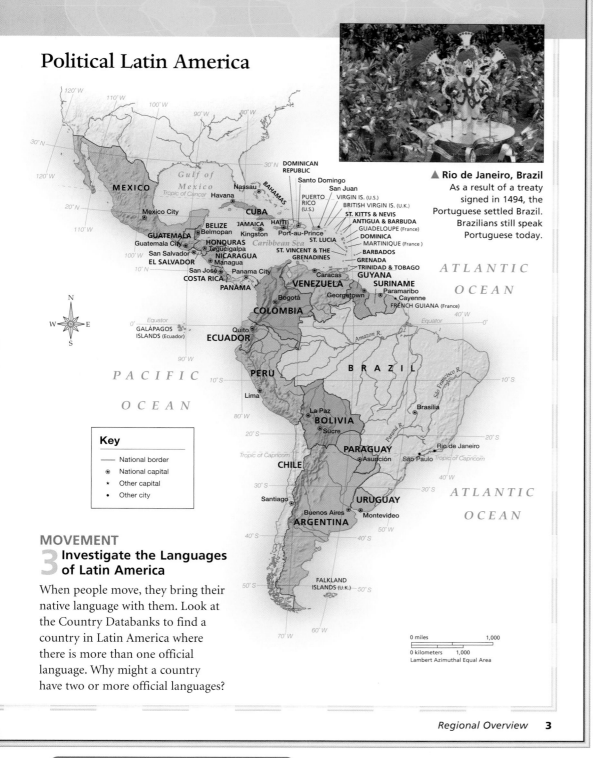

▲ **Rio de Janeiro, Brazil**
As a result of a treaty signed in 1494, the Portuguese settled Brazil. Brazilians still speak Portuguese today.

Key

— National border
⊕ National capital
★ Other capital
• Other city

0 miles 1,000
0 kilometers 1,000
Lambert Azimuthal Equal Area

MOVEMENT

3 Investigate the Languages of Latin America

When people move, they bring their native language with them. Look at the Country Databanks to find a country in Latin America where there is more than one official language. Why might a country have two or more official languages?

Regional Overview **3**

Political Latin America L2

Guided Instruction

- Read the Location paragraph. Ask students to discuss which countries they think are the two largest in area. Direct them to the Country Databanks on pages 98–101, 128–133, and 160–165 of their textbook to check their answers.

- Ask students to continue completing the Regional Overview worksheet.
  All in One Latin America Teaching Resources, *Regional Overview*, pp. 89–91

- Read the Movement paragraph. Refer students to the Country Databanks on pages 98–101, 128–133, and 160–165 to review the languages spoken in Latin America. Ask students to write on the board the countries that have more than one official language.

- Discuss why a country might have two or more official languages.

Independent Practice

Provide students with the *Outline Map 5: Latin America: Political.* Have students label each country in Latin America and color in the countries according to the official language spoken there. Remind them to include a key.
All in One Latin America Teaching Resources, *Outline Map 5: Latin America: Political,* p. 93

Monitor Progress

Circulate while students complete their maps and provide assistance where needed.

Answers

LOCATION Brazil and Argentina have the largest land area in Latin America.

MOVEMENT Haiti, Bolivia, and Peru all have more than one official language.

A country might have two or more official languages because its population might be bilingual; many people might speak one language, while many others speak another; it might have ties to a European language as well as an indigenous language

---

Differentiated Instruction

For Special Needs Students L2
If possible, show students the Latin America flyover segment on the Passport to the World CD-ROM. Ask students to list several of the region's major landforms on the board after viewing the segment.

⊙ *Flyover segment,* **Passport to the World CD-ROM**

Physical Latin America ▣

Guided Instruction
- Read the Location paragraph. Have students study the physical map of Latin America. Ask them to use the map key to determine the highest altitudes in Latin America, as well as the Amazon Basin's elevation.
- Ask students to continue completing the *Regional Overview* worksheet.
  All in One Latin America Teaching Resources, *Regional Overview*, p. 89–91

Independent Practice
- Have students explore the physical features of Latin America by creating a bar graph.
- Give them the following statistics:

Peak	Elevation
Aconcagua, Argentina	22,831ft [6,959m]
Ojos del Salado, Argentina-Chile	22,572 ft [6,880m]
Bonete, Argentina	22,546 ft [6872m]

Tell students that these are the three highest peaks in Latin America.

- Ask students to create a bar graph comparing the heights of these mounts to the highest peak in the United States: Mt. McKinley, Alaska, at an elevation of 20,320 ft [6,194m].
- Ask: **What do the bar graphs show?** *(Even the third highest peak in Latin America is taller than the highest peak in the United States.)*

Monitor Progress
Make sure students are creating their graphs correctly. If individuals are having trouble, guide them in setting up the graphs with the names of the mountains on the x-axis and the intervals of feet on the y-axis. Suggest they mark off intervals of 5,000 feet. Point out that they must plan ahead to have enough room on the y-axis to show the largest number of feet on their graphs.

Answers
LOCATION The Andes Mountains have the highest altitude in the Latin America. The Amazon Basin is zero to 650 feet above sea level. Climbing boots would probably not be necessary there.

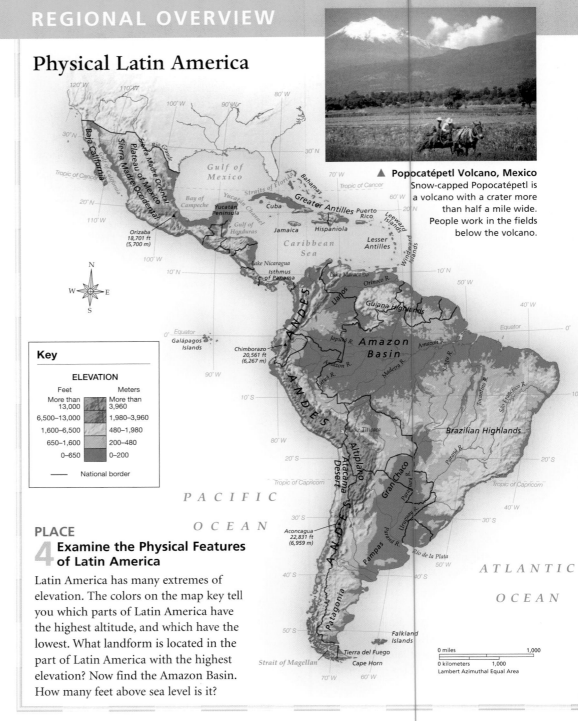

Physical Latin America

▲ **Popocatépetl Volcano, Mexico**
Snow-capped Popocatépetl is a volcano with a crater more than half a mile wide. People work in the fields below the volcano.

Key

ELEVATION

Feet	Meters
More than 13,000	More than 3,960
6,500–13,000	1,980–3,960
1,600–6,500	480–1,980
650–1,600	200–480
0–650	0–200

—— National border

PLACE
4 Examine the Physical Features of Latin America

Latin America has many extremes of elevation. The colors on the map key tell you which parts of Latin America have the highest altitude, and which have the lowest. What landform is located in the part of Latin America with the highest elevation? Now find the Amazon Basin. How many feet above sea level is it?

Background: Daily Life

Elevation Elevation is an important factor in everyday life in Latin America because elevation influences climate. Assuming that air is not moving, air is 3.5°F (1.9°C) cooler for every 1,000 feet (305 meters) one climbs. Thus, while the city of Guayaquil on the coast of Ecuador may be very hot and sticky, the city of Quito is almost cold. That is because Quito is located high in the Andes Mountains.

Major Hydroelectric Plants

Electricity generated from water power is called hydroelectricity. One way to build a hydroelectric plant is to dam a river. The dam creates a large lake. When the dam gates open, water gushes from the lake to the river, turning huge paddles that create electricity. If you live in a region near a large river, your electricity may be generated in this way.

▲ **Itaipú Dam, Brazil/Paraguay**
Water surges through the gate at the Itaipú Dam. This dam supplies electricity to large areas of Brazil and Paraguay.

LOCATION

5 Investigate Latin America's Use of Hydroelectricity

The world's largest hydroelectric plant is located on the border of Brazil and Paraguay. Look at the circle graph below. How much of its power does Latin America get from hydroelectricity? From what energy source does Latin America get most of its power?

Latin America: Sources of Energy

5%
18%
1%
1%
16%
59%

■ Petroleum
■ Hydroelectricity
■ Nuclear
■ Other
■ Natural Gas
■ Coal

SOURCE: Energy Information Administration

Key
— National border
■ Hydroelectric plant

0 miles 1,200
0 kilometers 1,200
Lambert Azimuthal Equal Area

PRACTICE YOUR GEOGRAPHY SKILLS

1 You are taking a trip through Latin America. You board your ship in Puerto Rico. You want to reach the Pacific Ocean by the most direct route. Which way must you sail to reach the Panama Canal?

2 You are traveling through the Andes in Peru, looking for a large lake. What is it called?

3 You have traveled north again. You are looking for a hydroelectric plant in the far north of Brazil, near the coast. What is the plant called?

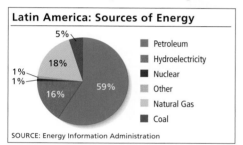

▲ **Surignui, Lake Titicaca, Peru**

Guided Instruction

■ Read the introductory paragraph and the Location paragraph and study the map.

■ Ask students: **What country has the most hydroelectric plants?** (*Brazil*)

■ Ask students: **Where do you think new hydroelectric plants could be built?** (*Possible answers: along the Amazon River in Brazil, where rivers drain in Ecuador*) **Which countries will be affected by the construction of these new plants?** (*Students should note that the new plants will affect the countries in which the river flows.*)

■ Ask students to study the circle graph. Ask: **What are the top three sources of energy in Latin America?** (*petroleum, natural gas, and hydroelectricity*) **How much more energy comes from petroleum than hydroelectricity?** (*43% more energy comes from petroleum than hydroelectricity*) Ask students to predict some of the benefits of hydroelectricity compared to the other top sources. (*renewable resource, less pollution*)

■ Direct students to finish the *Regional Overview* worksheet.

All in One Latin America Teaching Resources, *Regional Overview*, pp. 89–91

Independent Practice

Ask students to study the maps on pages 4 and 5 and write a brief statement on why Latin America is an ideal place for hydroelectric plants.

Monitor Progress

If students are having trouble with their statements, ask them: **Would you describe Latin America as "a region with plenty of rivers?"** (*Looking at the maps, yes. Almost every country in South America has at least one major river.*)

Differentiated Instruction

For Gifted and Talented L3
Challenge students to create a model of how a hydroelectric plant works. Have them research more details about how dams help create hydroelectric power, or explore alternate methods, such as harnessing the power of waterfalls or tides.

Answers

LOCATION sixteen percent; petroleum

PRACTICE YOUR GEOGRAPHY SKILLS

1. south southwest

2. Lake Titicaca

3. Tucuruí

Focus on Countries in Latin America

Guided Instruction
- Have students pick a number (1–5) from a hat and divide the class according to the numbers they selected.

- Have each group read the text on the country relative to their group number and note down important details.

Independent Practice
Have each group use the Country Databanks (pp. 98–101, 128–133, 160–165), DK Compact Atlas of the World, and the DK World Desk Reference Online (see student pages for web code) to research the country they have been assigned. Focus their efforts on the geography, climate, government and people of the countries. Then, have each group report to the class the information they have gathered.

Monitor Progress
If students' oral reports veer off the main topic, offer prompts to get them back on track.

Focus on Countries in Latin America

Now that you've investigated the geography of Latin America, take a closer look at some of the countries that make up this region. The map shows all the countries of Latin America. The ten countries that you will study in depth in the second half of this book are shown in yellow on the map.

Go Online PHSchool.com | Use Web Code lfp-1010 for the interactive maps on these pages.

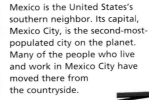

◄ **Mexico**
Mexico is the United States's southern neighbor. Its capital, Mexico City, is the second-most-populated city on the planet. Many of the people who live and work in Mexico City have moved there from the countryside.

▲ **Haiti**
Haiti lies on the western third of the island of Hispaniola. It is the only nation in the Americas formed as a result of a successful revolt by enslaved Africans.

◄ **Peru**
Peru is a mountainous country that is home to many species of animals, including the llama. Llamas thrive in the mountains and their wool is used for clothing.

6   Latin America

Background: Links Across Time

Place Names American Indian place names often describe a region's physical characteristics. For example, *Panama* meant "abundance of fish" to the people who lived there before Europeans arrived.

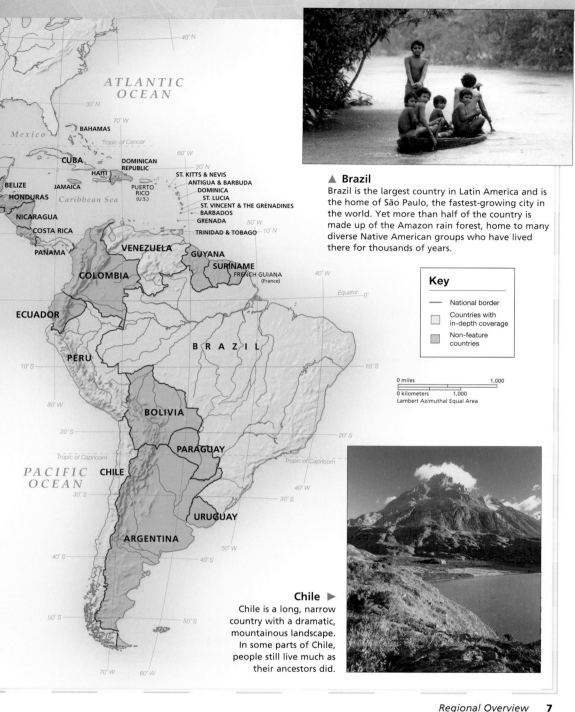

ATLANTIC OCEAN

Mexico

BAHAMAS

CUBA
HAITI
DOMINICAN REPUBLIC

BELIZE
JAMAICA
PUERTO RICO (U.S.)

HONDURAS
Caribbean Sea

ST. KITTS & NEVIS
ANTIGUA & BARBUDA
DOMINICA
ST. LUCIA
ST. VINCENT & THE GRENADINES
BARBADOS
GRENADA
TRINIDAD & TOBAGO

NICARAGUA

COSTA RICA

PANAMA

VENEZUELA
GUYANA
SURINAME
FRENCH GUIANA (France)

COLOMBIA

ECUADOR

PERU

B R A Z I L

BOLIVIA

PARAGUAY

PACIFIC OCEAN

CHILE

URUGUAY

ARGENTINA

Tropic of Cancer
Tropic of Capricorn
Equator

Key

— National border

☐ Countries with in-depth coverage

☐ Non-feature countries

0 miles 1,000
0 kilometers 1,000
Lambert Azimuthal Equal Area

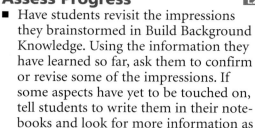

▲ **Brazil**
Brazil is the largest country in Latin America and is the home of São Paulo, the fastest-growing city in the world. Yet more than half of the country is made up of the Amazon rain forest, home to many diverse Native American groups who have lived there for thousands of years.

Chile ▶
Chile is a long, narrow country with a dramatic, mountainous landscape. In some parts of Chile, people still live much as their ancestors did.

Assess and Reteach

Assess Progress L2

- Have students revisit the impressions they brainstormed in Build Background Knowledge. Using the information they have learned so far, ask them to confirm or revise some of the impressions. If some aspects have yet to be touched on, tell students to write them in their notebooks and look for more information as they begin their study of Latin America.

- Ask students to complete Practice Your Geography Skills on p. 5.

Reteach L1

For more exploration of the region, have students view the Latin America portion of the Passport to the World CD-ROM and complete the Customs Quiz.

◉ *Latin America,* **Passport to the World CD-ROM**

Extend L3

Portfolio Activity One way of assessing student accomplishments is by having them build a portfolio of their best work. To begin their portfolios for Latin America, have students choose another of the Latin American countries mentioned on pages 6-7. Then, assign a project on this country. Students can choose what type of project they would like to do. Options include collages, maps, stories, paragraphs, dioramas, and more.

- Give students *Learning More About a Topic* to help them get started on their research.

All in One **Latin America Teaching Resources,** *Learning More About a Topic,* p. 94

Differentiated Instruction

For English Language Learners L2
Have students make a two-column chart, placing the English names for the five countries on this page on one side of the chart, and the word for that country in their native language on the other. Then have students share each country's non-English names with the class. Students watching the presentations should note any spelling or accent differences between the words.

Overview

Section 1

Land and Water
1. Learn where Latin America is located.
2. Discover the important landforms of Latin America.
3. Find out how Latin America's waterways have affected the region.

Section 2

Climate and Vegetation
1. Find out what kinds of climate Latin America has.
2. Learn what factors influence climate in Latin America.
3. Understand how climate and vegetation influence the ways people live.

Section 3

Resources and Land Use
1. Find out what Latin America's most important natural resources are.
2. Learn why depending on a one-resource economy has been a problem for Latin American nations.

Discovery CHANNEL SCHOOL Video

The Geography of Latin America
Length: 5 minutes
Use with Section 1
This segment gives a broad overview of the physical features, vegetation, and climates of Latin America. It also introduces how the people of Latin America interact with their environment.

Technology Resources

Go Online
PHSchool.com

Students use embedded Web codes to access internet activities, chapter self-tests, and additional map practice. They may also access Dorling Kindersley's Online Desk Reference to learn more about each country they study.

Interactive Textbook

Use the Interactive Textbook to make content and concepts come alive through animations, videos, and activities that accompany the complete basal text—online and on CD-ROM.

PRENTICE HALL
TeacherEXPRESS™
Plan • Teach • Assess

Use this complete suite of powerful teaching tools to make planning lessons and administering tests quicker and easier.

Reading and Assessment

Reading and Vocabulary Instruction

⟲ Model the Target Reading Skill

Reading Process Explain to students that reading actively will help them retain knowledge and become better readers. One way of reading actively is to preview and think about the text *before reading*.

Model this skill by thinking about this chapter aloud:

This chapter's title is *Latin America: Physical Geography*. So I'll be learning about what the physical features of Latin America are like when I read the chapter.

The first section is called *Land and Water*. I wonder how the land and water of Latin America are different from those of the United States? I'll read the section to find out.

The second section is called *Climate and Vegetation*. What does vegetation mean exactly? It sounds like the word "vegetable," so maybe it has something to do with plants. When I read that section, I'll find out what "vegetation" means.

The third section is called *Resources and Land Use*. I'm not sure about resources, but land use must mean how people use the land. I predict that in this section, I'll learn about interaction between humans and the environment in Latin America.

Use the following worksheets from All-in-One Latin America Teaching Resources, (pp. 110, 111, and 112) to support this chapter's Target Reading Skill.

Vocabulary Builder
High-Use Academic Words

Use these steps to teach this chapter's high-use words:

1. Have students rate how well they know each word on their Word Knowledge worksheets (All-in-One Latin America Teaching Resources, p. 113).
2. Pronounce each word and ask students to repeat it.
3. Give students a brief definition and sample sentence (provided on TE pp. 11, 16, and 25).
4. Work with students as they fill in the "Definition or Example" column of their Word Knowledge worksheets.

Assessment

Formal Assessment

Test students' understanding of core knowledge and skills.
> **Chapter Tests A and B,** All-in-One Latin America Teaching Resources, pp. 130–135

Customize the Chapter Tests to suit your needs.
> *ExamView® Test Bank CD-ROM*

Skills Assessment

Assess geographic literacy.
> **MapMaster Skills,** Student Edition, pp. 9, 11, 16, 20, 23, 25, 32

Assess reading and comprehension.
> **Target Reading Skills,** Student Edition, pp. 13, 19, 29, and in Section Assessments

> **Chapter 1 Assessment,** Latin America Reading and Vocabulary Study Guide, p. 15

Performance Assessment

Assess students' performance on this chapter's Writing Activities using the following rubric from All-in-One Latin America Teaching Resources.
> **Rubric for Assessing a Writing Assignment,** p. 129

Assess students' work through performance tasks.
> **Small Group Activity: Making a Relief Map,** All-in-One Latin America Teaching Resources, pp. 116–119

Online Assessment

Have students check their own understanding.
> **Chapter Self-Test**

Test Preparation

Assess students' skills and diagnose problems as students begin their study of this region.
> **Screening and Diagnosing Readiness Tests,** AYP Monitoring Assessments, pp. 1–63

Section 1 Land and Water

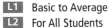 *1 periods, .5 block*

Social Studies Objectives

1. Learn where Latin America is located.
2. Discover the important landforms of Latin America.
3. Find out how Latin America's waterways have affected the region.

Reading/Language Arts Objective

Preview to set a purpose for reading.

Prepare to Read	Instructional Resources	Differentiated Instruction
Build Background Knowledge Name countries, landforms and waterways in Latin America. **Set a Purpose for Reading** Have students evaluate statements on the *Reading Readiness Guide.* **Preview Key Terms** Teach the section's Key Terms using a "See It—Remember It" chart. **Target Reading Skill** Introduce the section's Target Reading Skill of **previewing and setting a purpose for reading.**	**All in One Latin America Teaching Resources** L2 Reading Readiness Guide, p. 99 L2 Preview and Set a Purpose, p. 110 **World Studies Video Program** L2 The Geography of Latin America	**Spanish Reading and Vocabulary Study Guide** L2 Chapter 1, Section 1, pp. 6–7 ELL

Instruct	Instructional Resources	Differentiated Instruction
Where is Latin America? Using the map, discuss the location of Latin America. **Landforms of Latin America** Discuss landforms and their effects on the region's people. **Target Reading Skill** Review **previewing and setting a purpose for reading.** **Latin America's Waterways** Apply the target reading skill while discussing the waterways of Latin America.	**All in One Latin America Teaching Resources** L2 Guided Reading and Review, p. 100 L2 Reading Readiness Guide, p. 99 **Latin America Transparencies** L2 Section Reading Support Transparency LA 28	**Spanish Support** L2 Guided Reading and Review (Spanish), p. 4 ELL

Assess and Reteach	Instructional Resources	Differentiated Instruction
Assess Progress Evaluate student comprehension with the section assessment and section quiz. **Reteach** Assign the Reading and Vocabulary Study Guide to help struggling students. **Extend** Extend the lesson by assigning a map worksheet.	**All in One Latin America Teaching Resources** L2 Section Quiz, p. 101 L3 Reading a Physical Map, p. 122 Rubric for Assessing a Writing Assignment, p. 129 **Reading and Vocabulary Study Guide** L1 Chapter 1, Section 1, pp. 6–8	**Spanish Support** L2 Section Quiz (Spanish), p. 5 ELL

Key

L1 Basic to Average	L3 Average to Advanced	**LPR** Less Proficient Readers	**GT** Gifted and Talented
L2 For All Students		**AR** Advanced Readers	**ELL** English Language Learners
		SN Special Needs Students	

Section 2 Climate and Vegetation

2 periods, 1 block (includes Skills For Life)

Social Studies Objectives

1. Find out what kinds of climate Latin America has.
2. Learn what factors influence climate in Latin America.
3. Understand how climate and vegetation influence the way people live.

Reading/Language Arts Objective

Make predictions about a text to help set a purpose for reading.

Prepare to Read	Instructional Resources	Differentiated Instruction
Build Background Knowledge Discuss how climate affects people's lives. **Set a Purpose for Reading** Have students begin to fill out the *Reading Readiness Guide*. **Preview Key Terms** Teach the section's Key Terms. **Target Reading Skill** Introduce the section's Target Reading Skill of **previewing and predicting**.	**All in One Latin America Teaching Resources** L2 Reading Readiness Guide, p. 103 L2 Preview and Predict, p. 111	**Spanish Reading and Vocabulary Study Guide** L2 Chapter 1, Section 2, pp. 8–9 ELL

Instruct	Instructional Resources	Differentiated Instruction
The Climates of Latin America Have students consider effects of different climates. **What Factors Affect Climate?** Ask students key questions about factors affecting climate. **Target Reading Skill** Review **previewing and predicting**. **Climate, Plants, and People** Discuss the relationship between the climate and economy of Latin America.	**All in One Latin America Teaching Resources** L2 Guided Reading and Review, p. 104 L2 Reading Readiness Guide, p. 103 **Latin America Transparencies** L2 Section Reading Support Transparency LA 29 L2 Color Transparency LA 26: Mexico: Physical-Political	**All in One Latin America Teaching Resources** L2 Skills for Life, p. 115 AR, GT, LPR, SN **Teacher's Edition** L3 For Advanced Readers, TE p. 17 L1 For English Language Learners, p. 19 L3 For Gifted/Talented Students, TE p. 20 L1 For Special Needs Students, TE p. 23 **Spanish Support** L2 Guided Reading and Review (Spanish), p. 6 ELL

Assess and Reteach	Instructional Resources	Differentiated Instruction
Assess Progress Evaluate student comprehension with the section assessment and section quiz. **Reteach** Assign the Reading and Vocabulary Study Guide to help struggling students. **Extend** Extend the lesson by assigning a Small Group Activity.	**All in One Latin America Teaching Resources** L2 Section Quiz, p. 105 L3 Small Group Activity, pp. 116–119 Rubric for Assessing a Writing Assignment, p. 129 **Reading and Vocabulary Study Guide** L1 Chapter 1, Section 2, pp. 9–11	**All in One Latin America Teaching Resources** L3 Activity Shop Interdisciplinary, pp. 120–121 GT **Social Studies Skills Tutor CD-ROM** L1 Analyzing and Interpreting Special-Purpose Maps SN, LPR

Key

L1 Basic to Average
L2 For All Students

L3 Average to Advanced

LPR Less Proficient Readers
AR Advanced Readers
SN Special Needs Students

GT Gifted and Talented
ELL English Language Learners

Section 3 Resources and Land Use

2.5 periods, 1.25 blocks (includes Chapter Review and Assessment, and Literature)

Social Studies Objectives

1. Find out what Latin America's most important natural resources are.
2. Learn why depending on a one-resource economy has been a problem for Latin American nations.

Reading/Language Arts Objective

Create questions to help you understand and remember what you read.

Prepare to Read	Instructional Resources	Differentiated Instruction
Build Background Knowledge Discuss what students predict Latin America's natural resources might be. **Set a Purpose for Reading** Have students evaluate statements on the *Reading Readiness Guide*. **Preview Key Terms** Teach the section's Key Terms. **Target Reading Skill** Introduce the section's Target Reading Skill of **previewing and asking questions**.	**All in One Latin America Teaching Resources** L2 Reading Readiness Guide, p. 107 L2 Preview and Ask Questions, p. 112	**Spanish Reading and Vocabulary Study Guide** L2 Chapter 1, Section 3, pp. 10–11 ELL

Instruct	Instructional Resources	Differentiated Instruction
Latin America's Resources Ask students key questions about Latin America's resources. **Resources and the Economy** Discuss the relationship between the resources and economies of Latin American nations. **Target Reading Skill** Review **previewing and asking questions**.	**All in One Latin America Teaching Resources** L2 Guided Reading and Review, p. 108 L2 Reading Readiness Guide, p. 107 **Latin America Transparencies** L2 Section Reading Support Transparency LA 30	**All in One Latin America Teaching Resources** L3 Message from the Rain Forest Amerindians, p. 123 AR L2 Structuring Paragraphs, p. 126 AR, GT, LPR, SN L2 Creating Paragraph Outlines, p. 127 AR, GT, LPR, SN **Teacher's Edition** L1 For Less Proficient Readers, TE p. 26 L3 For Advanced Readers, TE p. 27 L1 For Special Needs Students, TE p. 29

Assess and Reteach	Instructional Resources	Differentiated Instruction
Assess Progress Evaluate student comprehension with the section assessment and section quiz. **Reteach** Assign the Reading and Vocabulary Study Guide to help struggling students. **Extend** Extend the lesson by assigning an Enrichment activity.	**All in One Latin America Teaching Resources** L2 Section Quiz, p. 109 L3 Enrichment, p. 114, Rubric for Assessing a Writing Assignment, p. 129 L2 Vocabulary Development, p. 128 L2 Word Knowledge, p. 113 L2 Chapter Tests A & B, pp. 130–135 **Reading and Vocabulary Study Guide** L1 Chapter 1, Section 3, pp. 12–14	**All in One Latin America Teaching Resources** L3 My Friend the Painter, pp. 124–125 AR, GT **Spanish Support** L2 Section Quiz (Spanish), p. 9 ELL L2 Chapter Summary (Spanish), p. 10 ELL L2 Vocabulary Development (Spanish), p. 11 ELL **Student Edition on Audio CD** L1 Chapter 1, Section 3 SN

Key

L1 Basic to Average   L3 Average to Advanced   LPR Less Proficient Readers   GT Gifted and Talented

L2 For All Students   AR Advanced Readers   ELL English Language Learners

                                                         SN Special Needs Students

Reading Background

Previewing and Prereading

This chapter's Target Reading Skill asks students to preview each section and set a purpose for reading. Students who do a brief, preliminary reading of complex material are in a strategic position to take control of their learning and comprehension.

Previewing helps students consider what they already know about a topic they will be studying and gives some idea of what a text selection is about before they read it. Previewing also helps students identify the text structure and develop a mental framework for ideas to be encountered in the text. This can help them in formulating a more realistic reading and study plan.

Follow the steps below to teach students how to preview and preread.

1. Tell students that previewing will help them identify the text structure and develop a mental outline of ideas they will encounter in the text.

2. List the various text features you will be previewing in the order in which you would like students to examine them: section title, text headings, introduction, list of key terms, questions or tasks in the reading selection, photographs, drawings, maps, charts and other visuals in the text. Focus students' attention on some of these items, or ask them to look at all of them.

3. Prompt students to reflect after examining various text features. They may ask themselves questions such as: What is this reading selection about? What are some key words I will learn? How should I tackle this reading and divide up the task?

Language Strategies for Predicting

In this chapter, students will use the ReQuest (Reciprocal Questioning) Procedure to share their ideas. As part of this activity, students are asked to make predictions about the reading. Students may feel more comfortable actively participating if they have some sample language strategies to use in framing their predictions. Offer students the following language strategies:

> *I guess/predict/imagine that . . .*
>
> *Based on . . . I infer that . . .*
>
> *I hypothesize that . . .*

Remind students that their predictions may differ from other students', and that they may build on others' predictions to help strengthen their own.

World Studies Background

Exploring the Amazon

The Amazon River has fascinated people for hundreds of years. Perhaps its most famous explorer was Theodore Roosevelt. In 1913, the former President was part of the first group to officially explore the rain forests of Brazil between the Amazon River and the Río de la Plata. For over 40 days, Roosevelt and his companions overcame insects, disease, lack of food, and high rapids in order to map this area.

Volcano of the Andes

The Andes Mountains contain many volcanoes, some of which are quite dangerous. On November 13, 1985, the Nevado del Ruiz volcano in northern Colombia erupted for the first time since 1845. This caused one of the worst natural disasters

in South American history. The heat of the volcanic eruption melted glacial ice that had accumulated on top of the volcano. As lahar, or volcanic mud, flowed furiously down from the volcano, 14 towns and villages in the area were destroyed, causing over 20,000 deaths.

The Silver River

The Río de la Plata, which means Silver River in Spanish, is the largest estuary in South America. An estuary is a partially enclosed area where seawater and fresh water meet, and a valuable environment for wildlife. The river provides a home to many species, including the La Plata, or Franciscana, dolphin, which is unique because it can live in the fresh water river and in the salt water of the ocean.

Infoplease® provides a wealth of useful information for the classroom. You can use this resource to strengthen your background on the subjects covered in this chapter. Have students visit this advertising-free site as a starting point for projects requiring research.

Use Web code **lfd-1100** for Infoplease.®

Latin America: Physical Geography

Guiding Questions

Remind students about the Guiding Questions introduced at the beginning of the book.

Section 1 relates to **Guiding Question 1**
What are the main physical features of Latin America? (*Latin America has mountains, plateaus, islands, tropical rain forests, and rivers.*)

Section 2 relates to **Guiding Question 5**
How has geography influenced the ways in which Latin Americans make a living? (*Temperature, rainfall, and elevation affect what kinds of crops Latin Americans can grow and sell.*)

Section 3 relates to **Guiding Question 5**
How has geography influenced the ways in which Latin Americans make a living? (*Some Latin American countries have many natural resources that can be sold, while others have limited resources to cultivate and sell.*)

Target Reading Skill

In this chapter, students will learn and apply the reading skill of compare and contrast. Use the following worksheets to help students practice this skill:

All in One **Latin America Teaching Resources**, *Preview and Set a Purpose*, p. 110; *Preview and Predict*, p. 111; *Preview and Ask Questions*, p. 112

Chapter Preview

This chapter will introduce you to the geography of Latin America and show how geography affects the people who live there.

Section 1
Land and Water

Section 2
Climate and Vegetation

Section 3
Resources and Land Use

Target Reading Skill

Reading Process In this chapter you will focus on the reading process by using previewing to help you understand and remember what you read.

▶ Stepping stones through a rain forest in Costa Rica

Differentiated Instruction

The following Teacher Edition strategies are suitable for students of varying abilities.

Advanced Readers, p. 17, 27
English Language Learners, p. 19
Gifted and Talented, p. 20
Less Proficient Readers, pp. 26, 36
Special Needs Students, pp. 23, 29

Bibliography

For the Teacher
The Eyewitness Atlas of the World. Dorling Kindersley, 1994.
Goulding, Michael. *Smithsonian Atlas of the Amazon*. Smithsonian Institution Press, 2003.
Schlessinger, Andrew. *The Rainforest*. Schlessinger, 1993. Video.

For the Student
L1 Albert, Toni. *The Remarkable Rainforest: An Active-Learning Book for Kids*. Trickle Creek Books, 1996.
L2 *National Geographic Student Atlas of the World*. National Geographic, 2001.
L3 Bernhard, Brendan. *Pizarro, Orellana, and the Exploration of the Amazon*. Chelsea, 1991.

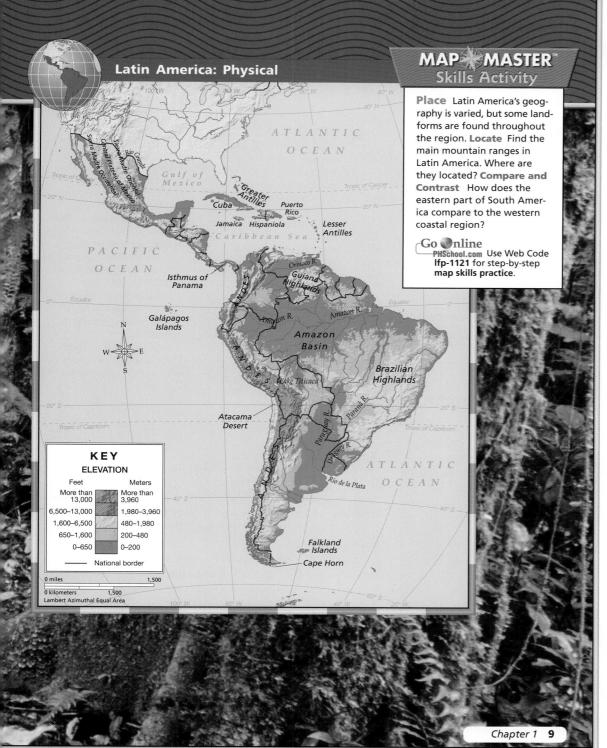

Latin America: Physical

MAP MASTER™ Skills Activity

ATLANTIC OCEAN

Rio Grande
Sierra Madre Oriental
Sierra Madre Occidental
Central Plateau of Mexico
Gulf of Mexico
Greater Antilles
Cuba
Jamaica   Hispaniola
Puerto Rico
Lesser Antilles
Caribbean Sea
PACIFIC OCEAN
Isthmus of Panama
Orinoco R.
Guiana Highlands
Galápagos Islands
Amazon R.   Amazon R.
Amazon Basin
Lake Titicaca
Brazilian Highlands
Atacama Desert
Paraguay R.
Paraná R.
Uruguay R.
Rio de la Plata
ATLANTIC OCEAN
Falkland Islands
Cape Horn

Tropic of Cancer
Equator
Tropic of Capricorn

KEY
ELEVATION

Feet	Meters
More than 13,000	More than 3,960
6,500–13,000	1,980–3,960
1,600–6,500	480–1,980
650–1,600	200–480
0–650	0–200

National border

0 miles 1,500
0 kilometers 1,500
Lambert Azimuthal Equal Area

Place Latin America's geography is varied, but some landforms are found throughout the region. **Locate** Find the main mountain ranges in Latin America. Where are they located? **Compare and Contrast** How does the eastern part of South America compare to the western coastal region?

Go Online PHSchool.com Use Web Code **lfp-1121** for step-by-step map skills practice.

Chapter 1   **9**

MAP MASTER™ Skills Activity

- Point out to students the shape of South America. Encourage students to trace the outline of the region, while describing its shape.

- Write Amazon Basin, Brazil Highlands, Atacama Desert, and Andes Mountains on the board. Call on students to write the elevation range of each physical feature on the board, using the map key.

Go Online PHSchool.com Students may practice their map skills using the interactive online version of this map.

Using the Visual   L2

Reach Into Your Background Ask students to study the photograph on pages 8 and 9, and read the caption on page 8. Ask them to note details about the image, then share their ideas with the class. Ask **Why do you think these stepping stones exist?** Point out that rain forests get a lot of rainfall. Some areas might be impassable after a heavy rain. Ask students if they can relate this image to their own lives. Allow them to share memories and ideas.

Answers

MAP MASTER™ Skills Activity **Locate** The Andes are on the Pacific coast of South America. The Sierra Madre Occidental and Sierra Madre Oriental cover much of Mexico.
Compare and Contrast The eastern part has a lower elevation than the western and coastal region.

Chapter Resources

Teaching Resources
Letter Home, p. 97
L2 Vocabulary Development, p. 128
L2 Skills for Life, p. 115
L2 Chapter Tests A and B, pp. 130–135

Spanish Support
Spanish Letter Home p. 3
L2 Spanish Chapter Summary, p. 10

L2 Spanish Vocabulary Development, p. 11

Media and Technology
L1 Student Edition on Audio CD
L1 Guided Reading Audiotapes, English and Spanish
L2 Social Studies Skills Tutor CD-ROM
ExamView® Test Bank CD-ROM

DISCOVERY CHANNEL SCHOOL World Studies Video Program

interactive Textbook

PRENTICE HALL
TeacherEXPRESS™ Plan · Teach · Assess

Objectives

Social Studies

1. Learn where Latin America is located.
2. Discover the important landforms of Latin America.
3. Find out how Latin America's waterways have affected the region.

Reading/Language Arts

Preview to set a purpose for reading.

Prepare to Read

Build Background Knowledge **L2**

Tell students that they will start their study of Latin America by learning about its land and water. Show the Discovery Channel School video. Ask students to note three to five facts about Latin America's land and water as they watch. Have students engage in a Give One, Get One activity (TE, p. T37) to share their answers.

📼 *The Geography of Latin America,* **World Studies Video Program**

Set a Purpose for Reading **L2**

■ Preview the Objectives.

■ Read each statement in the *Reading Readiness Guide* aloud. Ask students to mark the statements true or false.

Have students discuss the statements in pairs or groups of four, then mark their worksheets again. Use the Numbered Heads participation structure (TE, p. T36) to call on students to share their group's perspectives.

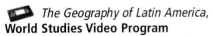 **Latin America Teaching Resources,** *Reading Readiness Guide,* p. 99

Vocabulary Builder

Preview Key Terms **L2**

Create a three-column "See It—Remember It" chart of the Key Terms on the board. Write a term in the first column, a short definition in the second column, and a sketch in the third column. Guide students as they copy and complete the chart.

Prepare to Read

Objectives

In this section you will
1. Learn where Latin America is located.
2. Discover the important landforms of Latin America.
3. Find out how Latin America's waterways have affected the region.

Taking Notes

As you read this section, look for the main ideas about the geography of Latin America. Copy the table below and record your findings in it.

Geography of Latin America		
Region	Landforms	Waterways
Middle America		
Caribbean		
South America		

🎯 Target Reading Skill

Preview and Set a Purpose When you set a purpose for reading, you give yourself a focus. Before you read this section, look at the headings, photos, and maps to see what the section is about. Then set a purpose for reading, such as learning about Latin America's geography. Now read to meet your purpose.

Key Terms

• **Middle America** (MID ul uh MEHR ih kuh) *n.* Mexico and Central America
• **plateau** (pla TOH) *n.* a large raised area of mostly level land
• **isthmus** (IS mus) *n.* a strip of land with water on both sides that joins two larger bodies of land
• **pampas** (PAM puz) *n.* flat grassland regions
• **rain forest** (rayn FAWR ist) *n.* a dense evergreen forest that has abundant rainfall year-round
• **Amazon River** (AM uh zahn RIV ur) *n.* a long river in northern South America
• **tributary** (TRIB yoo tehr ee) *n.* a river or stream that flows into a larger river

La Paz, Bolivia

10   Latin America

What would it be like to land at the highest major airport in the world? Many visitors to La Paz, Bolivia, do just that. They land at El Alto airport. *El Alto* (el AL toh) means "the high one" in Spanish. It is a good name for this airport, which is located more than 13,000 feet (3,962 meters) up in the Andes Mountains.

Shortly after leaving the plane, some visitors may get mountain sickness. The "thin" air of the Andes contains less oxygen than most people are used to. Oxygen starvation makes visitors' hearts beat faster and leaves them short of breath. Later on in the day, the visitors may get terrible headaches. It takes a few days for newcomers' bodies to get used to the mountain air. But the people who live in the Andes do not have these problems. Their bodies are used to the mountain environment.

🎯 Target Reading Skill **L2**

Preview and Set a Purpose for Reading

Point out the Target Reading Skill. Explain to students that passages containing new information are often easier if you have a reason for reading before you begin.

Model setting a purpose for reading using the heading and passage on page 14. Tell students that your purpose for reading Latin America's Waterways is to find out the names of the major waterways of Latin America.

Ask students to read the passage with this purpose in mind. While students are reading, write the waterways mentioned in the passage on the board. Allow students to ask questions about setting a purpose for reading if they are unsure of how to use the skill.

Give students *Preview and Set a Purpose.* Have them complete the activity in groups.

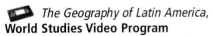 **Latin America Teaching Resources,** *Preview and Set a Purpose,* p. 110;

Where Is Latin America?

When visitors land in La Paz, Bolivia, they have arrived in South America, one of the regions of Latin America. Find Bolivia on the map titled Political Latin America on page 33. As you can see, Latin America is located in the Western Hemisphere, south of the United States. Notice that Latin America includes all the nations from Mexico to the tip of South America. It also includes the islands that dot the Caribbean (ka ruh BEE un) Sea.

Geographic features divide Latin America into three smaller regions, as you can see in the map below. They are Mexico and Central America, which is also called **Middle America;** the Caribbean; and South America. South America is so large that geographers classify it as a continent.

✓ **Reading Check** What three regions make up Latin America?

Learn about the geography of Latin America.

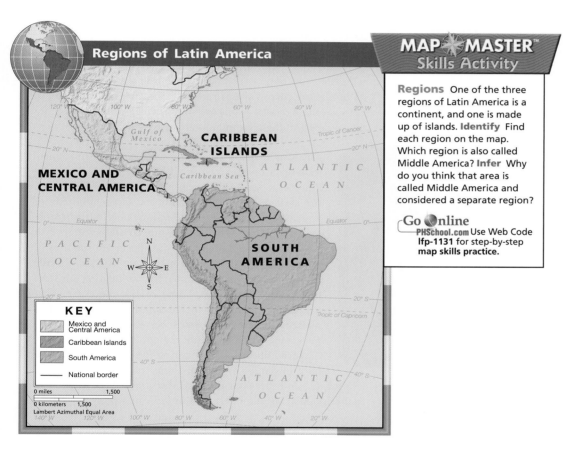

Regions of Latin America

CARIBBEAN ISLANDS

MEXICO AND CENTRAL AMERICA

SOUTH AMERICA

Caribbean Sea

ATLANTIC OCEAN

PACIFIC OCEAN

KEY
- Mexico and Central America
- Caribbean Islands
- South America
- National border

0 miles 1,500
0 kilometers 1,500
Lambert Azimuthal Equal Area

MAP MASTER Skills Activity

Regions One of the three regions of Latin America is a continent, and one is made up of islands. **Identify** Find each region on the map. Which region is also called Middle America? **Infer** Why do you think that area is called Middle America and considered a separate region?

Go Online
PHSchool.com Use Web Code lfp-1131 for step-by-step map skills practice.

Vocabulary Builder

Use the information below to teach students this section's high-use words.

High-Use Word	Definition and Sample Sentence
classify, p. 11	*v.* to arrange by putting into groups The librarian **classifies** books by author, title, and subject.
dominate, p. 12	*v.* to be most powerful or important; to tower over That huge building **dominates** the rest of the block.
impressive, p. 13	*adj.* having a strong effect on the mind or emotions The colorful display of fireworks was **impressive**.

Show students *The Geography of Latin America*. Ask **What geographic features would you find in Latin America?** (*grassy plains, rain forests, coral islands, high mountains, volcanoes*)

Where Is Latin America?   L2

Guided Instruction

- **Vocabulary Builder** Clarify the high-use word **classify** before reading.
- Read Where Is Latin America? using the Structured Silent Reading strategy (TE, p. T34).
- Ask students to use the map on this page to identify the continents spanned by Latin America, and the major bodies of water that border the three regions. (*North America and South America; Pacific Ocean, Caribbean Sea, Atlantic Ocean, and Gulf of Mexico*)

Independent Practice

Assign *Guided Reading and Review.*

All in One **Latin America Teaching Resources,** *Guided Reading and Review,* p. 100

Monitor Progress

As students begin *Guided Reading and Review,* circulate to answer questions and provide assistance as needed.

Answers

✓ **Reading Check** Middle America (Mexico and Central America), the Caribbean, and South America.

MAP MASTER Skills Activity **Identify** Mexico and Central America **Infer** The region falls in the middle of the Western Hemisphere between North America and South America. It has different characteristics from the other two Latin American regions.

Go Online
PHSchool.com Student may practice their map skills using the interactive online version of this map.

Links

Read the **Links Across Time** on this page. Ask students **What do the regions of Latin America have in common?** (*People from Latin America share a language based on the European language of Latin.*)

Landforms of Latin America

L2

Guided Instruction

- **Vocabulary Builder** Clarify the meaning of the high-use words **dominate** and **impressive** before reading.

- Ask students to read Landforms of Latin America. Circulate to make sure that students can answer the Reading Check question.

- Ask students **What landforms would they find in Central America?** (*an isthmus, coastal plains, mountains, and volcanoes*) **In South America?** (*huge mountains, rolling highlands, plains, rain forest*)

- Ask students **How does the mountainous land of Middle America affect the lives of people in the region?** (*Travel is difficult.*)

Independent Practice

Ask students to create the Taking Notes graphic organizer on a blank piece of paper. Then have them fill in the "Landforms" column with the information they have just learned. Briefly model how to choose details, reminding students that "Middle America" is another name for Mexico and Central America.

Monitor Progress

As students complete the "Landforms" column, walk around the room to ensure that students are recording the right details. Answer individual questions and offer help as needed.

Links Across Time

Why "Latin" America? Why are three distinct regions called by one name, Latin America? About 500 years ago, Europeans sailed to the Americas. Most of those who settled in what is now called Latin America came from Spain and Portugal. These European colonists brought their own languages and ways of life with them. Today, most Latin Americans speak Spanish, Portuguese, or French. These languages have their roots in the ancient European language of Latin. As a result, the entire region is known as Latin America.

A parrotfish swims by a coral reef in the Caribbean Sea.

Landforms of Latin America

Picture mountains that pierce the clouds, and grassy plains that never seem to end. Imagine wet, dense forests and sun-baked deserts. This is Latin America, a region of variety and contrast.

Mexico and Central America Mexico and Central America stretch 2,500 miles (4,023 kilometers) from the United States border to South America. This distance is almost equal to the width of the United States from Los Angeles to New York City. Mountains dominate Middle America. These mountains are part of a long system of mountain ranges that extends from Canada through the United States all the way to the tip of South America.

Mexico's central plateau lies between two mountain ranges. A **plateau** (pla TOH) is a large raised area of mostly level land. Most of Mexico's people live there. However, the surrounding mountains make it difficult for people to travel to and from the central plateau. Along the east and west coasts of Mexico are narrow coastal plains.

Central America, located south of Mexico and north of South America, is an isthmus. An **isthmus** (IS mus) is a strip of land with water on both sides that joins two larger bodies of land. As in Mexico, narrow plains run along Central America's coasts. Between these coastal plains are steep, rugged mountains. More than a dozen of these mountains are active volcanoes.

The Caribbean The Caribbean region of Latin America is made up of two types of islands located in the Caribbean Sea. Some of the smaller islands are made of coral, the skeletons of tiny sea animals. Over hundreds of years, the skeletons have melded together to form large reefs and islands. The Bahamas are coral islands.

The larger islands of the Caribbean are the tops of huge underwater mountains. These islands include Cuba, Jamaica (juh MAY kuh), Hispaniola (his pun YOH luh), and Puerto Rico. Some of the mountains that formed the islands of the Caribbean were once volcanoes, and a few of the volcanoes are still active. Earthquakes are common in this region.

In addition to mountain ranges, these islands also have lowlands, or plains, along their coasts. Beautiful landscapes, sandy beaches, and coral reefs make many Caribbean islands popular vacation destinations for tourists.

12 Latin America

Skills Mini Lesson

Making Valid Generalizations L2

1. A generalization is a conclusion based on a few examples. Generalizations help people to see patterns and similarities. To make a generalization, you must gather specific facts, identify similarities, and draw conclusions about the similarities.

2. Model the skill by reading Mexico and Central America on page 12. Note the sentences "Along the east and west coasts of Mexico are narrow coastal plains" and "As in Mexico, narrow plains run along Central America's coasts." A generalization could be: *Narrow plains are found along the coast of many countries in Middle America.*

3. Have students apply the skill by reading The Caribbean and South America and then creating a generalization about all of Latin America.

South America The continent of South America has many types of landforms, but the Andes Mountains are probably the most impressive. The Andes run some 5,500 miles (8,900 kilometers) along the western coast of South America. In some places, the Andes rise to heights of more than 20,000 feet (6,100 meters). That's about as high as twenty 100-story buildings stacked one on top of another. Except for the Himalayan Mountains in Asia, the Andes are the highest mountains in the world.

The Andes are steep and difficult to cross. Even so, many people farm in this region. East of the Andes are rolling highlands. These highlands spread across parts of Brazil, Venezuela (ven uh ZWAY luh), Guyana (gy AN uh), and other South American countries. Farther south are the pampas (PAM puz), a large plains area that stretches through Argentina (ahr jun TEE nuh) and Uruguay (YOOR uh gway). **Pampas** are flat grassland regions that are very similar to the Great Plains of the United States.

The eastern highlands and the Andes surround the Amazon River Basin. The Amazon River Basin contains the largest tropical rain forest in the world. A **rain forest** is a dense evergreen forest that has abundant rainfall throughout the year. This rain forest covers more than a third of the continent.

✓ **Reading Check** Describe the Andes mountain range.

Preview and Set a Purpose
If your purpose is to learn about the geography of Latin America, how does the paragraph at the left help you meet your goal?

Latin American Cowboys
These cowboys are herding cattle in the Patagonia region of Argentina. **Analyze Images** What details in the photo suggest that this scene is not taking place in the United States?

Chapter 1 Section 1 **13**

Background: Global Perspectives

Asia's Mighty Himalaya Mountains
Only the Himalaya, a mountain system in Asia, stand taller than the Andes. The Himalaya make up the tallest range in the world. They extend along the India-Tibet border and through Pakistan, Nepal, China, and Bhutan. The tallest peak of this range is the well-known—and often-climbed—Mount Everest. At 29,035 feet (8,850 meters) above sea level, Everest stands more than a mile higher than the tallest peak in the Andes (and the Western Hemisphere), Aconcagua, which is 22,835 feet (6,960 meters) high.

Assess and Reteach

Assess Progress [L2]

Have students complete the Section Assessment. Administer the *Section Quiz*.

 Latin America Teaching Resources, *Section Quiz,* p. 101

Reteach [L1]

For more instruction, have students read this section in the Reading and Vocabulary Study Guide.

 Chapter 1, Section 1, **Latin America Reading and Vocabulary Study Guide,** pp. 6–8

Extend [L3]

To extend the lesson, have students study the physical map of Latin America on *Reading a Physical Map*. Ask students to complete the worksheet individually or in pairs.

All in One Latin America Teaching Resources, *Reading a Physical Map,* p. 54

Answers

Infer The fishers will probably sell their catch locally because they are using small boats to transport a small number of fish.

✓ **Reading Check** The Paraná, Paraguay, and Uruguay Rivers form the Río de la Plata system.

Section 1 Assessment

Key Terms
Students' sentences should reflect knowledge of each Key Term.

Target Reading Skill
Students should be able to state a reasonable purpose for reading, such as "To learn about the landforms and waterways of Latin America" or "To be able to locate Latin America and name its regions." Students' answers will vary according to whether or not their purpose was accomplished. If not, students should be able to state a different, more appropriate purpose.

Comprehension and Critical Thinking
1. (a) Middle America, the Caribbean, and South America. **(b)** Middle America lies just south of the United States. The Caribbean is east of Middle America. South America is south of the Caribbean.

Fishing the Rivers of Brazil
The families of these Brazilian fishers could not survive without their catch. **Infer** *Do you think these fishers sell their catch locally or send it to other countries? Use details from the photo to explain your answer.*

Latin America's Waterways

Latin America has some of the longest and largest bodies of water in the world. These waterways are important to the people of the region. Rivers serve as natural highways in places where it is hard to build roads. Fish from the rivers provide food. Rushing water from large rivers provides power to generate electricity.

Latin America's **Amazon** (AM uh zahn) **River** is the second-longest river in the world. Only the Nile in Africa is longer. The Amazon flows 4,000 miles (6,437 kilometers) from Peru across Brazil into the Atlantic Ocean. It carries more water than any other river in the world—about 20 percent of all the fresh river water on Earth! The Amazon gathers power from more than 1,000 tributaries that spill into it. **Tributaries** are the rivers and streams that flow into a larger river. With its tributaries, the Amazon drains an area of more than two million square miles.

The Paraná (pah rah NAH), Paraguay, and Uruguay rivers form the Río de la Plata system, which separates Argentina and Uruguay. In Venezuela, people travel on the Orinoco River and Lake Maracaibo (mar uh KY boh). They also use Lake Titicaca, which is the highest lake in the world on which ships can travel. It lies 12,500 feet (3,810 kilometers) high in the Andes Mountains.

✓ **Reading Check** What rivers form the Río de la Plata system?

Section 1 Assessment

Key Terms
Review the key terms at the beginning of this section. Use each term in a sentence that explains its meaning.

Target Reading Skill
What was your purpose for reading this section? Did you accomplish it? If not, what might have been a better purpose?

Comprehension and Critical Thinking
1. (a) Name What are the three regions of Latin America?

(b) Synthesize Where are the regions located in relation to one another?
2. (a) Recall What are the main landforms of Latin America?
(b) Identify Cause and Effect How do mountain ranges affect life in Latin America?
3. (a) Identify Which is the largest river in Latin America?
(b) Analyze Information What are three important characteristics of that river?
(c) Generalize How do countries benefit from their waterways?

Writing Activity
If your family were planning to move to Latin America, which of its three regions would you prefer to live in? Write a paragraph explaining your choice.

Writing Tip Begin your paragraph with a topic sentence that states your main idea—your choice of region. Give at least two reasons for your choice. Support each reason with a specific detail.

14 Latin America

---

2. (a) The main landforms of Latin America are mountains, plains, rain forests, plateaus, highlands, and deserts. **(b)** Mountains make it difficult to travel, but some people are able to farm in the region.

3. (a) Amazon **(b)** It carries 20 percent of all fresh water on Earth, has more than 1,000 tributaries, and drains more than two million square miles. **(c)** People use rivers for travel, electricity, and as a source of food.

Writing Activity

Use the *Rubric for Assessing a Writing Assignment* to evaluate students' paragraphs.

All in One Latin America Teaching Resources, *Rubric for Assessing a Writing Assignment,* p. 129

Prepare to Read

Objectives

In this section you will
1. Find out what kinds of climate Latin America has.
2. Learn what factors influence climate in Latin America.
3. Understand how climate and vegetation influence the ways people live.

Taking Notes

As you read this section, look for the ways different factors affect climate and vegetation. Copy the table below and record your findings in it.

Factor	Effect on Climate	Effect on Vegetation

Target Reading Skill

Preview and Predict Making predictions about your text helps you set a purpose for reading and remember what you read. Before you begin, look at the headings, photos, and anything else that stands out. Then predict what the text might be about. For example, you might predict that this section will tell about Latin America's climate and plants. As you read, if what you learn doesn't support your prediction, revise your prediction.

Key Terms

- **El Niño** (el NEEN yoh) *n.* a warming of the ocean water along the western coast of South America
- **elevation** (el uh VAY shun) *n.* the height of land above sea level
- **economy** (ih KAHN uh mee) *n.* the ways that goods and services are produced and made available to people

---

Every few years, something strange happens off the western coast of South America. Fish that usually thrive in the cold waters of the Pacific Ocean are driven away. At the same time, other changes occur on land. Areas that usually have dry weather get heavy rains, and low-lying regions are flooded. In other parts of Latin America, drought plagues the land and the people.

What brings this disaster to Latin America? It is **El Niño** (el NEEN yoh), a warming of the ocean water along the western coast of South America. It occurs every few years and influences global weather patterns. El Niño is Spanish for "the Christ child." Latin Americans gave it this name because it usually strikes near Christmas time. El Niño is one of many factors that affect climate in Latin America.

The warm water current of El Niño appears red in this view from space.

Target Reading Skill

Preview and Predict Point out the Target Reading Skill. Tell students that to predict what the reading will be about, they should make an educated guess about the content based on clues. Clues might include photos, headings, maps, or even boldfaced words in the passage. Explain to students that once they make a prediction, they can read the passage with the purpose of finding out whether their prediction is correct or needs to be revised.

As an example, ask students to look at the head and the diagram on page 18 of the Student Edition. Using those clues, make this prediction: "This passage will explain what vertical climate zones are and how height affects climate."

Give students *Preview and Predict*. Have them complete the activity in groups.

All in One Latin America Teaching Resources, *Preview and Predict,* p. 111

Objectives

Social Studies

1. Find out what kinds of climate Latin America has.
2. Learn what factors influence climate in Latin America.
3. Understand how climate and vegetation influence the way people live.

Reading/Language Arts

Make predictions about a text to help set a purpose for reading.

Prepare to Read

Build Background Knowledge L2

In this section, students will learn about the climate and plant life of Latin America. Tell them that climate is a place's weather conditions over a number of years. Ask students to list examples of how climate affects their lives. Model a statement such as "When it is rainy, I don't like to sit outside." Conduct an Idea Wave (TE, p. T35) so that students can share their answers.

Set a Purpose for Reading L2

- Preview the Objectives.
- Form students into pairs or groups of four. Distribute the *Reading Readiness Guide*. Ask the students to fill in the first two columns of the chart. Use the Numbered Heads participation structure (TE, p. T36) to call on students to share one piece of information they already know and one piece of information they want to know.

All in One Latin America Teaching Resources, *Reading Readiness Guide,* p. 99

Vocabulary Builder
Preview Key Terms L2

Pronounce each Key Term, then ask the students to say the word with you. Provide a simple explanation for each term such as, "As you climb to the top of a mountain, the elevation increases."

The Climates of Latin America

L2

Guided Instruction

- **Vocabulary Builder** Clarify the meaning of the high-use word **vary** before reading.
- Read The Climates of Latin America with students, using the Oral Cloze technique (TE, p. T33).
- Have students look at the map on page 16 and tell which climate in Latin America most resembles the climate where they live and why. *(Answers will vary depending on where students live.)*

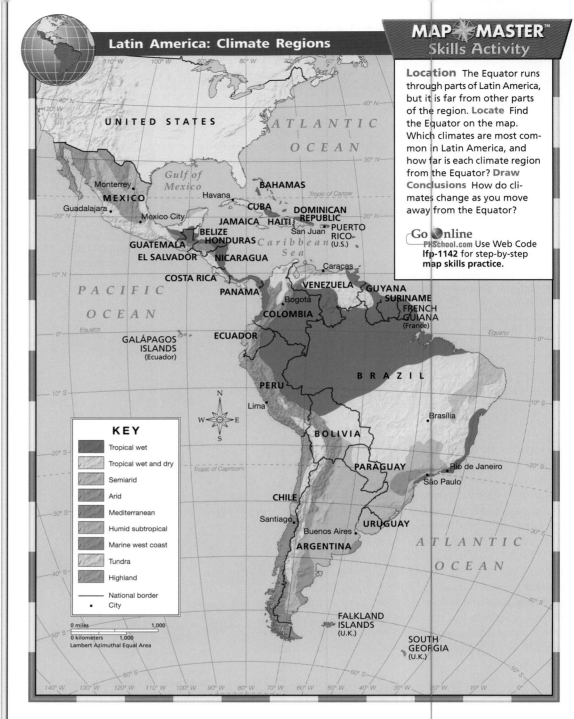

Latin America: Climate Regions

MAP MASTER™ Skills Activity

Location The Equator runs through parts of Latin America, but it is far from other parts of the region. **Locate** Find the Equator on the map. Which climates are most common in Latin America, and how far is each climate region from the Equator? **Draw Conclusions** How do climates change as you move away from the Equator?

Go Online
PHSchool.com Use Web Code lfp-1142 for step-by-step **map skills practice.**

KEY

- Tropical wet
- Tropical wet and dry
- Semiarid
- Arid
- Mediterranean
- Humid subtropical
- Marine west coast
- Tundra
- Highland
- ――― National border
- • City

0 miles 1,000
0 kilometers 1,000
Lambert Azimuthal Equal Area

Answers

MAP MASTER Skills Activity **Locate** The most common climates in Latin America are tropical wet, and tropical wet and dry. Both types of climate are found on or near the Equator. **Draw Conclusions** As you move farther away from the Equator, climates generally become cooler and drier.

Go Online
PHSchool.com Students may practice their map skills using the interactive online version of this map.

Vocabulary Builder

Use the information below to teach students this section's high-use words.

High-Use Word	Definition and Sample Sentence
vary, p. 17	*v.* to change The weather **varied** from hard rain to sunny skies.
moderate, p. 18	*adj.* not extreme A **moderate** breeze cooled her hot forehead.
abundant, p. 21	*adj.* existing in ample supply Her hair was thick and **abundant.**
irregular, p. 21	*adj.* not according to the usual pattern or rules; unpredictable The weather person could not predict the **irregular** weather.

The Climates of Latin America

What is the climate like where you live? Is it hot? Cold? Rainy? Dry? If you lived in Latin America, the climate might be any of these. Climate in Latin America can vary greatly even within the same country.

Hot, Cold, Wild, and Mild In parts of the Andes, below-zero temperatures can set your teeth chattering. Travel to the Amazon Basin, and you may be sweating in 90°F (32°C) heat. And don't forget your umbrella! This part of Latin America receives more than 80 inches (203 centimeters) of rain each year. If you prefer dry weather, visit the Atacama (ah tah KAH mah) Desert in Chile or the Sonoran Desert in Mexico. These areas are two of the driest places on Earth.

The weather in the Caribbean is usually sunny and warm. From June to November, however, the region is often hit with fierce hurricanes. In 1988, Hurricane Gilbert shattered the sunny Caribbean weather with a wild blast. Winds howled at more than 180 miles per hour (300 kilometers per hour). Waves nearly 20 feet (6 meters) high smashed into the coast. The storm tore roofs off houses, shattered windows, and yanked huge trees from the ground. Gilbert turned out to be the strongest hurricane to strike the Western Hemisphere in the twentieth century.

Hurricanes are a part of life for people living in the Caribbean. But people in other parts of Latin America have to deal with other climates. For example, people who live in the mountains need to protect themselves against the cold. That's because the higher up the mountains you go, the cooler it gets.

Climate Regions of Latin America Look at the map titled Latin America: Climate Regions. You will notice that many parts of Latin America have a tropical wet climate. A tropical wet climate means hot, humid, and rainy weather all year round.

Other parts of Latin America have a tropical wet and dry climate. These areas are equally hot, but the rainy season does not last all year long. Parts of Mexico and Brazil and most of the Caribbean have a tropical wet and dry climate.

Much of Argentina, Uruguay, and Paraguay has a humid subtropical climate, similar to that of parts of the southern United States. Here, the summers are hot and wet while the winters are cool and damp. Farther south, the climate turns arid, or dry. This colder, drier area is called Patagonia (pat uh GOH nee uh).

√ **Reading Check** Describe a tropical wet and dry climate.

Links to Science

What is a Hurricane? A hurricane is a strong tropical storm with winds of 73 miles per hour (117 kilometers per hour) or more. Hurricanes get their energy from warm, humid air at the ocean's surface. As the warm air rises and forms clouds, more air is pulled into the developing storm. The winds spiral inward. As the storm grows, it creates very high winds and heavy rains. At the center of the hurricane is the "eye," an area of calm. After the eye passes over an area, the hurricane resumes. It can still cause serious damage, as Hurricane Mitch did in Nicaragua in 1998 (photo below).

Guided Instruction (continued)

- Have students consider what life would be like in a region that is often hit hard by hurricanes, such as the Caribbean islands. Ask **What parts of life would be affected by a hurricane?** (*Hurricanes can destroy homes, devastate fields full of crops, cause roads to flood and become impassable, and knock down electrical wires.*)

- **How would you contrast the climate in northern Brazil with the climate in Patagonia?** (*The climate in northern Brazil is hot, humid, and rainy all year round, whereas the climate in Patagonia is cold and dry.*)

Independent Practice

Assign *Guided Reading and Review*.

All in One **Latin America Teaching Resources,** *Guided Reading and Review,* p. 104

Monitor Progress

Circulate among students as they begin the worksheet to answer questions and provide assistance as needed.

Links

Read the **Links to Science** on this page. Ask students **What makes hurricanes so dangerous?** (*The high winds of a hurricane can destroy homes and towns, and the heavy rains can cause flooding.*)

Differentiated Instruction

For Advanced Readers   L3

Have students read more about hurricanes using the library or approved Internet resources. Working in pairs or small groups, ask students to research one hurricane and its effect on the area it hit. Students can use the information they find to create a short oral report to present to the class.

Answers

√ **Reading Check** A tropical wet and dry climate has hot weather all year long, with a humid, rainy season and a drier season.

What Factors Affect Climate?

Guided Instruction

- **Vocabulary Builder** Clarify the meaning of the high-use word **moderate** before reading.

- Read about elevation, location, and wind patterns in What Factors Affect Climate? As students read, circulate and make sure that they can answer the Reading Check question.

- Ask students to apply the information they have just learned by answering these questions: **How do you think these three factors affect the climate in the region where we live? Is elevation an important factor? How far are we from the Equator? What kind of wind patterns do we have?** (*Answers will depend on region.*)

Independent Practice

Ask students to create the Taking Notes graphic organizer on a sheet of paper. Have them complete the "Factor" and "Effect on Climate" columns using the information in the reading. Model identifying a factor and an effect. Record each detail in the organizer.

Monitor Progress

As students work on the graphic organizer, walk around the classroom to answer questions and assist those who are having trouble identifying the correct details.

Answers

✓ **Reading Check** Regions near the Equator usually have a warm climate unless the region's elevation is high.

Diagram Skills Identify The elevation of the tree line is 10,000 feet (3,048 meters). Above 14,000 feet (4,267 meters) snow will not melt. **Draw Conclusions** Above the snow line, there is not sufficient grass for grazing, and below the tree line, farmers grow crops that they do not want the animals to eat.

What Factors Affect Climate?

Have you ever hiked in the mountains? If so, you've probably noticed that as you climbed higher the temperature dropped.

One key factor affecting the climate of mountainous Latin America is **elevation**, the height of land above sea level. Look at the diagram titled Vertical Climate Zones. It shows how elevation affects climate. As you can see, the higher the elevation, the colder the temperature. Near the Equator, it may be a warm 80°F (27°C) at sea level. But above 10,000 feet (3,048 meters), the temperature may remain below freezing—too cold for people to live.

Location also affects Latin America's climate. Regions close to the Equator are generally warmer than those farther away. Look at the map titled Latin America: Climate Regions on page 16. Find the Equator. Which parts of Latin America are closest to the Equator? These regions are likely to have the warmest weather.

Wind patterns affect climate too. Winds move cold air from the North and South poles toward the Equator. They also move warm air from the Equator toward the poles. In the Caribbean, sea breezes help to keep temperatures moderate. Winds also affect rainfall in the Caribbean. More rain falls on the sides of islands facing the wind than on the sides facing away.

✓ **Reading Check** How does nearness to the Equator affect climate?

■ Diagram Skills

Even near the Equator, temperature varies with elevation. Notice the tree line. Above the tree line, it is too cold and windy for trees to grow. **Identify** What is the elevation of the tree line? Above what elevation is there snow year-round? **Draw Conclusions** Why is land between the tree line and the snow line used for grazing?

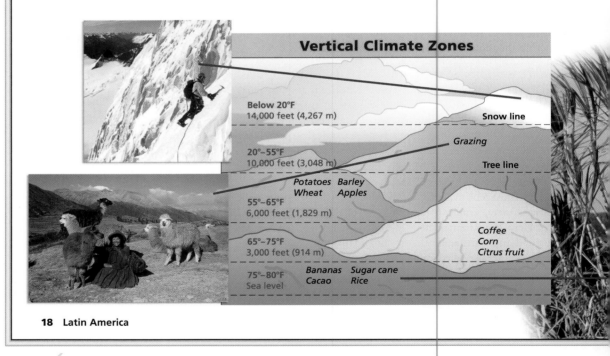

Vertical Climate Zones

Below 20°F 14,000 feet (4,267 m)		Snow line
20°–55°F 10,000 feet (3,048 m)	Grazing	Tree line
55°–65°F 6,000 feet (1,829 m)	Potatoes Barley Wheat Apples	
65°–75°F 3,000 feet (914 m)		Coffee Corn Citrus fruit
75°–80°F Sea level	Bananas Sugar cane Cacao Rice	

Skills Mini Lesson

Analyzing Photographs   L2

1. Point out that by examining a photograph closely and asking questions about it, students can gain more information about a topic.

2. Help students practice the skill by looking at the large photograph on page 19. Have them read the caption and ask them to identify what location is being shown.

3. Have students apply the skill by asking themselves other questions about the photo. (*For example: What feeling do I get from this photograph? What would life be like here?*)

Climate, Plants, and People

Imagine a forest so dense and lush that almost no sunlight reaches the ground. Broad green leaves, tangled vines, and thousands of species of trees and plants surround you. The air is hot and heavy with moisture. Welcome to the Amazon rain forest.

Now, suppose you have traveled to the coast of northern Chile. You're in the Atacama Desert. Winds carry no moisture to this barren land, and there are few signs of life. The Andes shield this parched region from rain. Parts of the desert have not felt a single raindrop in hundreds of years.

Vegetation Regions Latin America's varied climate and physical features make such extremes possible. Look at the map titled Latin America: Vegetation Regions on the next page. Notice which countries in Latin America have areas of tropical rain forest. Now, find these countries on the climate map. How do the tropical climate and heavy rainfall in these countries influence the vegetation that grows there?

Of course, not all of Latin America is either rain forest or desert. Many regions of Latin America with less extreme climates have different kinds of vegetation. For example, the pampas of Argentina and Uruguay are grassy plains where cattle are raised. Herding is also a way of life on grasslands high in the Andes Mountains, where Native Americans have raised llamas for centuries. Llamas are used mostly as pack animals. Their relatives, alpacas and vicuñas, provide fine wool.

Preview and Predict Based on what you've read so far, is your prediction on target? If not, revise or change your prediction now.

Life in the Climate Zones
A mountain climber ascends above the snow line in Argentina (facing page, top), and llamas graze above the tree line (facing page, bottom). In the photo on this page, a woman harvests sugar cane in Barbados. **Generalize** *At what elevations would you expect to find most farms? Explain why.*

Chapter 1 Section 2 **19**

Background: Links Across Time

Mummies of the Atacama Desert
The Chinchorro, a people who lived in what is today Chile more than 5,000 years ago, preserved their dead as mummies—long before the Egyptians did so. The Atacama Desert is so dry that the bodies could be preserved without decay for thousands of years.

Target Reading Skill L2
Preview and Predict As a follow up, ask students to answer the Target Reading Skill question in the Student Edition. (*Answers will vary, but students should be able to recognize whether their prediction is accurate.*)

Climate, Plants, and People L2

Guided Instruction
- **Vocabulary Builder** Clarify the meaning of the high-use words **abundant** and **irregular** before reading.
- Read Climate, Plants, and People with students.
- Engage students in a discussion about the relationship between climate and economy. Ask questions such as **What might happen to the gauchos of Argentina and Uruguay in a year of drought?** (*Gauchos would not be able to adequately feed their cattle in a year of drought and might lose income.*)
- **Why would a sugar cane farmer not want to live at the top of a mountain?** (*Sugar cane requires warm temperatures to grow, and temperatures would be too cool at high elevations.*)

Independent Practice
Have students complete the graphic organizer by filling in the "Effect on Vegetation" column using the information on pages 19–21.

Monitor Progress
- Show *Section Reading Support Transparency LA 29* and ask students to check their graphic organizers individually. Go over key concepts and clarify key vocabulary as needed.

  Latin America Transparencies, *Section Reading Support Transparency LA 29*

- Tell students to fill in the last column of *Reading Readiness Guide*. Probe for what they learned that confirms or invalidates each statement.

  All in One Latin America Teaching Resources, *Reading Readiness Guide*, p. 103

Answers
Generalize between sea level and 10,000 feet (3,048 meters)

Assess and Reteach

Assess Progress L2

Have students complete the Section Assessment. Administer the *Section Quiz*.

All in One **Latin America Teaching Resources**, *Section Quiz*, p. 105

Reteach L1

For more instruction, have students read this section in the Reading and Vocabulary Study Guide.

📖 Chapter 1, Section 2, **Latin America Reading and Vocabulary Study Guide**, pp. 9–11

Extend L3

Have students work together in small groups to complete the *Small Group Activity: Making a Relief Map*. Try to group students of varying abilities together.

All in One **Latin America Teaching Resources**, *Small Group Activity: Making a Relief Map*, pp. 116–119

Answers

MAP MASTER Skills Activity **Identify** The two largest vegetation regions in Latin America are tropical rain forest and tropical savanna.

Compare The outlines of vegetation regions are, in many cases, similar to climate regions. For example, the tropical wet climate region is also the region in which tropical rain forests are found.

Go Online PHSchool.com Students may practice their map skills using the interactive online version of this map.

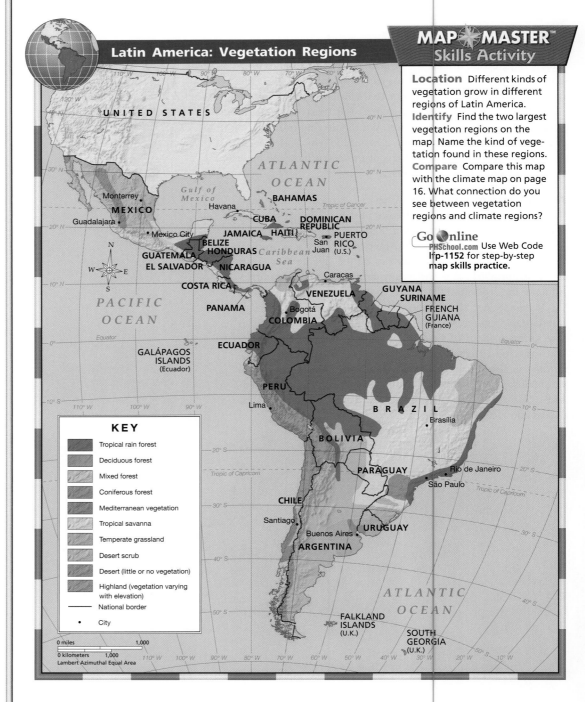

MAP MASTER™ Skills Activity

Latin America: Vegetation Regions

Location Different kinds of vegetation grow in different regions of Latin America. **Identify** Find the two largest vegetation regions on the map. Name the kind of vegetation found in these regions. **Compare** Compare this map with the climate map on page 16. What connection do you see between vegetation regions and climate regions?

Go Online PHSchool.com Use Web Code lfp-1152 for step-by-step map skills practice.

KEY

- Tropical rain forest
- Deciduous forest
- Mixed forest
- Coniferous forest
- Mediterranean vegetation
- Tropical savanna
- Temperate grassland
- Desert scrub
- Desert (little or no vegetation)
- Highland (vegetation varying with elevation)
- National border
- • City

0 miles 1,000
0 kilometers 1,000
Lambert Azimuthal Equal Area

20 Latin America

Differentiated Instruction

For Gifted and Talented L3

To help students expand their knowledge of the vegetation of Latin America, have them complete the *Activity Shop Interdisciplinary: Rain Forest Resources*.

All in One **Latin America Teaching Resources**, *Activity Shop Interdisciplinary: Rain Forest Resources*, pp. 120–121

Crops and Climate Temperature and rainfall affect not only what plants grow naturally in a region, but also what crops people can grow there. Sugar cane, coffee, and bananas require warm weather and abundant rainfall. These crops are important to the economies of many countries around the Caribbean Sea. The **economy** is the ways that goods and services are produced and made available to people. Look at the climate map. Why do you think the area around the Caribbean is well suited to growing these crops?

Elevation and Vegetation Elevation also affects vegetation. For example, palm trees and fruit trees that grow well in the coastal plains of Mexico and Central America would not survive high in the Andes. To grow at higher elevations, plants must be able to withstand cooler temperatures, chill winds, and irregular rainfall.

Look again at the diagram titled Vertical Climate Zones. Notice the tree line and the snow line. It is too cold and windy for trees to grow above the tree line, but plants that grow low to the ground are found in this area. What kinds of plants might be suited to this elevation? What kinds of animals might also be found there? Above the snow line of a mountain, snow does not melt. Do you think there is any vegetation above the snow line?

Harvesting bananas in Honduras

✓ Reading Check **Describe how elevation affects the vegetation of a region.**

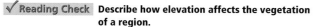

Section 2 Assessment

Key Terms
Review the key terms at the beginning of this section. Use each term in a sentence that explains its meaning.

Target Reading Skill
What did you predict about this section? How did your prediction guide your reading?

Comprehension and Critical Thinking
1. (a) Recall Describe Latin America's climate regions.

(b) Synthesize How does climate affect the ways that Latin Americans live?
2. (a) Identify Name three factors that affect climate.
(b) Apply Information Why might two areas near the Equator have very different climates?
3. (a) Name What two factors affect the kinds of vegetation that grow in a region?
(b) Infer Why do some farmers in Argentina raise apples while farmers in other parts of the country raise sheep?

Writing Activity
Would you pack differently for trips to the Atacama Desert and the Andes Mountains? Write a paragraph describing what you would take to each place and why.

For: An activity on the rain forest
Visit: PHSchool.com
Web Code: lfd-1102

Answers

✓ Reading Check Only vegetation that can withstand cold temperatures and irregular rainfall grows well at higher elevations; plants that need warm temperatures and steady rainfall thrive at lower elevations.

Section 2 Assessment

Key Terms
Students' sentences should reflect knowledge of each key term.

Target Reading Skill
Students' predictions should be appropriate to the section content, such as: "This section will contain information about how climate in Latin America influences the lives of people who live there." Thought-provoking predictions guide students' reading by helping them to stay focused. Students can read to find out if their predictions are on target or if they need to revise their predictions.

Comprehension and Critical Thinking
1. (a) The climate regions of Latin America include: tropical wet—hot, humid, and rainy all year; tropical wet and dry—hot and rainy during part of the year, and hot and dry the rest of the year; humid subtropical—hot and wet summers, cool and damp winters; and arid—dry. **(b)** Climate affects the variety and success of crops and the type of clothing and shelter needed to survive.

2. (a) elevation, location, and wind patterns **(b)** One area may have a higher elevation and thus a colder climate than the other.

3. (a) temperature and amount of rainfall **(b)** Apples grow best in the cool climate found in parts of northern and central Argentina, while sheep are raised in drier, colder climates in other parts of the country.

Writing Activity
Use the *Rubric for Assessing a Writing Assignment* to evaluate students' paragraphs.

All in One Latin America Teaching Resources, *Rubric for Assessing a Writing Assignment,* p. 129

Go Online
PHSchool.com Typing in the Web code when prompted will bring students directly to detailed instructions for this activity.

Objective

Learn how to analyze and interpret special-purpose maps.

Prepare to Read

Build Background Knowledge · L2

Ask students to think about times they have needed to use a map. Ask them what kinds of maps they have used. Create a list on the board.

Analyzing and Interpreting Special-Purpose Maps · L2

Guided Instruction

- Read the steps to analyze and interpret a special-purpose map as a class and write them on the board.

- Practice the skill by following the steps on p. 22 as a class. Model each step in the activity by choosing a sample vacation activity *(warm water surfing)*, identifying what climate the activity requires *(tropical wet, tropical wet and dry, or humid subtropical, located on the ocean)*, then find some locations on the map that meet your requirements *(any island in the Caribbean, most of the Atlantic coast of South America through the southern border of Uruguay, most of the Pacific and Atlantic coasts of Central America and parts of Mexico.)*

- Ask students to choose at least three of the vacation activities they brainstormed earlier. Then have students follow the steps to determine where in Latin America they should visit to do each activity.

Analyzing and Interpreting Climate Maps

> **Travel agent:** Thanks for calling South America Travel Service. May I help you?
>
> **Customer:** I'd like to visit South America, but I can't decide where to go. Could you send me brochures of places you recommend?
>
> **Travel agent:** Certainly. And you might want to visit our Web site, which features a climate map of South America. You'll see that the region has many climates, offering activities from water skiing to snow skiing.

A special purpose map shows information about a particular topic. The climate map on the next page is a type of special purpose map. The travel agent knows that for most people, climate is an important factor in deciding where to vacation.

Learn the Skill

Use these steps to analyze and interpret a climate map.

1. **Read the map title and look at the map to get a general idea of what it shows.** Notice the area for which climate is being shown.

2. **Read the key to understand how the map uses symbols, colors, and patterns.** A climate map usually uses colors to represent different climates.

3. **Use the key to interpret the map.** Look for the different colors on the map. Notice where different climates are located, and what landforms and waterways are also in those locations.

4. **Draw conclusions about what the map shows.** Facts you discover when you analyze a climate map can help you draw conclusions about a place: what kinds of plants and animals live there or how the people make a living.

22 Latin America

Independent Practice

Assign *Skills for Life* and have students complete it individually.

All in One **Latin America Teaching Resources,** *Skills for Life,* p. 115

Monitor Progress

As students are completing *Skills for Life*, circulate to make sure individuals are applying the skill steps effectively. Provide assistance as needed.

Practice the Skill

If you were the caller on page 22, where would you want to go on your vacation? List your favorite vacation activities, and then use the map on this page to identify several places you would like to visit.

1 Jot down the purpose of the map. What does it show?

2 Look at the key to see the different climates in South America. Identify the climates in which you could probably do the vacation activities on your list.

3 On the map, find the places that have the climates you have identified.

4 Use the climate map to draw conclusions about each place you found. Might the place have ocean views? Rock walls to climb? Forests with fascinating wildlife? Write your conclusions for each place, and choose a vacation destination.

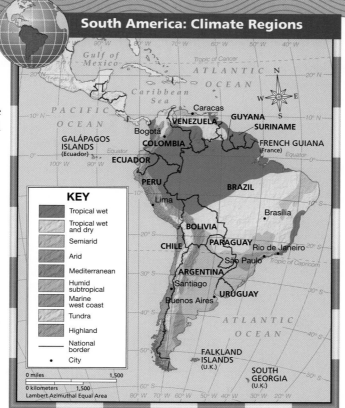

South America: Climate Regions

KEY
- Tropical wet
- Tropical wet and dry
- Semiarid
- Arid
- Mediterranean
- Humid subtropical
- Marine west coast
- Tundra
- Highland
- National border
- • City

0 miles 1,500
0 kilometers 1,500
Lambert Azimuthal Equal Area

Apply the Skill

Now take the role of the travel agent. You get an e-mail from an author. "I am writing a book that takes place in a desert region of South America that is also near the ocean. Where should I go to do my research?"

Turn to your map. **(a)** In what climate are you likely to find a desert? **(b)** What places in South America have that type of climate? **(c)** Among those places, which is closest to the ocean? Write a reply to the author. Suggest a location and explain why it will suit her needs.

Assess and Reteach

Assess Progress L2
Ask students to do the Apply the Skill activity.

Reteach L1
If students are having trouble applying the skill steps, have them review the skill using the interactive Social Studies Skills Tutor CD-ROM.

⊙ *Analyzing and Interpreting Special-Purpose Maps,* **Social Studies Skills Tutor CD-ROM**

Extend L3
■ To extend the lesson, ask students to apply the skill steps to the physical map of Mexico on *Color Transparency LA 26.* Instead of analyzing climate regions, however, the students will analyze Mexico's elevation.

■ Ask them to identify what the colors on the map key indicate *(the elevation of land).* Then ask them to identify what part of Mexico has an elevation of 5,000 to 10,000 feet *(the Plateau of Mexico).* What parts of Mexico have an elevation of 0 to 1,000 feet? *(both coasts)* Finally, remind students higher elevation usually causes lower temperatures. What conclusion can they draw about the temperature of the Plateau of Mexico? *(It will be cooler there than in areas with lower elevation.)*

📖 **Latin America Transparencies,** *Color Transparency LA 26: Mexico: Physical-Political*

Answers
Apply the Skill

(a) arid

(b) northern Mexico including Baja California; inland Argentina and the southern half of Argentina's Atlantic coast; a strip of land along the Pacific Coast in Peru and northern Chile

(c) Baja California; the southern part of Argentina's Atlantic coast; land along the Pacific Coast in Peru and northern Chile. Students' replies should describe the locations of these arid regions near the ocean.

Section 3
Step-by-Step Instruction

Objectives

Social Studies

1. Find out what Latin America's most important natural resources are.
2. Learn why depending on a one-resource economy has been a problem for Latin American nations.

Reading/Language Arts

Create questions to help you understand and remember what you read.

Prepare to Read

Build Background Knowledge L2

Tell students that they will learn about the natural resources of Latin America in this section. Ask students to briefly preview the headings and visuals, then predict what some of the region's natural resources might be. Conduct an Idea Wave (TE, p. T35) to elicit responses.

Set a Purpose for Reading L2

■ Preview the Objectives.

■ Read each statement in the *Reading Readiness Guide* aloud. Ask students to mark the statements true or false.

■ Have students discuss the statements in pairs or groups of four, and then mark their worksheets again. Use the Numbered Heads participation structure (TE, p. T36) to call on students to share their group's perspectives.

All in One **Latin America Teaching Resources,** *Reading Readiness Guide,* p. 107

Vocabulary Builder
Preview Key Terms L2

Pronounce each Key Term, and then ask the students to say the word with you. Provide a simple explanation, such as, "When you plant different kinds of crops instead of just one crop, you diversify your farming."

Section 3 Resources and Land Use

Prepare to Read

Objectives

In this section you will
1. Find out what Latin America's most important natural resources are.
2. Learn why depending on a one-resource economy has been a problem for Latin American nations.

Taking Notes

As you read this section, look for the major resources of each region of Latin America. Copy the chart below and record your findings in it.

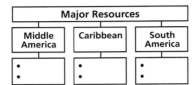

Major Resources		
Middle America	Caribbean	South America
•	•	•
•	•	•

Target Reading Skill

Preview and Ask Questions Before you read this section, preview the headings and illustrations to see what the section is about. Then write two questions that will help you understand or remember something important in the section. For example, you might ask, "What are the resources of Middle America?" Then read to answer your questions.

Key Terms

• **natural resources** (NACH ur ul REE sawrs uz) *n.* things found in nature that people can use to meet their needs
• **hydroelectricity** (hy droh ee lek TRIS ih tee) *n.* electric power produced by rushing water
• **one-resource economy** (wun REE sawrs ih KAHN uh mee) *n.* a country's economy based largely on one resource or crop
• **diversify** (duh VUR suh fy) *v.* to add variety

Quechua Indian women sort ore at a Bolivian tin mine.

Bolivia has long depended on its mineral resources for wealth. At first, silver helped to bring money into Bolivia's treasury. Soon, however, tin became even more important. For many years, Bolivia enjoyed the wealth that tin brought to the economy. Then, in the 1920s and 1930s, a worldwide economic crisis hit. Industries stopped buying tin, as well as other natural resources. Bolivia suffered as its main resource failed to bring in money. This economic crisis hit all of Latin America hard. It brought home a problem that many Latin American nations have: They rely too much on one resource.

Latin America's Resources

What do the following things have in common: fish, petroleum, water, silver, and forests? They are all natural resources of Latin America. **Natural resources** are things found in nature that people can use to meet their needs. Latin America's resources are as varied as its physical features and climate.

24 Latin America

Target Reading Skill L2

Preview and Ask Questions Point out the Target Reading Skill. Explain that creating questions about the reading is an effective way to read with a focus. Model previewing and asking questions using the subhead on page 27. Show students that South America: A Wealth of Resources can be rephrased as the question: "What resources are found in South America?"

Ask students to read the passage on page 27 with that question in mind. Then model answering the question by mentioning these resources: minerals, oil, forests, fish, rich soil.

Give students *Preview and Ask Questions*. Have them complete the activity in groups.

All in One **Latin America Teaching Resources,** *Preview and Ask Questions,* p. 112

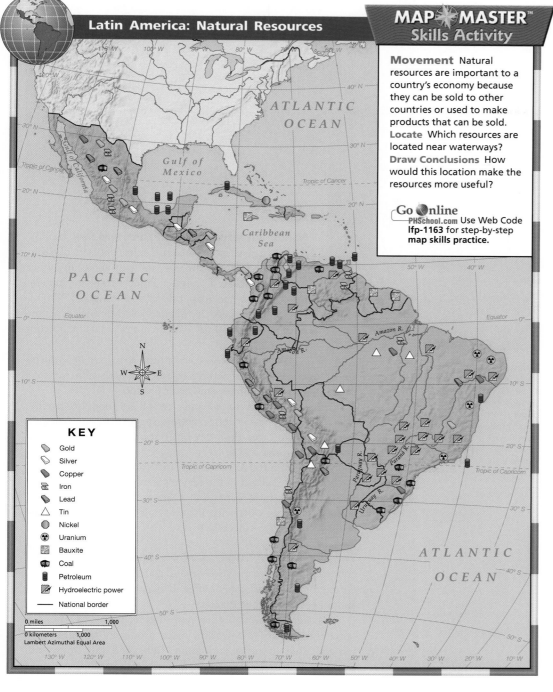

Latin America: Natural Resources

MAP MASTER™ Skills Activity

Movement Natural resources are important to a country's economy because they can be sold to other countries or used to make products that can be sold.

Locate Which resources are located near waterways?

Draw Conclusions How would this location make the resources more useful?

Go Online
PHSchool.com Use Web Code lfp-1163 for step-by-step map skills practice.

KEY

- Gold
- Silver
- Copper
- Iron
- Lead
- Tin
- Nickel
- Uranium
- Bauxite
- Coal
- Petroleum
- Hydroelectric power
- National border

0 miles 1,000
0 kilometers 1,000
Lambert Azimuthal Equal Area

Latin America's Resources L2

Guided Instruction

- **Vocabulary Builder** Clarify the meaning of the high-use word **deposit** before reading.

- Read Latin America's Resources using the ReQuest Procedure (TE, p. T35). As students engage in the silent reading portion of the technique, circulate to ensure that students are able to answer the Reading Check question.

- Ask students **What are some uses that you can think of for the different kinds of minerals found in Middle America and the Caribbean?** (*Coal and oil are used for fuel; copper and iron can be found in household items such as pots and pans; bauxite is used to make aluminum; gold and silver are precious metals sometimes found in jewelry.*)

- Ask students to identify three natural resources of the Caribbean. **Which resources does the Caribbean have in common with Mexico?** (*Three resources of the Caribbean are rich soil, minerals, and oil; all three are also found in Mexico.*)

Vocabulary Builder

Use the information below to teach students this section's high-use words.

High-Use Word	Definition and Sample Sentence
deposit, p. 26	*n.* a natural supply Finding the **deposit** of gold made the prospector rich.
factor, p. 29	*n.* something that actively brings about a result The heat of the sun was a **factor** in my decision to move inside.
dependence, p. 29	*n.* trust or reliance Nina's **dependence** on Jane for rides may be a problem if Jane is ever out sick.

Answers

MAP MASTER Skills Activity **Locate** All of the resources are located near waterways. **Draw Conclusions** because resources can be transported easily to other countries

Go Online
PHSchool.com Students may practice their map skills using the interactive online version of this map.

- Direct students' attention to the sentence on page 27 that says, "For example, coffee is a key crop in Brazil and Colombia." Ask students to discuss what they think "key crop" means. (*Students should suggest that a key crop is one that many farmers in those countries grow, and the sale of which accounts for a large piece of the economy in those countries.*)

- Ask students **Since there are so many possible uses for the trees in South America's rain forests, what problems or issues might come up in relation to this resource?** (*Possible answers: Some people want to cut down trees to use for firewood or to make furniture. Others want to protect the rain forests as a source of food and as a natural resource that is home to many kinds of unique plants and wildlife.*) **What would happen if all of the trees were cut down?** (*If the rain forests were cut down completely, it would affect plants, animals, and humans. Many species of plants and wildlife would be lost. Such a large change might also affect the climate.*)

Varied Resources
Countries depend on a variety of resources, from commercially grown cabbage in the Dominican Republic (upper photo) to hydroelectric power produced by this dam in Brazil (lower photo). **Generalize** *Explain how each resource could benefit a country's economy.*

Middle America: Riches of Land and Sea Mexico is a treasure chest of minerals. It has deposits of silver, gold, copper, coal, iron ore, and just about any other mineral you can name. Find Mexico's mineral resources on the map titled Latin America: Natural Resources on page 25. Mexico also has huge amounts of oil and natural gas. Where are Mexico's petroleum resources located?

In addition, trees cover nearly a quarter of Mexico's land. Trees are another natural resource. Wood from Mexico's trees is turned into lumber and paper products.

Central America's climate and rich soil are good for farming. The people there grow coffee, cotton, sugar cane, and bananas. They also plant cacao (kuh KAY oh) trees. Cacao seeds are made into chocolate and cocoa.

Not all of Central America's resources are on land. The people catch fish and shellfish in the region's waters. Central Americans also have built huge dams that harness the power of rushing water to produce electricity. Electric power created by rushing water is called **hydroelectricity.**

The Caribbean: Sugar, Coffee, and More Caribbean countries also have rich soil and a good climate for farming. Farmers grow sugar cane, coffee, bananas, cacao, citrus fruits, and other crops on the islands.

The Caribbean has other resources as well. For example, Jamaica is one of the world's main producers of bauxite—a mineral used to make aluminum. Cuba and the Dominican Republic have nickel deposits. Trinidad is rich in oil.

Answers

Generalize The commercially grown cabbage is exported to other countries, bringing money into the Dominican Republic. Hydroelectric power created by the dam in Brazil could be used in Brazil, or exported to other countries for a profit.

Commercial Fishing
Workers unload their catch at a dock in Argentina. The fish shown below are tuna.
Compare and Contrast
How is this example of fishing different from that shown on page 14?

page 14?

South America: A Wealth of Resources Like Mexico, South America is rich in minerals. It has gold, copper, tin, bauxite, and iron ore. Look again at the map titled Latin America: Natural Resources on page 25. Where are these resources located? South America also has oil. Much of South America's oil is found in Venezuela.

South America's plants and fish are natural resources, too. Forests cover about half the continent. Trees from these forests provide everything from wood for building to coconuts for eating. Mahogany and rosewood are used to make fine furniture. Some woods are used by local people for fuel. The rain forests of South America contain a wide variety of trees and other vegetation. Some of these plants are used to make medicines. Scientists are studying other plants to see if they, too, might have medical uses.

The people of South America harvest many kinds of fish. Tuna, anchovies, and other species of fish are plentiful in the waters off the Pacific coast. Shellfish, such as shrimp, are also important to the region's economy. Freshwater fish, those found in rivers, are an important food source in South America.

Like other parts of Latin America, South America has rich soil. Farmers grow many different crops there. For example, coffee is a key crop in Brazil and Colombia. Wheat is important in Argentina. Many South American economies rely on the production of sugar cane, cotton, and rice.

✓ **Reading Check** **What kinds of products are made from South America's forests?**

Independent Practice

Have students create the Taking Notes graphic organizer on a blank piece of paper. Ask them to fill in the information for "Middle America" and "Caribbean." Briefly model how to choose the correct details. Then have students complete the graphic organizer by filling in the "South America" section.

Monitor Progress

Show *Section Reading Support Transparency LA 30* and ask students to check their graphic organizers individually. Go over key concepts and clarify key vocabulary as needed.

📖 **Latin America Transparencies,** *Section Reading Support Transparency LA 30*

Differentiated Instruction

For Advanced Readers   L3

Have these students continue learning about the important natural resources of the Latin American forests by reading the primary source *Message from the Rain Forest Amerindians*. Ask these students to share what they have learned with the class, as well as any opinions they may have developed as a result of the reading.

All in One **Latin America Teaching Resources,** *Message from the Rain Forest Amerindians,* p. 123

Answers

✓ Reading Check Trees and plants from South America's forests are used to make buildings and furniture, supply coconuts and other food products, as a source of medicines, and for research. **Compare and Contrast** A large quantity of fish are being packed and loaded onto large ships, while on page 14, fewer fish are placed into a small boat for transport.

Resources and the Economy

Guided Instruction

- **Vocabulary Builder** Clarify the meaning of the high-use words **factor** and **dependence** before reading.

- Read Resources and the Economy with students, asking them to pay special attention to the vocabulary in the section.

- Ask students why a nation might develop a one-resource economy. *(When a country is rich in one resource, many people and companies may want to profit from that resource. If all of the companies turn to one industry, the nation slips into a one-resource economy.)*

- Ask students **Which resources and crops have some countries become too dependent on in Latin America?** *(oil, coffee, bananas, sugar)*

- Ask students how weather can affect a country's economy if it is too dependent on one crop. *(For example, if El Niño kills plants that fish depend on, a country that is too dependent on fishing can suffer.)*

World Coffee Prices, 1960–2000

Prices adjusted for inflation, using U.S. dollars.
SOURCE: World Bank

Graph Skills

World coffee prices affect not only the economies of many Latin American countries but also ordinary people, such as this Guatemalan coffee-picker. **Describe** What is the pattern of coffee prices over the 40 years shown in the graph above? **Analyze Information** What years were good years for coffee growers? What year might have been the worst? Explain your answer.

Resources and the Economy

Not every country shares equally in the wealth of Latin America's resources. Some Latin American countries have many resources, while others have few. Some countries do not have the money they need to develop all of their resources. Even when countries do develop their resources, not everyone in that country always enjoys the benefits. And sometimes countries rely too much on one resource or crop.

Problems of a One-Resource Economy Sometimes having a great deal of a valuable resource can lead to economic problems. That's because some countries then develop what is called a **one-resource economy,** an economy that depends largely on one resource or crop. Why is this a problem? Here is an example: When world copper prices are high, the copper mining industry is very successful. But suppose copper prices drop sharply. Then copper exports are not worth as much. When this happens, the mining industry loses money. Mining workers may lose their jobs. People and businesses—even a whole country—can go into debt. Chile is the leading producer of copper in the world. When prices plunge, Chile's whole economy suffers.

Answers

Graph Skills **Describe** Prices have gone down over the 40 years shown on the graph, with many highs and lows. **Analyze Information** The spans 1965–1970 and 1980–1985 were good years for coffee growers. The year 1990 was probably the worst, because the prices dropped quickly after a number of good years.

The World Economy Oil is one of Latin America's most valuable resources. But world oil prices go up and down, sometimes very suddenly. Mexico and Venezuela are major oil producers. In the mid-1980s, oil companies produced more oil than the world needed. As a result, prices dropped. Mexico earned much less income than it had expected.

Many people in Latin America make their living by farming. Some Latin American countries depend on only one or two crops, such as coffee, bananas, or sugar. Certain factors outside the country—such as increased production of coffee by other countries—may cause the price of the crop to drop. When the price of a crop goes down, exports of that crop bring less money into the country.

Weather Effects Weather brings challenges, too. Hurricanes, droughts, and plant diseases may damage crops. Weather can also hurt the fishing industry. Usually, the cold water of the Pacific supports a large number of small water plants on which fish feed. But when El Niño strikes, the warm water kills the plants and the fish die or move to other areas. The fishing industry of Peru has suffered great economic losses due to El Niño effects.

In each case described above, dependence on a particular resource—copper, oil, one particular crop, or fishing—has hurt the economy of the country that depended on it. That is because, if something unexpected happens to the major resource of a country with a one-resource economy, that country is left with few other sources of income.

 Preview and Ask Questions
Ask a question that will help you learn something important from the paragraph at the left. Now read the paragraph and answer your question.

At the Mercy of the Weather
In 2001, a severe drought in Guatemala caused many crops to dry up. This man is sowing beans on top of his failed corn crop. **Predict** *What might be the result if this farmer depended only on corn?*

Chapter 1 Section 3 **29**

Assess and Reteach

Assess Progress `L2`

Have students complete the Section Assessment. Administer the *Section Quiz.*

 Latin America Teaching Resources, *Section Quiz,* p. 109.

Reteach `L1`

For more instruction, have students read this section in the Reading and Vocabulary Study Guide.

📖 Chapter 1, Section 3, **Latin America Reading and Vocabulary Study Guide,** pp. 12–14

Extend `L3`

Have students learn more about crops grown in Latin America by completing the *Enrichment* activity.

 Latin America Teaching Resources, *Enrichment,* p. 114

Answers

✓ Reading Check Brazil is diversifying its economy by making machinery, steel, and chemicals and encouraging cotton farming to support a weaving industry.

Section 3 Assessment

Key Terms
Students' sentences should reflect knowledge of each key term.

🎯 **Target Reading Skill**
Students' questions and answers will vary, but should reflect an understanding of the section's important concepts.

Comprehension and Critical Thinking
1. (a) *Middle America*: minerals, oil, natural gas, trees, rich soil, fish, rushing water. *Caribbean*: fertile soil, bauxite, nickel, oil; *South America*: minerals, oil, trees, plants, fish, fertile soil. **(b)** Middle America and South America both have minerals, oil, trees, and fertile soil. **(c)** They enable a region to grow crops like coffee, corn, citrus fruit, potatoes, barley, wheat, and apples, which all benefit an economy.

2. (a) Venezuela has depended on oil, while El Salvador depended mainly on coffee. **(b)** No—both Venezuela's and El Salvador's economies were hurt by depending on one resource. **(c)** If a disease destroyed El Salvador's coffee crop, coffee plantation workers

An automobile factory in Quito, Ecuador

Latin America Begins to Diversify

Because Latin American nations have learned the risks of depending on one resource or crop, they are diversifying their economies. To **diversify** is to add variety. Many Latin American nations are building factories. Factories make products that can be sold to bring more money into the economy. Factories also provide jobs.

Rather than depending so much on oil, Venezuela has been creating more factories and farms. Venezuela is also improving its bauxite and iron mines. Brazil, too, has been building up its industries so that it does not have to depend so much on agriculture. Brazil now exports machinery, steel, and chemicals. Brazil has also encouraged cotton farming. As a result, cotton weaving has become a successful industry there.

El Salvador used to depend too heavily on its coffee crop. Now, cotton, sugar, corn, and other crops play an important role in the nation's economy. Trinidad has also encouraged its farmers to raise a greater variety of crops. The governments of Latin America continue to look for ways to protect their nations against the hazards of a one-resource economy.

✓ Reading Check **How is Brazil diversifying its economy?**

⭐ Section 3 Assessment

Key Terms
Review the key terms at the beginning of this section. Use each term in a sentence that explains its meaning.

🎯 **Target Reading Skill**
What questions helped you learn something important from this section? What are the answers to your questions?

Comprehension and Critical Thinking
1. (a) Identify Name the important natural resources of each region of Latin America.

(b) Compare How are the resources of South America similar to those of Middle America?
(c) Draw Conclusions How can rich soil and a mild climate benefit the economy of a region?
2. (a) Recall What resources have Venezuela and El Salvador depended on in the past?
(b) Synthesize Was depending on these resources good for the economies of these countries?
(c) Identify Cause and Effect Suppose a disease destroyed El Salvador's coffee crop. How would this loss affect coffee-plantation workers and the economy of El Salvador? Explain your answer.

Writing Activity
Suppose you are the president of a Latin American country. Your nation depends on sugar cane for nearly all of its income. Outline the arguments you would use in a speech to persuade your people of the need to diversify. Then write an introduction to your speech.

> **Writing Tip** A persuasive speech is like a persuasive essay. Be sure you have three reasons to support your main idea. Use persuasive language to introduce those ideas in your opening paragraph.

would suffer, but El Salvador's economy as a whole would not be harmed as much as in the past, because the country has diversified and grows other crops.

Writing Activity
Use the *Rubric for Assessing a Writing Assignment* to evaluate students' paragraphs.

 Latin America Teaching Resources, *Rubric for Assessing a Writing Assignment,* p. 129

Review and Assessment

◆ Chapter Summary

Section 1: Land and Water
- Latin America is located south of the United States and is made up of three regions.
- Mountain ranges and rain forests dominate Latin America, but there are also islands, plains, plateaus, and deserts.
- Waterways such as the Amazon River provide transportation, food, and electric power to the people of Latin America.

Section 2: Climate and Vegetation
- Latin America has a wide range of climate regions.
- Climate is shaped by elevation, nearness to the Equator, and wind patterns.
- Latin America's diverse climate regions affect vegetation patterns and how people live.

Section 3: Resources and Land Use
- Latin America's resources include minerals, good farmland, forests, and fish.
- Depending on only a few resources, such as one crop or mineral, can lead to economic problems.
- Latin American countries are now diversifying their economies.

Argentina

Honduras

Brazil

◆ Key Terms

Each of the statements below contains a key term from the chapter. Decide whether each statement is true or false. If it is true, write *true*. If it is false, rewrite the sentence to make it true.

1. A plateau is a narrow strip of land that has water on both sides and joins two larger bodies of land.

2. A tributary is smaller than the river into which it flows.

3. Pampas are flat grassland regions.

4. Rain forests thrive in hot, dry climates.

5. Elevation is the distance from the Equator.

6. The goods a country produces are its natural resources.

7. Hydroelectricity is electric power produced from rushing water.

8. To diversify an economy is to produce more of one resource.

┌ Vocabulary Builder

Revisit this chapter's high-use words:

classify	dominate	impressive
vary	moderate	deposit
abundant	irregular	
factor	dependence	

Ask students to review the definitions they recorded on their *Word Knowledge* worksheets.

All in One **Latin America Teaching Resources,** *Word Knowledge,* p. 113

Consider allowing students to earn extra credit if they use the words in their answers to the questions in the Chapter Review and Assessment. The words must be used correctly and in a natural context to win the extra points.

Review and Assessment

Review Chapter Content

- Review the important themes of this chapter by asking students to classify what Guiding Question each bulleted statement in the Chapter Summary answers. Have students do this activity together as a class. Refer to page 1 in the Student Edition for the text of the Guiding Questions.

- Assign *Vocabulary Development* for students to review Key Terms.

All in One **Latin America Teaching Resources,** *Vocabulary Development,* p. 128

Answers

Key Terms

1. False. A plateau is a large raised area of mostly level land.

2. True

3. True

4. False. Rain forests thrive in hot, wet climates.

5. False. Elevation is the altitude above sea level.

6. False. The things found in nature that people can use are its natural resources.

7. True

8. False. To diversify an economy is to add variety by producing more than one kind of product or resource.

Review and Assessment

Comprehension and Critical Thinking

9. (a) on the central plateau **(b)** That part of Mexico is a raised area of level land surrounded by mountains. **(c)** The region has rich soil and a warm climate.

10. (a) the Andes Mountains **(b)** The high elevation causes some parts of South America to have a very cold climate; only vegetation that can withstand cooler or cold temperatures can survive. The Andes are difficult for people to cross, but many people farm there. **(c)** Possible answers: Help—the Andes are a fertile farming area and a sight that attracts tourists. Hurt—the Andes have isolated some communities of South America.

11. (a) a warming of the ocean water along the western coast of South America that occurs every few years and influences global weather patterns **(b)** El Niño drives cold-water fish away, causes heavy rains in dry areas, floods in low-lying areas, and drought. **(c)** Commercial fisherman cannot work, property is destroyed through flooding, and tourism declines.

12. (a) the higher the elevation, the cooler the temperatures **(b)** Possible answer: Hot, wet, tropical regions give rise to rain forests; arid regions are usually deserts with little vegetation; areas with more moderate temperatures and rainfall contain grasslands or other kinds of vegetation. **(c)** People's jobs often depend on climate and vegetation: for example, farmers can only raise crops that tolerate the climate.

13. (a) minerals, oil, natural gas, trees, rich soil for farming, and abundant waters that produce electricity and contain fish and shell fish **(b)** The rushing waters of rivers are harnessed to produce hydroelectric power. **(c)** The prices of the resource fall sharply and economies that depend solely on that resource go into crisis.

14. (a) one that depends largely on one resource or crop **(b)** Possible answers: Venezuela is creating more factories and farms and improving its mines. Brazil is exporting machinery, steel, and chemicals and encouraging cotton farming to promote a weaving industry. El Salvador and Trinidad are encouraging farmers to diversify their crop production. **(c)** One-resource economies are vulnerable to outside factors that can leave the country with few or no sources of income.

Review and Assessment (continued)

◆ Comprehension and Critical Thinking

9. **(a) Recall** In what part of Mexico do most Mexicans live?
(b) Describe What is this part of Mexico like?
(c) Identify Causes Why are so many Central Americans farmers?

10. **(a) Identify** What is the major mountain range in South America?
(b) Identify Effects Describe two effects this mountain range has on the climate, the vegetation, or the people.
(c) Evaluate Do you think that the mountains help or hurt South America? Explain.

11. **(a) Define** What is El Niño?
(b) Identify Effects What are some of El Niño's effects on land and sea?
(c) Synthesize How can El Niño affect the economy of Latin America?

12. **(a) Recall** How does elevation affect climate?
(b) Contrast How are the different vegetation regions in Latin America shaped by their climates?
(c) Infer How do climate and vegetation affect how people live and work?

13. **(a) Identify** What are the major resources of Middle America?
(b) Categorize Which of these resources helps produce power?
(c) Analyze Explain what happens when too much of one resource is produced worldwide.

14. **(a) Define** What is a one-resource economy?
(b) Summarize Describe how one Latin American country is diversifying its economy.
(c) Generalize Why is it important for countries to diversify their economies?

◆ Skills Practice

Analyzing and Interpreting Climate Maps
In the Skills for Life activity in this chapter, you analyzed and interpreted a climate map. The skill you learned can be applied to other special-purpose maps.

Review the steps you followed to learn the skill. Then turn to the map titled Latin America: Vegetation Regions on page 20. Take the role of the travel agent again. This time respond to two

people: one who wants to visit a rain forest and another who wants to visit grassy plains to observe Latin American cowboys.

◆ Writing Activity: Science

Suppose you are the television meteorologist for a small Caribbean island. As part of your weather report, you are doing an overview of the weather for the past three months. Explain to your broadcast audience why one side of your island has been rainy and the other side has been sunny. You can create a mental picture or a map of the geography of your island (including mountains and rivers) to aid in your explanation.

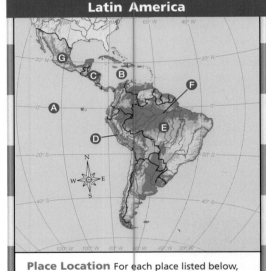

MAP★MASTER™
Skills Activity

Latin America

Place Location For each place listed below, write the letter from the map that shows its location.

1. South America
2. Caribbean Sea
3. Amazon River
4. Equator
5. Mexico
6. Central America
7. Andes Mountains

Go Online
PHSchool.com Use Web Code **lfp-1123** for an **interactive map**.

Skills Practice

Possible response to someone who wants to visit a rain forest: Visit the Amazon rain forest.

Possible response to someone who wants to visit grassy plains: Visit the pampas of Argentina or Uruguay.

Writing Activity: Science

Students' answers should note that more rain falls on the side of an island that faces the wind than on the side that faces away from the wind.

Use the *Rubric for Assessing a Writing Assignment* to evaluate students' overviews.

All in One **Latin America Teaching Resources,** *Rubric for Assessing a Writing Assignment,* p. 129

Standardized Test Prep

Test-Taking Tips

Some questions on standardized tests ask you to make mental maps. Read the passage below. Then follow the tips to answer the question.

TIP Try to picture the locations of the Southern Hemisphere and the Amazon River in your mind. Think of maps you have seen.

Pick the letter that best answers the question.

Zach's geography teacher asked his class to write clues for a game called What Country Is It? Zach wrote the following set of clues:

This country is mostly in the Southern Hemisphere. The Amazon River runs through it. It is larger than Argentina.

A ~~Mexico.~~
B Brazil.
C ~~Canada.~~
D Peru.

TIP First rule out answer choices that don't make sense. Pick the BEST answer from the remaining choices.

Think It Through Canada and Mexico are both in the Northern Hemisphere, so you can rule out answers A and C. The Amazon River runs across northern South America, including both Peru and Brazil. But Peru is smaller than Argentina. That leaves Brazil, answer B.

Practice Questions

Choose the letter of the best answer.

1. What two bodies of land does the isthmus of Central America connect?
   A the Caribbean and South America
   B Mexico and the United States
   C Mexico and the Caribbean
   D South America and North America

2. Which of the following factors does NOT affect a region's climate?
   A hurricanes
   B elevation
   C location
   D wind patterns

3. Throughout much of Latin America, people use rushing water to create
   A wells.
   B swimming pools.
   C water parks.
   D hydroelectricity.

4. The largest tropical rain forest in the world is located in
   A Mexico's central plateau.
   B the Amazon River Basin.
   C the isthmus of Central America.
   D the coral reefs of the Caribbean.

Read the following passage and answer the question that follows.

Yoshi is writing clues for a game called Name That Region. He wrote the following set of clues:
This region in Latin America is located in the Northern Hemisphere. It is made up of islands. Farming is especially good in this region.

5. What region do Yoshi's clues describe?
   A South America
   B the Caribbean
   C Mexico
   D North America

Use Web Code **lfa-1101** for a **Chapter 1 self-test.**

MAP MASTER Skills Activity

1. E
2. B
3. F
4. A
5. G
6. C
7. D

Go Online PHSchool.com Students may practice their map skills using the interactive online version of this map.

Standardized Test Prep

Answers

1. D
2. A
3. D
4. B
5. B

Go Online PHSchool.com Students may use the Chapter 1 self-test on PHSchool.com to prepare for the Chapter Test.

Assessment Resources

Use *Chapter Tests A and B* to assess students' mastery of chapter content.

All in One Latin America Teaching Resources, *Chapter Tests A and B,* pp. 130–135

Tests are also available on the *ExamView*® *Test Bank CD-ROM.*

○ *ExamView*® *Test Bank CD-ROM*

Objectives

1. Discover how a story from the past can shape the present.
2. Learn how geography can have an important effect on people's lives.
3. Analyze the effectiveness of plot elements such as setting, conflict, and resolution.

Prepare to Read

Build Background Knowledge `L2`

Ask students to read the title of the story and the definition of *surveyor* in the margin. Invite students to predict what the story will be about and how geography might affect it. Point out that the title "The Surveyor" could have more than one meaning. Lead an Idea Wave (TE, p. T35) to help students share their ideas.

The Surveyor `L2`

Guided Instruction

- Point out that some potentially unfamiliar words are defined for students in the margin. Clarify the meanings of the words before reading.

- Partner students and have them read the selection. Ask them to write the answers to each Reading Check as they read. Do a brief survey of their answers to make sure they understand the passage as they read.

- Ask students **What distinction does the author make about Latin American family life?** (*The author explains that Latin American families tend to expand family boundaries to include people who share time and significant experiences with the family.*) **Félix Caballero is not related by blood or marriage to the author, but Ada considers him part of her family. Why?** (*Felix spends a lot of time with the family, so he is part of the author's extended family.*)

The Surveyor
By Alma Flor Ada

Prepare to Read

Background Information
Do people in your family tell you stories about their past? Are some of those stories repeated many times? What stories do you remember the best? What do you learn from these stories?

The stories that family members tell each other become a part of a family's history. They are important because they teach us about our cultural heritage. They connect us to events, to places, and to people. They show us the world from a particular, personal point of view.

Alma Flor Ada (AL muh flawr AY duh) grew up in Cuba. The following selection shows what Ada learned from one of the stories her father used to tell her.

Objectives
In this selection you will

1. Discover how a story from the past can shape the present.
2. Learn how geography can have an important effect on people's lives.

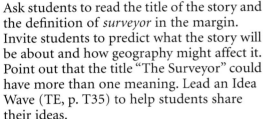

surveyor (sur VAY ur) *n.* a person who measures land and geographic features

Small farmers in Cuba live in villages like this one.

My father, named Modesto after my grandfather, was a <u>surveyor</u>. Some of the happiest times of my childhood were spent on horseback, on trips where he would allow me to accompany him as he plotted the boundaries of small farms in the Cuban countryside. Sometimes we slept out under the stars, stringing our hammocks between the trees, and drank fresh water from springs. We always stopped for a warm greeting at the simple huts of the neighboring peasants, and my eyes would drink in the lush green forest crowned by the swaying leaves of the palm trees.

Read Fluently

Partner students and have them choose a paragraph from the selection. Have students take turns reading the paragraph aloud. Ask them to underline words that give them trouble as they read. Then, have them decode the problem words with their partner. Provide assistance as needed. Have them reread the paragraph two more times to improve their reading speed. Remind them to stop at the commas and periods and to read with expression.

Since many surveying jobs called for dividing up land that a family had inherited from a deceased parent or relative, my father's greatest concern was that justice be achieved. It was not enough just to divide the land into equal portions. He also had to ensure that all parties would have access to roads, to water sources, to the most fertile soil. While I was able to join him in some trips, other surveying work involved large areas of land. On these jobs, my father was part of a team, and I would stay home, eagerly awaiting to hear the stories from his trip on his return.

Surveyors use instruments like this one to help them take measurements.

Latin American families tend not to limit their family boundaries to those who are born or have married into it. Any good friend who spends time with the family and shares in its daily experiences is welcomed as a member. The following story from one of my father's surveying trips is not about a member of my blood family, but instead concerns a member of our extended family.

Félix Caballero, a man my father always liked to <u>recruit</u> whenever he needed a team, was rather different from the other surveyors. He was somewhat older, unmarried, and he kept his thoughts to himself. He came to visit our house daily. Once there, he would sit silently in one of the living room's four rocking chairs, listening to the lively conversations all around him. An occasional nod or a single word were his only contributions to those conversations. My mother and her sisters sometimes made fun of him behind his back. Even though they never said so, I had the impression that they questioned why my father held him in such high regard.

recruit (rih KROOT) *v.* to enlist or hire to join a group

Then one day my father shared this story.

"We had been working on foot in mountainous country for most of the day. Night was approaching. We still had a long way to go to return to where we had left the horses, so we decided to cut across to the other side of the mountain, and soon found ourselves facing a deep <u>gorge</u>. The gorge was <u>spanned</u> by a railroad bridge, long and narrow, built for the sugarcane trains. There were no side rails or walkways, only a set of tracks resting on thick, heavy crossties suspended high in the air.

"We were all upset about having to climb down the steep gorge and up the other side, but the simpler solution, walking across the bridge, seemed too dangerous. What if a cane train should appear? There would be nowhere to go. So we all began the long descent . . . all except for Félix. He decided to risk

gorge (gawrj) *n.* a narrow canyon with steep walls
span (span) *v.* to extend across a space

✓ Reading Check

What kind of work does Ada's father do?

Literature **35**

Guided Instruction (continued)

■ Ask students: **What is Ada's father's profession?** (*He is a surveyor.*) **How is his profession related to geography?** (*He measures land and geographic features.*)

■ Ask students to describe the setting of the story. (*rural Cuba, a mountainous gorge with a railroad bridge*)

■ Ask **What are the two main problems in the story?** (*Félix is in danger when a train comes as he is crossing the railroad bridge above the gorge; Félix's inclusion in the family is awkward and not understood.*)

■ Ask **How is Félix's problem on the bridge resolved?** (*To survive, Félix rests his surveyor poles on the ties and hangs below the railroad tracks until the train passes.*)

■ **How does the story about Félix's past adventure affect Ada's opinion about him?** (*She decides that underneath Félix's quiet manner is a very courageous man. She understands why her father admires Félix.*)

Answers

✓ Reading Check Ada's father is a surveyor. He measures land and geographic features.

Independent Practice

Partner students and ask them to write a brief paragraph explaining how the saying "Actions speak louder than words" relates to this story. Instruct them to brainstorm ideas together before writing, and then write their paragraphs individually. Give them *Structuring Paragraphs* and *Creating Paragraph Outlines* to help them get started.

All in One **Latin America Teaching Resources,** *Structuring Paragraphs*, p. 126; *Creating Paragraph Outlines*, p. 127

Monitor Progress

As students brainstorm, circulate and make sure the partners are communicating effectively. If some are having trouble brainstorming, ask them the following questions: **What does Félix say in the story?** *(not very much)* **What does Félix do in Ada's father's story?** *(He thinks quickly and acts bravely in a dangerous situation.)*

dissuade (dis SWAYD) *v.* to persuade not to do something

ominous (AHM uh nus) *adj.* threatening

resilient (rih ZIL yunt) *adj.* able to withstand shock and bounce back from changes

walking across the railroad bridge. We all tried to <u>dissuade</u> him, but to no avail. Using an old method, he put one ear to the tracks to listen for vibrations. Since he heard none, he decided that no train was approaching. So he began to cross the long bridge, stepping from crosstie to crosstie between the rails, balancing his long red-and-white surveyor's poles on his shoulder.

"He was about halfway across the bridge when we heard the <u>ominous</u> sound of a steam engine. All eyes rose to Félix. Unquestionably he had heard it, too, because he had stopped in the middle of the bridge and was looking back.

"As the train drew closer, and thinking there was no other solution, we all shouted, 'Jump! Jump!', not even sure our voices would carry to where he stood, so high above us. Félix did look down at the rocky riverbed, which, as it was the dry season, held little water. We tried to encourage him with gestures and more shouts, but he had stopped looking down. We could not imagine what he was doing next, squatting down on the tracks, with the engine of the train already visible. And then, we understood. . . .

"Knowing that he could not manage to hold onto the thick wooden crossties, Félix laid his thin but <u>resilient</u> surveyor's poles across the ties, parallel to the rails. Then he let his body slip down between two of the ties, as he held onto the poles. And there he hung, below the bridge, suspended over the gorge but safely out of the train's path.

A train on a narrow railroad bridge travels high above the trees.

Differentiated Instruction

For Less Proficient Readers   **L1**
Explain to students that "The Surveyor" contains a story within a story. The story that forms the framework of the selection is about Ada's family, particularly her father. The story within the story describes Félix Caballero's courageous actions. To help students with this concept, have them create a chart and label one column "Framework story" and the other "Internal story," then have them take notes in the appropriate column as they read.

"The cane train was, as they frequently are, a very long train. To us, it seemed interminable. . . . One of the younger men said he counted two hundred and twenty cars. With the approaching darkness, and the smoke and shadows of the train, it was often difficult to see our friend. We had heard no human sounds, no screams, but could we have heard anything at all, with the racket of the train crossing overhead?

"When the last car began to curve around the mountain, we could just make out Félix's lonely figure still hanging beneath the bridge. We all watched in relief and amazement as he pulled himself up and at last finished walking, slowly and calmly, along the tracks to the other side of the gorge."

After I heard that story, I saw Félix Caballero in a whole new light. He still remained as quiet as ever, prompting a smile from my mother and her sisters as he sat silently in his rocking chair. But in my mind's eye, I saw him crossing that <u>treacherous</u> bridge, stopping to think calmly of what to do to save his life, emerging all covered with soot and smoke but triumphantly alive—a lonely man, hanging under a railroad bridge at dusk, suspended from his surveyor's poles over a rocky gorge.

If there was so much courage, such an ability to calmly confront danger in the quiet, aging man who sat rocking in our living room, what other wonders might lie hidden in every human soul?

About the Selection

"The Surveyor" appears in a collection of real-life stories set in Cuba, *Where the Flame Trees Bloom,* by Alma Flor Ada.

treacherous (TRECH ur us) *adj.* dangerous

✓ **Reading Check**

What makes Félix think he will be safe?

About the Author

Alma Flor Ada (b. 1938) was born in Camagüey (kah mah GWAY), Cuba. Her relatives were great storytellers. Their stories—part truth, part fiction—and her own childhood experiences are woven into her writing. Dr. Ada now lives in California where she is a professor at the University of San Francisco and an author and translator.

Review and Assessment

Thinking About the Selection

1. (a) Respond What is your reaction to what Félix did?
(b) Infer What qualities did Ada's father see in Félix that shaped his opinion of the man?
2. (a) Recall How did Ada's mother and her sister treat Félix?
(b) Analyze Why did the women have such a response to Félix?
3. (a) Recall What parts of the story tell us about Ada and her father?

(b) Evaluate Information What has Ada learned and from whom did she learn it? What did you learn?

Writing Activity

Write a Short Story Choose a story you have heard from a friend or a family member, or a story that you have told about an event that was important or meaningful to you. Write the story. Include an introduction and a conclusion that explain why the story is important to you.

Literature **37**

Assess and Reteach

Assess Progress [L2]

Have students answer the assessment questions.

Reteach [L1]

■ If students are having trouble analyzing and interpreting the actions of the characters in the story, have them list each character and the information they know about them. *(Ada's father—works as a surveyor, tries to divide land fairly, respects Félix; Félix Caballero—works with Ada's father, his quietness hides courage and the ability to take decisive action; Ada's mother—makes fun of Félix behind his back, wonders why her husband admires him; Ada—loves her father's stories, has a new appreciation of Félix after her father's story)*

■ Work with the students until their lists are complete, and then ask them to answer the assessment questions again.

Extend [L3]

To extend the lesson, ask students to read the selection *My Friend the Painter* and answer the questions at the end.

All in One Latin America Teaching Resources, *My Friend the Painter,* pp. 124–125

Answers

✓ **Reading Check** Felix trusts the strength of his surveyor's poles to hold him suspended under the bridge.

Review and Assessment

Thinking About the Selection

1. (a) Students may say they admire Félix for his actions, as Ada did, or they think he made a bad decision to cross the bridge instead of climbing down the gorge. **(b)** Ada's father saw that Félix was brave and resourceful.

2. (a) Ada's mother and her sisters made fun of Félix behind his back. **(b)** Félix visited every day, but was very quiet.

3. (a) In the beginning of the story, Ada shares memories of accompanying her father on surveying trips and listening to his stories. **(b)** Ada learns to look beneath the surface of people to get a true measure of their characters from her father; student answers will vary.

Writing Activity

Use *Rubric for Assessing a Writing Assignment* to evaluate students' stories.

All in One Latin America Teaching Resources, *Rubric for Assessing a Writing Assignment,* p. 129

CHAPTER 2

Latin America: Shaped by Its History

Chapter Overview

Overview

  Section 1

Early Civilizations of Middle America
1. Find out what Mayan civilization was like.
2. Learn how the Aztecs built their empire and understand what kind of society they created.

 Section 2

The Incas: People of the Sun
1. Find out how the Incas created their empire.
2. Understand what Incan civilization was like.
3. Learn how the descendants of the Incas live today.

 Section 3

European Conquest
1. Learn why Europeans sailed to the Americas.
2. Find out how the conquistadors conquered the Aztecs and the Incas.
3. Understand how the Spanish empire was organized and how colonization affected the Americas.

 Section 4

Independence
1. Learn what events inspired revolutions in Latin America.
2. Find out how Mexico gained its independence.
3. Discover how Bolívar and San Martín helped bring independence to South America.

 Section 5

From Past to Present
1. Learn how Latin American caudillos and foreign involvement contributed to the region's troubled past.
2. Find out how Latin American nations are struggling to improve their economies and the welfare of their people.

 DISCOVERY CHANNEL SCHOOL™ Video

Pizarro and the Empire of Gold

Length: 3 minutes, 24 seconds
Use with Section 3

This segment portrays Pizarro's discovery and domination of the Inca people. It will introduce the Inca empire and reveal how Pizarro and his small army were able to defeat the large army of the Incas.

 # Technology Resources

 Go Online
PHSchool.com

Students use embedded Web codes to access Internet activities, chapter self-tests, and additional map practice. They may also access Dorling Kindersley's Online Desk Reference to learn more about each country they study.

 Interactive Textbook

Use the Interactive Textbook to make content and concepts come alive through animations, videos, and activities that accompany the complete basal text—online and on CD-ROM.

 PRENTICE HALL
TeacherEXPRESS™
Plan • Teach • Assess

Use this complete suite of powerful teaching tools to make planning lessons and administering tests quicker and easier.

38a

Reading and Assessment

Reading and Vocabulary Instruction

🔄 Model the Target Reading Skill

Clarifying Meaning When rereading and reading ahead, students look within the text for the meaning of unfamiliar words and terms. Paraphrasing helps students restate ideas in words they better understand and remember. When summarizing, students state the main points of the passage.

Model techniques for clarifying meaning by thinking aloud about this text from page 41:

The Great Mystery of the Mayas *About A.D. 900 the Mayas suddenly left their cities. No one knows why. Crop failures, war, disease, drought, or famine may have killed many Mayas. Or perhaps people rebelled against the control of the priests and nobles. The Mayas stayed in the region, however. Millions of Mayas still live in Mexico, Belize, Guatemala, Honduras, and El Salvador.*

I'm not sure what the mystery in the subhead is. I'll read ahead to find out. In the first two sentences, I see the mystery—no one is sure why the Mayas suddenly left their cities. The third sentence lists many possible explanations, so I'll reread it and think about each one. The fourth sentence seems complicated, so I'll restate it: "Maybe the Mayas got tired of the rules made by their leaders." Finally, I'll finish the paragraph and summarize it: "No one is sure why Mayas suddenly left their cities in A.D. 900, but their descendants still live in the area."

Use the following worksheets from All-in-One Latin America Teaching Resources, (pp. 159, 160, and 161) to support this chapter's Target Reading Skill.

Vocabulary Builder
High-Use Academic Words

Use these steps to teach this chapter's High-Use Words:

1. Have students rate how well they know each word on their Word Knowledge worksheets (All-in-One Latin America Teaching Resources, p. 162).
2. Pronounce each word and ask students to repeat it.
3. Give students a brief definition or sample sentence (provided on TE pp. 41, 46, 51 and 65).
4. Work with students as they fill in the "Definition or Example" column of their Word Knowledge worksheets.

Assessment

Formal Assessment

Test students' understanding of core knowledge and skills.

Chapter Tests A and B, All-in-One Latin America Teaching Resources, pp. 177–182

Customize the Chapter Tests to suit your needs.

ExamView Test Bank CD-ROM

Skills Assessment

Assess geographic literacy.

MapMaster Skills, Student Edition pp. 39, 70

Assess reading and comprehension.

Target Reading Skills, Student Edition, pp. 42, 46, 54, 59, 66 and in Section Assessments

Chapter 4 Assessment, Latin America Reading and Vocabulary Study Guide, p. 31

Performance Assessment

Assess students' performance on this chapter's Writing Activities using the following rubrics from All-in-One Latin America Teaching Resources.

Rubric for Assessing a Writing Assignment, p. 174

Rubric for Assessing a Student Poster, p. 175

Assess students' work through performance tasks.

Small Group Activity: Mayan Math Bowl, All-in-One Latin America Teaching Resources, pp. 165–168

Online Assessment

Have students check their own knowledge.

Chapter Self-Test

Section 1 Early Civilizations of Middle America

 *1 period, .5 block*

Social Studies Objectives

1. Find out what Mayan civilization was like.

2. Learn how the Aztecs built their empire and understand what kind of society they created.

Reading/Language Arts Objective

Reread to better understand words and ideas in the text.

Prepare to Read	Instructional Resources	Differentiated Instruction
Build Background Knowledge Discuss the meaning of civilization. **Set a Purpose for Reading** Have students evaluate statements on the *Reading Readiness Guide*. **Preview Key Terms** Teach the section's Key Terms using a "See It—Remember It" chart. **Target Reading Skill** Introduce the section's Target Reading Skill of **rereading**.	**All in One** **Latin America Teaching Resources** **L2** Reading Readiness Guide, p. 140 **L2** Reread or Read Ahead, p. 159	**Spanish Reading and Vocabulary Study Guide** **L1** Chapter 2, Section 1, pp. 13–14 ELL

Instruct	Instructional Resources	Differentiated Instruction
The Mayas Discuss aspects of Mayan civilization. **The Aztec Empire** Discuss how the Aztec empire worked. **Target Reading Skill** Review **rereading**. **Eyewitness Technology** Have students read about and discuss Aztec Farming.	**All in One** **Latin America Teaching Resources** **L2** Guided Reading and Review, p. 141 **L2** Reading Readiness Guide, p. 140 **Latin America Transparencies** **L2** Section Reading Support Transparency LA 31	**Teacher's Edition** **L3** For Gifted and Talented Students, TE p. 43 **Spanish Support** **L2** Guided Reading and Review (Spanish), p. 12 ELL

Assess and Reteach	Instructional Resources	Differentiated Instruction
Assess Progress Evaluate student comprehension with the section assessment and section quiz. **Reteach** Assign the Reading and Vocabulary Study Guide to help struggling students. **Extend** Extend the lesson by assigning a small group activity.	**All in One** **Latin America Teaching Resources** **L2** Section Quiz, p. 142 **L3** Small Group Activity: Mayan Math Bowl, pp. 165–168 Rubric for Assessing a Writing Assignment, p. 174 **Reading and Vocabulary Study Guide** **L1** Chapter 2, Section 1, pp. 16–18	**Spanish Support** **L2** Section Quiz (Spanish), p. 13 ELL

Key

L1 Basic to Average	**L3** Average to Advanced	**LPR** Less Proficient Readers	**GT** Gifted and Talented
L2 For All Students		**AR** Advanced Readers	**ELL** English Language Learners
		SN Special Needs Students	

Section 2 The Incas: People of the Sun

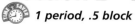 *1 period, .5 block*

Social Studies Objectives

1. Find out how the Incas created their empire.
2. Understand what Incan civilization was like.
3. Learn how the descendants of the Incas live today.

Reading/Language Arts Objective

Read ahead to help clarify a word or an idea.

Prepare to Read	Instructional Resources	Differentiated Instruction
Build Background Knowledge Discuss uses of interstate highways. **Set a Purpose for Reading** Have students begin to fill out the *Reading Readiness Guide.* **Preview Key Terms** Teach the section's Key Terms. **Target Reading Skill** Introduce the section's Target Reading Skill of **reading ahead.**	**All in One Latin America Teaching Resources** L2 Reading Readiness Guide, p. 144 L2 Reread or Read Ahead, p. 159	**Spanish Reading and Vocabulary Study Guide** L1 Chapter 2, Section 2, pp. 15–16 ELL

Instruct	Instructional Resources	Differentiated Instruction
The Rise of the Incas Discuss how the Incan empire developed. **Target Reading Skill** Review **reading ahead.** **Incan Civilization** Discuss aspects of Incan civilization. **The Quechua: Descendants of the Incas** Ask students how the Quechua continue Incan traditions.	**All in One Latin America Teaching Resources** L2 Guided Reading and Review, p. 145 L2 Reading Readiness Guide, p. 144 **Latin America Transparencies** L2 Section Reading Support Transparency LA 32	**Teacher's Edition** L3 For Gifted and Talented Students, TE p. 47 **Spanish Support** L2 Guided Reading and Review (Spanish), p. 14 ELL

Assess and Reteach	Instructional Resources	Differentiated Instruction
Assess Progress Evaluate student comprehension with the section assessment and section quiz. **Reteach** Assign the Reading and Vocabulary Study Guide to help struggling students. **Extend** Extend the lesson by assigning a Long-Term Integrated Project.	**All in One Latin America Teaching Resources** L2 Section Quiz, p. 146 Rubric for Assessing a Writing Assignment, p. 174 **Reading and Vocabulary Study Guide** L1 Chapter 2, Section 2, pp. 19–21	**Spanish Support** L2 Section Quiz (Spanish), p. 15 ELL **PHSchool.com** L3 For: Long-Term Integrated Projects: Building Models of Housing Around the World Web code: lfd-1206

Key

 Basic to Average   Average to Advanced   **LPR** Less Proficient Readers   **GT** Gifted and Talented

L2 For All Students   **AR** Advanced Readers   **ELL** English Language Learners

SN Special Needs Students

Section 3 European Conquest

 1 period, .5 block

Social Studies Objectives

1. Learn why Europeans sailed to the Americas.
2. Find out how the conquistadors conquered the Aztecs and the Incas.
3. Understand how the Spanish empire was organized and how colonization affected the Americas.

Reading/Language Arts Objective

Paraphrase to understand and remember what you have read.

Prepare to Read	**Instructional Resources**	**Differentiated Instruction**
Build Background Knowledge Discuss reasons for exploring the unknown. **Set a Purpose for Reading** Have students begin to fill out the *Reading Readiness Guide.* **Preview Key Terms** Teach the section's Key Terms. **Target Reading Skill** Introduce the section's Target Reading Skill of **paraphrasing**.	**All in One Latin America Teaching Resources** L2 Reading Readiness Guide, p. 148 L2 Paraphrase, p. 160	**Spanish Reading and Vocabulary Study Guide** L2 Chapter 2, Section 3, pp. 17–18 ELL

Instruct	**Instructional Resources**	**Differentiated Instruction**
Europeans Arrive in the Americas Ask students key questions about the beginnings of American exploration. **The Success of the Conquistadors** Discuss the actions of the conquistadors with students. **Colonization** Discuss the colonization of Latin America. **Target Reading Skill** Review **paraphrasing**.	**All in One Latin America Teaching Resources** L2 Guided Reading and Review, p. 149 L2 Reading Readiness Guide, p. 148 **Latin America Transparencies** L2 Section Reading Support Transparency LA 33	**All in One Latin America Teaching Resources** L3 The Talking Stone, pp. 169–171 **Teacher's Edition** L2 For English Language Learners, TE p. 53 L2 For Advanced Readers, TE p. 53 **Spanish Support** L2 Guided Reading and Review (Spanish), p. 16 ELL

Assess and Reteach	**Instructional Resources**	**Differentiated Instruction**
Assess Progress Evaluate student comprehension with the section assessment and section quiz. **Reteach** Assign the Reading and Vocabulary Study Guide to help struggling students. **Extend** Extend the lesson by showing and discussing a video.	**All in One Latin America Teaching Resources** L2 Section Quiz, p. 150 Rubric for Assessing a Writing Assignment, p. 174 **Reading and Vocabulary Study Guide** L1 Chapter 2, Section 3, pp. 22–24 **World Studies Video Program** L2 Pizarro and the Empire of Gold	**Spanish Support** L2 Section Quiz (Spanish), p. 17 ELL

Key

L1 Basic to Average	L3 Average to Advanced	LPR Less Proficient Readers	GT Gifted and Talented
L2 For All Students		AR Advanced Readers	ELL English Language Learners
		SN Special Needs Students	

Section 4 Independence

 2 periods, 1 block (includes Skills for Life)

Social Studies Objectives

1. Learn what events inspired revolutions in Latin America.
2. Find out how Mexico gained its independence.
3. Discover how Bolívar and San Martín helped bring independence to South America.

Reading/Language Arts Objective

Summarize to understand the main points you have read in the correct order.

Prepare to Read	**Instructional Resources**	**Differentiated Instruction**
Build Background Knowledge Discuss the ideas behind the Fourth of July. **Set a Purpose for Reading** Have students evaluate statements on the *Reading Readiness Guide*. **Preview Key Terms** Teach the section's Key Terms. **Target Reading Skill** Introduce the section's Target Reading Skill of **summarizing**.	**All in One Latin America Teaching Resources** L2 Reading Readiness Guide, p. 152 L2 Summarize, p. 161	**Spanish Reading and Vocabulary Study Guide** L2 Chapter 2, Section 4, pp. 19–20 ELL

Instruct	**Instructional Resources**	**Differentiated Instruction**
The Seeds of Revolution Discuss the events that inspired revolutions in Latin America. **Independence in Mexico** Teach students how Mexico gained its independence. **South American Independence** Discuss how revolutionary leaders brought about independence in Latin America. **Target Reading Skill** Review **paraphrasing**.	**All in One Latin America Teaching Resources** L2 Guided Reading and Review, p. 153 L2 Reading Readiness Guide, p. 152 **Latin America Transparencies** L2 Section Reading Support Transparency LA 34	**All in One Latin America Teaching Resources** Rubric for Assessing a Student Poster, p. 175 AR L2 Skills for Life, p. 164 GT, AR, LPR, SN **Teacher's Edition** L1 For Less Proficient Readers, TE p. 59 L3 For Advanced Readers, TE p. 59 **Reading and Vocabulary Study Guide** L1 Chapter 2, Section 4, pp. 25–27 LPR

Assess and Reteach	**Instructional Resources**	**Differentiated Instruction**
Assess Progress Evaluate student comprehension with the section assessment and section quiz. **Reteach** Assign the Reading and Vocabulary Study Guide to help struggling students. **Extend** Assign students to groups to prepare a talk show based on Latin American revolutionary leaders.	**All in One Latin America Teaching Resources** L2 Section Quiz, p. 154 Rubric for Assessing a Writing Assignment, p. 174 **Reading and Vocabulary Study Guide** L1 Chapter 2, Section 4, pp. 25–27	**Teacher's Edition** L2 For Special Needs Students, TE p. 63 **Spanish Support** L2 Section Quiz (Spanish), p. 19 ELL **Social Studies Skills Tutor CD-ROM** L1 Sequencing SN, LPR, ELL

Key

L1 Basic to Average	L3 Average to Advanced	LPR Less Proficient Readers	GT Gifted and Talented
L2 For All Students		AR Advanced Readers	ELL English Language Learners
		SN Special Needs Students	

Section 5 **From Past to Present**

 2.5 periods, 1.25 blocks (includes Chapter Review and Assessment)

Social Studies Objectives

1. Learn how Latin American caudillos and foreign involvement contributed to the region's troubled past.
2. Find out how Latin American nations are struggling to improve their economies and the welfare of their people.

Reading/Language Arts Objective

Reread or read ahead to help understand words and ideas in the text.

Prepare to Read

Build Background Knowledge
Have students predict the problems Latin America faced after independence.

Set a Purpose for Reading
Have students evaluate statements on the *Reading Readiness Guide*.

Preview Key Terms
Teach the section's Key Terms.

Target Reading Skill
Introduce the section's Target Reading Skill of **rereading or reading ahead**.

Instructional Resources

All in One Latin America Teaching Resources

- L2 Reading Readiness Guide, p. 156
- L2 Reread or Read Ahead, p. 159

Differentiated Instruction

Spanish Reading and Vocabulary Study Guide

- L2 Chapter 2, Section 5, pp. 21–22 ELL

Instruct

A Troubled Past
Discuss how caudillos and foreign involvement affected the newly independent Latin America.

The Struggle Continues
Discuss the economic challenges of Latin America.

Target Reading Skill
Review **rereading or reading ahead**.

Instructional Resources

All in One Latin America Teaching Resources

- L2 Guided Reading and Review, p. 157
- L2 Reading Readiness Guide, p. 156

Latin America Transparencies

- L2 Section Reading Support Transparency LA 35

Differentiated Instruction

Spanish Support

- L2 Guided Reading and Review (Spanish), p. 20 ELL

Assess and Reteach

Assess Progress
Evaluate student comprehension with the section assessment and section quiz.

Reteach
Assign the Reading and Vocabulary Study Guide to help struggling students.

Extend
Extend the lesson by assigning an Enrichment worksheet.

Instructional Resources

All in One Latin America Teaching Resources

- L2 Section Quiz, p. 158
- L3 Enrichment, p. 163
  Rubric for Assessing a Writing Assignment, p. 174
- L2 Vocabulary Development, p. 173
- L2 Word Knowledge, p. 162
- L2 Chapter Tests A and B, pp. 177–182

Reading and Vocabulary Study Guide

- L1 Chapter 2, Section 5, pp. 28–30

Differentiated Instruction

Teacher's Edition

- L1 For Special Needs Students, TE p. 67
- L1 For English Language Learners, TE p. 67

Spanish Support

- L2 Section Quiz (Spanish), p. 21 ELL
- L2 Chapter Summary (Spanish), p. 22 ELL
- L2 Vocabulary Development (Spanish), p. 23 ELL

Student Edition on Audio CD

- L1 Chapter 2, Section 5 SN, LPR, ELL

Key

L1 Basic to Average	L3 Average to Advanced	LPR Less Proficient Readers	GT Gifted and Talented
L2 For All Students		AR Advanced Readers	ELL English Language Learners
		SN Special Needs Students	

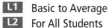

Reading Background

Using the Choral Reading Technique Effectively

The Choral Reading Technique ensures participation by all learners, including English Language Learners, because it provides a non-threatening reading environment. To ensure success with this technique, choose shorter passages (less than 500 words), and encourage students to stay with your voice, so that everyone reads at the same rate. When students have finished reading in unison, allow time for students to reread the passage silently, focusing on new or unfamiliar words.

Pre-Teaching Vocabulary

Research literature on academic vocabulary instruction indicates that effective strategies require students to go beyond simply looking up dictionary definitions or examining the context. Vocabulary learning must be based on the learner's dynamic engagement in constructing understanding.

If students are not retaining the meaning of the Key Terms or high-use words, use this extended vocabulary sequence to engage them in learning new words.

1. Present the word in writing and point out the part of speech.
2. Pronounce the word and have students pronounce the word.
3. Provide a range of familiar synonyms (or "it's like" words) before offering definitions.
4. Provide an accessible definition and concrete examples, or "showing sentences."
5. Rephrase the simple definition or example sentence, asking students to complete the statement by substituting the word aloud.
6. Check for understanding by providing an application task/question requiring critical thinking.

Sample instructional sequence:

1. *Dictator* is a noun, a word that names a person, place, or thing.
2. Say the word *dictator* after me. (Students repeat.)
3. A *dictator* is like a *tyrant* or a *despot*.
4. The word *dictator* means *a ruler with complete power*. The *dictator* declared that every Friday would be a holiday celebrating his rule.
5. By the _____'s order, every Friday was a holiday celebrating his rule. (Students substitute missing word.)
6. Is the president of the United States a *dictator*? Yes-No-Why? (Students answer the question.)

World Studies Background

Uncovering the World of the Maya

A huge volcanic eruption that occurred around the year A.D. 595 in modern-day El Salvador covered Cerén, a Mayan village, with volcanic ash and left it frozen in time. Archaeologists have found mud-preserved adobe buildings that were once homes, kitchens, and ceremonial buildings. Objects such as deer skull headdresses and red paste were probably used in religious ceremonies. Food that the Maya ate, such as corn and squash, has been found. Even footprints in the dirt were preserved. As they discover more clues in Cerén, researchers become more convinced of the sophistication of the Mayan civilization.

Brazil's Revolution

Although Brazil's fight for independence lacked the violence of other Latin American revolutions, freedom did not come easily. Groups of Brazilian rebels began working toward independence in the late 1700s, but the Portuguese government stopped them. In 1817, a northeastern region of Brazil tried to form its own colony, but again, the rebels were stopped. Brazilians were finally able to move toward independence when the Emperor Pedro I came to rule Portugal. Despite pressure from many Portuguese officials to keep Brazil as a colony, Pedro refused. Instead, he set Brazil free in September 1822, with a written statement titled "Independence or Death."

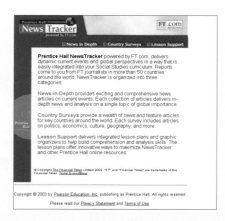

Get in-depth information on topics of global importance with **Prentice Hall Newstracker**, powered by FT.com.

Use Web Code **lfd-1200** for **Prentice Hall Newstracker.**

Guiding Questions

Remind students about the Guiding Questions introduced at the beginning of the book.

Section 1 relates to **Guiding Question** ❷ **How has Latin America been shaped by its history?** *(The Mayas and the Aztecs made scientific and agricultural discoveries that are still important in Latin America today.)*

Section 2 relates to **Guiding Question** ❸ **What factors have affected cultures in Latin America?** *(Descendants of the Incas still use farming methods similar to those of their ancestors.)*

Section 3 relates to **Guiding Question** ❷ **How has Latin America been shaped by its history?** *(The European conquest helped lead to the decline of the Native American population and increased European cultural influence in Latin America.)*

Section 4 relates to **Guiding Question** ❹ **What types of governments have existed in Latin America?** *(In the early 1800s, many countries in Latin America struggled to become independent of European rule.)*

Section 5 relates to **Guiding Question** ❹ **What types of government have existed in Latin America?** *(In the 1960s and 1970s, military regimes seized power in many Latin American countries. By the 1980s, some of these were replaced by elected governments.)*

⤷ Target Reading Skill

In this chapter, students will learn and apply the reading skill of clarifying meaning. Use the following worksheets to help students practice this skill:

All in One Latin America Teaching Resources, *Reread or Read Ahead,* p. 159; *Paraphrase,* p. 160; *Summarize,* p. 161

Differentiated Instruction

The following Teacher Edition strategies are suitable for students of varying abilities.

Advanced Readers, pp. 53, 59
English Language Learners, pp. 53, 67
Gifted and Talented, pp. 43, 47
Less Proficient Readers, p. 59
Special Needs Students, pp. 63, 67

Chapter Preview

This chapter presents the history of Latin America and shows how that history affects the region to this day.

Section 1
Early Civilizations of Middle America

Section 2
The Incas: People of the Sun

Section 3
European Conquest

Section 4
Independence

Section 5
From Past to Present

⤷ Target Reading Skill

Clarifying Meaning In this chapter you will focus on skills you can use to clarify meaning as you read.

▶ **Decorated wall of a Mayan building at Uxmal, Mexico**

38 Latin America

Bibliography

For the Teacher

Arnold, Caroline. *City of the Gods: Mexico's Ancient City of Teotihuacán.* Clarion, 1994.

Baquedano, Elizabeth. *Aztec, Inca, and Maya* (Eyewitness Books). Knopf, 1993.

Thomson, Hugh. *The White Rock: An Exploration of the Inca Heartland.* Overlook Press, 2003.

For the Student

L1 Defrates, Joanna. *What Do We Know About the Aztecs?* Bedrick, 1995.

L2 Kimmel, Eric. *Montezuma and the Fall of the Aztecs.* Holiday House, 2000.

L3 Green, Jen. *The Encyclopedia of the Ancient Americans: Explore the Wonders of the Aztec, Maya, Inca, North American Indian and Arctic Peoples.* Southwater, 2001.

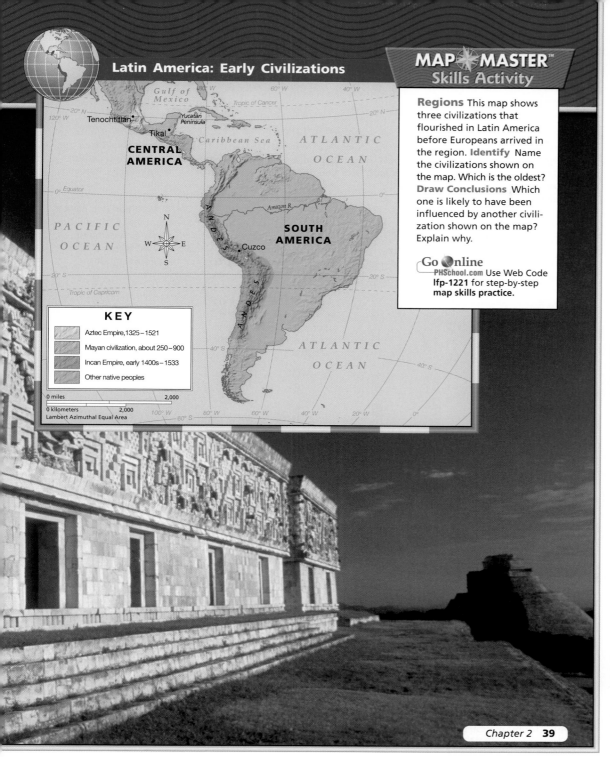

Latin America: Early Civilizations

CENTRAL
AMERICA

Gulf of
Mexico

Yucatán
Peninsula

Tenochtitlán

Tikal

Caribbean Sea

ATLANTIC
OCEAN

Equator

PACIFIC
OCEAN

Amazon R.

ANDES

SOUTH
AMERICA

Cuzco

ANDES

N
W   E
S

Tropic of Cancer

Tropic of Capricorn

ATLANTIC
OCEAN

KEY

Aztec Empire, 1325–1521

Mayan civilization, about 250–900

Incan Empire, early 1400s–1533

Other native peoples

0 miles   2,000
0 kilometers   2,000
Lambert Azimuthal Equal Area

Regions This map shows three civilizations that flourished in Latin America before Europeans arrived in the region. **Identify** Name the civilizations shown on the map. Which is the oldest? **Draw Conclusions** Which one is likely to have been influenced by another civilization shown on the map? Explain why.

Go Online
PHSchool.com Use Web Code **lfp-1221** for step-by-step **map skills practice.**

Chapter 2   **39**

- Point out to students that each shaded area on the map represents a different civilization. Call on students to identify the colors and which civilizations they represent.

- Ask students to use the map's scale to measure the approximate length of the territory held by each civilization, and compare them. Ask **Which civilization had the largest area?** *(Incan Empire)* **Which had the smallest?** *(Mayan civilization)* **How do you think size of a civilization might have affected its inhabitants?** *(Possible answer: Larger civilizations might have needed more rulers in different areas; smaller civilizations might have needed less.)*

Go Online
PHSchool.com Students may practice their map skills using the interactive online version of this map.

Using the Visual   L2

Reach Into Your Background Draw students' attention to the caption and photo on pages 38–39. Discuss the visual with students, and have them identify the items in the photo. Ask **Do you think that these are modern buildings? Why or why not? What kinds of clues can they see in the photo that might tell them what the building was used for or where it was located?**

Answers

MAP MASTER™ **Identify** Aztec, Mayan, and Incan; Mayan **Draw Conclusions** The Aztec and Mayan Empires likely influenced one another since they existed in nearby areas.

Chapter Resources

Teaching Resources
- L2 Vocabulary Development, p. 173
- L2 Skills for Life, p. 164
- L2 Chapter Tests A and B, pp. 177–182

Spanish Support
- L2 Spanish Chapter Summary, p. 22
- L2 Spanish Vocabulary Development, p. 23

Media and Technology
- L1 Student Edition on Audio CD
- L1 Guided Reading Audiotapes, English and Spanish
- L2 Social Studies Skills Tutor CD-ROM
  ExamView Test Bank CD-ROM

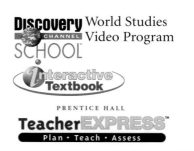

Discovery World Studies
CHANNEL Video Program
SCHOOL

Interactive
Textbook

PRENTICE HALL
TeacherEXPRESS™
Plan • Teach • Assess

Objectives

Social Studies

1. Find out what Mayan civilization was like.
2. Learn how the Aztecs built their empire and understand what kind of society they created.

Reading/Language Arts

Reread to better understand words and ideas in the text.

Prepare to Read

Build Background Knowledge L2

Tell students that they will now study the history of Latin America, starting with the oldest civilizations we know about. Ask students to name some features of American civilization. Model the thought process by encouraging them to think about cities, the arts, the sciences, and the system of education. Use the Give One and Get One participation strategy (TE, p. T37) to generate a list.

Set a Purpose for Reading L2

- Preview the Objectives.
- Read each statement in the *Reading Readiness Guide* aloud. Ask students to mark the statements true or false.

  All in One Latin America Teaching Resources, *Reading Readiness Guide,* p. 140

- Have students discuss the statements in pairs or groups of four, then mark their worksheets again. Use the Numbered Heads participation structure (TE, p. T36) to call on students to share their group's perspectives.

Vocabulary Builder
Preview Key Terms L2

Create a three column "See It—Remember It" chart of the Key Terms on the board. Write a term in the first column, a short definition in the second column, and a sketch in the third column. Guide students as they copy and complete the chart.

Prepare to Read

Objectives

In this section you will
1. Find out what Mayan civilization was like.
2. Learn how the Aztecs built their empire and understand what kind of society they created.

Taking Notes

As you read this section, look for similarities and differences in the Mayan and Aztec civilizations. Copy the diagram below and record your findings in it.

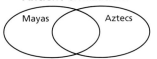

Ancient Civilizations

Mayas   Aztecs

Target Reading Skill

Reread Rereading can help you understand words and ideas in the text. If you do not understand a sentence or a paragraph, read it again to look for connections among the words and sentences. For example, rereading the first paragraph below can make it clear that the game being described took place long ago. Now you can better understand the surprising comparison of pok-ta-tok to basketball.

Key Terms

- **hieroglyphics** (hy ur oh GLIF iks) *n.* a system of writing using signs and symbols
- **maize** (mayz) *n.* corn
- **Tenochtitlán** (teh nawch tee TLAHN) *n.* capital city of the Aztec empire, located where Mexico City now stands

Fans cheered as the players brought the ball down the court. Suddenly, the ball flew into the air and sailed through the hoop. Fans and players shouted and screamed. Although this may sound like a championship basketball game, it is actually a moment in a game played more than 1,000 years ago. The game was called pok-ta-tok.

Pok-ta-tok was a game played by the ancient Mayas. Using only their leather-padded hips and elbows, players tried to hit a four-pound (1.9 kilogram), six-inch (15.2 centimeter) rubber ball through a stone hoop mounted 30 feet (9.1 meters) above the ground.

The Mayas

How do we know about this ancient game? Crumbling ruins of pok-ta-tok courts and ancient clay statues of players have been found at sites in Central America and southern Mexico. In these areas, Mayan civilization thrived from about A.D. 250 to A.D. 900. By studying ruins, scientists have learned much about Mayan civilization.

Target Reading Skill L2

Reread Point out the Target Reading Skill. Tell students that rereading a sentence or a paragraph will help them to better understand words and ideas in the text.

Model rereading by reading and rereading the first paragraph on page 41. Tell students that rereading can help them better under-

stand where Mayan cities were located and how they served as religious centers.

Give students *Reread or Read Ahead.* Have them complete the activity in groups.

All in One Latin America Teaching Resources, *Reread or Read Ahead,* p. 159

Mayan Civilization The Mayas built great cities, such as Copán (koh PAHN) in the present-day country of Honduras, and Tikal (tee KAHL) in present-day Guatemala. Mayan cities were religious centers. Large pyramid-shaped temples often stood in the middle of Mayan cities. The Mayas worshipped their gods there, and performed rituals including human sacrifice, or the offering of human life to their gods.

Mayan priests studied the stars and planets. They designed an accurate calendar, which they used for deciding when to hold religious ceremonies. The Mayan calendar was more accurate than any used in Europe until the 1700s. The Mayas also developed a system of writing using signs and symbols called **hieroglyphics** (hy ur oh GLIF iks). Mayan books were made of paper created from the bark of fig trees. Hieroglyphics found in these books and in carvings have helped scientists understand Mayan culture.

Farmers worked in fields surrounding the cities. Their most important crop was **maize,** or corn, the main food of the Mayas. They also grew beans, squash, peppers, avocados, and papayas.

The Great Mystery of the Mayas About A.D. 900, the Mayas suddenly left their cities. No one knows why. Crop failures, war, disease, drought, or famine may have killed many Mayas. Or perhaps people rebelled against the control of the priests and nobles. The Mayas stayed in the region, however. Millions of Mayas still live in Mexico, Belize, and Guatemala.

✔ Reading Check **What is the "great mystery of the Mayas"?**

Links to Math

The Concept of Zero
The Mayas created a number system that included zero. Zero is important in math because it is a symbol that shows that there is none of something. For example, to write the number 308, you need a symbol to show that there are no tens. The idea of zero is considered to be one of the greatest inventions in mathematics. In the Mayan book above, the zero looks like a shell. Other numbers are made up of bars and dots.

Mayan Ruins
The Mayan city of Chichén Itzá had a pok-ta-tok court as well as this huge temple. **Infer** *What does this great temple suggest about Mayan culture and technology?*

Vocabulary Builder

Use the information below to teach students this section's high-use words.

High-Use Word	Definition and Sample Sentence
ritual, p. 41	*n.* a ceremony or regularly performed practice Going to the baseball game had become a **ritual** in her family.
garment, p. 42	*n.* any article of clothing He had to wash the **garment** by hand.

Links

Read the **Links to Math** on this page. Ask students **Why would an easy-to-use number system be important to Mayan civilization?** (*It would help people to keep track of the size of the population and the amount of crops that were harvested. It was also needed for an accurate calendar.*)

Instruct

The Mayas

Guided Instruction

■ **Vocabulary Builder** Clarify the high-use word **ritual** before reading.

■ Read The Mayas with students, using the Choral Reading technique (TE, p. T34). As students read, circulate and make sure individuals can answer the Reading Check question.

■ Discuss some aspects of Mayan civilization. (*Mayan cities were religious centers; Mayan priests studied the stars and planets and designed an accurate calendar; the Mayas developed a system of writing called hieroglyphics; Mayan farmers grew crops, such as maize, in fields surrounding the cities.*)

■ Ask students **What types of jobs did the Mayas have? Are they similar to or different from jobs that people have today?** (*builders, priests, and farmers; similar*)

Independent Practice

Ask students to create the Taking Notes graphic organizer on a blank piece of paper. Then have them fill in the "Mayas" circle with the information they have just learned. Briefly model how to identify which details to record.

Monitor Progress

As students fill in the graphic organizer, circulate and make sure individuals are choosing the correct details. Provide assistance as needed.

Answers

✔ Reading Check The "great mystery of the Mayas" is why they suddenly left their cities about A.D. 900.

Infer The great temple suggests that the Mayas had an advanced culture and technology.

The Aztec Empire

Guided Instruction
- **Vocabulary Builder** Clarify the high-use word **garment** before reading.
- Read The Aztec Empire with students.
- Discuss how the Aztecs built their empire. (*The Aztecs gained land and riches from the people they conquered.*)
- Have students describe the different roles and positions in Aztec society. (*The Aztec emperor ruled over all Aztec lands; nobles helped the emperor govern; soldiers fought in wars to expand the empire and protected trade routes; priests were religious leaders and were important in government; many Aztecs were farmers.*)

Independent Practice
Have students complete the graphic organizer by filling in the "Aztecs" circle and then adding the aspects common to both civilizations in the overlapping circle.

Monitor Progress
- Show *Section Reading Support Transparency LA 31* and ask students to check their graphic organizers individually. Go over key concepts and clarify key vocabulary as needed.
  Latin America Transparencies, *Section Reading Support Transparency LA 31*
- Tell students to fill in the last column of the *Reading Readiness Guide.* Probe for what they learned that confirms or invalidates each statement.
  All in One Latin America Teaching Resources, *Reading Readiness Guide,* p. 140

Target Reading Skill
Reread As a follow up, ask students to answer the Target Reading Skill question in the Student Edition. (*Aztec astronomers predicted eclipses and the movements of planets, and kept records using hieroglyphics.*)

Aztec sun calendar

Reread
Read the paragraph at the right again to find out two things Aztec astronomers did.

42 Latin America

The Aztec Empire

In the 1400s, another great civilization arose in Middle America. It was created by the Aztecs, who had arrived in the Valley of Mexico in the 1100s.

The Aztecs settled on an island in Lake Texcoco in 1325. They changed the swampy lake into a magnificent city. **Tenochtitlán** (teh nawch tee TLAHN), the Aztec capital, stood on the site of present-day Mexico City. When Europeans explored the area in the 1500s, they found the Aztecs ruling a rich empire from the city of Tenochtitlán.

Building an Empire In the 1400s, Aztec warriors began conquering the other people in the region. They forced the conquered people to pay tribute, or taxes. Tribute could be paid in food, cotton, gold, or slaves. The Aztecs grew rich from the tribute.

The Aztec emperor ruled over all Aztec lands. Nobles helped the emperor to govern. Soldiers fought in wars to expand the empire. They also protected the empire's trade routes. Priests were not only religious leaders, but were also important in society. People of the upper classes wore feathered garments and carried feathered fans as symbols of their status.

Farming Most of the people in the Aztec empire were farmers. Like the Mayas, the Aztecs used irrigation to water their crops. As you can see in Eyewitness Technology: Aztec Farming on the next page, they also "created" new farmland by constructing artificial floating gardens. Aztec farmers grew corn, squash, and beans on these floating islands.

Culture and Religion Tenochtitlán was a magnificent capital city. It had huge temples, busy markets, wide streets and canals, and floating gardens. It even had a zoo. The markets were filled with food, gold and silver jewelry, feathers, and fine crafts. The emperor and nobles lived in splendid palaces and had many slaves to serve them.

In the temples, priests performed ceremonies, including human sacrifice, to please their gods. Like the Mayas, Aztec priests used their knowledge of astronomy to create an accurate calendar. Aztec astronomers also predicted eclipses and the movements of planets. They kept records using hieroglyphics similar to those used by the Mayas.

42 Latin America

Background: Global Perspectives

Hieroglyphics The term *hieroglyph*, meaning "sacred carving," was used by the Greeks to describe the characters on Egyptian monuments. Eventually, *hieroglyphic* was applied to the picture-writing of other cultures, such as the Mayas. The Mayan writing system is pictorial, but bears no other relation to Egyptian hieroglyphics.

Aztec Farming

The Aztec city of Tenochtitlán, in central Mexico, grew quickly. The Aztecs soon used up all the farmland that was available on the island. To grow more crops, they learned how to create new farmland. At the outskirts of town, Aztec farmers dug canals through the marshy land to make small plots called *chinampas*, or "floating beds." People could paddle canoes through the many canals running among the chinampas.

The Floating City: Tenochtitlán
This painting shows what Tenochtitlán looked like. Built on a small island in the middle of a lake, it grew to a city of 200,000 people.

2 Mud and vegetation are piled onto mats that rest on the water's surface.

1 Wooden posts are set up to hold the sides of each plot in place.

3 Willow trees are planted to keep the mud in place. Over time, their roots will anchor the chinampas to the bottom of the lake.

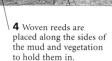

4 Woven reeds are placed along the sides of the mud and vegetation to hold them in.

5 More layers of mud and fertile manure are added until the land is ready to plant.

6 Maize grows tall on a fully developed chinampa.

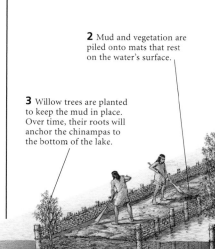

Modern-Day Living
Today, most of the lakes used by the Aztecs have been drained and covered by city growth. However, some chinampas are still used as farmland. The photo at the left shows Mexicans farming chinampas today.

ANALYZING IMAGES
How did the planting of willow trees make the Aztecs' chinampas more stable?

Aztec Farming

Guided Instruction   L2

Have students read the first paragraph on this page. As a class, look at the diagram and read the numbered captions. Then have students discuss their answers to the Analyzing Images question. Then direct students' attention to the photos and their captions.

Independent Practice

Have students work in pairs to create an "Instruction Manual" for growing a crop using the Aztec Farming method. Students should create a list of the numbered steps, and include drawings of each step.

Assess and Reteach

Assess Progress   L2

Have students complete the Section Assessment. Administer the *Section Quiz.*

All in One **Latin America Teaching Resources,** *Section Quiz,* p. 142

Reteach   L1

If students need more instruction, have them read this section in the Reading and Vocabulary Study Guide.

Chapter 2, Section 1, **Latin America Reading and Vocabulary Study Guide,** pp. 16–18

Differentiated Instruction

For Gifted and Talented   L3

Read the following quotation from Bernal Díaz del Castillo, one of the first Spaniards to see Tenochtitlán:

"Some of the soldiers among us who had been in many parts of the world, in Constantinople, and all over Italy, and in Rome, said that so large a market place and so full of people . . . they had never beheld before."

Ask students **What can you conclude about the population of the Aztec capital from this eyewitness account? How do you think the Spanish might have felt when they first saw the city of Tenochtitlán?** *(The population must have been very large. The Spanish might have been in awe of the city, impressed by its wealth, or might have felt intimidated by so many people.)*

Answers

ANALYZE IMAGES Over time, the roots of the willow trees anchored the chinampas to the bottom of the lake.

Extend

L3

Have students further explore the Mayan civilization by doing this chapter's *Small Group Activity* about the Mayan mathematic system.

All in One Latin America Teaching Resources, *Small Group Activity: Mayan Math Bowl,* p. 165–168

Answers

Generalize Students may answer that people are fascinated by the ancient culture.

✓ **Reading Check** The Aztecs traded crops, crafts, weapons, tools and luxury goods. Porters carried the goods because the Aztecs had no pack animals. Trade was usually done by barter.

Section 1 Assessment

Key Terms
Students' sentences should reflect knowledge of each Key Term.

↻ **Target Reading Skill**
Students should be able to identify a difficult or unfamiliar word or unclear idea and explain how rereading helped their comprehension.

Comprehension and Critical Thinking

1. (a) Mayas built great cities, many of which were religious centers. Mayan farmers grew many crops; the most important was maize. Mayas designed an accurate calendar and wrote using hieroglyphics. **(b)** Their civilization was advanced with highly educated people in science and technology. **(c)** Although the ancient Maya left their cities, they remained in the region.

2. (a) The emperor ruled over the people; nobles and priests helped the emperor rule; warriors fought battles; traders carried goods; craftspersons created works of art. Most people were farmers. It was successful because it was very organized and everyone had a role in the society. **(b)** 1100s—the Aztec arrived in the Valley of Mexico; 1325 —they settled on an island in Lake Texcoco, and built the city of Tenochtitlán; 1400s— warriors began conquering other people in the region; 1500s —Aztecs were ruling a rich empire **(c)** Answers will vary but should include that conquered people were probably unhappy about being forced to work for and pay tribute to the Aztecs.

Past Meets Present
This girl is sketching an Aztec statue at the site of the Great Temple of the Aztecs in Mexico City. **Generalize** *Why do you think people still flock to see and study Aztec ruins?*

Aztec Medicine Aztec doctors were able to make more than 1,000 medicines from plants. They used the medicines to lower fevers, cure stomachaches, and heal wounds. Aztec doctors also set broken bones and practiced dentistry.

Trade Because of the power of the Aztec army, traders could travel long distances in safety. Crops from distant parts of the empire were brought to the capital and to other cities. Crafts, weapons, and tools were also carried throughout the empire and beyond. Luxury goods such as jaguar skins, cacao beans, and fine jewelry were also traded. These goods were carried by people called porters, because the Aztecs did not have pack animals to carry loads. Trade was usually done by barter, or the exchange of goods without the use of money.

The End of the Aztec Empire The Aztecs did not abandon their fine cities as the Mayas had done. Instead, they were conquered by newcomers from a faraway land. You will read about how the Aztec empire fell later in this chapter.

✓ **Reading Check** How was trade carried out in the Aztec empire?

Section 1 Assessment

Key Terms
Review the key terms at the beginning of this section. Use each term in a sentence that explains its meaning.

↻ **Target Reading Skill**
What word or idea were you able to clarify by rereading? Explain how rereading helped.

Comprehension and Critical Thinking
1. (a) Identify Describe the main features of Mayan civilization.

(b) Conclude What do the facts that Mayas created accurate calendars and great cities tell about their civilization?
(c) Infer Why do Mayas still live in Middle America?
2. (a) Describe How was Aztec society organized and why was it successful?
(b) Sequence Tell how the Aztecs created their large and powerful empire.
(c) Infer How do you think the conquered peoples felt about being ruled by the Aztecs? Explain your answer.

Writing Activity
If you could interview an ancient Maya or Aztec about his or her life, what would you ask? Write some questions that would help you understand one of these civilizations. Organize your questions into at least three different topics.

Writing Tip First decide which civilization to focus on. Then use the blue headings in the section to help you decide on topics. Reread the text under the headings to get ideas for your questions.

Writing Activity
Use the *Rubric for Assessing a Writing Assignment* to evaluate students' interview questions.

All in One Latin America Teaching Resources, *Rubric for Assessing a Writing Assignment,* p. 174

The Incas: People of the Sun

Prepare to Read

Objectives

In this section you will
1. Find out how the Incas created their empire.
2. Understand what Incan civilization was like.
3. Learn how the descendants of the Incas live today.

Taking Notes

As you read this section, look for details of Incan civilization. Copy the web below and fill in the ovals with information about the Incas.

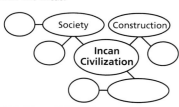

Target Reading Skill

Read Ahead Reading ahead can help you understand something you are not sure of in the text. If you do not understand a certain word or passage, keep reading. The word or idea may be clarified further on. For example, at first you may not understand why a second runner begins running beside the first one in the first paragraph below. Read the second paragraph to find the term *relay runners*. That will help you understand the idea in paragraph one.

Key Terms

- **Cuzco** (KOOS koh) *n.* capital of the Incan empire
- **Topa Inca** (TOH puh ING kuh) *n.* emperor of the Incas, who expanded their empire
- **census** (SEN sus) *n.* an official count of all the people in an area and how they make a living
- **quipu** (KEE poo) *n.* knotted strings on which the Incas recorded information
- **aqueduct** (AK wuh dukt) *n.* a pipe or channel that carries water from a distant source

The runner sped along the mountain road. He lifted a horn made from a shell to his lips and blew. A second runner appeared and began running beside him. Without stopping, the first runner gave the second runner the message he carried. The second runner was gone like the wind. He would not stop until he reached the next runner.

The Incas used relay runners to spread news from one place in their empire to another. Incan messengers carried news at a rate of 250 miles (402 kilometers) a day. Without these runners, controlling the vast empire would have been very difficult.

An Incan runner blowing a conch shell and carrying a quipu

Chapter 2 Section 2 **45**

Objectives

Social Studies

1. Find out how the Incas created their empire.
2. Understand what Incan civilization was like.
3. Learn how the descendants of the Incas live today.

Reading/Language Arts

Read ahead to help clarify a word or an idea.

Prepare to Read

Build Background Knowledge [L2]

In this section, students will learn about an ancient civilization located in South America. Ask students to quickly preview the headings and visuals in the section with this question in mind: **How does the Incan civilization differ from the Mayan and Aztec civilizations?** Provide a few simple examples to get students started. Conduct an Idea Wave (TE, p. T35) to generate a list.

Set a Purpose for Reading [L2]

- Preview the Objectives.
- Form students into pairs or groups of four. Distribute the *Reading Readiness Guide*. Ask students to fill in the first two columns of the chart. Use the Numbered Heads participation structure (TE, p. T36) to call on students to share one piece of information they already know and one piece of information they want to know.

   All in One Latin America Teaching Resources, *Reading Readiness Guide*, p. 144

Vocabulary Builder

Preview Key Terms [L2]

Pronounce each Key Term, then ask students to say the word with you. Provide a simple explanation such as "Every ten years the United States takes a census to count how many people live in our country and learn how they make a living."

Target Reading Skill [L2]

Read Ahead Point out the Target Reading Skill. Tell students to keep reading if a word or an idea in a paragraph is not clear because it may be clarified further on.

Model reading ahead by reading the first sentence under the subhead Government and Records from p. 47: "The government of the Incan empire was carefully organized." Tell students to read ahead to the next paragraph to clarify how the emperor governed and kept track of his empire.

Give students *Reread or Read Ahead*. Have them complete the activity in their groups.

   All in One Latin America Teaching Resources, *Reread or Read Ahead,* p. 159

Instruct

The Rise of the Incas L2

Guided Instruction

- **Vocabulary Builder** Clarify the high-use words **conquest** and **loyalty** before reading.

- Have students read The Rise of the Incas using the Partner Paragraph Shrinking technique. (TE, p. T34). As students read, circulate and make sure individuals can answer the Reading Check question.

- Discuss how the Inca were able to acquire a vast empire. *(through wars and conquest, by demanding loyalty from conquered peoples)*

- Ask students **Why do you think it was important to Pachacuti that conquered peoples were loyal to the Incas?** *(If conquered people were disloyal, they might rebel and try to fight against Pachacuti and the Incas. Pachacuti would then have to divide his forces to fight the rebellions.)*

Independent Practice

Ask students to create the Taking Notes graphic organizer on a blank piece of paper. Then have them fill in a few of the circles with the information they have just learned. Briefly model how to identify which details to record.

Monitor Progress

As students fill in the graphic organizer, circulate and make sure individuals are choosing the correct details. Provide assistance as needed.

🎯 Target Reading Skill L2

Read Ahead As a follow up, ask students to answer the Target Reading Skill question in the Student Edition. *(The Incan Empire was over 2,500 miles [4,023 kilometers] long and had 12 million people. The answer is found in the third paragraph on the page.)*

Answers

✔ **Reading Check** by forcing those who were disloyal to leave their land and replacing them with people who were loyal

Chart Skills Identify The Mayan civilization lasted more than 600 years, the Incan civilization only 97 years. **Analyze Information** The two early dates show important milestones in the growth of the Aztec civilization before it became an empire.

46 *Latin America*

🎯 **Read Ahead**
The paragraph at the right says that the Incan empire was "large and powerful." Read ahead to find out how big it was. Where did you find the answer?

▋ Timeline Skills

Three great civilizations are shown on the timeline. Vertical lines indicate specific events. Horizontal brackets show periods of time. **Identify** Which civilization lasted the longest? Which empire lasted the shortest time? **Analyze Information** Why does the timeline show two dates for the Aztecs before the beginning of their empire?

The Rise of the Incas

The large and powerful empire of the Incas had small beginnings. In about 1200, the Incas settled in **Cuzco** (KOOS koh), a village in the Andes that became the Incan capital city. It is now a city in the country of Peru. Most Incas were farmers. They grew maize and other crops. Through wars and conquest, the Incas won control of the entire Cuzco Valley, one of many valleys that dot the Andes Mountains.

In 1438, Pachacuti (pahch ah KOO tee) became ruler of the Incas. The name Pachacuti means "he who shakes the earth." Pachacuti conquered the people of the Andes and the Pacific coast, from Lake Titicaca north to the city of Quito in present-day Ecuador. Pachacuti demanded loyalty from the people he conquered. If they were disloyal, he forced them off their land. He replaced them with people loyal to the Incas.

Later, Pachacuti's son, **Topa Inca,** became emperor of the Incas. He expanded the empire. In time, it stretched some 2,500 miles (4,023 kilometers) from what is now Ecuador south along the Pacific coast through Peru, Bolivia, Chile, and Argentina. The 12 million people ruled by the Incas lived mostly in small villages.

✔ **Reading Check** **How did Pachacuti make sure conquered peoples were loyal to the Incas?**

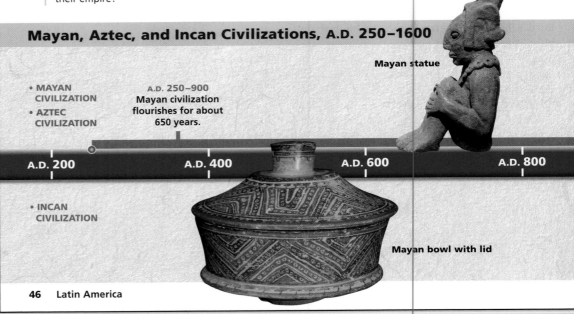

Mayan statue

Mayan, Aztec, and Incan Civilizations, A.D. 250–1600

- **MAYAN CIVILIZATION**
- **AZTEC CIVILIZATION**

A.D. 250–900
Mayan civilization flourishes for about 650 years.

- **INCAN CIVILIZATION**

A.D. 200   A.D. 400   A.D. 600   A.D. 800

Mayan bowl with lid

46   Latin America

┌ Vocabulary Builder ─────────────

Use the information below to teach students this section's high-use words.

High-Use Word	Definition and Sample Sentence
conquest, p. 46	*n.* the act of gaining something by using force After its **conquest,** the Spanish had to rebuild the country.
loyalty, p. 46	*n.* the quality or state of being faithful Her dog showed his **loyalty** by barking when the doorbell rang.
descendant, p. 49	*n.* a person who comes from an ancestor or group of ancestors The Quechuas are **descendants** of the ancient Incas.

Incan Civilization

The Incas were excellent farmers, builders, and managers. The Incan capital, Cuzco, was the center of government, trade, learning, and religion. In the 1500s, one of the first Spaniards to visit Cuzco described it as "large enough and handsome enough to compare to any Spanish city."

The emperor, along with the nobles who helped him run the empire, lived in the city near the central plaza. Nobles wore special headbands and earrings that showed their high rank. Most of the farmers and workers outside Cuzco lived in adobe mud huts.

Government and Records The government of the Incan empire was carefully organized. The emperor chose nobles to govern each province. Each noble conducted a census so that people could be taxed. A **census** is an official count of all the people in an area and how they make a living. Local officials collected some of each village's crops as a tax. The villagers also had to work on government building projects. However, the government took care of the poor, the sick, and the elderly.

The Incas did not have a written language. Incan government officials and traders used **quipus** (KEE pooz), knotted strings on which they recorded information. Each quipu had a main cord with several colored strings attached to it. Each color represented a different item, and knots of different sizes at certain distances stood for numbers.

Keeping Count
Incan quipus like this one recorded information about births, deaths, trade, and taxes. **Generalize** What would be some advantages and disadvantages of this system of record keeping?

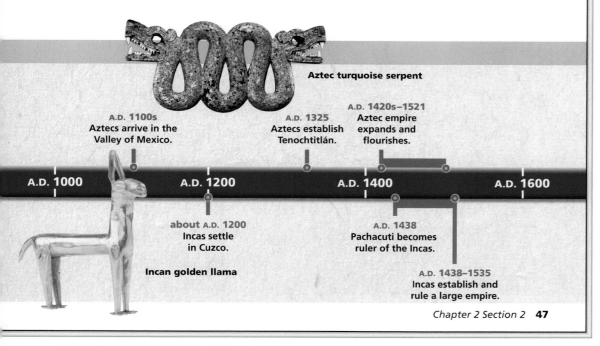

Aztec turquoise serpent

Incan golden llama

A.D. 1000 — A.D. 1200 — A.D. 1400 — A.D. 1600

A.D. 1100s
Aztecs arrive in the Valley of Mexico.

A.D. 1325
Aztecs establish Tenochtitlán.

A.D. 1420s–1521
Aztec empire expands and flourishes.

about A.D. 1200
Incas settle in Cuzco.

A.D. 1438
Pachacuti becomes ruler of the Incas.

A.D. 1438–1535
Incas establish and rule a large empire.

Chapter 2 Section 2 **47**

Incan Civilization `L2`

Guided Instruction

- Read about the achievements of the Inca in Incan Civilization.

- Ask students to discuss what aspects of Incan civilization are similar to the community in which they live. (*The government is responsible for conducting a census, collecting taxes, and taking care of the poor, the sick, and the elderly; public buildings are used as government or religious centers; roads and bridges transport goods, information, and people; aqueducts carry water to city centers and farms.*)

- Have students discuss the most important aspects of Incan religion. (*The Incas worshipped many gods and practiced human sacrifice; Inti and Viracocha were two important Inca gods.*)

Independent Practice

Have students complete the graphic organizer by filling in the remaining circles about Incan civilization.

Monitor Progress

- Show *Section Reading Support Transparency LA 32* and ask students to check their graphic organizers individually. Go over key concepts and clarify key vocabulary as needed.

  Latin America Transparencies, *Section Reading Support Transparency LA 32*

Answers

Generalize Advantages—could record a lot of information on quipus, quipus might last longer than paper; Disadvantages—quipus take up a lot of space, hard to learn

The Quechua: Descendants of the Incas L2

Guided Instruction

- **Vocabulary Builder** Clarify the high-use word **descendant** before reading.
- Read how Incan descendants combine ancient and modern traditions in The Quechua: Descendants of the Incas.
- Ask students **What traditions do the Quechua maintain that reflect their Incan heritage?** (*farming methods, spinning and weaving, distinctive clothing style*)

Independent Practice

Assign *Guided Reading and Review*.

All in One **Latin America Teaching Resources,** *Guided Reading and Review,* p. 145

Monitor Progress

Tell students to fill in the last column of the *Reading Readiness Guide*. Ask them to evaluate if what they learned was what they had expected to learn.

All in One **Latin America Teaching Resources,** *Reading Readiness Guide,* p. 144

Answers

✓ Reading Check Incan buildings were constructed without modern tools. Stoneworkers cut stones so that they fit together perfectly without mortar or cement.

Links to Science

Earthquake-Proof Buildings
The land under the Incan empire was often shaken by earthquakes. Incan buildings swayed but did not collapse. That is because their walls tilt in at about an 80° angle rather than standing straight up at 90°. The doors and windows are shaped like trapezoids, wider at the base than at the top. This gives them stability when the ground shakes. The Spanish conquerors of the Incas built in the European style—and when earthquakes hit Cuzco, the Spanish buildings collapsed while the Incan stonework remained.

48 Latin America

Roads, Bridges, and Aqueducts The Incas built more than 14,000 miles (22,530 kilometers) of roads. The roads went over some of the most mountainous land in the world. The road system helped the Incas to govern their vast empire. Not only did runners use the roads to deliver messages, but Incan armies and trade caravans also used the roads for speedy travel.

In addition to roads, the Incas needed bridges to span the deep gorges of the Andes Mountains. Gorges are narrow passes or valleys between steep cliffs. In the Andes, swift-moving rivers often flow through gorges. The Incas developed rope bridges to carry people safely over these dangerous spaces. The bridges were made of braided vines and reeds. Similar bridges are still in use today in the Andes.

The Incas also built canals and aqueducts to carry water to dry areas. An **aqueduct** is a pipe or channel that carries water from a distant source. One stone aqueduct carried water from a mountain lake almost 500 miles (805 kilometers) to its destination. The system of canals and aqueducts allowed the Incas to irrigate land that was otherwise too dry to grow crops.

Incan Buildings The Incas were masters of building with stone. They constructed cities, palaces, temples, and fortresses without the use of modern tools. Using only hammers and chisels, Incan stoneworkers cut large stones so precisely that they fit together without mortar or cement. The stones fit together so tightly that even today a piece of paper cannot be slipped between them. Many Incan structures can still be seen in Peru. The most famous Incan ruin is Machu Picchu (MAH choo PEEK choo), a city that includes buildings, stairs carved into the side of the mountain, and roads cut into bare rock.

Religion Like the Mayas and the Aztecs, the Incas worshipped many gods and practiced human sacrifice. The sun god, Inti, was one of their most important gods. The Incas believed that Inti was their parent, and they referred to themselves as "children of the sun." Another important Incan god was Viracocha (vee ruh KOH chuh), the creator of all the people of the Andes.

✓ Reading Check Describe Incan stone buildings.

The Quechua: Descendants of the Incas

The Spanish conquered the Incan empire in the 1500s. However, descendants of the Incas still live in present-day Peru, Ecuador, Bolivia, Chile, and Colombia. They speak Quechua (KECH wuh), the Incan language.

Today, many of the Quechua live high in the Andes. Although they are isolated from many aspects of modern life, they have been influenced by it. For example, their religion combines elements of Roman Catholic and traditional practices.

Most Quechua who live in the mountains grow only enough food to feed their families. They continue to use farming methods similar to those of the ancient Incas. They also continue the weaving traditions of the Incas. They spin wool and weave fabric much as their ancestors did. They use this brightly colored cloth with complex patterns for their own clothing and also sell it to outsiders. Their clothing styles, such as the distinctive poncho, also reflect their Incan heritage.

Terrace Farming
The Incas built terraces into the sides of steep slopes to increase their farmland and to keep soil from washing down the mountains. **Infer** *Why do you think terrace farming is still used in the Andes Mountains today?*

✓ **Reading Check** How do the Quechua preserve Incan culture?

Section 2 Assessment

Key Terms
Review the key terms at the beginning of this section. Use each term in a sentence that explains its meaning.

↻ **Target Reading Skill**
What word or idea were you able to clarify by reading ahead? Where did you find this clarification?

Comprehension and Critical Thinking
1. (a) Recall Where and when did the Incas create their empire?

(b) Sequence List the major events in the creation of the Incan empire in order.
2. (a) Identify What were the major achievements of Incan civilization?
(b) Draw Conclusions Why were a good network of roads and record keeping important to the Incan empire?
3. (a) Describe How do the descendants of the Incas live now?
(b) Infer Why do you think the Quechua still do many things the way their ancestors did?

Writing Activity
Which of the Incan achievements do you think was most important in creating their large and rich empire? Explain your choice in a paragraph. Give at least two reasons for your choice.

For: An activity on the Incas
Visit: PHSchool.com
Web Code: lfd-1202

Assess and Reteach

Assess Progress `L2`
Have students complete the Section Assessment. Administer the *Section Quiz*.

📄 **Latin America Teaching Resources,** *Section Quiz, p. 146*

Reteach `L1`
If students need more instruction, have them read this section in the Reading and Vocabulary Study Guide.

📄 Chapter 2, Section 1, **Latin America Reading and Vocabulary Study Guide,** pp. 19–21

Extend `L3`
Have students discover more about Incan building methods by completing the *Long Term Integrated Project: Building Models of Housing Around the World*. Assign students to work groups to work on the project.

Go Online PHSchool.com **For:** Long Term Integrated Project: *Building Models of Housing Around the World*
Visit: PHSchool.com
Web Code: lfd-1206

Answers

Infer The people of the Andes still need to farm as much land as possible.

✓ **Reading Check** The Quechua preserve their Incan culture by continuing to use farming methods and weaving traditions similar to those of the ancient Incas.

Writing Activity
Use the *Rubric for Assessing a Writing Assignment* to evaluate students' paragraphs.

📄 **Latin America Teaching Resources,** *Rubric for Assessing a Writing Assignment,* p. 174

Section 2 Assessment

Key Terms
Students' sentences should reflect knowledge of each Key Term.

↻ Target Reading Skill
Students should identify a word or idea they were uncertain about and indicate where they found clarification.

Comprehension and Critical Thinking
1. (a) The Incas created their empire in about 1200 in Cuzco, a village in the Andes of what is today Peru. **(b)** 1200—settled in Cuzco; 1438—Pachacuti conquered the people of the Andes and the Pacific coast; later Topa Inca expanded the empire even more; 1500s—the Spaniards conquered the Incas.

2. (a) a well-organized government; earthquake-proof buildings; roads and bridges;

canals and aqueducts; the quipu **(b)** Roads connected all parts of the empire and made travel easier. Good record keeping made the government efficient.

3. (a) The Quechua live in the Andes and practice farming and weaving traditions similar to those of the ancient Incas. **(b)** The Quechua are subsistence farmers who are isolated from many aspects of modern life.

Section 3
Step-by-Step Instruction

Objectives
Social Studies

1. Learn why Europeans sailed to the Americas.
2. Find out how the conquistadors conquered the Aztecs and the Incas.
3. Understand how the Spanish empire was organized and how colonization affected the Americas.

Reading/Language Arts

Paraphrase to understand and remember what you have read.

Prepare to Read

Build Background Knowledge `L2`
Tell students that in this section they will learn about the Europeans' effect on the history of Latin America. Show *Pizarro and the Empire of Gold*, then ask students what they think will happen when Europeans arrive in Latin America. Use an Idea Wave (TE, p. T35) to solicit answers.

Pizarro and the Empire of Gold, **World Studies Video Program**

Set a Purpose for Reading `L2`
- Preview the Objectives.
- Form students into pairs or groups of four. Distribute the *Reading Readiness Guide*. Ask students to fill in the first two columns of the chart. Use the Numbered Heads participation structure (TE, p. T36) to call on students to share one piece of information they already know and one piece of information they want to know.

All in One Latin America Teaching Resources, *Reading Readiness Guide,* p. 148

Vocabulary Builder
Preview Key Terms
Pronounce each Key Term, then ask students to say the word with you. Provide a simple explanation such as, "In Brazil, farmers grow banana trees or coffee beans on large haciendas made up of hundreds of acres of land."

Section 3 — European Conquest

Prepare to Read

Objectives
In this section you will
1. Learn why Europeans sailed to the Americas.
2. Find out how the conquistadors conquered the Aztecs and the Incas.
3. Understand how the Spanish empire was organized and how colonization affected the Americas.

Taking Notes
As you read this section, look for the major events in the European conquest of Latin America. Copy the timeline below, and record the events in the proper places on it.

Columbus arrives in the Americas.

1490 1492

Target Reading Skill
Paraphrase When you paraphrase, you restate what you have read in your own words. This process can help you understand and remember what you read.

Key Terms
- **Moctezuma** (mahk tih ZOO muh) *n.* ruler of the Aztecs
- **Christopher Columbus** (KRIS tuh fur kuh LUM bus) *n.* Italian explorer sponsored by Spain who landed in the West Indies in 1492
- **conquistador** (kahn KEES tuh dawr) *n.* one of the conquerors who claimed and ruled land in the Americas for the Spanish government in the 1500s
- **Hernán Cortés** (hur NAHN kohr TEZ) *n.* conquistador who conquered the Aztec empire
- **Francisco Pizarro** (frahn SEES koh pea SAHR oh) *n.* conquistador who conquered the Incas
- **mestizo** (meh STEE zoh) *n.* a person of mixed Spanish and Native American ancestry
- **hacienda** (hah see EN dah) *n.* a large farm or plantation

Moctezuma meets Cortés, in a 1976 mural by Roberto Cueva del Rio.

50 Latin America

One day in 1519, the Aztec ruler **Moctezuma** (mahk tih ZOO muh) received startling news. Something strange had appeared offshore. He sent spies to find out about it. The spies reported back to Moctezuma:

> **We must tell you that we saw a house in the water, out of which came white men, with white hands and faces, and very long, bushy beards, and clothes of every color: white, yellow, red, green, blue, and purple, and on their heads they wore round hats.**
>
> —*An Aztec spy*

The white men with round hats were a Spanish military force. They had sailed to the coast of Mexico in search of treasure. They would bring great changes to the land of the Aztecs.

Target Reading Skill `L2`
Paraphrase Point out the Target Reading Skill. Tell students that paraphrasing, or restating what they have read in their own words, can help them understand and remember what they have read.

Model using paraphrasing by restating the quotation in the second paragraph of this page. (*The spies said they saw what looked like a house in water and strange white men with colorful clothes and round hats.*)

Give students *Paraphrase*. Have them complete the activity in groups.

All in One Latin America Teaching Resources, *Paraphrase,* p. 160

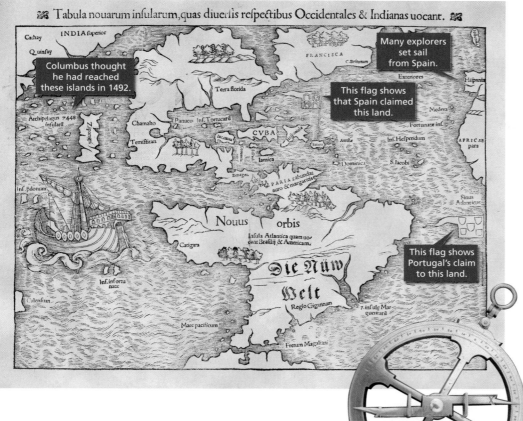

Tabula nouarum infularum, quas diuerlis respectibus Occidentales & Indianas uocant.

Columbus thought he had reached these islands in 1492.

Many explorers set sail from Spain.

This flag shows that Spain claimed this land.

This flag shows Portugal's claim to this land.

Europeans Arrive in the Americas

In the 1400s, the European nations of Spain and Portugal were searching for new trade routes to Asia. They knew that in Asia they would find goods such as spices and silks. These goods could be traded for huge profits in Europe.

Columbus Reaches America Christopher Columbus, an Italian explorer, thought he could reach Asia by sailing west across the Atlantic Ocean. Columbus knew the world was round, as did most educated Europeans. But Columbus believed the distance around the world was shorter than it is. First Columbus asked Portugal to sponsor his voyage. Portugal refused. Then he asked Spain. Queen Isabella of Spain finally agreed.

Columbus set sail in early August, 1492. Some 10 weeks later, on October 12, he spotted land. Columbus thought he had reached the East Indies in Asia, so he called the people he met Indians.

Mapping the Americas
This 1540 map is based on information supplied by Columbus and other explorers. Also shown is an astrolabe, a navigational instrument from the 1500s. **Infer** *Find the islands Columbus was looking for, and the Caribbean islands he found instead. Why do you think he thought they were the same?*

Instruct

Europeans Arrive in the Americas   L2

Guided Instruction
- **Vocabulary Builder** Clarify the high-use word **profit** before reading.
- Read Europeans Arrive in the Americas using the Structured Silent Reading technique (TE, p. T34).
- Ask students **Why did European nations begin exploring other parts of the world?** *(They were searching for new trade routes to Asia.)*
- Ask students **How did Spain and Portugal divide the continent of South America?** *(The Treaty of Tordesillas set the Line of Demarcation that gave Spain land and the right to trade west of the line and Portugal the same east of the line.)*
- Ask students to locate the Line of Demarcation on the map on p. 54. Then ask **What country benefited the most from the Line of Demarcation? Why?** *(Spain; it received the right to settle and trade on much more land than Portugal.)*

Independent Practice
Ask students to create the Taking Notes graphic organizer on a blank piece of paper. Then have them fill in the time line with dates and events they have just learned.

Monitor Progress
As students fill in the graphic organizer, circulate and make sure individuals did not miss any dates or events and that they are written in chronological order.

Vocabulary Builder

Use the information below to teach students this section's high-use words.

High-Use Word	Definition and Sample Sentence
profit, p. 51	*n.* a gain or benefit We made a **profit** from the sale.
supernatural, p. 52	*adj.* not explainable by known forces or laws of nature Most of the students were frightened by **supernatural** events.
fearless, p. 52	*adj.* unafraid The **fearless** hiker thought nothing of climbing up the cliff.
superior, p. 54	*adj.* better The new computer was **superior** to the old one.

Answers

Infer Columbus may have thought he had found the right islands because the ones he did find were in a similar harbor.

The Success of the Conquistadors

Guided Instruction

- **Vocabulary Builder** Clarify the high-use words **supernatural** and **fearless** before reading.

- Ask students to read about how Cortés and Pizarro defeated two of the most powerful empires in the Americas in The Success of the Conquistadors. As students read, circulate and make sure individuals can answer the Reading Check question.

- Ask students **Why were Spanish explorers interested in conquering kingdoms in the Americas?** (*They were in search of gold and other treasures.*)

- Ask students to predict what might have happened if Moctezuma and the Aztecs defeated Cortés and his army. Allow students to share answers with a partner before responding. (*Possible answers include: Cortés and his men may have been forced to pay tribute to Moctezuma; more Spaniards may have come from Spain to continue fighting the Aztecs.*)

Dividing a Continent Spain and Portugal each sent explorers to the Americas and tried to stop the other country from claiming land there. In 1494, the two nations signed an important treaty. (A treaty is an agreement in writing made between two or more countries.) The Treaty of Tordesillas (tawr day SEE yahs) set an imaginary line from the North Pole to the South Pole at about 50°W longitude, called the Line of Demarcation. It gave Spain the right to settle and trade west of the line. Portugal could do the same east of the line. The only part of South America that is east of the line is roughly the eastern half of present-day Brazil. Because of the Treaty of Tordesillas, the language and background of Brazil are Portuguese.

✓ **Reading Check** Why did Spain and Portugal become rivals?

The Success of the Conquistadors

Spanish explorers heard stories of wealthy kingdoms in the Americas. They hoped to find gold and other treasures there. Spanish rulers did not pay for the expeditions of the explorers. Instead, they gave the **conquistadors** (kahn KEES tuh dawrs), or conquerors, the right to hunt for treasure and to settle in the Americas. In exchange, conquistadors agreed to give Spain one fifth of any treasures they found.

Cortés Conquers the Aztecs Aztec rulers demanded heavy tribute from the peoples they had conquered. When the conquistador **Hernán Cortés** arrived in Mexico in 1519, he found many of these groups willing to help him against the Aztecs.

Cortés headed for Tenochtitlán with 500 soldiers and 16 horses. Aztec spies saw them coming. They had never seen horses before. Moctezuma's spies described the Spanish as "supernatural creatures riding on hornless deer, armed in iron, fearless as gods."

Moctezuma thought Cortés might be the god Quetzalcoatl (ket sahl koh AHT el). Quetzalcoatl had promised to return and rule the Aztecs. With a heavy heart, Moctezuma welcomed Cortés and his soldiers. Cortés tried to convince Moctezuma to surrender to Spain and then seized him as a hostage. After a brief period of peace, Spanish soldiers killed some Aztecs. Then the Aztecs rebelled against the Spanish. By the end of the fighting, Moctezuma was dead, and Cortés and his army barely escaped.

With the help of the Aztecs' enemies, Cortés defeated the Aztecs in 1521. By then, about 240,000 Aztecs had been killed and so had 30,000 of Cortés's allies. Tenochtitlán and the Aztec empire lay in ruins, but the region had been claimed for Spain.

Sculpture of the Aztec god Quetzalcoatl

Answers

✓ **Reading Check** Spain and Portugal became rivals because each country sent explorers to the Americas and tried to stop one another from claiming land there.

(Skills for Life) Skills Mini Lesson

Analyzing Primary Sources

1. Teach the skill by telling students that a primary source is an eyewitness account or observation of an event. It can include facts as well as opinions. Primary sources include letters, diaries, interviews, speeches, photographs, paintings, and newspapers.

2. Have students practice this skill by analyzing the second paragraph on page 50.

Ask students if they think this is a primary source and why. Have students identify the eyewitnesses to this event and explain how they know.

3. Have students apply the skill by reading Christopher Columbus' *Journal Entry*. Ask them to identify and analyze the primary source.

All in One Latin America Teaching Resources, *Journal Entry,* p. 172

Pizarro Conquers the Incas Francisco Pizarro (frahn SEES koh pea SAHR oh) was also a Spanish conquistador. He heard stories about the rich Incan empire. In 1531, Pizarro sailed to the Pacific coast of South America with a force of 180 Spanish soldiers. The Spanish captured and killed the Incan emperor and many other Incan leaders. By 1535, Pizarro had conquered most of the Incan empire, including the capital, Cuzco.

In only 15 years, the conquistadors had defeated the two most powerful empires in the Americas. How did they do it? The Spanish had guns and cannons and horses, all of which the Native Americans had never seen. The Europeans also carried diseases such as smallpox, measles, and chicken pox. The Native Americans had never been exposed to these diseases, and entire villages got sick and died. Also, because of local rivalries, some Native Americans were eager to help the Spanish conquistadors.

✓ Reading Check **What are two reasons the conquistadors were able to conquer the Aztecs and the Incas?**

Advantages of the Conquistadors
This illustration shows conquistadors using guns ➊ to fight Aztec soldiers armed with spears ➋. For protection, the Spanish have helmets, ➌ while the Aztecs use feather shields ➍.
Contrast *What other items in the picture might have contributed to the Spanish victory?*

Differentiated Instruction

For English Language Learners L2
Students may have difficulty pronouncing some of the longer words in this section, such as *supernatural, surrounded, surrendered,* and *diseases.* Encourage students to break down these words into smaller parts and sound out the pronunciations.

For Advanced Readers L3
Give students the Aztec story *The Talking Stone* to learn more about Moctezuma and the Aztec culture.

All in One **Latin America Teaching Resources,** *The Talking Stone,* pp. 169–171

Guided Instruction (continued)
■ Ask students **How were the Spanish able to defeat the Native Americans?** *(They had guns and horses, which the Native Americans had never seen; they carried diseases that sickened and killed entire villages; they were able to use local rivalries to enlist the help of some Native American groups.)*

Independent Practice
Have students continue to fill in the graphic organizer with dates and events from The Success of the Conquistadors.

Monitor Progress
As students fill in the graphic organizer, circulate and make sure individuals are choosing the correct details. Provide assistance as needed.

Answers

Contrast The picture shows that the conquistadors also have full body armor and a crossbow. Both items would have helped the conquistadors to defeat the Aztecs.

✓ Reading Check Possible answers: The conquistadors had guns, cannons, and horses; they carried diseases that wiped out entire villages; they received help from enemies of the Aztecs and Incas.

Colonization

Guided Instruction

- **Vocabulary Builder** Clarify the meaning of the high-use word **superior** before reading.

- Ask students to read Colonization and review the map and diagram on pages 54 and 55.

- Ask students to explain how Spain organized its territory. *(The territory was divided into provinces that were ruled by viceroys appointed by the king.)*

- Discuss with students how Spain's colonization of Latin America affected the region. *(European culture became an influence in the region; Christianity was introduced; Native Americans were enslaved and affected by disease; new industries were introduced; the new products influenced trade.)*

Independent Practice

Have students complete the graphic organizer with dates and events from Colonization.

🎯 Target Reading Skill   L2

Paraphrase As a follow up, ask students to answer the Target Reading Skill question in the Student Edition. *(Possible answer: Settlers from many European nations came to Latin America to 1) spread the Christian religion, 2) find gold and riches, 3) farm. The settlers created colonies that would benefit them.)*

Answers

MAP MASTER Skills Activity   **Locate** Cortés started in present-day Cuba; Pizarro in present-day Panama. **Identify Causes** The coasts were accessible by sailing vessel; the Spanish may have used rivers to extend inland.

Go Online
PHSchool.com Students may practice their map skills using an online version of this map.

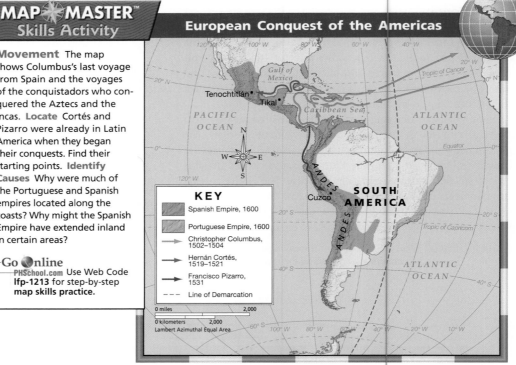

MAP MASTER™ Skills Activity — European Conquest of the Americas

Movement The map shows Columbus's last voyage from Spain and the voyages of the conquistadors who conquered the Aztecs and the Incas. **Locate** Cortés and Pizarro were already in Latin America when they began their conquests. Find their starting points. **Identify Causes** Why were much of the Portuguese and Spanish empires located along the coasts? Why might the Spanish Empire have extended inland in certain areas?

Go Online
PHSchool.com Use Web Code **lfp-1213** for step-by-step **map skills practice.**

KEY

- Spanish Empire, 1600
- Portuguese Empire, 1600
- Christopher Columbus, 1502–1504
- Hernán Cortés, 1519–1521
- Francisco Pizarro, 1531
- Line of Demarcation

0 miles 2,000
0 kilometers 2,000
Lambert Azimuthal Equal Area

Colonization

By the 1600s, Spain claimed land throughout much of the Americas. Spain's lands stretched from the tip of South America all the way north into the present-day United States, and included some islands in the Caribbean Sea. Later, the French and English also claimed some Caribbean islands. Portugal claimed Brazil.

European Settlers Arrive Settlers from Spain, Portugal, and other European nations began arriving in what came to be called Latin America. Some of them were missionaries, sent by the Catholic Church to spread Christianity to the peoples of the Americas. Others came to look for gold and other mineral riches. Still others wanted to settle and farm the land. If the Native American people resisted, the newcomers used their superior force to suppress them. The Europeans created the kinds of colonies that would benefit them and the countries from which they had come.

🎯 **Paraphrase**
Read the paragraph at the right carefully and then paraphrase it, or restate it in your own words. In your paraphrase, you might number the reasons people came to the Americas.

54 Latin America

🛠 Skills for Life — Skills Mini Lesson

Recognizing Bias

1. Teach the skill by telling students that bias, or prejudice, involves judging what a person is like based on assumptions or a stereotype, rather than on that person's individual qualities.

2. Practice the skill by discussing how European actions, such as demanding taxes or labor from Native Americans, show that Europeans prejudged the Native Americans.

3. Apply the skill by asking **What kinds of biases or opinions might the Spanish have had about the Native Americans that led to this treatment?** *(Europeans might have thought that their culture and ways of life were superior to that of the Native Americans.)*

Spain Organizes Its Empire Spain controlled the largest portion of the Americas south of what is now the United States. The king of Spain wanted to keep strict control over his empire, so the territory was divided into provinces. The king appointed viceroys, or representatives who ruled the provinces in the king's name. Other settlers who had been born in Spain helped the viceroys rule. Meanwhile, a council in Spain supervised the colonial officials to make sure they did not become too powerful.

The two most important provinces in Spain's American empire were New Spain and Peru. The capital of New Spain was Mexico City. Lima became the capital of Peru.

Spanish social classes determined where people lived in Lima. The most powerful citizens lived in the center of the city. They either came from Spain or had Spanish parents. **Mestizos,** people of mixed Spanish and Native American ancestry, lived on the outskirts of Lima. Many mestizos were poor, but some were middle class or even quite wealthy. Native Americans were the least powerful class. Most Native Americans continued to live in the countryside. The Spanish forced them to work on haciendas. A **hacienda** (hah see EN dah) was a plantation owned by Spaniards or the Catholic Church.

Learn how Pizarro conquered the Incan empire.

Show students *Pizarro and the Empire of Gold.* Ask **What political event within the Incan empire aided Pizarro in his conquest of the Inca?** *(the death of the emperor and thus the bloody rivalry between his sons for control of the empire)*

Monitor Progress

- Show *Section Reading Support Transparency LA 33* and ask students to check their graphic organizers individually. Go over key concepts and clarify key vocabulary as needed.

    Latin America Transparencies, *Section Reading Support Transparency LA 33*

- Tell students to fill in the last column of the *Reading Readiness Guide.* Ask them to evaluate if what they learned was what they had expected to learn.

    All in One **Latin America Teaching Resources,** *Reading Readiness Guide,* p. 148

Assess and Reteach

Assess Progress [L2]

Have students complete the Section Assessment. Administer the *Section Quiz.*

All in One **Latin America Teaching Resources,** *Section Quiz,* p. 150

Reteach [L1]

If students need more instruction, have them read this section in the Reading and Vocabulary Study Guide.

Chapter 2, Section 3, **Latin America Reading and Vocabulary Study Guide,** pp. 22–24

Extend [L3]

Show students *Pizarro and the Empire of Gold.* Have them paraphrase how Pizarro and his small army were able to defeat the much larger Incan army.

Pizarro and the Empire of Gold, **World Studies Video Program**

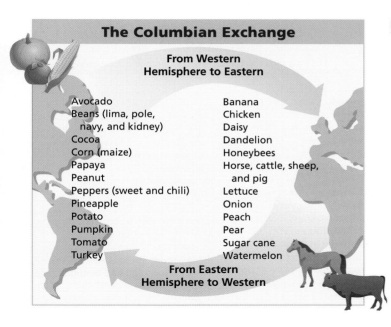

The Columbian Exchange

From Western Hemisphere to Eastern

Avocado	Banana
Beans (lima, pole, navy, and kidney)	Chicken
	Daisy
Cocoa	Dandelion
Corn (maize)	Honeybees
Papaya	Horse, cattle, sheep, and pig
Peanut	
Peppers (sweet and chili)	Lettuce
Pineapple	Onion
Potato	Peach
Pumpkin	Pear
Tomato	Sugar cane
Turkey	Watermelon

From Eastern Hemisphere to Western

■ **Diagram Skills**
Goods, as well as people, crossed the Atlantic Ocean in the years after Columbus's voyages. **Identify** Which animals were part of the exchange? **Infer** Which animal had the potential for making the greatest change in its new home? Explain your answer.

Background: Biography

Defender of the Indians

Bartolomé de Las Casas, born in Seville, Spain, in 1474, was a Spanish missionary and historian who spoke out against the Europeans' harsh treatment of Native Americans. He had witnessed the abuses that Native Americans had suffered and worked to improve their conditions. Las Casas' work helped Spain pass the New Laws in 1542, which brought about some improvements in the lives of the Native Americans in the Spanish colonies. Las Casas also contributed to our knowledge of Spanish colonies in America through his writings in *History of the Indies.* He died in Madrid in July 1566.

Answers

Diagram Skills Identify Chickens, honeybees, horses, cattle, sheep, pigs **Infer** Horses had the potential to make great changes because the people in the Western Hemisphere had no domesticated animals capable of carrying people and goods as well as horses.

Answers

Explain Diseases weakened Native American resistance to Spanish rule.

✓ **Reading Check** The Native American population declined because of overwork, malnutrition, and European diseases.

Section 3 Assessment

Key Terms
Students' sentences should reflect knowledge of each Key Term.

⟳ Target Reading Skill
During the first 50 years of Spanish rule the Native American population declined greatly. Because they needed more workers, the Spanish began importing enslaved Africans. Meanwhile, European demand for products from the Americas grew.

Comprehension and Critical Thinking
1. (a) Europeans reached the Americas while searching for new trade routes to Asia; once in the Americas they searched for gold and other treasures, and wanted to spread Christianity. **(b)** It divided the land; land west of the line was settled by Spain; land east of the line was settled by Portugal.

2. (a) Hernán Cortés conquered the Aztecs; Francisco Pizarro conquered the Incas. **(b)** Similar: Both were conquered by the Spanish; their enemies helped the conquistadors; their emperors were killed; Different: At first Cortés was welcomed by Moctezuma, but then the Aztecs revolted and were ultimately defeated by Cortés; the Incan emperor was immediately killed by Pizarro and his men; Tenochtitlán was in ruins after it was conquered; Cuzco was preserved. **(c)** Answers will vary, but possible answers include: The conquistadors had weapons and horses; they carried diseases that wiped out entire villages; they received help from both empires' enemies.

3. (a) The territory was divided into provinces; the king of Spain appointed viceroys to rule the provinces; Spanish settlers helped the viceroys rule; a council in Spain supervised the colonial officials to curb their power. **(b)** The Spanish forced Native Americans to work on haciendas and in mines. Many died from overwork, malnutrition, and disease. Then the Spanish brought millions of enslaved Africans to work in the Americas.

Devastating Diseases
This 1500s illustration shows a medicine man treating an Aztec for smallpox. Native Americans had never been exposed to European diseases. **Explain** *How did these diseases contribute to the success of Spanish rule?*

The Effect of European Rule Spain gave its settlers encomiendas (en koh mee EN dahs), which were rights to demand taxes or labor from Native Americans. At first, the Native Americans were forced to work only on the haciendas. But when silver was discovered in Mexico and Peru, the Spanish forced them to work in the mines as well. Many Native Americans died from overwork, malnutrition, and European diseases. Others rebelled unsuccessfully against the Spanish.

In the first 50 years of Spanish rule, the Native American population of New Spain declined from an estimated 25 million to 3 million. The Spanish now needed more workers for their haciendas and mines. They began importing enslaved Africans in large numbers. In Europe, the demand for products from the Americas continued to grow. Even more workers were needed. Millions more slaves were brought from Africa.

Brazil The situation was somewhat different in Brazil, which was a colony of Portugal. Most settlers remained near the coast. They took land from the Native Americans for sugar plantations and cattle ranches. Brazil also came to depend on the forced labor of Indians and enslaved Africans.

✓ **Reading Check** Why did the Native American population decline?

Section 3 Assessment

Key Terms
Review the key terms at the beginning of this section. Use each term in a sentence that explains its meaning.

⟳ **Target Reading Skill**
Paraphrase the second paragraph on this page. Present ideas in the order they appear in the paragraph.

Comprehension and Critical Thinking
1. (a) Recall Explain why Europeans came to the Americas in the 1500s.

(b) Identify Cause and Effect How did the Treaty of Tordesillas affect the European settlement of the Americas?
2. (a) Identify Which conquistadors conquered the Aztecs and the Incas?
(b) Compare In what ways were the defeats of the Aztec and Incan empires similar, and in what ways were they different?
(c) Evaluate Information What was the most important reason for the conquistadors' success? Explain.
3. (a) Describe How was Spain's empire organized?
(b) Draw Conclusions How did the Spanish conquest affect Native Americans and Africans?

Writing Activity
Review how Moctezuma's spies described the Spanish when they saw them for the first time. How do you think those spies might have described you and your friends? Write a brief description from their point of view.

> **Writing Tip** Notice the details in the description by Moctezuma's spies. Then focus on similar details. Use descriptive words for color, size, texture, and sound. Remember the point of view of the speaker: a Native American of the 1500s.

Writing Activity
Use the *Rubric for Assessing a Writing Assignment* to evaluate students' descriptions.

All in One **Latin America Teaching Resources,** *Rubric for Assessing a Writing Assignment,* p. 174

Section 4 — Independence

Prepare to Read

Objectives

In this section you will
1. Learn what events inspired revolutions in Latin America.
2. Find out how Mexico gained its independence.
3. Discover how Bolívar and San Martín helped bring independence to South America.

Taking Notes

As you read the section, look for the ways revolutionary leaders helped bring independence to Latin America. Copy the table below and use it to record the name and accomplishments of each person.

Leader	Country	Accomplishment

Target Reading Skill

Summarize When you summarize, you restate the main points you have read in the correct order. Because you leave out less important details, a summary is shorter than the original text. Summarizing is a good technique to help you comprehend and study. As you read, pause to summarize occasionally.

Key Terms

• **Toussaint L'Ouverture** (too SAN loo vehr TOOR) *n.* leader of Haiti's fight for independence

• **revolution** (rev uh LOO shun) *n.* overthrow of a government, with another taking its place
• **criollo** (kree OH yoh) *n.* a person with Spanish parents who was born in Latin America
• **Simón Bolívar** (see MOHN boh LEE vahr) *n.* a South American revolutionary leader
• **José de San Martín** (hoh SAY deh sahn mahr TEEN) *n.* a South American revolutionary leader
• **caudillo** (kaw DEE yoh) *n.* a military officer who rules a country very strictly

---

On August 24, 1791, the night sky over Saint-Domingue (san duh MAYNG) glowed red and gold. The French Caribbean colony was on fire. The slaves were sick of being mistreated by their white masters. They finally had rebelled. Now they were burning every piece of white-owned property they could find. This Night of Fire was the beginning of the first great fight for freedom in Latin America. **Toussaint L'Ouverture** (too SAN loo vehr TOOR), a former slave, led the people of Saint-Domingue in this fight for independence for more than 10 years. Eventually they won, and they founded the independent country of Haiti (HAY tee) in 1804.

The Seeds of Revolution

The flame of liberty lit in Haiti soon spread across Latin America. By 1825, most of the region was independent. Latin Americans would no longer be ruled by Europe.

Toussaint L'Ouverture

Chapter 2 Section 4 **57**

Target Reading Skill L2

Summarize Point out the Target Reading Skill. Tell students that when summarizing a paragraph or section they should include only the main points in the correct order and omit the less important details.

Model the skill by summarizing the first paragraph on this page. "The Night of Fire was the first battle for independence in Latin America. Toussaint L'Ouverture led the people of Saint-Domingue in their fight for independence for more than 10 years. Eventually Haiti became an independent country in 1804."

Give students *Summarize*. Have them complete the activity in their groups.

All in One Latin America Teaching Resources, *Summarize,* p. 161

Section 4
Step-by-Step Instruction

Objectives
Social Studies

1. Learn what events inspired revolutions in Latin America.
2. Find out how Mexico gained its independence.
3. Discover how Bolívar and San Martín helped bring independence to South America.

Reading/Language Arts

Summarize to understand the main points you have read in the correct order.

Prepare to Read

Build Background Knowledge L2

Tell students that they will learn how the countries of Latin America won their independence in this section. Remind students about how Americans celebrate their independence on the Fourth of July. Ask **Why is independence so important to Americans?** Use the Idea Wave participation strategy (TE, p. T35) to generate a list.

Set a Purpose for Reading L2

■ Preview the Objectives.

■ Read each statement in the *Reading Readiness Guide* aloud. Ask students to mark the statements true or false.

   All in One Latin America Teaching Resources, *Reading Readiness Guide,* p. 152

■ Have students discuss the statements in pairs or groups of four, then mark their worksheets again. Use the Numbered Heads participation structure (TE, p. T36) to call on students to share their group's perspectives.

Vocabulary Builder
Preview Key Terms L2

Pronounce each Key Term, then ask students to say the word with you. Provide a simple explanation such as, "The American colonists fought the American Revolution to free themselves from British rule."

Chapter 2 Section 4 **57**

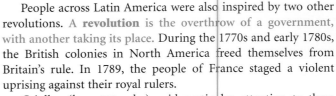

Instruct

The Seeds of Revolution `L2`

Guided Instruction
- Read The Seeds of Revolution using the Re Quest Procedure (TE, p. T35).
- Ask students **Who were the criollos?** *(Latin Americans who had Spanish parents; they were often the wealthiest and best-educated people in the Spanish colonies, but had little political power.)*
- Ask students **What effect did the American and French revolutions have on Latin Americans?** *(They inspired ideas of independence in many Latin Americans.)*

Independent Practice
Ask students to create the Taking Notes table on a blank piece of paper. Then have them fill in the columns with information about Toussaint L'Ouverture.

Monitor Progress
As students fill in the table, circulate and make sure individuals summarize L'Ouverture's accomplishments, omitting the less important details.

People across Latin America were also inspired by two other revolutions. A **revolution** is the overthrow of a government, with another taking its place. During the 1770s and early 1780s, the British colonies in North America freed themselves from Britain's rule. In 1789, the people of France staged a violent uprising against their royal rulers.

Criollos (kree OH yohz) paid particular attention to these events. A **criollo** had Spanish parents, but had been born in Latin America. Criollos often were the best-educated and wealthiest people in the Spanish colonies, but they had little political power. Only people born in Spain could hold government office. Many criollos attended school in Europe. There, they learned about the ideas that inspired revolution in France and the United States.

The criollos especially liked the idea that people had the right to govern themselves. However, they were frightened by the slave revolt in Haiti. The criollos wanted independence from Spain but power for themselves.

✓ **Reading Check** Which revolutions inspired ideas of independence in Latin America?

Independence in Mexico

Mexico began its struggle for self-government in 1810. That's when Miguel Hidalgo (mee GEL hee DAHL goh), a criollo priest, began planning the Mexican revolution. He appealed to local mestizos and Native Americans.

Cry of Dolores
This section of a mural by Juan O'Gorman shows Hidalgo and his followers. **Analyze Images** *Look carefully at the people behind Hidalgo. What does the painter suggest about the Mexican Revolution by showing these people?*

The "Cry of Dolores" In September 1810, the Spanish government discovered Hidalgo's plot. But before the authorities could arrest him, Hidalgo took action. He wildly rang the church bells in the town of Dolores. A huge crowd gathered. "Recover from the hated Spaniards the land stolen from your forefathers," he shouted.

Hidalgo's call for revolution became known as the "Cry of Dolores." It attracted some 80,000 fighters, mostly mestizos and Native Americans. The rebels won some victories, but their luck soon changed. By the beginning of 1811, they were in full retreat. Hidalgo tried to flee the country, but government soldiers soon captured him. He was convicted of treason and then executed by firing squad in July 1811.

58   Latin America

Answers

✓ **Reading Check** The American and French Revolutions inspired ideas of independence in Latin America. **Analyze Images** Some of the people behind Hidalgo seem to be Native Americans, while others are dressed as farmers or soldiers. The painter may be suggesting that Hidalgo was supported by many different groups of people.

Vocabulary Builder

Use the information below to teach students this section's high-use words.

High-Use Word	Definition and Sample Sentence
authorities, p. 58	*n.* persons in command The **authorities** looked into the incident.
forefathers, p. 58	*n.* ancestors My **forefathers** came from Spain.

South American Independence

MAP ★ MASTER™
Skills Activity

Regions After freeing themselves from Spain, several former colonies formed Gran Colombia, modeled after the United States. **Identify** Which modern nations were part of Gran Colombia? **Compare** Look at the map of South America on page 3. Compare Peru's modern borders to those of 1831.

Go Online
PHSchool.com Use Web Code
lfp-1214 for step-by-step
map skills practice.

Mexico Becomes Independent The Spanish could execute the revolution's leaders, but they could not kill its spirit. Small rebel groups kept fighting. Then a high-ranking officer in the Spanish army, Agustín de Iturbide (aw guh STEEN deh ee toor BEE day), joined the rebels. Many wealthy people who had viewed Hidalgo as a dangerous hothead trusted Iturbide to protect their interests. He was a criollo and an army officer. They decided to support the rebellion. In 1821, Iturbide declared Mexico independent.

✓ Reading Check **What groups made up most of Hidalgo's army?**

South American Independence

Simón Bolívar (see MOHN boh LEE vahr), one of South America's most important revolutionary leaders, was born in Venezuela in 1783. His family was one of the richest and most important families in Latin America. When Bolívar was at school in Spain, he met Prince Ferdinand, the heir to the Spanish throne. He played a game similar to present-day badminton with the prince. Custom required that Bolívar show respect for the prince by losing. Instead, Bolívar played hard and tried to win. He even knocked the prince's hat off with his racquet! The angry prince demanded an apology. Bolívar refused. He claimed it was an accident.

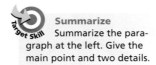

Summarize
Summarize the paragraph at the left. Give the main point and two details.

Chapter 2 Section 4 **59**

Independence in Mexico and South American Independence L2

Guided Instruction

- **Vocabulary Builder** Clarify the high-use words **authorities** and **forefathers** before reading.

- Read how Latin America became free from Spain's rule in Independence in Mexico and South American Independence. As students read, circulate and make sure individuals can answer the Reading Check questions.

- Ask students **What was the "Cry of Dolores?"** *(Miguel Hidalgo's call for revolution against Spain in Mexico)*

- Ask students **How did Mexico become independent in 1821?** *(Agustín de Iturbide, a criollo leader in the Spanish army, joined with mestizo and Native American rebel forces to declare independence.)*

- Ask students to brainstorm what qualities they think make a hero. Do the qualities of a hero fit the description of the leaders they have read about? Who? Why? Use a Numbered Heads participation strategy (TE, p. T36) to have students answer these questions.

- Ask students **What challenges might the newly independent countries face?** *(Possible challenges: remaining unified, organizing their governments, finding good leaders, rebuilding their economies.)*

⟳ Target Reading Skill L2

Summarize As a follow up, ask students to answer the Target Reading Skill question in the Student Edition. *(Possible answer: Símon Bolívar as a young man defied authority. He refused to lose a game to Prince Ferdinand and even knocked Ferdinand's hat off.)*

Differentiated Instruction

For Less Proficient Readers L1
Have students read the section in the Reading and Vocabulary Study Guide. This version provides basic-level instruction in an interactive format with questions and write-on lines.

📖 Chapter 2, Section 4, **Latin America Reading and Vocabulary Study Guide,** pp. 25–27

For Advanced Readers L3
Have students work in pairs to create posters for or against seeking independence from Spanish rule. The posters should urge people to support their position. Use the *Rubric for Assessing a Student Poster* to evaluate students' posters.

All in One Latin America Teaching Resources, *Rubric for Assessing a Student Poster,* p. 175

Answers

✓ Reading Check Mestizo and Native American groups made up most of Hidalgo's army.

MAP ★ MASTER Skills Activity **Identify** the modern nations of Colombia, Panama, Venezuela, and Ecuador **Compare** Peru used to extend further inland, but had less land along the coast to the South.

Independent Practice

Have students complete the table of leaders and their accomplishments.

Monitor Progress

- Show *Section Reading Support Transparency LA 34* and ask students to check their graphic organizers individually. Go over key concepts and clarify key vocabulary as needed.

  📖 **Latin America Transparencies,** *Section Reading Support Transparency LA 34*

- Tell students to fill in the last column of the *Reading Readiness Guide*. Probe for what they learned that confirms or invalidates each statement.

  All in One **Latin America Teaching Resources,** *Reading Readiness Guide,* p. 152

Citizen Heroes

Read **Citizen Heroes** on this page. Ask students **How do Martí's efforts to free his country from Spain compare to those of San Martín?** *(Martí, like San Martín, dedicated his life to fighting for independence from Spanish rule.)*

Assess and Reteach

Assess Progress L2

Have students complete the Section Assessment. Administer the *Section Quiz.*

  All in One **Latin America Teaching Resources,** *Section Quiz,* p. 154

Reteach L1

If students need more instruction, have them read this section in the Reading and Vocabulary Study Guide.

  📖 Chapter 2, Section 4, **Latin America Reading and Vocabulary Study Guide,** pp. 25-27

Citizen Heroes ★

To Be a Leader: José Martí
José Martí grew up in Cuba when it was still a Spanish colony. At the age of 16, he started a newspaper dedicated to Cuban independence. After he supported an 1868 uprising, Martí was sent to prison. He spent many years in exile, working for Cuban freedom by writing and publishing, and by helping to form a revolutionary party. In 1895, Martí led an invasion of Cuba to free the island from Spanish rule. He was killed on the battlefield a month later—seven years before Cuba achieved independence. This statue of Martí is in New York City's Central Park.

60 Latin America

Bolívar, The Liberator Many years later, Bolívar and Ferdinand faced off again. This time, Bolívar knocked Spanish America right out from under Ferdinand's feet. Bolívar joined the fight for Venezuelan independence in 1807. Six years later he became its leader. His confidence, courage, and daring inspired his soldiers. They enjoyed victory after victory. By 1822, Bolívar's troops had freed a large area from Spanish rule (the future countries of Colombia, Venezuela, Ecuador, and Panama).

This newly liberated region formed Gran Colombia. Bolívar became its president. Even though his country was free, Bolívar did not give up the cause of independence. "The Liberator," as he was now known, turned south toward Peru.

San Martín Fights for Freedom Another important revolutionary leader was **José de San Martín** (hoh SAY deh sahn mahr TEEN). He was an Argentine who had lived in Spain and served in the Spanish army. When Argentina began its fight for freedom, he quickly offered to help. San Martín took good care of his troops. He shared each hardship they had to suffer, and they loved him for it. Many said they would follow San Martín anywhere—even over the snow-capped Andes Mountains.

In 1817, his soldiers had to do just that. San Martín led them through high passes in the Andes into Chile. This bold action took the Spanish completely by surprise. In a matter of months, Spain was defeated. San Martín declared Chile's independence. Then he, too, turned his attention to Peru.

Again, San Martín planned a surprise. This time, he attacked from the sea. The Spanish were not prepared, and their defenses quickly collapsed. In July 1821, San Martín pushed inland and seized Lima, the capital of Peru.

An Important Meeting A year later, San Martín met with Bolívar to discuss the fight for independence. Historians do not know what happened in that meeting. But afterward, San Martín suddenly gave up his command. He left Bolívar to continue the fight alone. Eventually, Bolívar drove the remaining Spanish forces out of South America altogether. By 1825, only Cuba and Puerto Rico were still ruled by Spain.

Background: Links Across Time

African Independence Although Europe is closer to Africa than Latin America, most Europeans began to colonize Africa later. Many Europeans established formal colonies in Africa in the late 1800s. Like the people of Latin America, many people in Africa later were inspired by the ideas of self-government and independence. African countries began to achieve independence in the 1950s, 1960s, and 1970s.

Brazil Takes a Different Route Portugal's colony, Brazil, became independent without fighting a war. In the early 1800s, during a war in Europe, French armies invaded Spain and Portugal. Portugal's royal family fled to Brazil for safety. The king returned to Portugal in 1821. However, he left his son, Dom Pedro, to rule the colony. Dom Pedro took more power than the king expected. He declared Brazil independent in 1822. Three years later, Portugal quietly admitted that Brazil was independent.

Independence Brings Challenges Simón Bolívar dreamed of uniting South America as one country, a "United States of South America." Gran Colombia was the first step. But Bolívar found that his dream was impossible. Latin America was a huge area, divided by the Andes and dense rain forests. Also, the leaders of the countries in Gran Colombia wanted little to do with Bolívar. In poor health, he retired from politics.

Even though he did not remain in office, Bolívar set the standard for Latin American leaders. Most were **caudillos** (kaw DEE yohz), military officers who ruled very strictly. Bolívar cared about the people he governed. However, many caudillos did not. These later caudillos only wanted to stay in power and get rich. You will read about how these caudillos affected the nations they governed in the next section.

✓ **Reading Check** What are two reasons that South America was not united into one country?

This July 2000 parade in Bogotá celebrates 181 years of Colombian independence.

Section 4 Assessment

Key Terms
Review the key terms at the beginning of this section. Use each term in a sentence that explains its meaning.

⟳ **Target Reading Skill**
Write a summary of the last two paragraphs on this page. Include a main point and several details from each paragraph.

Comprehension and Critical Thinking
1. (a) **Identify** What events inspired independence movements in Latin America?

(b) **Identify Cause and Effect** Why were many criollos in favor of independence?
2. (a) **Describe** How did Hidalgo begin the Mexican Revolution?
(b) **Analyze Information** Explain why Iturbide was successful and Hidalgo was not.
3. (a) **Recall** What were the achievements of Bolívar, San Martín, and Dom Pedro?
(b) **Infer** What do you think Bolívar had in mind when he wanted to create the "United States of South America"?

Writing Activity
Suppose you are a soldier in Bolívar's or San Martín's army. Describe what you are doing, why you are doing it, and how you feel about your commander.

> **Writing Tip** Remember to write your description in the first person, using the pronouns *I* or *we*. Use vivid words, such as *terrified, exhausted,* or *thrilled,* to describe your feelings.

Writing Activity
Use the *Rubric for Assessing a Writing Assignment* to evaluate students' descriptions.

All in One **Latin America Teaching Resources,** *Rubric for Assessing a Writing Assignment,* p. 174

Extend L3

Assign students to work groups to prepare a talk show featuring the heroes of the Latin American independence movement as guests. Individual group members should: prepare questions to ask the heroes, create props, write the script, assign roles for heroes and talk show host, and rehearse the show. Call on groups to present their shows to the class.

Answers

✓ **Reading Check** South America was a huge area, divided by the Andes and dense rain forests. Also, the leaders of the countries in Gran Colombia did not want to unite South America as one country.

Section 4 Assessment

Key Terms
Students' sentences should reflect an understanding of each Key Term.

⟳ **Target Reading Skill**
Bolívar dreamed of uniting South America as one country, but found his dream was impossible. South America was too large, and leaders of the Gran Colombia countries did not want to have anything to do with him. Bolívar became the model for Latin American leaders. He was a caudillo, but he cared about the people he governed. Other caudillos that followed only wanted to have power and get rich.

Comprehension and Critical Thinking
1. (a) the American and French Revolutions (b) The criollos wanted independence from Spain because they wanted political power.
2. (a) In 1810 Hidalgo's "Cry of Dolores" attracted 80,000 fighters, mostly mestizos and Native Americans. (b) Many people viewed Hidalgo as dangerous, but they trusted Iturbide who was a criollo and a high-ranking officer in the Spanish army. As a result, they supported the rebellion.
3. (a) Bolívar and San Martín were liberators who fought against the Spanish for the independence of countries in South America. Dom Pedro peacefully gained independence for Brazil from Portugal. (b) Possible answers: Bolívar wanted to unite all the countries under one central government; he also might have wanted to create a government like that of the United States.

Objective

Learn how to sequence and make a timeline.

Prepare to Read

Build Background Knowledge L2

Ask students to think about one activity they have done each day over the last five days. Then ask how they might show these activities in the order in which they occurred.

Instruct

Sequencing Making a Timeline L2

Guided Instruction

■ Read the steps to make a timeline as a class and write them on the board.

■ Practice the skill by following the steps on p. 63 as a class. If students are uncomfortable disclosing events from their past, tell them that they are free to make up entries. No one will call them on incorrect events. Model each step in the activity by suggesting a name for the timeline (*History of the First 10 Years of My Life*) and providing simple examples of events. (*moving to a new place, starting a new school, or learning to ride a bicycle*)

■ Have students write their events on separate index cards. Make sure that students choose beginning and end dates that will encompass all their entries. Ask students to put all their events in chronological order. Then have students construct their timelines on a sheet of paper. Before students mark their entries on their timelines, make sure that their dates are evenly spaced.

Skills for Life — Making a Timeline

If you want to show where cities and towns are located along a certain route, you can draw a road map. But how do you show when events occurred? In that case, you can draw a timeline.

You might say that a timeline is a map of time. It has a beginning date and an ending date. It shows when events occurred during that time period, and in what order. Look at pages 46 and 47 for an example of a historical timeline. Use a timeline whenever you need to organize a series of dates.

Golden bird made by the Incas

Learn the Skill

Use these steps to make a timeline.

1 **Create a title for your timeline.** Decide what your timeline will show. It might be "History of the Incas" or "The Life of Simón Bolívar."

2 **Put events in order.** On sticky notes or index cards, write down four or five important events. They will be the entries for your timeline. Put one entry on each sticky or card. Write the date and a short description of the event. Now arrange the entries in chronological order—that is, from the earliest to the latest date.

3 **Select a time span.** Choose a starting date that is earlier than your first entry. Choose an ending date that is later than your last entry.

4 **Build your timeline.** On a sheet of paper, draw a straight line across the page. Make a large dot on the line at each end, and label those dots with the starting and ending dates of your timeline.

5 **Mark the divisions of time periods.** Divide your timeline into equal time periods. Label each one.

6 **Put your entries on the timeline.** Put a dot at the appropriate place on the timeline for each entry. From each dot, draw a straight line upward or downward. Write the text of the entry next to the straight line.

Portrait of Simón Bolívar

62 Latin America

Independent Practice

Assign *Skills for Life* and have students complete it individually.

All in One **Latin America Teaching Resources,** *Skills for Life,* p. 164

Monitor Progress

As students are completing *Skills for Life*, circulate to make sure individuals are applying the skill steps effectively. Provide assistance as needed.

Practice the Skill

Now make a timeline of your own life, the life of someone you know, or the life of someone famous. Create the timeline by following the steps below.

1 Your timeline can cover an entire life or some portion of it. Choose a title that reflects the topic and the time span.

2 Decide which important events you want to include. Write the events with their dates on sticky notes or index cards, and arrange them chronologically, that is, from the earliest to the latest date.

3 Choose starting and ending dates that include all your entries.

4 Draw your timeline and mark the starting and ending dates.

5 Add the time periods to your drawing. For instance, if you used 1995 as your starting date, your next date might be 1998 or 2000. Make sure the dates are equally spaced along the line.

6 Add your entries to the appropriate places on your timeline.

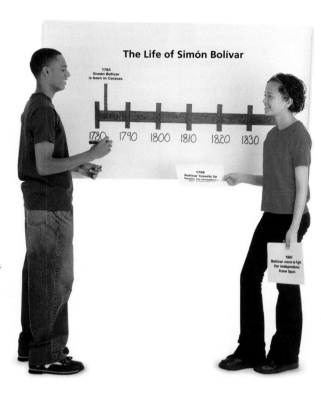

The Life of Simón Bolívar

1783
Simón Bolívar
is born in Caracas.

1780 1790 1800 1810 1820 1830

1799
Bolívar travels to
Spain to complete...

1804
Bolívar vows to fight
for independence
from Spain.

Apply the Skill

Identify what you think are the most important events in Section 4, Independence. Then create a timeline of the major events in the section, using no more than five entries.

Assess Progress   **L2**

Ask students to do the Apply the Skill activity.

Reteach   **L1**

If students are having trouble applying the skill steps, have them review the skill using the interactive Social Studies Skills Tutor CD-ROM.

 Sequencing, Social Studies Skills Tutor CD-ROM

Extend   **L3**

To extend the lesson, ask students to research the life of one of the people they read about in Section 4. Then have them make a timeline of up to eight events in that person's life.

Differentiated Instruction

For Special Needs Students   **L1**

Partner special needs students with more proficient students to do Level 1 of the Sequencing lesson on the Social Studies Skills Tutor CD-ROM together. When students feel more confident, they can move onto Level 2 alone.

 Sequencing, Social Studies Skills Tutor CD-ROM

Answers
Apply the Skill

Answers will vary, but students' timelines should include dates and events from Section 4 in chronological order.

Objectives
Social Studies

1. Learn how Latin American caudillos and foreign involvement contributed to the region's troubled past.

2. Find out how Latin American nations are struggling to improve their economies and the welfare of their people.

Reading/Language Arts

Reread or read ahead to help understand words and ideas in the text.

Prepare to Read

Build Background Knowledge L2

In this section, students will read about Latin America's history from independence to the present. Write this statement on the board: After independence, the biggest problems facing Latin American nations were _____. Have students preview the section, then predict answers to the statement. Conduct an Idea Wave (TE, p. T35) to generate a list.

Set a Purpose for Reading L2

- Preview the Objectives.
- Read each statement in the *Reading Readiness Guide* aloud. Ask students to mark the statements true or false

  All in One **Latin America Teaching Resources,** *Reading Readiness Guide,* p. 156

- Have students discuss the statements in pairs or groups of four, then mark their worksheets again. Use the Numbered Heads participation structure (TE, p. T36) to call on students to share their group's perspectives.

Vocabulary Builder
Preview Key Terms L2

Pronounce each Key Term, then ask students to say the word with you. Provide a simple explanation such as, "The dictator took away people's right to freedom of speech and freedom of religion."

Prepare to Read

Objectives
In this section you will
1. Learn how Latin American caudillos and foreign involvement contributed to the region's troubled past.
2. Find out how Latin American nations are struggling to improve their economies and the welfare of their people.

Taking Notes
As you read the section, look for the main ideas and details. Copy the format below, and use it to outline the section.

> I. A troubled past
>   A. Colonial legacy
>   1.
>   2.
>   3.
>   B. Foreign involvement

Target Reading Skill

Reread or Read Ahead Both rereading and reading ahead can help you understand words and ideas in the text. If you do not understand a word or passage, use one or both of these techniques. In some cases, you may wish to read ahead first to see if the word or idea is clarified later on. If not, try going back and rereading the original passage.

Key Terms
- **dictator** (DIK tay tur) *n.* a ruler with complete power
- **export** (eks PAWRT) *v.* to send products from one country to be sold in another
- **import** (im PAWRT) *v.* to bring products into one country from another
- **foreign debt** (FAWR in det) *n.* money owed by one country to other countries
- **regime** (ruh ZHEEM) *n.* a particular administration or government

Slaves building a street in Rio de Janeiro, from an 1824 lithograph

64 Latin America

Before independence, when Latin America was ruled by European nations, many of the ordinary people of the region were very poor. In the Spanish colonies, people born in Spain held government office. Criollos were often wealthy and owned large haciendas, or plantations. However, most mestizos and Native Americans owned little land. African Americans were slaves.

A Troubled Past

Latin America has changed a great deal since the nations of the region became independent. On the other hand, many problems with their roots in the colonial past still remain today.

Colonial Legacy After Spain's Latin American colonies became independent, the criollos gained political power. However, most mestizos and Native Americans remained poor. Many continued to work on the haciendas as they had before. Even after slavery was ended, former slaves had little opportunity for a better life.

Target Reading Skill L2

Reread or Read Ahead Point out the Target Reading Skill. Tell students to reread or read ahead to help them understand unfamiliar words or clarify ideas.

Model rereading using the second paragraph on page 67. Tell students that rereading can help clarify what reformers in South American countries wanted to do. Then tell students that reading ahead to the next paragraph will help them understand what happened as reformers made their demands to the governments of South American countries.

Give students *Reread or Read Ahead*. Have them complete the activity in their groups.

All in One **Latin America Teaching Resources,** *Reread or Read Ahead,* p. 159

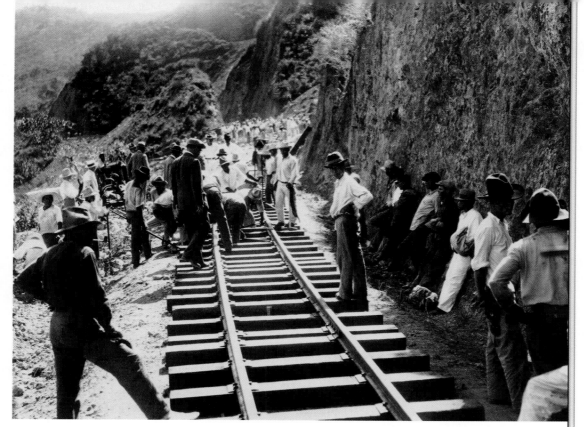

Many of the new Latin American countries were ruled by caudillos. These "strongmen" ignored the democratic constitutions that had been established by their new nations. They became **dictators**, or rulers with complete power. There were revolts, and some dictators were overthrown. Often they were replaced by other caudillos. Life changed little for the ordinary people.

Before independence, Latin American colonies exported farm products, minerals, and other resources to Spain and Portugal. To **export** is to send products from one country to be sold in another. The colonies bought manufactured products from the European countries that ruled them. After independence, the new nations of Latin America were free to trade with other countries. The United States became an important trading partner for Latin America. But Latin American countries still relied on exporting farm products and minerals. And they still imported manufactured goods. To **import** is to bring products into one country from another.

Working on the Railroad
This railroad linking San Salvador to Guatemala was built in the 1920s by an American company, using local laborers. **Identify Causes** *Why do you think an American company was interested in building a railroad there?*

Instruct

A Troubled Past L2

Guided Instruction

- **Vocabulary Builder** Clarify the meaning of the high-use words **legacy** and **intervene** before reading.

- Have students read A Troubled Past using the Structured Silent Reading technique (TE, p. T34). As students read, circulate and make sure individuals can answer the Reading Check question.

- Ask students **What problems arose under the rule of the Latin American caudillos, and what happened to the ordinary people as a result?** *(They ignored the democratic constitutions established by their new nations and became dictators; as a result, independence changed little for ordinary people.)*

- Ask students **How did foreign involvement affect the newly independent countries of Latin America?** *(Latin American countries were free to trade with other countries; foreign governments also became involved in Latin American policies.)*

Independent Practice

Ask students to create the Taking Notes outline on a blank piece of paper. Then have them fill in the main ideas and details from the information they have just learned. Briefly model how to identify which details to record.

Monitor Progress

As students fill in the outline, circulate and make sure individuals are choosing the correct details. Provide assistance as needed.

Vocabulary Builder

Use the information below to teach students this section's high-use words.

High-Use Word	Definition and Sample Sentence
legacy, p. 64	*n.* anything handed down from an ancestor The ring was a **legacy** from her grandmother.
intervene, p. 66	*v.* to come or be in between His mother **intervened** and stopped the fight between him and his brother.
censor, p. 67	*v.* to remove or suppress material The government **censored** some of the official papers.

Answers

Identify Causes to transport goods between San Salvador and Guatemala

Reread or Read Ahead As a follow up, ask students to answer the Target Reading Skill question in the Student Edition. (*Answers will vary, but students should either indicate that rereading or reading ahead helped them clarify what they read.*)

The Struggle Continues L2

Guided Instruction

■ **Vocabulary Builder** Clarify the high-use word **censor** before reading.

■ Together with students, read about the challenges faced by Latin American countries as they strive to advance their economies in The Struggle Continues.

■ Help students to recognize the cycle that is perpetuated by borrowing and owing money. Ask students **How does the inability to pay back foreign debt make it difficult for countries to improve their economies?** (*To pay their debts countries must cut back on some services; foreign ownership of business increases, sending revenue outside of the country.*)

■ Ask students to brainstorm ways in which the people in Latin American countries might address these challenges in the future. Conduct a Give One, Get One participation strategy (TE, p. T37) to generate a list of possibilities. (*Answers will vary but might include borrowing less money from other countries, increasing trade between countries, trying to export more goods and import fewer manufactured goods, and creating more jobs.*)

Answers

✓**Reading Check** President Roosevelt thought that the United States should keep law and order in Latin America and force Latin American nations to pay their foreign debt.

Graph Skills Identify highest – Brazil, lowest – Paraguay; **Identify Cause and Effect** The industrialized countries might have borrowed large sums of money to help them industrialize.

⊘ **Reread or Read Ahead**
Reread or read ahead to see why the United States became involved in Latin America. Which technique helped you clarify what you reread?

Foreign Involvement Foreign companies began to buy large farms, mines, and other land in Latin America. They built seaports and railroads that made it easier to export their products. These companies were interested in taking resources out of Latin America. The United States and other foreign nations supported Latin American governments that helped these companies.

In 1903, the United States wanted to build a canal across the Isthmus of Panama, in the nation of Colombia. A canal would benefit American trade and the American navy. When Colombia refused permission to build a canal, President Theodore Roosevelt backed a revolt by the people of Panama against Colombia. Once Panama was independent, it allowed the United States to build the Panama Canal.

As owner of the Panama Canal, the United States had even more interest in Latin America. In 1904, President Roosevelt claimed that the United States had a right to keep law and order there. He also said the United States could force Latin American nations to pay their **foreign debt,** or money they owed to other countries. For the next 20 years, the United States used Roosevelt's policy to intervene in Latin America.

✓**Reading Check** What role did President Roosevelt think the United States should have in Latin America?

▓ Graph Skills

Many Latin American nations have gone into debt to foreign countries and to world organizations. **Identify** Which country in the graph has the highest foreign debt? Which has the lowest? **Identify Cause and Effect** Brazil, Mexico, and Argentina are among the most industrialized Latin American countries. Why might there be a connection between industrializing and debt?

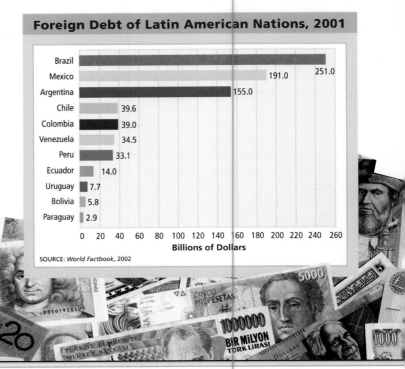

Foreign Debt of Latin American Nations, 2001

Country	Billions of Dollars
Brazil	251.0
Mexico	191.0
Argentina	155.0
Chile	39.6
Colombia	39.0
Venezuela	34.5
Peru	33.1
Ecuador	14.0
Uruguay	7.7
Bolivia	5.8
Paraguay	2.9

SOURCE: *World Factbook*, 2002

66 Latin America

Skills Mini Lesson

Analyzing Graphic Data

1. Tell students that charts and graphs can help them see information quickly, and can also help them draw conclusions.

2. Refer students to the bar graph *Foreign Debt of Latin American Nations, 2001* on this page. Have them practice the skill by identifying the title of the graph, the labels, and any similarities or differences they notice in the information being pre-sented in the graph. Then have them draw a conclusion about the countries and their foreign debts shown on the graph. (*Larger countries such as Brazil, Mexico, and Argentina have larger amounts of foreign debt than smaller countries.*)

3. Have students apply the skill by identifying the parts of the graph on page 77 entitled *The World's Five Largest Cities, 2000* and drawing conclusions from the information illustrated on the graph.

The Struggle Continues

In the mid-1900s, there were still big gaps between the few who were rich and the many who were poor. Most of Latin America's land was owned by a small percentage of the people. Many businesses were owned by foreign companies.

The Beginnings of Reform At the same time, some groups wanted to improve conditions for the poor. Reformers of the 1930s and 1940s wanted to divide the land more equally and to diversify the economies of their countries. Some Latin American countries did begin to make reforms.

As demands for reform continued in the 1960s and 1970s, military regimes seized power in many Latin American countries. A regime is a particular administration or government. These military regimes ruled harshly. They censored the press, outlawed political parties, and imprisoned—or even killed—those who opposed them.

By the 1980s, however, some of these harsh regimes were replaced by elected governments. But problems still remained. Some elected leaders abused their power. President Alberto Fujimori of Peru, for example, dissolved Peru's legislature and later dismissed the high court justices when they disagreed with him. And many Latin American nations still had huge economic problems. One of these problems was foreign debt.

Foreign Debt Latin American countries had borrowed money to improve their economies. In the 1980s, oil prices went up at the same time that prices of many Latin American products fell. Latin American countries had to spend more money, but they were making less and less. To make up the difference, they borrowed money from wealthy countries such as the United States. Then they had to borrow more money to pay off their debts.

Although Mexico was a major oil producer, it too suffered an economic crisis. In the 1970s, Mexico began to rely more and more on oil exports to fuel its economy. But in the 1980s, more oil was being produced than the world needed. In 1982, Mexico found that it could not repay its debt.

Protests in Buenos Aires
In Argentina, foreign debt contributed to an economic crisis. In this 2003 protest, unemployed Argentines lift shovels as they march to demand jobs. **Apply Information** *Use the text to help explain how foreign debt might lead to unemployment.*

Chapter 2 Section 5 **67**

Independent Practice

Have students complete their outlines by adding main ideas and details. Tell them to continue their outlines with "II. The struggle continues," and items that fall underneath that heading.

Monitor Progress

- Show *Section Reading Support Transparency LA 35* and ask students to check their graphic organizers individually. Go over key concepts and clarify key vocabulary as needed.

   📖 **Latin America Transparencies,** *Section Reading Support Transparency LA 35*

- Tell students to fill in the last column of the *Reading Readiness Guide*. Probe for what they learned that confirms or invalidates each statement.

   All in One **Latin America Teaching Resources,** *Reading Readiness Guide,* p. 156

Assess and Reteach

Assess Progress `L2`
Have students complete the Section Assessment. Administer the *Section Quiz*.

   All in One **Latin America Teaching Resources,** *Section Quiz,* p. 158

Reteach `L1`
If students need more instruction, have them read this section in the Reading and Vocabulary Study Guide.

   📖 Chapter 2, Section 5, **Latin America Reading and Vocabulary Study Guide,** pp. 28–30

Extend `L3`
Have students learn more about the history of Latin America by completing the *Enrichment* worksheet in the Latin America Teaching Resources.

   All in One **Latin America Teaching Resources,** *Enrichment,* p. 163

Answers

Apply Information Foreign debt may lead the government to cut jobs.

Answers

When Mexico could not pay its debt, two international organizations, the World Bank and the International Monetary Fund, lent Mexico money under strict conditions.

Section 5 Assessment

Key Terms
Students' sentences should reflect knowledge of each Key Term.

↻ Target Reading Skill
Students should identify any unfamiliar words or unclear ideas that they clarified by rereading or reading ahead.

Comprehension and Critical Thinking
1. (a) Caudillos often ignored the democratic constitutions adopted by their countries and ruled as dictators. **(b)** Latin American governments that allowed foreign companies to remove resources from Latin America were supported by the United States and other foreign countries. The United States helped Panama become independent from Colombia in order to gain permission to build the Panama Canal. **(c)** After gaining independence, the new Latin American nations were free to trade with other countries. However, they still relied on exporting farm products and minerals, and importing manufactured goods.

2. (a) Mexico borrowed money to improve its economy. When Mexico could not pay its foreign debt, it borrowed more money from the World Bank and the International Monetary Fund. As a result, the debt grew larger. **(b)** Powerful groups probably resist reform because they do not want to risk losing any of their power, wealth, or land.

Writing Activity
Use the *Rubric for Assessing a Writing Assignment* to evaluate students' paragraphs.

All in One Latin America Teaching Resources, *Rubric for Assessing a Writing Assignment,* p. 174.

Plaza in Montevideo, Uruguay

Two international organizations stepped in. The World Bank and the International Monetary Fund lent Mexico money—but there were strict conditions. Mexico found that it had to cut back on programs that helped the poor. Other Latin American countries also borrowed under these strict conditions. They had to allow more foreign ownership of businesses and farms. In Argentina, debt, unemployment, and other economic problems caused riots in the streets. In 2000, the president of Argentina was forced to resign.

Looking Toward the Future Recently, Latin American countries have tried to improve their economies by cooperating with one another in trade organizations. In 1994, another trade treaty was signed, the North American Free Trade Agreement (NAFTA). It made trade easier among Mexico, the United States, and Canada.

Efforts to improve the economies and the welfare of people in Latin America continue. You will read more about these efforts in the Focus on Countries chapters later in this book.

✓ **Reading Check** What happened when Mexico could not pay its debt?

Section 5 Assessment

Key Terms
Review the key terms at the beginning of this section. Use each term in a sentence that explains its meaning.

↻ Target Reading Skill
What words or ideas in this section were you able to clarify by rereading or reading ahead?

Comprehension and Critical Thinking
1. (a) Describe How did caudillos rule their countries?
(b) Explain Describe foreign involvement in Latin America.
(c) Compare and Contrast How did Latin America's economy change after independence? How did it remain the same?
2. (a) Recall How did Mexico end up with a large foreign debt?
(b) Draw Conclusions The powerful groups that own the most land also run the governments of some Latin American countries. Why do you think these groups resist reform?

Writing Activity
What do you think is the most important challenge facing Latin America today? Write a paragraph explaining your choice.

Go Online PHSchool.com
For: An activity on Venezuela
Visit: PHSchool.com
Web Code: lfd-1205

Go Online PHSchool.com Typing in the Web code when prompted will bring students directly to detailed instructions for this activity.

◆ Chapter Summary

Section 1: Early Civilizations of Middle America

- The Mayas built great cities, created an advanced number system and calendar, and then mysteriously abandoned their cities.
- The Aztecs of central Mexico ruled a rich empire from their capital at Tenochtitlán, which was a center of trade and learning.

Mexico

Section 2: The Incas

- The Incas built a huge empire based in what is now Peru.
- The Incas built excellent roads and aqueducts, and used quipus rather than a written language to manage their empire.
- The descendants of the Incas still live in the Andes Mountains.

Section 3: European Conquest

- Europeans came to the Americas for riches and for land.
- The conquistadors conquered the Aztecs and Incas in 15 years.
- Spain ruled a large empire in the Americas, bringing disease and enslavement to the Native Americans and importing enslaved Africans.

Section 4: Independence

- Revolutions in North America, France, and Haiti helped inspire Latin Americans to seek independence.
- Mexico's revolution began with Hidalgo's "Cry of Dolores" and was completed by Iturbide.
- Bolívar and San Martín were the liberators of South America.

Section 5: From Past to Present

- Many problems in Latin America are the result of the region's colonial past, foreign involvement, and undemocratic governments.
- Reform movements are working to help the poor, elected governments have replaced military ones, and nations are struggling with their foreign debt.

◆ Key Terms

Define each of the terms below.

1. hieroglyphics
2. maize
3. census
4. regime
5. conquistador
6. mestizo
7. hacienda
8. revolution
9. criollo
10. caudillo
11. import
12. foreign debt

┌ **Vocabulary Builder** ─

Revisit this chapter's high-use words:

ritual	profit	forefathers
garment	supernatural	legacy
conquest	fearless	intervene
loyalty	superior	censor
descendant	authorities	

Ask students to review the definitions they recorded on their *Word Knowledge* worksheets.

All in One **Latin America Teaching Resources,** *Word Knowledge,* p. 162

Consider allowing students to earn extra credit if they use the words in their answers to the questions in the Chapter Review and Assessment. The words must be used correctly and in a natural context to earn extra points.

Chapter 2
Review and Assessment

Review Chapter Content

- Review and revisit the major themes of this chapter by asking students to classify what Guiding Question each bulleted statement in the Chapter Summary answers. Have students work together in groups to classify the sentences. Refer to page 1 in the Student Edition for the text of the Guiding Questions.

- Assign *Vocabulary Development* for students to review Key Terms.

  All in One **Latin America Teaching Resources,** *Vocabulary Development,* p. 173

Answers

Key Terms

1–12. Make sure students' definitions accurately reflect the definition of each Key Term.

Comprehension and Critical Thinking

13. (a) Mayans built great cities, designed an accurate calendar and used a system of writing. **(b)** Similar: Both groups conquered other groups to build large empires, used irrigation to water their crops, used nobles to help the emperors govern, and were conquered by the Spanish. Different: Aztecs constructed artificial floating gardens, while Incas farmed the surrounding land; Incas built roads, bridges, tunnels and aqueducts; Aztecs had a written language, the Incas did not; descendants of the Incas live in the Andes today. **(c)** having strong leaders and large and powerful armies to conquer other groups and control vast lands

14. (a) Christopher Columbus, Hernán Cortés, and Francisco Pizarro **(b)** They hoped to find gold and other treasures. **(c)** They disliked the Aztecs because they demanded heavy tribute from them.

15. (a) The territory was divided into provinces. Viceroys appointed by the Spanish King ruled the provinces. Other settlers who had been born in Spain helped the viceroys rule. A council in Spain supervised the colonial officials to make sure they did not become too powerful. **(b)** rights given to the Spanish settlers to demand taxes or labor from Native Americans; Native Americans were forced to work on haciendas and later in mines. **(c)** The Native American population dropped from 25 million to 3 million and the Spanish needed more workers. European demand for more products from the Americas meant that more enslaved workers were needed.

16. (a) Miguel Hidalgo **(b)** People of each country wanted to be free to govern themselves. Enslaved or poor workers who were oppressed supported the revolutions. **(c)** After independence criollos gained political power while life for Native Americans remained the same as before.

17. (a) Caudillos were "strongmen" who often ignored the democratic constitutions established by their new nations and instead became dictators. **(b)** Railroads and seaports made it easier for foreign companies to export their products. **(c)** When it borrows money to improve its economy, prices for its products fall, and it has to borrow more money to pay off existing debts.

◆ Comprehension and Critical Thinking

13. (a) Recall Describe Mayan civilization.
(b) Compare How were the Aztec and Incan civilizations similar and different?
(c) Generalize What lessons in empire-building can be learned from the Aztecs and the Incas?

14. (a) Name Which Europeans were the first to explore Central and South America?
(b) Identify Causes Why did the Spanish want to explore the Americas?
(c) Conclude Why did many Native Americans help Hernán Cortés defeat the Aztecs?

15. (a) Recall How did Spain organize its empire?
(b) Explain What were encomiendas and what effect did they have on Native Americans?
(c) Identify Causes Why did the Spanish start to import enslaved Africans to the Americas? Why did this practice increase over time?

16. (a) Identify Who led the Mexican Revolution?
(b) Compare Compare the ways Mexico, Haiti, and Peru gained their independence.
(c) Draw Conclusions How did independence affect criollos? Native Americans?

17. (a) Recall Describe how caudillos ruled their countries.
(b) Identify Causes Why did foreign nations build seaports and railroads in Latin America?
(c) Explain What is one way a nation can develop foreign debt?

◆ Writing Activity: Math

Look again at the photo of the quipu on page 47. Suppose you have five strings of different colors to record the number of people in your class: girls, boys, and the teacher. How would you show this information? Use string or make a drawing with colored pencils. Now write directions for using the mathematical system you just invented. Have another student read and follow your directions. Evaluate how well your partner used your mathematical system.

◆ Skills Practice

Making a Timeline In the Skills for Life activity in this chapter, you learned to create a timeline. Review the steps you followed to learn the skill.

Use an encyclopedia or other reliable source to research one of the people you read about in this chapter. Then make a timeline of the important events in that person's life.

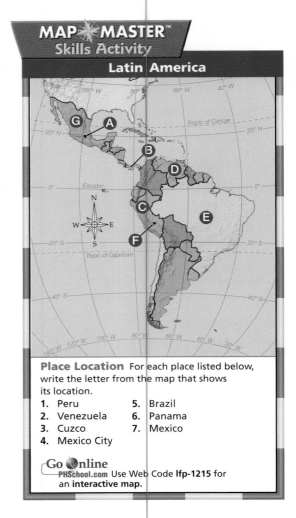

MAP MASTER™ Skills Activity

Latin America

Place Location For each place listed below, write the letter from the map that shows its location.
1. Peru
2. Venezuela
3. Cuzco
4. Mexico City
5. Brazil
6. Panama
7. Mexico

Go Online
PHSchool.com Use Web Code lfp-1215 for an interactive map.

Skills Practice
Students' timelines should accurately reflect the dates and events of the life of the person they chose.

Writing Activity: Math
Students' drawings and directions for their mathematical system will vary, but should accurately record the number of people in the class.

Standardized Test Prep

Test-Taking Tips

Some questions on standardized tests ask you to analyze a point of view. Read the paragraph below. Then follow the tips to answer the sample question.

Pick the letter that best answers the question.
In 1519, the Spanish conquistador Hernán Cortés marched toward the great Aztec capital, Tenochtitlán, with 500 soldiers. Somebody watching the troops whispered: *This is a happy day! These white gods could mean the end to Moctezuma and his bloodthirsty followers. Let us help them on their way.*

Which onlooker might have made those comments?
- **A** a spy of Moctezuma
- **B** a soldier of Francisco Pizarro
- **C** a Native American neighbor of the Aztecs
- **D** a wife of Moctezuma

Think It Through Moctezuma's own spies would not want an end to him or call themselves bloodthirsty. The same would be true for his wife. Francisco Pizarro was a conqueror who didn't arrive in South America until years after Cortés. A neighbor of the Aztecs might have been happy to see Cortés, because Moctezuma was a powerful enemy who conquered many of his neighbors. So the best answer is C.

TIP Make sure you understand the question. Restate it in your own words: *The person who said those words was probably _____.*

TIP Use what you know about history along with common sense to choose the BEST answer.

Practice Questions

Choose the letter of the best answer.

1. Unlike the Incas and Aztecs, the Mayas did NOT have
   - **A** an emperor.
   - **B** a calendar.
   - **C** cities.
   - **D** a form of writing.

2. Brazil's language and culture—Portuguese—were established by
   - **A** the voyage of Columbus.
   - **B** Pizarro's conquest.
   - **C** the Treaty of Tordesillas.
   - **D** the encomienda system.

3. What is one way that Latin American countries have been trying to improve their economies?
   - **A** by cooperating with one another
   - **B** by increasing their foreign debt
   - **C** by giving more land to large companies
   - **D** by depending on one resource

Read the following passage and answer the question that follows.

The following is taken from a speech made by someone living in Latin America in the early 1800s: "I love my country, but I deserve to govern myself. I learned plenty about governing when I attended school in Europe!"

4. Who most likely made this speech?
   - **A** the king of Spain
   - **B** a criollo
   - **C** a poor mestizo
   - **D** a Native American

Go Online PHSchool.com
Use Web Code lfa-1201 for a **Chapter 2 self-test.**

---

1. C
2. D
3. F
4. A
5. E
6. B
7. G

Go Online PHSchool.com Students may practice their map skills using the interactive online version of this map.

Standardized Test Prep

Answers

1. A
2. C
3. A
4. B

Go Online PHSchool.com Students may use the Chapter 2 self-test on PHSchool.com to prepare for the Chapter Test

---

Assessment Resources

Use *Chapter Tests A and B* to assess students' mastery of chapter content.

Tests are also available on the *ExamView® Test Bank CD-ROM.*

All in One **Latin America Teaching Resources,** *Chapter Tests A and B,* pp. 177-182

⊙ *ExamView Test Bank CD-ROM*

Overview

Section 1 — Cultures of Mexico and Central America
1. Discover the cultural heritage of the people of Middle America.
2. Find out why many people in this region have been moving away from the countryside.

Section 2 — The Cultures of the Caribbean
1. Find out what ethnic groups make up the people of the Caribbean.
2. Learn how the different cultures of the region blended to create Caribbean food, music, and celebrations.

Section 3 — The Cultures of South America
1. Find out what ethnic groups are represented in the four cultural regions of South America.
2. Learn what life is like in the countryside and in the cities of South America.

DISCOVERY CHANNEL SCHOOL Video

Caribbean Music: It's All in the Mix
Length: 6 minutes, 23 seconds
Use with Section 2
This segment explores three distinct types of Caribbean music: Bomba from Puerto Rico, Merengue from the Dominican Republic, and Mambo from Cuba. Students will get a sense of each type of music's cultural and historical heritage while watching instrumental and dance performances.

Technology Resources

Go Online PHSchool.com

Students use embedded Web codes to access Internet activities, chapter self-tests, and additional map practice. They may also access Dorling Kindersley's Online Desk Reference to learn more about each country they study.

Interactive Textbook

Use the Interactive Textbook to make content and concepts come alive through animations, videos, and activities that accompany the complete basal text—online and on CD-ROM.

PRENTICE HALL
TeacherEXPRESS
Plan • Teach • Assess

Use this complete suite of powerful teaching tools to make planning lessons and administering tests quicker and easier.

Reading and Assessment

Reading and Vocabulary Instruction

🔊 Model the Target Reading Skill

Cause and Effect Explain to students that understanding cause and effect will help them to better understand the events that they read about. By identifying causes and effects, understanding that some effects are the results of multiple causes, and analyzing effects in context, students become more adept at seeing patterns both within and beyond the reading.

Model this skill by thinking aloud about these statements concerning the cultures of the Caribbean from page 83 of the Student Edition:

> *Many people came to the Caribbean as colonists, slaves, or immigrants.*
>
> *The area has great ethnic variety.*

One of these sentences states a cause, and the other one states an effect. How will I decide which is which? Let me set up the statements in two ways, using a connection word like "because," to see which makes more sense. 1) "Because many people came to the Caribbean as colonists, slaves, or immigrants, the Caribbean now has great ethnic variety." 2) "Because the Caribbean has great ethnic variety, many people came to the Caribbean as colonists, slaves, or immigrants."

My first statement makes more sense. People coming to the Caribbean as colonists, slaves, and immigrants happened first, and it caused the variety of ethnicities, which is the effect.

Use the following worksheets from All-in-One Latin America Teaching Resources (pp. 199, 200, and 201) to support this chapter's Target Reading Skill.

Vocabulary Builder
High-Use Academic Words

Use these steps to teach this chapter's high-use words:

1. Have students rate how well they know each word on their Word Knowledge worksheets (All-in-One Latin America Teaching Resources, p. 202.)

2. Pronounce each word and ask students to repeat it.

3. Give students a brief definition or sample sentence (provided on TE pp. 75, 83, and 88.)

4. Work with students as they fill in the "Definition or Example" column of their Word Knowledge worksheets.

Assessment

Formal Assessment

Test students' understanding of core knowledge and skills.

> **Chapter Tests A and B,** All-in-One Latin America Teaching Resources, pp. 218–223

Customize the Chapter Tests to suit your needs.

> *ExamView Test Bank CD-ROM*

Skills Assessment

Assess geographic literacy.

> **MapMaster Skills,** Student Edition pp. 73, 94

Assess reading and comprehension.

> **Target Reading Skills,** Student Edition, pp. 77, 83, 88, and in Section Assessments

> **Chapter 3 Assessment,** Reading and Vocabulary Study Guide, p. 41

Performance Assessment

Assess students' performance on this chapter's Writing Activities using the following rubrics from All-in-One Latin America Teaching Resources.

> **Rubric for Assessing a Journal Entry,** p. 215
>
> **Rubric for Assessing a Writing Assignment,** p. 216
>
> **Rubric for Assessing a Newspaper Article,** p. 217

Assess students' work through performance tasks.

> **Small Group Activity: Share the Music,** All-in-One Latin America Teaching Resources, pp. 205–208

Online Assessment

Have students check their own understanding.
> **Chapter Self-Test**

Test Preparation

> **Latin America Benchmark Test 1,** AYP Monitoring Assessments, pp. 97–100

Section 1 Cultures of Mexico and Central America

 2 periods, 1 block (includes Skills for Life)

Social Studies Objectives

1. Discover the cultural heritage of the people of Middle America.

2. Find out why many people in this region have been moving away from the countryside.

Reading/Language Arts Objective

Identify causes and effects to understand the relationships among situations and events.

Prepare to Read

Build Background Knowledge
Brainstorm things that represent culture.

Set a Purpose for Reading
Have students evaluate statements on the *Reading Readiness Guide*.

Preview Key Terms
Teach the section's Key Terms.

Target Reading Skill
Introduce the section's Target Reading Skill of **identifying causes and effects**.

Instructional Resources

All in One Latin America Teaching Resources
- **L2** Reading Readiness Guide, p.188
- **L2** Identify Causes and Effects, p. 199

Differentiated Instruction

Spanish Reading and Vocabulary Study Guide
- **L2** Chapter 3, Section 1, pp. 24–25 ELL

Instruct

Cultural Heritage
Discuss the different elements that make up Middle American culture.

Leaving the Countryside
Discuss why people are leaving rural areas.

Target Reading Skill
Review **identifying causes and effects**.

Instructional Resources

All in One Latin America Teaching Resources
- **L2** Guided Reading and Review, p. 189
- **L2** Reading Readiness Guide, p. 188

Latin America Transparencies
- **L2** Section Reading Support Transparency LA 36

Differentiated Instruction

All in One Latin America Teaching Resources
- **L3** We Live in Mexico (Lugo), pp. 209–210 AR, GT
- **L3** A Huge Black Umbrella, pp. 211–213 AR, GT
- **L2** Skills for Life, p. 204 GT, AR, LPR, SN

Teacher's Edition
- **L1** For Less Proficient Readers, TE p. 77
- **L3** For Advanced Readers, TE p. 77

Spanish Support
- **L2** Guided Reading and Review (Spanish), p. 24 ELL

Assess and Reteach

Assess Progress
Evaluate student comprehension with the section assessment and section quiz.

Reteach
Assign the Reading and Vocabulary Study Guide to help struggling students.

Extend
Extend the lesson by assigning an activity from *Environmental and Global Issues*.

Instructional Resources

All in One Latin America Teaching Resources
- **L2** Section Quiz, p. 190
  Rubric for Assessing a Journal Entry, p. 215

Reading and Vocabulary Study Guide
- **L1** Chapter 3, Section 1, pp. 32–34

PHSchool.com
- **L3** For: Environmental and Global Issues, *Nickel-and-Diming*
  Web code: lfd-1304

Differentiated Instruction

Spanish Support
- **L2** Section Quiz (Spanish), p. 25 ELL

Teacher's Edition
- **L1** For Special Needs Students, p. 81
- **L1** For Less Proficient Readers, p. 81

Social Studies Skills Tutor CD-ROM
- **L1** Distinguishing Fact from Opinion SN, LPR, ELL

Key

L1 Basic to Average

L2 For All Students

L3 Average to Advanced

LPR Less Proficient Readers
AR Advanced Readers
SN Special Needs Students

GT Gifted and Talented
ELL English Language Learners

Section 2 The Cultures of the Caribbean

 1 periods, .5 block

Social Studies Objectives

1. Find out what ethnic groups make up the people of the Caribbean.
2. Learn how the different cultures of the region blended to create Caribbean food, music, and celebrations.

Reading/Language Arts Objective

Recognize multiple causes to understand the development of complex events.

Prepare to Read	Instructional Resources	Differentiated Instruction
Build Background Knowledge Fill in a word web with information about the Caribbean. **Set a Purpose for Reading** Have students evaluate statements on the *Reading Readiness Guide.* **Preview Key Terms** Teach the section's Key Terms. **Target Reading Skill** Introduce the section's Target Reading Skill of **recognizing multiple causes.**	**All in One Latin America Teaching Resources** **L2** Reading Readiness Guide, p. 192 **L2** Recognize Multiple Causes, p. 200	**Spanish Reading and Vocabulary Study Guide** **L2** Chapter 3, Section 2, pp. 26–27 ELL

Instruct	Instructional Resources	Differentiated Instruction
The People of the Caribbean Discuss the major ethnic groups of the Caribbean. **Target Reading Skill** Review **recognizing multiple causes.** **A Blend of Cultures** Identify how cultures blended in the Caribbean.	**All in One Latin America Teaching Resources** **L2** Guided Reading and Review, p. 193 **L2** Reading Readiness Guide, p. 192 **Latin America Transparencies** **L2** Section Reading Support Transparency LA 37	**Spanish Support** **L2** Guided Reading and Review (Spanish), p. 26 ELL

Assess and Reteach	Instructional Resources	Differentiated Instruction
Assess Progress Evaluate student comprehension with the section assessment and section quiz. **Reteach** Assign the Reading and Vocabulary Study Guide to help struggling students. **Extend** Extend the lesson by having students watch a Discovery Channel World Studies Video.	**All in One Latin America Teaching Resources** **L2** Section Quiz, p. 194 Rubric for Assessing a Writing Assignment, p. 216 **Reading and Vocabulary Study Guide** **L1** Chapter 3, Section 2, pp. 35–37 **World Studies Video Program** **L3** Caribbean Music: It's All in the Mix	**Spanish Support** **L2** Section Quiz (Spanish), p. 27 ELL

Key

L1 Basic to Average
L2 For All Students
L3 Average to Advanced

LPR Less Proficient Readers
AR Advanced Readers
SN Special Needs Students

GT Gifted and Talented
ELL English Language Learners

Section 3 The Cultures of South America

2.5 periods, 1.25 blocks (includes Chapter Review and Assessment)

Social Studies Objectives

1. Find out what ethnic groups are represented in the four cultural regions of South America.
2. Learn what life is like in the countryside and in the cities of South America.

Reading/Language Arts Objective

Understand how one cause can bring about multiple effects.

Prepare to Read	Instructional Resources	Differentiated Instruction
Build Background Knowledge Have students predict the cultural elements shared by South America and other regions of Latin America. **Set a Purpose for Reading** Have students evaluate statements on the *Reading Readiness Guide*. **Preview Key Terms** Teach the section's Key Terms. **Target Reading Skill** Introduce the section's Target Reading Skill of **understanding effects**.	**All in One Latin America Teaching Resources** L2 Reading Readiness Guide, p. 196 L2 Understand Effects, p. 201	**Spanish Reading and Vocabulary Study Guide** L2 Chapter 3, Section 3, pp. 28–29 ELL

Instruct	Instructional Resources	Differentiated Instruction
The People of South America Ask students about the four cultural regions of South America. **Target Reading Skill** Review **understanding effects**. **Country and City Life** Discuss country and city life in South America.	**All in One Latin America Teaching Resources** L2 Guided Reading and Review, p. 197 L2 Reading Readiness Guide, p. 196 **Latin America Transparencies** L2 Section Reading Support Transparency LA 38	**Teacher's Edition** L3 For Gifted and Talented Students, TE p. 90 L1 For Less Proficient Readers, p. 90 L1 For Special Needs Students, TE p. 91 L2 For English Language Learners, p. 91 L1 **Passport to the World CD-ROM** LPR, SN, ELL **Student Edition on Audio CD** L1 Chapter 3, Section 1, SN, LPR, ELL **Spanish Support** L2 Guided Reading and Review (Spanish), p. 28 ELL

Assess and Reteach	Instructional Resources	Differentiated Instruction
Assess Progress Evaluate student comprehension with the section assessment and section quiz. **Reteach** Assign the Reading and Vocabulary Study Guide to help struggling students. **Extend** Extend the lesson by assigning an activity about art in Latin America.	**All in One Latin America Teaching Resources** L2 Section Quiz, p. 198 Rubric for Assessing a Newspaper Article, p. 217 L2 Vocabulary Development, p. 214 L2 Word Knowledge, p. 202 L2 Chapter Tests A and B, pp. 218–223 **Reading and Vocabulary Study Guide** L1 Chapter 3, Section 3, pp. 38–40	**Spanish Support** L2 Section Quiz (Spanish), p. 9 ELL L2 Chapter Summary (Spanish), p. 30 ELL L2 Vocabulary Development (Spanish), p. 31 ELL

Key

L1 Basic to Average   L3 Average to Advanced

L2 For All Students

LPR Less Proficient Readers
AR Advanced Readers
SN Special Needs Students

GT Gifted and Talented
ELL English Language Learners

Reading Background

Mapping Word Definitions

Mapping definitions can extend students' understanding of vocabulary and high-use words. Have students create word maps by answering each of these questions about each word: What is it? What is it like or not like? What are some examples?

Model mapping the key term *cash crop* from section 3 of this chapter:

What is it? *(a crop grown for sale or export rather than for the farmer's own use)* What is it like? *(It is the opposite of subsistence farming, in which farmers grow only enough to use themselves.)* What are some examples? *(coffee, sugar, cocoa, and bananas)*

Another way to map words is to develop a graphic organizer that shows the word, its definition, a synonym, and a sentence using the word. Put this example of an organizer on the board:

Term	*cash crop*
Definition	*crop grown for sale or export rather than for the farmer's own use*
Synonym	*profitable harvest*
Sentence	*Farmers in South America grow bananas as a cash crop to export to other countries.*

Summarizing

Help students to engage with the text by asking them to summarize as they read. Model how to summarize by using the B-head section "Leaving the Countryside" on page 77 of this chapter. Ask students to read silently and actively take notes. At the same time, write notes about the section on the board, such as "rapid population growth"; "seeking work in factories"; and "growing cities have trouble providing services." Have students add to the notes on the board. Then ask students to choose which sentence provides a better summary of the passage based on the notes written on the board:

1. Because of rapid population growth in Mexico and Central America, many people must leave rural areas to find jobs in cities. The cities are growing so fast that there are often not enough services for all of the people.

2. The population of Mexico and Central America will double in 30 years. Some people in Mexico move to the border with the United States to work in factories.

Students should recognize that option 1 provides a more effective summary, because it applies more of the information in the passage.

World Studies Background

The Children of Mexico

As the population of Mexico rapidly increases, children under 18 become a greater percentage of the population. In fact, about 40 percent of Mexico's total population is now under 18 years of age.

Because youth makes up such a large part of the population, in 2000 and 2003 children were invited by UNICEF to participate in a survey about how to improve their country. Their main concerns were violence and poverty.

Sharing Caribbean Culture

The poetry and plays of Nobel Prize winner Derek Walcott have helped teach the world about the Caribbean. His work focuses on themes of his Caribbean heritage—slavery (his ancestors were slaves), violence, and finding identity in a country that was once a colony. Born in St. Lucia, Walcott writes in English but sometimes includes other languages, such as Creole.

Cash Crops in South America

In much of South America, the processing and exporting of cash crops creates jobs for city dwellers. For this reason, many crops are grown on large farms closer to cities where they can be immediately processed. Agriculture made up only 12 percent of the gross domestic product in the 1990s, but workers involved in the agriculture industry made up more than 20 percent of the total workforce.

Infoplease® provides a wealth of useful information for the classroom. You can use this resource to strengthen your background on the subjects covered in this chapter. Have students visit this advertising-free site as a starting point for projects requiring research.

Use Web Code **lfd-1300** for **Infoplease®**

Guiding Questions

Remind students about the Guiding Questions introduced at the beginning of the book.

Section 1 relates to **Guiding Question** ➌ **What factors have affected cultures in Latin America?** *(The cultures of Mexico and Central America have been affected by the regions' ethnic diversity, religion, and the migration of much of the population from the countryside to towns and cities.)*

Section 2 relates to **Guiding Question** ➋ **How has Latin America been shaped by its history?** *(The Caribbean is ethnically and culturally diverse because of the many groups that settled there as colonists, immigrants, or slaves.)*

Section 3 relates to **Guiding Question** ➌ **What factors have affected culture in Latin America?** *(The cultures of South America have been affected by the ethnic variety, geography, and local history of the different cultural regions.)*

⟳ Target Reading Skill

In this chapter, students will learn and apply the reading skill of cause and effect. Use the following worksheets to help students practice this skill:

All in One **Latin America Teaching Resources,** *Identify Causes and Effects,* p. 199; *Recognize Multiple Causes,* p. 200; *Understand Effects,* p. 201

Cultures of Latin America

Chapter Preview

This chapter will introduce you to the cultures of the three regions of Latin America.

Section 1
The Cultures of Mexico and Central America

Section 2
The Cultures of the Caribbean

Section 3
The Cultures of South America

⟳ Target Reading Skill

Cause and Effect In this chapter you will focus on recognizing cause and effect in the text you are reading. Recognizing cause and effect will help you understand relationships among situations or events.

▶ A boy playing steel drums during a Carnival celebration in St. Thomas

72 Latin America

Differentiated Instruction

The following Teacher Edition strategies are suitable for students of varying abilities.

Advanced Readers, p. 77
English Language Learners, p. 91
Gifted and Talented Students, p. 90
Less Proficient Readers, pp. 77, 81, 90
Special Needs Students, pp. 81, 91

Bibliography

For the Teacher

Barlow, Genevieve. *Stories from Latin America: Historias de Latinoamerica.* McGraw Hill/Contemporary Books, 1995.

Gutmann, Matthew C. *Perspectives on Las Americas: A Reader in Culture, History, and Representation.* Blackwell Publishers, 2003.

Machado, Ana Maria. *Exploration into Latin America.* New Discovery, 1995.

For the Student

L1 Dorros, Arthur. *Tonight Is Carnaval.* Dutton, 1992.

L2 Despain, Pleasant. *The Emerald Lizard: Fifteen Latin American Tales to Tell in English and Spanish.* August House, 1999.

L3 Hernandez, Romel. *Caribbean Islands: Facts and Figures.* Mason Crest Publishers, 2002.

Latin America: Languages

MAP MASTER™
Skills Activity

Regions Notice that many languages are spoken in Latin America and that language regions do not follow political boundaries. **Locate** Where in the region do people speak English? Spanish? Portuguese? **Conclude** Why are those languages spoken in those places?

Go Online
PHSchool.com Use Web Code lfp-1321 for step-by-step map skills practice.

ATLANTIC OCEAN

Gulf of Mexico

Tropic of Cancer

Caribbean Sea

PACIFIC OCEAN

Equator

Equator

Tropic of Capricorn

ATLANTIC OCEAN

KEY

- Spanish
- Portuguese
- Native American languages
- English
- Creole
- Dutch
- French
- National border

0 miles 1,500
0 kilometers 1,500
Lambert Azimuthal Equal Area

Chapter 3 **73**

MAP MASTER™
Skills Activity

- Point out to students the map title, key, and scale. Encourage students to study the map and list the languages spoken in Latin America.

- Refer students to the political map of Latin America on page 3 of the Student Edition. They can use the map to help them with the MapMaster Skills Activity.

Go Online
PHSchool.com Students may practice their map skills using the interactive online version of this map.

Using the Visual   L2

Reach Into Your Background Draw students attention to the caption accompanying the picture on pages 72–73. Discuss the photograph with students. Have them discuss what details stand out to them. Can they relate the celebration pictured to their own lives? Encourage students to share their ideas with the class.

Answers

Locate English is spoken in parts of Central America, parts of the Caribbean islands, and a small area in northern South America. Spanish is spoken in Mexico, much of Central America, the Caribbean, and parts of South America, especially in the south. Portuguese is spoken mainly in Brazil. **Conclude** The languages spoken in a region are affected by its history, culture, and the ethnic groups who live there.

Chapter Resources

Teaching Resources
- L2 Vocabulary Development, p. 214
- L2 Skills for Life, p. 204
- L2 Chapter Tests A and B, pp. 218–223

Spanish Support
- L2 Spanish Chapter Summary, p. 10
- L2 Spanish Vocabulary Development, p. 11

Media and Technology
- L1 Student Edition on Audio CD
- L1 Guided Reading Audiotapes, English and Spanish
- L2 Social Studies Skills Tutor CD-ROM
- *ExamView Test Bank CD-ROM*

DISCOVERY World Studies
CHANNEL Video Program
SCHOOL

Interactive Textbook

PRENTICE HALL
TeacherEXPRESS™
Plan • Teach • Assess

Objectives

Social Studies

1. Discover the cultural heritage of the people of Middle America.
2. Find out why many people in this region have been moving away from the countryside.

Reading/Language Arts

Identify causes and effects to better understand the relationships among situations and events.

Prepare to Read

Build Background Knowledge **L2**

Tell students that knowing about the geography and history of Latin America will help them as they learn about the region's cultures. Ask students to quickly preview the section headings and photographs with this question in mind: **What makes up a culture?** Point out the artwork on p. 75 and explain that art is one facet of culture. Use the Give One and Get One strategy (TE, p. 37) to generate a list.

Set a Purpose for Reading **L2**

- Preview the Objectives.
- Read each statement from the *Reading Readiness Guide* aloud. Ask students to mark the statements true or false.

  All in One Latin America Teaching Resources, *Reading Readiness Guide*, p. 188

- Have students discuss the statements in pairs or groups of four, then mark their worksheets again. Use the Numbered Heads participation structure (TE, p. T36) to call on students to share their group's perspectives.

Vocabulary Builder

Preview Key Terms

Pronounce each Key Term, and then ask students to say the word with you. Provide a simple explanation such as, "Native American groups, such as the Cherokee and Sioux, are indigenous people living in the United States."

Prepare to Read

Objectives

In this section you will
1. Discover the cultural heritage of the people of Middle America.
2. Find out why many people in this region have been moving away from the countryside.

Reading to Learn

As you read this section, look for information on the cultures of Middle America. Copy the web diagram below and record information about ancestry, religion, and language.

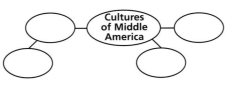

Target Reading Skill

Identify Causes and Effects A cause makes something happen. An effect is what happens. Determining causes and effects helps you understand relationships among situations and events. As you read this section, think of the cultures of Middle America as effects. What are the causes of these effects?

Key Terms

- **campesino** (kahm peh SEE noh) *n.* a poor Latin American farmer or farm worker
- **indigenous people** (in DIJ uh nus PEA pul) *n.* descendants of the people who first lived in a region
- **maquiladora** (mah kee luh DOHR ah) *n.* a Mexican factory that assembles parts to make products for export
- **emigrate** (EM ih grayt) *v.* to leave one country to settle in another
- **immigrant** (IM uh grunt) *n.* a person who comes into a foreign country to make a new home

---

A Honduran boy at work

74 Latin America

Seven nations form the narrow, crooked isthmus of Central America. Together with Mexico, these nations make up Middle America. The nations of Middle America share a cultural heritage, but there are also differences among them.

In Middle America, many people are **campesinos** (kahm peh SEE nohz), or poor farmers. Most of them have little or no land of their own. Therefore, it is hard for them to make enough money to support their families. Today, organizations of campesinos help farmers get loans to buy seeds and farm machinery.

Cultural Heritage

There is much diversity, or variety, among the people of Middle America. Many people are mestizo. That means they have both Spanish and indigenous ancestors. **Indigenous people** are descendants of the people who first lived in a region. In Latin America, indigenous people are also called Native Americans or Indians.

Target Reading Skill **L2**

Identify Causes and Effects Point out the Target Reading Skill. Tell students that being able to identify causes and effects will help them to understand how and why events occur or situations develop.

Model identifying the causes and effect in this passage on p. 76: "The Spanish settlers who came to the region were Roman Catholic. In the 1500s and 1600s, Spanish missionaries converted many Native Americans to Christianity. The Catholic Church has been important to this region every since." *(Causes—Spanish settlers were Catholic and Catholic missionaries converted many Native Americans. Effect—The Catholic Church has long been important to the region.)*

Give students *Identify Causes and Effects.* Have them complete the activity in groups.

All in One Latin America Teaching Resources, *Identify Causes and Effects*, p. 199

One Region, Many Faces In Honduras, most of the people are mestizo. About one third of Guatemala's people are mestizo. Another 60 percent are indigenous. Many Costa Ricans are direct descendants of Spaniards. And more than 40 percent of the people of Belize are of African or mixed African and European descent.

The countries of Central America have many languages, too. Guatemala is home to more than 20 languages. Spanish is the language of government and business, but the indigenous people in Guatemala speak their own languages. So do indigenous people in Panama, El Salvador, and Nicaragua. Spanish is the main language in six of the seven countries. People in Belize speak English.

Mexico also blends Native American and Spanish influences. Spanish is the first language for most Mexicans, but some Mexicans speak Native American languages as well. About 30 percent of the people of Mexico are indigenous, and about 60 percent of the population are mestizos.

Art of Middle America The art of Mexico reflects both its Spanish and its Native American cultures. In the 1920s, the government invited Mexican artists to create murals on public buildings. Murals are large pictures painted directly on walls. The murals by Diego Rivera (dee AY goh rih VEHR uh), José Clemente Orozco (ho SAY kleh MEN teh oh ROHS koh), and David Alfaro Siqueiros (dah VEED ahl FAH roh see KEH rohs) show the history of Mexico and the struggles of its people for freedom. They include the contributions of the indigenous people to the Mexican nation. Because the Aztecs and Mayas had done mural painting, these new artworks also revived an ancient Native American art form.

This 1930 self-portrait is by the Mexican artist Frida Kahlo.

Mexican History
This detail of *Sugar Cane* (1931) by Diego Rivera shows some people hard at work. **Infer** *Which people are not hard at work? What do you learn about Mexican history from these details?*

Vocabulary Builder

Use the information below to teach students this section's high-use words.

High-use Word	Definition and Sample Sentence
heritage, p. 74	*n.* culture or traditions handed down from one's ancestors or the past He was very proud of his **heritage**.
influence, p. 75	*n.* the power of persons or things to affect others She hoped her sister would not use her **influence** to get her into the club.
rural, p. 77	*adj.* of, or related to, the countryside I love the **rural** atmosphere of the farm.
urban, p. 77	*adj.* of, or related to, the city Living in an **urban** area can be exciting.

Cultural Heritage　L2

Guided Instruction

- **Vocabulary Builder** Clarify the high-use words **heritage** and **influence** before reading.

- Read Cultural Heritage using the Structured Silent Reading technique (TE, p. T34).

- Ask students to identify and discuss the main "ingredients" that blended to create the culture of Middle America. *(Native American beliefs, customs, languages, and art mixed with those of the Spanish settlers to form a unique and diverse cultural blend. The Catholic Church has also been an important influence on the culture of this region.)*

Answers

Infer The man in the hammock and the guards are not hard at work. The man in the hammock is probably a Spanish settler who owns the sugar-cane plantation. The guards are probably mestizo. This shows that Spanish settlers took over Mexico and had more power than the indigenous people. They had to hire guards to force people to work. It also shows that Mexican society was split into classes based on a person's ancestry.

Independent Practice

Ask students to create the Taking Notes graphic organizer on a blank piece of paper. Then have them label the ovals "Ancestry," "Art," "Religion," and "Language." Students can then fill in the ovals with information they have just learned. Briefly model labeling the ovals and recording details.

Monitor Progress

As students fill in the graphic organizer, circulate and make sure that individuals are choosing the correct details. Provide assistance as needed.

Show *Section Reading Support Transparency LA 36* and ask students to check their graphic organizers individually. Go over key concepts and clarify key vocabulary as needed.

Latin America Transparencies, *Section Reading Support Transparency LA 36*

A Blend of Cultures
Indigenous people attend a church service in the Mexican state of Chiapas. **Infer** *What evidence is there in the photo that these people have blended Christianity with their traditional culture?*

Art made by Native Americans before the arrival of Europeans is called Pre-Columbian art. Archaeologists have found beautiful wall paintings and painted vases, sculptures, and metalwork in Mexico and Central America. Gold jewelry was a specialty of the Mixtec people, while the Olmecs created huge stone heads and lovely figures made of jade.

The Church Religion is important to the people of Mexico and Central America. The Spanish settlers who came to the region were Roman Catholic. In the 1500s and 1600s, Spanish missionaries converted many Native Americans to Christianity. The Catholic Church has been important to this region ever since. Most of the people are Catholic. Native Americans have blended many elements of their religions with Christianity.

Fighting Injustice In Middle America, priests and bishops have spoken out against injustice. Following the Church's lead, many citizens have taken their own steps to end poverty and injustice. Ordinary people have started health clinics, farms, and organizations.

Elvia Alvarado (el VEE uh al vuh RAH doh) works for one of these organizations, and her work is not easy. "The communities we work in are hard to get to," she says. "Sometimes I don't eat all day, and in the summertime the streams dry up and there's often no water to drink." Sometimes Alvarado does not get paid. "But I couldn't be happy if my belly was full while my neighbors didn't have a plate of beans and tortillas to put on the table," she says.

√ **Reading Check** Name two ways people have worked to fight poverty and injustice.

76 Latin America

Background: Biography

Oscar Arnulfo Romero y Galdamez
Oscar Arnulfo Romero y Galdamez, archbishop of El Salvador, was born in Ciudad Barrios, El Salvador, in 1917. Ordained as a priest in 1942, he was appointed archbishop in 1977. At first, Romero avoided political affairs. Later, he thought the church should help its people obtain social justice. Romero spoke out against the human rights abuses and violence committed against the poor by the military regime. In 1980, while celebrating mass, Romero was assassinated.

Answers

Infer The people in the photo are wearing brightly colored traditional clothing as they head into the Christian church to worship.

√ **Reading Check** Officials of the Catholic Church have spoken out against injustice, and ordinary citizens have started organizations to help the poor, such as health clinics and farms.

Leaving the Countryside

The population of Mexico and Central America is growing rapidly. This rapid population growth has made it hard for young people in rural areas to find jobs. Many have left their homes to look for work in the cities. Today, most people in Middle America live in cities.

In Mexico, some people move to towns and cities along the border with the United States. There, they can work in factories owned by American companies. These companies place their factories in Mexico because wages and other costs are lower there. Border factories that assemble imported parts to make products for export are called **maquiladoras** (mah kee luh DOHR ahs).

Other urban areas in Middle America also offer jobs and other opportunities. Many rural people have moved to large cities such as Mexico City in Mexico, Panama City and Colón in Panama, and San José, the capital of Costa Rica. As a result, these cities have grown rapidly and often have trouble providing housing and services for new arrivals.

Identify Causes and Effects

What factor makes it difficult for young people in rural areas to find jobs? List that as a cause. What is the result of this unemployment? List that as an effect.

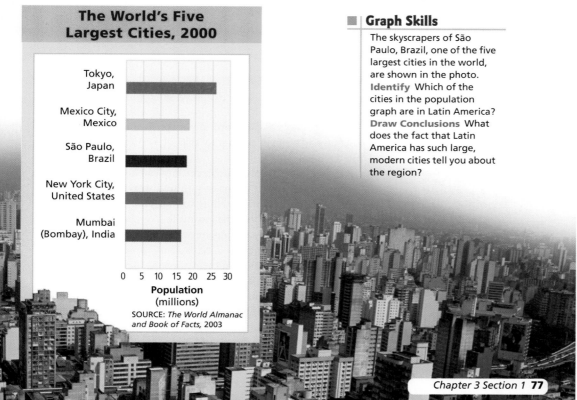

The World's Five Largest Cities, 2000

- Tokyo, Japan
- Mexico City, Mexico
- São Paulo, Brazil
- New York City, United States
- Mumbai (Bombay), India

Population (millions): 0 5 10 15 20 25 30

SOURCE: *The World Almanac and Book of Facts*, 2003

Graph Skills

The skyscrapers of São Paulo, Brazil, one of the five largest cities in the world, are shown in the photo. **Identify** Which of the cities in the population graph are in Latin America? **Draw Conclusions** What does the fact that Latin America has such large, modern cities tell you about the region?

Target Reading Skill L2

Identify Causes and Effects As a follow up, ask students to answer the Target Reading Skill question in the Student Edition. *(Cause—rapid population growth; Effect—Many young people have left their homes in the countryside to find work in the cities.)*

Leaving the Countryside L2

Guided Instruction

- **Vocabulary Builder** Clarify the high-use words **rural** and **urban** before reading.

- With students, read about the changes in population distribution in Middle America in Leaving the Countryside. As students read, circulate and make sure that individuals can answer the Reading Check question.

- Ask students **Why are many rural people in Middle America moving to the cities? What might be some drawbacks to living in the cities?** *(Because of a huge growth in population, there are few jobs in the countryside. This forces many young people to leave their homes to look for work in the cities. The cities provide jobs and a better education than the countryside does. However, many people who go to the cities end up living in crowded conditions and in poverty.)*

- Discuss with students the reasons why some people from Middle America emigrate to other countries. *(because they want a better life in a new land or to earn good money before returning home)*

Answers

Graph Skills **Identify** Mexico City, São Paulo **Draw Conclusions** It is an urbanized region, with a large percentage of the population living in cities.

Independent Practice

Assign *Guided Reading and Review.*

All in One **Latin America Teaching Resources**, *Guided Reading and Review*, p. 189

Monitor Progress

Tell students to fill in the last column of the *Reading Readiness Guide.* Probe for what they learned that confirms or invalidates each statement.

All in One **Latin America Teaching Resources**, *Reading Readiness Guide*, p. 188

Assess and Reteach

Assess Progress L2

Have students complete the Section Assessment. Administer the *Section Quiz.*

All in One **Latin America Teaching Resources**, *Section Quiz*, p. 190

Reteach L1

If students need more instruction, have them read this section in the Reading and Vocabulary Study Guide.

 Chapter 3, Section 1, **Latin America Reading and Vocabulary Study Guide,** pp. 32–34

Extend L3

Have students investigate the challenges of living in a growing city by completing *Nickel-and-Diming* from Environmental and Global Issues. After they discuss the questions in pairs, have volunteers share their ideas with the class.

Go Online PHSchool.com **For:** Environmental and Global Issues: *Nickel-and-Diming*
Visit: PHSchool.com
Web Code: lfd-1304

Answer

Analyze Images The men are wearing hats and boots, which appear to be of Middle American style. One building has a Spanish or Mexican tile roof. The figure in the wagon and the figures hanging from the stall look Mexican. The smaller, hanging items might be piñatas.

A Plaza in California
When immigrants come to the United States, they bring many aspects of their culture with them.
Analyze Images *What details in this photo of a market in Los Angeles reflect Middle American culture?*

Life in the City In many cities in the region, there are sharp contrasts between the lives of the wealthy and the lives of the poor. Wealthy people live in big houses on wide streets. They go to good schools and can afford to pay for medical care. Many of them have a lifestyle similar to that of wealthy people in the United States.

For the poor, however, life in the city can be hard. There is a shortage of housing. It is not easy to find work. Sometimes, the only way to make a living is selling fruit or soda on street corners. It is hard to feed a family on the income that can be earned this way.

Nevertheless, many people are willing to live with the hardships they find in the cities. Cecilia Cruz can explain why. She moved with her husband and their two sons to Mexico City from the southern state of Oaxaca (wah HAH kah). They live in a two-room house made of cinder blocks. It is on the outermost boundary of the city. "We came here for the schools," says Cruz. "There are more choices here. The level of education is much higher." Most newcomers to the city would agree.

 Skills Mini Lesson

Making Predictions L2

1. Point out to students that if they understand how certain causes produce certain effects, they can use that knowledge to make predictions.

2. Help students practice the skill by reading the following pair of sentences and determining which is the cause and which is the effect.

   ■ Thousands of young people in the countryside cannot find jobs. *(cause)*

   ■ Thousands move to cities to find work. *(effect)*

3. Have students apply the skill by answering these questions: People moved away from the countryside because they could not find jobs. What if new industries developed in the countryside? What might happen to the population? *(People might move back to the countryside to get jobs in the new industries.)*

Moving to the United States Most people in Mexico and Central America move somewhere else within their own country if they cannot find work. However, there are also thousands of people who emigrate. To **emigrate** is to leave one country and settle in another. Most leave to find jobs. Many of them emigrate to the United States.

Fermin Carrillo (fehr MEEN kah REE yoh) is one worker who did just that. He left his home town of Huaynamota (wy nah MOH tah), Mexico. There were no more jobs at home, and his parents needed food and medical care. Carrillo moved to a town in Oregon. Now he works in a fish processing plant. He sends most of the money he earns home to his parents. Carrillo hopes one day to become an American citizen.

Other immigrants are different. An **immigrant** is a person who has moved into one country from another. These immigrants want to return home after earning some money to help their families.

Building a Better Life Many Mexicans and Central Americans, like Fermin Carrillo, have left the region in search of a better life. Many more have followed Elvia Alvarado's example. You read about Alvarado's work with community groups in Honduras. She helps poor farmers get seeds, farm machinery, and more land. Like Alvarado, many Middle Americans have stayed at home and begun to build a better life for themselves and their neighbors.

A modern Tarahumara Indian of Mexico wearing traditional clothing

✓ **Reading Check** Why do many Mexicans move to the United States?

![Section 1 Assessment]

Section 1 Assessment

Key Terms
Review the key terms at the beginning of this section. Use each term in a sentence that explains its meaning.

Target Reading Skill
What are three effects of the Spanish colonization of Middle America?

Comprehension and Critical Thinking
1. (a) Identify What are the main languages and religions of the people of Middle America?

(b) Identify Cause and Effect How do the languages and religions of Middle America reflect the region's history?
(c) Predict How might this diversity lead to challenges for the region?
2. (a) Recall Describe life in the countryside and in the city.
(b) Identify Causes What is one reason that rural people in Mexico and Central America are moving to the cities?
(c) Predict What impact might the emigration of many Mexicans have on their country?

Writing Activity
Write a journal entry from the point of view of one of the people you read about in this section. Think about what life is like for that person. Include his or her hopes, dreams, and experiences.

For: An activity on indigenous peoples
Visit: PHSchool.com
Web Code: lfd-1301

Writing Activity
Use the *Rubric for Assessing a Journal Entry* to evaluate students' journal entries.

All in One Latin America Teaching Resources, *Rubric for Assessing a Journal Entry, p. 215*

Go Online PHSchool.com Typing in the Web code when prompted will bring students directly to detailed instructions for this activity.

Answers

✓ **Reading Check** Many Mexicans come to the United States to improve their way of life, to earn money to help support their families, and to find better jobs than they could find at home.

Section 1 Assessment

Key Terms
Students' sentences should reflect an understanding of each Key Term.

Target Reading Skill
Three effects of Spanish colonization of Middle America are: Spanish is the major language in the region; Catholicism is the main religion in the region; and a large number of the people are of Spanish descent or of mixed Spanish and Native-American descent.

Comprehension and Critical Thinking
1. (a) Although some indigenous languages still exist, Spanish is the main language in the region. Catholicism, with some elements of Native American beliefs, is the main religion in the region. **(b)** The languages and religions vary within the region, reflecting the fact that different groups have lived there over time. However, the fact that Spanish and Catholicism are the main language and main religion reflects that the Spanish conquered the indigenous people. **(c)** Some groups of indigenous people might want to gain back their lands or fight to have other rights. Indigenous groups may resent people of Spanish descent. People of Spanish descent might be prejudiced against mestizo or indigenous people.

2. (a) In the countryside, the population is growing rapidly. This is leading to unemployment. Young people leave their towns to go to the cities to find work. In the cities, people are crowded together and often live in poverty, although there are more jobs and schools are usually better than in the countryside. **(b)** The rapid rise in the population is leading to unemployment in the rural areas, forcing people to move to the cities to find jobs. **(c)** If too many people emigrate from Mexico, the country would lose people with skills that are important for its economy. Also, if people work in other countries, they pay taxes there, so Mexico loses tax money when workers leave the country.

Objective

Learn how to distinguish fact and opinion.

Prepare to Read

Build Background Knowledge   L2

On the board, write a statement of fact and a statement of opinion. (For example: *Fact*— "Our community's population is 15,000." *Opinion*— "Our community is the prettiest in the state.") Ask volunteers to identify which statement is a fact and which is an opinion, and then label each statement accordingly. Discuss what makes each statement a fact or an opinion, and then ask students to write short definitions of fact and opinion.

Instruct

Distinguishing Fact and Opinion   L2

Guided Practice

- Read the steps to analyze statements in the sample paragraph and determine if the statements are facts or opinions.

- Practice the skill by following the steps on p. 80 as a class. Model each step in the activity by choosing a sample fact from the paragraph (*Urbanization takes place when people move from rural areas to urban areas*), and explaining how that fact could be proven true (*by looking the word up in a dictionary*). Then identify a word in the paragraph that judges (*bad*), and any words that signal personal feeling in that statement (*I believe*), and decide if the statement could be proven true or false. (*The words* I believe *signal that this is an opinion, not a fact. However, it might be possible to prove that the belief is a fact if enough evidence can be found that supports that opinion.*)

Distinguishing Fact and Opinion

> Kate was excited. She was going to Papantla, Mexico. Lila had just been there. "The bus ride is very long and boring," she told Kate. "The town is not interesting. You should skip that trip!"
>
> Kate's guidebook said that Papantla is near the ruins of an ancient Indian city and that traditional dances are still performed there. The bus schedule said it was a three-hour ride. Her map showed that the bus traveled through the mountains.
>
> Kate hurried off to buy a ticket. She relied on facts rather than opinions. That the bus ride is three hours long is a **fact**. Lila's statement that the bus ride "is very long and boring" is an **opinion**.

Distinguishing fact from opinion is something you need to do almost every day. You do it as you—like Kate—reach your own decisions.

Learn the Skill

To distinguish fact from opinion, use the following steps.

1. **Look for facts by asking what can be proved true or false.** A fact usually tells who, what, when, where, or how much.

2. **Ask how you could check whether each fact is true.** Could you do your own test by measuring or counting? Could you find information in an encyclopedia?

3. **Look for opinions by identifying personal beliefs or value judgments.** Look for words that signal personal feelings, such as *I think*. Look for words that judge, such as *beautiful* and *ugly* or *should* and *ought to*. An opinion cannot be proved true *or* false.

4. **Ask whether each opinion is supported by facts or good reasons.** A well-supported opinion can help you make up your own mind—as long as you recognize it as an opinion and not a fact.

Independent Practice

Assign *Skills for Life* and have students complete it individually.

All in One Latin America Teaching Resources, *Skills for Life*, p. 204

Monitor Progress

As students complete the *Skills for Life* worksheet, circulate to make sure they understand the skills steps.

Practice the Skill

Read the paragraph in the box at the right until you are sure that you understand its meaning. Then read for facts and opinions.

1 Identify facts in the paragraph that tell how much, what, where, or when.

2 Explain how each fact you identified could be proven true or false.

3 (a) Identify two words that judge. Could the statements containing these words be proved true or false? (b) Identify one example of words that signal personal feelings. Could this statement be proved true or false?

4 The second sentence of the paragraph expresses an opinion. Is the opinion well supported with facts and reasons?

> Urbanization takes place when people move from rural areas to urban areas. I believe that urbanization in Mexico is bad. First, the cities are already too crowded. There are thousands of homeless people in urban areas. Many people can't find jobs. Second, the city streets were not designed for so many cars. Traffic jams are a huge headache. Finally, the water and electrical systems do not have the capacity to serve more people. I think the time has come for the government to stop urbanization.

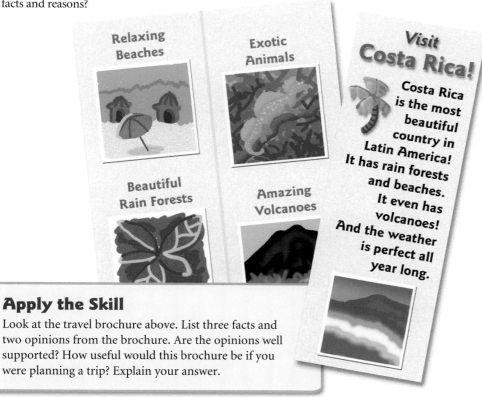

Relaxing Beaches

Exotic Animals

Beautiful Rain Forests

Amazing Volcanoes

Visit Costa Rica!

Costa Rica is the most beautiful country in Latin America! It has rain forests and beaches. It even has volcanoes! And the weather is perfect all year long.

Apply the Skill

Look at the travel brochure above. List three facts and two opinions from the brochure. Are the opinions well supported? How useful would this brochure be if you were planning a trip? Explain your answer.

Assess and Reteach

Assess Progress L2

Ask students to do the Apply the Skill activity.

Reteach L1

If students are having trouble applying the skill steps, have them review the skill using the interactive Social Studies Skills Tutor CD-ROM.

⊙ *Distinguishing Fact and Opinion,* **Social Studies Skills Tutor CD-ROM**

Extend L3

To extend the lesson, ask students to apply the skill steps to identify fact and opinion in a short newspaper or magazine article. Ask students to identify at least three facts in the article and explain how each one could be proven true or false. Then ask students to identify at least two opinions, if applicable. They should point out any words that signal a personal feeling, and tell if and how, the statements could be proven true or false. Point out to students that when reporters write straight news articles, they try to avoid expressing their personal opinion. An editorial, on the other hand, is an expression of someone's opinion.

Answers

Apply the Skill

Facts: 1. Costa Rica has rain forests and beaches. **2.** Costa Rica has volcanoes. **3.** The weather is warm all year round.

Opinions: 1. Costa Rica is the most beautiful country in Latin America. **2.** Costa Rica's beaches are "relaxing;" the rain forests are "beautiful;" the volcanoes are "amazing."

The opinions are not well supported, since there are no facts provided to back them up. Some students may feel that the brochure would be helpful in planning a vacation; others may feel that the brochure does not offer enough facts to be useful.

Section 2
Step-by-Step Instruction

Objectives
Social Studies

1. Find out what ethnic groups make up the people of the Caribbean.
2. Learn how the different cultures of the region blended to create Caribbean food, music, and celebrations.

Reading/Language Arts

Recognize multiple causes to understand the development of complex events.

Prepare to Read

Build Background Knowledge   **L2**

In this section, students will learn about Caribbean cultures. Draw the beginnings of a word web on the board. In the center oval write "Caribbean." Ask students to quickly preview the section then ask them what they know about the Caribbean. Conduct an Idea Wave (TE, p. T35) to elicit student ideas, and add relevant responses to the word web.

Set a Purpose for Reading   **L2**

■ Preview the Objectives.

■ Read each statement from the *Reading Readiness Guide* aloud. Ask students to mark the statements true or false.

All in One **Latin America Teaching Resources,** *Reading Readiness Guide,* p. 192

■ Have students discuss the statements in pairs or groups of four, then mark their worksheets again. Use the Numbered Heads participation structure (TE, p. T36) to call on students to share their group's perspectives.

Vocabulary Builder
Preview Key Terms   **L2**

Pronounce each Key Term, and then ask students to say the word with you. Provide a simple explanation such as, "The West Indies is another name for the region called the Caribbean."

Section 2

The Cultures of the Caribbean

Prepare to Read

Objectives
In this section you will
1. Find out what ethnic groups make up the people of the Caribbean.
2. Learn how the different cultures of the region blended to create Caribbean food, music, and celebrations.

Taking Notes
As you read the section, look for the main ideas and details about Caribbean culture. Copy the format below and use it to outline the section.

> I. The people of the Caribbean
>   A. The first people of the Caribbean
>   1.
>   2.
>   3.
>   B. People in the Caribbean today

Target Reading Skill

Recognize Multiple Causes A cause makes something happen. An effect is what happens. Sometimes an effect can have more than one cause. For example, the distinctive quality of Caribbean food is an effect with several causes, including local fishing and farming as well as the cultural heritage of the West Indian people. As you read this section, identify multiple causes for other characteristics of Caribbean culture.

Key Terms
- **West Indies** (west IN deez) *n.* the Caribbean islands
- **ethnic group** (ETH nik groop) *n.* a group of people who share the same ancestry, language, religion, or cultural traditions
- **Carnival** (KAHR nuh vul) *n.* a lively annual celebration just before Lent in Latin America

The Caribbean islands are spread across more than 2,000 miles (3,219 kilometers), from Florida to the northeast coast of South America. There are more than a dozen different nations in the Caribbean region. As you might expect, a variety of peoples with many different cultures live within this large area.

This watercolor showing the Arawaks was painted in the 1800s.

The People of the Caribbean

The Caribbean islands are also called the **West Indies** because Christopher Columbus, when he first arrived there, thought he had reached the Indies in Asia. That's why he called the people of the islands *Indians.*

82 Latin America

Target Reading Skill   **L2**

Recognize Multiple Causes Point out the Target Reading Skill. Tell students that, often, an event or problem has more than one cause. To understand a complex situation, it is important to recognize if it has various causes and what they might be.

Model recognizing multiple causes using this passage on p. 83: "Because so many people came to the Caribbean as colonists, slaves, or immigrants, the area has a rich ethnic variety." (*Effect*—The Caribbean has great ethnic diversity. *Causes*—Colonists from European countries settled in the region; Africans were brought to the region as slaves; immigrants from countries such as China arrived.)

Give students *Recognize Multiple Causes.* Have them complete the activity in groups.

All in One **Latin America Teaching Resources,** *Recognize Multiple Causes,* p. 200

The First People of the Caribbean Long before Columbus arrived, the first people to live on these islands were a Native American group called the Ciboney (see buh NAY). The Ciboney lived in the region for thousands of years. In about 300 B.C., they were joined by another indigenous group, the Arawaks (AH rah wahks), who came from South America. In about 1000, the Caribs (KAR ibz), another South American group, arrived.

The Caribs gave the region its name. They lived in the Caribbean for more than 400 years before the first Europeans arrived. Christopher Columbus and other Spaniards enslaved the Native Americans. Almost all of the Caribs, Arawaks, and other indigenous groups died either of overwork or of diseases the Spanish brought with them. Today, there are just a few hundred Caribs. They live on the island of Dominica.

Other Europeans followed the Spanish. They hoped to make money from the region's wealth of natural resources. In the 1600s, Dutch, French, and English colonists began claiming territory. They built large sugar plantations and brought many enslaved Africans to work on them.

Most of the Caribbean people today are descended from these Africans. Immigrants from China, India, and the Middle East have also come to the region to work.

People in the Caribbean Today Because so many people came to the Caribbean as colonists, slaves, or immigrants, the area has a rich ethnic variety. An **ethnic group** is a group of people who share the same ancestry, language, religion, or cultural traditions. The ethnic groups of the Caribbean are Native American, African, European, Asian, and Middle Eastern.

Recognize Multiple Causes
There are very few Native Americans left on the Caribbean islands. What causes of this effect are given in the paragraph at the left?

Caribbean Diversity
These teenagers are students in the French West Indies. **Generalize** *How does this group reflect the population of the Caribbean?*

Vocabulary Builder

Use the information below to teach students this section's high-use words.

High-Use Word	Definition and Sample Sentence
fertile, p. 84	*adj.* rich in resources The **fertile** soil of the garden led to a large harvest.
require, p. 84	*v.* to order or command The school **requires** students to take tests in every subject.
festival, p. 85	*n.* a time or day of feasting or celebration Many different types of food were for sale at the **festival**.
distinctive, p. 86	*adj.* not alike; different. The fish casserole had a **distinctive** odor.

The People of the Caribbean L2

Guided Instruction

- **Vocabulary Builder** Clarify the high-use words **fertile** and **require** before reading.

- Read The People of the Caribbean using the Structured Silent Reading technique (TE, p. T34).

- Ask students to describe the main groups of people that make the Caribbean so ethnically diverse. *(Native Americans, Africans, Europeans, Asians)* Discuss the general history of the settlement of the islands and the origins of the major ethnic groups. *(The first people to live in the Caribbean were Native Americans. Most of them died in colonial times from overwork or European diseases. Today, the population of the Caribbean is mostly made up of the descendants of Africans brought there as slaves. Other major groups include descendants of Spanish, Dutch, French, and English colonists, as well as modern-day immigrants from China, India, and the Middle East.)*

Target Reading Skill L2
Recognize Multiple Causes As a follow up, ask students to answer the Target Reading Skill question in the Student Edition. *(Most of the Native Americans in the Caribbean died of overwork during enslavement or of diseases brought by the Spanish.)*

Answers

Generalize The population of the Caribbean is very diverse. The teenagers in the photo appear to come from several different ethnic groups.

Independent Practice

Ask students to create the Taking Notes outline on a blank piece of paper. Then have students fill the outline in with the information they have just read. Briefly model the outlining by filling in the first numbered item.

Monitor Progress

As students fill in the outline, circulate and make sure that individuals are choosing useful details and are putting them in the correct order. Provide assistance as needed.

A Blend of Cultures L2

Guided Instruction

■ **Vocabulary Builder** Clarify the high-use words **festival** and **distinctive** before reading.

■ With students, read about the colorful and diverse cultural aspects of the Caribbean in A Blend of Cultures. As students read, circulate and make sure that individuals can answer the Reading Check question.

Answers

✓ **Reading Check** The right of Jamaican women to equal opportunities in education is protected by law. Equality for women is important in Jamaica because so many women are independent farmers and business owners.

V. S. Naipaul: Trinidad and Beyond When V. S. Naipaul was born in Trinidad in 1932, more than one third of the island's population was from India. Like many other Indian immigrants, Naipaul's grandparents had come to Trinidad to work on sugar plantations owned by Europeans. Naipaul grew up knowing people from Africa, China, South America, and Europe. For him, the culture of Trinidad was a mix of languages, religions, and customs. When he was 18, Naipaul won a scholarship to study in England, where he still lives. Naipaul has written about life in Trinidad, about England, and about his worldwide travels. In 2001, he was awarded the Nobel Prize for Literature.

Depending on their island's history, the people of a Caribbean island may speak one of several European languages. Their language may also be a mixture of European and African languages. For example, two countries and two cultures exist on the island of Hispaniola. On the eastern half is one country, the Dominican Republic. Its population is Spanish-speaking and mostly mestizo. West of the Dominican Republic is the country of Haiti. Nearly all of Haiti's people are descended from Africans. They speak French and Haitian Creole, a French-based language with some African and Spanish words.

Most West Indians are Christians, but there are also small groups of Hindus, Muslims, and Jews. Some people practice traditional African religions.

Life on the Islands Most of the Caribbean islands have very fertile soil, and many people in the region make their living farming. Dorothy Samuels is a ten-year-old from Jamaica, one of the Caribbean islands. Her family are farmers. They plant yams and other vegetables and fruits. They also plant cacao beans. Every Saturday, Dorothy's mother and grandmother take their fruits and vegetables to the market to sell. All the traders at their market are women.

Dorothy is a good student. She hopes one day to go to college in Kingston, Jamaica's capital city. Jamaican laws require that women have as much opportunity for education as men have. Equality for women is important in Jamaican culture because many Jamaican women are independent farmers and business owners.

✓ **Reading Check** How are women's rights and opportunities protected in Jamaica?

A Blend of Cultures

The rich culture of the Caribbean has a variety of sources. West Indians enjoy many kinds of music and dance, celebrations, and food. They also play a variety of sports. Baseball, soccer, and track and field are popular. On some islands, people also play cricket, which is a British game similar to baseball. Dominoes—although not a sport—is a popular game throughout the region.

Carnival Many people in the Caribbean observe the Roman Catholic tradition of Lent, which is the period of 40 days before Easter Sunday. Because Lent is a very solemn time, these people have a lively public festival called **Carnival** just before Lent.

Different countries celebrate Carnival in different ways. In Trinidad and Tobago, for example, people spend all year making costumes and floats for the celebration. Lent always starts on a Wednesday. At 5 A.M. the Monday before, people go into the streets in their costumes. Calypso bands play. Thousands of fans follow the bands through the streets, dancing and celebrating. At the stroke of midnight on Tuesday, the party stops. Lent has begun.

Explore three types of Caribbean music.

Carnival Celebration
The dancers below are Carnival performers in Port of Spain, Trinidad, while the girl on the facing page has dressed up for the celebration. **Draw Inferences** *What do the costumes and props indicate about how much time and effort goes into preparing for this celebration?*

┌ Background: Links Across Time ─

Calypso In the early 1800s, enslaved West Africans in Trinidad developed the Caribbean musical style *calypso*. Often forbidden to communicate with each other, the enslaved Africans developed a folk form using a call-and-response style brought from Africa. The songs expressed the slaves' feelings about slave masters and other local figures. After the abolition of slavery in 1838, calypso groups began competing during the Carnival season before Lent.

In the 1940s and 1950s, calypso moved on to the world stage, via popular recordings. An example of a very famous calypso recording is Harry Belafonte's *Banana Boat Song (Day-O)*. Calypso was also the basis for more recent Caribbean musical styles, such as reggae and soca.

Show *Caribbean Music: It's All in the Mix*. Ask students **How does the Bomba reflect the survival of African traditions in the Caribbean?** *(Enslaved Africans brought the music and dance style of the Bomba to Puerto Rico from Ghana.)*

Guided Instruction (continued)

- Have students identify elements of blended Caribbean culture in religion, food, and music. *(Religion—Carnival is celebrated before Lent, which is a Roman Catholic practice brought from Europe. The celebration has characteristics of other cultures, such as Calypso music, which has African roots. Food—Caribbean cooking blends local foods and recipes from various cultures, including African, Indian, British, and Chinese. Music—Caribbean music is a blend of both African and European musical traditions.)*

Independent Practice

Have students complete the Taking Notes outline by jotting down details from A Blend of Cultures.

Monitor Progress

- When students are finished with their outlines, show *Section Reading Support Transparency LA 37* and ask students to check their outlines individually. Go over key concepts and clarify key vocabulary as needed.

  Latin America Transparencies, *Section Reading Support Transparency LA 37*

- Tell students to fill in the last column of the *Reading Readiness Guide*. Probe for what they learned that confirms or invalidates each statement.

  All in One Latin America Teaching Resources, *Reading Readiness Guide,* p. 192

Answers

Draw Inferences The props and costumes show that a lot of time and effort went into preparing for the celebration.

Assess and Reteach

Assess Progress [L2]

Have students complete the Section Assessment. Administer the *Section Quiz.*

 Latin America Teaching Resources, *Section Quiz,* p. 194

Reteach [L1]

If students need more instruction, have them read this section in the Reading and Vocabulary Study Guide.

Chapter 3, Section 2, **Latin America Reading and Vocabulary Study Guide,** pp. 35–37

Extend [L3]

Remind students about the different types of music they learned about in the video *Caribbean Music: It's All in the Mix.* Make the music of Latin America come alive for students by having them create simple percussion instruments. *Small Group Activity: Share the Music* gives students complete instructions for creating some instruments used in the region.

Caribbean Music: It's All in the Mix, **World Studies Video Program**

 Latin America Teaching Resources, *Small Group Activity: Share the Music,* pp. 205–208

Answers

✓ **Reading Check** Calypso songs have humorous lyrics and a distinctive beat. Reggae from Jamaica has a strong rhythm with a "chunking" sound at the end of each measure, and the lyrics are sometimes political.

Section 2 Assessment

Key Terms
Students' sentences should reflect an understanding of each Key Term.

Target Reading Skill
Causes include: Europeans colonizing islands in the region; Africans being brought to the islands as slaves to work on plantations; more recently, new groups, such as Chinese, Indians, and people from the Middle East immigrating to the Caribbean.

Comprehension and Critical Thinking
1. (a) The Ciboney, Aranaks, and Caribs. **(b)** They died of overwork or Spanish diseases.

This waiter in Grenada shows a variety of Caribbean dishes.

Food Caribbean food is a mixture that represents the different cultures of the islands. It also makes use of the rich natural resources of the region. Caribbean people can enjoy many types of seafood that are not found in United States waters. For instance, the people of Barbados love to eat flying fish and sea urchin eggs. Bammy—a bread made from the cassava plant—is still made the way the African slaves made it. West Indians also cook spicy curries from India, sausages from England, and Chinese dishes. Many tropical fruits grow on the islands. The fruits are used to make many juices and other drinks that are not readily available in the United States.

Music Caribbean music, which has both African and European sources, is famous around the world. Calypso is a form of song that uses humorous lyrics and has a distinctive beat. Reggae (REHG ay) music and ska come from Jamaica. Reggae songs have a strong rhythm with a "chunking" sound at the end of each measure. The lyrics of traditional reggae songs often have political messages.

Another distinctive Caribbean musical sound is that made by steel drums. These instruments are made from recycled oil drums. A steel drum can be tuned so that different parts of it play different notes. Players strike the instruments with rubberized drumsticks.

✓ **Reading Check** Describe two types of Caribbean music.

Section 2 Assessment

Key Terms
Review the key terms at the beginning of this section. Use each term in a sentence that explains its meaning.

Target Reading Skill
What are three reasons, or causes, for the diversity of ethnic groups and cultures in the Caribbean?

Comprehension and Critical Thinking
1. (a) Identify Who were the first inhabitants of the Caribbean islands?

(b) Explain What happened to those people? Why?
(c) Identify Causes Why do West Indians speak a variety of languages today?
2. (a) Recall What kinds of activities do Caribbean people enjoy?
(b) Categorize Which traditions have these activities come from?
(c) Draw Conclusions Why is there more of a cultural blend in the Caribbean than in Middle America?

Writing Activity
Select one aspect of Caribbean culture, such as food, music, or celebrations. Write a paragraph comparing and contrasting that aspect of Caribbean culture with the cultural practices where you live.

> **Writing Tip** Before you begin, decide how you will organize your paragraph. One way is to cover all the similarities first and then all the differences.

86 Latin America

(c) West Indians speak a variety of languages because so many different groups came to live there.

2. (a) Caribbean people enjoy festivals, cooking and eating, music and dance, and sports and games. **(b)** Most of these activities are a blend of African and European traditions, but also include traditions from Chinese, Indian, and other cultures. **(c)** because many more types of people came to the Caribbean

to conquer the area, to farm it, and to work there, than came to Middle America

Writing Activity
Use the Rubric for *Assessing a Writing Assignment* to evaluate students' paragraphs.

 Latin America Teaching Resources, *Rubric for Assessing a Writing Assignment,* p. 216

Prepare to Read

Objectives

In this section you will
1. Find out what ethnic groups are represented in the different cultural regions of South America.
2. Learn what life is like in the countryside and the cities of South America.

Taking Notes

As you read this section, look for information about the cultural regions of South America. Copy the table below and record your findings in it.

Location of Region	Countries	Characteristics
Caribbean Coast		

Target Reading Skill

Understand Effects An effect is what happens as the result of a specific cause or factor. For example, you can see in the paragraph below that the geography of the Lake Titicaca region has had several effects on the way the Native Americans there live. This section discusses the effects of geography and colonization on different regions of South America. As you read, note the effects of each of these factors on the way South Americans live today.

Key Terms

- **gauchos** (GOW chohz) *n.* cowboys of the pampas of Argentina
- **subsistence farming** (sub SIS tuns FAHR ming) *n.* growing only enough food to meet the needs of the farmer's family
- **cash crop** (kash krahp) *n.* a crop grown mostly for sale rather than for the farmer's own use

Between Peru and Bolivia is the deep lake called Lake Titicaca. It lies high in the Andes Mountains. This area is cool and dry. There are few trees. Native Americans here make their living from totora reeds, a kind of thick, hollow grass that grows on the lakeshore. They use these reeds to make houses, mats, hats, ropes, sails, toys, roofs, and floors. They eat the reeds, feed them to livestock, and brew them into tea. Totora reeds can even be made into medicine.

Long ago, a number of Native American groups built floating islands with totora reeds. They used the islands to hide from the Incas. Today, some Native Americans still live on floating islands on Lake Titicaca.

Native Americans who live on Lake Titicaca make their boats out of totora reeds.

Chapter 3 Section 3 **87**

Target Reading Skill L2

Understand Effects Point out the Target Reading Skill. Tell students that it is important to understand what the effects of different causes are, and how those effects change and shape the world.

Model understanding effects using this passage on p. 91: "Export farming uses so much land for cash crops that South America has to import food for its own people to eat." (*The effect of South American countries using so much farm land for growing cash crops is that many South American countries import food to eat.*)

Give students *Understand Effects*. Have them complete the activity in groups.

All in One Latin America Teaching Resources, *Understand Effects,* p. 201

Objectives

Social Studies

1. Find out what ethnic groups are represented in the four cultural regions of South America.
2. Learn what life is like in the countryside and in the cities of South America.

Reading/Language Arts

Understand how one cause can bring about multiple effects.

Prepare to Read

Build Background Knowledge L2

In this section, students will learn about the cultures of South America. Explain that, along with Middle America and the Caribbean, the Spanish also colonized much of South America. Based on what they have learned from Sections 1 and 2 of this chapter, have students predict what South American cultures might have in common with the other regions of Latin America. Conduct an Idea Wave (TE, p. T35) to elicit responses.

Set a Purpose for Reading L2

- Preview the Objectives.
- Distribute the worksheet and read each statement from the *Reading Readiness Guide* aloud. Ask students to mark the statements true or false.

  All in One Latin America Teaching Resources, *Reading Readiness Guide,* p. 196

- Have students discuss the statements in pairs or groups of four, then mark their worksheets again. Use the Numbered Heads participation structure (TE, p. 36) to call on students to share their group's perspectives.

Vocabulary Builder

Preview Key Terms L2

Pronounce each Key Term, and then ask students to say the word with you. Provide a simple explanation such as, "A cash crop is something people grow purposely not to eat themselves but to sell."

Understand Effects As a follow up, ask students to answer the Target Reading Skill question in the Student Edition. (*Many people in South America speak Spanish and are Catholic.*)

Instruct

The People of South America `L2`

Guided Instruction

- **Vocabulary Builder** Clarify the high-use words **official** and **style** before reading.

- Read The People of South America using the Structured Silent Reading technique (TE, p. T34).

- Ask students **What are the five cultural regions of South America?** (*northern South America; the Andean region; Argentina, Chile, Paraguay, and Uruguay; the pampas; and Brazil.*)

- Ask students **How has history influenced the culture of the Caribbean coast?** (*The languages, religions, and ethnic groups of each country have been influenced by the countries that colonized the area.*)

Answers

Conclude The land in the photo seems to be suitable for raising llamas, but might be difficult to farm.

⟲ **Understand Effects**
Target Skill
What two effects of Spanish colonization are described in the paragraph at the right?

An Ancient Way of Life
Toco Indians in Peru wear traditional clothing and herd llamas much as their ancestors did. **Conclude** *Look at the setting of the photo. How do you think geography has contributed to these people keeping their traditional way of life?*

88 Latin America

The People of South America

Most South Americans today are descended from Native Americans, Africans, or Europeans. In this way, they are like the people of Mexico and Central America. Like its neighbors to the north, South America, too, was colonized mainly by Spain. Today, many South Americans speak Spanish and are Catholic, yet different regions within South America have their own unique cultures.

The Caribbean Coast There are five cultural regions in South America. The first region includes Colombia, Venezuela, Guyana, Suriname, and French Guiana, all of which are in the northern part of South America. They all border the Caribbean Sea, and their cultures are similar to those of the Caribbean islands.

Local history has also influenced the cultures of each nation. Colombia and Venezuela were Spanish colonies, and their people are mainly mestizo. Their official language is Spanish, and most of the people are Roman Catholic. On the other hand, Guyana, Suriname, and French Guiana were colonized by different European nations. Guyana was once an English colony, and its official language is English. Suriname was a Dutch colony until 1975, and the people there still speak Dutch. In both countries, many people are Muslim or Hindu. French Guiana is not an independent nation; it is an overseas department of France. While its official language is French, many of its people are of mixed African and European descent.

Vocabulary Builder

Use the information below to teach students this section's high-use words.

High-Use Word	Definition and Sample Sentence
official, p. 88	*adj.* lawful; having authority The document had an **official** seal on it.
style, p. 90	*n.* way or manner She wore her hair in an attractive **style.**
vast, p. 91	*adj.* very large and wide The auditorium was so **vast** that it could have seated a thousand people.
interior, p. 92	*n.* remote, inner part or area, especially of a country If you dislike the coast, try visiting the **interior** of the country.

- Ask students **How do the Quechua and the Aymara keep their cultural traditions alive?** (*They speak their own languages and follow the ways of their ancestors.*)

- Discuss Chile's geographic diversity with students. (*Chile has mountains, beaches, deserts, forests, and polar regions.*)

- Ask students **How is the traditional lifestyle of the gauchos changing?** (*Cattle ranching is still important, but wheat fields are begin to replace grazing lands.*)

- Ask students **What ethnic groups live in Brazil?** (*Native Americans, people of African and European descent, and people of mixed descent*)

The Andean Countries and the South To the south and west, the culture is very different. Peru, Ecuador, and Bolivia are Andean countries. Many Native Americans live high in the Andes Mountains. In Bolivia, there are more indigenous people than mestizos. The Quechua and Aymara (eye muh RAH) peoples speak their own languages and follow the traditional ways of their ancestors.

The third cultural region consists of Chile, Argentina, Paraguay, and Uruguay. The long, narrow country of Chile has mountains, beaches, deserts, forests, and even glaciers. Although its geography is diverse, its people are not. Most people in Chile are mestizos. In Argentina and Uruguay, however, the big cities are very diverse. Many different ethnic groups live there.

Another culture exists on Argentina's pampas, or plains. The pampas are the traditional home of the **gauchos** (GOW chohz), the Argentinean cowboys. While cattle raising is still important, wheat fields are beginning to replace grazing lands on the pampas, and the day of the gaucho may be coming to an end.

Brazil South America's largest country was once a colony of Portugal, and today its people speak Portuguese. However, Brazil is culturally diverse. Many Native Americans live in Brazil, as do people of African and European descent. Some Brazilians are of mixed descent. Many people have moved to Brazil from other countries. Brazil's largest city, São Paulo (sow PAW loh), is home to more Japanese than any other place in the world except Japan.

Cityscapes
This avenue in Buenos Aires, Argentina (left photo) is said to be the widest boulevard in the world. Signs in São Paulo, Brazil, (right photo) are in Portuguese and Japanese. **Draw Conclusions** *What can you conclude about South America's cities and culture from these two photos?*

Chapter 3 Section 3 **89**

Background: Links Across Place

Pampas Beef Industry The pampas, like the Great Plains in the United States, is an important source of beef for countries around the world. Argentina exports its beef to the European Union (its largest customer), the United States, and Canada, among many other countries. In 2002, the United States imported over 20,000 metric tons of processed beef from Argentina, worth $128 million, and representing 9 percent of Argentina's production. Argentina exported a total of 223,403 tons of beef in 2002, making it the eighth largest beef exporter in the world.

Answers

Draw Conclusions The left photo shows a large and modern city. The right photo shows signs in different languages. From these photos, one can conclude that South America's cities are large, modern, and diverse.

Read **Citizen Heroes** with students. Ask **How did these women achieve their leadership role?** (*The Mothers of the "Disappeared" became leaders by continuing to protest when their government refused to account for their children's disappearances.*)

Guided Instruction (continued)

- Ask students **How are South American women fighting for their rights?** (*Some are getting bank loans to start small businesses.*)

- Ask students to list the South American writers discussed in the text along with what country they are from. (*Possible answers: Gabriela Mistral, Chile; Pablo Neruda, Chile; Gabriel Garcia Marquez, Colombia; Isabel Allende, Chile*)

Independent Practice

Ask students to create the Taking Notes chart on a blank piece of paper. Students then fill the chart in with information they have just read. Briefly model by filling in the first box.

Monitor Progress

As students fill in the graphic organizer, circulate and make sure that individuals are choosing the correct details. Provide assistance as needed.

Show *Section Reading Support Transparency LA 38* and ask students to check their graphic organizers individually. Go over key concepts and clarify key vocabulary as needed.

Latin America Transparencies, *Section Reading Support Transparency LA 38*

Answers

✓ Reading Check South American women are fighting for equal rights in the areas of education, jobs, access to health care, and political power.

Citizen Heroes

Mothers of the "Disappeared"

In 1976, a military government took control of Argentina and began arresting people who opposed their regime. Other opponents of the government simply "disappeared"—kidnapped by unidentified armed men. Fourteen mothers of these "disappeared" demanded information about their children. When the government did not respond, the women began to march in front of the presidential palace every Thursday at 3:30 P.M. They became know as the Mothers of Plaza de Mayo (PLAH zuh day MY oh). Their peaceful protests brought worldwide attention to their cause. As one observer put it, "These are women who moved from being housewives in Argentina to being global leaders for justice."

South American Literature South America has produced many famous writers. Gabriela Mistral (gah bree AY lah mees TRAHL), a poet from Chile, was the first Latin American to win the Nobel Prize for Literature. Her poetry reflects her love of children, and so does her second career as a teacher. When she was a school principal, she encouraged the young Chilean poet Pablo Neruda (PAH bloh neh ROO duh). He went on to win the Nobel Prize in 1971. When he was a young man, Neruda composed complex poems. Toward the end of his life, however, he wrote about simple, everyday objects, such as onions and socks.

Another South American winner of the Nobel Prize for Literature was the Colombian novelist Gabriel García Márquez (gah bree EL gahr SEE ah MAHR kes). He is best known for novels in the style of magic realism, which mixes fantasy with historical facts and realistic stories. Isabel Allende (EES uh bel ah YEN day), a novelist from Chile, also uses magic realism in many of her novels and stories. She is also known for her "letters" to members of her family, which were published as books.

The Role of Women In some ways, women do not yet play a role equal to that of men in South America. Women in South America are more likely than men to be poor. They also do not attend school for as many years as men do.

More and more women in South America today are fighting to make a living for themselves and their children. They are demanding equal rights. Women are struggling for the rights to go to school, to work in all types of jobs, to have good health care, and to have a voice in government. Some women are getting bank loans to start small businesses. These businesses are sometimes based on traditional skills such as sewing, weaving, or preparing food.

✓ Reading Check **What rights are women fighting for?**

Differentiated Instruction

For Gifted and Talented   L3
Have students research and write a biography of one of the authors mentioned on Student Edition p. 90. Have students give brief outlines of their subjects' lives as oral reports to the class, including a poem or brief excerpt of the author's work. If students are Spanish speakers, have them read the work in Spanish first and then in English.

For Less Proficient Readers   L1
Have students use the Passport to the World CD-ROM to enrich and extend their knowledge of Brazil. They can take the Photo Tour and examine the Timeline of the country.

Brazil, **Passport to the World CD-ROM**

Country and City Life

South America has cities with millions of people, but it also has vast areas with almost no people at all. Many South Americans still live in the countryside, but others are leaving farms and moving to cities.

Farming in South America Outside of Argentina, Chile, and Uruguay, most rural people with land of their own do **subsistence farming.** That means they grow only enough food to meet their families' needs. They have only small plots of land. These farmers plant corn, beans, potatoes, and rice.

Very large farms grow crops to export to other countries. The main export cash crops of South America are coffee, sugar, cacao, and bananas. **Cash crops** are crops grown mostly for sale rather than for the farmer's own use. Export farming uses so much land for cash crops that South America has to import food for its own people to eat.

South America's Cities The cities of South America illustrate the region's mix of cultures. Many major cities—Lima, Peru, and Buenos Aires, Argentina, for example—were founded by Spanish colonists more than 400 years ago. Much of their architecture is Spanish in style. Some buildings in even older cities follow Native American designs.

Two Ways to Farm
The top photo shows a banana processing plant on a plantation in Ecuador. Below is a small family-owned coffee farm in Colombia. **Infer** *Why might plantation owners not be interested in farming the area in the lower photo? How easy do you think it is to make a living there?*

Differentiated Instruction

For Special Needs Students L1
Have students read the section as they listen to the recording on the Student Edition on Audio CD. Check for comprehension by pausing the CD and asking students to share their answers to the Reading Check questions.

⊙ Chapter 3, Section 3, **Student Edition on Audio CD**

For English Language Learners L2
Before students read, have them skim the section and select two to four words which are unfamiliar to them, or which interest them. Have students write each word with its part of speech and definition, and then write a sentence using the word. Partner them with native English speakers to review the information and sentences.

Country and City Life L2

Guided Instruction

- **Vocabulary Builder** Clarify the high-use words **vast** and **interior** before reading.

- With students, read about the characteristics of the urban and rural experience in South America in Country and City Life. As students read, circulate and make sure that individuals can answer the Reading Check question.

- Ask students to list the characteristics of South America's countryside and the characteristics of South America's cities. *(Countryside—Many people still live there, but some areas have almost no people; in most countries rural people practice subsistence farming; cash crops use much of the land and keep countries from growing enough food to feed the people. Cities— have a cultural mix; architecture is Spanish and modern, with some Native-American buildings; some cities have slums called favelas or ranchos; rural people are moving to cities; cities are crowded and resources are under great pressure; some governments cannot provide enough water and electricity.)*

Independent Practice

Assign *Guided Reading and Review.*

All in One **Latin America Teaching Resources,** *Guided Reading and Review,* p. 197

Monitor Progress

Tell students to fill in the last column of the *Reading Readiness Guide.* Probe for what they learned that confirms or invalidates each statement.

All in One **Latin America Teaching Resources,** *Reading Readiness Guide,* p. 196

Answer

Infer because the area is hilly and looks inaccessible; it is probably hard to make a living there

Assess and Reteach

Assess Progress
Have students complete the Section Assessment. Administer the *Section Quiz.*

All in One **Latin America Teaching Resources,** *Section Quiz,* p. 198

Reteach L1
If students need more instruction, have them read this section in the Reading and Vocabulary Study Guide.

Chapter 3, Section 3, **Latin America Reading and Vocabulary Study Guide,** pp. 38–40

Extend L3
Have students learn more about the art of Latin America by completing the *Enrichment* activity.

All in One **Latin America Teaching Resources,** *Enrichment,* p. 203

Answers

 Reading Check buildings in the Spanish colonial style, new, modern structures of concrete, steel, and glass; and some of Native American design

Infer electricity, plumbing, sewers

Section 3 Assessment

Key Terms
Students' sentences should reflect an understanding of each Key Term.

Target Reading Skill
Many still follow the traditional ways of their ancestors and speak their own languages.

Comprehension and Critical Thinking
1. (a) Cultural regions of South America: Northern—very diverse area; includes many different groups and colonial histories. Andean—many indigenous people still live here and ancient languages and traditions are still alive. Chile, Argentina, Paraguay, and Uruguay—mostly mestizos and Spanish speaking, although large cities are diverse. Brazil—official language is Portuguese; Native Americans, people of African and European descent, and Japanese live there. **(b)** Native Americans have been able to maintain their cultures in remote areas like the Andes Mountains. Argentineans developed a ranching culture on the plains of the pampas.

City of Contrasts
This view of Buenos Aires shows poor neighborhoods in the foreground while the modern downtown rises in the distance. **Infer** *What city services do the people in the foreground seem to lack?*

In contrast, modern office blocks and apartment buildings of concrete, steel, and glass tower above the downtown areas of many South American cities. One or two cities were built quite recently. Brasília, the Brazilian capital, was constructed in the 1950s. It was a completely planned city, designed to draw people to the country's interior.

On the other hand, the slums of many South American cities have certainly been unplanned. They are called *favelas* (fuh VEH lus) in Brazil and *ranchos* in Venezuela. The population of South America is booming. Like Mexicans and Central Americans, South Americans cannot find enough jobs in rural areas. Every day, thousands of rural people move to the cities looking for work. Usually they end up in poor neighborhoods. City governments try to provide electricity and running water to everyone. But people move into cities so quickly that it is hard for city governments to keep up.

✓ **Reading Check** **What types of buildings are found in South American cities?**

Section 3 Assessment

Key Terms
Review the key terms at the beginning of this section. Use each term in a sentence that explains its meaning.

Target Reading Skill
What are two effects of the fact that many Native Americans still live high in the Andes Mountains?

Comprehension and Critical Thinking
1. (a) Recall Describe two cultural regions of South America.

(b) Identify Cause and Effect Explain two ways in which the geography of South America has shaped how people live.
2. (a) Identify Describe two different kinds of farms in South America.
(b) Compare and Contrast How are city life and rural life similar and different?
(c) Analyze Information How does the movement of people from the countryside to urban areas put pressure on cities?

Writing Activity
Suppose you were a newspaper reporter visiting Argentina in 1976. Write a short article about the Mothers of Plaza de Mayo for your American readers.

For: An activity on South America
Visit: PHSchool.com
Web Code: lfd-1303

2. (a) Subsistence farming is done by individual families to raise food to survive. Cash crops are raised on large farms to be sold. **(b)** Similar—the poor struggle to survive on very little; different—some areas of the countryside are empty, while the cities are crowded. **(c)** Cities must increase services such as water and electricity. Housing can be in short supply, leading to the development of slums and homelessness.

Writing Activity
Use the *Rubric for Assessing a Newspaper Article* to evaluate students' articles.

All in One **Latin America Teaching Resources,** *Rubric for Assessing a Newspaper Article,* p. 217

Go Online PHSchool.com Typing in the Web code when prompted will bring students directly to detailed instructions for this activity.

Review and Assessment

Review and Assessment

Review Chapter Content

- Revisit the Guiding Questions on p.1 of the Student Edition. Then have students review the major themes of this chapter by deciding what Guiding Question each bulleted statement in the Chapter Summary answers. Write the statements on the board and have students work in groups to classify them.

- Assign *Vocabulary Development* for students to review Key Terms.

  All in One Latin America Teaching Resources, *Vocabulary Development,* p. 214

◆ Chapter Summary

Section 1: The Cultures of Middle America

- Many different cultural groups live in Middle America, and the languages and arts of the region reflect this diversity.
- Population growth and lack of jobs have caused many rural Middle Americans to move to the cities or to emigrate to the United States.

Section 2: The Cultures of the Caribbean

- The people of the Caribbean are made up of many ethnic groups, including descendants of Africans and Europeans.
- West Indian sports, food, music, and celebrations reflect the blend of cultures in the Caribbean.

Section 3: The Cultures of South America

- Life in the different cultural regions of South America is influenced by geography and by the ethnic groups that settled there.
- South America has both large farms that export their crops and small subsistence farms.
- South American cities are overcrowded with poor rural people coming to look for work.

Mexico

French West Indies

Ecuador

◆ Key Terms

Match the definitions in Column I with the key terms in Column II.

Column I
1. a group of people who share ancestry, language, religion, or cultural traditions
2. descendants of the people who first lived in a region
3. growing only enough food to meet the needs of their families
4. a person who has moved from one country to settle in another
5. a poor farmer who owns little or no land

Column II
A indigenous people

B campesino

C immigrant

D ethnic group

E subsistence farming

Chapter 3 **93**

Answers

Key Terms

1. **D, ethnic group** (*a group of people who share ancestry, language, religion, or cultural traditions*)

2. **A, indigenous people** (*descendants of the people who first lived in a region*)

3. **E, subsistence farming** (*growing only enough food to meet the needs of their families*)

4. **C, immigrant** (*a person who has moved from one country to another*)

5. **B, campesino** (*a poor farmer who owns little or no land*)

┌─ **Vocabulary Builder** ─────

Revisit this chapter's high-use words:

heritage	influence	rural
urban	fertile	require
distinctive	festival	tradition
official	style	vast
interior		

Ask students to review the definitions they recorded on their *Word Knowledge* worksheets.

All in One Latin America Teaching Resources, *Word Knowledge,* p. 202

Consider allowing students to earn extra credit if they use the words in their answers to the questions in the chapter Review and Assessment. The words must be used correctly and in a natural context to earn extra points.

Comprehension and Critical Thinking

6. (a) In general, the population is rising in Middle America. **(b)** The rise in population is making jobs scarce, especially in rural areas, so many people in those regions are moving to cities.

7. (a) The Ciboney were the first people to live in the Caribbean; later the Arawak and Carib people also populated the region. **(b)** When the Spanish colonized the Caribbean, most Native Americans were enslaved and died of overwork or from European diseases. **(c)** The Caribbean has been colonized by many different European groups, who also brought enslaved Africans there to work on plantations. In modern times, people from other parts of the world, such as China, India, and the Middle East, have also come to the Caribbean to live and work.

8. (a) Carnival is a festival celebrated by Roman Catholics just before the fasting period of Lent. **(b)** In the Caribbean, this festival occurs before Lent and includes elements of West Indian cultures, such as African-influenced music and costumes.

9. (a) Chile is a long, narrow country on the Pacific Ocean, with mountains, beaches, deserts, forests, and polar regions. **(b)** Unlike the rest of South America, which was mainly colonized by Spain, Brazil was colonized by Portugal, and Brazil's language and culture reflect this.

10. (a) *Ranchos* is the word for "slums" in Brazil; *favelas* is the word for "slums" in Venezuela. **(b)** Many rural people have gone to the cities to look for jobs, and they often end up in these very poor areas. **(c)** Because there are not enough jobs in the countryside, people flock to the cities, where governments have a difficult time keeping up with the demand for services, such as water and electricity.

11. (a) Cash crops are crops that are grown to sell, not to feed a farm family. **(b)** Huge amounts of land are used to grow cash crops for export, and not to grow food to feed the people.

Skills Practice

Facts: "There is so much variety from the different cultures in the area."; "There are also lots of tropical fruits and juices."; "A lot of food is quite spicy"; "The Carib Heaven Restaurant will give you a chance to try. . . cuisine."

◆ Comprehension and Critical Thinking

6. (a) Recall Describe population growth in Middle America.
(b) Identify Effects How has population growth affected the movement of people in that region?

7. (a) Identify Who were the first people to inhabit the Caribbean islands?
(b) Identify Cause and Effect What happened to those people, and why?
(c) Draw Conclusions Why is there such cultural diversity in the Caribbean today?

8. (a) Define What is Carnival?
(b) Identify Cause and Effect How does Carnival reflect both West Indian culture and Roman Catholic traditions?

9. (a) Describe What is the geography of Chile like?
(b) Identify Effects Why are Brazil's culture and language different from the rest of South America's?

10. (a) Define What are *ranchos* and *favelas*?
(b) Identify Causes Why are they growing?
(c) Draw Conclusions How do conditions in the countryside affect these city neighborhoods?

11. (a) Define What are cash crops?
(b) Conclude Why does export farming cause problems for some South American countries?

◆ Skills Practice

Distinguishing Fact and Opinion In the Skills for Life activity in this chapter, you learned how to distinguish facts from opinions. You also learned how to use facts and well-supported opinions to help you make decisions.

Read the paragraph below. List the facts and the opinions. Explain how this paragraph could help you decide whether to try the Carib Heaven Restaurant.

> Caribbean food is the best in the world. There is so much variety from the different cultures of the area. There are also lots of tropical fruits and juices. A lot of the food is quite spicy—just the way I like it! The Carib Heaven Restaurant will give you a chance to try this great cuisine.

◆ Writing Activity: Geography

Suppose you are a writer for a travel magazine. Write an article about one of the places you "visited" in this chapter. Include descriptions of the landforms, waterways, climate, and vegetation. Explain how geography has affected the way people live in that place.

Refer to the maps in the Regional Overview and in Chapter 1 as well as to the information in this chapter. You can also do additional research if you wish.

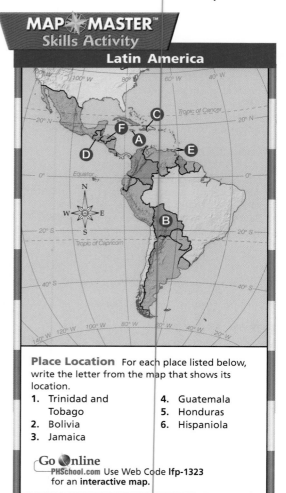

MAP MASTER Skills Activity

Latin America

Place Location For each place listed below, write the letter from the map that shows its location.
1. Trinidad and Tobago
2. Bolivia
3. Jamaica
4. Guatemala
5. Honduras
6. Hispaniola

Go Online
PHSchool.com Use Web Code lfp-1323 for an **interactive map**.

Opinions: "Caribbean food is the best in the world"; "just the way I like it (spicy)"; "this great cuisine"

Students' answers will vary. Students may focus on a particular detail about food served by the restaurant, such as the fact that the food is spicy, in deciding whether they would want to try eating there.

Writing Activity: Geography
Students' answers will vary, but should focus on one of the places described in the chapter, and include information about landforms, waterways, climate, and vegetation.

Use *Rubric for Assessing a Newspaper Article* to evaluate students' reports.

All in One Latin America Teaching Resources, *Rubric for Assessing a Newspaper Article,* p. 217

Standardized Test Prep

Test-Taking Tips

Some questions on standardized tests ask you to analyze graphs and charts. Look at the circle graph at the right. Then follow the tips to answer the sample question.

Think It Through Because only one percent of Mexicans are Protestant, you can eliminate answer D. You can also eliminate A easily, because England had little influence on Mexico. You know from the text that the Aztec influence was important, but you can see from the graph that the Aztec religion does not play a large role in Mexico today. That leaves the Roman Catholic country of Spain, which makes sense when you consider Mexico's history. Therefore, the correct answer is B.

TIP Draw your own conclusions about the graph before you look at the answer choices.

Mexico Today: Religious Groups

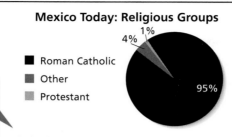

- ■ Roman Catholic
- ■ Other
- ■ Protestant

95% / 4% / 1%

Pick the letter that best answers the question.

The information in the graph could be used to show the influence of

A England on the development of modern Mexico.
B Spain on the development of modern Mexico.
C Ancient Aztecs on the development of modern Mexico.
D Protestantism on the development of modern Mexico.

TIP Look for the BEST answer, as more than one answer choice may seem to fit.

Practice Questions

Choose the letter of the best answer.

1. Most of the people of Mexico and Central America are
   A indigenous or of mixed ancestry.
   B European or Spanish.
   C indigenous or European.
   D Spanish or of mixed ancestry.

2. Rapid population growth in Mexico and Central America has caused all of the following EXCEPT
   A migration to cities.
   B emigration to other countries.
   C fewer jobs for everyone.
   D better living conditions in the cities.

3. The Andean countries of South America include
   A Bolivia, Peru, and Ecuador.
   B Peru, Brazil, and Bolivia.
   C Brazil, Argentina, and Chile.
   D Bolivia, Ecuador, and Argentina.

Study the circle graphs and answer the question that follows.

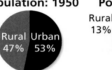

Venezuela Population: 1950
Rural 47% / Urban 53%

Venezuela Population: 2002
Rural 13% / Urban 87%

4. Which sentence best describes the population trend in Venezuela?
   A The rural population has steadily increased.
   B The urban and rural populations have remained the same.
   C The urban population has steadily increased.
   D The urban population has steadily decreased.

Go Online
PHSchool.com
Use Web Code lfa-1301 for a **Chapter 3 self-test.**

---

1. E	**2.** B
3. A	**4.** D
5. F	**6.** C

Go Online
PHSchool.com Students may practice their map skills using the interactive online version of this map.

Standardized Test Prep
Answers

1. A
2. D
3. A
4. C

Go Online
PHSchool.com Students may use the Chapter 3 self-test on PHSchool.com to prepare for the Chapter Test.

Assessment Resources

Use *Chapter Tests A and B* to assess students' mastery of chapter content.

All in One **Latin America Teaching Resources,** *Chapter Tests A and B,* pp. 218–223

Tests are also available on the *ExamView Test Bank CD-ROM.*

⊙ *ExamView Test Bank CD-ROM*

Use a benchmark test to evaluate students' cumulative understanding of what they have learned in Chapters 1 through 3.

📄 *Latin America Benchmark Test 1,* **AYP Monitoring Assessments,** pp. 97–100

Overview

Video

 Introducing Mexico and Central America
1. Use data to compare countries.
2. Learn what characteristics Mexico and most Central American countries share.
3. Name some key differences among the countries.

Mexico and Central America: Navigating the Highs and Lows
Length: 5 minutes, 51 seconds
Explores the region's geography.

 Section 1 **Mexico: Moving to the City**
1. Learn what life is like for people in rural Mexico.
2. Find out why many Mexicans have been moving from the countryside to the cities.
3. Understand why the growth of Mexico City presents challenges for the people and the environment.

Living in Mexico: Natural Hazards
Length: 5 minutes, 16 seconds
Explains the destructive natural forces at work in Mexico.

 Section 2 **Guatemala: Descendants of an Ancient People**
1. Learn why there is a struggle for land in Guatemala.
2. Find out how the Mayas lost their land.
3. Discover how groups are working to improve the lives of Guatemala's indigenous people.

Guatemala's Coffee Economy
Length: 4 minutes, 23 seconds
Visits a coffee plantation in Guatamala.

 Section 3 **Panama: An Important Crossroads**
1. Find out why people wanted to build a canal across the Isthmus of Panama.
2. Learn how the Panama Canal was built.
3. Understand how the canal has affected the nation of Panama.

Changing Panama's Landscape
Length: 4 minutes, 15 seconds
Examines how humans interact with the environment of Panama.

 # Technology Resources

Go Online
PHSchool.com

Students use embedded web codes to access internet activities, chapter self-tests, and additional map practice. They may also access Dorling Kindersley's Online Desk Reference to learn more about each country they study.

Interactive Textbook

Use the Interactive Textbook to make content and concepts come alive through animations, videos, and activities that accompany the complete basal text—online and on CD-ROM.

PRENTICE HALL
TeacherEXPRESS
Plan • Teach • Assess

Use this complete suite of powerful teaching tools to make planning lessons and administering tests quicker and easier.

Reading and Assessment

Reading and Vocabulary Instruction

🔁 Model the Target Reading Skill

Context Understanding how to derive meaning from context clues can help students become more confident and better readers.

Model using context clues to better understand unfamiliar words by thinking aloud about this sentence from page 102: *Mexico's population has risen dramatically over the last 30 years.*

This sentence uses the word *dramatically*. I think this is an important word, but I'm not completely sure of its meaning. Because it is right next to the word *risen*, I am going to guess that *dramatically* describes how or how much the population of Mexico has risen. Maybe something in the next sentence will give me another clue. The next sentence says: *The country's population is growing at one of the highest rates in the world.* That's a great clue. Now I can see that *dramatically* in this context must mean a lot, or a great deal.

Use the following worksheets from All-in-One Latin America Teaching Resources (pp. 239–241) to support this chapter's Target Reading Skill.

Vocabulary Builder
High-Use Academic Words

Use these steps to teach this chapter's high-use words:

1. Have students rate how well they know each word on their Word Knowledge worksheets (All-in-One Latin America Teaching Resources, p. 242).

2. Pronounce each word and ask students to repeat it.

3. Give students a brief definition or sample sentence (provided in TE pp. 103, 110, and 117.)

4. Work with students as they fill in the "Definition or Example" column of their Word Knowledge worksheets.

Assessment

Formal Assessment

Test students' understanding of core knowledge and skills.

Chapter Tests A and B, All-in-One Latin America Teaching Resources, pp. 265–270

Customize the Chapter Tests to suit your needs.

ExamView Test Bank CD-ROM

Skills Assessment

Assess geographic literacy.

MapMaster Skills, Student Edition pp. 97, 106, 117, 124

Country Profile Map and Chart Skills, Student Edition pp. 104, 111, 118

Assess reading and comprehension.

Target Reading Skills, Student Edition, pp. 107, 110, 120 and in Section Assessments

Chapter 4 Assessment, Reading and Vocabulary Study Guide, p. 51

Performance Assessment

Assess students' performance on this chapter's Writing Activities using the following rubrics from All-in-One Latin America Teaching Resources.

Rubric for Assessing a Bar Graph, p. 260
Rubric for Assessing a Journal Entry, p. 261
Rubric for Assessing a Report, p. 262
Rubric for Assessing a Writing Assignment, p. 263
Rubric for Assessing a Newspaper Article, p. 264

Assess students' work through performance tasks.

Small Group Activity: Simulation: Who Should Control the Panama Canal? All-in-One Latin America Teaching Resources, pp. 245–248

Portfolio Activity, Teacher Edition, p.101

Online Assessment

Have students check their own understanding.

Chapter Self-Test

Section 1 **Mexico: Moving to the City**

 2 periods, 1 block (includes Country Databank)

Social Studies Objectives

1. Learn what life is like for people in rural Mexico.
2. Find out why many Mexicans have been moving from the countryside to the cities.
3. Understand why the growth of Mexico City presents challenges for people and the environment.

Reading/Language Arts Objective

Use context clues to determine the meaning of unfamiliar words.

Prepare to Read

Build Background Knowledge
Discuss city life vs. country life.

Set a Purpose for Reading
Have students evaluate statements on the *Reading Readiness Guide*.

Preview Key Terms
Teach the section's Key Terms.

Target Reading Skill
Introduce the section's Target Reading Skill of **using context clues**.

Instructional Resources

All in One Latin America Teaching Resources

- **L2** Reading Readiness Guide, p. 228
- **L2** Use Context Clues: Definition/Description, p. 239

Differentiated Instruction

Spanish Reading and Vocabulary Study Guide

- **L2** Chapter 4, Section 1, pp. 31–32 ELL

World Studies Video Program

- **L2** Mexico and Central America: Navigating the Highs and Lows ELL, LPR, SN

Instruct

Life in Rural Mexico
Ask students key questions about life in rural Mexico.

Country Profile
Direct students to derive information from maps, charts, and graphs.

Moving to Mexico City
Discuss why people are moving to Mexico City.

Opportunities and Challenges
Discuss pollution in Mexico City.

Target Reading Skill
Review **using context clues**.

Instructional Resources

All in One Latin America Teaching Resources

- **L2** Guided Reading and Review, p. 229
- **L2** Reading Readiness Guide, p. 228
- **L2** Reading a Population Distribution Map, p. 251

Latin America Transparencies

- **L2** Section Reading Support Transparency LA 39

World Studies Video Program

- **L2** Living in Mexico: Natural Hazards

Differentiated Instruction

All in One Latin America Teaching Resources

- **L2** Outline Map 6: Mexico, p. 253 AR, GT, LPR, SN
- **L2** Outline Map 7: Central America and the Caribbean, p. 254 AR, GT, LPR, SN

Latin America Teacher's Edition

- **L1** For Special Needs Students, TE p. 100, 105
- **L1** For Less Proficient Readers, TE p. 100, 105
- **L3** For Advanced Readers, TE p. 106

Student Edition on Audio CD

- **L1** Chapter 4, Section 1 SN, ELL, LPR
- **L1** **Passport to the World CD-ROM** SN, LPR, ELL

Assess and Reteach

Assess Progress
Evaluate student comprehension with the section assessment and section quiz.

Reteach
Assign the Reading and Vocabulary Study Guide to help struggling students.

Extend
Extend the lesson by assigning an *Enrichment* activity.

Instructional Resources

All in One Latin America Teaching Resources

- **L2** Section Quiz, p. 230
- **L3** Enrichment, p. 243
  Rubric for Assessing a Journal Entry, p. 261

Reading and Vocabulary Study Guide

- **L1** Chapter 4, Section 1, pp. 42–44

Differentiated Instruction

All in One Latin America Teaching Resources

  Rubric for Assessing a Bar Graph, p. 260

Spanish Support

- **L2** Section Quiz (Spanish), p. 33 ELL

Key

- **L1** Basic to Average
- **L2** For All Students
- **L3** Average to Advanced
- LPR Less Proficient Readers
- AR Advanced Readers
- SN Special Needs Students
- GT Gifted and Talented
- ELL English Language Learners

Section 2 Guatemala: Descendants of an Ancient People

🕐 *2.5 periods, 1.25 blocks (includes Skills for Life)*

Social Studies Objectives

1. Learn why there is a struggle for land in Guatemala.
2. Find out how the Mayas lost their land.
3. Discover how groups are working to improve the lives of Guatamala's indigenous people.

Reading/Language Arts Objective

Use context clues that show contrast to determine the meaning of unfamiliar words.

Prepare to Read	**Instructional Resources**	**Differentiated Instruction**
Build Background Knowledge Use photographs to brainstorm about the Maya. **Set a Purpose for Reading** Have students evaluate statements on the *Reading Readiness Guide.* **Preview Key Terms** Teach the section's Key Terms. **Target Reading Skill** Introduce the section's Target Reading Skill of **using context clues.**	**All in One Latin America Teaching Resources** L2 Reading Readiness Guide, p. 232 L2 Use Context Clue: Compare and Contrast, p. 240	**Spanish Reading and Vocabulary Study Guide** L2 Chapter 4, Section 2, pp. 33–34 ELL

Instruct	**Instructional Resources**	**Differentiated Instruction**
The Struggle for Land Discuss the ownership and distribution of land. **Target Reading Skill** Review **using context clues.** **The Mayas Lose Their Land** Discuss the challenges facing the Mayas' ownership of land. **Country Profile** Direct students to derive information from maps, charts, and graphs. **Working for a Better Life** Discuss how the Mayas are improving their situation.	**All in One Latin America Teaching Resources** L2 Guided Reading and Review, p. 233 L2 Reading Readiness Guide, p. 232 L2 Reading a Circle Graph, p. 252 **Latin America Transparencies** L2 Section Reading Support Transparency LA 40 **World Studies Video Program** L2 Guatemala's Coffee Economy	**All in One Latin America Teaching Resources** L2 Skills for Life, p. 244 AR, GT, LPR, SN **Latin America Teacher's Edition** L1 For English Language Learners, TE p. 112 L3 For Gifted and Talented Students, TE p. 112 **Student Edition on Audio CD** L1 Chapter 4, Section 2 ELL, LPR, SN **Spanish Support** L2 Guided Reading and Review (Spanish), p. 34 ELL

Assess and Reteach	**Instructional Resources**	**Differentiated Instruction**
Assess Progress Evaluate student comprehension with the section assessment and section quiz. **Reteach** Assign the Reading and Vocabulary Study Guide to help struggling students. **Extend** Extend the lesson by assigning a Book Project.	**All in One Latin America Teaching Resources** L2 Section Quiz, p. 234 L3 Book Project: Latin America in the News, pp. 76–78 Rubric for Assessing a Report, p. 262 **Reading and Vocabulary Study Guide** L1 Chapter 4, Section 2, pp. 45–47	**Latin America Teacher's Edition** L1 For Special Needs Students, p. 115 L3 For Gifted and Talented, TE p. 115 **Social Studies Skills Tutor CD-ROM** L1 Drawing Inferences and Conclusions LPR, SN, ELL

Key

L1 Basic to Average	L3 Average to Advanced	**LPR** Less Proficient Readers **GT** Gifted and Talented
L2 For All Students		**AR** Advanced Readers **ELL** English Language Learners
		SN Special Needs Students

Section 3 Panama: An Important Crossroads

 3 periods, 1.5 blocks (includes Chapter Review and Assessment)

Social Studies Objectives

1. Find out why people wanted to build a canal across the Isthmus of Panama.
2. Learn how the Panama Canal was built.
3. Understand how the canal has affected the nation of Panama.

Reading/Language Arts Objective

Use context clues and your own knowledge to determine the meaning of unfamiliar words.

Prepare to Read	Instructional Resources	Differentiated Instruction
Build Background Knowledge Discuss aspects of Panama. **Set a Purpose for Reading** Have students begin to fill out the *Reading Readiness Guide*. **Preview Key Terms** Teach the section's Key Terms. **Target Reading Skill** Introduce the section's Target Reading Skill of **using context clues**.	**All in One Latin America Teaching Resources** L2 Reading Readiness Guide, p. 236 L2 Use Context Clues: General Knowledge, p. 241 **World Studies Video Program** L2 Changing Panama's Landscape	**Spanish Reading and Vocabulary Study Guide** L2 Chapter 4, Section 2, pp. 33–34 ELL

Instruct	Instructional Resources	Differentiated Instruction
Why Build a Canal? Discuss the reasons for building the Panama Canal. **Country Profile** Direct students to derive information from maps, charts, and graphs. **Building the Canal: A Heroic Effort** Ask questions about how the canal was built. **Target Reading Skill** Review **using context clues**. **Panama and Its Canal** Ask questions about the control of the Panama Canal. **Eyewitness Technology** Teach students more about the Panama Canal.	**All in One Latin America Teaching Resources** L2 Guided Reading and Review, p. 237 L2 Reading Readiness Guide, p. 236 L2 Outline Map 7: Central America and the Caribbean, p. 254 L2 Doing Searches on the Internet, p. 258 L2 Activity Shop Lab: Making a Model Canal Lock, pp. 249–250 **Latin America Transparencies** L2 Section Reading Support Transparency LA 41	**All in One Latin America Teaching Resources** L3 Locks, Crocs, and Skeeters, pp. 255–256 AR, GT L3 Beyond the Chagres, p. 257 AR, GT **Latin America Teacher's Edition** L1 For Less Proficient Readers, TE p. 119 L3 For Advanced Readers, TE p. 119 L1 For Special Needs Students, TE p. 120 **Spanish Support** L2 Guided Reading and Review (Spanish), p. 36 ELL

Assess and Reteach	Instructional Resources	Differentiated Instruction
Assess Progress Evaluate student comprehension with the section assessment and section quiz. **Reteach** Assign the Reading and Vocabulary Study Guide to help struggling students. **Extend** Extend the lesson by assigning a Small Group Activity about who should control the Panama Canal.	**All in One Latin America Teaching Resources** L2 Section Quiz, p. 238 L3 Small Group Activity: pp. 245–248 Rubric for Assessing a Newspaper Article, p. 264 L2 Vocabulary Development, p. 259 L2 Chapter Tests A and B , p. 265–270	**Spanish Support** L2 Section Quiz (Spanish), p. 37 ELL L2 Chapter Summary (Spanish), p. 38 ELL L2 Vocabulary Development (Spanish), p. 39 ELL **Reading and Vocabulary Study Guide** L2 Chapter 4, Section 3, pp. 48–58

Key

L1 Basic to Average	L3 Average to Advanced	LPR Less Proficient Readers	GT Gifted and Talented
L2 For All Students		AR Advanced Readers	ELL English Language Learners
		SN Special Needs Students	

Reading Background

Applying New Words Outside the Classroom

Expand students' understanding of this chapter's vocabulary by assigning an activity which applies the chapter's Key Terms and high-use words to real life. Choose five or six vocabulary words from the chapter, such as *plaza, support, political movement, erosion,* and *benefit,* and ask students to list them in their notebooks.

Next, ask students where they might *see* these words outside of their textbook. List the responses on the board. Suggestions might include signs, newspapers, magazines, history books, fiction books, and biographies. Then ask students where they might *hear* these words. Answers might include television or radio news broadcasts, conversations with parents or other adults, and political speeches. Finally, ask students how they might *use* these words. Students can suggest sample sentences or topics of conversation.

Have students keep a log for one week in which they record where and how they see their selected words printed or spoken. Have students share their logs at the end of the week.

Encourage Active Participation

In this chapter, students will use an Idea Wave to share their ideas. Remind students that if their idea is closely related to another person's idea, they should acknowledge the other person's idea when they share theirs. Below are some language strategies for active classroom participation:

> *My idea is similar to _____'s idea.*
>
> *As _____ already pointed out, it seems like . . .*
>
> *I don't agree with _____ because . . .*

Be sure that students understand that it is acceptable and desirable for them to build on their classmates' ideas, using these strategies.

World Studies Background

Mexico's Cities

Mexico City is one of the biggest cities in the world, alongside Tokyo, Japan, São Paolo, Brazil, and New York City. Besides Mexico City, Mexico has two other large metropolitan areas—Guadalajara and Monterrey. Guadalajara is called "the most Mexican of cities." It has a rich history and plentiful cultural events. Monterrey, in the Sierra Madres, is considered Mexico's industrial powerhouse.

Political Unrest in Guatemala

Civil war erupted in Guatemala in the 1960s when leftist guerrilla movements challenged the harsh military regime. During the civil war, the government ruled through the heavy hand of "death squads" that routinely tortured and murdered critics, including students and labor leaders. More than 150,000 people were killed and another 40,000 "disappeared." The civil war finally ended in 1996.

Malaria

Although the malaria problem that plagued the building of the Panama Canal was eventually resolved by technological advancements, the disease is still a growing problem. Some three million people die each year as a result of malaria. Quinine was effective in treating malaria for many years. However, some strains of malaria have now grown resistant to the quinine cure. This factor, among others, is one cause of the latest rise of malaria.

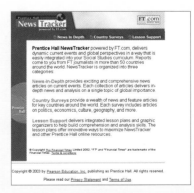

Prentice Hall **NewsTracker** powered by FT.com, delivers dynamic current events and global perspectives in a way that is easily integrated into your Social Studies curriculum. Reports come to you from FT journalists in more than 50 countries around the world. NewsTracker is organized into three categories:

News-In-Depth provides exciting and comprehensive news articles on current events. Each collection of articles delivers in-depth news and analysis on a single topic of global importance.

Country Surveys provide a wealth of news and feature articles for key countries around the world. Each survey includes articles on politics, economics, culture, geography, and more.

Lesson Support delivers integrated lesson plans and graphic organizers to help build comprehension and analysis skills. The lesson plans offer innovative ways to maximize NewsTracker and other Prentice Hall online resources.

© Copyright The Financial Times Limited 2002. "FT" and "Financial Times" are trademarks of the Financial Times. Terms & Conditions

Copyright © 2003 by Pearson Education, Inc. publishing as Prentice Hall. All rights reserved.
Please read our Privacy Statement and Terms of Use.

Get in-depth information on topics of global importance with **Prentice Hall NewsTracker®,** powered by FT.com.

Use Web Code **lfd-1400** for **NewsTracker®**.

Chapter 4
Mexico and Central America

Guiding Questions

Remind students about the Guiding Questions introduced at the beginning of the book.

Section I relates to **Guiding Question** ⑤ **How has geography influenced the ways in which Latin Americans make a living?** (*The dependence of rural Mexicans on farming is changing as more Mexicans move to cities.*)

Section 2 relates to **Guiding Question** ② **How has Latin America been shaped by its history?** (*The Mayas of Guatemala have been struggling to keep their land and their culture intact for five hundred years.*)

Section 3 relates to **Guiding Question** ⑤ **How has geography influenced the ways in which Latin Americans make a living?** (*The location of the isthmus in Panama spurred the building of the canal, which is a large part of Panama's economy.*)

⤺ Target Reading Skill

In this chapter, students will learn and apply the reading skill of using context clues. Use the following worksheets to help students practice this skill:

> **All in One** **Latin America Teaching Resources,** *Use Context Clues: Definition/ Description,* p. 239; *Use Context Clues: Compare and Contrast,* p. 240; *Use Context Clues: General Knowledge,* p. 241

Chapter Preview

This chapter will introduce you to the northernmost region of Latin America: Mexico and Central America.

Country Databank
The Country Databank provides data and descriptions of each of the countries in the region: Belize, Costa Rica, El Salvador, Guatemala, Honduras, Mexico, Nicaragua, and Panama.

Section 1
  Mexico
  Moving to the City

Section 2
  Guatemala
  Descendants of an Ancient People

Section 3
  Panama
  An Important Crossroads

⤺ Target Reading Skill

Context In this chapter you will focus on using context to help you understand unfamiliar words. Context includes the words, phrases, and sentences surrounding the word.

▶ A Guatemalan woman walking home from a rural market

Differentiated Instruction

The following Teacher Edition strategies are suitable for students of varying abilities.

Advanced Readers, pp. 106, 119
English Language Learners, p. 112
Gifted and Talented Students, pp. 112, 115
Less Proficient Readers, pp. 100, 105, 119
Special Needs Students, pp. 100, 105, 115, 120

Bibliography

For the Teacher
Ancona, George. *The Piñata Maker: El Piñatero.* Harcourt, 1994.
Nye, Naomi Shihab, ed. *The Tree is Older Than You Are: A Bilingual Gathering of Poems and Stories from Mexico with Paintings by Mexican Artists.* Simon, 1995.
St. George, Judith. *Panama Canal: Gateway to the World.* Putnam, 1989.

For the Student
L1 Herrera, Juan Felipe. *Calling the Doves/El canta de las palomas.* Children's Book Press, 1995.
L2 Rummel, Jack. *Mexico.* Chelsea, 1990.
L3 Castañada, Omar S. *Among the Volcanoes.* Lodestar, 1992.

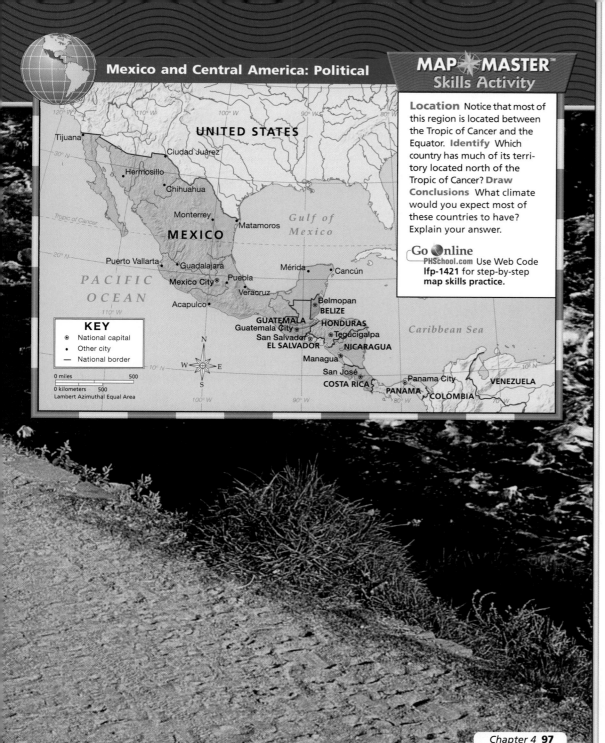

Mexico and Central America: Political

UNITED STATES

Tijuana
Ciudad Juárez
Hermosillo
Chihuahua
Monterrey
Matamoros
Gulf of Mexico
MEXICO
Tropic of Cancer
Puerto Vallarta
Guadalajara
Puebla
Mérida
Cancún
Mexico City
Veracruz
Acapulco
PACIFIC OCEAN
Belmopan
BELIZE
GUATEMALA
Guatemala City
HONDURAS
San Salvador
Tegucigalpa
EL SALVADOR
NICARAGUA
Managua
San José
Panama City
COSTA RICA
PANAMA
COLOMBIA
VENEZUELA
Caribbean Sea

KEY
⊛ National capital
• Other city
— National border

0 miles 500
0 kilometers 500
Lambert Azimuthal Equal Area

N W E S

MAP MASTER™
Skills Activity

Location Notice that most of this region is located between the Tropic of Cancer and the Equator. **Identify** Which country has much of its territory located north of the Tropic of Cancer? **Draw Conclusions** What climate would you expect most of these countries to have? Explain your answer.

Go Online
PHSchool.com Use Web Code **lfp-1421** for step-by-step map skills practice.

MAP MASTER™
Skills Activity

- Point out to students the shape of Mexico and Central America. Encourage students to trace the outline of the region, while describing its funnel shape.

- Write *Mexico* and the names of each country in Central America on the board. Then call on students to write the names of the capital cities next to the appropriate countries on the board. Point out that the map key provides a symbol for national capitals.

Go Online
PHSchool.com Students may practice their map skills using the interactive online version of this map.

Using the Visual [L2]

Reach Into Your Background Draw students' attention to the caption accompanying the picture on pages 96–97. Discuss the visual with students. What interests them about this photo? Encourage students to share details about the woman and the landscape. Have them describe the scene in the photo. Why are markets important in all countries? Have students share their ideas.

Answers

MAP MASTER™
Skills Activity
Identify Mexico
Draw Conclusions Most of the countries have a warm climate because they are close to the Equator.

Chapter Resources

Teaching Resources
[L2] Vocabulary Development, p. 259
[L2] Skills for Life, p. 244
[L2] Chapter Tests A and B, pp. 265–270

Spanish Support
[L2] Spanish Chapter Summary, p. 38
[L2] Spanish Vocabulary Development, p. 39

Media and Technology
[L1] Student Edition on Audio CD
[L1] Guided Reading Audiotapes, English and Spanish
[L2] Social Studies Skills Tutor CD-ROM
ExamView Test Bank CD-ROM

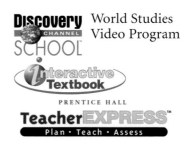

DISCOVERY CHANNEL SCHOOL — World Studies Video Program

Interactive Textbook

PRENTICE HALL

TeacherEXPRESS™
Plan • Teach • Assess

Objectives

- Use data to compare countries.
- Learn what characteristics Mexico and most Central American countries share.
- Name some key differences among the countries.

Show *Mexico and Central America: Navigating the Highs and Lows.* Ask **What are some common features of the region?** *(Most of the countries are somewhat mountainous and have a history of either earthquakes or volcanic eruptions.)* **How does Panama's location affect its role in the region?** *(Panama's location was ideal for building the Panama Canal. Trade goods moving through the canal affect the economy of the entire region.)*

Prepare to Read

Build Background Knowledge L2

Tell students that they will learn about Mexico and each country in Central America as they read the Country Databank. Show the World Studies video, telling students to note two or three facts about Mexico and Central America as they watch. Ask students to share what they know about Mexico and Central America and what they found interesting in the World Studies Video Overview. List the students' ideas on the board. Tell them that what they learn in this chapter may overturn some of their ideas about the region.

Mexico and Central America: Navigating the Highs and Lows, **World Studies Video Program**

Guide for Reading

This section provides an introduction to the eight countries that make up the region of Mexico and Central America.

- Look at the map on the previous page and then read the paragraphs below to learn about each nation.
- Analyze the data to compare the countries.
- What are the characteristics that most of the countries share?
- What are some key differences among the countries?

Viewing the Video Overview

View the World Studies Video Overview to learn more about each of the countries. As you watch, answer this question:

- Seven countries make up Central America. How were the borders of many countries determined?

Explore the geography of Mexico and Central America.

Belize

Capital	Belmopan
Land Area	8,805 sq mi; 22,806 sq km
Population	262,999
Ethnic Group(s)	mestizo, Creole, Maya, Garifuna
Religion(s)	Roman Catholic, Protestant
Government	parliamentary democracy
Currency	Belizean dollar
Leading Exports	sugar, bananas, citrus, clothing, fish products, molasses, wood
Language(s)	English (official), English Creole, Spanish, Mayan, Garifuna (Carib)

Belize (buh LEEZ) is a small country on the Caribbean coast of Central America. It is bordered on the north by Mexico and on the south and west by Guatemala. Much of Belize is rain forest. After a 1961 hurricane severely damaged the former capital, Belize City, the new capital of Belmopan was built. However, Belize City is still the country's largest and most important city. Formerly known as British Honduras, Belize was the last British colony in North America. It didn't become independent until 1981. Today, its government is based on the British model.

Jaguar in Belize

Costa Rica

Capital	San José
Land Area	19,560 sq mi; 50,660 sq km
Population	3.8 million
Ethnic Group(s)	white, mestizo, black, indigenous Indian, East Asian
Religion(s)	Roman Catholic, Protestant
Government	democratic republic
Currency	Costa Rican colón
Leading Exports	coffee, bananas, sugar, pineapples, textiles, electronics
Language(s)	Spanish (official), English Creole, Bribri, Cabecar

Costa Rica (KAHS tah REE kuh) is a narrow country located between the Pacific Ocean and the Caribbean Sea. It is bordered by Nicaragua and Panama. Even though its name means "rich coast," few riches were found there, and the Spanish colony grew slowly. Costa Rica gained its independence in 1838. Today it is known for its stable government, democratic traditions, and the fact that its army was abolished in 1948. Wealth is more evenly divided in Costa Rica than in other countries in the region, and more government resources go to education and public welfare.

El Salvador

Capital	San Salvador
Land Area	8,000 sq mi; 20,720 sq km
Population	6.4 million
Ethnic Group(s)	mestizo, indigenous Indian, white
Religion(s)	Roman Catholic, Protestant
Government	republic
Currency	Salvadoran colón, U.S. dollar
Leading Exports	offshore assembly exports, coffee, sugar, shrimp, textiles, chemicals, electricity
Language(s)	Spanish (official)

Small and densely populated, El Salvador (el SAL vuh dawr) is one of the poorest countries in the region. It is bordered by Guatemala, Honduras, and the Pacific Ocean. A row of volcanoes runs through El Salvador. In 2001, violent earthquakes killed many people and shattered the economy. El Salvador also suffered from political unrest and a bloody civil war from 1979 to 1992. For much of its history, El Salvador's economy depended on coffee, but manufacturing increased in the 1960s when El Salvador joined the Central American Common Market.

Guatemala

Capital	Guatemala City
Land Area	41,865 sq mi; 108,430 sq km
Population	13.3 million
Ethnic Group(s)	mestizo, indigenous Indian, white
Religion(s)	Roman Catholic, Protestant, traditional beliefs
Government	constitutional democratic republic
Currency	quetzal
Leading Exports	coffee, sugar, bananas, fruits and vegetables, cardamom, meat, apparel, petroleum, electricity
Language(s)	Spanish (official), Quiché, Cakchiquel, Kekchi

One third of the people in Central America live in Guatemala (gwaht uh MAH luh), and Guatemala City is the largest city in Central America. Guatemala is bordered by Mexico, Belize, Honduras, and El Salvador as well as the Caribbean Sea and the Pacific Ocean. Earthquakes, volcanic eruptions, and hurricanes have caused repeated disasters. Guatemala was once home to the ancient Mayan civilization. More recently, it has suffered from harsh military dictatorships, civil war, and discrimination against its large Indian population.

Instruct

Introducing Mexico and Central America L2

Guided Instruction

■ Read each country paragraph as a class using the Oral Cloze strategy (TE, p. T33). Then, ask students to read through each data table.

■ Ask **Which country has the largest land area?** (*Mexico, with 742,486 sq mi/ 1,923,040 sq km*) **Which has the smallest land area?** (*El Salvador, with 8,000 sq mi/ 21,720 sq km*)

■ Discuss the religions listed for each country. **What religions do almost all of the countries share?** (*Roman Catholic and Protestant*) **What countries are exceptions?** (*Some Guatemalans hold traditional beliefs.*)

■ Ask **Which country does not use Spanish as its official language?** (*The official language of Belize is English.*) Have students study the information on Belize, then speculate why Belize uses English instead of Spanish. (*Belize has strong ties to Great Britain. It was a British colony rather than a Spanish colony, and did not become independent until 1981.*)

■ Ask **How is Costa Rica different from other countries in the region?** (*Costa Rica gained independence early; has abolished its army; and allows wealth to be distributed more evenly.*)

Background: Links Across Time

The Quiché Maya of Guatemala

The Quiché Maya lived in Guatemala as early as 1500 B.C. During that time they had an advanced civilization that included political, social, and class structures. Their history and beliefs are written in the Quiché language in the *Popol Vuh,* which includes a list of their kings until 1550. Today, the Quiché language is spoken by about 700,000 people, more than any other Mayan language.

Independent Practice

■ Give students *Outline Maps 6 and 7.*

All in One Latin America Teaching Resources, *Outline Map 6: Mexico; Outline Map 7: Central America and the Caribbean,* pp. 253–254

■ Ask them to choose one type of data in the Country Databank (such as Government or Official Language) and express it on their maps. Guide them to avoid Ethnic Groups and Leading Exports. Refer them to p. 97 for a map of the region.

■ Remind them to create a map key that clearly explains the meaning of any colors or symbols on their maps.

■ Students should also include the capital of each country on their maps.

Monitor Progress

Circulate to make sure students have chosen appropriate data and are expressing it correctly.

Introducing Mexico and Central America

Honduras

Capital	Tegucigalpa
Land Area	43,201 sq mi; 111,890 sq km
Population	6.6 million
Ethnic Group(s)	mestizo, indigenous Indian, black, white
Religion(s)	Roman Catholic, Protestant
Government	democratic constitutional republic
Currency	Lempira
Leading Exports	coffee, bananas, shrimp, lobster, meat, zinc, lumber
Language(s)	Spanish (official), Black Carib, English Creole

Honduras (hahn DOOR us) stretches from the Caribbean Sea to the Pacific Ocean. It is also bordered by Guatemala, El Salvador, and Nicaragua. Much of the country is mountainous, and the Mosquito Coast on the Caribbean has few people. Most of the population lives in the central highlands. During the early 1900s, foreign-owned banana plantations dominated the economy, and Honduras was ruled by a series of military governments. There was a return to democracy in 1984, and diversification of the economy began. In 1998, the country was devastated by Hurricane Mitch, and it is still recovering from this disaster.

Mayan statue at Copán in Honduras

***The Flower Carrier* (1935) by Mexican artist Diego Rivera**

Mexico

Capital	Mexico City
Land Area	742,486 sq mi; 1,923,040 sq km
Population	103.4 million
Ethnic Group(s)	mestizo, Amerindian, European
Religion(s)	Roman Catholic, Protestant
Government	federal republic
Currency	Mexican peso
Leading Exports	manufactured goods, oil and oil products, silver, fruits, vegetables, coffee, cotton
Language(s)	Spanish (official), Nahuatl, Mayan, Zapotec, Mixtec

Mexico (MEK sih koh) is located south of the United States and northwest of Central America. It stretches from the Pacific Ocean to the Gulf of Mexico and the Caribbean Sea. Like the United States, Mexico is a federal republic. It has 31 states. In 1995, a rebellion by Native Americans in the state of Chiapas was put down by the government. President Vicente Fox, elected in 2000, moved quickly to bring peace to Chiapas. Mexico is a major oil producer, but also has considerable foreign debt.

100 Latin America

Differentiated Instruction

For Special Needs Students L1

Have students become more familiar with the region through the flyover, time line, and photographs for this region on the Passport to the World CD ROM.

◉ **Passport to the World CD-ROM**

For Less Proficient Readers L1

If students are having trouble comparing the data, have them create a chart that will show all of the information in one place. Have them complete the charts in groups of two or three.

Nicaragua

Capital	Managua
Land Area	46,430 sq mi; 120,254 sq km
Population	5.2 million
Ethnic Group(s)	mestizo, white, black, indigenous Indian
Religion(s)	Roman Catholic, Protestant
Government	republic
Currency	Córdoba oro
Leading Exports	coffee, shrimp and lobster, cotton, tobacco, beef, sugar, bananas, gold
Language(s)	Spanish (official), English Creole, Miskito

Nicaragua (nik uh RAH gwuh) stretches across Central America from the Caribbean Sea to the Pacific Ocean. It is bordered on the north by Honduras and on the south by Costa Rica. Like its neighbors, Nicaragua has a row of volcanoes and has experienced many eruptions and earthquakes. After the overthrow of a 40-year dictatorship in 1979, Nicaragua was plunged into civil war, which ended in 1990. In 1998, the country was devastated by Hurricane Mitch and is still recovering from the aftermath of the hurricane and the years of civil war.

Panama

Capital	Panama City
Land Area	29,340 sq mi; 75,990 sq km
Population	2.9 million
Ethnic Group(s)	mestizo, mixed black and indigenous Indian, white, indigenous Indian
Religion(s)	Roman Catholic, Protestant
Government	constitutional democracy
Currency	Balboa
Leading Exports	bananas, shrimp, sugar, coffee, clothing
Language(s)	Spanish (official), English Creole, indigenous Indian languages

The narrow country of Panama (PAN uh mah) has been both a barrier and a bridge between the Atlantic and Pacific oceans. It is bordered on the west by Costa Rica and on the east by the South American nation of Colombia. At first, Panama's rough terrain and rain forests hindered travel across the isthmus. The Panama Canal, which opened in 1914, made Panama a main shipping route and led to its economic growth. Most Panamanians live near the canal. Panama City is located at the canal's Pacific entrance. Another major city, Colón, is found near the Caribbean entrance to the canal.

SOURCES: DK World Desk Reference Online; *CIA World Factbook,* 2002; *The World Almanac,* 2003

Assessment

Comprehension and Critical Thinking

1. Compare and Contrast Compare the physical size and the population size of Honduras and Guatemala.

2. Draw Conclusions What are the characteristics that most of the countries share?

3. Compare and Contrast What are some key differences among the countries?

4. Categorize What kinds of products are the major exports of this region?

5. Infer What can you infer about a country if many of its exports are made in factories?

6. Make a Bar Graph Create a bar graph showing the population of the countries in the region.

Keeping Current

Access the **DK World Desk Reference Online** at **PHSchool.com** for up-to-date information about all eight countries in this chapter.

Go Online
PHSchool.com

Web Code: lfe-1410

Assess and Reteach

Assess Progress

- Ask students to return to the list of their impressions about Mexico and Central America. How many of them turned out to be untrue?
- Ask students to answer the Assessment questions.

Reteach L1

If students are having trouble analyzing the data, ask them to concentrate on only two countries. Have them create a simple table with the following heads: **Similarities** and **Differences.** Have them study the two countries they have chosen and record similarities between them in one column and differences in another. Then ask them to write one sentence summarizing the similarities and another sentence explaining the differences.

Extend L3

 Have students choose one country in the Country Databank. Ask them to research the country, using the DK World Desk Reference Online as a starting point. Then, have them create a paragraph, short story, chart, graph, map, or illustration about the country to add to their portfolios.

Answers

Assessment

1. The two countries are roughly the same size, but Guatemala has 6.7 million more people.

2. Most of the countries share the Roman Catholic and Protestant religions and have had political upheavals.

3. Belize uses English as its official language; Costa Rica has had less political turmoil.

4. crops such as coffee or bananas

5. The country is fairly industrialized.

6. Students' bar graphs should reflect the countries' populations accurately. Use *Rubric for Assessing a Bar Graph* to evaluate students' work.

   Latin America Teaching Resources, *Rubric for Assessing a Bar Graph,* p. 260

Objectives
Social Studies
1. Learn what life is like for people in rural Mexico.
2. Find out why many Mexicans have been moving from the countryside to the cities.
3. Understand why the growth of Mexico City presents challenges for the people and the environment.

Reading/Language Arts
Use context clues to determine the meaning of unfamiliar words.

Prepare to Read

Build Background Knowledge L2
Tell students that they will learn about life in Mexico in this section. Ask students to list two ideas about country life and two ideas about city life. Model the thought process by encouraging them to think about housing, transportation, jobs, and schools. Conduct an Idea Wave (TE, p. T35) to generate a list.

Set a Purpose for Reading L2
- Preview the Objectives.
- Read each statement in the *Reading Readiness Guide* out loud. Ask students to mark the statements true or false.

  All in One Latin America Teaching Resources, *Reading Readiness Guide,* p. 228

- Have the groups discuss the statements in pairs or groups of four, then mark their guides again. Use the Numbered Heads participation structure (TE, p. T36) to call on students to share their group's perspectives.

Vocabulary Builder
Preview Key Terms L2
Pronounce each Key Term and then ask the students to say the word with you. Provide a simple explanation, such as "A migrant worker might be hired to pick tomatoes in one place and apples in another."

Prepare to Read

Objectives
In this section you will
1. Learn what life is like for people in rural Mexico.
2. Find out why many Mexicans have been moving from the countryside to the cities.
3. Understand why the growth of Mexico City presents challenges for people and the environment.

Taking Notes
As you read this section, look for ways that life is similar and different in rural and in urban Mexico. Copy the Venn diagram below and record your findings in it.

Life in Mexico

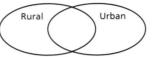

Rural   Urban

🎯 Target Reading Skill
Use Context Clues When you come across an unfamiliar word, you can often figure out its meaning from clues in the context. The context refers to the surrounding words, phrases, and sentences. Sometimes the context will define the word. In this example, the phrase in italics explains what smog is: "Smog, *a low-lying layer of polluted air,* hung over the city."

Key Terms
- **migrant worker** (MY grunt WUR kur) *n.* a laborer who travels from one area to another, picking crops that are in season
- **plaza** (PLAH zuh) *n.* a public square at the center of a village, a town, or a city
- **squatter** (SKWAHT ur) *n.* a person who settles on someone else's land without permission

---

Using oxen to plow a field

Most farm families in Mexico are poor. Many are campesinos. Some work their own small farms. They often plow the land and harvest their crops by hand because they cannot afford expensive farm machinery. Other campesinos do not own land. They work on large farms owned by rich landowners. These **migrant workers** travel from one area to another, picking the crops that are in season.

Mexico's population has risen dramatically over the last 30 years. The country's population is growing at one of the highest rates in the world. There is not enough farm work for so many people. A large family cannot support itself on a small farm. And there are not enough jobs for all the migrant workers.

Many rural Mexicans are moving from the countryside to Mexico City. Why are they making this move? How does moving to the city change their lives? How is this trend changing the country of Mexico?

🎯 Target Reading Skill L2
Use Context Clues Point out the Target Reading Skill. Tell students that information surrounding an unknown word can provide clues to the word's meaning.

Model using context clues to find the meaning of the word *support* in this sentence: "Ramiro works to support, or provide for, his family." (The phrase *or provide for* explains what support means.)

Give students *Use Context Clues: Definition/Description.* Have them complete the activity in their groups.

All in One Latin America Teaching Resources, *Use Context Clues: Definition/ Description,* p. 239

Life in Rural Mexico

Find the Plateau of Mexico on the map titled Physical Latin America on page 4. The southern part of the plateau has Mexico's best farmland. Throughout much of this region, life has changed little over many years.

Rural Villages Nearly every village in the Mexican countryside has a church and a market. At the center of most villages is a public square called a **plaza.** Farm families grow their own food. If they have extra food, they sell it at the market in the plaza. Rural people buy nearly everything they need—clothing, food, toys, and housewares—at the market rather than in stores.

Farm Work Ramiro Avila (rah MEE roh ah VEE luh) grew up in the state of Guanajuato (gwah nah HWAH toh), in central Mexico. In his small village, Ramiro knew everyone and everyone knew him.

Ramiro's family were campesinos who owned no land. Even as a young child, Ramiro had to work to help support his family. He and his father had jobs as farm laborers. They worked on someone else's farm. They made less than a dollar a day. When Ramiro was 13, his parents decided to move to Mexico City. They joined many other Mexicans who were making this move.

✔ **Reading Check** What is life like in rural Mexican villages?

A Village Market in Mexico
Like many Mexican markets, this one sells a wide variety of goods. **Infer** *Why do you think markets like this one become the center of village life?*

Vocabulary Builder

Use the information below to teach students this section's high-use words.

High-Use Word	Definition and Sample Sentence
support, p. 103	*v.* to hold up or provide for The table legs **support** the tabletop.
afford, p. 105	*v.* to be able to do without serious risks (usually used in terms of money) I could not **afford** to buy a ticket to the movie.
sturdy, p. 105	*adj.* strongly built, firm I packed the heavy books in a strong, **sturdy** box.

Instruct

Life in Rural Mexico L2

Guided Instruction

- **Vocabulary Builder** Clarify the high-use word **support** before reading.
- Read Life in Rural Mexico, using the Oral Cloze technique (TE p. T33).
- Discuss good aspects of living in the country, then possible reasons for leaving. Use the Numbered Heads participation strategy to elicit responses. *(Good—good farmland so families can grow their own food, community gatherings at plaza, everyone knows each other; Reasons for leaving—hard work, can't own their own land, poor wages as farm laborers)*
- Ask students: **Do you think the good aspects of life in rural Mexico outweigh the bad? Why?** *(Possible answers: Good—living in a community where people know you; Bad—staying poor even if you work hard, not having enough food or medicine to keep your family healthy)*

Independent Practice

Ask students to create the Taking Notes graphic organizer on a blank piece of paper. Then have them fill in the "Rural" circle with the information they have just learned. Briefly model how to identify which details to record.

Monitor Progress

As students fill in the graphic organizer, circulate and make sure individuals are choosing the correct details. Provide assistance as needed.

Answers

Infer People can get many of the things they need there; it is a central place where the community gathers.

✔ **Reading Check** Life in rural areas is good because people can grow their own food and people know each other. However, life can be difficult because many people work as farm laborers and do not make much money.

Guided Instruction L2

Ask students to study the Country Profile on this page. As a class, answer the Map and Chart Skills questions. Allow students to briefly discuss their responses with a partner before sharing answers.

Independent Practice

■ Distribute *Reading a Population Distribution Map.* Have students work with partners to complete the worksheet.

All in One Latin America Teaching Resources, *Reading a Population Distribution Map,* p. 251

■ Tell students that the map of Mexico on the worksheet shows where the people of Mexico live. Ask them to compare the map on this page of the Student Edition with the map on the worksheet. Coach students to see that the population distribution map shows that more people live in Mexico's cities, where the industrial businesses are located.

Answers

Map and Chart Skills

1. in and around cities

2. Mexico exports the most goods to the United States. The location of the United States along Mexico's border fosters this trade partnership.

3. People tend to live near where they can get jobs to support themselves. If most economic activity takes place in a country's cities, jobs and people will follow.

Go Online PHSchool.com Students can find more information about this topic on the DK World Desk Reference Online.

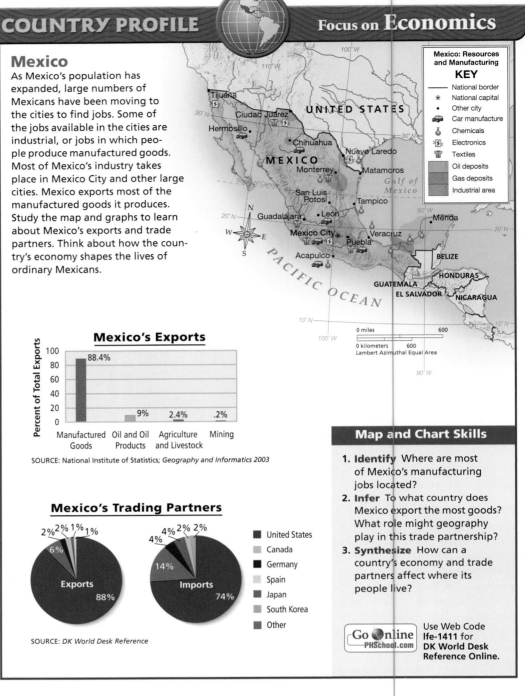

Mexico

As Mexico's population has expanded, large numbers of Mexicans have been moving to the cities to find jobs. Some of the jobs available in the cities are industrial, or jobs in which people produce manufactured goods. Most of Mexico's industry takes place in Mexico City and other large cities. Mexico exports most of the manufactured goods it produces. Study the map and graphs to learn about Mexico's exports and trade partners. Think about how the country's economy shapes the lives of ordinary Mexicans.

Mexico: Resources and Manufacturing KEY
- National border
- National capital
- Other city
- Car manufacture
- Chemicals
- Electronics
- Textiles
- Oil deposits
- Gas deposits
- Industrial area

Mexico's Exports

Percent of Total Exports

- Manufactured Goods 88.4%
- Oil and Oil Products 9%
- Agriculture and Livestock 2.4%
- Mining .2%

SOURCE: National Institute of Statistics; *Geography and Informatics 2003*

Mexico's Trading Partners

Exports 88% — 6%, 2%, 2%, 1%, 1%
Imports 74% — 14%, 4%, 4%, 2%, 2%

- United States
- Canada
- Germany
- Spain
- Japan
- South Korea
- Other

SOURCE: *DK World Desk Reference*

Map and Chart Skills

1. Identify Where are most of Mexico's manufacturing jobs located?

2. Infer To what country does Mexico export the most goods? What role might geography play in this trade partnership?

3. Synthesize How can a country's economy and trade partners affect where its people live?

Go Online PHSchool.com Use Web Code lfe-1411 for DK World Desk Reference Online.

104 Latin America

 Skills for Life Skills Mini Lesson

Using Cartographer's Tools L2

1. Teach the skill by pointing out to students that there are certain elements common to most maps. These include a scale and a compass rose.

2. Help students practice the skill by looking at the map on this page and determining how many miles Ciudad Juarez is from Chihuahua. *(a little over 200 miles or 320 kilometers)*

3. Have students apply the skill by answering this question: How far is Hermosillo from the United States border? *(about 175 miles or 280 kilometers)*

Life in the City
New arrivals to Mexico City often live in temporary houses (left). But the children still have a chance to attend school (right). **Infer** *Using clues from the photos, describe what life is like for the family shown washing clothes outdoors.*

Moving to Mexico City

Many rural people move to the cities because they cannot find work in the countryside. They hope they can make a better living in urban areas such as Mexico City. They also hope that their children will get a better education in city schools. Although city life will be very different from life in the countryside, these families leave their familiar villages behind to make a new start in the city.

Housing in the City Like thousands of other campesino families coming to the city, Ramiro's family did not have much money. When they arrived in Mexico City, they could not afford a house. They went to live in Colonia Zapata, one of many neighborhoods where poor people become squatters. A **squatter** is a person who settles on someone else's land without permission.

Many small houses built by squatters cling to the sides of a steep hill in the Colonia. The older houses near the bottom of the hill are built of concrete. However, most people cannot afford to make sturdy houses when they first arrive. Therefore many of the newer houses higher up the hill are constructed of scrap metal. Most squatter families hope that they will soon be able to buy land from the government. Then they can build their own permanent houses and even have a garden and a patio.

Work and School Once they settle in Mexico City, many families discover that it is still difficult to find work. Sometimes the men of the family look for jobs across the border, in the United States. They often work as farm laborers in states near the Mexican border, such as Texas and California. These men leave their families behind in Mexico, but many of them send money home every month.

Guided Instruction

- **Vocabulary Builder** Clarify the high-use words **afford** and **sturdy** before reading.
- Read the portrait of life in Mexico City presented in Moving to Mexico City with students. As students read, circulate and make sure individuals can answer the Reading Check question.
- Ask students to list reasons why many rural people move to the cities. *(to find better jobs, to get a better education for their children)*

Independent Practice

Have students complete the graphic organizer by filling in the "Urban" circle and adding the aspects common to rural and urban life where the circles overlap.

Monitor Progress

Show *Section Reading Support Transparency LA 39* and ask students to check their graphic organizers individually. Go over key concepts and clarify key vocabulary as needed.

📖 **Latin America Transparencies,** *Section Reading Support Transparency LA 39*

Differentiated Instruction

For Less Proficient Readers ▫L1
Have students read the section in the Reading and Vocabulary Study Guide. This version provides basic-level instruction in an interactive format with questions and write-on lines.

📖 Chapter 4, Section 1, **Latin America Reading and Vocabulary Study Guide,** pp. 42–44

For Special Needs Students ▫L1
Have students read the section as they listen to the recorded version on the Student Edition on Audio CD. Check for comprehension by pausing the CD and asking students to share their answers to the Reading Checks.

💿 Chapter 4, Section 1, **Student Edition on Audio CD**

Answer

Infer Life looks difficult for these people. They look like they are crowded into a very small space. They must use the small space around their temporary house to clean, cook, and dry their clothes after washing.

Show students *Living in Mexico: Natural Hazards.* Ask **How might Mexico's natural hazards affect families like Ramiro's?** *(A natural disaster could hit families like Ramiro's hard by endangering their lives, and destroying their makeshift housing or some of their possessions, which would be hard to replace.)*

Learn how natural hazards affect life in Mexico.

Opportunities and Challenges [L2]

Guided Instruction

- Ask students to read Opportunities and Challenges. Review the map and diagram on pp. 106 and 107 with students.

- Ask students **On the site of what city was Mexico City built?** *(the Aztec capital Tenochtitlán)* **When was Mexico city the capital of New Spain?** *(during colonial times)* **Have students describe Mexico City today.** *(It is the capital of Mexico. About 20 million people live there, and it is one of the largest cities in the world.)*

Answer

✓ Reading Check Older children may have to hold down jobs when they move from the country to the city. They may also have to cope with fathers being away for much of the year.

Use the Map Key purple **Synthesize** Students may respond that the increased size of Mexico City adds to the city's transportation problems.

Go Online PHSchool.com Students may practice their map skills using the interactive online version of this map.

Children in these families not only have to get used to city life. They must also adjust to being without their fathers for months at a time. The older children have many new responsibilities. Sometimes they care for the younger children. Or they may work at low-paying jobs in the daytime to help support their families and then go to school at night.

✓ Reading Check What new responsibilities might older children face when they move to Mexico City?

Opportunities and Challenges

Large cities in Mexico—and around the world—share many problems as well as many advantages. Even so, each city is unique. Take a closer look at Mexico City.

Mexico's Capital City Mexico City was built on the site of the Aztec capital, Tenochtitlán. During colonial times, it was the capital of New Spain. Today, it is the capital of the modern nation of Mexico.

Much of Mexico's urban population lives in Mexico City. If you count the people in outlying areas, Mexico City has nearly 20 million people. It is one of the largest cities in the world.

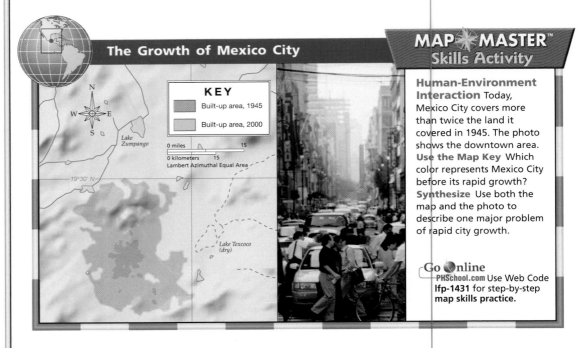

The Growth of Mexico City

KEY
- Built-up area, 1945
- Built-up area, 2000

0 miles 15
0 kilometers 15
Lambert Azimuthal Equal Area

Lake Zumpango

19°30' N

Lake Texcoco (dry)

MAP★MASTER™ Skills Activity

Human-Environment Interaction Today, Mexico City covers more than twice the land it covered in 1945. The photo shows the downtown area. **Use the Map Key** Which color represents Mexico City before its rapid growth? **Synthesize** Use both the map and the photo to describe one major problem of rapid city growth.

Go Online PHSchool.com Use Web Code lfp-1431 for step-by-step map skills practice.

Differentiated Instruction

For Advanced Readers [L3]
Have students choose one aspect about Mexico City that intrigues them. The aspect could be daily life in the city, the history of the place, or its geographical make-up. Ask them to read more about their chosen angle, and create a brief oral report to deliver to the class.

Smog in Mexico City

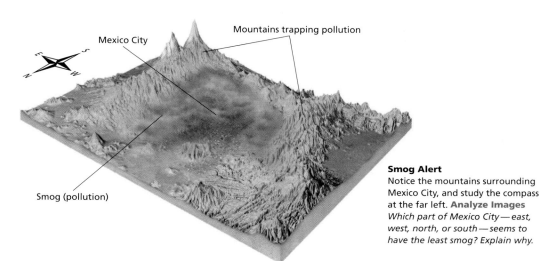

Mexico City

Mountains trapping pollution

Smog (pollution)

Smog Alert
Notice the mountains surrounding Mexico City, and study the compass at the far left. **Analyze Images** *Which part of Mexico City—east, west, north, or south—seems to have the least smog? Explain why.*

Old and New, Rich and Poor Mexico City has both modern skyscrapers and older, historic areas with two- and three-story buildings. Wide avenues and highways along with narrower side streets can barely handle the traffic of this sprawling city. The subway, the underground railroad system, carries more than four million people each day.

Small neighborhoods of very wealthy people are tucked away from the rest of the city. But most of Mexico City's residents are not wealthy. The poorest live on the outskirts of the city. Some of them must travel several hours a day just to get to their jobs.

Pollution and Geography Because of their rapid population growth, many of Mexico's large cities face problems of traffic, pollution, and water shortages. In Mexico City, millions of cars and trucks jam the streets. They compete with taxis, trolleys, and buses. The exhaust fumes from these vehicles pollute the air. Mexico City has also outgrown its fresh water supply. The city must now pump in water from sources as far as 100 miles away.

Mexico City's geography makes its pollution problem worse. The city spreads across a bowl-shaped valley. The surrounding mountains trap automobile exhaust, factory smoke, and other kinds of pollution near the city. The resulting smog cannot blow away, and it hangs over Mexico City as a brown cloud.

Target Skill — Use Context Clues
If you do not know what a subway is, look in the surrounding words for a context clue. Here, the phrase following *subway* is a definition of the term. What is a subway?

Background: Global Perspectives

Earthquakes in Urban Centers
Although the volcanoes that ring Mexico City are dormant, the land is still seismically active. One of Mexico's most destructive earthquakes occurred in Mexico City in 1985. Other cities that are located on earthquake faults include San Francisco; Tokyo, Japan; and Kathmandu, Nepal.

Guided Instruction (continued)
- Ask students to describe the factors contributing to air pollution in Mexico City. Allow students to share answers with a partner before responding. (*growing population, traffic, pollution, mountains*)
- Ask students to brainstorm ways in which the people of Mexico could address the challenges of air pollution. Conduct an Idea Wave (TE, p. T35) to generate a list of possibilities. (*improve public transportation, improve the roads, better emission standards*)
- Ask students **How do people make a living in large cities such as Mexico City?** (*working in factories or offices, selling goods from stalls on the street*)
- Ask students **What effects has NAFTA had in Mexico?** (*NAFTA increased manufacturing and exports in Mexico, but new industrial development has increased pollution in cities.*)

Independent Practice
Assign *Guided Reading and Review*.
All in One Latin America Teaching Resources, *Guided Reading and Review*, p. 229

Monitor Progress
Tell students to fill in the last column of the *Reading Readiness Guide*. Probe for what they learned that confirms or invalidates each statement.
All in One Latin America Teaching Resources, *Reading Readiness Guide*, p. 228

Target Reading Skill L2
Use Context Clues As a follow up, ask students to answer the Target Reading Skill question in the Student Edition. (*A subway is an underground railroad system.*)

Answers

Analyze Images The northern part of Mexico City has less smog because the northern edge of the city is not hemmed in by mountains.

Assess and Reteach

Assess Progress L2
Have students complete the Section Review. Administer the *Section Quiz*.

 Latin America Teaching Resources, *Section Quiz,* p. 230

Reteach L1
If students need more instruction, have them read this section in the Reading and Vocabulary Study Guide.

📖 Chapter 4, Section 1, **Latin America Reading and Vocabulary Study Guide,** pp. 42–44

Extend L3
Have students learn more about Mexico today by completing the *Enrichment* activity. Assign students to work groups to complete the project.

 Latin America Teaching Resources, *Enrichment,* p. 243

Answers

✓ Reading Check Mexico recently became a member of NAFTA, and elected Vicente Fox president. Fox promised many changes to improve life for ordinary Mexicans.

Section 1 Assessment

Key Terms
Students' sentences should reflect knowledge of each Key Term.

Target Reading Skill
Because the text says that Tenochtitlán was the capital of the Aztec civilization and also of New Spain, you can assume that it was a particularly important city.

Comprehension and Critical Thinking
1. (a) Most people who live in Mexican villages are farmers. They buy most of their goods at the village market. (b) Most people are poor and do not own the land they farm. Farming is hard work. People can earn more money working in a city.

2. (a) Poor people in Mexico City live in temporary housing and work as much as possible to make ends meet. (b) Rural Mexicans face housing problems, transportation problems, and possible separation from family members.

Vicente Fox campaigning for president

Making a Living In spite of all their problems, large cities offer many ways to make a living. Millions of people work in factories and offices. Thousands more sell goods from stalls in the street. These street vendors are an important part of city life. For example, some vendors sell bottled water while others get up early in the morning to make fresh juice.

Looking to the Future Two events have recently brought changes to Mexico. One of these was the signing of the North American Trade Agreement (NAFTA) in 1994. As you read in Chapter 2, the purpose of NAFTA was to improve the economies of Canada, the United States, and Mexico by making it easier for these countries to trade with one another.

In Mexico, manufacturing and exports did increase. So did foreign investment. But some say that poor Mexican farmers and factory workers did not benefit from NAFTA. Their incomes actually went down. What's more, new industrial development has increased pollution in Mexico's cities.

In 2000, Mexicans elected Vicente Fox president. Until Fox's election, one political party had ruled Mexico for 71 years. Fox ran against that party and promised many changes, from stamping out corruption to improving the income of Mexican workers. Fox hopes to improve life for ordinary Mexicans.

✓ Reading Check What changes has Mexico recently gone through?

Section 1 Assessment

Key Terms
Review the key terms at the beginning of this section. Use each term in a sentence that explains its meaning.

Target Reading Skill
Find the word *Tenochtitlán* on page 106. Use context to figure out its meaning. What clue helped you figure out its meaning?

Comprehension and Critical Thinking
1. (a) Recall Describe life in a Mexican village.

(b) Identify Causes Why do so many rural Mexicans move to the cities?
2. (a) Describe How do poor people live in Mexico City?
(b) Synthesize What new problems do rural Mexicans face when they move to the city?
3. (a) Describe What is Mexico City like?
(b) Identify Causes What factors cause pollution in Mexico City?
(c) Evaluate Information Identify the benefits and drawbacks of moving to Mexico City.

Writing Activity
Write an entry in your journal comparing Mexico City with your hometown. How are the two places similar and how are they different? How would your life be different if you lived in a place like Mexico City?

For: An activity on Mexico City
Visit: PHSchool.com
Web Code: lfd-1401

108 Latin America

---

3. (a) Mexico City is large, with a huge population and pollution problems.
(b) Traffic volume, high emissions, and geographic factors cause pollution in Mexico City. (c) Benefits—more jobs, better pay, more opportunities for education; Drawbacks—crowding, inadequate housing, and pollution.

Writing Activity
Use the *Rubric for Assessing a Journal Entry* to evaluate students' journal entries.

Latin America Teaching Resources, *Rubric for Assessing a Journal Entry,* p. 261

Go Online PHSchool.com Typing in the web code when prompted will bring students directly to detailed instructions for this activity.

Prepare to Read

Objectives
In this section you will
1. Learn why there is a struggle for land in Guatemala.
2. Find out how the Mayas lost their land.
3. Discover how groups are working to improve the lives of Guatemala's indigenous people.

Taking Notes
As you read this section, look for details about the Mayas' struggle for their rights. Copy the chart below, and record your findings in it.

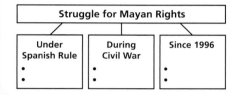

```
          Struggle for Mayan Rights

   Under         During        Since 1996
Spanish Rule   Civil War
   •              •              •
   •              •              •
```

Target Reading Skill

Use Context Clues
Context, the words and phrases surrounding a word, can help you understand a new word. One context clue is contrast, a word or words that have the opposite meaning of the unfamiliar word. In this example, the contrast with the newly arrived Spanish helps explain the word *indigenous:* "The struggle of the indigenous people of Guatemala to keep their land began when the Spanish first arrived."

Key Terms
- **ladino** (luh DEE noh) *n.* a mestizo, or person of mixed Spanish and Native American ancestry in Guatemala
- **land reform** (land ree FAWRM) *n.* the effort to distribute land more equally and fairly
- **political movement** (puh LIT ih kul MOOV munt) *n.* a large group of people who work together for political change
- **strike** (stryk) *n.* a refusal to work until certain demands of workers are met

I n Guatemala, Native Americans make up the majority of the population. They form 23 ethnic groups. Even though the indigenous groups of Guatemala are related to one another, each group is different. Each one has its own language and customs. The largest group is the Quiché Maya.

Mayan families are often poor. They raise corn on tiny plots of land, but can barely earn enough money to survive. Children often work to help support their families. Mayan girls do weaving to bring in extra money. One Mayan girl described her childhood as similar to the childhoods of "all Indian girls, at the side of my mother, making tortillas and learning to weave and embroider."

Like many other indigenous people, the Mayas have found it difficult to get an education and escape poverty. They have also struggled to preserve their traditional culture as they become part of modern Guatemala.

Modern Mayan women weave much as their ancestors did.

Chapter 4 Section 2 **109**

Target Reading Skill

Use Context Clues Point out the Target Reading Skill. Tell students that information surrounding an unfamiliar word can provide clues to the word's meaning. Explain that sometimes a paragraph may contain words that contrast, or are opposite in meaning to, an unfamiliar word in the paragraph.

Model how to use context clues to figure out the meaning of the word *rebel* in this sentence from page 112: "Then government military forces fought **rebel** groups that were living in the highlands." (The word *rebel* contrasts with *government military forces*.)

Give students *Use Context Clues: Compare and Contrast.* Have them complete the activity in their groups.

All in One Latin America Teaching Resources, *Use Context Clues: Compare and Contrast,* p. 240

Objectives
Social Studies
1. Learn why there is a struggle for land in Guatemala.
2. Find out how the Mayas lost their land.
3. Discover how groups are working to improve the lives of Guatemala's indigenous people.

Reading/Language Arts
Use context clues that show contrast to determine the meaning of unfamiliar words.

Prepare to Read

Build Background Knowledge L2
Ask students to preview the photographs in this section and to write down what these photographs show about the Mayas. Conduct an Idea Wave (TE, p. T35) to allow students to share their ideas.

Set a Purpose for Reading L2
- Preview the Objectives.
- Read each statement in the *Reading Readiness Guide* aloud. Ask students to mark the statements true or false.

  All in One Latin America Teaching Resources, *Reading Readiness Guide,* p. 232

- Have students discuss the statements in pairs or groups of four, then mark their worksheets again. Use the Numbered Heads participation structure (TE, p. T36) to call on students to share their group's perspectives.

Vocabulary Builder
Preview Key Terms L2
Pronounce each Key Term, then ask the students to say the word with you. Provide a simple explanation such as, "During a strike, workers may stop working until they get better wages or working conditions."

Instruct

The Struggle for Land L2

Guided Instruction

- **Vocabulary Builder** Clarify the high-use words **resource** and **erosion** before reading.

- Read The Struggle for Land using the Structured Silent Reading technique (TE, p. T34).

- Discuss with students why Mayan families in Guatemala are unable to produce good crops on their land. *(Much of the land in Guatemala belongs to a few rich families and the only land available to the Mayas is in the mountains. The soil of the Guatemalan highlands is not very good and soil erosion makes farming difficult.)*

- Ask students **Why do you think that wealthy landowners have resisted land reform?** *(The wealthy landowners probably do not want to give up their land to poorer farmers. They may want to protect what they have.)*

Independent Practice

Assign *Guided Reading and Review.*

■ **All in One Latin America Teaching Resources,** *Guided Reading and Review,* p. 233

Monitor Progress

Make sure that students are correctly completing the *Guided Reading and Review* worksheet. Provide assistance as necessary.

⟳ Target Reading Skill L2

Use Context Clues As a follow up, ask students to answer the Target Reading Skill question in the Student Edition. *(A hacienda is a big farm, or plantation, where crops are grown to sell abroad.)*

Answers

Analyze Images The people who live on this farm may be able to raise only enough food for themselves, possibly with some left over to sell to others.

✓ Reading Check The best land is used for haciendas, where crops are grown to sell abroad. Campesinos and Native Americans grow crops on small farms in the highlands. These crops are often sold locally.

Farming in the Mountains
This small Mayan farm clings to a Guatemalan hillside. **Analyze Images** Look carefully at the buildings and the fields. What do these details tell you about making a living on this farm?

Use Context Clues
If you do not remember what *hacienda* means, consider these context clues. A hacienda is "where crops are grown to sell abroad." Haciendas are also contrasted with small farms. Therefore a hacienda is _____.

The Struggle for Land

Land is a valuable resource in Guatemala, as it is in all of Latin America. Fair distribution of the land is a serious problem throughout the region.

The People and the Land Much of the land in Guatemala belongs to a few rich families. The rich landowners of Guatemala are **ladinos** (luh DEE nohz), mestizos who are descended from Native Americans and Spaniards. Native Americans who follow European ways are also considered to be ladinos.

For many years, most Mayas have lived in the mountains because it was the only land available to Native Americans. Although Mayan families work hard on their farms, they often fail to produce good crops. The soil of the Guatemalan highlands is not very good. Soil erosion makes farming even more difficult.

Land Distribution In many Latin American countries, the best land is used for haciendas where crops are grown to sell abroad. Guatemalan haciendas produce coffee, cotton, sugar cane, and bananas. In contrast, campesinos and Native Americans grow maize, beans, and squash on small farms in the highlands. These crops are often sold in village markets and provide food for the local population.

Since the 1930s, **land reform,** the effort to distribute land more equally, has been a major goal of many reform and political groups. The wealthy landowners, who have the greatest political power in many Latin American countries, have often resisted these reforms. Clashes between those in favor of reform and those against it have even led to violence and civil war. You will read about the Guatemalan civil war later in this section.

✓ Reading Check How is land distributed in many Latin American countries?

Vocabulary Builder

Use the information below to teach students this section's high-use words.

High-Use Word	Definition and Sample Sentence
resource, p. 110	*n.* a supply of something useful Iron is a useful natural **resource.**
erosion, p. 110	*n.* the slow wearing away by water and wind Tree roots hold down soil and stop **erosion.**
civilian, p. 112	*n.* a person who is not a member of the armed forces I am a **civilian,** not a soldier.
violation, p. 113	*n.* the breaking of a rule, law, or promise Speeding is a **violation** of the law.

The Mayas Lose Their Land

In order to get enough land to make a living—or even to keep the land they have—the Mayas of Guatemala have faced many challenges. One challenge relates to their culture. Indigenous people do not always think of themselves as citizens of the country in which they live. A Mayan woman is more likely to think of herself as a Maya than as a Guatemalan.

Discovery SCHOOL Video
Learn about growing coffee in Guatemala.

Show *Guatemala's Coffee Economy.* Ask **Why is Guatemala a good place for growing coffee?** *(It has the high altitude, tropical climate, and rich volcanic soil needed to grow high quality coffee beans.)*

COUNTRY PROFILE · Focus on **Culture**

Guatemala

Guatemala today has two distinct cultures: Indian and ladino. Ladinos speak Spanish, the country's official language, and live mainly in the cities. The majority of Guatemala's population, however, is Mayan Indian. Most Mayas live in villages and towns in the country's highlands. From town to town, Mayan groups speak slightly different languages and create unique art. Their art includes distinctive fabric patterns woven by each group. Study the map and charts to learn more about Guatemalan culture.

Guatemala: Languages
KEY
- Spanish
- Native American
- ⊛ National capital
- • Other city

MEXICO
BELIZE
GUATEMALA
San Juan Cotzal · Cobán
Rabinal
Chichicastenango
Patzún
Guatemala City
HONDURAS
Puerto Barrios
Caribbean Sea
San José
EL SALVADOR
PACIFIC OCEAN

0 miles 100
0 kilometers 100
Mercator

Ethnic Groups

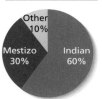
Other 10%
Mestizo 30%
Indian 60%

SOURCE: *DK World Desk Reference*

Mayan Towns

Town Name	Language	Sample Fabric
Patzún	Cakchiquel	
Cobán	Kekchí	
Chichicastenango	Quiché	
San Juan Cotzal	Ixil	
Rabinal	Pokomchi	

Map and Chart Skills

1. **Identify** In what parts of the country is Spanish spoken? What language would you expect the people in Rabinal to speak?
2. **Infer** What advantages and disadvantages result from having so many languages in one country?

Go Online PHSchool.com Use Web Code lfe-1412 for **DK World Desk Reference Online.**

Skills Mini Lesson

Problem Solving

1. Teach the skill by reviewing with students the problem of unfair distribution of land in Guatemala.
2. Have students practice the skill by brainstorming possible solutions to the problem.

L2 3. Have students apply the skill by evaluating the possible solutions. Which would be the most effective? Why? Have them choose the most effective solution.

The Mayas Lose Their Land **L2**

Guided Instruction

- **Vocabulary Builder** Clarify the high-use word **civilian** before reading.
- Read The Mayas Lose Their Land.
- Discuss with students why Native Americans were left with little political power or land after the Spanish invasion. *(The Spanish conquistadors claimed the country's land. The Spanish had political power.)*

Independent Practice

Ask students to create the Taking Notes graphic organizer on a blank piece of paper. Have them fill in the first two segments.

Monitor Progress

As students fill in the graphic organizer, circulate and make sure that individuals are choosing the correct details.

COUNTRY PROFILE
Focus on **Culture**

Guided Instruction **L2**

Ask students to study the Country Profile on this page. As a class, answer the Map and Chart Skills questions.

Independent Practice

For practice in reading circle graphs, have students complete *Reading a Circle Graph* in pairs.

All in One Latin America Teaching Resources, *Reading a Circle Graph,* p. 252

Answers

Map and Chart Skills

1. in northern Guatemala and in southern Guatemala; Pokomchi.
2. Advantages: Creates diversity and keeps traditions alive. Disadvantages: Causes communication problems.

Read the **Citizen Heroes** text on this page. **Ask students How has Tzoc worked for change in Guatemala?** *(She has helped Mayan women fight for their rights.)*

Working for a Better Life L2

Guided Instruction
- **Vocabulary Builder** Clarify the high-use word **violation** before reading.
- Have students read Working for a Better Life. As students read, circulate and make sure they can answer the Reading Check question.
- Have students look at the photo on this page. Ask how these demonstrators are voicing their opinion. *(by organizing in a group and carrying signs)*
- Ask **Why are Mayan language radio programs, books, and newspapers important?** *(They give the Mayas access to current events, literature, and information.)*

Independent Practice
Ask students to fill in the last segment of their graphic organizers.

Monitor Progress
- Show *Section Reading Support Transparency LA 40* and ask students to check their graphic organizers individually. Go over key concepts and clarify key vocabulary as needed.

  📖 **Latin America Transparencies,** *Section Reading Support Transparency LA 40*

- Tell students to fill in the last column of the *Reading Readiness Guide.* Probe for what they learned that confirms or invalidates each statement.

  All in One **Latin America Teaching Resources,** *Reading Readiness Guide,* p. 232

Answers

✓ Reading Check Some Mayas were killed or forced to leave the country. Soldiers claimed their land and many Mayas lost their belongings.

Citizen Heroes ★

Justina Tzoc: A Voice for Change

For many years, Justina Tzoc (hoo STEE nah tsohk) has worked to help Mayan women in remote areas of Guatemala. She calls her effort "the kind of work that has no beginning and no end." During the Guatemalan civil war, Tzoc faced many dangers as she helped these women organize to fight for their rights. Although the civil war is over, Tzoc's work goes on. According to Tzoc, the indigenous women of Guatemala will continue to work "so that we are recognized—have a voice and a vote."

112 Latin America

In addition, the majority of Native Americans in Guatemala cannot read or write. For these two reasons, most Mayas have not filed any papers with the government showing that they own land. Even after they have worked hard for many years to grow crops on a piece of land, a Mayan family often has no way to prove that their land belongs to them.

A 500-Year-Old Struggle The indigenous people of Guatemala have fought to keep both their land and their culture for more than 500 years. This struggle began when the Spanish first arrived in the Americas.

The Spanish conquistadors conquered the Native Americans by force. Many were killed. Others died of hunger or the hardships of slavery. Still others died from European diseases. In many Latin American countries, there are few indigenous people left. In contrast, Guatemala is largely Native American. However, the Native Americans have little political power or land.

Civil War Beginning around 1960, a civil war raged in Guatemala for more than 30 years. First, an elected leader who favored land reform was overthrown by the military. Then government military forces fought rebel groups that were living in the highlands. Armed fighters were not the only ones killed in the fighting. Thousands of civilians were also killed, and many others fled the country. Those who fought for human rights or opposed the government were treated harshly by a series of military rulers.

The Mayas suffered during the civil war. In hundreds of villages throughout Guatemala, soldiers came to claim the Mayas' land. Many Mayas lost all of their belongings and were forced out of their villages. Some had to move to other countries to live.

✓ Reading Check **What happened to the Mayas during the civil war?**

Working for a Better Life

Some Mayas remained in Guatemala during the civil war. They started **political movements,** which are large groups of people who work together for political change. One such movement, called Nukuj Akpop (nooh KOO ahk POHP), still works to fight poverty and bring human rights to Mayas.

A political demonstration in Guatemala City

Differentiated Instruction

For English Language Learners L1
Pair students with a partner who is a native English speaker to read the section while listening to the Student Edition on Audio CD. Students should pause the CD frequently to allow the English speaker to help the English learner with any questions.

 Chapter 4, Section 2, **Student Edition on Audio CD**

For Gifted and Talented L3
Ask students to research the culture of the Mayas. Have each student choose one aspect of Mayan culture, such as food, clothing, or ceremonies. Have students create a poster about their topic to display for the class.

Defending Campesino Rights Today, Mayan political movements seek to defend campesino rights. They help villages plan ways to protect themselves. They teach people the history of their land and how to read. They also help organize meetings, protests, and strikes. A **strike** is a refusal to work until certain demands of workers are met. Above all, these political movements defend Native American land rights.

Changes Come to Guatemala These efforts brought change in Guatemala. For the first time, Mayas gained a voice in their government. Mayan priests were appointed to advise government officials about Mayan culture. Radio programs were broadcast in Mayan languages, and Mayan-language books and newspapers also appeared.

In 1996, agreements were signed ending the civil war. Among these was a promise that indigenous communities would be rebuilt. However, not all of these agreements have been carried out. Violations of human rights by the government increased again in 2000, and many Guatemalans protested in the streets. The fight for the rights of the Mayas—and for all the ordinary people of Guatemala—continues.

✔ **Reading Check** How do political movements try to help the Mayas?

An Indian man selling vegetables at a Guatemalan market

⭐ Section 2 Assessment

Key Terms
Review the key terms at the beginning of this section. Use each term in a sentence that explains its meaning.

◑ Target Reading Skill
Find the word *civilians* on page 112. Look for a contrast near the word. How does this contrast help you define *civilians*?

Comprehension and Critical Thinking
1. (a) **Describe** How is land used in Guatemala?
(b) **Identify Causes** Why do the Mayas often fail to earn a living from their land?

2. (a) **Recall** What are two reasons the Mayas lost their land?
(b) **Synthesize** Explain how the Mayas have been at a disadvantage in their struggle against their rulers.
3. (a) **Identify** What are two ways that political movements work to help the Mayas?
(b) **Summarize** What kinds of changes have these groups brought about?
(c) **Predict** Do you think life will improve for the Mayas in the decades ahead? Explain.

Writing Activity
Suppose you are a reporter for a radio news program. Write a report on the situation of the Mayas in Guatemala. Present background information about Mayan culture and history. Then tell your listeners about current conditions. Be sure that your report can be read in two to three minutes.

> **Writing Tip** Introduce your report with a "hook," an interesting event or observation that will make your listeners stay tuned.

Chapter 4 Section 2 **113**

Section 2 Assessment

Key Terms
Students' sentences should reflect knowledge of each Key Term.

◑ Target Reading Skill
A contrast near the word *civilians* is *armed fighters*. This contrast shows that a civilian is someone who is not a member of the armed forces.

Comprehension and Critical Thinking
1. (a) Guatemalan haciendas produce crops to sell abroad, while campesinos and Native Americans grow crops on small farms. (b) Poor soil and erosion make farming difficult.

2. (a) Possible answers: the invasion of the Spanish conquistadors; civil war in the 1950s; lack of proper paperwork. (b) The Mayas have a historical disadvantage; also many cannot read or write.

3. (a) Possible answers: defending campesino rights and Native American land rights; teaching people their history and how to read; organizing meetings, protests, and strikes. (b) Mayas have gained a voice in their government; Mayan-language books and newspapers have been created. (c) Students' opinions will vary, but should reflect what they have learned in this section.

Assess and Reteach

Assess Progress [L2]
Have students complete the Section Assessment. Administer the *Section Quiz.*

All in One Latin America Teaching Resources, *Section Quiz, p. 234*

Reteach [L1]
If students need more instruction, have them read this section in the Reading and Vocabulary Study Guide.

Chapter 4, Section 2, **Latin America Reading and Vocabulary Study Guide,** pp. 45–47

Extend [L3]
Have students extend their knowledge by completing the *Book Project: Latin America in the News.*

All in One Latin America Teaching Resources, *Book Project: Latin America in the News,* pp. 76–78

Answers

✔ **Reading Check** by seeking to defend their rights, especially land rights.

Writing Activity
Use the *Rubric for Assessing a Report* to evaluate students' reports.

All in One Latin America Teaching Resources, *Rubric for Assessing a Report,* p. 262

Objective
Learn how to infer and draw conclusions.

Prepare to Read

Build Background Knowledge L2
Ask students to suppose that a friend has asked them on an outing to a surprise location, telling them to bring a towel, sunscreen, sunglasses, and a bathing suit. Then ask what they can infer from these items and how these inferences help them to conclude where their friend is taking them. *(A towel and bathing suit indicate swimming; sunglasses and sunscreen indicate outdoors; therefore they are probably going to the beach or an outdoor pool.)*

Instruct

Drawing Inferences and Conclusions L2

Guided Instruction
- Read the passage, then read the steps to drawing inferences and conclusions as a class and write them on the board.
- Practice the skill by following the steps on p. 115 as a class. Model each step in the activity by walking through how to build inferences from facts about the Mayas in Guatemala, use the facts to draw inferences, and come to a conclusion from those inferences.

Independent Practice
Assign *Skills for Life* and have students complete it individually.

All in One **Latin America Teaching Resources,** *Skills for Life,* p. 244

Monitor Progress
Check to make sure students understand the skill steps as they complete the *Skills for Life* worksheet.

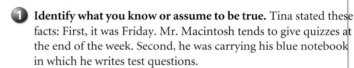

When Mr. Macintosh walked into the classroom, Tina watched him carefully.

"Uh-oh," she said quietly. "Looks like a pop quiz." Tina started flipping through the pages of last night's homework assignment.

Miguel heard Tina. "Why do you think there's going to be a quiz?" he whispered to Tina.

"For starters, it's Friday. He tends to give quizzes at the end of the week. And do you see that blue notebook he's got in his hand?" Miguel saw it. "He always writes test questions in it. Whenever he pulls it out, we have a test."

Just then Mr. Macintosh said, "Good morning, class. Please close your books for a pop quiz."

Tina was correct that the class would have a pop quiz. You can understand why. She drew good inferences and a strong conclusion.

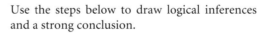

An inference is an educated guess based on facts or evidence. A conclusion is a judgment. Conclusions are often based on several inferences.

Learn the Skill
Use the steps below to draw logical inferences and a strong conclusion.

1. **Identify what you know or assume to be true.** Tina stated these facts: First, it was Friday. Mr. Macintosh tends to give quizzes at the end of the week. Second, he was carrying his blue notebook in which he writes test questions.

2. **Use the facts to draw inferences.** Inferences can usually be stated as an "if . . . then" sentence. The "if" part is the facts you know. The "then" part is an educated guess that follows logically from the facts.

3. **Use two or more inferences to draw a reasoned judgment or conclusion.** From her two inferences, Tina was able to draw this conclusion: The class was about to have a pop quiz.

A protest by Mayas in
Guatemala City

Practice the Skill

Read the passage titled Working for a Better Life on pages 112 and 113. Then use the steps below to draw inferences and a conclusion about the situation of the Mayas in Guatemala.

1 Answer these questions in order to help you find facts: What have political movements done to improve life for Guatemalans? What changes have occurred in Guatemala?

2 Use the facts to create at least two inferences, or educated guesses. State your inferences as "if . . . then" sentences. For example: If Mayas learn to read, then they will be more successful at defending their rights.

3 Using the inferences you have written, what conclusion can you draw about the Mayas in Guatemala?

Apply the Skill

Turn to Section 1 of Chapter 4 and reread the passage titled Opportunities and Challenges on pages 106 and 107. Use the steps of this skill to draw inferences and a conclusion about some aspect of life in Mexico City, such as traffic or pollution.

Smog in Mexico City

Chapter 4 **115**

Assess Progress   L2
Ask students to do the Apply the Skill activity.

Reteach   L1
If students are having trouble applying the skills steps, have them review the skill using the interactive Social Studies Skills Tutor CD-ROM.

 Drawing Inferences and Conclusions, **Social Studies Skills Tutor CD-ROM**

Extend   L3
Have students find an article in a newspaper or magazine about current events and use the skill steps to draw inferences and conclusions from facts in the article.

Differentiated Instruction

For Special Needs Students   L1
Pair special needs students with more proficient students to do Level 1 of the Social Studies Skills Tutor CD-ROM. When students feel more confident, they can move onto Level 2 alone.

Drawing Inferences and Conclusions, **Social Studies Skills Tutor CD-ROM**

For Gifted and Talented   L3
Have students write a short mystery story, about one page long. Instead of revealing the conclusion at the end, tell students that they should include enough facts so the reader can make inferences, and then from those inferences try to solve the mystery. Students can then read their stories aloud while the rest of the class predicts the conclusion.

Answers
Apply the Skill

A possible answer is that because the underground railroad carries more than four million people a day *(fact)*, and roads cannot handle the amount of traffic the city has *(fact)*, you can infer that the underground railroad is very crowded and traffic on the roads moves slowly. Therefore, it must take a long time to travel from one place to another in Mexico City *(conclusion)*.

Objectives

Social Studies

1. Find out why people wanted to build a canal across the Isthmus of Panama.
2. Learn how the Panama Canal was built.
3. Understand how the canal has affected the nation of Panama.

Reading/Language Arts

Use context clues and your own knowledge to determine the meaning of unfamiliar words.

Prepare to Read

Build Background Knowledge L2

Tell students that they will learn how Panama became an important crossroads in this section. Ask students to quickly preview the headings, photos, and maps in the section. As they preview, ask students to note two or three ideas about Panama. Then ask **What makes Panama different from Guatemala and Mexico?** Use the Idea Wave participation strategy (TE, p. T35) to allow students to share their ideas.

Set a Purpose for Reading L2

- Preview the Objectives.
- Form students into pairs or groups of four. Distribute the *Reading Readiness Guide*. Ask students to fill in the first two columns of the chart. Use the Numbered Heads participation structure (TE, p. T36) to call on students to share one piece of information they already know and one piece of information they want to know.

  All in One Latin America Teaching Resources, *Reading Readiness Guide*, p. 236

Vocabulary Builder

Preview Key Terms L2

Pronounce each Key Term, and then ask students to say the word with you. Provide a simple explanation such as, "Ecotourism has sprung up because many people like to travel to different places to learn about and observe wildlife."

Panama
An Important Crossroads

Prepare to Read

Objectives

In this section you will
1. Find out why people wanted to build a canal across the Isthmus of Panama.
2. Learn how the Panama Canal was built.
3. Understand how the canal has affected the nation of Panama.

Taking Notes

As you read this section, look for the problems the builders of the Panama Canal faced and how they solved those problems. Copy the table below, and record your findings in it.

Building the Panama Canal

Problem	Solution

🎯 Target Reading Skill

Use Context Clues
Sometimes you come across a word you know that is being used in an unfamiliar way. You can use context clues and your own general knowledge to understand the new use of the word. For example, you may know that *vessel* often means "ship," and that a cargo ship carries cargo. Therefore, a water vessel is probably a container that holds, or carries, water.

Key Terms

- **Panama Canal** (PAN uh mah kuh NAL) *n.* a shipping canal across the Isthmus of Panama, linking the Atlantic Ocean to the Pacific Ocean
- **lock** (lahk) *n.* a section of waterway in which ships are raised or lowered by adjusting the water level
- **Canal Zone** (kuh NAL zohn) *n.* a 10-mile strip of land along the Panama Canal, once governed by the United States
- **ecotourism** (ek oh TOOR iz um) *n.* travel to unspoiled areas in order to learn about the environment

Statue of Vasco Nuñez de Balboa in Panama City, Panama

116 Latin America

Ever since Christopher Columbus first explored the Isthmus of Panama, the Spanish had been looking for a water route through it. They wanted to be able to sail west from Spain all the way to Asia. The Spanish were also looking for gold. In 1513, the conquistador Vasco Nuñez de Balboa heard of "a mighty sea beyond the mountains" of what is now Panama. He also heard that the streams flowing into that sea were filled with gold.

Balboa organized an expedition of Spaniards and Indians. They struggled across the isthmus, through very difficult country, for over a month. Finally Balboa waded into the Pacific Ocean, which he claimed for Spain. Balboa went on to explore the Pacific coast and found gold and other treasure there.

Balboa still hoped that a water route could be found through the isthmus. But if not, he said, "it might not be impossible to make one." The effort to create this waterway has shaped the history of the isthmus and led to the creation of the nation of Panama. Even today, geography has a major effect on Panama.

🎯 Target Reading Skill L2

Use Context Clues Point out the Target Reading Skill. Tell students that information surrounding an unknown word as well as their own knowledge can provide clues to that word's meaning.

Model using context clues to find the meaning of the word *hub* in this sentence from p. 122: "Panama is also a communications *hub.* Five international fiber-optic networks cross through Panama. Fiber-optic networks are used for long-distance telephone lines and computer networks." (*Panama is a communications center because five fiber-optic networks cross through the country. Hub must mean the center or core of something.*)

Give students *Use Context Clues: General Knowledge.* Have them complete the activity in groups.

All in One Latin America Teaching Resources, *Use Context Clues: General Knowledge,* p. 241

Why Build a Canal?

The **Panama Canal,** a manmade waterway across the Isthmus of Panama, is a shortcut through the Western Hemisphere. It is the only way to get from the Pacific Ocean to the Atlantic Ocean by ship without going all the way around South America. Sailors had dreamed of a canal through Central America since the 1500s. A canal could shorten the trip from the Atlantic to the Pacific by 7,800 miles (12,553 kilometers), saving both time and money. But it was not until the 1900s that engineers had the technology to make such a canal.

Crossing the Isthmus By 1534, the Spanish had acted on a suggestion in Balboa's report to the king of Spain. They had built a seven-foot-wide stone road across the isthmus. It was used to carry treasure to the Atlantic coast for shipment to Spain. More than 300 years later, during the California Gold Rush, prospectors wanted to get from the east coast of the United States to California as quickly as possible. An American company built a railroad to transport them across the isthmus. The first major attempt to build a canal came in 1881, when Panama was part of Colombia. Colombia gave a French company the rights to build a canal.

Passing Through the Canal
Special Panama Canal pilots steer ships through the canal. Here, the captain and first mate of a ship consult with a pilot. **Infer** *Why do you think the passage of ships through the canal is controlled so carefully?*

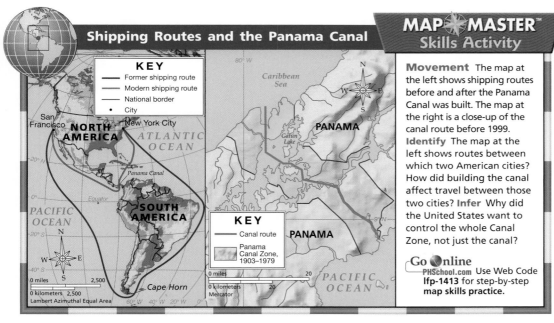

Shipping Routes and the Panama Canal

MAP MASTER™ Skills Activity

KEY
— Former shipping route
— Modern shipping route
— National border
• City

San Francisco, NORTH AMERICA, New York City, ATLANTIC OCEAN, Panama Canal, PACIFIC OCEAN, SOUTH AMERICA, Equator, Cape Horn

Caribbean Sea, PANAMA, Gatún Lake

KEY
— Canal route
Panama Canal Zone, 1903–1979
PANAMA

0 miles 2,500
0 kilometers 2,500
Lambert Azimuthal Equal Area

0 miles 20
0 kilometers 20
Mercator

Movement The map at the left shows shipping routes before and after the Panama Canal was built. The map at the right is a close-up of the canal route before 1999. **Identify** The map at the left shows routes between which two American cities? How did building the canal affect travel between those two cities? **Infer** Why did the United States want to control the whole Canal Zone, not just the canal?

Go Online
PHSchool.com Use Web Code **lfp-1413** for step-by-step map skills practice.

Vocabulary Builder

Use the information below to teach students this section's high-use words.

High-Use Word	Definition and Sample Sentence
bankrupt, p. 118	*adj.* unable to pay one's debts, or bills The **bankrupt** company could not pay its bills and went out of business.
benefit, p. 119	*v.* to be good for A good night's rest would **benefit** the team before the game.
crossroads, p. 120	*n.* a place where roads meet Meet me at the **crossroads.**
finance, p. 120	*n.* the management and use of money She was good with money, so she chose a career in **finance.**

Instruct

Why Build a Canal? L2

Guided Instruction

■ **Vocabulary Builder** Clarify the high-use words **bankrupt** and **benefit** before reading.

■ Have students read Why Build a Canal? using the Oral Cloze strategy (TE, p. T33). Review the map on p. 117 with students.

■ Discuss with students why President Roosevelt wanted to build a canal across the Isthmus of Panama. *(It would speed trade between the Atlantic and Pacific coasts and allow the American navy mobility.)*

■ Ask students **Do you think that the United States should have helped Panama to revolt against Colombia? Why or why not?** *(Yes: The United States needed to help Panama so that it could be a free country and so that the United States could build the canal. No: The United States should not have interfered with Panama and Colombia just so that it could build a canal. It should have tried further negotiations with Colombia.)*

Independent Practice

Ask students to create the Taking Notes graphic organizer on a blank piece of paper. Then have them fill in the "Problem" column with the information they have just learned.

Monitor Progress

As students fill in the graphic organizer, circulate and make sure individuals are choosing the correct details. Provide assistance as needed.

Answers

Infer probably to avoid delays and damage to the canal and to ships

MAP MASTER™ Skills Activity **Identify** New York City and San Francisco; it shortened the shipping routes between them **Infer** perhaps to protect the canal, control who used the canal, and to charge admittance fees

Go Online
PHSchool.com Students may practice their map skills using the interactive online version of this map.

Guided Instruction L2

Ask students to study the Country Profile. Point out the map, chart, and circle graph. As a class, answer the Map and Chart Skills questions. Allow students to briefly discuss their responses with a partner before sharing answers.

Independent Practice

Distribute *Outline Map 7: Central America and the Caribbean.* Have students locate and label Panama, the Atlantic Ocean, and the Pacific Ocean on their maps. Then, using the map on p. 118 as a reference, have students mark and label the approximate location of the Panama Canal on their outline maps. Assist students as necessary.

All in One Latin America Teaching Resources, *Outline Map 7: Central America and the Caribbean,* p. 254

The French Begin a Canal Digging a canal through Panama posed enormous problems. The builders had to struggle with mud slides, and a mountain range blocked the way. Much of Panama was covered with dense tropical forest. Tropical diseases killed many workers. After several years of digging and blasting, the French company went bankrupt. Work on the canal stopped.

In 1902, the United States government bought the French company's equipment. Then, the United States began negotiating with Colombia for the rights to continue building a canal.

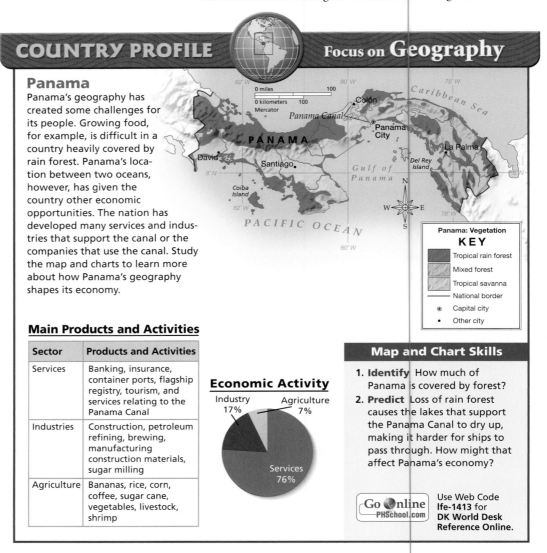

COUNTRY PROFILE — Focus on Geography

Panama

Panama's geography has created some challenges for its people. Growing food, for example, is difficult in a country heavily covered by rain forest. Panama's location between two oceans, however, has given the country other economic opportunities. The nation has developed many services and industries that support the canal or the companies that use the canal. Study the map and charts to learn more about how Panama's geography shapes its economy.

Panama: Vegetation
KEY
- Tropical rain forest
- Mixed forest
- Tropical savanna
- — National border
- ⊛ Capital city
- • Other city

Main Products and Activities

Sector	Products and Activities
Services	Banking, insurance, container ports, flagship registry, tourism, and services relating to the Panama Canal
Industries	Construction, petroleum refining, brewing, manufacturing construction materials, sugar milling
Agriculture	Bananas, rice, corn, coffee, sugar cane, vegetables, livestock, shrimp

Economic Activity
- Industry 17%
- Agriculture 7%
- Services 76%

Map and Chart Skills

1. **Identify** How much of Panama is covered by forest?
2. **Predict** Loss of rain forest causes the lakes that support the Panama Canal to dry up, making it harder for ships to pass through. How might that affect Panama's economy?

Go Online PHSchool.com Use Web Code **Ife-1413** for **DK World Desk Reference Online.**

118 Latin America

Answers

Map and Chart Skills

1. About three-quarters to two-thirds of Panama's land is covered by forest.
2. Industries related to the canal would suffer financially.

Go Online PHSchool.com Students can find more information about this topic on the DK World Desk Reference Online.

Skills for Life — Skills Mini Lesson

Using Reliable Information L2

1. Point out to students that some sources are more reliable than others. To evaluate reliability, one must consider the source's accuracy, time period, authority, and bias.
2. Help students practice the skill by comparing two Internet or print sources

about the Panama Canal.

3. Have students apply the skill by asking them to complete *Doing Searches on the Internet.* Ask them to evaluate the reliability of some of their favorite Web sites.

All in One Latin America Teaching Resources, *Doing Searches on the Internet,* p. 258

The New Nation of Panama Colombia refused to grant the United States rights to build a canal. But business people in Panama thought a canal would benefit the local economy. Also, many Panamanians wanted to be free of Colombia's rule. They saw the canal as an opportunity to win independence.

At the same time, President Theodore Roosevelt felt that the canal was important for the United States. It would speed trade between the Atlantic and Pacific coasts. It would also allow the American navy to move back and forth in case of war. Roosevelt did not wait for events to unfold. He took action. In November 1903, the United States helped Panama revolt against Colombia. Two weeks after Panama declared its independence, the United States received the rights to build the canal.

✓ Reading Check **Why did Panamanians want a canal?**

Building the Canal: A Heroic Effort

The Americans faced the same challenges of moving earth and rock that the French had faced. In addition, the project called for a dam to be built to form a lake. There were locks to design and build. A **lock** is a section of waterway in which ships are raised or lowered by adjusting the water level.

While the work on the canal was difficult and slow, by far the biggest problem was disease. Some 20,000 workers had died of malaria and yellow fever while the French worked on the canal. Scientists did not know what caused these diseases, so they could do little to prevent them.

Digging the Canal
Canal workers wore the badges shown above. In the photo at the left, they use steam shovels and trains to build the Panama Canal.
Draw Conclusions *From what you see in the photo, how were trains used in the construction?*

Show students *Changing Panama's Landscape.* Ask **What is one problem occurring in the rain forests of Panama?** *(deforestation)*

Building the Canal: A Heroic Effort L2

Guided Instruction
- Have students read Building the Canal: A Heroic Effort.
- Ask students **Why did workers need to build a dam and locks in order for the canal to work?** *(A dam stops the flow of water across a river or stream and creates a reservoir; locks allow ships to be raised and lowered to compensate for the different water levels connected by the canal.)*
- Ask students **What challenges were faced by the workers building the canal?** *(The French faced mudslides, diseases, difficulty clearing the forest, bankruptcy; Americans faced disease and resistance from Colombia for the rights to build the canal.)*

Independent Progress
Have students complete the graphic organizer by filling in the "Solution" column.

Monitor Progress
Show *Section Reading Support Transparency LA 41* and ask students to check their graphic organizers individually. Go over key concepts and clarify key vocabulary as needed.

   Latin America Transparencies, *Section Reading Support Transparency LA 41*

Differentiated Instruction

For Less Proficient Readers L1
Ask students to find photographs of words or terms with which they may not be familiar, such as "dams" and "locks," in print or on the Internet. To search for terms on the Internet, have students type in the unfamiliar word along with the word "photograph" to get the best results.

For Advanced Readers L3
Have students read *Locks, Crocs, and Skeeters* and *Beyond the Chagres*. Then, ask students to create their own dictionaries of the selections' key words or terms, with illustrations.

   Latin America Teaching Resources, *Locks, Crocs, and Skeeters,* pp. 255–256; *Beyond the Chagres,* p. 257

Answer

✓ Reading Check Panamanians wanted a canal because they thought that it would benefit the local economy. Some Panamanians wanted a canal because they saw it as a way to win independence from Colombia.
Draw Conclusions The trains in the photograph appear to be hauling supplies to the building site, or carrying rubble out of the building site.

Use Context Clues As a follow up, ask students to answer the Target Reading Skill question in the Student Edition. (*Standing water is water that does not move.*)

Panama and Its Canal L2

Guided Instruction

- **Vocabulary Builder** Clarify the meaning of the high-use words **crossroads** and **finance** before reading.

- Read Panama and Its Canal. As students read, circulate and make sure individuals can answer the Reading Check question.

- Ask students **Why did Panamanians riot in the 1960s and 1970s?** (*They rioted to protest American control of the Panama Canal and the Canal Zone.*)

- Ask students **Do you think the United States should have given Panama control of the canal? Why or why not?** (*Yes—The people of Panama deserve control over their own land. No—Panama's original treaty with the United States was forever. The United States needs to be near to the canal to protect it.*)

- Discuss how the canal has affected Panama's economy. (*It has made Panama a hub for communication and international trade, increased the numbers of factories, boosted ecotourism.*)

Independent Practice

Assign *Guided Reading and Review*.

All in One **Latin America Teaching Resources,** *Guided Reading and Review,* p. 237

Monitor Progress

Tell students to fill in the last column of the *Reading Readiness Guide*. Ask them to evaluate if what they learned was what they expected to learn.

All in One **Latin America Teaching Resources,** *Reading Readiness Guide,* p. 236

Answer

✔ **Reading Check** Workers fought the mosquitoes by burning sulfur in houses, covering water vessels with mesh, and filling in swampy breeding grounds with dirt.

Use Context Clues You know that *standing* often refers to a person "staying still in an upright position." Use part of that definition to help you understand *standing water*. Ask yourself, can water stand still? What does *standing* mean in this context? What is *standing water*?

In the early 1900s, doctors discovered that malaria and yellow fever were both carried by mosquitoes. The mosquitoes bred in standing water. In 1904, the Panama Canal Company hired a doctor and a large crew to deal with the mosquito problem. It took more than a year to complete the job. Workers burned sulfur in every house to kill mosquitoes. They covered every water vessel with mesh to keep mosquitoes out. They filled in swampy breeding grounds with dirt. Without these efforts, the Panama Canal probably could not have been built.

It took eight years and more than 70,000 workers, mostly Caribbean islanders, to build the Panama Canal. It remains one of the greatest engineering feats of modern times.

✔ **Reading Check** How did workers fight the mosquitoes?

Panama and Its Canal

When the United States gained the rights to build a canal, it signed a treaty with Panama. The treaty gave the United States the right to build the Panama Canal and to control it forever.

The Canal Zone The United States also controlled an area called the Canal Zone. The **Canal Zone** was an area containing the canal, the land on either side of the canal, the ports, the port cities, and the railroad. The treaty allowed the United States to govern the Canal Zone according to its laws and gave the United States the right to invade Panama to protect the canal. The United States built 14 military bases in the Canal Zone and stationed thousands of soldiers there.

Many Panamanians felt the United States had too much power in Panama. For years, Panama held talks with the United States about transferring control of the canal to Panama. In the 1960s and 1970s, angry Panamanians rioted to protest American control.

A Change of Ownership In 1977, after years of talks, President Jimmy Carter signed two new treaties with Panama's government. These treaties gave Panama more control over the canal. In 1999, Panama finally gained full control of the Panama Canal.

Panama Today The Panama Canal dominated life in Panama for much of the 1900s, and it continues to be extremely important today. Because of the canal, Panama has become an international crossroads for trade. The ships that pass through the Panama Canal each day pay tolls according to their weight. International trade is very important to Panama's economy. The canal has made Panama a leading banking and finance center.

Panama City at night

120 Latin America

Differentiated Instruction

For Special Needs Students L1
Help students review the major events that led to Panamanian control of the canal by creating time lines. Have pairs draw a line on a piece of paper. Ask students to look for dates on this page under "The Canal Zone" and "A Change of Ownership" and to write them on their time lines. Then have students look for the events that go with the dates, and write those events next to the dates on their time lines. (*1960s—Panamanians protest American control of the canal; 1970s—Panamanians continue to protest; 1978—President Carter signs new treaties giving Panama more control; 1999—Panama gains control of the canal.*)

The Panama Canal

Every day, an average of 33 ships pass through the Panama Canal. It takes each ship around nine hours to cross from one ocean to the other. The Panama Canal is like a water elevator with lakes. Ships are raised and lowered in the locks as they travel from one ocean to the other.

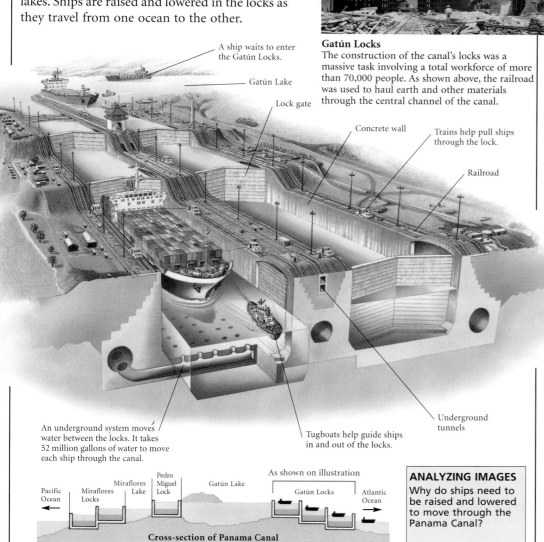

Gatún Locks
The construction of the canal's locks was a massive task involving a total workforce of more than 70,000 people. As shown above, the railroad was used to haul earth and other materials through the central channel of the canal.

A ship waits to enter the Gatún Locks.

Gatún Lake

Lock gate

Concrete wall

Trains help pull ships through the lock.

Railroad

An underground system moves water between the locks. It takes 52 million gallons of water to move each ship through the canal.

Tugboats help guide ships in and out of the locks.

Underground tunnels

Pacific Ocean — Miraflores Locks — Miraflores Lake — Pedro Miguel Lock — Gatún Lake — As shown on illustration — Gatún Locks — Atlantic Ocean

Cross-section of Panama Canal

ANALYZING IMAGES
Why do ships need to be raised and lowered to move through the Panama Canal?

Chapter 4 Section 3 **121**

The Panama Canal L2

Guided Instruction
Ask students to study the diagrams of the Panama Canal on this page. Help students to see which parts of the detailed diagram on the top of the page correspond to the cross section below it. As a class, answer the question at the bottom of the page. Allow students to briefly discuss their responses with a partner before sharing their ideas.

Independent Practice
Have students learn more about how the Panama Canal works by completing the *Activity Shop Lab: Making a Model Canal Lock.*

All in One **Latin America Teaching Resources,** *Activity Shop Lab: Making a Model Canal Lock,* pp. 249–250

Background: Links Across Place

The Suez Canal Like the Panama Canal, the Suez Canal is one of the world's busiest canals. The Suez Canal, which extends across the Isthmus of Suez in Egypt, connects the Mediterranean and the Red Seas and is a major link between Europe and Asia. Unlike the Panama Canal, which contains many locks, the Suez Canal does not contain locks because the levels of the Mediterranean and Red Seas are similar. Before the Suez Canal was built, ships from Great Britain and other parts of Europe had to travel around the southern coast of Africa to get to India.

Answer
ANALYZING IMAGES The Gatún Lake, in the middle of the canal, has a higher elevation than the sea on both sides of the canal. People designed locks to allow the ships to pass from sea level to Gatún Lake and back to sea level again.

Assess and Reteach

Assess Progress `L2`

Have students complete the Section Assessment. Administer the *Section Quiz.*

> **All in One** **Latin America Teaching Resources,** *Section Quiz,* p. 238

Reteach `L1`

If students need more instruction, have them read this section in the Reading and Vocabulary Study Guide.

> Chapter 4, Section 3, **Latin America Reading and Vocabulary Study Guide,** pp. 48–50

Extend `L3`

Have students learn more about issues surrounding the Panama Canal works by completing the *Small Group Activity: Simulation: Who Should Control the Panama Canal?*

> **All in One** **Latin America Teaching Resources,** *Small Group Activity: Simulation: Who Should Control the Panama Canal?,* pp. 245–248

Answers

✓ **Reading Check** Because of the canal, Panama is an international trading center, a leading banking and finance center, and a communications and tourist center.

Section 3 Assessment

Key Terms
Students' sentences should reflect knowledge of each Key Term.

Target Reading Skill
The word *unfold* means "to become known." The words *wait* and *took action* provide clues to the word's meaning. The fact that Roosevelt *took action,* not waiting for events to *unfold,* shows that *unfold* has a less active meaning.

Comprehension and Critical Thinking
1. (a) It shortens the trip between the Atlantic and Pacific Oceans, saving both time and money. **(b)** Possible answer: Colombia refused to grant the United States permission to build the canal; the United States helped Panama revolt against Colombia to gain independence; Panama gave the United States the right to build the canal.

2. (a) Difficulties included: moving earth and rock, building a dam to form a lake, designing and building locks, and battling disease. **(b)** The discovery that mosquitoes carried malaria and yellow fever allowed workers to take measures to control mosquitoes, which lessened disease.

3. (a) an area containing the Panama Canal, the land on either side of the canal, the ports, the port cities, and the railroad **(b)** according to United States laws **(c)** Many Panamanians believed that the United States had too much power in Panama.

An ecotourist riding through Panama's rain forest

New Industries Traffic through the canal has also encouraged warehousing and manufacturing. Many factories in Panama are similar to the maquiladoras in Mexico. They assemble parts imported from abroad and then export the finished products. Materials for these factories come from Hong Kong, the United States, and Japan as well as other countries. Most finished products are shipped to Latin American nations or are sold within Panama itself.

Panama is also a communications hub. Five international fiber-optic networks cross through Panama. Fiber-optic networks are used for long-distance telephone lines and computer networks.

Tourism Another important industry in Panama is tourism. Many tourists come to travel through the canal. They also visit Panama's rain forests. Look at the map in the Country Profile on page 118 to see how much of Panama is covered by rain forests. Tourism in unspoiled areas to observe wildlife and learn about the environment is called **ecotourism.** Ecotourists come to see the wide variety of plants and animals in the rain forest. These include howler monkeys, sloths, harpy eagles, and capybaras—huge rodents that look like guinea pigs. Panama's government has recently invested millions of dollars to promote ecotourism in its rain forests.

 ✓ **Reading Check** Why is the canal important to Panama today?

Section 3 Assessment

Key Terms
Review the key terms at the beginning of this section. Use each term in a sentence that explains its meaning.

Target Reading Skill
Find the word *unfold* on page 119. Use your own knowledge and the surrounding words and phrases to explain what *unfold* means in this context.

Comprehension and Critical Thinking
1. (a) Recall What are the benefits of a canal across the Isthmus of Panama?

(b) Sequence List three events, in order, that led to the building of the canal.
2. (a) Describe What kinds of difficulties did the builders of the canal face?
(b) Identify Cause and Effect How did advances in medicine lead to the successful completion of the Panama Canal?
3. (a) Define What was the Canal Zone?
(b) Explain How was the Canal Zone governed?
(c) Draw Conclusions Why was it so important to Panamanians to gain control of the canal?

Writing Activity
Suppose you are an American newspaper editor in the 1970s. Write an editorial either for or against giving control of the Panama Canal and the Canal Zone to Panama. State your position clearly. Be sure to support your position with reasons and facts.

For: An activity on Panama
Visit: PHSchool.com
Web Code: lfd-1403

122 Latin America

Writing Activity
Use the *Rubric for Assessing a Newspaper Article* to evaluate students' editorials.

> **All in One** **Latin America Teaching Resources,** *Rubric for Assessing a Newspaper Article,* p. 264

> **Go Online** PHSchool.com Typing in the web code when prompted will bring students directly to detailed instructions for this activity.

Review and Assessment

Review Chapter Content

- Review and revisit the major themes of this chapter by asking students to classify what Guiding Question each bulleted statement in the Chapter Summary answers. Form students into groups of three or four to complete the activity. Refer to page 1 in the Student Edition for the text of the Guiding Questions.

- Assign *Vocabulary Development* to help students review the Key Terms.

    All in One Latin America Teaching Resources, *Vocabulary Development,* p. 259

◆ Chapter Summary

Section 1: Mexico
- Many farmers in Mexico are poor, and jobs in the countryside are scarce.
- Many rural Mexicans move to the cities to look for work, but they find that city life is hard and very different from life in the countryside.
- Mexico City is a huge city that is facing overcrowding and pollution problems.

Section 2: Guatemala
- Most of the land in Guatemala is owned by only a few wealthy ladino families who grow crops for export.
- The Mayas lost much of their land to their Spanish conquerors and later they lost more land during the civil war.
- Today, political movements are working to improve life for the Mayas.

Section 3: Panama
- The Panama Canal shortens sea travel between the Atlantic Ocean and the Pacific Ocean.
- After the French could not complete the canal, the United States overcame engineering challenges and disease to build it.
- The Panama Canal is a key water route today and is important to Panama's economy.

Mexico

Guatemala

Panama

◆ Key Terms

Each of the statements below contains a key term from the chapter. If the statement is true, write *true*. If it is false, rewrite the statement to make it true.

1. A migrant worker is a person who settles on someone else's land without permission.

2. A plaza is an open field in the countryside.

3. A canal uses a series of locks to raise and lower ships by adjusting the water level.

4. Land reform is a new and better way of farming the land.

5. When people strike, they stop working in order to achieve a goal.

6. Ecotourism can involve visiting the rain forest to learn about its environment.

7. A ladino is any person from Latin America.

8. The Panama Canal shortens the route ships must travel between the Atlantic Ocean and the Pacific Ocean.

Chapter 4 **123**

Answers

Key Terms
1. False. A migrant worker is a laborer who travels from one area to another, picking crops that are in season.

2. False. A plaza is a public square at the center of a village, a town, or a city.

3. True.

4. False. Land reform is the effort to distribute land more equally and fairly.

5. True.

6. True

7. False. A ladino is a mestizo, or person of mixed Spanish and Native America ancestry in Guatemala.

8. True.

┌ **Vocabulary Builder** ─

Revisit this chapter's High-Use Words:

support	erosion	benefit
afford	civilian	crossroads
sturdy	violation	finance
resource	bankrupt	

Ask students to review the definitions they recorded on their *Word Knowledge* worksheets.

 **Latin America Teaching Resources,** *Word Knowledge,* p. 242

Consider allowing students to earn extra credit if they use the words in their answers to the questions in the Chapter Review and Assessment. The words must be used correctly and in a natural context to win the extra points.

Review and Assessment

Comprehension and Critical Thinking

9. (a) Mexico City and the United States **(b)** because it is difficult to support their families in the country

10. (a) Mexico's population is growing rapidly. **(b)** Population growth causes crowding and increased pollution in Mexico's cities.

11. (a) The Mayas lost more of their land. **(b)** Good farmland in Guatemala is scarce. Powerful people have tried to force Mayas off their land because the Mayas have little political power.

12. (a) Political movements are working to improve life for Mayas. **(b)** The political movements use protests and strikes as methods to bring about change. These methods bring about changes by forcing authorities to recognize the Mayas' rights.

13. (a) France **(b)** Difficulties such as disease and thick vegetation caused France's efforts to fail. **(c)** The canal saves time and money for travelers by shortening the trip from the Atlantic Ocean to the Pacific Ocean by almost 8,000 miles.

14. (a) Many Panamanians wanted the United States to build the canal, but Colombia blocked the negotiations. The United States helped Panama become independent from Colombia. **(b)** Panamanians thought that the canal would benefit the local economy. **(c)** The canal brings international trade to Panama and encourages many other businesses, including tourism.

Skills Practice

Students answers will vary.

Possible inferences Panama was unhappy as part of Colombia. The opportunities the canal presented were more important to some Panamanians than remaining part of Colombia. The United States helped Panama gain independence to win the right to build the canal.

Possible conclusion The United States and Panama fought jointly for Panamanian independence because leaders in both countries felt that building the canal would serve their country's interests.

Writing Activity: Science

Student answers will vary, but should include the scientific discovery that mosquitoes carried malaria and yellow fever.

◆ Comprehension and Critical Thinking

9. (a) Identify Name two places many rural Mexicans go when they leave the countryside. **(b) Generalize** Why do so many people make these moves?

10. (a) Recall Describe population growth in Mexico. **(b) Identify Effects** How does population growth affect Mexico's cities?

11. (a) Summarize What happened to the Mayas during the Guatemalan civil war? **(b) Synthesize** Why have so many Mayas been forced from their land?

12. (a) Identify What groups are working to improve life for the Mayas? **(b) Identify Cause and Effect** What are two methods these groups use, and how might these methods bring about change?

13. (a) Identify What country first tried to build a canal across Panama? **(b) Identify Causes** Why did that country fail to complete the canal? **(c) Draw Conclusions** How does the whole world benefit from the Panama Canal?

14. (a) Summarize How did Panama become an independent nation? **(b) Identify Causes** Why did Panama want the United States to build the Panama Canal? **(c) Identify Effects** What benefits has the Panama Canal brought to Panama?

◆ Skills Practice

Drawing Inferences and Conclusions In the Skills for Life activity in this chapter, you learned how to draw inferences. You also learned how to draw a conclusion, or make a reasoned judgment, using two or more inferences.

Review the steps you followed to learn this skill. Then reread The New Nation of Panama on page 119. List several inferences you can draw about the events described there. Finally, use your inferences to draw a conclusion about those events.

◆ Writing Activity: Science

Suppose you were the science reporter for a newspaper covering the building of the Panama Canal. Write a brief report about how advances in science contributed to the successful completion of the Panama Canal.

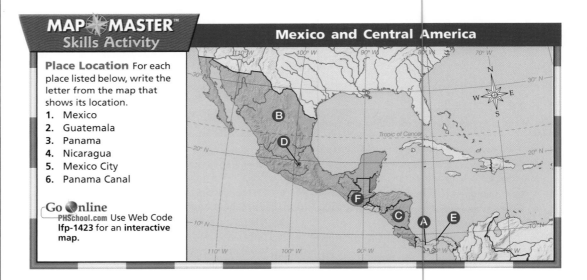

MAP MASTER™
Skills Activity

Mexico and Central America

Place Location For each place listed below, write the letter from the map that shows its location.
1. Mexico
2. Guatemala
3. Panama
4. Nicaragua
5. Mexico City
6. Panama Canal

Go Online
PHSchool.com Use Web Code lfp-1423 for an **interactive map.**

Use Rubric for Assessing a Newspaper Article to evaluate students' reports. Tell students how many sources you would like them to use, if any beyond the textbook.

All in One Latin America Teaching Resources, *Rubric for Assessing a Newspaper Article,* p. 264

Standardized Test Prep

Test-Taking Tips

Some questions on standardized tests ask you to analyze a reading selection. Study the passage below. Then follow the tips to help you answer the sample question.

> Many people have moved to Mexico City to find jobs in factories. Cars and buses clog the city streets. In addition, the city is located in a valley surrounded by mountains, and pollution gets trapped there. <u>Because</u> of its geography and heavy traffic, Mexico City has one of the worst cases of air pollution in the world.

TIP Look for words that signal causes or reasons, such as the word *because* in the last sentence.

Pick the letter that best completes the statement.

Mexico City's air pollution problem is made worse by

A ~~smog from South America.~~

B its location.

C its textile factories.

D ~~its lack of rain.~~

TIP First cross out answers that you know are wrong. Then consider each remaining choice before selecting the best answer.

Think It Through Look at the remaining answer choices. Answer C might be correct, but the passage does not mention textile factories. Remember the signal word *because*. The sentence beginning with *because* gives geography as one reason for Mexico City's pollution. Geography includes location, so B is the correct answer.

Practice Questions

Use the tips above and other tips in this book to help you answer the following questions.

1. Which of the following was not a problem for the builders of the Panama Canal?
   A disease carried by mosquitoes
   B mudslides
   C blizzards
   D a mountain range blocking the route

2. In Guatemala, most of the land is owned by
   A Native Americans.
   B Spanish conquerors.
   C a few wealthy ladino families.
   D the Mayas.

3. What is one result of rapid population growth in Mexico?
   A Farms are getting overcrowded.
   B The economy is improving because there are more people to buy things.
   C Rural people are moving to the cities to find work.
   D Factories are shutting down.

Use the circle graph below to answer Question 4. Choose the letter of the best answer to the question.

Population of Guatemala

- Native American
- Ladino
- Other

10%
30%
60%

4. According to the circle graph, which of the following statements is true?
   A Most people in Guatemala are descended from Europeans and Native Americans.
   B Half of Guatemala's population is ladino.
   C Most Guatemalans are Native American.
   D There are more Spaniards than ladinos in Guatemala.

Go Online
PHSchool.com

Use Web Code lfa-1401
for a **Chapter 4 self-test.**

Chapter 4 **125**

Standardized Test Prep
Answers

1. C

2. C

3. C

4. C

Assessment Resources

Use *Chapter Tests A and B* to assess students' mastery of chapter content.

All in One Latin America Teaching Resources, *Chapter Tests A and B,* pp. 265–270

Tests are also available on the **ExamView Test Bank CD-ROM.**

⊙ *ExamView Test Bank CD-ROM*

Overview

Introducing The Caribbean

1. Find out the location and important facts about each country.
2. Analyze the data to compare countries.
3. Learn what characteristics countries share.
4. Discover key differences among countries.

The Caribbean: Dynamic Lands and Cultures
Length: 4 minutes, 48 seconds
Gives an overview of the Caribbean islands' geography, development, and climate.

Section **1**

Cuba: Clinging to Communism

1. Find out how Cuba's history led to thousands of Cubans leaving their homeland.
2. Discover how Cuban exiles feel about their lives in the United States and about their homeland.
3. Learn what changes have recently come to Cuba.

Baseball and Cuba Go Hand in Glove
Length: 3 minutes, 33 seconds
Discusses the importance of baseball in Cuba.

Section **2**

Haiti: A Democracy in Progress

1. Find out how democracy has been threatened in Haiti.
2. Learn what life is like for the people of Haiti, both in the countryside and in the cities.

Haiti: A Striving Nation
Length: 5 minutes, 37 seconds
Briefly details the people, geography, and history of Haiti.

Section **3**

Puerto Rico: An American Commonwealth

1. Understand how the people of Puerto Rico are both American and Puerto Rican.
2. Find out what life is like on the island of Puerto Rico.
3. Learn about the three kinds of political status Puerto Ricans are considering for their future.

Puerto Rico: Past and Present
Length: 4 minutes, 38 seconds
Contrasts the urban and rural regions of Puerto Rico, with a focus on San Juan and the diverse geography of the island.

Technology Resources

Go Online
PHSchool.com

Students use embedded Web codes to access Internet activities, chapter self-tests, and additional map practice. They may also access Dorling Kindersley's Online Desk Reference to learn more about each country they study.

Interactive Textbook

Use the Interactive Textbook to make content and concepts come alive through animations, videos, and activities that accompany the complete basal text—online and on CD-ROM.

PRENTICE HALL
TeacherEXPRESS
Plan · Teach · Assess

Use this complete suite of powerful teaching tools to make planning lessons and administering tests quicker and easier.

Reading and Assessment

Reading and Vocabulary Instruction

🔄 Model the Target Reading Skill

Main Idea Tell students that finding the main idea can help them understand their reading and remember key concepts. The main idea is the most important point in the reading. It is supported by the details in the passage. Model this skill by thinking aloud about the main idea of Section 2 of this chapter.

I am going to look for clues to the main idea on the first page of the section. The title of the section is *Haiti: A Democracy in Progress*. This probably means that the main idea will have to do with the ongoing political issues in Haiti.

The first sentence of the section says: *Jean Bertrand Aristide was elected president of Haiti in 1990, but he served for only seven months!* Because this sentence includes very specific details about one person, it is a detail, not the main idea.

The next paragraph starts like this: *Haiti's history has been a continuing struggle for democracy.* This sentence is more general. It talks about all of Haiti and about a process that is continuing. It also relates to the title of the section. I think I have found the main idea.

Use the following worksheets from All-in-One Latin America Teaching Resources, (pp. 287, 288, and 289) to support this chapter's Target Reading Skill.

Vocabulary Builder

High-Use Academic Words

Use these steps to teach this chapter's high-use words:

1. Have students rate how well they know each word on their Word Knowledge worksheets (All-in-One Latin America Teaching Resources, p. 290).
2. Pronounce each word and ask students to repeat it.
3. Give students a brief definition or sample sentence (provided on TE pp. 135, 143, and 149.)
4. Work with students as they fill in the "Definition or Example" column of their Word Knowledge worksheets.

Assessment

Formal Assessment

Test students' understanding of core knowledge and skills.

Chapter Tests A and B, All-in-One Latin America Teaching Resources, pp. 306–311

Customize the Chapter Tests to suit your needs.

ExamView Test Bank CD-ROM

Skills Assessment

Assess geographic literacy.

MapMaster Skills, Student Edition pp. 127, 156

Country Profile Map and Chart Skills, Student Edition pp. 137, 144, 151

Assess reading and comprehension.

Target Reading Skills, Student Edition, pp. 136, 146, 150, and in Section Assessments

Chapter 5 Assessment, Reading and Vocabulary Study Guide, p. 61

Performance Assessment

Assess students' performance on this chapter's Writing Activities using the following rubrics from All-in-One Latin America Teaching Resources.

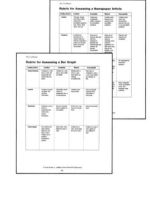

Rubric for Assessing a Bar Graph, p. 302

Rubric for Assessing a Writing Assignment, p. 303

Rubric for Assessing a Newspaper Article, p. 304

Rubric for Assessing a Journal Entry, p. 305

Assess students' work through performance tasks.

Small Group Activity: Creating a Magazine Story, All-in-One Latin America Teaching Resources, pp. 293–296

Portfolio Activity, Teacher Edition, p. 132

Online Assessment

Have students check their own understanding.

Chapter Self-Test

Section 1 Cuba: Clinging to Communism

 3 periods, 1.5 blocks (includes Country Databank and Skills for Life)

Social Studies Objectives
1. Find out how Cuba's history led to thousands of Cubans leaving their homeland.
2. Discover how Cuban exiles feel about their lives in the United States and about their homeland.
3. Learn what changes have recently come to Cuba.

Reading/Language Arts Objective
Identify main ideas in each section or paragraph.

Prepare to Read	**Instructional Resources**	**Differentiated Instruction**
Build Background Knowledge Preview the section and then brainstorm how Cuba's government affects life in Cuba. **Set a Purpose for Reading** Have students begin to fill out the *Reading Readiness Guide*. **Preview Key Terms** Teach the section's Key Terms. **Target Reading Skill** Introduce the section's Target Reading Skill of **identifying main ideas**.	**All in One Latin America Teaching Resources** L2 Reading Readiness Guide, p. 276 L2 Identify Main Ideas, p. 287	**Spanish Reading and Vocabulary Study Guide** L2 Chapter 5, Section 1, pp. 38–39 ELL **World Studies Video Program** L2 The Caribbean: Dynamic Lands and Cultures ELL, LPR, SN

Instruct	**Instructional Resources**	**Differentiated Instruction**
Cuba's History Discuss Castro's government. **Target Reading Skill** Review **identifying main ideas**. **Cuban Exiles** Discuss successes and difficulties faced by Cuban exiles. **Country Profile** Ask students to derive and use information from maps, charts, and graphs. **Changes Come to Cuba** Describe changes in Cuba since the 1990s.	**All in One Latin America Teaching Resources** L2 Guided Reading and Review, p. 277 L2 Reading Readiness Guide, p. 276 **Latin America Transparencies** L2 Section Reading Support Transparency LA 42 **World Studies Video Program** L2 Baseball and Cuba Go Hand in Glove	**All in One Latin America Teaching Resources** L3 Morning Girl, pp. 298–300 L2 Outline Map 7: Central America and the Caribbean, p. 297 AR, GT, LPR, SN L2 Skills for Life, p. 292 AR, GT, LPR, SN **Latin America Teacher's Edition** L1 For Less Proficient Readers, TE p. 129, 136 L3 For Advanced Readers, TE p. 129 L1 For Special Needs Students, TE p. 136

Assess and Reteach	**Instructional Resources**	**Differentiated Instruction**
Assess Progress Evaluate student comprehension with the section assessment and section quiz. **Reteach** Assign the Reading and Vocabulary Study guide to help struggling students. **Extend** Extend the lesson by assigning an *Enrichment* activity.	**All in One Latin America Teaching Resources** L2 Section Quiz, p. 278 L3 Enrichment, p. 291 　　Rubric for Assessing a Writing Assignment, p. 303 **Reading and Vocabulary Study Guide** L1 Chapter 5, Section 1, pp. 52–54	**All in One Latin America Teaching Resources** 　　Rubric for Assessing a Bar Graph, p. 302 **Latin America Transparencies** L1 Color Transparency LA 23: Central America and the Caribbean: Political LPR, SN, ELL **Social Studies Skills Tutor CD-ROM** L1 Comparing and Contrasting SN, LPR, ELL

Key

L1 Basic to Average	L3 Average to Advanced	LPR Less Proficient Readers	GT Gifted and Talented
L2 For All Students		AR Advanced Readers	ELL English Language Learners
		SN Special Needs Students	

Section 2 Haiti: A Democracy in Progress

1.5 periods, .75 block

Social Studies Objectives

1. Find out how democracy has been threatened in Haiti.

2. Learn what life is like for the people of Haiti, both in the countryside and in the cities.

Reading/Language Arts Objective

Identify supporting details of a main idea.

Prepare to Read	Instructional Resources	Differentiated Instruction
Build Background Knowledge Have students list countries where people speak French. **Set a Purpose for Reading** Have students evaluate statements on the *Reading Readiness Guide*. **Preview Key Terms** Teach the section's Key Terms. **Target Reading Skill** Introduce the section's Target Reading Skill of **identifying supporting details.**	**All in One Latin America Teaching Resources** **L2** Reading Readiness Guide, p. 280 **L2** Identify Supporting Details, p. 288 **World Studies Video Program** **L2** Haiti: A Striving Nation	**Spanish Reading and Vocabulary Study Guide** **L2** Chapter 5, Section 2, pp. 40–41 ELL

Instruct	Instructional Resources	Differentiated Instruction
Democracy in Danger Ask questions about the hardships with which Haitians have struggled. **Country Profile** Ask students to derive information from maps, charts, and graphs. **The People of Haiti** Discuss the people of Haiti. **Target Reading Skill** Review **identifying supporting details.**	**All in One Latin America Teaching Resources** **L2** Outline Map 7: Central America and the Caribbean, p. 297 **L2** Guided Reading and Review, p. 281 **L2** Reading Readiness Guide, p. 280 **Latin America Transparencies** **L2** Section Reading Support Transparency LA 43	**Latin America Teacher's Edition** **L3** For Gifted and Talented, TE p. 144 **L3** For Advanced Readers, TE p. 144 **L1** For English Language Learners, TE p. 145 **L1** For Special Needs Students, TE p. 145 **Student Edition on Audio CD** **L1** Chapter 5, Section 2 SN, LPR, ELL **Spanish Support** **L2** Guided Reading and Review (Spanish), p. 40 ELL

Assess and Reteach	Instructional Resources	Differentiated Instruction
Assess Progress Evaluate student comprehension with the section assessment and section quiz. **Reteach** Assign the Reading and Vocabulary Study Guide to help struggling students. **Extend** Extend the lesson by assigning a *Small Group Activity.*	**All in One Latin America Teaching Resources** **L2** Section Quiz, p. 282 **L3** Small Group Activity: Creating a Magazine Story, pp. 293–296 Rubric for Assessing a Newspaper Article, p. 304 **Reading and Vocabulary Study Guide** **L1** Chapter 5, Section 2, pp. 55–57	**Spanish Support** **L2** Section Quiz (Spanish), p. 41 ELL

Key

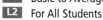 Basic to Average

  For All Students

L3 Average to Advanced

LPR Less Proficient Readers
AR Advanced Readers
SN Special Needs Students

GT Gifted and Talented
ELL English Language Learners

126d

Section 3 Puerto Rico: An American Commonwealth

 3 periods, 1.5 blocks (includes Chapter Review and Assessment)

Social Studies Objectives
1. Understand how the people of Puerto Rico are both American and Puerto Rican.
2. Find out what life is like on the island of Puerto Rico.
3. Learn about the three kinds of political status Puerto Ricans are considering for their future.

Reading/Language Arts Objective
Identify implied main ideas in the text.

Prepare to Read	Instructional Resources	Differentiated Instruction

Build Background Knowledge
Think about Latin American countries' struggle for independence.

Set a Purpose for Reading
Have students begin to fill out the *Reading Readiness Guide*.

Preview Key Terms
Teach the section's Key Terms.

Target Reading Skill
Introduce the section's Target Reading Skill of **identifying implied main ideas**.

All in One Latin America Teaching Resources
- **L2** Reading Readiness Guide, p. 284
- **L2** Identify Implied Main Ideas, p. 289

Spanish Reading and Vocabulary Study Guide
- **L2** Chapter 5, Section 3, pp. 42–43 ELL

Instruct	Instructional Resources	Differentiated Instruction

Puerto Rican and American
Compare and contrast Puerto Ricans and citizens who live in the United States.

Life on the Island
Discuss what the island of Puerto Rico is like.

Country Profile
Ask students to derive information from maps, charts, and graphs.

Seeking a New Direction
Discuss the possibility of Puerto Rico becoming part of the United States.

Target Reading Skill
Review **identifying implied main ideas**.

All in One Latin America Teaching Resources
- **L2** Guided Reading and Review, p. 285
- **L2** Reading Readiness Guide, p. 284

Latin America Transparencies
- **L2** Section Reading Support Transparency LA 44

World Studies Video Program
- **L2** Puerto Rico: Past and Present

Latin America Teacher's Edition
- **L3** For Advanced Readers, TE p. 150
- **L1** For English Language Learners, TE p. 150
- **L1** For Less Proficient Readers, TE p. 153
- **L3** For Gifted and Talented, TE p. 153

Reading and Vocabulary Study Guide
- **L1** Chapter 5, Section 3, pp. 58–60 LPR, SN, ELL

Spanish Support
- **L2** Guided Reading and Review (Spanish), p. 44 ELL

Assess and Reteach	Instructional Resources	Differentiated Instruction

Assess Progress
Evaluate student comprehension with the section assessment and section quiz.

Reteach
Assign the Reading and Vocabulary Study Guide to help struggling students.

Extend
Extend the lesson by analyzing information from a Discovery Channel World Studies video.

All in One Latin America Teaching Resources
- **L2** Section Quiz, p. 286
  Rubric for Assessing a Journal Entry, p. 305
- **L2** Vocabulary Development, p. 301
- **L2** Word Knowledge, p. 290
- **L2** Chapter Tests A and B, pp. 306–311

Reading and Vocabulary Study Guide
- **L1** Chapter 5, Section 3, pp. 56–60

Spanish Support
- **L2** Section Quiz (Spanish), p. 45 ELL
- **L2** Chapter Summary (Spanish), p. 46 ELL
- **L2** Vocabulary Development (Spanish), p. 47 ELL

Key
- **L1** Basic to Average
- **L2** For All Students
- **L3** Average to Advanced
- LPR Less Proficient Readers
- AR Advanced Readers
- SN Special Needs Students
- GT Gifted and Talented
- ELL English Language Learners

Reading Background

Summarizing

Showing students how to summarize can help them comprehend and recall text.

Good summarizers make notes on the text and reread as they write. Poor summarizers read the text once and begin writing. Share this information with your students, then model how to create a one-sentence summary. In this type of summary, students must organize their ideas in the briefest possible way.

Use the following steps to model how to write a one-sentence summary:

1. Read the selection aloud.

2. List four or five ideas from the selection.

3. Show how to combine these ideas into one sentence.

4. Take out any extra words to make the sentence as short as possible.

If students are new to summarizing this way, give them the following sentence frames:

Section 1: *Compare and Contrast*

Cuba's government and economy in the 1800s and in 1994 are similar in that they both _____, but in the 1800s, _____ while in 1994, _____.

Section 2: *Description*

Haiti's political situation has always been _____.

Section 3: *Problem/Solution*

Puerto Rico is_____, but_____, so_____.

Seed Discussions

Give students the opportunity to lead their own discussions about what they are reading in the chapter. Tell students that in order to lead a discussion with their classmates, they will need a strong "seed" to start with. Have the class list ideas for strong seeds, such as questions or opinions about what they have learned, or things in the chapter that surprised them.

Model a strong seed versus a weak seed. A strong seed might be an opinion, such as: "I believe Puerto Rico should become a state of the United States." A weak seed might be a restatement of fact, such as: "Puerto Ricans adopted their constitution in 1951."

Once students are comfortable with the concept of a strong seed, have each student write a seed on a sheet of paper. Then have students form small groups. In each group, students should take turns leading a discussion from the seed they have written. Divide time equally so every person gets an equal opportunity as leader.

World Studies Background

The Spanish-American War

In the late 1800s, when Cuba was fighting for independence from Spain, the American government sent the battleship *Maine* to Cuba to protect Americans living there. On February 15, 1898, the *Maine* exploded and 266 people died. Although no one knew what caused the explosion, many Americans called for the President to "Remember the *Maine*!" and go to war with Spain. The Spanish-American War ended after four months, with Spain having to give up its colonies.

The Island of Hispaniola

The nations of Haiti and the Dominican Republic have had intertwined histories. The countries began as Spanish colonies.

Later, Spain and France traded possession back and forth for years. Haiti declared its independence from France in 1804, and the Dominican Republic won its independence from Spain 40 years later.

Puerto Rico's Baseball Hero

Roberto Clemente, from Puerto Rico, was one of the first Latin American superstars in baseball. He was famous not only for baseball but also for his desire to help others. In 1972 Clemente was on his way to assist with earthquake relief efforts in Nicaragua when his plane crashed, killing everyone aboard. A sports center was built in Puerto Rico as a reminder of Clemente's contributions.

Infoplease® provides a wealth of useful information for the classroom. You can use this resource to strengthen your background on the subjects covered in this chapter. Have students visit this advertising-free site as a starting point for projects requiring research.

Use Web Code **lfd-1500** for **Infoplease**.

Chapter 5

Guiding Questions

Remind students about the Guiding Questions introduced at the beginning of the book.

Section 1 relates to **Guiding Question** ❹ **What types of government have existed in Latin America?** *(After Fidel Castro took power in 1959, Cuba became a communist country.)*

Section 2 relates to **Guiding Question** ❷ **How has Latin America been shaped by its history?** *(Haiti, the only nation in the Americas formed from a successful revolt of enslaved Africans, has struggled through years of dictatorship while striving toward democracy.)*

Section 3 relates to **Guiding Question** ❸ **What factors have affected cultures in Latin America?** *(Puerto Rico's relationship with the United States as a commonwealth has resulted in a mix of cultures between the two places.)*

⟳ Target Reading Skill

In this chapter, students will learn and apply the reading skill of identifying the main idea. Use the following worksheets to help students practice this skill.

All in One **Latin America Teaching Resources,** *Identify Main Ideas,* p. 287; *Identify Supporting Details,* p. 288; *Identify Implied Main Ideas,* p. 289

The Caribbean

Chapter Preview

This chapter will introduce you to 13 island nations and one commonwealth of the Caribbean.

Country Databank
The Country Databank provides data and descriptions of the commonwealth and each of the countries in the region: Antigua and Barbuda, The Bahamas, Barbados, Cuba, Dominica, Dominican Republic, Grenada, Haiti, Jamaica, Saint Kitts and Nevis, Saint Lucia, Saint Vincent and the Grenadines, and Trinidad and Tobago.

Section 1
Cuba
Clinging to Communism

Section 2
Haiti
A Democracy in Progress

Section 3
Puerto Rico
An American Commonwealth

⟳ Target Reading Skill

Main Idea In this chapter you will focus on finding and remembering the main idea, or the most important point, of sections and paragraphs.

▶ Rowboats on a Curaçao beach

Differentiated Instruction

The following Teacher Edition strategies are suitable for students of varying abilities.

Advanced Readers, pp. 129, 150
English Language Learners, pp. 145, 150
Gifted and Talented, pp. 144, 153
Less Proficient Readers, pp. 129, 136, 153

Bibliography

For the Teacher
Arthur, Charles. *Haiti in Focus: A Guide to the People, Politics, and Culture.* Interlink Publishing Group, 2002.
Martinez-Fernandez, Luis et al. *Encyclopedia of Cuba: People, History, Culture* (2 Volumes). Oryx Press, 2003.
Trias, Monge. *Puerto Rico: The Trials of the Oldest Colony in the World.* Yale University Press, 1999.

For the Student
L1 Banting, Erinn. *Puerto Rico: The People and Culture (Lands, Peoples, Cultures).* Crabtree Publishing, 2003.
L2 Crouch, Clifford W. *Cuba (Major World Nations).* Chelsea House Publishers, 1997.
L3 Ngcheong-Lum. *Haiti (Cultures of the World).* Benchmark Books, 1997.

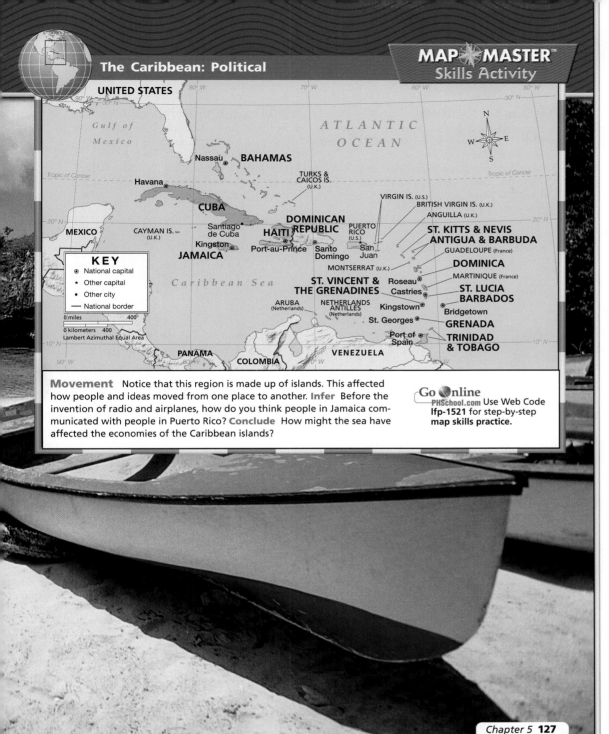

The Caribbean: Political

MAP✦MASTER™
Skills Activity

KEY
- ⊛ National capital
- ★ Other capital
- • Other city
- — National border

0 miles 400
0 kilometers 400
Lambert Azimuthal Equal Area

UNITED STATES

Gulf of Mexico

ATLANTIC OCEAN

Nassau • BAHAMAS

TURKS & CAICOS IS. (U.K.)

Havana • CUBA

MEXICO

CAYMAN IS. (U.K.)

Santiago de Cuba •

Kingston •

JAMAICA

DOMINICAN REPUBLIC

HAITI

Port-au-Prince • Santo Domingo

PUERTO RICO (U.S.)

San Juan

VIRGIN IS. (U.S.)

BRITISH VIRGIN IS. (U.K.)

ANGUILLA (U.K.)

ST. KITTS & NEVIS

ANTIGUA & BARBUDA

GUADELOUPE (France)

MONTSERRAT (U.K.)

DOMINICA

MARTINIQUE (France)

Caribbean Sea

ST. VINCENT & THE GRENADINES

Roseau ⊛

Castries ⊛

ST. LUCIA

BARBADOS

Kingstown ⊛

Bridgetown ⊛

GRENADA

St. Georges ⊛

Port of Spain ⊛

TRINIDAD & TOBAGO

ARUBA (Netherlands)

NETHERLANDS ANTILLES (Netherlands)

PANAMA

COLOMBIA

VENEZUELA

Movement Notice that this region is made up of islands. This affected how people and ideas moved from one place to another. **Infer** Before the invention of radio and airplanes, how do you think people in Jamaica communicated with people in Puerto Rico? **Conclude** How might the sea have affected the economies of the Caribbean islands?

Go Online
PHSchool.com Use Web Code lfp-1521 for step-by-step map skills practice.

MAP✦MASTER™
Skills Activity

- Point out the map of the Caribbean on page 127. Tell students that the words in capital letters show the names of the countries, while the words with upper and lower case letters identify cities in the countries, mostly the capitals. Show students how the leaders, or lines, connect a label with a place on the map. Point out that when a country's name appears in parentheses, it means that it has a connection to the place under whose name it appears. Ask students to find examples of places on the map with connections to other countries.

Go Online
PHSchool.com Students may practice their map skills using the interactive online version of this map.

Using the Visual L2

Reach Into Your Background Draw students' attention to the caption accompanying the picture on pages 126–127.

Have students share details about the scene. What might the weather in this region be like? How might the boats be used? Have students provide examples of ways that location and climate can affect a nation's economy.

Answers

MAP✦MASTER™
Skills Activity **Infer** in person or by mail
Conclude People of the Caribbean islands may have traded products found in the sea, such as fish.

Chapter Resources

Teaching Resources
- L2 Vocabulary Development, p. 301
- L2 Skills for Life, p. 292
- L2 Chapter Tests A and B, pp. 306–311

Spanish Support
- L2 Spanish Chapter Summary, p. 46
- L2 Spanish Vocabulary Development, p. 47

Media and Technology
- L2 Student Edition on Audio CD
- L2 Guided Reading Audiotapes, English and Spanish
- L2 Social Studies Skills Tutor CD-ROM
ExamView Test Bank CD-ROM

DISCOVERY World Studies
CHANNEL Video Program
SCHOOL

interactive Textbook

PRENTICE HALL
TeacherEXPRESS™
Plan • Teach • Assess

COUNTRY DATABANK

Objectives

- Learn about the nations of the Caribbean.
- Analyze data to compare Caribbean countries.
- Identify characteristics that countries share.
- Discover key differences among countries.

Show students *The Caribbean: Dynamic Lands and Cultures.* Ask **What is the climate of the Caribbean?** *(tropical)* **How were the Caribbean islands formed?** *(volcanic activity)*

Prepare to Read

Build Background Knowledge L2

Tell students that in this section they will be learning about the countries that make up the Caribbean region of Latin America. Show the World Studies video. Ask students to note three to five facts about the Caribbean countries as they watch. Have students engage in a Give One, Get One activity (TE, p. T37) to share the facts they noted.

The Caribbean: Dynamic Lands and Cultures, **World Studies Video Program**

COUNTRY DATABANK

Introducing The Caribbean

Guide for Reading

This section provides an introduction to the 13 countries and one commonwealth that make up the Caribbean region.

- Look at the map on the previous page and then read the paragraphs to learn about each nation.
- Analyze the data to compare countries.
- What are the characteristics that most of these countries share?
- What are some key differences among the countries?

Viewing the Video Overview

View the World Studies Video Overview to learn more about each of the countries. As you watch, answer these questions:

- How did the islands of the Caribbean form?
- What factors influence the cultural diversity of these islands?

Explore the lands and cultures of the Caribbean.

Antigua and Barbuda

Capital	Saint John's
Land Area	171 sq mi; 442 sq km
Population	67,448
Ethnic Group(s)	black, white, Southwest Asian
Religion(s)	Protestant, Roman Catholic, traditional beliefs
Government	constitutional monarchy
Currency	East Caribbean dollar
Leading Exports	petroleum products, manufactured goods, machinery and transport equipment, food and live animals
Language(s)	English (official), English Creole

The tiny nation of Antigua and Barbuda (an TIG wuh and bahr BOO dah) is made up of three islands located in the eastern Caribbean Sea. Christopher Columbus landed on the main island, Antigua, in 1493. English settlers began arriving there in the 1630s. They raised tobacco and then sugar cane. Enslaved Africans were imported to work on the plantations. However, slavery was abolished in the British colony in 1834. In 1981, Antigua joined with neighboring Barbuda and with Redonda, a nearby uninhabited island, to become an independent nation. Today, tourism is the nation's main source of income.

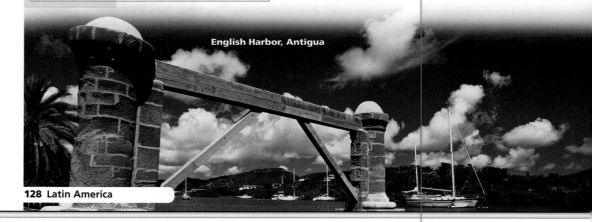

English Harbor, Antigua

128 Latin America

The Bahamas

Capital	Nassau
Land Area	3,888 sq mi; 10,070 sq km
Population	308,529
Ethnic Group(s)	black, white, Asian, Hispanic
Religion(s)	Anglican, Baptist, Roman Catholic, Methodist, Church of God
Government	constitutional parliamentary democracy
Currency	Bahamian dollar
Leading Exports	fish and crawfish, rum, salt, chemicals, fruits and vegetables
Language(s)	English (official), English Creole, French Creole

More than 700 islands make up the nation called The Bahamas (buh HAH muz), but fewer than 30 of them are inhabited. The island chain stretches southward off the east coast of Florida to within 50 miles (80.5 kilometers) of Cuba. It is thought that Christopher Columbus first landed in the Americas on the Bahamian island of San Salvador. The Bahamas are generally flat, with a mild climate and beautiful beaches, so it is not surprising that tourism is a major industry. Banking has also become important. Once a British colony, The Bahamas now has a government based on the British parliamentary model.

Barbados

Capital	Bridgetown
Land Area	166 sq mi; 431 sq km
Population	276,607
Ethnic Group(s)	black, white, mixed white and black
Religion(s)	Protestant, Roman Catholic
Government	parliamentary democracy
Currency	Barbados dollar
Leading Exports	sugar and molasses, rum, other foods and beverages, chemicals, electrical components, clothing
Language(s)	English (official), Bajan

Barbados (bahr BAY dohs) is a triangular-shaped island in the eastern Caribbean Sea. It was settled by the British in the 1600s and gained its independence in 1966. Today, both the culture and the government of Barbados reflect its British colonial heritage. In the past, much of Barbados was used for sugar plantations. Today, the government promotes smaller farms that grow food for the local population. The government spends approximately 20 percent of its budget on education, and 98 percent of the people can read and write.

Cuba

Capital	Havana
Land Area	42,803 sq mi; 110,860 sq km
Population	11.2 million
Ethnic Group(s)	mixed white and black, white, black, East Asian
Religion(s)	Roman Catholic, Protestant
Government	communist state
Currency	Cuban peso
Leading Exports	sugar, nickel, tobacco, fish, medical products, citrus, coffee
Language(s)	Spanish

Cuba (KYOO buh) is the largest country in the Caribbean region. Its main island lies south of Florida in the Caribbean Sea near the Gulf of Mexico. The island has many beaches, bays, and harbors. In 1903, the United States leased Guantánamo Bay from Cuba for use as a naval base, and it is still under American control today. The rest of the island is a communist state headed by Fidel Castro, who has governed Cuba since the revolution of 1959. Cuban culture reflects its Spanish colonial past and African influences.

Chapter 5 **129**

- Ask students to identify the different types of governments of the Caribbean nations. **Which country is a commonwealth?** *(Puerto Rico)* **Which country has a communist government?** *(Cuba)* **Which countries have governments that are constitutional monarchies?** *(Antigua and Barbuda, Grenada, Saint Kitts and Nevis)* **What form of government do most of the other countries have?** *(some type of democracy)*

- Ask **What language do Dominica and the Dominican Republic share?** *(French Creole)*

- Ask **Why is Grenada sometimes called the Isle of Spice?** *(It produces nutmeg, cinnamon, cloves, ginger, and vanilla.)*

COUNTRY DATABANK

Introducing The Caribbean

Dominica

Capital	Roseau
Land Area	291 sq mi; 754 sq km
Population	73,000
Ethnic Group(s)	black, mixed white and black, white, Southwest Asian, Carib
Religion(s)	Roman Catholic, Protestant
Government	parliamentary democracy
Currency	East Caribbean dollar
Leading Exports	bananas, soap, bay oil, vegetables, grapefruit, oranges
Language(s)	English (official), French Creole

Dominica (dahm uh NEE kuh) lies between Guadeloupe and Martinique in the Caribbean Sea. The island was formed by volcanic activity. Hot springs, such as those that feed Boiling Lake, are still active. In spite of its rich soil and pleasant climate, Dominica is very poor. Hurricanes often destroy crops. Tourism is hampered by poor transportation and lack of hotels. Dominica is one of the few Caribbean islands on which Carib Indians still live and continue to practice the cultural traditions of their ancestors.

Dominican Republic

Capital	Santo Domingo
Land Area	18,679 sq mi; 48,380 sq km
Population	8.7 million
Ethnic Group(s)	mixed white and black, white, black
Religion(s)	Roman Catholic
Government	representative democracy
Currency	Dominican Republic peso
Leading Exports	ferronickel, sugar, gold, silver, coffee, cocoa, tobacco, meats, consumer goods
Language(s)	Spanish (official), French Creole

The Dominican Republic (doh MIN ih kun rih PUB lik) occupies the eastern two thirds of Hispaniola. The island was first colonized by Spain. In 1697, France acquired the western third of Hispaniola. That part of the island became the independent country of Haiti in 1804. The remaining portion—which later became the Dominican Republic—was controlled by France, Spain, and Haiti at various times. It also suffered many revolutions and dictatorships. Today, its government is stable. Agriculture and tourism are important to the economy of the Dominican Republic.

Grenada

Nutmeg, Grenada

Capital	Saint George's
Land Area	133 sq mi; 344 sq km
Population	89,211
Ethnic Group(s)	black, mixed white and black, white, South Asian, Carib
Religion(s)	Roman Catholic, Protestant
Government	constitutional monarchy
Currency	East Caribbean dollar
Leading Exports	bananas, cocoa, nutmeg, fruits and vegetables, clothing, mace
Language(s)	English (official), English Creole

Grenada (gruh NAY duh) is an oval-shaped island in the eastern Caribbean Sea. It has forested mountains as well as highlands with many rivers and streams. Bays, natural harbors, and beaches dot the southern coast. Grenada is sometimes called the Isle of Spice because of its production of nutmeg, cinnamon, cloves, ginger, and vanilla. Agricultural exports and tourism support the economy. Once governed by France and later by Great Britain, Grenada is now an independent state within the British Commonwealth.

130 Latin America

Background: Links Across Place

Reggae This popular music dates to the 1960s when it developed among poor Jamaicans in Kingston, the country's capital. Its roots include ska, a Jamaican and British dance-hall music, traditional Jamaican and African folk music, and American soul music. Reggae features strong accents off the beat and instrumentation including electric guitars, organ, piano, and drums. The words to many reggae songs reflect Rastafarian beliefs. The singer Bob Marley and his group, the Wailers, helped to spread reggae, and it gained international popularity.

Haitian postage stamps

Haiti

Capital	Port-au-Prince
Land Area	10,641 sq mi; 27,560 sq km
Population	7.1 million
Ethnic Group(s)	black, mixed white and black, white
Religion(s)	Roman Catholic, Protestant, traditional beliefs
Government	elected government
Currency	gourde
Leading Exports	manufactured goods, coffee, oils, cocoa
Language(s)	French (official), French Creole (official)

Occupying the western third of the island of Hispaniola, Haiti (HAY tee) was once heavily forested. Today, there are few woodlands left, and much of the land is no longer able to support farming due to soil erosion. Even so, most of Haiti's people are farmers, although they have little modern machinery or fertilizers. Haiti is one of the most densely populated nations in the world and the poorest in the Western Hemisphere. Numerous revolutions and dictatorships have plagued Haiti since its hopeful beginning as the first independent nation in Latin America.

Jamaica

Capital	Kingston
Land Area	4,182 sq mi; 10,831 sq km
Population	2.7 million
Ethnic Group(s)	black, mixed white and black, South Asian, white, East Asian
Religion(s)	Protestant, Roman Catholic, traditional beliefs
Government	constitutional parliamentary democracy
Currency	Jamaican dollar
Leading Exports	alumina, bauxite, sugar, bananas, rum
Language(s)	English (official), English Creole

Jamaica (juh MAY kuh) is a mountainous island located 90 miles (145 kilometers) south of Cuba in the Caribbean Sea. Tourism is vital to the economy of this beautiful island. Most of the population lives on the coastal plains, and more than half of Jamaicans live in cities. The island was first colonized by the Spanish and then by the British. Enslaved Africans were brought to Jamaica to work on the sugar and coffee plantations. Today, Jamaica's population is diverse, including Asian and Arab immigrants as well as people of European and African descent.

Puerto Rico

Capital	San Juan
Land Area	3,459 sq mi; 8,959 sq km
Population	4.0 million
Ethnic Group(s)	white, black, indigenous Indian, Asian, mixed white and black
Religion(s)	Roman Catholic, Protestant
Government	commonwealth
Currency	U.S. dollar
Leading Exports	pharmaceuticals, electronics, apparel, canned tuna, beverage concentrates, medical equipment
Language(s)	Spanish and English (official)

The self-governing commonwealth of Puerto Rico (PWEHR tuh REE koh) lies approximately 50 miles (80 kilometers) east of the Dominican Republic in the Caribbean Sea. The northern shore of the main island faces the Atlantic Ocean. Several smaller islands are also part of the commonwealth. The island's economy originally depended on sugar. In the mid-1900s, however, industry and trade became more important. Today, Puerto Rico has a more diverse economy than any of the other Caribbean islands.

Chapter 5 **131**

- Ask **What are some characteristics of the population of Haiti?** *(They are black, mixed white and black, and white; belong to Roman Catholic or Protestant religions or practice traditional beliefs. Most are farmers.)*

- Ask students **How does the size and make-up of the population of Haiti compare with those of Puerto Rico?** *(Sample answer: Puerto Rico's population is slightly less than half the size of Haiti's, but it has more ethnic groups.)*

Independent Practice

- Provide students with *Outline Map 7: Central America and the Caribbean.*

   All in One Latin America Teaching Resources, *Outline Map 7: Central America and the Caribbean,* p. 297

- Have students put the capital of each country on the map. Students can refer to the map on page 127.

- Next, have students choose one of the following types of data—religion, government, or language(s)—to show on their maps. Remind them to make a map key with colors or symbols that match the information on their maps.

Monitor Progress

As students work, circulate to make sure they are converting the data to use on their maps in an appropriate way.

Assess and Reteach

Assess Progress [L2]

- Recall with students the information they volunteered about countries in the Caribbean before reading the Country Databank. Ask **How have you added to your knowledge?**

- Ask students to answer the Assessment questions.

Reteach [L1]

Use *Color Transparency LA 23: Central America and the Caribbean: Political* to help students locate the countries they have read about. As students locate each country, go over the key information given in the Databank. If students are having difficulty, review only one or two countries at a time.

 Latin America Transparencies, *Color Transparency LA 23: Central America and the Caribbean: Political*

Extend [L3]

Portfolio Activity

Have students choose one country in the Country Databank. Ask students to learn more about one or two aspects of the country, using the Internet or other reference sources. Then ask students to imagine that they have visited this country and are writing a letter to a friend about their observations. Students can add their letter to their portfolios.

Introducing The Caribbean

St. Kitts and Nevis

Capital	Basseterre
Land Area	101 sq mi; 261 sq km
Population	38,736
Ethnic Group(s)	black, white, Southwest Asian
Religion(s)	Roman Catholic, Protestant
Government	constitutional monarchy
Currency	East Caribbean dollar
Leading Exports	machinery, food, electronics, beverages, tobacco
Language(s)	English (official), English Creole

Two small islands located in the eastern Caribbean Sea make up the Federation of St. Kitts and Nevis (saynt kits and NEE vis). They gained their independence from Great Britain in 1983, and are now part of the British Commonwealth. The islands are of volcanic origin, and a dormant volcano is the highest point on St. Kitts. The beaches of that island have black, volcanic sands. Nevis is known for its hot and cold springs, and is surrounded by coral reefs. St. Kitts and Nevis have become popular tourist destinations.

St. Lucia

Capital	Castries
Land Area	234 sq mi; 606 sq km
Population	160,145
Ethnic Group(s)	black, mixed white and black, South Asian, white
Religion(s)	Roman Catholic, Protestant
Government	parliamentary democracy
Currency	East Caribbean dollar
Leading Exports	bananas, clothing, cocoa, vegetables, fruits, coconut oil
Language(s)	English (official), French Creole

The island nation of St. Lucia (saynt LOO shuh) is located in the eastern Caribbean Sea. Its geography is marked by wooded mountains and fertile valleys as well as by two huge pyramids of rock, called the Twin Pitons, which rise more than 2,400 feet (731.5 kilometers) from the sea. In the crater of a dormant volcano are boiling sulphur springs, which attract many tourists. St. Lucia's rain forests are also a major tourist attraction. Sugar cane was the most important crop on the island until 1964, when most of the land was converted to raising bananas.

St. Vincent and the Grenadines

Capital	Kingstown
Land Area	150 sq mi; 389 sq km
Population	116,394
Ethnic Group(s)	black, mixed white and black, South Asian, Carib
Religion(s)	Protestant, Roman Catholic, Hindu
Government	parliamentary democracy
Currency	East Caribbean dollar
Leading Exports	bananas, eddoes and dasheen, arrowroot starch, tennis racquets
Language(s)	English (official), English Creole

The nation of St. Vincent and the Grenadines (saynt VIN sunt and thuh GREN uh deenz) is made up of the island of St. Vincent and a string of islands called the Grenadines. They are located in the eastern Caribbean Sea, between St. Lucia and Grenada. St. Vincent has forested volcanic mountains. Its tallest volcano, Soufrière, last erupted in 1979, causing extensive damage. However, the volcanic ash has also made the soil fertile. The Grenadines are made up of coral reefs and have fine beaches. Therefore, it is not surprising that agriculture and tourism play important roles in the nation's economy.

132 Latin America

Trinidad and Tobago

Capital	Port-of-Spain
Land Area	1,980 sq mi; 5,128 sq km
Population	1.2 million
Ethnic Group(s)	black, South Asian, mixed white and black, white, East Asian
Religion(s)	Roman Catholic, Hindu, Muslim, Protestant
Government	parliamentary democracy
Currency	Trinidad and Tobago dollar
Leading Exports	petroleum and petroleum products, chemicals, steel products, fertilizer, sugar, cocoa, coffee, citrus, flowers
Language(s)	English (official), English Creole, Hindi, French, Spanish

SOURCES: DK World Desk Reference Online; *CIA World Factbook*, 2002; *World Almanac*, 2003

Trinidad and Tobago (TRIN ih dad and toh BAY goh) are located close to the South American coast, northeast of Venezuela. Trinidad, the larger island, has mountains with spectacular waterfalls as well as swampy areas. Tobago is surrounded by coral reefs. The reefs have rich marine life, and are popular tourist attractions. The bird sanctuary at Caroni Swamp also attracts tourists. Trinidad has a very diverse population, with Spanish, French, African, English, East Indian, and Chinese influences, and many languages are spoken there. Trinidad is known for its calypso and steel-drum music.

Green honeycreeper, Trinidad and Tobago

Assessment

Comprehension and Critical Thinking

1. Compare and Contrast Compare the physical size and population of Cuba to those of the Dominican Republic.

2. Draw Conclusions What are the characteristics that most Caribbean countries share?

3. Compare and Contrast What are some key differences among the countries?

4. Categorize Which countries rely on agricultural products as their major exports? Which rely on other products?

5. Infer How has geography influenced the economies of the Caribbean countries?

6. Make a Bar Graph Use your answer to Question 1 to make a bar graph. What does the graph reveal about the population densities of Cuba and the Dominican Republic?

Keeping Current

Access the **DK World Desk Reference Online** at **PHSchool.com** for up-to-date information about all the countries in this chapter.

Go Online
PHSchool.com

Web Code: lfe-1510

Answers

Assessment

1. Cuba has more than twice the land area of the Dominican Republic and has almost three million more people.

2. They are islands; they are small in land size, have fine beaches and tourist appeal; most have a democratic government, English as an official language, and Roman Catholicism and Protestantism as main religions.

3. Possible answers: Some countries are made up of more than one island, while others consist of only one island; their people speak different languages such as English, French, and Spanish; they use different forms of money such as the East Caribbean dollar, the Bahamian dollar, or the Dominican Republic peso; they have different forms of government such as constitutional monarchies, a communist state, and a representative democracy.

4. Answers will vary because most countries have a combination of agricultural and other products for export. Mostly agricultural: Dominica, Grenada, St. Lucia, Saint Vincent and the Grenadines; Mostly other products: Antigua and Barbuda, Bahamas, Barbados, Cuba, Dominican Republic, Haiti, Jamaica, Puerto Rico, Saint Kitts and Nevis, Trinidad and Tobago.

5. Many rely on tourism because of their climate, beaches, and beautiful waters. The climate is also an asset for growing crops.

6. Students should conclude that the Dominican Republic is more densely populated because it is a much smaller country in terms of land. Use *Rubric for Assessing a Bar Graph* to evaluate students' work.

All in One Latin America Teaching Resources, *Rubric for Assessing a Bar Graph*, p. 302

Section 1
Step-by-Step Instruction

Objectives

Social Studies
1. Find out how Cuba's history led to thousands of Cubans leaving their homeland.
2. Discover how Cuban exiles feel about their lives in the United States and about their homeland.
3. Learn what changes have recently come to Cuba.

Reading/Language Arts
Identify main ideas in a section or paragraph.

Prepare to Read

Build Background Knowledge `L2`
In this section, students will learn about the political and economic history of Cuba. Ask students to preview the headings and visuals in the section with this question in mind: **How has the government in Cuba affected the lives of the Cuban people?** Provide a few simple examples to get students started. Have students engage in a Think-Pair-Share activity (TE, p. T36) to share their answers.

Set a Purpose for Reading `L2`
- Preview the Objectives.
- Form students into pairs or groups of four. Distribute the *Reading Readiness Guide*. Ask students to fill in the first two columns of the chart. Use the Numbered Heads participation structure (TE, p. T36) to call on students to share one piece of information they already know and one piece of information they want to know.

All in One Latin America Teaching Resources, *Reading Readiness Guide,* p. 276

Vocabulary Builder
Preview Key Terms `L2`
Pronounce each Key Term, then ask students to say the word with you. Provide a simple explanation, such as, "Someone who is illiterate cannot read a newspaper or a book."

Section 1
Cuba
Clinging to Communism

Prepare to Read

Objectives
In this section you will
1. Find out how Cuba's history led to thousands of Cubans leaving their homeland.
2. Discover how Cuban exiles feel about their lives in the United States and about their homeland.
3. Learn about recent changes in Cuba.

Taking Notes
As you read this section, look for details about life in communist Cuba. Copy the web diagram below, and record your findings in it.

Target Reading Skill
Identify Main Ideas It is impossible to remember every detail that you read. Good readers identify the main idea in every section or paragraph. The main idea is the most important point—the one that includes all the other points. For example, the first sentence under the red heading Cuban Exiles states the main idea of that portion of text.

Key Terms
- **Fidel Castro** (fih DEL KAS troh) *n.* the leader of Cuba's government
- **communism** (KAHM yoo niz um) *n.* an economic system in which the government owns all large businesses and most of the country's land
- **illiterate** (ih LIT ur ut) *adj.* unable to read and write
- **ally** (AL eye) *n.* a country joined to another country for a special purpose
- **exile** (EK syl) *n.* a person who leaves his or her homeland for another country, often for political reasons

Cubans in a makeshift raft set out for the United States.

134 Latin America

In the summer of 1994, more than 20,000 Cubans took to the sea. They sailed on anything that would float—rubber tires, old boats, and homemade rafts. One hope kept them going. It was the thought of making it to the United States. They wanted desperately to live in the United States as immigrants.

These Cubans left their homeland for two main reasons. One reason was Cuba's struggling economy. People often did not have enough to eat. Clothing, medicine, and other basic necessities were also hard to get. A desire for freedom was even more important to many Cubans. Cuba's leader, **Fidel Castro** (fih DEL KAS troh), was a dictator. He did not allow Cubans to speak out against government policies they disagreed with.

Political and economic changes in Cuba caused many of its citizens to leave their country. How and why did these changes occur? How has Cuba changed since then?

Target Reading Skill `L2`
Identifying Main Ideas Draw attention to the Target Reading Skill. Remind students that the main idea is the most important point in a section or paragraph. The other information in the section or paragraph tells more about the main idea.

Model identifying the main idea using the first paragraph on page 136. The main idea is the first sentence: "At the same time, Castro's

government brought some improvements to Cuba." (The rest of the paragraph gives two examples of these improvements—improved literacy and access to health care.)

Give students *Identify Main Ideas*. Have them complete the activity in their groups.

All in One Latin America Teaching Resources, *Identify Main Ideas,* p. 287

Cuba's History

Cuba's government and economy had once been very different than they were in 1994. Although it is a small country, Cuba has many advantages. It has fertile farmland. It is located at the entrance to the Gulf of Mexico, and has excellent harbors. The map titled The Caribbean: Political, at the beginning of this chapter, shows why Cuba's location makes it a good place for trade with the United States and other parts of the Caribbean.

Cuban Independence When the United States won the Spanish-American War in 1898, Cuba gained its independence from Spain. In the years that followed, Cuba became the richest country in the Caribbean. Sugar planters made money selling to people in the United States. Hotels were built, and tourists came to Cuba to enjoy its beautiful beaches and wonderful climate. Many Cubans became businesspeople, teachers, doctors, and lawyers.

Not all Cubans shared in the country's wealth, however. Most farm and factory workers earned low wages. Cuba also had many harsh leaders who ruled as dictators. In the 1950s, Fulgencio Batista (fool HEN see oh bah TEE stah) ruled Cuba. Rebel groups began forming. They wanted to remove the corrupt Batista regime and change the country.

Communism in Cuba A young lawyer named Fidel Castro led one of these small rebel groups. After two attempts to overthrow the government, he was finally successful in 1959.

Fidel Castro still holds power in Cuba today. Castro's government is communist. Under **communism,** the government owns all large businesses and most of the country's land. After Castro took power, the Cuban government nationalized, or took over, private businesses and land. Further, Castro said that newspapers and books could print only information supporting his government. Anyone who disagreed with government policy was put in jail. Huge numbers of Cubans fled the island. Many settled in Miami, Florida, in a neighborhood that came to be called Little Havana, named after the capital of Cuba.

An Important Vote
Fulgencio Batista, "strong man" of Cuba, casts his vote in the 1940 presidential election. **Infer** *Why do you think dictators hold "elections"?*

Learn about baseball in Cuba.

Chapter 5 Section 1 **135**

Instruct

Cuba's History L2

Guided Instruction

- **Vocabulary Builder** Clarify the high-use words **dictator**, **corrupt**, and **missile** before reading.
- Read Cuba's History, using Partner Paragraph Shrinking (TE, p. T34).
- Discuss the changes that Fidel Castro's government brought to Cuba. *(Many Cubans fled the country. Castro's government took over the land and businesses of people, suppressed information that didn't support the government, and jailed those who opposed it. The government also improved literacy and provided health care.)*
- Ask students: **Why do you think Castro has been able to stay in power for so long?** *(Possible answer: Castro has a tight hold on Cuba. The government owns most of the businesses. Castro was backed by the Soviet Union with money and supplies for a long time.)*

Independent Practice

Have students create the Taking Notes graphic organizer on a blank piece of paper. Then have them begin to fill in the circles on the web with information about life in communist Cuba.

Monitor Progress

As students fill in the graphic organizer, circulate and make sure individuals are choosing relevant details. Provide assistance as needed.

Answers

Infer Possible answer: Dictators may hold elections to give the impression that the government is democratic.

Vocabulary Builder

Use the information below to teach students this section's high-use words.

High-Use Word	Definition and Sample Sentence
dictator, p. 134	*n.* a ruler with complete power The **dictator** would not allow any kind of music to be played in his country.
corrupt, p. 135	*adj.* dishonest, crooked We do not do business with them because they seem **corrupt**.
missile, p. 136	*n.* a weapon that shoots into the air The **missile** soared overhead as it flew to reach its target.
collapse, p. 139	*n.* breakdown The **collapse** of the bridge occurred when the support columns crumbled.

Identify Main Ideas As a follow-up, ask students to answer the Target Reading Skill question in the Student Edition. *(The United States viewed communist Cuba as a threat to American interests in the region.)*

Cuban Exiles   **L2**

Guided Instruction

- Read the stories in Cuban Exiles with students. Then ask students to read Links Across the World.

- Ask students to name some successes and difficulties faced by Cuban exiles in the United States. *(Successes—Many have become successful in business in Florida, serve as elected officials, and influence government policy. Difficulties—At times, exiles have been unable to communicate with their families in Cuba; some have disturbing memories of their former lives and trips to the United States.)*

Independent Practice

Have students continue to fill in their graphic organizers.

Monitor Progress

Circulate to make sure students are filling in their graphic organizers correctly. Provide assistance as needed.

The Cold War Heats Up
The photo at the left shows Fidel Castro and Nikita Khrushchev, the Soviet premier. At the right, an American patrol plane flies over a Soviet freighter during the Cuban Missile Crisis. **Infer** *What kind of relationship did Cuba and the Soviet Union have in the 1960s?*

 Identify Main Ideas What sentence states the main idea of the text headed Cold War Crisis?

At the same time, Castro's government brought some improvements to Cuba. In the 1960s and 1970s, many Cubans were **illiterate**, or unable to read and write. Castro sent teachers into the countryside, and literacy improved dramatically. Today, about 97 percent of Cubans can read and write. The government also provides basic health care for all.

As a communist country, Cuba became an ally of the Soviet Union. An **ally** is a country joined with another country for a special purpose. The Soviet Union was the most powerful communist nation in the world. It wanted to spread communism worldwide. The Soviets sent money and supplies to Cuba. Relations between Cuba and the United States grew worse when the United States openly welcomed the people who fled from Cuba.

Cold War Crisis The United States viewed communist Cuba as a threat to American interests in the region. This was a period of tension between the United States and the Soviet Union and their allies. It was called the Cold War because the conflict did not involve "hot," or military, action.

In the 1960s, the Soviets began sending military support to Cuba. Then, in 1962, photographs taken by American aircraft revealed the construction of Soviet atomic-missile sites in Cuba. Those missiles would be able to reach the United States.

President John F. Kennedy demanded the missiles be removed, and sent the American navy to prevent Soviet ships from going to Cuba. He said that an attack from Cuba would be viewed as an attack by the Soviet Union. After a week of tension called the Cuban Missile Crisis, Soviet Premier Nikita Khrushchev agreed to remove the missiles if the United States promised not to invade Cuba. A "hot" war was prevented, but the Cold War continued.

✓ **Reading Check** What was the Cuban Missile Crisis?

Answers

Infer Possible answer: Cuba and the Soviet Union were allies against the United States.

✓ **Reading Check** It was a situation created when the United States learned that the Soviet Union had sent atomic missiles to Cuba, a country within striking distance of the United States. The United States called out its navy to prevent Soviet ships from going to Cuba, and after a week of tension the Soviet Union agreed to remove the missiles if the United States would promise not to invade Cuba.

Differentiated Instruction

For Less Proficient Readers   **L1**
Students who are less proficient readers may have trouble absorbing the information in this section. Have students work in pairs to create an outline of the material. They should use the headings in the section as a framework.

For Special Needs Students   **L1**
Partner students with more able students. Have students write on a sheet of paper the three headings of Cuba's History. As each pair reads this section, have them determine the main idea of the text related to the heading. Then have students write a sentence on their sheet of paper stating the main idea for each.

Cuban Exiles

Cubans have been leaving their country ever since Castro took power. They have become exiles. An **exile** is a person who leaves his or her homeland for another country, usually for political reasons. A large number of Cuban exiles have come to the United States to live.

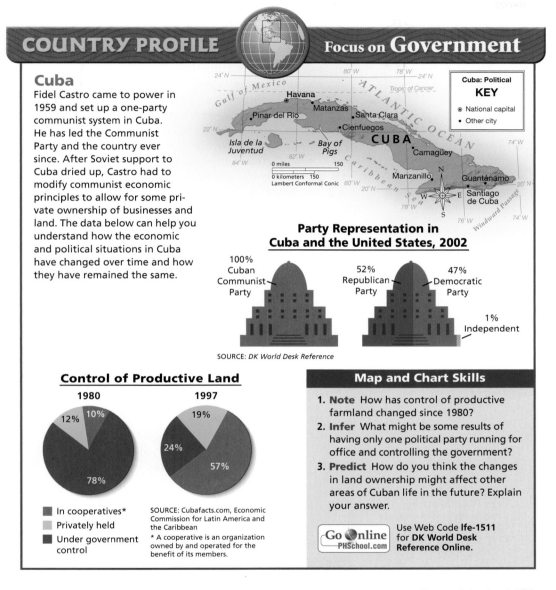

COUNTRY PROFILE
Focus on **Government**

Cuba

Fidel Castro came to power in 1959 and set up a one-party communist system in Cuba. He has led the Communist Party and the country ever since. After Soviet support to Cuba dried up, Castro had to modify communist economic principles to allow for some private ownership of businesses and land. The data below can help you understand how the economic and political situations in Cuba have changed over time and how they have remained the same.

Cuba: Political KEY
- ⊛ National capital
- • Other city

Party Representation in Cuba and the United States, 2002

- 100% Cuban Communist Party
- 52% Republican Party
- 47% Democratic Party
- 1% Independent

SOURCE: *DK World Desk Reference*

Control of Productive Land

1980
- 12%
- 10%
- 78%

1997
- 19%
- 24%
- 57%

- ■ In cooperatives*
- ▨ Privately held
- ■ Under government control

SOURCE: Cubafacts.com, Economic Commission for Latin America and the Caribbean
* A cooperative is an organization owned by and operated for the benefit of its members.

Map and Chart Skills

1. **Note** How has control of productive farmland changed since 1980?
2. **Infer** What might be some results of having only one political party running for office and controlling the government?
3. **Predict** How do you think the changes in land ownership might affect other areas of Cuban life in the future? Explain your answer.

Go Online PHSchool.com
Use Web Code **lfe-1511** for **DK World Desk Reference Online.**

 Skills Mini Lesson

Decision Making L2

1. Point out to students that they often make decisions. First, they identify the problem. Then they think of possible options. Next they evaluate each option. Finally, they choose an option.
2. Have students practice the skill by reading the Links Across the World feature

on page 138. Tell them to identify the problem facing some Cuban baseball players. *(Should they defect to the U.S.?)* Ask students to list options and note the pros and cons for each.

3. Have students apply the skill by deciding what they would do if they were a Cuban baseball player.

COUNTRY PROFILE
Focus on **Government**

Guided Instruction L2

Ask students to study the text and visuals in the Country Profile on this page. As a class, answer the Map and Chart Skills questions. Allow students to discuss their responses with a partner before sharing.

Independent Practice

Ask students to represent on a circle graph the number of people in 2003's National Assembly of the People's Power who belonged to the Cuban Communist Party. *(It would show one circle with no sections to represent 100 percent.)*

Answers

Map and Chart Skills

1. Less is under government control and more is in cooperatives or is privately held.
2. There would be little opposition to government policies in a one-party system.
3. As people gain more control in one area, they might want it in others.

Go Online PHSchool.com Students can find more information about this topic on the DK World Desk Reference Online.

Changes Come to Cuba L2

Guided Instruction

- **Vocabulary Builder** Clarify the high-use word **collapse** before reading.

- Ask students to read about and describe the changes in Cuba beginning in the 1990s. Allow students to share answers with a partner before responding. *(Private ownership of some businesses has been allowed; tourism has been encouraged; the United States has loosened travel restrictions; American businesspeople and farmers hope to trade in Cuba; the Cuban economy is improving and there is more interest in trade.)*

Independent Practice

Have students complete the graphic organizer.

Monitor Progress

- Show *Section Reading Support Transparency 5.1* and ask students to check their graphic organizers individually. Go over key concepts and clarify key vocabulary as needed. Provide assistance as needed.

  📖 **Latin America Transparencies,** *Section Reading Support Transparency LA 42*

- Tell students to fill in the last column of the *Reading Readiness Guide.* Ask them to evaluate if what they learned was what they had expected to learn.

  All in One Latin America Teaching Resources, *Reading Readiness Guide,* p. 276

Links Across The World

The Baseball Connection
You've probably heard that baseball is "America's pastime," but did you know that it is also the national pastime of Cuba? Baseball has been played on the island since the 1860s, and major league teams used Cuba for spring training until Castro took power. Cubans also played in the major leagues. Today, however, the Cuban government regards baseball stars who leave the country as traitors. Nevertheless, many Cuban players have defected, or come to the United States. Orlando Hernandez, called El Duque (el DOO kay), or "The Duke," fled Cuba by boat in 1997. He became a starring pitcher for the New York Yankees as shown above.

A New Life Lydia Martin left Cuba in 1970 when she was only six years old. Her mother had grown tired of the limits on freedom and lack of opportunity in communist Cuba. She wanted to take Lydia to the United States. Lydia's father begged them to stay. He asked them, "Have you stopped to think you may never see me again?"

Like Lydia, many Cuban exiles left family members behind. They dream of returning to Cuba—once it is no longer a communist country. Meanwhile, many Cubans have made successful new lives in the United States. A large number have settled in Miami, Florida. In the Cuban neighborhood of Little Havana, they keep their language and their culture alive. At the same time, they have become important in the economic, cultural, and political life of Miami and the state of Florida. They own successful businesses, serve as elected officials, and influence government policy.

When relations between the United States and Cuba grew worse in the 1970s, Cuban exiles suffered. They could not even write to the families they had left behind. Castro's government might punish people who got a letter from the United States. What's more, the United States did not allow Americans to visit Cuba.

Cuban exiles playing dominoes in Little Havana, Miami, Florida

138 Latin America

┌─ Background: Link Across Time ─

Cash Crop The chief crop grown in Cuba is sugar cane, the plant from which refined sugar and cane sugar come. Sugar cane plants, originally from Asia, were introduced to the Americas by Spanish and Portuguese explorers in the fifteenth and sixteenth centuries. In a tropical climate, such as that of Cuba, the plant, once a costly luxury or medicine, thrived. Today, Cuba and India produce a large percentage of the world's cane sugar.

Another Wave of Exiles In 1991, the government of the Soviet Union collapsed and could no longer help Cuba. Food, medicine, tools, and other necessities became even more scarce in Cuba. Many families had little more than rice to eat.

As the situation in Cuba worsened, more people wanted to leave the island. Vanesa Alonso (vah NES uh ah LOHN soh) was one of them. In 1994, Vanesa and her family left Cuba on a rickety raft. Today, Vanesa lives in Miami, just a few miles from the ocean, but she hardly ever goes to the beach. The blue waves and roaring surf remind her of her terrifying trip from Cuba to the United States. That memory still gives her bad dreams.

✓ **Reading Check** What caused another wave of exiles?

Changes Come to Cuba

In the 1990s, when Cuba's economy was near collapse, Castro began allowing private ownership of some businesses. In addition, the Cuban government began encouraging tourism. The United States also loosened some restrictions on travel to Cuba. American businesspeople and farmers have begun to visit Cuba, hoping to sell their products there. The Cuban economy is improving. Castro has ruled Cuba for more than 40 years. Many Cuban exiles hope that the regime that follows Castro's will encourage better relations with the United States. They hope that they will be able to return home or to visit there in freedom.

✓ **Reading Check** What changes did Castro make in the 1990s?

New Visitors
Tourism increased in Cuba during the 1990s. **Analyze Images** *Judging from this photo of Havana, why might tourists want to visit Cuba?*

Section 1 Assessment

Key Terms
Review the key terms at the beginning of this section. Use each term in a sentence that explains its meaning.

🔄 **Target Reading Skills**
One important main idea of this section is stated on the first page. What is it?

Comprehension and Critical Thinking
1. (a) **Describe** How did Castro come to power in Cuba?

(b) **Identify Effects** How did life for Cubans change—for better and for worse—under Castro's rule?
(c) **Synthesize** What role did the Soviet Union play in Cuba?
2. (a) **Define** What is Little Havana?
(b) **Find Main Ideas** How have many Cubans adapted to life in the United States?
3. (a) **Recall** What do Cuban exiles hope will happen in Cuba in the near future?
(b) **Predict** What changes do you think are in store for Cuba? Explain your answer.

Writing Activity
Write a letter to a relative in Cuba from the point of view of a Cuban exile in the United States. Have another student write a response from the point of view of the Cuban relative. The relatives should exchange information about their daily lives and their hopes for the future.

> **Writing Tip** Before you begin, decide on the age, gender, and personality of the person writing the letter.

Assess Progress
Have students complete the Section Assessment. Administer the *Section Quiz.*

> 🔲 **Latin America Teaching Resources,** *Section Quiz,* p. 278

Reteach
If students need more instruction, have them read this section in the *Reading and Vocabulary Study Guide.*

> 📖 Chapter 5, Section 1, **Latin America Reading and Vocabulary Study Guide,** pp. 52–54

Extend
Have students learn more about the Caribbean pastime—baseball— as well as the history of the game in the region, the players, and the Pan American Games by completing the *Enrichment* activity.

> 🔲 **Latin America Teaching Resources,** *Enrichment,* p. 291

Answers

Analyze Images Tourists may be attracted to Cuba's nice weather, shopping areas, and history.

✓ **Reading Check** More people wanted to leave Cuba because food and other necessities became scarce after the Soviet Union collapsed so Castro allowed private ownership of some businesses and encouraged tourism.

Writing Activity
Use the *Rubric for Assessing a Writing Assignment* to evaluate students' journal entries.

> 🔲 **Latin America Teaching Resources,** *Rubric for Assessing a Writing Assignment,* p. 303

Section 1 Assessment

Key Terms
Students' sentences should reflect knowledge of each Key Term.

🔄 **Target Reading Skill**
Political and economic changes in Cuba caused many of its citizens to leave their country.

Comprehension and Critical Thinking
1. (a) He led a rebel group to overthrow the government of Batista. (b) Better—Cubans were taught to read and given health care. Worse—Many people lost their land, businesses, and freedom of speech. (c) It became an ally and sent money and supplies to Cuba.

2. (a) a Cuban neighborhood in Miami, Florida (b) Many have made successful new lives.

3. (a) They hope the regime that follows Castro will have better relations with the United States. (b) Students' predictions should be based on information they have acquired.

Objective

Learn how to compare and contrast information.

Prepare to Read

Build Background Knowledge `L2`

Ask students to think of the variety of countries in the Caribbean region and have them select two or three that they might like to visit. Then ask how comparing and contrasting these places might help them decide where to go.

Instruct

Comparing and Contrasting `L2`

Guided Instruction

- Read the steps as a class to learn how to compare and contrast. Then write them on the board.

- Practice the skill by following the steps on page 141 as a class. Model each step in the activity. Show students how to choose a topic and categories for comparison, note details about each place, identify similarities and differences, and draw a conclusion about which vacation spot they might prefer.

Independent Practice

Assign *Skills for Life* and have students complete it individually.

All in One Latin America Teaching Resources, *Skills for Life,* p. 292

Monitor Progress

The teacher should monitor the students doing the *Skills for Life* worksheet, checking to make sure they understand the skills steps.

Skills for Life — Comparing and Contrasting

"Come to the Caribbean," say the TV ads. But which Caribbean will you choose: an island with a Spanish culture or one with Native American, African, British, or French heritage? Do you want a luxury resort or a small village?
To plan your trip, you'd have to think about what you want to see and do and about which islands have these characteristics.
Then you would use the skill of comparing and contrasting to decide which country to visit.

To compare and contrast means to look for similarities and differences. It is a skill you use often, but you can learn to use it even more effectively by following the steps below.

Learn the Skill

Follow the steps below to learn the skill of comparing and contrasting.

 1 **Identify a topic and purpose.** What do you want to compare, and why? Some examples of a purpose are to make a choice, to understand a topic, and to discover patterns.

2 **Select some categories for comparison.** For example, if you wanted to choose between two cars, your categories might be model, cost, and power seats.

3 **Make notes or a chart about the categories you're comparing.** A category such as power seats calls for a *yes* or a *no*. For other categories, such as model or cost, you need to note specific details.

4 **Identify the similarities and differences.** For each category, are the things you are comparing the same or different? What are the differences? Which differences are most important for your purpose?

5 **Draw conclusions.** Use the similarities and differences you found to answer an important question about your topic or to make a choice.

Democracy in Danger

The year after Aristide's election, thousands of his supporters fled Haiti's capital, Port-au-Prince (pawrt oh PRANS). Some squeezed into trucks by the dozen and went to hide in the hills. Others tore their homes apart to make rafts. Then they took to the sea.

The Boat People The Haitians who fled by sea became known as the Haitian boat people. Because they left their homeland to protect their own personal safety and escape persecution, they are called **refugees.** Many Haitian boat people headed for the United States.

The Beaubrun (boh BRUN) family was among those refugees. Bazelais (bah zuh LAY) Beaubrun had spoken out against the military government in Haiti. Soldiers had threatened Bazelais, and he knew his life was in danger if he stayed. First Bazelais went into hiding. Then he took his family onto a crowded boat that was headed for the United States.

The United States Coast Guard stopped the boat and took the Haitians to an American military base. United States officials wanted to make sure that Bazelais was really in danger for his political beliefs. If so, he and his family could immigrate to the United States. After three months, the Beaubruns were allowed to enter the United States. Some families were not as lucky as the Beaubruns. United States officials sent them back to Haiti.

The Birth of Haiti The military takeover in 1991 does not mean that most Haitians did not want democracy. Their country was born out of a desperate struggle for freedom. Haiti is the only nation in the Americas formed from a successful revolt of enslaved Africans.

As you can see on the map of Haiti on the next page, Haiti lies on the western third of the island of Hispaniola. It was once a colony of France. Europeans brought enslaved Africans to Haiti to work on sugar cane and coffee plantations. In the 1790s, slave revolts began. The Haitian leader Toussaint L'Ouverture helped banish slavery from Haiti in 1801. He also offered Haitians a new way of life, based on the idea that all people could live as equals.

Refugees
The Beaubrun family escaped from Haiti and now live in Brooklyn, New York. **Infer** *Why would it be particularly difficult for a family like the Beaubruns, with young children, to make the journey described here?*

Learn about everyday life in Haiti.

Democracy in Danger L2

Guided Instruction

- **Vocabulary Builder** Clarify the high-use words **prosperity** and **fraud** before reading.

- Read Democracy in Danger using the Oral Cloze technique (TE, p. T33).

- Discuss the problems that the Beaubruns faced in leaving Haiti and immigrating to the United States. *(They were threatened by Haitian soldiers and had to go into hiding; they took a crowded boat to the United States and waited three months for approval for entry.)*

- Ask **Why do you think Haitians have been willing to undergo hardships to get to the United States?** *(The constant military struggles and harsh dictators have caused upheaval and persecution and have ruined the economy.)*

Show students *Haiti: A Striving Nation.* Ask students for examples from the video that support the concept of Haiti as a striving nation. *(Students might mention farmers working, women carrying water and goods, children learning in school, or examples from Haiti's history as the only nation in the Americas to be formed from a successful revolt of enslaved Africans).*

Vocabulary Builder

Use the information below to teach students this section's high-use words.

High-Use Word	Definition and Sample Sentence
prosperity, p. 145	*n.* the condition of being wealthy, successful
	The increase in employment illustrates the company's **prosperity**.
fraud, p. 145	*n.* a deception for unlawful gain
	The defendant was found guilty of **fraud** for cheating on his taxes.
dispute, p. 147	*n.* a quarrel or argument
	A **dispute** developed between the umpire and the batter.

Answer

Infer Possible answer: Rafts may be unsafe for ocean travel and some children may not know how to swim.

Guided Instruction   L2

Ask students to study the Country Profile on this page. Have them read the text and study the visual material. As a class, answer the Map and Chart Skills questions. Allow students to discuss their responses with a partner before sharing answers.

Independent Practice

- Distribute *Outline Map 7: Central America and the Caribbean.* Have students work with partners to label the bodies of water, Haiti, the Dominican Republic, the Bahamas, and the United States. Ask students to trace possible routes that boat people from Haiti might take as they try to reach the United States.

  All in One Latin America Teaching Resources, *Outline Map 7: Central America and the Caribbean,* p. 297

- Have partners write a statement suggesting how events listed on the timeline may have caused hardships for Haitians.

Answers

Map and Chart Skills

1. Dominican Republic

2. to the United States, Canada, the Bahamas, France, and the Dominican Republic

3. The western part of Hispaniola was acquired by France in 1697.

4. Unemployment is high, the ratio of doctors to people is low, and life expectancy is low.

5. Students may answer that Haitians might want to return to Haiti if there were peace, opportunities to work, and improved health conditions.

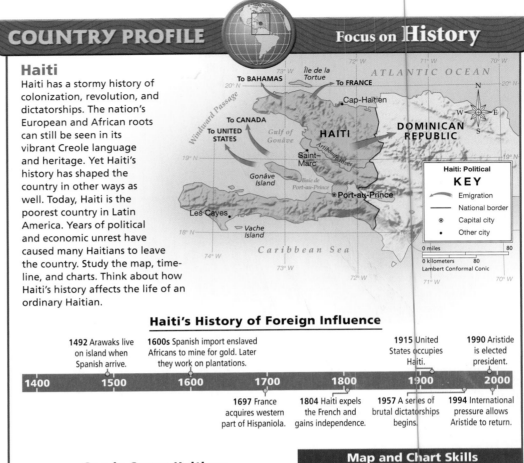

COUNTRY PROFILE — Focus on History

Haiti

Haiti has a stormy history of colonization, revolution, and dictatorships. The nation's European and African roots can still be seen in its vibrant Creole language and heritage. Yet Haiti's history has shaped the country in other ways as well. Today, Haiti is the poorest country in Latin America. Years of political and economic unrest have caused many Haitians to leave the country. Study the map, timeline, and charts. Think about how Haiti's history affects the life of an ordinary Haitian.

Haiti: Political — KEY
- Emigration
- National border
- ⊛ Capital city
- • Other city

Haiti's History of Foreign Influence

1492 Arawaks live on island when Spanish arrive.

1600s Spanish import enslaved Africans to mine for gold. Later they work on plantations.

1915 United States occupies Haiti.

1990 Aristide is elected president.

| 1400 | 1500 | 1600 | 1700 | 1800 | 1900 | 2000 |

1697 France acquires western part of Hispaniola.

1804 Haiti expels the French and gains independence.

1957 A series of brutal dictatorships begins.

1994 International pressure allows Aristide to return.

One in Seven Haitians Has Emigrated

Haiti Today

Unemployment	Ratio of Doctors to People	Life Expectancy
70%	1 doctor per 5,000 people	52 years

SOURCE: DK World Desk Reference

Map and Chart Skills

1. **Identify** Haiti shares an island with which country?
2. **Locate** Where do Haitians go when they leave their country?
3. **Identify Causes** What information in the timeline helps explain why Haiti's culture has many French influences?
4. **Infer** What data in the table show why some Haitians choose to leave?
5. **Predict** What changes in Haiti might encourage Haitians who have emigrated to return to their country?

Differentiated Instruction

For Gifted and Talented   L3

Have students choose one of Haiti's past leaders. Ask students to learn more about this person and his or her impact on the country. Have students prepare a brief oral report to deliver to the class.

Years of Dictatorship In the years that followed, Toussaint L'Ouverture's goal of freedom and equality was never fully realized. Most of Haiti's presidents became dictators once they got into power. One of the worst was François Duvalier (frahn SWAH doo vahl YAY), who took power in 1957. Because Duvalier had been a country doctor, Haitians called him "Papa Doc." Papa Doc was followed by his son, Jean-Claude Duvalier (zhan KLAWD doo vahl YAY), or "Baby Doc." Both were cruel leaders who stole government funds and used violence to keep power.

In 1986, rebels forced Baby Doc to leave the country. Many Haitians thought a period of freedom and prosperity was about to begin. Instead, Haiti was ruled by one military dictator after another.

A Brief Period of Hope Aristide's election in 1990 briefly brought hope to Haitians. However, these hopes were dashed when yet another military uprising forced Aristide to flee the country. The United States and other nations pressured the military to give power back to Aristide. In 1994, Aristide returned to Haiti, restoring democratic government. Haitians rejoiced, believing that peace and progress would follow.

In national elections held in 2000, it seemed that Aristide's supporters had won control of the legislature, and Aristide again assumed the presidency. But the election results were challenged. Many people claimed that there had been cheating and fraud. Because of the disputed election, international aid to Haiti stopped, and the weak Haitian economy got worse. Many Haitians began to call for Aristide to resign. In early 2004, after rebel groups gained control of much of Haiti, Aristide resigned and left the country. Democracy in Haiti was threatened again.

✓ **Reading Check** What were the results of the 2000 elections?

Citizen Heroes

Loune Viaud: Winner of Human Rights Award

Loune Viaud (loon vee OH) has been fighting injustice for a long time. During "Baby Doc's" regime, she courageously spoke out for human rights. Today she fights for all Haitians to have the right to healthcare—no matter how poor or sick they are. Viaud runs a clinic and works to ensure safe drinking water. When she received the 2002 Robert F. Kennedy Human Rights Award, Viaud called herself "a humble foot soldier in the struggle for health and human rights."

Haitians cheer for Jean-Bertrand Aristide upon his return in 1994.

Guided Instruction (continued)

■ Ask students **What has been a main cause of Haiti's lack of success in achieving democracy?** (*Haiti hasn't had the right kind of leadership for a democracy. The military holds too much power.*)

Independent Practice

Ask students to copy the Taking Notes graphic organizer on a blank piece of paper. Then have them fill in events that they have read about. Briefly model how to decide which events to include.

Monitor Progress

■ Show *Section Reading Support Transparency LA 43* and have students check their graphic organizers individually. Go over key concepts and clarify key vocabulary as needed.

📖 **Latin America Transparencies,** *Section Reading Support Transparency LA 43*

Links

Read the **Citizen Heroes** on this page. Ask students **Why do you think Viaud was courageous during "Baby Doc's" regime?** (*She was probably in danger because she spoke out for human rights.*)

Answers

✓ **Reading Check** The election was disputed amid accusations of cheating and fraud, and as a result, international aid was withdrawn, causing Haiti's economy to worsen.

Identify Supporting Details As a follow-up, ask students to answer the Target Reading Skill question in the Student Edition. (*Most Haitians are descended from enslaved Africans, and Creole, based on French and African languages, is spoken in Haiti.*)

The People of Haiti L2

Guided Instruction

- **Vocabulary Builder** Clarify the high-use word **dispute** before reading.

- Read The People of Haiti with students. As students read, circulate and make sure individuals can answer the Reading Check question.

- Ask students **Which traditions blend to create the culture of Haiti?** (*French, African, and West Indian traditions*)

- Ask students to explain how people in rural parts of Haiti often trade one kind of poverty for another when they move to the city. (*People in the countryside are usually farmers who struggle to grow enough food on small plots. When they go to the city looking for work, they end up in poor neighborhoods.*)

Independent Practice

Assign *Guided Reading and Review.*

All in One Latin America Teaching Resources, *Guided Reading and Review,* p. 281

Monitor Progress

Have students fill in the last column of the *Reading Readiness Guide.* Probe for what they learned that confirms or invalidates each statement.

All in One Latin America Teaching Resources, *Reading Readiness Guide,* p. 280

Answer

Synthesize Rural Haitians use resources from the sea and build their homes with local resources.

Identify Supporting Details
What details in the paragraph at the right are examples that support this idea: Haitian culture blends African, French, and West Indian traditions?

The People of Haiti

The Haitian people have suffered a great deal. Nevertheless, Haitian refugees remember many good things about their homeland: the warm weather, children playing soccer with their friends, dressing up for church, and many festivals. Haitian culture blends African, French, and West Indian traditions. Nearly all of Haiti's people are descended from the enslaved Africans who were brought to Haiti during colonial times. Haitians of mixed African and European ancestry are referred to as **Creole.** They are a minority in Haiti, but they have much of the wealth and power. Creole also refers to the language spoken in Haiti, which is based on both French and African languages.

Rural Life Today, Haiti is the poorest country in the Western Hemisphere. About two thirds of the people struggle to make a living farming small plots of land. But the land has been overused. Most trees have been cut. Rains wash the topsoil into the sea. When farmer Pierre Joseph stands on his small farm, he can see the calm waters of the Caribbean. When he looks down, he sees the dry, cracked earth of his one-acre field. Joseph is thin because he rarely gets enough to eat. "The land just doesn't yield enough," he says. He points to the few rows of corn and beans that he can grow on his one acre.

Fishing and Farming
A rural fisherman casts his net (above). The homes in the photo at the right have adobe walls and thatched roofs.
Synthesize *What can you learn about rural life in Haiti from these photos?*

146 Latin America

Skills Mini Lesson

Supporting a Position L2

1. Point out that people generally have a position, or view, on subjects. Explain that reasons, supported by evidence such as facts, statistics, and statements from experts, help to support a position.

2. Have students practice the skill by taking a position on whether or not Haitians should leave the countryside for the city. Have students list evidence for their position.

3. Have students apply the skill by writing a paragraph stating a position and supporting it with evidence.

City Life Because of rural poverty, many people have left the countryside for the cities. They come to Port-au-Prince looking for work. Most poor people from the country cannot afford decent housing. They live in the poorest neighborhoods. These areas are dirty and crowded. The streets are not paved, so the rain turns them to mud. Many of the tiny homes are made of crumbling concrete. At the same time, the wealthy live in large wooden houses on the hills overlooking the city. There is also a small middle class of doctors, lawyers, teachers, and owners of small businesses. These people live fairly well. But the overwhelming majority of Haitians—in the city as well as in the countryside—are poor.

What Lies Ahead Recent election disputes and political violence have put Haitian democracy at risk once again. And these conditions have hurt the economy as well. Most people in Haiti are still poor. Many live in cities where violence is common. And many still try to leave their homeland, in search of a better life.

✔ **Reading Check** Describe the poor neighborhoods of Port-au-Prince.

Colorful Culture
Haitians often decorate buses and trucks in bright colors. **Analyze Images** What can you learn about city life in Haiti from this photo of Port-au-Prince?

Section 2 Assessment

Key Terms
Review the key terms at the beginning of this section. Use each term in a sentence that explains its meaning.

🎯 Target Reading Skills
State the details that support the main idea on page 145: *Toussaint L'Ouverture's goal of freedom and equality was never fully realized.*

Comprehension and Critical Thinking
1. (a) Define Who are the Haitian boat people?

(b) Sequence List the major events of Haiti's history in the order they occurred.
(c) Identify Cause and Effect How did the events of Haiti's history lead to the migration of the boat people?
2. (a) Describe What is rural life like for many Haitians?
(b) Compare and Contrast How is life in the city similar to and different from life on a farm?
(c) Find Main Ideas What are the major problems facing Haiti today?

Writing Activity
Suppose you were an American newspaper reporter in Haiti in 1991. Write an article about conditions in Haiti immediately after President Aristide was forced from power. Include the experiences of individual Haitians.

Go Online
PHSchool.com

For: An activity on Haiti
Visit: PHSchool.com
Web Code: lfd-1502

Chapter 5 Section 2 **147**

Section 2 Assessment

Key Terms
Students' sentences should reflect knowledge of each Key Term.

🎯 Target Reading Skill
Most of Haiti's presidents became dictators. François Duvalier and his son, Jean-Claude, were cruel leaders who used violence to stay in power. After Jean-Claude was forced to leave Haiti, more dictators came to power.

Comprehension and Critical Thinking
1. (a) refugees from Haiti who fled Haiti by sea **(b)** Arawaks live in Haiti when Spanish arrive; Spanish bring enslaved Africans; Toussaint L'Ouverture helps Haiti become independent; United States occupies Haiti; a series of dictatorships beginning with Papa Doc; President Aristide forced to leave by military but returns in 1994; disputed elections continue to trouble Haiti; Aristide forced to leave again after rebel groups gain control. **(c)** In 1990, the military forced out

Assess and Reteach

Assess Progress   L2
Have students complete the Section Assessment. Then administer the *Section Quiz.*

All in One **Latin America Teaching Resources,** *Section Quiz, p. 282*

Reteach   L1
If students need more instruction, have them read this section in the Reading and Vocabulary Study Guide.

📖 Chapter 5, Section 2, **Latin America Reading and Vocabulary Study Guide,** pp. 55–57

Extend   L3
Have students learn more about the countries of the Caribbean by completing the *Small Group Activity: Creating a Magazine Story.*

All in One **Latin America Teaching Resources,** *Small Group Activity: Creating a Magazine Story, pp. 293–296*

Answers

✔ **Reading Check** They are dirty and crowded with no decent housing. The streets are unpaved, and the concrete homes are tiny and crumbling.

Analyze Images Port-au-Prince is very crowded with much traffic.

Writing Activity
Use the *Rubric for Assessing a Assessing a Newspaper Article* to evaluate students' articles.

All in One **Latin America Teaching Resources,** *Rubric for Assessing a Newspaper Article, p. 304*

Go Online
PHSchool.com Typing in the web code when prompted will bring students directly to detailed instructions for this activity.

an elected ruler. Some of the ruler's supporters fled Haiti.

2. (a) It is a struggle to make a living farming on small overused plots of poor land. **(b)** Alike—poor people live in bad conditions; Different—those in the country are farmers; city dwellers look for other kinds of work. **(c)** election disputes, a poor economy, poverty, and violence.

Section 3
Step-by-Step Instruction

Objectives

Social Studies

1. Understand how the people of Puerto Rico are both American and Puerto Rican.

2. Find out what life is like on the island of Puerto Rico.

3. Learn about the three kinds of political status Puerto Ricans are considering for their future.

Reading/Language Arts

Identify implied main ideas in the text.

Prepare to Read

Build Background Knowledge L2

In this section, students will learn about Puerto Rico and the benefits and detriments of being a commonwealth of the United States. Remind students about the variety of struggles for independence fought by the countries of Latin America. Have students engage in a Think-Pair-Share activity (TE, p. T36) to create a list of reasons why a country would desire to be independent.

Set a Purpose for Reading L2

■ Preview the Objectives.

■ Form students into pairs or groups of four. Distribute the *Reading Readiness Guide*. Ask students to fill in the first two columns of the chart. Use the Numbered Heads participation structure (TE, p. T36) to call on students to share one piece of information they already know and one piece of information they want to know.

All in One Latin America Teaching Resources, *Reading Readiness Guide,* p. 284

Vocabulary Builder
Preview Key Terms L2

Pronounce each Key Term, then ask students to say the word with you. Provide an example such as, "A citizen of the United States enjoys many rights and privileges under our government."

Section 3 Puerto Rico
An American Commonwealth

Prepare to Read

Objectives

In this section you will

1. Understand why the people of Puerto Rico are both American and Puerto Rican.
2. Find out what life is like on the island of Puerto Rico.
3. Learn about the three kinds of political status Puerto Ricans are considering for their future.

Taking Notes

As you read this section, look for ways that life is similar and different in Puerto Rico and on the mainland United States. Copy the Venn diagram below, and record your findings in it.

Puerto Rican Life

In Puerto Rico / On the mainland

Target Reading Skill

Identify Implied Main Ideas Identifying main ideas can help you remember the most important points you read. Sometimes the main idea is not stated directly. All the details in that portion of text add up to a main idea, but you must state the main idea yourself. For example, you could state the main idea of the text headed A Mix of Cultures this way: *Puerto Rico shows influences of Spanish, African, Caribbean, and United States mainland culture.*

Key Terms

■ **constitution** (kahn stuh TOO shun) *n.* a statement of a country's basic laws and values
■ **citizen** (SIT uh zun) *n.* a person with certain rights and responsibilities under a particular government
■ **commonwealth** (KAHM un welth) *n.* a self-governing political unit that has strong ties to a particular country

A government building in Puerto Rico

148 Latin America

Puerto Rico was once a Spanish colony. When the United States defeated Spain in the Spanish-American War, Spain ceded, or gave, Puerto Rico to the United States. The United States slowly granted Puerto Rico more control of its own government and affairs. In 1951, Puerto Ricans voted to adopt their own constitution. A **constitution** is a statement of a country's basic laws and values. This gave Puerto Rico its own lawmakers. But it was still connected to the United States.

What is the nature of Puerto Rico's connection to the United States? How does that relationship affect life in Puerto Rico? And why do some Puerto Ricans want to change the nature of their island's relationship to the United States?

Target Reading Skill L2

Identify Implied Main Ideas Point out the Target Reading Skill. Review what students have learned about main ideas, then explain that sometimes the main idea is not stated directly, but is implied by details in a passage. In this case a reader must determine the main idea from the details.

Model identifying implied main ideas with this sentence about the first paragraph on this page: *Although it has its own constitution, Puerto Rico is still connected to the United States.* Point out the details in the paragraph that support this idea, even though it is not explicitly stated.

Give students *Identify Implied Main Ideas.* Have them complete the activity in their groups.

All in One Latin America Teaching Resources, *Identify Implied Main Ideas,* p. 289

Puerto Ricans in the Mainland United States, 2000

Population	
Total	3,406,178
Northeast	2,074,574
South	759,305
Midwest	325,363
West	246,936

Distribution by Region

7.2%
9.6%
22.3%
60.9%

- Northeast
- South
- Midwest
- West

SOURCE: United States Census Bureau

Puerto Rican and American

People move from Puerto Rico to the United States mainland and back again very easily because Puerto Rico is part of the United States. Puerto Ricans are American citizens. **Citizens** are individuals with certain rights and responsibilities under a particular government. But Puerto Rico is not a state of the Union. It has a different status.

The Commonwealth of Puerto Rico Today, Puerto Rico is a commonwealth of the United States. A **commonwealth** is a self-governing political unit that has strong ties to a particular country. Although Puerto Ricans are American citizens, they cannot vote in presidential elections. They do not pay United States taxes. And they have only a nonvoting representative in the United States Congress. However, Puerto Ricans do serve in the armed forces of the United States.

Puerto Ricans on the Mainland Many Puerto Ricans have moved to the mainland United States. Most settle in cities in the Northeast. Life is very different there. While Puerto Rico has a warm Caribbean climate, winters in Northern cities can be cold and harsh. And cities like New York are much bigger than any city in Puerto Rico. The language of the mainland is English, while people speak Spanish in Puerto Rico. There is a lot to get used to.

Chart Skills

This market is in an area of New York City called Spanish Harlem, where many Puerto Ricans have settled. **Identify** According to the graph, which region has the largest Puerto Rican population? The smallest? **Infer** Why do you think that people tend to settle in areas where there are already many people from their former homes?

Instruct

Puerto Rican and American L2

Guided Instruction

- **Vocabulary Builder** Clarify the high-use words **grant** and **status** before reading.
- Read about the people of Puerto Rico in Puerto Rican and American, using the Choral Reading technique (TE, p. T34).
- Ask students **What are three ways that Puerto Ricans living in Puerto Rico are different from Americans who live in the United States mainland?** *(People living in Puerto Rico can't vote in presidential elections, don't pay United States taxes, and only have a non-voting representative in Congress.)*
- Ask students **Suppose that you are moving from the mainland United States to Puerto Rico. What would you like about moving there? What would you dislike?** *(Answers will vary. Students may say that they would like the warm weather, but would have trouble learning Spanish and miss their friends.)*

Independent Practice

Ask students to create the Taking Notes graphic organizer on a blank piece of paper. Then have them begin to fill in the sections of the Venn diagram. Briefly model how to fill in the diagram.

Monitor Progress

While students fill in the graphic organizer, move around the room and make sure individuals are choosing the correct details. Provide assistance as needed.

Vocabulary Builder

Use the information below to teach students this section's high-use words.

High-Use Word	Definition and Sample Sentence
grant, p. 148	*v.* to allow to have The principal **granted** the students use of the gym for the dance.
status, p. 149	*n.* state of affairs or condition Due to the **status** of the injury, he will not be able to compete.
luxury, p. 152	*n.* great comfort It was a **luxury** driving to the prom in a limousine.
restore, p. 152	*v.* to bring back to an earlier condition The museum **restored** the damaged painting.

Answers

Chart Skills Identify Northeast; West **Infer** Possible answer: It may be easier to adjust to new surroundings with people who share the same language and traditions.

Life on the Island L2

Guided Instruction

- **Vocabulary Builder** Clarify the high-use words **luxury** and **restore** before reading.
- Read Life on the Island with students.
- Ask students to explain why they think people have moved back to Puerto Rico from the United States mainland. *(Possible answer: Puerto Rico was their original homeland and they miss the mountains, sea, vegetation, and Puerto Rican lifestyle.)*

Esmeralda Santiago

Coming to New York City Esmeralda Santiago (ez mehr AHL dah sahn tee AH goh) moved from Puerto Rico to New York City when she was 13 years old. At first, she found life on the mainland strange and confusing. One problem was that to succeed in school, she had to improve her English. She also found that Puerto Ricans living in New York were different from her friends on the island. Instead of the salsa and merengue music she loved, they preferred rock music. Most of the time they spoke neither pure Spanish nor English, but a mixture of the two that they called "Spanglish." Although they were Puerto Rican, Esmeralda felt different from them. Eventually, she learned their ways. She became more like them and thought less about her old life on the island.

✓ **Reading Check** **When Puerto Ricans move to New York City, what kinds of differences do they find?**

Life on the Island

Many people travel back and forth between the mainland and Puerto Rico. They live for a while in each place. Many Puerto Ricans moved to the mainland during the 1950s. However, since 1965, just as many Puerto Ricans have been moving back to their island as are leaving it.

Returning Home Julia de Jesus Chaparro (HOO lee ah day HAY soos chah PAH roh) moved back to a small mountain village in Puerto Rico after spending more than 14 years in Boston, Massachusetts. To explain why, she takes visitors to her back porch. From there, she can see a row of steep mountains. Peeking between them is the bright blue of the Caribbean Sea. The mountain slopes steeply down from Julia's back porch, but she has managed to clear some land. Her garden of mangoes, coconuts, grapefruit, and lemons thrives in the sun. Behind a nearby tree, a hen and six chickens are pecking in the dirt.

Puerto Rican Hillside
This hilly region is in the Central Mountains of Puerto Rico. **Draw Conclusions** *What can you learn about the geography, climate, and land use of this region from the photograph?*

Differentiated Instruction

For Advanced Readers L3
Have students choose one of the following famous Puerto Ricans in the United States and prepare a biographical sketch of him or her to share with the class: Raúl Julia, Rita Moreno, Juan "Chichi" Rodriquez, José Ferrer, José Feliciano, Chita Rivera, Roberto Clemente, Angel Cordero.

For English Language Learners L1
Use the photographs in the Student Edition to help students relate English nouns and verbs to pictures. Encourage students to use each word in an oral sentence.

Answers

✓ **Reading Check** There are differences in climate, population density, language, music, and customs.

Draw Conclusions This region has hills, has a warm climate, and is used for farming.

Much of Puerto Rico is made up of hills and mountains—the kind of landscape you would see from Julia's back porch. In the hills, Puerto Rican cowhands, called *jíbaros* (HEE bahr ohs), raise cattle. They also hunt, fish, and raise chickens and pigs. On other parts of the island, farmers ride horses through fields of tall sugar cane. To the southwest, where the land is lower, fishing villages dot the coast.

Discovery CHANNEL SCHOOL Video
Learn about Puerto Rico, past and present.

Discovery SCHOOL Video
Show students *Puerto Rico: Past and Present*. Ask **What kinds of landforms and bodies of water make up Puerto Rico's geography?** *(Students' answers should reflect landforms and bodies of water described in the video.)*

COUNTRY PROFILE — Focus on Government

Puerto Rico

Since becoming a United States Territory in 1898, Puerto Rico has been slowly gaining self-government. In 1917, the people of Puerto Rico were given American citizenship. In 1948, they elected their own governor, and in 1951, they adopted their own constitution. Today, Puerto Rico is a commonwealth of the United States with one nonvoting commissioner in the House of Representatives. As you study the charts below, think about how Puerto Rico's commonwealth status affects the lives of its people.

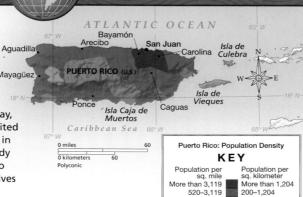

Puerto Rico: Population Density KEY

Population per sq. mile	Population per sq. kilometer
More than 3,119	More than 1,204
520–3,119	200–1,204
260–519	100–199
130–259	50–99

Urban Areas
- 500,000–999,999
- Less than 500,000

Citizen Status in Iowa versus Puerto Rico

	If Born in Iowa	If Born in Puerto Rico
Citizen of United States	Yes	Yes
Vote for U.S. president	Yes	No
Pay income taxes	Yes	No
Serve in military	Yes	Yes
Representatives in U.S. Congress	Five	One (with no vote)
Senators in U.S. Congress	Two	None

2000 Puerto Rico Election Results

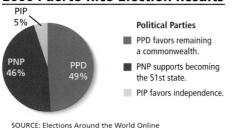

PIP 5%
PNP 46%
PPD 49%

Political Parties
- PPD favors remaining a commonwealth.
- PNP supports becoming the 51st state.
- PIP favors independence.

SOURCE: Elections Around the World Online

Map and Chart Skills

1. **Identify** What two rights do people born in Iowa have that someone born in Puerto Rico does not have?
2. **Analyze** What do the results of the 2000 elections tell you about how Puerto Ricans feel about their relationship with the United States?
3. **Draw Conclusions** Why do you think political opinion is divided the way it is?

Go Online PHSchool.com Use Web Code **Ife-1513** for **DK World Desk Reference Online.**

Chapter 5 Section 3 **151**

COUNTRY PROFILE — Focus on Government

Guided Instruction   L2

Direct students to read the Country Profile text about Puerto Rico and to study the visuals on this page. As a class, answer the Map and Chart Skills questions. Allow students to discuss their responses with a partner before sharing answers.

Independent Practice

Ask students to use the information in the text on this page to create a timeline showing how the government in Puerto Rico has changed over time.

Answers

Map and Chart Skills

1. the right to vote for President and to have voting representatives in Congress
2. Most favor remaining a commonwealth or becoming a state; only a small percentage want to end their relationship with the United States.
3. Possible answer: There are compelling advantages and disadvantages to Puerto Rico becoming a state.

Go Online PHSchool.com Students can find useful information about this topic on the DK World Desk Reference Online.

Guided Instruction (continued)

■ Ask students **How do some people living in Puerto Rico's cities make their living?** (*They work in factories and hotels and restaurants that draw tourists.*)

Independent Practice

Have students complete the graphic organizer by filling in the Venn diagram.

Monitor Progress

Show *Section Reading Support Transparency LA 44* and ask students to check their graphic organizers individually. Go over key concepts and clarify key vocabulary as needed

📖 **Latin America Transparencies,** *Section Reading Support Transparency LA 44*

This guitar maker is playing a cuatro, Puerto Rico's national instrument.

A Mix of Cultures As people travel back and forth, they bring customs and products with them. If you visited Puerto Rico, you would see many influences from the United States mainland. You would also see that in Puerto Rico, there is a strong cultural connection to the Caribbean. Most people are a mix of Spanish and African ancestry.

Puerto Rican cities show influences of Spanish, Caribbean, and United States mainland culture. About 75 percent of Puerto Ricans live in cities. Many city people work in factories. Others work in the hotels and restaurants that draw many tourists. Puerto Rico's capital, San Juan (san HWAHN), has a large waterfront area known as the Condado (kohn DAH do). It is packed with luxury hotels. Not far away, modern skyscrapers pierce the brilliant sky.

In the old section of San Juan, Spanish-style buildings are everywhere. A 450-year-old Catholic church built by the Spanish has been carefully restored. Not far from the church sit ancient houses graced with iron balconies in lacy Spanish style.

✓ **Reading Check** Compare old and new San Juan.

Old and New
The San Geronimo Fortress, built in the 1500s by the Spanish, stands in sharp contrast to the modern hotels of San Juan. **Infer** *How do you think the fortress might contribute to the current economy of San Juan?*

152 Latin America

Answers

✓ **Reading Check** San Juan, Puerto Rico's capital, is on a waterfront called the Condado. It has many luxury hotels and skyscrapers. It also has an old section with Spanish-style buildings, including a 450-year-old Catholic church and old houses with Spanish-style iron balconies.

Infer Many tourists may come to Puerto Rico to see the fortress and other examples of Puerto Rico's Spanish history.

Seeking a New Direction

Puerto Rico is bound by many United States laws, and Puerto Ricans have many questions about this situation. Is it good for Puerto Rico? Should Puerto Rico become independent? Or should it become a state of the United States?

Commonwealth or Statehood? Puerto Ricans have many disagreements over what the status of their island should be. Many feel that having "one foot" in Puerto Rico and "one foot" in the United States can lead to problems. Others point out how the relationship with the United States has helped Puerto Rico. American businesses on the island have raised the standard of living. Each year, the United States government sends millions of dollars to the island to help people in need.

Some people still feel that Puerto Rico is at a disadvantage because Puerto Ricans cannot vote in United States elections. They say Puerto Rico should try to become a state. But if it does, it will become the poorest state in the union. Puerto Ricans earn more money than people in other Caribbean countries. However, they earn less than people on the United States mainland. Also, if Puerto Rico becomes a state, Puerto Ricans will have to pay United States taxes. This could lower the earnings of many people who have little to spare. For these reasons, in 1993 and again in 1998, Puerto Ricans voted not to become the 51st state of the United States.

Statehood Now!
These people are rallying for Puerto Rican statehood in a 1996 demonstration. **Transfer Information** *What arguments in favor of statehood might these demonstrators give?*

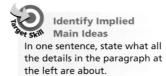 **Identify Implied Main Ideas**
In one sentence, state what all the details in the paragraph at the left are about.

Guided Instruction

- Read Seeking a New Direction with students. As students read, circulate and make sure that individuals can answer the Reading Check question.

- Discuss with students how life would change for Puerto Ricans if Puerto Rico became a state of the United States. *(Puerto Ricans would be allowed to vote in the United States elections, but would have to pay taxes.)*

- Ask students **Do you think Puerto Rico should become the fifty-first state? Why or why not?** *(Answers will vary. Yes—If Puerto Rico becomes a state, its citizens will have all the benefits of American citizenship. Paying taxes is worth the advantage. No— Puerto Ricans should wait until their economy improves before joining the United States so that taxation will not be a hardship on people.)*

Independent Practice
Assign *Guided Reading and Review.*

All in One Latin America Teaching Resources, *Guided Reading and Review,* p. 285

Monitor Progress
Tell students to fill in the last column of the *Reading Readiness Guide.* Ask them to evaluate if what they learned was what they had expected to learn.

All in One Latin America Teaching Resources, *Reading Readiness Guide,* p. 284

Target Reading Skill [L2]
Identify Implied Main Ideas As a follow up, ask students to answer the Target Reading Skill question in the Student Edition. *(So far economic reasons have kept Puerto Ricans from voting to become a state.)*

Differentiated Instruction

For Less Proficient Readers [L1]
Have students read the section in the Reading Vocabulary and Study Guide. This version provides basic-level instruction in an interactive format with questions and write-on lines.
Chapter 5, Section 3, **Latin America Reading and Vocabulary Study Guide,** pp. 58–60

For Gifted and Talented [L3]
Ask students to find photographs of various aspects of life and scenery in Puerto Rico. Encourage students to prepare short captions or statements about the photos and share these with the class.

Answer

Transfer Information They might argue that statehood would give them more influence over laws in the United States.

Assess and Reteach

Assess Progress `L2`

Have students complete the Section Assessment. Administer the *Section Quiz*.

 Latin America Teaching Resources, *Section Quiz,* p. 286

Reteach `L1`

If students need more instruction, have them read this section in the Reading and Vocabulary Study Guide.

📖 Chapter 5, Section 3, **Latin America Reading and Vocabulary Study Guide,** pp. 58–60

Extend `L3`

Remind students of the World Studies video, *Puerto Rico: Past and Present,* that they watched earlier. Have students make a chart comparing either rural or urban regions of Puerto Rico or New and Old San Juan. You may wish to reshow the video if students are having trouble recalling data.

📼 *Puerto Rico: Past and Present,* **World Studies Video Program**

Answers

Predict Answers will vary but should reflect knowledge of facts from the lesson.

 Reading Check They feel Puerto Rico's identity as a Caribbean nation with Spanish culture is threatened by its association with the United States.

Section 3 Assessment

Key Terms

Students' sentences should reflect knowledge of each Key Term.

Target Reading Skill

Answers will vary, but should reflect important main ideas from the section.

Comprehension and Critical Thinking

1. (a) It is a commonwealth of the United States. **(b)** Puerto Ricans adopted their own constitution in 1951.

2. (a) Possible answer: In the mountains and hills people hunt, fish, and raise animals; in other parts of the island farmers grow sugar cane; along the coast people fish. **(b)** Most people are of African and Spanish ancestry, speak Spanish, and live in cities with skyscrapers.

3. (a) commonwealth, statehood, and a separate nation **(b)** commonwealth benefit—helped by American businesses and government, drawback—cannot vote in U.S. elections; statehood benefit—people can vote, drawback—will be poorest state, have to pay taxes; separate nation benefit—clear identity, drawback—might lose some U.S. aid

Writing Activity

Use the *Rubric for Assessing a Journal Entry* to evaluate students' journal entries.

 Latin America Teaching Resources, *Rubric for Assessing a Journal Entry,* p. 305

Go Online PHSchool.com Typing in the web code when prompted will bring students directly to detailed instructions for this activity.

Rally for Independence
This rally of the Independenista Party was held in 1980. **Predict** *Do you think these demonstrators or those on the previous page will ever get their wish for Puerto Rico? Explain your answer.*

The Question of Independence Some people who voted against statehood have even bigger dreams for Puerto Rico. They want it to become a separate nation. If it does not, they fear that Puerto Ricans will become confused about their identity. They stress Puerto Rico's connection to other Caribbean nations. They want to make sure that Puerto Ricans always identify with the Spanish language and Spanish culture. But for now, Puerto Rico will keep its links to the mainland. Many Puerto Ricans hope that their relationship with the United States will lead to a profitable and peaceful future.

✓ **Reading Check** **Why do some people favor Puerto Rican independence?**

Section 3 Assessment

Key Terms

Review the key terms at the beginning of this section. Use each term in a sentence that explains its meaning.

Target Reading Skills

State two main ideas of Section 3.

Comprehension and Critical Thinking

1. (a) Explain What is Puerto Rico's relationship to the United States?
(b) Sequence How did Puerto Rico gain more control over its own affairs?

2. (a) Describe List three different regions of Puerto Rico, and tell how people earn a living in each one.
(b) Synthesize How does Puerto Rican culture show Spanish, Caribbean, and mainland influences?
3. (a) List What are the three options Puerto Ricans consider for the future of their relationship with the United States?
(b) Analyze What are the benefits and drawbacks of each option?

Writing Activity

Write a journal entry from the point of view of either Julia or Esmeralda. Discuss your feelings about life on the mainland and in Puerto Rico. Explain where you would prefer to live and why.

For: An activity on San Juan
Visit: PHSchool.com
Web Code: lfd-1503

154 Latin America

Review and Assessment

◆ Chapter Summary

Section 1: Cuba

- Cuba became a communist country under Fidel Castro and then became an ally of the Soviet Union.
- During the Cold War, relations between Cuba and the United States worsened.
- Many Cubans have fled Cuba for the United States, where they have made successful new lives, but some dream of returning to a free and democratic Cuba.
- Recently Castro has allowed some private ownership of businesses and is encouraging tourism and trade.

Cuba

Section 2: Haiti

- Haiti has struggled for democracy since independence, but has enjoyed only short periods of elected government.
- The election of President Aristide brought a brief period of hope, but then a military takeover caused many Haitians to flee their country.
- The people of Haiti are poor. Farmers struggle on land that has been overused, crowded city slums do not have basic services, and political violence is a fact of life.

Section 3: Puerto Rico

- Puerto Rico is a commonwealth of the United States. Puerto Ricans are American citizens, and many of them move to the United States mainland.
- Life in Puerto Rico blends Caribbean and mainland influences.
- Puerto Ricans disagree over whether they should become a state, become independent, or remain a commonwealth.

◆ Key Terms

Match the definitions in Column I with the key terms in Column II.

Column I

1. a statement of a country's basic laws and values
2. a country joined to another country for a special purpose
3. a place that has its own government but also has strong ties to another country
4. those who leave their homeland for their own personal safety and to escape persecution
5. individuals with certain rights and responsibilities under a particular government

Column II

A citizens
B ally
C commonwealth
D constitution
E refugees

─ Vocabulary Builder ─

Revisit this chapter's high-use words:

dictator	prosperity	status
corrupt	fraud	luxury
missile	dispute	restore
collapse	grant	

Ask students to review the definitions they recorded on their *Word Knowledge* worksheets.

 Latin America Teaching Resources, *Word Knowledge,* p. 290

Consider allowing students to earn extra credit if they use the words in their answers to the questions in the Chapter Review and Assessment. The words must be used correctly and in a natural context to win the extra points.

Chapter 5

Review and Assessment

Review Chapter Content

- Review and revisit the major themes of this chapter by asking students to classify what Guiding Question each bulleted statement in the Chapter Summary answers. Have students complete this activity as a class. Refer to page 1 in the Student Edition for the text of the Guiding Questions.

- Assign *Vocabulary Development* for students to review Key Terms.

 Latin America Teaching Resources, *Vocabulary Development,* p. 301

Answers

Key Terms

1. D
2. B
3. C
4. E
5. A

Review and Assessment

Comprehension and Critical Thinking

6. (a) Possible answers: fertile farmland, located at entrance to the Gulf of Mexico, excellent harbors, good beaches, pleasant climate. **(b)** Its location made it a good place for trade with the United States and other parts of the Caribbean; its farmland provided money from sugar cane; its beaches and climate drew tourists. **(c)** Castro's communist government took over private businesses and land.

7. (a) During Batista's rule many farm and factory workers earned low wages and didn't share the country's wealth. **(b)** The government took over businesses and land; people couldn't speak out against government; many people fled the island; literacy and healthcare improved. **(c)** The country's economy and living conditions worsened without the help of the Soviet Union. Castro allowed some private ownership of businesses and encouraged tourism to bolster the economy.

8. (a) France **(b)** L'Overture wanted all people to live as equals and enjoy freedom. His ideals were not fulfilled during the rule of the Duvaliers, cruel dictators who used violence to keep power and who stole government money.

9. (a) a Catholic priest who was elected president of Haiti **(b)** elected in 1990, forced to leave the country by the military, returned in 1994, elected again in 2000 under cloud of cheating and fraud resulting in the halt of international aid, called on to resign by some Haitians in 2002 **(c)** People who supported Aristide had to hide because they were attacked by the military. Many fled; some became boat people and headed for the United States.

10. (a) Puerto Ricans can move easily between Puerto Rico and the mainland, serve in armed forces, have nonvoting representative in Congress **(b)** Many move to the mainland for jobs and services but move back to the island for the beautiful geography and because of family and cultural ties.
(c) Advantages: self-government, U.S. government aid, no taxes, better standard of living. Disadvantages: nonvoting representative in Congress, unable to vote in presidential elections.

◆ Comprehension and Critical Thinking

6. (a) Name What are two advantages Cuba has because of its geography?
(b) Identify Cause and Effect How did these advantages lead to Cuba's prosperity?
(c) Synthesize Information How did Cuba change from a prosperous country to a poor one?

7. (a) Recall Why did revolutionary leaders like Fidel Castro gain support in Cuba?
(b) Describe What is life like under Castro's communist government of Cuba?
(c) Identify Effects What happened in Cuba when the communist regime of the Soviet Union collapsed? Explain why.

8. (a) Name Haiti was a colony of which European country?
(b) Synthesize Describe Toussaint L'Ouverture's ideals for Haiti, and explain whether or not the rule of the Duvaliers fulfilled those ideals.

9. (a) Identify Who is Jean-Bertrand Aristide?
(b) Sequence What are the main events of Aristide's struggle for power?
(c) Draw Conclusions How did what happened to Aristide affect ordinary people who supported him? Explain why.

10. (a) List What rights and responsibilities of United States citizenship do Puerto Ricans have?
(b) Find Main Ideas Explain why so many Puerto Ricans move back and forth between their island and the mainland.
(c) Compare What are the advantages and disadvantages of commonwealth status for Puerto Rico?

◆ Skills Practice

Comparing and Contrasting In the Skills for Life activity in this chapter, you learned how to compare and contrast. Review the steps of this skill.

Now look again at the first two sections of this chapter. As you recall, people from both Cuba and Haiti have fled their countries to come to the United States. What kinds of countries did they leave behind? How are Cuba and Haiti similar and different? Use a chart to compare the two countries. Then write a conclusion sentence on the topic.

◆ Writing Activity: Math

Review the charts in Country Profile: Haiti on page 144. Also consider the current population of Haiti, which is approximately 8 million. Use this information and your math skills to write a paragraph about Haiti's loss of population. You may wish to convert numbers into percentages or explain ratios in your paragraph.

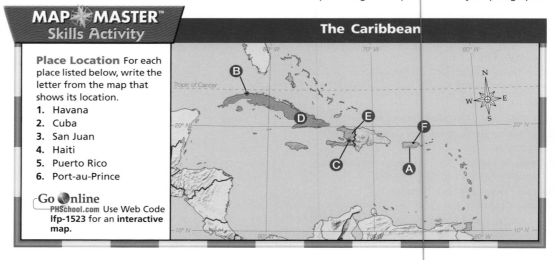

MAP MASTER™ Skills Activity

The Caribbean

Place Location For each place listed below, write the letter from the map that shows its location.
1. Havana
2. Cuba
3. San Juan
4. Haiti
5. Puerto Rico
6. Port-au-Prince

Go Online PHSchool.com Use Web Code lfp-1523 for an interactive map.

Skills Practice
Students should create a chart comparing and contrasting Cuba and Haiti using appropriate information from the text.

Possible conclusion: Both are former colonies that were ruled by dictators and have poor economies. Haiti is poorer and more volatile than Cuba.

Standardized Test Prep

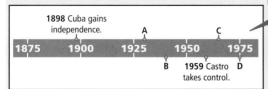

Test-Taking Tips

Some questions on standardized tests ask you to sequence information. Study the timeline below. Then follow the tips to answer the sample question.

TIP Notice that the leader lines connect events to their dates on the timeline. See which dates are closest to each answer choice.

```
1898 Cuba gains
independence.        A              C
|———————————————————————————————————|
1875   1900   1925   1950   1975
                    B    1959 Castro  D
                         takes control.
```

Pick the letter that best answers the question.

At which point on the timeline did large numbers of Cuban exiles <u>begin</u> going to the United States?

- A point A
- B point B
- C point C
- D point D

TIP Preview the question first. Look for information relating to the question as you examine the timeline.

Think It Through Notice the key word *begin* in the question. You know that many Cubans left Cuba for the United States because they opposed Castro's government. Therefore, they must have *started* leaving after Castro came to power. So you can rule out choices A and B. Although exiles may still have been leaving Cuba in 1975, the exile movement most likely *began* shortly after Castro's new government was formed. So the correct answer is C.

Practice Questions

Choose the letter of the best answer.

1. Before Cuba gained independence, it was a colony of
   - A France.
   - B Spain.
   - C the United States.
   - D Portugal.

2. Which of the following nations was formed from a revolt of enslaved Africans?
   - A Haiti
   - B Cuba
   - C Puerto Rico
   - D Hispaniola

3. Which of the following statements best describes Puerto Rico's relationship with the United States?
   - A It is a colony of the United States.
   - B It is a state of the United States.
   - C It is a country with special ties to the United States.
   - D It is a commonwealth of the United States.

Study the timeline below and answer the question that follows.

```
1898 Spain
cedes Puerto
Rico to the
A  United States.          C              D
|———————————————————————————————————————|
1875   1900   1925   1950   1975   2000
         B                        1993 Puerto
                                  Ricans vote
                                  against statehood.
```

4. At which point on the timeline did Puerto Rico become a commonwealth?
   - A point A
   - B point B
   - C point C
   - D point D

Go Online
PHSchool.com
Use Web Code lfa-1501
for a **Chapter 5 self-test.**

Writing Activity: Math
Answers will vary, but students should mention the flight of Haitians in their paragraph as one reason for population loss.

Use *Rubric for Assessing a Writing Assignment* to evaluate students' paragraphs. Tell students how many sources you would like them to use, if any, beyond the textbook.

All in One **Latin America Teaching Resources,** *Rubric for Assessing a Writing Assignment,* p. 303

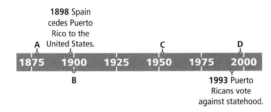
MAP MASTER
Skills Activity

1. B	**2.** D
3. F	**4.** E
5. A	**6.** C

Go Online
PHSchool.com Students may practice their map skills online using the interactive version of this map.

Standardized Test Prep

Answers

1. B

2. A

3. D

4. C

Go Online
PHSchool.com Students may use the Chapter 5 self-test on PHSchool.com to prepare for the Chapter Test.

Assessment Resources

Use *Chapter Tests A and B* to assess students' mastery of chapter content.

All in One **Latin America Teaching Resources,** *Chapter Tests A and B,* pp. 306–311

Tests are also available on the **Exam*View*®** **Test Bank CD-ROM.**

⊙ *ExamView Test Bank CD-ROM*

Overview

Introducing South America
1. Use data to compare countries.
2. Learn what characteristics the countries of South America share.
3. Name some key differences among the countries.

South America: Adapting to a Varied Landscape
Length: 5 minutes, 30 seconds
Uses maps to provide an overview of South America's geography and major cities.

Brazil: Geography Shapes a Nation
Section 1
1. Learn about the geography of Brazil.
2. Discover why the rain forests are important to Brazil and to the whole world.
3. Find out what groups make up the people of Brazil and how they live.

Brazil's Carnival
Length: 3 minutes, 36 seconds
Discusses origins and traditions of the Carnival celebration.

Peru: An Ancient Land Looks to the Future
Section 2
1. Learn how geography has affected the way people live in the three regions of Peru.
2. Discover what life is like in the cities and towns of the Altiplano.

Making a Living in Peru
Length: 5 minutes, 52 seconds
Shows the lives of three Peruvians who make a living working with natural resources.

Chile: Land of Contrasts
Section 3
1. Find out how the geography of Chile creates regions where people live very differently.
2. Learn how Chile's people live and what products they produce.
3. Find out how Chile restored democracy.

Santiago, Chile: Between the Andes and the Sea
Length: 4 minutes, 44 seconds
Visits Santiago, the capital of Chile, and provides a glimpse of its people and culture.

Venezuela: Oil Powers the Economy
Section 4
1. Find out how Venezuela was made wealthy by oil.
2. Learn how the ups and downs of oil prices affected the economy and people of Venezuela.
3. Understand how Venezuela is changing.

The Liberator, Simón Bolívar
Length: 4 minutes, 41 seconds
Recounts the history of Simón Bolívar and how he liberated many countries in Latin America.

Technology Resources

Students use embedded web codes to access internet activities, chapter self-tests, and additional map practice. They may also access Dorling Kindersley's Online Desk Reference to learn more about each country they study.

Use the Interactive Textbook to make content and concepts come alive through animations, videos, and activities that accompany the complete basal text—online and on CD-ROM.

Use this complete suite of powerful teaching tools to make planning lessons and administering tests quicker and easier.

Reading and Assessment

Reading and Vocabulary Instruction

🔄 Model the Target Reading Skill

Compare and Contrast Tell students that comparing and contrasting can be a helpful tool both for clarifying and remembering information. Comparing allows students to see patterns of similarities, and contrasting elucidates patterns of difference.

Model comparing and contrasting by thinking aloud about the following paragraph:

There are three distinct geographic regions in Peru. The mountain region is often very cold. Native Americans live in the mountains, surviving by farming and selling wool. The coastal region is dry. It was once home to Native Americans, but is now an urban region, with a mixture of cultural groups. The forests are hot and humid. Some Native Americans live in the forests, but there are few towns or roads.

Think aloud: The subject of this paragraph is the three geographic regions in Peru. To be more specific, the paragraph discusses the climate and people of these geographic regions. How are these regions similar? At one point in time, Native Americans lived in all three regions. How are these regions different? They have different climates.

Use the following worksheets from All-in-One Latin America Teaching Resources, (pp. 331, 332, and 333) to support this chapter's Target Reading Skill.

Vocabulary Builder
High-Use Academic Words

Use these steps to teach this chapter's High-Use words:

1. Have students rate how well they know each word on their Word Knowledge worksheets (All-in-One Latin American Teaching Resources, p. 334).
2. Pronounce each word and ask students to repeat it.
3. Give students a brief definition or sample sentence (provided on TE pp. 167, 174, 180, and 189.)
4. Work with students as they fill in the "Definition or Example" column of their Word Knowledge worksheets.

Assessment

Formal Assessment

Test students' understanding of core knowledge and skills.

> **Chapter Tests A and B**, All-in-One Latin America Teaching Resources, pp. 353–358

Customize the Chapter Tests to suit your needs.

ExamView Test Bank CD-ROM

Skills Assessment

Assess geographic literacy.

> **MapMaster Skills,** Student Edition pp. 159, 196
> **Country Profile Map and Chart Skills,** Student Edition pp. 170, 174, 180, 190

Assess reading and comprehension.

> **Target Reading Skills,** Student Edition, pp. 169, 177, 181, 191, and in Section Assessments
> **Chapter 6 Assessment,** Latin Americae Reading and Vocabulary Study Guide, p. 74

Performance Assessment

Assess students' performance on this chapter's Writing Activities using the following rubrics from All-in-One Latin America Teaching Resources.

> **Rubric for Assessing a Bar Graph,** p. 348
> **Rubric for Assessing a Timeline,** p. 351

Assess students' work through performance tasks.

> **Small Group Activity: Making a Mural,** All-in-One Latin America Teaching Resources, pp. 337–340
> **Portfolio Activity,** Teacher Edition, p. 165

Online Assessment

Have students check their own understanding.

> **Chapter Self-Test**

Test Preparation

> **Latin America Practice Tests A, B and C,** Test Prep Workbook, pp. 61–72
> **Latin America Benchmark Test 2 and Outcome Test,** AYP Monitoring Assessments, pp. 101–104, 182–187

Section 1 Brazil: Geography Shapes a Nation

 2 periods, 1 blocks (includes Country Databank)

Social Studies Objectives

1. Learn about the geography of Brazil.
2. Discover why the rain forests are important to Brazil and to the whole world.
3. Find out what groups make up the people of Brazil and how they live.

Reading/Language Arts Objective

Compare and contrast things to analyze and sort out information.

Prepare to Read	Instructional Resources	Differentiated Instruction

Build Background Knowledge
Have students discuss the effects of Brazil's geography on its people.

Set a Purpose for Reading
Have students evaluate statements on the *Reading Readiness Guide*.

Preview Key Terms
Teach the section's Key Terms.

Target Reading Skill
Introduce the section's Target Reading Skill of **comparing and contrasting**.

All in One Latin America Teaching Resources
- **L2** Reading Readiness Guide, p. 316
- **L2** Compare and Contrast, p. 331

Spanish Reading and Vocabulary Study Guide
- **L2** Chapter 6, Section 1, pp. 45–46 ELL

World Studies Video Program
- **L2** South America: Adapting to a Varied Landscape LPR, SN, ELL

Latin America Transparencies
- **L1** Transparency B16: Venn Diagram LPR, SN, ELL

Instruct	Instructional Resources	Differentiated Instruction

The Geography of Brazil
Discuss the geography of Brazil.

The Importance of the Rain Forest
Discuss the dangers threatening the Amazon rain forest.

Target Reading Skill
Review **comparing and contrasting**.

Country Profile
Direct student to derive information from maps, charts, and graphs, followed by an activity and a discussion.

The People of Brazil
Discuss Brazil's people and how they live.

All in One Latin America Teaching Resources
- **L2** Guided Reading and Review, p. 317
- **L2** Reading Readiness Guide, p. 316
- **L2** Reading a Population Density Map, p. 341

Latin America Transparencies
- **L2** Section Reading Support Transparency LA 45

World Studies Video Program
- **L2** Brazil's Carnival

All in One Latin America Teaching Resources
- **L3** Enrichment, p. 335 AR, GT
- **L1** Outline Map 8: South America, p. 343 AR, GT, LPR, SN

Latin America Teacher's Edition
- **L1** For Less Proficient Readers, TE p. 161
- **L1** For English Language Learners, TE p. 161, 168
- **L3** For Gifted and Talented Students, TE p. 164, 168
- **L3** For Advanced Readers, TE p. 162, 169
- **L1** For Special Needs Students, TE p. 169

Assess and Reteach	Instructional Resources	Differentiated Instruction

Assess Progress
Evaluate student comprehension with the section assessment and section quiz.

Reteach
Assign the Reading and Vocabulary Study Guide to help struggling students.

Extend
Extend the lesson by assigning a Small Group Activity.

All in One Latin America Teaching Resources
- **L2** Section Quiz, p. 318
- **L3** Small Group Activity: Making a Mural, pp. 337–340
  Rubric for Assessing a Writing Assignment, p. 349

Reading and Vocabulary Study Guide
- **L1** Chapter 6, Section 1, pp. 62–64

All in One Latin America Teaching Resources
  Rubric for Assessing a Bar Graph, p. 348 AR, GT, ELL

Spanish Support
- **L2** Section Quiz (Spanish), p. 49 ELL

Key

- **L1** Basic to Average
- **L2** For All Students
- **L3** Average to Advanced
- LPR Less Proficient Readers
- AR Advanced Readers
- SN Special Needs Students
- GT Gifted and Talented
- ELL English Language Learners

Section 2 Peru: An Ancient Land Looks to the Future

 1.5 periods, .75 block

Social Studies Objectives
1. Learn how geography has affected the way people live in the three regions of Peru.
2. Discover what life is like in the cities and towns of the altiplano.

Reading/Language Arts Objective
Contrast two regions to find out how they are different.

Prepare to Read	**Instructional Resources**	**Differentiated Instruction**
Build Background Knowledge Show a video to help students brainstorm about life in Peru. **Set a Purpose for Reading** Have students evaluate statements on the *Reading Readiness Guide.* **Preview Key Terms** Teach the section's Key Terms. **Target Reading Skill** Introduce the section's Target Reading Skill of **identifying contrasts**.	**All in One Latin America Teaching Resources** L2 Reading Readiness Guide, p. 320 L2 Identify Contrasts, p. 332 **World Studies Video Program** L2 Making a living in Peru	**Spanish Reading and Vocabulary Study Guide** L2 Chapter 6, Section 2, pp. 47–48 ELL

Instruct	**Instructional Resources**	**Differentiated Instruction**
Country Profile Ask students to derive information from maps, charts, and graphs. **The Regions and People of Peru** Discuss why the people of Peru live where they do. **Life in the Altiplano** Discuss how the altiplano reflects the past. **Target Reading Skill** Review **identifying contrasts**.	**All in One Latin America Teaching Resources** L2 Guided Reading and Review, p. 321 L2 Reading Readiness Guide, p. 320 L2 Reading a Table, p. 342 **Latin America Transparencies** L2 Section Reading Support Transparency LA 46	**All in One Latin America Teaching Resources** L3 A Women's Prison in London, pp. 344–345 GT, AR **Latin America Teacher's Edition** L3 For Gifted and Talented Students, TE p. 175 L1 For Less Proficient Readers, TE p. 176 L3 For Advanced Readers, TE p. 176 **Spanish Support** L2 Guided Reading and Review (Spanish), p. 50 ELL

Assess and Reteach	**Instructional Resources**	**Differentiated Instruction**
Assess Progress Evaluate student comprehension with the section assessment and section quiz. **Reteach** Assign the Reading and Vocabulary Study Guide to help struggling students. **Extend** Extend the lesson by showing a Discovery Channel School Video.	**All in One Latin America Teaching Resources** L2 Section Quiz, p. 322 Rubric for Assessing a Writing Assignment, p. 349 **Reading and Vocabulary Study Guide** L1 Chapter 6, Section 2, pp. 65–67 **World Studies Video Program** L3 Making a Living in Peru	**Spanish Support** L2 Section Quiz (Spanish), p. 51 ELL

Key

L1 Basic to Average	L3 Average to Advanced	LPR Less Proficient Readers AR Advanced Readers SN Special Needs Students	GT Gifted and Talented ELL English Language Learners

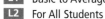

Section 3 Chile: Land of Contrasts

 2.5 periods, 1.25 block (includes Skills for Life)

Social Studies Objectives

1. Find out how the geography of Chile creates regions where people live very differently.
2. Learn how Chile's people live and what products they produce.
3. Find out how Chile restored democracy.

Reading/Language Arts Objective

Compare and contrast things to analyze and sort out information.

Prepare to Read

Build Background Knowledge
Discuss with students how geography has influenced the cultures of Chile.

Set a Purpose for Reading
Have students evaluate statements on the *Reading Readiness Guide*.

Preview Key Terms
Teach the section's Key Terms.

Target Reading Skill
Introduce the section's Target Reading Skill of **comparing and contrasting**.

Instructional Resources

All in One Latin America Teaching Resources

- **L2** Reading Readiness Guide, p. 324
- **L2** Compare and Contrast, p. 331

Differentiated Instruction

Spanish Reading and Vocabulary Study Guide

- **L2** Chapter 6, Section 3, pp. 49–50 ELL

Instruct

Country Profile
Ask students to derive information from maps, charts, and graphs.

Target Reading Skill
Review **comparing and contrasting**.

The Geography of Chile
Discuss the differences between Chile's regions.

Chile's People and Products
Have students describe how Chile's natural resources affect its economy.

Restoring Democracy
Discuss Chile's political struggles.

Instructional Resources

All in One Latin America Teaching Resources

- **L2** Guided Reading and Review, p. 325
- **L2** Reading Readiness Guide, p. 324

Latin America Transparencies

- **L2** Section Reading Support Transparency LA 47

All in One Latin America Teaching Resources

- **L2** Skills for Life, p. 336 AR, GT, LPR, SN

Differentiated Instruction

Latin America Teacher's Edition

- **L3** For Advanced Readers, TE p. 181, 183
- **L1** For Less Proficient Readers, TE p. 182
- **L1** For Special Needs Students, TE p. 182
- **L1** For English Language Learners, TE p. 183

PHSchool.com

- **L3** For: Environmental and Global Issues: *Trade in a Global Economy*
Web code: lfd-1606 AR, GT

Student Edition on Audio CD

- **L1** Chapter 6, Section 3 SN, LPR, ELL

Assess and Reteach

Assess Progress
Evaluate student comprehension with the section assessment and section quiz.

Reteach
Assign the Reading and Vocabulary Study Guide to help struggling students.

Extend
Extend the lesson by assigning an online activity.

Instructional Resources

All in One Latin America Teaching Resources

- **L2** Section Quiz, p. 326
  Rubric for Assessing a Journal Entry, p. 350

Reading and Vocabulary Study Guide

- **L1** Chapter 6, Section 3, pp. 68–70

PHSchool.com

- **L3** For: Environmental and Global Issues: *Analysis of Human Rights Violations*
Web code: lfd-1607

Differentiated Instruction

Latin America Transparencies

- **L2** Color Transparency LA 9: The World: Annual Precipitation AR, GT, LPR, SN

Spanish Support

- **L2** Section Quiz (Spanish), p. 53 ELL

Social Studies Skills Tutor CD-ROM

- **L1** Synthesizing Information SN, LPR, ELL

Key

L1 Basic to Average	**L3** Average to Advanced	**LPR** Less Proficient Readers	**GT** Gifted and Talented
L2 For All Students		**AR** Advanced Readers	**ELL** English Language Learners
		SN Special Needs Students	

Section 4 Venezuela: Oil Powers the Economy

 3 periods, 1.5 blocks (includes Chapter Review and Assessment)

Social Studies Objectives
1. Find out how Venezuela was made wealthy by oil.
2. Learn how the ups and downs of oil prices affected the economy and people of Venezuela.
3. Understand how Venezuela is changing.

Reading/Language Arts Objective
Make comparisons to find out how two things are alike.

Prepare to Read

Build Background Knowledge
Discuss the economy of Venezuela.

Set a Purpose for Reading
Have students evaluate statements on the *Reading Readiness Guide*.

Preview Key Terms
Teach the section's Key Terms.

Target Reading Skill
Introduce the section's Target Reading Skill of **making comparisons**.

Instructional Resources

All in One Latin America Teaching Resources
- **L2** Reading Readiness Guide, p. 328
- **L2** Make Comparisons, p. 333

Differentiated Instruction

Spanish Reading and Vocabulary Study Guide
- **L2** Chapter 6, Section 4, pp. 51–52 ELL

Instruct

A Land Made Wealthy by Oil
Ask questions about how oil has affected Venezuela's economy.

Country Profile
Ask students to derive information from maps, charts, and graphs.

Target Reading Skill
Review **making comparisons**.

The Economy and the People
Ask questions about how oil has affected the people of Venezuela.

Venezuela in Crisis
Discuss Venezuela's economic and political crises.

Instructional Resources

All in One Latin America Teaching Resources
- **L2** Guided Reading and Review, p. 329
- **L2** Reading Readiness Guide, p. 328

Latin American Transparencies
- **L2** Section Reading Support Transparency LA 48

World Studies Video Program
- **L2** The Liberator: Simón Bolivar

Differentiated Instruction

All in One Latin America Teaching Resources
Rubric for Assessing a Timeline, p. 351 LPR, SN, ELL

Latin America Teacher's Edition
- **L1** For Less Proficient Readers, TE p. 191, 193
- **L1** For Special Needs Students, TE p. 91, 193
- **L2** For English Language Learners, TE p. 192

Reading and Vocabulary Study Guide
- **L1** Chapter 6, Section 4, pp. 71–73 SN, ELL, LPR

Assess and Reteach

Assess Progress
Evaluate student comprehension with the section assessment and section quiz.

Reteach
Assign the Reading and Vocabulary Study Guide to help struggling students.

Extend
Extend the lesson by assigning a writing activity.

Instructional Resources

All in One Latin America Teaching Resources
- **L2** Section Quiz, p. 330
- **L3** Writing to Persuade, p. 346
  Rubric for Assessing a Writing Assignment, p. 349
- **L2** Vocabulary Development, p. 347
- **L2** Word Knowledge Rating Form, p. 334
  Rubric for Assessing a Report, p. 352
- **L2** Chapter Tests A and B, pp. 353–358

Differentiated Instruction

Spanish Support
- **L2** Section Quiz (Spanish), p. 55 ELL
- **L2** Chapter Summary (Spanish), p. 56 ELL
- **L2** Vocabulary Development (Spanish), p. 57 ELL

Key

- **L1** Basic to Average
- **L2** For All Students
- **L3** Average to Advanced
- **LPR** Less Proficient Readers
- **AR** Advanced Readers
- **SN** Special Needs Students
- **GT** Gifted and Talented
- **ELL** English Language Learners

Reading Background

Numbered Heads Strategy

In this chapter, students will use the Numbered Heads engagement strategy to come up with and share their responses to questions. Numbered Heads allows students to become more confident of their individual responses by sharing them with a smaller group before facing the whole class. Because students are then called on at random to speak for the group, they alternate opportunities to take on a leadership role, and all students are responsible for paying attention to the team's ideas.

Remind students that it is a good idea to compare and contrast their responses with those of other teams. Below are sample language strategies to help students achieve this goal.

Our answer was (similar to/different from) that of team _____ because _____.

We agree with team _____ that...

As team _____ already pointed out, it seems like...

Team _____ already mentioned..., but I would like to add that...

Evaluating similarities and differences between the teams' responses is also a good way to practice this chapter's Target Reading Skill of comparing and contrasting.

Author's Craft

Encourage students to notice not only the *what* of the reading, but the *how*. That is, ask them to pay special attention to how the author presents information. Explain that by exploring the structure of the reading, they can better analyze and remember the information presented. As an example, present the following paragraph from page 189 of the Student Edition:

During the 1970s, the price of oil went up. An oil boom began. The standard of living of many Venezuelans went up, too. That is when the government started spending huge sums of money. Many people were hired to run government-owned businesses. The government built expensive subways and high-quality roads. Then the government began to borrow money so that it could spend even more.

Guide students toward recognizing a framework for these sentences by asking questions. *Did the author use dates or present a chronological sequence? Is the author comparing one thing to another? Can you see a cause and effect relationship?* Students should recognize a chronological sequence. One clue is the fact that the author begins by setting up a time frame: *During the 1970s....* Other clues are the use of the words *That is when* and *Then*. These are all phrases that have to do with time.

Have students work individually or in pairs as they reread sections of the chapter. As they read, have them identify different techniques the author used by asking the same kinds of questions

World Studies Background

Fighting for the Brazilian Rain Forest

Tensions over how best to use the Brazilian rain forest have sometimes led to violence. Francisco "Chico" Mendes lived his entire life in the forest, and made his living by collecting rubber from rubber trees. He led the Rural Workers Union, a group whose purpose was to stop ranchers and other people from cutting down trees. In December 1988, Mendes was shot and killed by a rancher with whom Mendes had previously argued. The rancher had hoped to clear a road to his property, and the Rural Workers Union had protested. Brazil continues to work to find a balance between the need to use the forest's resources to support the nation's economy and maintaining the forest and the way of life of its indigenous peoples.

The Quechua Language

It is estimated that about 10 million people in South America speak the Quechua language—more than any other native language on the continent. So many Peruvians speak Quechua that in 1975, the government made Quechua and Spanish both official languages of the country. Quechua spread across the continent as a trade language before the early 1400s, when the Inca adopted it. When the Spanish colonists arrived, they integrated some Quechua words into their own speech. Variations on some of those words have entered into the English we speak today, such as *condor* (a type of bird), *puma* (cougar), and *jerky* (dried meat.)

Infoplease® provides a wealth of useful information for the classroom. You can use this resource to strengthen your background on the subjects covered in this chapter. Have students visit this advertising-free site as a starting point for projects requiring research.

Use Web Code **lfd-1600** for **Infoplease**.

of themselves. When students have finished taking notes, have the class discuss what techniques they have found.

Questions and Answers

Encourage students to be aware of the fact that there are many different kinds of questions. Questions that require you to:

1. remember a specific fact from the reading

2. synthesize or analyze information from different places in the reading

3. think beyond the reading to make an inference or assumption

4. find the answer somewhere completely outside of the reading

Model this concept by listing the following questions on the board and asking students to state what type of question each is, and where the answer could be found in relation to this chapter.

■ What is the largest country in South America?

(Specific fact; Brazil: page 167)

■ What are some threats to the Brazilian rain forest?

(Synthesize or analyze; Cutting down timber, smuggling, and pollution: page 169)

■ Why might Daniel Monteiro Costa want to be called Daniel Munduruku?

(Inference or assumption; To raise people's awareness about the culture and heritage of Munduruku Indians: inference from information on page 171)

■ How has Brazil recently been featured in the news?

(Outside the reading; could be answered by looking at recent newspapers and magazines)

After discussing these examples, have students work in teams to develop one question of each type based on the information in each chapter. Challenge students to trade their finished questions with another group and try to identify each type of question and how to answer it.

The Chilean Government

After the 1988 election in which the people of Chile voted to end the reign of military leader Augusto Pinochet, the government was returned to a democratic structure set out in a constitution of 1981. Like the United States, the government of Chile has an executive, legislative, and judicial branch. The president is elected for a four-year term, the National Congress has two houses, and a 17-member Supreme Court presides over the judicial system. Although political parties were outlawed under Pinochet, they were brought back in 1987 and now are an integral part of the democratic process.

Tourism in Venezuela

Although a distant second to the oil industry, on which Venezuela's economy heavily relies, tourism is the next-most profitable industry in the country. Just as is true of oil prices, income from tourism is vulnerable to change. Because of recent political turmoil in Venezuela, tourism— along with the rest of the nation's economy—has suffered, dropping almost 10 percent between 1995 and 2000.

One possible way to expand tourism in Venezuela would be to promote ecotourism, or environmental and adventure trips that promote sensitivity for local people and environments.

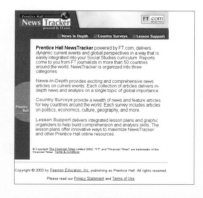

Get in-depth information on topics of global importance with **Prentice Hall NewsTracker,** powered by FT.com.

 Use Web Code **lfd-1605** for **Prentice Hall NewsTracker.**

Chapter 6

Guiding Questions

Remind students about the Guiding Questions introduced at the beginning of the book.

Section 1 relates to **Guiding Question** ❶ **What are the main physical features of Latin America?** *(The Amazon rain forest takes up more than one third of Brazil.)*

Section 2 relates to **Guiding Question** ❷ **How has Latin America been shaped by its history?** *(Many Quechuas, Uros, and other Native Americans living in Peru follow traditions that are hundreds of years old. The ruins of Incan cities still stand in parts of Peru.)*

Section 3 relates to **Guiding Question** ❸ **What factors have affected cultures in Latin America?** *(Chile's geography creates three regions in which people have very different cultures.)*

Section 4 relates to **Guiding Question** ❺ **How has geography influenced the ways in which Latin Americans make a living?** *(Venezuela's land is rich with oil. Many Venezuelans make a living in the oil industry.)*

⤳ Target Reading Skill

In this chapter, students will learn and apply the reading skill of comparison and contrast. Use the following worksheets to help students practice this skill.

All in One **Latin America Teaching Resources,** *Compare and Contrast,* p. 331; *Identify Contrasts,* p. 332; *Make Comparisons,* p. 333

Differentiated Instruction

The following Teacher Edition strategies are suitable for students of varying abilities.

Advanced Readers, pp. 162, 169, 176, 181, 183
English Language Learners, pp. 161, 168, 183, 192
Gifted and Talented, pp. 164, 168, 175, 187
Less Proficient Readers, pp. 161, 176, 182, 191, 193
Special Needs Students, pp. 169, 182, 185, 191, 193

Chapter 6 South America

Chapter Preview

This chapter will introduce you to the countries of the continent of South America.

Country Databank
The Country Databank provides data and descriptions of each of the countries in the region: Argentina, Bolivia, Brazil, Chile, Colombia, Ecuador, Guyana, Paraguay, Peru, Suriname, Uruguay, and Venezuela.

Section 1
Brazil
Geography Shapes a Nation

Section 2
Peru
An Ancient Land Looks to the Future

Section 3
Chile
Land of Contrasts

Section 4
Venezuela
Oil Powers the Economy

⤳ Target Reading Skill

Comparison and Contrast In this chapter you will focus on using comparison and contrast to help you sort out and analyze information.

▶ A plaza in Rio de Janeiro, Brazil

Bibliography

For the Teacher
Allende, Isabel and Margaret Sayers Peden. *My Invented Country: A Nostalgic Journey Through Chile.* HarperCollins Publishers, 2003.
Bishop, Nathaniel H. *The Pampas and Andes: A Thousand Miles Walk Across South America.* The Narrative Press, 2003.

For the Student
L1 Goodman, Susan E. *Adventures in the Amazon Rain Forest (Ultimate Field Trip 1).* Bt Bound, 1999.
L1 Handau, Elaine. *Peru (True Book).* Children's Book Press, 2000.
L2 Black, Carolyn and Malika Hollander. *Brazil: The Land.* Crabtree Publishing, 2003.

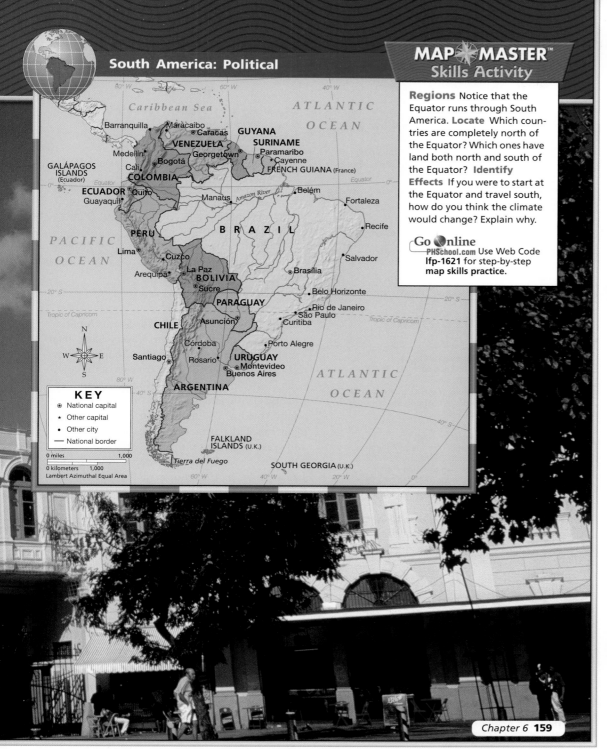

South America: Political

Regions Notice that the Equator runs through South America. **Locate** Which countries are completely north of the Equator? Which ones have land both north and south of the Equator? **Identify Effects** If you were to start at the Equator and travel south, how do you think the climate would change? Explain why.

Go Online
PHSchool.com Use Web Code lfp-1621 for step-by-step map skills practice.

KEY
⊛ National capital
★ Other capital
• Other city
— National border

0 miles 1,000
0 kilometers 1,000
Lambert Azimuthal Equal Area

■ Have students locate the mountain chain in the western part of the continent. Point out that these are the Andes Mountains. Ask students **How do you think the Andes Mountains may have affected political boundaries in South America?** *(Some political boundaries seem to have been drawn along the mountains. For example, the mountains separate Argentina and Chile.)* **L3**

Go Online
PHSchool.com Students may practice their map skills using the interactive online version of this map.

Using the Visual **L2**

Reach Into Your Background Draw students' attention to the photograph (pp. 158-159) and its caption (p. 158). Discuss the visual. What interests students about this photograph? Is the scene something they would or would not expect to find in Rio de Janeiro, Brazil? Ask students to observe details in the photograph and share them with the class. Ask them to reach into their own background: have they ever seen buildings similar to those shown in the photograph? If so, where? Encourage students to discuss ideas.

Answers

Locate Venezuela, Guyana, Suriname, French Guiana; Ecuador, Colombia, Brazil
Identify Effects The climate would get cooler the farther south you traveled from the Equator.

Chapter Resources

Teaching Resources
L2 Vocabulary Development, p. 347
L2 Skills for Life, p. 336
L2 Chapter Tests A and B, pp. 353–358

Spanish Support
L2 Spanish Chapter Summary, p. 56
L2 Spanish Vocabulary Development, p. 57

Media and Technology
L1 Student Edition on Audio CD
L1 Guided Reading Audiotapes, English and Spanish
L2 Social Studies Skills Tutor CD-ROM
ExamView Test Bank CD-ROM

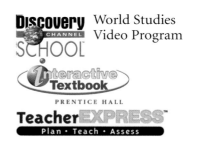

Discovery CHANNEL **SCHOOL** World Studies Video Program

interactive Textbook PRENTICE HALL

TeacherEXPRESS™
Plan • Teach • Assess

Objectives

■ Use data to compare countries.

■ Learn what characteristics South American countries share.

■ Identify some key differences among the countries.

Show *South America: Adapting to a Varied Landscape.* Ask students to name some of the major geographical features of South America. *(Andes Mountains, Amazon River, Amazon rain forest)*

Prepare to Read

Build Background Knowledge   L2

Invite students to share what they know about South America and what they learned about the continent's geography from watching the World Studies Video Overview. Write the following headings on the chalkboard: *Climate, Vegetation, Population, Natural Resources.* Conduct an Idea Wave (TE, p. T35) to generate a list of what students learned or know about each topic. Write their responses under the appropriate heading on the board.

Guide for Reading

This section provides an introduction to the 12 countries of South America.

• Look at the map on the previous page and then read the paragraphs to learn about each nation.

• Analyze the data to compare the countries.

• What characteristics do most of these countries share?

• What are some key differences among the countries?

Viewing the Video Overview

View the World Studies Video Overview to learn more about each of the countries. As you watch, answer these questions:

• What topographical feature has a major influence on the climate of South America?

• What topographical features influence the climate where you live?

Explore the varied landscape of South America.

Argentina

Capital	Buenos Aires
Land Area	1,056,636 sq mi; 2,736,690 sq km
Population	37.8 million
Ethnic Group(s)	white, mestizo, indigenous Indian
Religion(s)	Roman Catholic, Protestant, Jewish
Government	republic
Currency	Argentine peso
Leading Exports	edible oils, fuels and energy, cereals, feed, motor vehicles
Language(s)	Spanish (official), Italian, indigenous Indian languages

The second-largest country in South America, Argentina (ahr jun TEE nuh) covers more than 1 million square miles (2.7 million square kilometers). It is located in the southern part of the continent, between the Andes Mountains and the Atlantic Ocean, and extends to the southern tip of South America. The Andes slope down to a fertile plain called the pampas, where raising livestock and wheat dominates the culture and the economy. Argentina has suffered from a series of harsh military regimes. In 1983, however, the nation established a democratic government.

Albatross chicks, Diego Ramirez Islands, Chile

160 Latin America

Bolivia

Capitals	La Paz and Sucre
Land Area	418,683 sq mi; 1,084,390 sq km
Population	8.5 million
Ethnic Group(s)	Quechua, mestizo, Aymara, white
Religion(s)	Roman Catholic, Protestant
Government	republic
Currency	boliviano
Leading Exports	soybeans, natural gas, zinc, gold, wood
Language(s)	Spanish (official), Quechua (official), Aymara (official)

Bolivia (buh LIV ee uh) is a landlocked country in central South America. Much of its population lives in the Altiplano, or high plateau region, which Bolivia shares with Peru. This plain lies between two ranges of the Andes Mountains. Mountains and rain forests isolate the Altiplano from the sea and from the rest of South America. Although Bolivia has rich mineral resources, mining is difficult at high altitudes. It is also difficult to transport the minerals to market. So, in spite of its resources, Bolivia has remained poor. More than half of Bolivians are Indians.

Brazil

Capital	Brasília
Land Area	3,265,059 sq mi; 8,456,510 sq km
Population	176 million
Ethnic Group(s)	white, mixed white and black, black, Asian, Arab, indigenous Indian
Religion(s)	Roman Catholic
Government	federal republic
Currency	real
Leading Exports	manufactured goods, iron ore, soybeans, footwear, coffee, autos
Language(s)	Portuguese (official), German, Italian, Spanish, Polish, Japanese, indigenous Indian languages

Brazil (bruh ZIL) is the largest country in South America. It occupies the eastern-central region of the continent, bordering the Atlantic Ocean. Brazil is known as the home of the huge Amazon rain forest and for its vibrant culture. The influence of its Portuguese colonial past can still be seen in Brazil's language, culture, and architecture. However, other groups have also made contributions to a distinctive Brazilian culture. These groups include the native Indians, Africans originally brought to Brazil as slaves, and immigrants from northern Europe and Japan.

Chile

Capital	Santiago
Land Area	289,112 sq mi; 748,800 sq km
Population	15.5 million
Ethnic Group(s)	white, mestizo, indigenous Indian
Religion(s)	Roman Catholic, Protestant
Government	republic
Currency	Chilean peso
Leading Exports	copper, fish, fruits, paper and pulp, chemicals
Language(s)	Spanish (official), indigenous Indian languages

Chile (CHIL ee) is a long, narrow country. It lies along the western coast of South America, from its northern border with Peru to the southern tip of the continent. Chile has varied landforms and climates, from deserts in the north and central fertile plains, to its rainy, stormy southern tip. Mountains, lakes, and glaciers complete the picture. Most Chileans live in the fertile valley of central Chile. About one third of Chile's people live in the vibrant capital of Santiago.

Chapter 6 **161**

Instruct

Introducing South America   L2

Guided Instruction

- Read each country paragraph as a class using the Structured Silent Reading technique (TE, p. T34). Then, ask students to read through each data table.

- Ask students **What groups have contributed to Brazil's culture?** *(Portuguese, native Indians, Africans, northern Europeans, and Asians)*

- Have students identify the similarities between Argentina and Bolivia. Remind them to use both the paragraphs and the data beside them. *(Similarities: Spanish as their official language, whites and mestizos as major ethnic groups, Roman Catholicism and Protestantism as major religions, and located near the Andes Mountains)*

- Ask students **How is Chile's long seacoast reflected in its economy?** *(The data shows that ocean resources are important to Chile's economy—fish is one of Chile's leading exports.)*

Differentiated Instruction

For English Language Learners   L1
Students may find it difficult to pronounce some of the words on these pages, such as *established*, *isolate*, and *vibrant*. Show students how to break down these words into smaller parts to help them sound out the pronunciations. Also, check to make sure students understand the meanings of the words.

For Less Proficient Readers   L1
Have students create a Venn Diagram to show the similarities and differences between Brazil and Chile. Display the *Venn Diagram* transparency to show students how to sketch the organizer.

📖 **Latin America Transparencies,** *Transparency B16: Venn Diagram*

Guided Instruction (continued)

- Ask **Where is Colombia located? Why do you think its location would be important to its economy?** *(Colombia is located at the intersection of Central and South America. People and goods traveling by land between Central America and South America must pass through Colombia. Colombia's economy can benefit from the traffic of tourists and trade.)*

- Ask students **What leading exports do Colombia and Ecuador have in common?** *(petroleum and coffee)* Have students look at the map on p. 159. Discuss why the two countries might both produce and export these products. *(Ecuador and Colombia are located next to each other, therefore the resources found in the ground such as petroleum are similar. They are both located on the Equator so they both a have a warm, wet climate that is good for growing coffee beans.)*

Introducing South America

Colombia

Capital	Bogotá
Land Area	401,042 sq mi; 1,038,700 sq km
Population	41 million
Ethnic Group(s)	mestizo, white, mixed white and black, mixed black and indigenous Indian, indigenous Indian
Religion(s)	Roman Catholic
Government	republic
Currency	Colombian peso
Leading Exports	petroleum, coffee, coal, apparel, bananas, cut flowers
Language(s)	Spanish (official), indigenous Indian languages

Located on the northwest corner of South America, Colombia (kuh LUM bee uh) has coastlines on both the Pacific Ocean and the Caribbean Sea. To the northwest, it is bordered by Panama, which was once part of its territory. Colombia is located at the intersection of Central and South America and near the Panama Canal. This location makes it important to transportation and communication between the regions. Three ranges of the Andes Mountains divide the country. Most of Colombia's people live in the central valley or the hot, wet western region.

Ecuador

Capital	Quito
Land Area	106,888 sq mi; 276,840 sq km
Population	13.5 million
Ethnic Group(s)	mestizo, indigenous Indian, white, black
Religion(s)	Roman Catholic
Government	republic
Currency	U.S. dollar
Leading Exports	petroleum, bananas, shrimp, coffee, cocoa, cut flowers, fish
Language(s)	Spanish (official), Quechua, other indigenous Indian languages

Once part of the Incan empire, Ecuador (EK wuh dawr) was colonized by Spain in 1533 and became independent in 1830. A small country on the Pacific Coast, Ecuador has three regions. The lowland coastal region is the industrial center as well as the farm belt of Ecuador. Subsistence farming is the main economic activity in the highlands of the Andes Mountains. This is the region where the descendants of the Incas live and struggle to maintain their languages and traditional ways of life. The inland region benefits from large deposits of oil.

Giant tortoise, Ecuador

162 Latin America

Differentiated Instruction

For Advanced Readers   L3
Have students do Internet or library research to learn more about how Incas in Ecuador are struggling to maintain their traditional ways of life. What are their traditional ways of life? What is threatening them? Have students write a short essay summarizing their findings.

Guyana

Capital	Georgetown
Land Area	76,004 sq mi; 196,850 sq km
Population	698,209
Ethnic Group(s)	South Asian, black, indigenous Indian, white, East Asian, mixed white and black
Religion(s)	Christian, Hindu, Muslim
Government	republic
Currency	Guyanese dollar
Leading Exports	sugar, gold, bauxite/alumina, rice, shrimp, molasses, rum, timber
Language(s)	English (official), English Creole, Hindi, Tamil, indigenous Indian languages

Guyana (gy AN uh) lies on the northeast coast of South America. It is similar to its Caribbean island neighbors. Guyana was originally colonized by the Dutch, who imported enslaved Africans to work on their plantations. It became a British colony in 1814. After slavery ended in 1838, the British brought workers from India to do farm work. The descendants of these Africans and Indians form the largest ethnic groups in Guyana today. Most of the population lives on the narrow, wet coastal plain. The interior of the country is covered with dense rain forests.

Paraguay

Capital	Asunción
Land Area	153,398 sq mi; 397,300 sq km
Population	5.9 million
Ethnic Group(s)	mestizo
Religion(s)	Roman Catholic, Protestant
Government	constitutional republic
Currency	guaraní
Leading Exports	soybeans, feed, cotton, meat, edible oils, electricity
Language(s)	Spanish (official), Guaraní (official)

A small landlocked country, Paraguay (PA ruh gway) is bordered by Brazil, Argentina, and Bolivia. The Paraguay River divides the country into two sections. Much of the population is clustered in the fertile plains and hills of the eastern region. The west is sparsely populated. Most of the people of Paraguay are descended from the Spanish and the Guaraní, an indigenous group. In the cities, both Spanish and Guaraní are spoken, but in the countryside most people speak Guaraní.

Peru

Capital	Lima
Land Area	494,208 sq mi; 1,280,000 sq km
Population	28 million
Ethnic Group(s)	indigenous Indian, mestizo, white, black, East Asian
Religion(s)	Roman Catholic
Government	constitutional republic
Currency	nuevo sol
Leading Exports	fish and fish products, gold, copper, zinc, crude petroleum and byproducts, lead, coffee, sugar, cotton
Language(s)	Spanish (official), Quechua (official), Aymara

Peru (puh ROO) lies along the Pacific coast of South America, south of Colombia and Ecuador, and north of Chile. The Andes Mountains run the length of the country. A high plateau called the Altiplano is home to descendants of the Incas and other indigenous groups. Many of them live much as their ancestors did and speak Indian languages. The economic center of Peru is Lima, on the coast. Peru has been slow to modernize and industrialize. It has also suffered from military dictatorships and government corruption, but today it has an elected democratic government.

Chapter 6 **163**

Independent Practice

■ Distribute the outline map of South America.

All in One **Latin America Teaching Resources,** *Outline Map 8: South America,* p. 343

■ Have students create a map that shows the types of government of all of the South American countries. Tell students to choose a color to represent each government that will be displayed on the map. They should explain what each color represents in the map key. Then have students fill in each country with the color that corresponds to its type of government and have them locate and name the country's capital on the map.

■ Tell students to give the map an appropriate title.

Monitor Progress

■ Circulate to be sure students are making the map key, coloring in the countries, and locating the capitals correctly and that they have chosen an appropriate map title.

Assess and Reteach

Assess Progress   L2

Direct students attention back to the lists on the chalkboard. Encourage them to suggest more information to fill in under each topic based on what they learned from the Country Databank.

Introducing South America

Suriname

Capital	Paramaribo
Land Area	62,344 sq mi; 161,470 sq km
Population	436,494
Ethnic Group(s)	South Asian, Creole, Javanese, Maroon, indigenous Indian, East Asian, white
Religion(s)	Christian, Hindu, Muslim, traditional beliefs
Government	constitutional democracy
Currency	Suriname guilder or florin
Leading Exports	alumina, crude oil, lumber, shrimp and fish, rice, bananas
Language(s)	Dutch (official), Sranan, Javanese, Sarnami Hindi, Saramaccan, Chinese, Carib

Suriname (soor ih NAHM) is a small country on the northern coast of South America. Mountains and rain forest dominate its geography. Most of the people live on a narrow coastal plain. Suriname was settled by the Dutch, who imported enslaved Africans to work their coffee and sugar cane plantations. After slavery ended, workers from India, Java, and China were brought to work in the fields. The result is an ethnically mixed population. Suriname became independent in 1975. A series of military regimes followed, but democratic rule was established in 1987.

Gaucho, Uruguay

Uruguay

Capital	Montevideo
Land Area	67,108 sq mi; 173,620 sq km
Population	3.4 million
Ethnic Group(s)	white, mestizo, black
Religion(s)	Roman Catholic, Protestant, Jewish
Government	constitutional republic
Currency	Uruguayan peso
Leading Exports	meat, rice, leather products, wool, vehicles, dairy products
Language(s)	Spanish (official)

Uruguay (YOOR uh gway) is a small country located between two large ones: Brazil to the north and Argentina to the west. The capital, Montevideo, is situated where the River Platte empties into the Atlantic Ocean, making the city an important port for international trade. Most of Uruguay is made up of grassy plains and low hills. Raising cattle and sheep are the main occupations of that region. Tourism has become important along the country's sandy coastal beaches. Banking and other service industries also contribute to the economy.

164 Latin America

Differentiated Instruction

For Gifted and Talented   L3

To learn more about the coat of arms of the countries of Bolivia, Brazil, and Peru, have students complete the *Enrichment* worksheet in the Latin America Teaching Resources.

All in One **Latin America Teaching Resources,** *Enrichment,* p. 335

Venezuela

Capital	Caracas
Land Area	340,560 sq mi; 882,050 sq km
Population	24.3 million
Ethnic Group(s)	white, Southwest Asian, black, indigenous Indian
Religion(s)	Roman Catholic, Protestant
Government	federal republic
Currency	bolívar
Leading Exports	petroleum, bauxite and aluminum, steel, chemicals, agricultural products, basic manufactured goods
Language(s)	Spanish (official), indigenous Indian languages

Venezuela (ven uh ZWAY luh) is located on the northern coast of South America, along the Caribbean Sea. The government has encouraged both agriculture and industry in an effort to diversify the economy. However, Venezuela still depends largely on its huge deposits of oil. Most of Venezuela's people live in cities, primarily in the northern part of the country. Some of the country's indigenous population lives in isolated areas of rain forest. Once a Spanish colony, Venezuela freed itself from Spain in 1821 and then became part of Gran Colombia. Venezuela became an independent republic in 1830.

SOURCES: DK World Desk Reference Online; *CIA World Factbook,* 2002; *World Almanac,* 2003

Caraballeda, Venezuela

Assessment

Comprehension and Critical Thinking

1. Compare and Contrast Which is the largest country in South America? Which is the smallest? What do these two countries have in common, in spite of their difference in size?

2. Categorize What characteristics do the countries south of the Equator share?

3. Contrast How have such contrasting geographic features as rolling, grassy plains and high altitudes affected the cultures and economies of the countries in which they are found?

4. Draw Conclusions Which countries have the most diverse populations? Explain how you reached that conclusion.

5. Make a Bar Graph Create a population graph of the five most populous countries of South America.

Keeping Current

Access the **DK World Desk Reference Online** at **PHSchool.com** for up-to-date information about all the countries in this chapter.

PHSchool.com

Web Code: lfe-1433

Reteach L2

Ask students to create a table on a large piece of poster board that shows the data for all of the countries in the Country Databank. Have them list the categories across the top of the table and the names of the countries along the side. Model filling in the information for one country on the chalkboard.

Extend L2

Portfolio Activity

Have students choose two countries in the Country Databank. Ask them to do library or Internet research to learn more about each country. Then have them write a short essay or create a table to explain the differences and similarities between the two countries. Have students add their work to their portfolios.

Answers

Assessment

1. Brazil is the largest country and Suriname is the smallest country. Both have rain forests and a diverse population.

2. They all have a form of republican government, and Roman Catholicism is a major religion in all countries.

3. Answers will vary. Students' responses should reflect that the geography of an area affects how people make a living and influences local traditions and cultures.

4. Guyana, Suriname, and Brazil have the most diverse populations. The data show that these countries have the largest numbers of ethnic groups. The text also explains that these countries are very diverse.

5. Students' bar graphs should reflect the correct populations of each country. Use *Rubric for Assessing a Bar Graph* to evaluate students' graphs.

All in One **Latin America Teaching Resources,** *Rubric for Assessing a Bar Graph,* p. 348

Section 1
Step-by-Step Instruction

Objectives

Social Studies

1. Learn about the geography of Brazil.
2. Discover why the rain forests are important to Brazil and to the whole world.
3. Find out what groups make up the people of Brazil and how they live.

Reading/Language Arts

Compare and contrast things to analyze and sort out information.

Prepare to Read

Build Background Knowledge L2

In this section, students will learn about the people and resources of Brazil. Ask students to preview the headings and visuals in the section with this question in mind: **How have the people of Brazil been affected by the country's natural resources?** Provide a few examples to get students started. Have students engage in a Think-Pair-Share activity (TE, p. T36) to generate their list of possible effects.

Set a Purpose for Reading L2

- Preview the Objectives.
- Read each statement in the *Reading Readiness Guide* aloud. Ask students to mark the statements true or false.

  All in One **Latin America Teaching Resources,** *Reading Readiness Guide,* p. 316

- Have students discuss the statements in pairs or groups of four, then mark their worksheets again. Use the Numbered Heads participation structure (TE, p. T36) to call on students to share their group's perspectives.

Vocabulary Builder
Preview Key Terms L2

Pronounce each Key Term, then ask students to say the word with you. Provide a simple explanation such as, "The canopy of the rain forest is made up of the leaves and branches at the very top of the forest."

Section 1
Brazil
Geography Shapes a Nation

Prepare to Read

Objectives

In this section you will
1. Learn about the geography of Brazil.
2. Discover why the rain forests are important to Brazil and to the whole world.
3. Find out what groups make up the people of Brazil and how they live.

Taking Notes

As you read this section, look for information about the rain forest. Copy the flowchart below and record your findings in it.

Amazon Rain Forest		
Importance	**Dangers**	**Efforts to Protect It**
•	•	•
•	•	•

A toucan from Brazil's rain forest

 Target Reading Skill

Compare and Contrast
When you compare, you examine the similarities between things. When you contrast, you look at the differences. Comparing and contrasting can help you sort out and analyze information. As you read this section, look for similarities and differences in the geographic regions, cultures, and cities of Brazil.

Key Terms

- **canopy** (KAN uh pea) *n.* the dense mass of leaves and branches that form the top layer of a rain forest
- **Amazon rain forest** (AM uh zahn rayn FAWR ist) *n.* a large tropical rain forest occupying the Amazon Basin in northern South America
- **Rio de Janeiro** (REE oh day zhuh NEHR oh) *n.* a large city in Brazil
- **Brasília** (bruh ZIL yuh) *n.* Brazil's new capital city
- **savanna** (suh VAN uh) *n.* a flat, grassy region, or plain

Deep in Brazil's rain forest, the light barely penetrates. At the top of the trees, the leaves form a dense mass called a **canopy.** Sun and rain beat down upon the canopy. But on the ground, it is almost chilly. The cool, moist air is filled with sounds, such as the calls of birds, monkeys, and insects.

The **Amazon rain forest** is a large area of abundant rainfall and dense vegetation in northern Brazil. It occupies the Amazon Basin, the land drained by the Amazon River and its tributaries. Find the Amazon River and the Amazon Basin on the map titled Physical Latin America on page 4. The Amazon rain forest gets more than 80 inches (200 centimeters) of rain each year and has an average temperature of 80°F (27°C). It has millions of species of plants and animals, including orchids, jaguars, and toucans.

The dense foliage makes travel through the rain forest difficult, and few people live there. Even so, the Amazon rain forest is very important to the people of Brazil. It is also important to the rest of the world. Find out what Brazil is doing to protect and develop its rain forest resources.

Target Reading Skill L2

Compare and Contrast Point out the Target Reading Skill. Explain to students that you look for similarities when you compare things, and you look for differences when you contrast things. Tell them that comparing and contrasting can help them analyze information.

Model the skill by comparing and contrasting Brazil's interior and coast from the information given on p. 167. Point out a similarity (*Both are inhabited by people, although the coast has more.*) and a difference. (*The interior is mostly covered with rain forest, while the coast is a flat plateau.*)

Give students *Compare and Contrast.* Have them complete the activity in groups.

All in One **Latin America Teaching Resources,** *Compare and Contrast,* p. 331

The Geography of Brazil

Brazil, the largest country in South America, is nearly as big as the United States. It is also one of the richest countries in the world in land and resources. Until recently, its immense rain forests remained undisturbed. Only the few indigenous groups that had lived in them for centuries ever explored them.

Rain Forest and More Brazil's rain forests take up more than a third of the country. Look at the map titled Latin America: Vegetation Regions on page 20. In the southeast, the forests give way to a large plateau divided by mountain ranges and river valleys. The plateau reaches Brazil's long coast. Many harbors lie along the coast. **Rio de Janeiro** (REE oh day zhuh NEHR oh), Brazil's former capital, is one of many Brazilian cities that grew up around these coastal harbors. Most of Brazil's people live near the coast, far from the rain forests.

Brazil's New Capital: Brasília In the 1950s, the government of Brazil wanted to develop Brazil's interior region using the resources of the rain forest. But few Brazilians wanted to move to the interior of the country. How could the government tempt Brazilians to move?

The government's solution was to build a new capital city called **Brasília** in the interior, near the rain forest. They chose a site on the vast interior plain, or **savanna,** called the Cerrado (suh RAH doh). Work started in 1957, and the government began to move to the partly-completed capital in 1960. Today, Brasília has a population of nearly 2 million people, and many of Brazil's companies and organizations have their headquarters there.

✓ **Reading Check** Why was Brasília built?

Links to Science

The Photosynthesis "Factory" What is the source of the oxygen we breathe? The food we eat? The fuels we burn? They all begin with photosynthesis. This process is carried out by green plants. They transform water, sunlight, carbon dioxide, and other minerals into energy-rich substances. Plants store these substances for their own nourishment. But animals eat the plants as food. And people eat those animals, as well as eating plants directly. At the same time, the process of photosynthesis releases oxygen into the air. The Amazon rain forest, with its wealth of green plants, is such an important source of oxygen that it is sometimes called "the lungs of Earth."

And there's more. Fuels such as coal and oil are the remains of ancient plants. So photosynthesis, in a way, powers the world.

Chapter 6 Section 1 **167**

Vocabulary Builder

Use the information below to teach students this section's high-use words.

High-Use Word	Definition and Sample Sentence
dense, p. 166	*adj.* packed tightly together
	The **dense** crowd made it hard to get a good view of the parade.
occupy, p. 166	*v.* to take up or fill up, such as time or space
	Studying for the test **occupied** our entire evening.
community, p. 171	*n.* a group of people forming a smaller social unit within a larger one, and sharing common interests, work, identity, and location
	The athletic **community** was thrilled about the new gym.

Guided Instruction

- **Vocabulary Builder** Clarify the high-use words **dense** and **occupy** before reading.
- Read The Geography of Brazil, using the Partner Paragraph Shrinking technique (TE, p. T34).
- Ask students **Why do you think many Brazilians live on the coast?** (*Many Brazilians live along the coast because the harbors provide access to people and goods from other places. The interior does not offer that access.*)
- Discuss the features that make up Brazil's interior. (*The rain forest covers more than a third of the country. It gives way to a plateau in the southeast that is divided by mountains and river valleys.*)

Independent Practice

Have students create the Taking Notes graphic organizer on a blank piece of paper. Then have them begin to fill in a few details about the Amazon rain forest. Briefly model how to identify which details to record.

Monitor Progress

As students fill in the graphic organizer, circulate and make sure individuals are choosing the correct details. Encourage students to add bullets as needed. Provide assistance as needed.

Links

Read the **Links to Science** on this page. Have students explain why some people say that photosynthesis powers the world. (*Photosynthesis provides the necessary energy and nutrients for vegetation to survive. In turn, the oxygen created by photosynthesis and the vegetation itself provides the air and nutrients for animals and humans to survive.*)

Answers

✓ **Reading Check** Brasília was built because the government thought that having a capital city in the interior of the country would encourage Brazilians to move to that region.

Show students *Brazil's Carnival*. Then have them identify some of the traditions that make Brazil's Carnival unique. *(Students' answers will vary, but should highlight the parades, costumes, and music of Carnival.)*

The Importance of the Rain Forest L2

Guided Instruction

■ Read about the importance of the Amazon rain forest in Brazil and on Earth in The Importance of the Rain Forest. As students read, circulate and make sure individuals can answer the Reading Check question.

■ Ask students **What makes the Amazon rain forest so important?** *(The Amazon rain forest helps provide about one third of the world's oxygen; it is home to several million species of plants, animals, and insects; many modern medicines have been made from its plants; and it holds about one fifth of the world's fresh water.)*

■ Discuss the dangers against which Brazil's government has to protect the Amazon rain forest. Ask students to consider the reasons why these dangers exist. *(The Amazon rain forest is in danger of having too many trees cut down, too many animals smuggled out, and too much pollution created within it. These dangers exist because people, such as loggers, furniture-makers, and miners, want to use the resources of the rain forest in their industries.)*

Answers

Graph Skills Transfer Information
Manaus; Manaus **Contrast** Possible answer: Brasília and Manaus would be surrounded by different types of vegetation, which could lead to different industries being based in each city.

■ **Graph Skills**

Differences in temperature and rainfall create different environments for plants, animals, and people. **Transfer Information** Which city shown in the graphs gets more rainfall? Which has the higher temperatures? **Contrast** Use these climate differences to infer how life might be different in Brasília and Manaus.

Brasília

The Importance of the Rain Forest

The rain forest is very important to life all over the world. Scientists estimate that rain forests produce about one third of the world's oxygen. They also calculate that the Amazon rain forest has several million different species of plants, animals, and insects—some that have not even been discovered yet. That is more species than any other region in the world.

Using Rain Forest Resources Many modern medicines have been made from rain forest plants, and scientists hope to discover even more species that have practical uses. The rain forest also holds about one fifth of the world's fresh water. But many scientists think that when people begin to use the resources of the rain forest, they upset the delicate balance of nature.

For example, in the past, Brazil made efforts at land reform by moving poor farmers to the Amazon rain forest and giving them land there. The farmers burned down trees to clear the land for their crops. After a few years, the soil in the rain forest became unfit for farming.

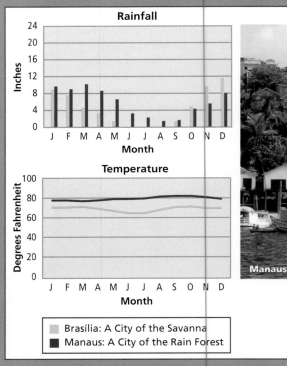

Two Cities, Two Climates

Rainfall

Inches (24, 20, 16, 12, 8, 4, 0)

Month J F M A M J J A S O N D

Temperature

Degrees Fahrenheit (100, 80, 60, 40, 20, 0)

Month J F M A M J J A S O N D

☐ Brasília: A City of the Savanna
■ Manaus: A City of the Rain Forest

Manaus

Differentiated Instruction

For English Language Learners L2
Pair students with native English speakers to read the Links to Science on page 167. Then have the students work together to draw a diagram showing the process of photosynthesis.

For Gifted and Talented L3
Have students make posters showing the process of photosynthesis in which plants, animals, and people transform water, sunlight, carbon dioxide, and minerals into oxygen. Encourage them to do further reading on the subject if they want to add details beyond those given in the text to their poster.

Threats to the Amazon Rain Forest

Today, Brazil's leaders are trying to control development of the rain forest. They want to find ways to help the economy and the farmers while protecting this important resource. They are working to protect the rain forest from the following dangers:

First, if too much timber is cut down, there will not be enough trees to absorb the carbon dioxide in the atmosphere. The buildup of carbon dioxide may trap heat near Earth's surface, altering the world's climate. When part of the forest is destroyed, the animals and plants that live there may not survive. Plants that might produce important medicines could be destroyed before they are even discovered.

Smuggling is another problem. Approximately 12 million animals are smuggled out of Brazil each year. Many are endangered, and it is illegal to capture or kill them. There are also laws to slow down the logging of mahogany, a wood used to make furniture. But these laws are being broken. Illegal logging continues to threaten the rain forest.

Pollution caused by mining is a third problem. In the late 1980s, the mercury used in gold mining polluted streams in the forest. It made people in several Native American villages sick. The government of Brazil passed strict laws about mining in the rain forest. Sometimes the government insisted that the miners leave. At times, military police had to be called in to make sure they did.

Threats to Traditional Ways of Life Threats to the Amazon rain forest are also threats to the people who have traditionally lived there. The difficulty of traveling in the rain forest had kept many indigenous peoples isolated. They continued their ancient ways of life. Once the rain forest was opened to development, however, miners, farmers, and land speculators arrived. These newcomers brought diseases the Indians had not been exposed to before, and many died. Conflicts between the developers and the Indians were sometimes violent, and Indians were killed. And the isolated culture of the indigenous people began to change as it was brought into contact with modern ways.

√ Reading Check   **Describe three dangers threatening the rain forest.**

Illegal Logging
The small boat is towing a long raft of illegally cut logs down the Amazon River. **Analyze Images** *Which details in the photo suggest why logging might be difficult in the rain forest? Which details suggest why it might be easy?*

 Compare and Contrast What are some differences between the way the indigenous people lived before the development of the rain forest and the way they live now?

Chapter 6 Section 1 **169**

Differentiated Instruction

For Special Needs Students L1
Have students read the section as they listen to the recorded version on the Student Edition on Audio CD. Pause the CD after each subsection and ask the students if they have any questions about what they have read.

⊙ Chapter 6, Section 1, **Student Edition on Audio CD**

For Advanced Readers L3
Ask students to consider the three threats to the rain forest discussed in the text. Then have them write a possible solution to each problem. Encourage them to solve the problem while still allowing the rain forest's vast resources to be used.

Independent Practice
Have students complete the graphic organizer.

Monitor Progress
Show *Section Reading Support Transparency LA 45* and ask students to check their graphic organizers individually. Go over key concepts and clarify key vocabulary as needed.

📖 **Latin America Transparencies,** *Section Reading Support Transparency LA 45*

🎯 Target Reading Skill L2
Compare and Contrast As a follow up, ask students to answer the Target Reading Skill question in the Student Edition. *(Many still live in traditional communities, but their way of life is threatened. Modern ways have been introduced to the people there. Some have moved to the cities.)*

Answers

Analyze Images Dense foliage makes getting trees out of the forest difficult, but the wide river makes passage easy.

√ Reading Check   The dangers threatening the Amazon rain forest include too much logging, the smuggling of animals out of the rain forest, and pollution caused by mining.

Guided Instruction L2

Ask students to study the Country Profile on this page. Remind them to read the map key to help them understand the population density map. Also encourage them to study each photograph on the page and think about the information it provides. As a class, answer the Map and Chart Skills questions. Allow students to briefly discuss their responses with a partner before sharing answers.

Independent Practice

- Distribute *Reading a Population Density Map.* Have students work in pairs to complete the worksheet.

  All in One **Latin America Teaching Resources,** *Reading a Population Density Map,* p. 341

- Now ask students to consider the map on p. 170. It, too, shows a country in which most of the population lives along or near the coastline and rivers. Ask students to use this knowledge as well as the other information given in the Country Profile to discuss reasons why the indigenous Indian culture is distinct from the culture of Brazil's cities.

Answers

Map and Chart Skills

1. Most Brazilians live near the coast or the major rivers.

2. Possible answer: Many Brazilians live on the coast because it provides access to harbors, and the flat, coastal plateau provides for easier living conditions than the dense rain forest of the country's interior.

3. Possible answer: Most of Brazil's population lives in coastal cities. People who come to Brazil from other countries probably feel there are more opportunities in these cities than in the rain forests of the interior.

Go Online PHSchool.com Students can find more information about this topic in the DK World Desk Reference Online.

Brazil

Brazil's culture is vibrant and diverse. Portuguese and African influences are evident in Brazilian architecture, religion, music, and food. They also shape the culture of Brazil's cities, where 81 percent of the people live. The indigenous Indian culture, however, has remained largely separate from the rest of Brazil, isolated in the interior of the Amazon rain forest. As you study the map and charts, consider how geography and settlement patterns shape a nation's culture.

Brazil: Population Density
KEY

Population per sq. mile	Population per sq. kilometer
More than 519	More than 199
260–519	100–199
130–259	50–99
25–129	10–49
1–24	1–9
Less than 1	Less than 1

Urban Areas
- ■ More than 9,999,999
- □ 5,000,000–9,999,999
- ◉ 1,000,000–4,999,999
— National border

0 miles 1,000
0 kilometers 1,000
Lambert Azimuthal Equal Area

Cultural Regions of Brazil

The Northeast
Sugar plantations shaped the culture of the northeast. Enslaved Africans imported to work on the plantations brought their culture with them. Today, the area is rich in art and music. The dance called the samba (shown above) began here.

SOURCE: *The World Today Series, Latin America 2002*

The South
European immigrants shaped the culture of the south. People mainly of Portuguese descent brought cattle ranching, wheat farming, and coffee production to the region. A distinct diet based on meat products developed here.

The Rain Forests
European immigrants had little contact with Brazil's indigenous peoples. These peoples continued to lead traditional lives, isolated in Brazil's rain forests. Some 200 groups live here today. Among them, the Yanomami, who are hunter-gatherers.

The Cities
In urban centers such as Rio de Janeiro (above) and São Paulo, African and European cultures blended together. One example is the Brazilian party called Carnival, which mixes Catholic and African traditions.

Brazil's Ethnic Groups

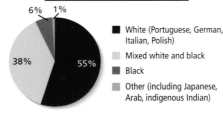

- 6%
- 1%
- 38%
- 55%

- ■ White (Portuguese, German, Italian, Polish)
- Mixed white and black
- ■ Black
- Other (including Japanese, Arab, indigenous Indian)

SOURCE: *CIA World Factbook, 2002*

Map and Chart Skills

1. **Identify** Where do most Brazilians live?
2. **Identify Causes** What are some of the reasons why Brazilians live where they do?
3. **Draw Conclusions** Why do you think Brazil's cities are more culturally diverse than the interior rain forest?

Go Online PHSchool.com Use Web Code lfe-1611 for DK World Desk Reference Online.

Skills for Life **Skills Mini Lesson**

Transferring Information from One Medium to Another L2

1. Teach the skill by pointing out that sometimes you need to transfer information from one form to another to present ideas more clearly.

2. Help students practice the skill by suggesting another way to present the information shown on the population density map. *(A table is a good option.)*

3. Have students apply the skill by compiling a table that shows the name of each city on the map and the population range it is in.

The People of Brazil

The Native Americans living in the rain forest were some of the first people to live in Brazil. Today, many Brazilians are a mix of Native American, African, and European heritages. The Yanomami (yah noh MAH mee) are one of the larger Native American groups. They still live in traditional communities in the rain forest. As the rain forest is threatened, however, so too is the Yanomami way of life. Some Native Americans have left the rain forest for the cities.

The Different Cultures of Brazil Daniel Monteiro Costa is a writer and teacher who lives in São Paulo, Brazil. He is also known as Daniel Munduruku (mun duh ROO koo). Daniel is a Munduruku Indian. Many Munduruku still live in small villages in the rain forest. Daniel was born in the city of Belém (buh LEM), but he often visited his relatives in a nearby village. There, he heard stories the Munduruku people told about their history and culture. When he was growing up, Daniel saw that Indians were often treated with disrespect. He began studying the indigenous peoples of Brazil and became proud of his heritage. Now, Daniel works to keep Munduruku stories alive and to end discrimination against Indians in Brazil.

Native Americans are not the only cultural groups in Brazil. Many features of African culture also flourish there. The most African of Brazilian cities, Salvador, lies on the coastal plain. Most of the people who live here are descendants of the millions of Africans brought to Brazil as slaves.

Many Brazilians also have a European heritage. Some are descended from the Portuguese who colonized the area. Other more recent immigrants come from countries such as Italy. There are also Asian immigrants from Japan.

Working on Farms and in Factories In Brazil, most of the land that is suitable for growing crops is owned by only a few people. Sometimes they choose not to farm their land. About one third of Brazil's farmland, approximately 300 million acres (122 million hectares), is unused.

In the 1990s, Brazil's government gave some of this unused land to poor farmers. People began starting small farms just north of Rio de Janeiro. The farms allow them to support themselves.

Modern and Traditional
In the top photo, Brazilian soccer star Sissi participates in the 1999 Women's World Cup competition. The photo above shows a Kaiapo Indian from the rain forest.
Synthesize *Use the text to help you describe the two very different Brazilian ways of life represented by the photos.*

Background: Daily Life

Capoeira Capoeira, a Brazilian combination of dance and martial arts, developed in the northeastern part of the country. The dance form was created by enslaved Africans. Forbidden to fight each other, the slaves developed a form of fighting to music that looked like dancing. Music was played on drums and on a *beribau* made from a bow and gourd. Today, boys and some girls study capoeira, just as American young people study karate, judo, and other martial arts.

Instruct

The People of Brazil L2

Guided Instruction

- **Vocabulary Builder** Clarify the high-use word **community** before reading.

- Ask students to read about the lives of Brazilians in The People of Brazil.

- Have students list the various heritages of people in Brazil. *(People in Brazil have Native American, African, European, and Asian heritages.)*

- Engage students in a discussion about possible reasons why Brazil's government gave some of the country's unused land to poor farmers. *(The government was probably trying to help poor families support themselves and earn money from their crops.)*

Independent Practice
Assign *Guided Reading and Review*.

All in One Latin America Teaching Resources, *Guided Reading and Review,* p. 317

Monitor Progress
Tell students to fill in the last column of the *Reading Readiness Guide.* Probe for what they learned that confirms or invalidates each statement.

All in One Latin America Teaching Resources, *Reading Readiness Guide,* p. 316

Answers
Synthesize Many Brazilians enjoy a very modern lifestyle, while some Native Americans still maintain traditional ways of life.

Assess and Reteach

Assess Progress `L2`

Have students complete the Section Assessment. Then administer the *Section Quiz*.

 Latin America Teaching Resources, *Section Quiz,* p. 318

Reteach `L1`

If students need more instruction, have them read this section in the Reading and Vocabulary Study Guide.

 Chapter 6, Section 1, **Latin America Reading and Vocabulary Study Guide,** pp. 62–64

Extend `L3`

Have students work together in small groups to complete the *Small Group Activity: Making a Mural.* Try to group students of varying abilities together.

Latin America Teaching Resources, *Small Group Activity: Making a Mural,* pp. 337–340

Answers

✔ **Reading Check** Rio de Janeiro is a city on the coast that is surrounded by mountains. Parts of the city are wealthy, with hotels, shops, and old palaces and government buildings. Other parts are poor; some homes have no electricity or running water.

Section 1 Assessment

Key Terms

Students' sentences should reflect knowledge of each Key Term.

🎯 **Target Reading Skill**

Both Brasília and Rio de Janeiro are large cities that are home to both the rich and the poor. Both are also home to many of Brazil's factories and businesses. The cities are different in that Rio de Janeiro is located on the coast while Brasília is located inland, and the population of Rio de Janeiro is about 10 million people while the population of Brasília is smaller at about two million people.

Comprehension and Critical Thinking

1. (a) rain forest, a large plateau, mountain ranges, and river valleys **(b)** Possible answer: Brazilians may have thought there would be

---

Rio de Janeiro

The plantations, or large farms, of Brazil produce crops for export. Brazil is the largest coffee producer in the world. But Brazilians know that they cannot depend on only one or two crops. The government has discouraged coffee production and tried to diversify the economy by building more factories. Today, Brazil produces iron and steel, cars, and electrical equipment. Since 1960, about 30 million people have left farms and plantations and moved into the cities to get jobs in these new industries.

A Brazilian City: Rio de Janeiro Brazilian cities are home to both the rich and the very poor. Rio de Janeiro is a good example of these contrasts. It lies on the Atlantic coast, surrounded by huge mountains that dip to the sea. If you climbed to the top of one, you could see the whole city. To the south, you would see expensive hotels and shops for tourists. In the downtown area, you would see old palaces and government buildings. Rio de Janeiro was Brazil's capital from 1822 to 1960.

But to the north, you would see clusters of small houses where factory workers live. On the slopes of the mountains are neighborhoods crowded with homes that have no electricity or running water. About 20 percent of Rio's more than 10 million people live in these *favelas,* or slums. However, most of Rio's people live in well-built houses with electricity and running water.

✔ **Reading Check** What is Rio de Janeiro like?

 Section 1 Assessment

Key Terms

Review the key terms at the beginning of this section. Use each term in a sentence that explains its meaning.

🎯 **Target Reading Skills**

What are two ways Brasília and Rio de Janeiro are similar? What are two ways they are different?

Comprehension and Critical Thinking

1. (a) Name What are the main features of Brazil's geography?

(b) Infer Why do you think many people moved to Brasília?
2. (a) Identify Effects Why are Brazil's rain forests important to the whole world?
(b) Analyze Explain why it is difficult for Brazil to protect its rain forest and improve its economy at the same time.
3. (a) Identify What is the cultural heritage of Brazilians?
(b) Draw Conclusions How does unequal land distribution affect the economy and people of Brazil?

Writing Activity

Suppose you lived in a Brazilian city, such as Rio de Janeiro or Salvador, in 1960. Would you have moved to the new city of Brasília if you had been given the chance? Write a letter to a friend explaining why you are planning to move to Brasília or why you are not moving there.

> **Writing Tip** State your choice clearly. Then give three reasons to support your choice.

---

new opportunities in a new city and in a new region.
2. (a) Brazil's rain forests help provide much of the world's oxygen, are home to several million species of plants, animals, and insects, and are the source of many medicines. **(b)** Many of the activities that would help the economy hurt the rain forest.

3. (a) Native American, African, European, with some Asian immigrants **(b)** Many poor Brazilians have no land to farm—and thus

aren't growing food for their families to eat or sell—while many rich Brazilians have land they could farm but do not.

Writing Activity

Use the *Rubric for Assessing a Writing Assignment* to evaluate students' letters to their friends.

Latin America Teaching Resources, *Rubric for Assessing a Writing Assignment,* p. 349

Prepare to Read

Objectives
In this section you will
1. Learn how geography has affected the way people live in the three regions of Peru.
2. Discover what life is like in the cities and towns of the Altiplano.

Taking Notes
As you read this section, look for the ways that people live in the three regions of Peru. Copy the table below and record your findings in it.

Region	Geography	How People Live
	• •	• •

Target Reading Skill

Identify Contrasts When you contrast two regions, you examine how they are different. In this section you will read about the three geographic regions of Peru and about the ways people have adapted to them. As you read, list the differences between the regions and the ways people live there.

Key Terms
- **Altiplano** (al tih PLAH noh) *n.* a high plateau in the Andes Mountains
- **sierra** (see EHR uh) *n.* the mountain region of Peru
- **oasis** (oh AY sis) *n.* a fertile area in a desert that has a source of water

When people on Tribuna, an island in Lake Titicaca, play soccer, they are very careful. That's because the island is made of straw. The ground is uneven, and when they walk on it they can feel the water shifting below. "It seems crazy to play soccer on water," says Luis Colo, who lives on Tribuna. "We don't jump on each other after a goal, or we'd probably fall through the field."

Tribuna is one of about 70 islands made by the Uros (oo ROHS). The Uros have adapted to the geography of Lake Titicaca. As you read in Chapter 3, they make their islands out of totora reeds. They join the floating roots together and then lay cut reeds on top. This process creates an island that is firm enough to support small communities of people with huts and livestock. When the Uros need more land, they simply build another island.

From the time of the Incas, the people of Peru—like people everywhere—have adapted to their geography. The Uros are only one example. You will read about other examples of how geography has affected culture in this section.

Reed boats moored by a totora-reed island

Chapter 6 Section 2 **173**

Target Reading Skill
Identify Contrasts Point out the Target Reading Skill. Explain that students can contrast two regions to see how they are different.

Model the skill by helping students identify a contrast between the sierra and the selva using the information on p. 175. (*The sierra is cold while the selva is hot and humid.*)

Give students *Identify Contrasts*. Have them complete the activity in their groups.

 Latin America Teaching Resources, *Identify Contrasts,* p. 332

Objectives
Social Studies
1. Learn how geography has affected the way people live in the three regions of Peru.
2. Discover what life is like in the cities and towns of the Altiplano.

Reading/Language Arts
Contrast two regions to find out how they are different.

Prepare to Read

Build Background Knowledge `L2`
Tell student that in this section they will learn how the geography and cultures of Peru have influenced the way Peruvians live. Show the World Studies video. Ask students to note three to five facts about the way people earn a living in Peru as they watch the video. Have students engage in a Give One, Get One activity (TE, p. T37) to share the information that have collected.

 Making a Living in Peru, **World Studies Video Program**

Set a Purpose for Reading `L2`
- Preview the Objectives.
- Read each statement in the *Reading Readiness Guide* aloud. Ask students to mark the statements true or false.

  Latin America Teaching Resources, *Reading Readiness Guide,* p. 320

- Have students discuss the statements in pairs or groups of four, then mark their worksheets again. Use the Numbered Heads participation structure (TE, p. T36) to call on students to share their group's perspectives.

Vocabulary Builder
Preview Key Terms `L2`
Pronounce each Key Term, then ask students to say the word with you. Provide a simple explanation such as, "Someone walking in the desert might feel great relief if he came across an oasis where there is water."

Guided Instruction L2

Ask students to study the Country Profile on this page. Remind them to read the map key to understand what the different colors on the map mean. Also encourage them to study the table and line graph carefully. As a class, answer the Map and Chart Skills questions. Allow students to briefly discuss their responses with a partner before sharing answers.

Independent Practice

- Distribute *Reading a Table*. Have students work in pairs to complete the worksheet.

  All in One Latin America Teaching Resources, *Reading a Table,* p. 342

- Now ask students to consider the table on p. 174. It gives information about the physical geography and the people of Peru. Help students identify the relationship between the geographic information and the cultural information. *(Geography influences aspects of culture, such as how people earn a living.)*

Answers

Map and Chart Skills

1. In the coastal region, people earn a living with professional jobs or jobs in manufacturing, refining, and agriculture. In the sierra, people have jobs in farming, herding, and tourism. In the selva, people earn a living by fishing, hunting, and gathering.

2. the coastal region; the sierra

3. The sierra may have lost population because of the lack of variety in occupations.

Go Online PHSchool.com Students can find additional useful information about this topic on the DK World Desk Reference Online.

Peru

Peru is a country of geographic extremes. In the high mountains of the sierra, the air is almost too thin to breathe. The coast is largely desert except for scattered oases where rivers flow down from the mountains to the Pacific. Rain forest covers much of the eastern half of the country, or selva. As you study the map and charts below, think about how geography and climate affect the lives of Peruvians.

Peru: Three Regions
KEY
ELEVATION

Feet	Meters
More than 13,000	More than 3,960
6,500–13,000	1,980–3,960
1,600–6,500	480–1,980
650–1,600	200–480
0–650	0–200

Division between regions

—— National border
⊙ National capital
• Other city

0 miles 500
0 kilometers 500
Lambert Azimuthal Equal Area

Characteristics of Three Regions

Characteristic	Coastal Region	Sierra	Selva
Land area	11%	26%	63%
Dominant feature	Desert and oases	Mountains	Rain forest
Yearly precipitation	2 inches	Varies	75–125 inches
Main language	Spanish	Quechua	Varied indigenous languages
Major occupations	Professional; manufacturing and refining; agriculture	Farming and herding; tourism	Fishing; hunting and gathering

SOURCES: *Peru, Country Study, Department of the Army Handbook,* 1981; *Encyclopaedia Britannica; The World Today Series, Latin America 2002;* Library of Congress online

Peru's Population

Percent of People: 60%, 40%, 20%, 0%
Years: 1960, 1980, 2000*

* estimated
SOURCE: Instituto Nacional de Estadística e Informática, Perú

— Coastal region
— Sierra
— Selva

Map and Chart Skills

1. **Identify** How do people earn a living in different parts of Peru?
2. **Analyze** What region of Peru has the most people? What region has lost population?
3. **Infer** What information in the map and charts indicates why these changes in population might have occurred?

 Use Web Code lfe-1612 for DK World Desk Reference Online.

174 Latin America

Vocabulary Builder

Use the information below to teach students this section's high-use words.

High-Use Word	Definition and Sample Sentence
dwell, p. 176	*v.* to live as a resident
	Many fishermen in the northeast **dwell** along the Atlantic coast.
foundation, p. 176	*n.* the base on which something rests
	The house is more secure because its **foundation** is made of concrete.
adapt, p. 178	*v.* to make fit by changing or adjusting
	Animals **adapt** to the winter weather by growing a heavier coat of fur.

The Regions and People of Peru

The Uros live on Lake Titicaca. Find Lake Titicaca on the map of Peru in the Country Profile. Lake Titicaca is in Peru's **Altiplano** (al tih PLAH noh), a high plateau in the Andes Mountains. The Altiplano is about 12,000 feet (3,658 meters) above sea level. It is located in southern Peru near the Bolivian border.

Peru's Three Geographic Regions The Andes Mountains, which run from northwest to southeast Peru, divide the country into three geographic regions. The mountain region, including the Andes and the Altiplano, is known as the **sierra**. Much of this region is so high that lower layers of the soil remain frozen all year. This kind of treeless plain, which supports only low-growing vegetation, is called tundra. Even so, people have lived in this region for centuries. The Incas built their empire in the Altiplano, with Cuzco as its capital. Today, some descendants of the Incas live much as their ancestors did. In addition to farming, these Native Americans herd sheep, cattle, llamas, and alpacas. Wool is one of the major products of the region.

The coastal region of Peru is very different from the sierra. This dry area is dotted with oases. An **oasis** is a fertile area in a desert that has a source of water. Before Europeans arrived, indigenous groups settled by these oases. Later, the Spanish also built cities along the coast. Today, this area is the economic center of Peru. In Lima (LEE muh), Peru's capital, historic Spanish buildings from the 1600s and 1700s stand next to modern skyscrapers. More than 6 million people—more than a quarter of Peru's population—live in Lima.

The third region of Peru is the large forested area that stretches from the lower slopes of the mountains to the lowlands of northeast Peru. Here, the weather is hot and humid all year. This isolated region is called the selva. It has few roads connecting it to the sierra and the coast. Little modern development has occurred here. Some Native American groups live in this rain forest much as their ancestors did.

A modern skyscraper stands beside a Spanish-style home in Lima.

A Peruvian Oasis
This small fertile area is surrounded by desert. **Draw Inferences** *Why do you think people settled by oases in this area of Peru?*

Differentiated Instruction

For Gifted and Talented `L3`
Have students read the primary source reading *A Women's Prison in London* to learn more about the experiences of Flora Tristan, the niece of one of Peru's presidents.

All in One **Latin America Teaching Resources,** *A Women's Prison in London,* p. 344–345

Instruct

The Regions and People of Peru `L2`

Guided Instruction
- Read The Regions and People of Peru, using the Structured Silent Reading technique (TE, p. T34).
- Ask students **Why do you think many people live in Peru's coastal region?** *(The climate of the coastal region is not as harsh as the other regions; the land is fertile for farming; people have access to ports on the coast.)*
- Ask students to consider which regions of Peru are mainly inhabited only by Native Americans. Then ask **Why do you think Native Americans live in these regions but most other Peruvians do not?** *(The sierra and the selva are mainly inhabited only by Native Americans. Native Americans probably live there because that is where their ancestors lived and their culture developed. Other Peruvians probably have not moved there because the high mountains and cold air of the sierra, the rain forest, and few roads of the selva make them harder places to live than the coastal region.)*

Independent Practice
Ask students to create the Taking Notes graphic organizer on a blank piece of paper. Then ask them to fill in the table with the information they have just learned about how people live in Peru's three regions. Briefly model how to fill in information in the appropriate column.

Monitor Progress
As students fill in the graphic organizer, circulate and make sure individuals are choosing the correct details and placing them in the correct columns of the table. Help students as needed.

Answers
Draw Inferences The surrounding area is dry desert so they needed to settle in a place where water was available.

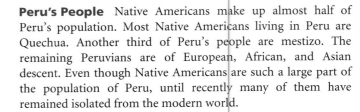
Explore how people make a living in Peru.

Show students *Making a Living in Peru.* Ask **How does the geography of Peru affect the lives of the people you have just seen?** *(All three use the natural resources of Peru to make a living.)*

Life in the Altiplano L2

Guided Instruction

- **Vocabulary Builder** Clarify the high-use words **dwell**, **foundation**, and **adapt** before reading.

- Read Life in the Altiplano. As students read, circulate and make sure individuals can answer the Reading Check question.

- Have students describe one difference and one similarity between the Altiplano's cities and its villages. *(Possible answer: A difference is that in the cities, most people have telephones; in the villages, there are no telephones. A similarity is that there are Incan ruins in both places.)*

- Ask students **How do you think Peruvians today feel about encountering Incan remains in their daily life?** Encourage students to think of a variety of responses Peruvians might have to this evidence of the past. *(While some Peruvians may not care strongly about remains from the past, many Peruvians probably respond to these remains by feeling pride about their heritage. As more Peruvians move to cities and as the villages of the Altiplano change, the physical remains of the past help people remember their cultural origins. Also, some Peruvians may see these remains as inspiration for their own ideas and pursuits—for example, the Incan suspension bridges offer a good method of crossing the deep gorges of the Altiplano.)*

Answers

√ **Reading Check** Native Americans and mestizos make up the majority of Peruvians.
Conclude They built staircases to travel up and down the mountain and built an aqueduct to transport water there.

Peru's People Native Americans make up almost half of Peru's population. Most Native Americans living in Peru are Quechua. Another third of Peru's people are mestizo. The remaining Peruvians are of European, African, and Asian descent. Even though Native Americans are such a large part of the population of Peru, until recently many of them have remained isolated from the modern world.

√ **Reading Check** **Which two groups make up the majority of Peruvians?**

Life in the Altiplano

Many Quechuas, Uros, and other Native Americans living on the Altiplano follow traditions that are hundreds of years old. Their communities, however, are slowly changing. Thousands of Native Americans have left for jobs in the city. And life is changing even for those who stay in their villages.

Old and New The past is constantly present in the Altiplano. The ruins of Incan cities, such as Machu Picchu, are found in the countryside. Even in modern cities, the old mixes with the new. Most city dwellers in the Altiplano have electricity. The streets are paved, and there are telephones. But there are also remnants of the past. In Cuzco, for example, parts of the old Incan wall that once surrounded the city are still standing. Modern houses are made of adobe and have red tile roofs, but their foundations are the remains of Incan stonework. There are also buildings constructed by the Spanish colonists.

Lost City of the Incas
The ruins of Machu Picchu were "discovered" in 1911 when a local guide led American scholars to the site. It has stone buildings, walkways, and staircases, as well as agricultural terraces that were once watered by an aqueduct. **Conclude** *How did the Incan builders adapt their city to the mountain site?*

176 Latin America

Differentiated Instruction

For Less Proficient Readers L1
Have students write a letter to Modesto Mamani describing their own daily life. Encourage them to include all the same details about themselves that the text gives about Modesto—how old they are, what they eat, what they do during the day, what they hope to do for a career, and what they do for fun.

For Advanced Readers L3
Challenge students to find a book or Internet or magazine article about the Quechua, Aymara, or Uro people. Ask them to read at least a portion of the book or article and write a summary of what they learned.

A Day in a Quechua Village Village life is very different from city life. In the isolated towns of the Altiplano, there are no telephones. Few buses drive through the villages. Most people are Quechua or Aymara.

Like their Incan ancestors, many Quechua rely on raising animals for their wool. The Incas tamed wild llamas and alpacas, and then they raised them to use as pack animals and as a source of wool. Today, many Quechua families keep sheep instead. Sheep are not native to the region but were brought to the Americas by European settlers.

Modesto Mamani (moh DES toh MUH mahn ee) is a 13-year-old Quechua boy. He wakes before dawn to the freezing mountain air and eats breakfast as soon as the sun comes up. Breakfast is always the same: a few rolls, coffee with sugar, and whole wheat kernels that can be eaten like popcorn. His only other meal may be lunch. It is usually potato and barley soup with *chunos*—freeze-dried potato skins.

On some days, Modesto spends much of his time working in the field with his father and brothers. On other days, he looks after the sheep or goes with his mother to the market. Even with school and chores, Modesto finds time to play soccer on the tundra in back of his house.

Like many other children who live in Altiplano villages, Modesto's life mixes the modern and the traditional. He wants to study to become an engineer so he can bring technology to the Altiplano. Meanwhile, much of his time revolves around the sheep his family raises. Not only does Modesto tend the sheep, he also uses their wool to knit sweaters.

School, Work, and Play
Modesto attends school—with his soccer ball! (left), and shows off one of his family's sheep (right). **Infer** *Why do you think people raise sheep in the region seen in the photo?*

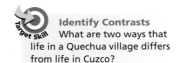
Identify Contrasts
What are two ways that life in a Quechua village differs from life in Cuzco?

Chapter 6 Section 2 **177**

Independent Practice
Have students complete the graphic organizer by filling in any new information about the Altiplano that they have just learned.

Monitor Progress
- Show *Section Reading Support Transparency LA 46* and ask students to check their graphic organizers individually. Go over key concepts and clarify key vocabulary as needed.

  Latin America Transparencies, *Section Reading Support Transparency LA 46*

- Tell students to fill in the last column of the *Reading Readiness Guide*. Probe for what they learned that confirms or invalidates each statement.

  All in One Latin America Teaching Resources, *Reading Readiness Guide*, p. 320

Target Reading Skill　L2
Identify Contrasts As a follow up, ask students to answer the Target Reading Skill question in the Student Edition. *(Possible answers: In Cuzco, people have telephones, there is a lot of traffic, and most people are not Quechua or Aymara.)*

Skills Mini Lesson

Identifying Frame of Reference and Point of View　L2

1. Teach the skill by explaining that point of view is an opinion or perspective on a topic and frame of reference is a person's background. Frame of reference often affects point of view.

2. Help students practice the skill by identifying the point of view of Modesto in the following scenario: Modesto's father tells Modesto to spend more time tending the sheep. Modesto is unhappy about this decision.

3. Have students apply the skill by identifying Modesto's frame of reference in the same scenario.

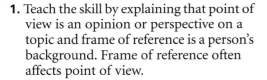

Answer
Infer The land looks suited to sheep grazing.

Assess and Reteach

Assess Progress   `L2`
Have students complete the Section Assessment. Then administer the *Section Quiz*.

📘 **Latin America Teaching Resources,** *Section Quiz,* p. 322

Reteach   `L1`
If students need more instruction, have them read this section in the Reading and Vocabulary Study Guide.

📖 Chapter 6, Section 2, **Latin America Reading and Vocabulary Study Guide,** pp. 65–67

Extend   `L3`
If you have not already done so, show students *Making a Living in Peru*. After students watch the video, ask them to write a brief summary describing the experiences of one of the Peruvians featured.

📼 *Making a Living in Peru,* **World Studies Video Program**

Answers

✔ **Reading Check** Possible answer: Quechua families have adapted to the tundra by raising sheep, animals that are well-suited to that environment.

Analyze The bridge helps people travel across the gorges of the Altiplano.

Section 2 Assessment

Key Terms
Students' sentences should reflect knowledge of each Key Term.

🔁 **Target Reading Skill**
The selva is hot while the sierra is cool. The coast is much drier than the sierra. The coastal region is more populated than both the sierra and the selva.

Comprehension and Critical Thinking
1. (a) The three regions of Peru are the mountain region, or sierra, the coastal region, and the forested region, or selva. Students should draw their descriptions from information provided on pp. 175–176 of the text.
(b) The coastal plain has easy access to the outside world. It is an easier region to live in than the mountains or the rain forest.

Modern Suspension Bridge
Tourists stand on a modern suspension bridge that is based on a design developed by the Incas. **Analyze** *How does this type of bridge suit its environment?*

Geography and Culture You have seen how the Uros adapted to their environment by living on islands they create themselves, much as their ancestors did. But they are also modern people who play soccer. In another part of the Altiplano, Quechua families raise sheep, animals that are suited to the tundra. But their children learn about technology in school.

Long ago, the Incas solved a problem of their mountain environment: how to cross the deep gorges between mountain peaks. They invented suspension bridges. Modern versions of these bridges are still used in the Andes today. They are one more example of how geography and the past influence the present in Peru.

✔ **Reading Check** Explain how one group of Peruvians has adapted to their environment.

 Section 2 Assessment

Key Terms
Review the key terms at the beginning of this section. Use each term in a sentence that explains its meaning.

🔁 **Target Reading Skills**
How are the three geographic regions of Peru different?

Comprehension and Critical Thinking
1. (a) Describe What are the three regions of Peru, and what are they like?

(b) Identify Cause and Effect Why is the coastal plain the economic center of Peru?
2. (a) Describe How does Cuzco represent both old and new?
(b) Compare How is life for the Quechua similar to and different from life for the Uros?
(c) Predict Do you think the Uros and Quechua will preserve their traditional ways of life in this century? Explain.

Writing Activity
Write a letter that Modesto might send to a friend in Cuzco, inviting the friend to visit him in his village. Have Modesto describe what his friend might see and do on his visit.

For: An activity on Peru
Visit: PHSchool.com
Web Code: lfd-1602

---

2. (a) Cuzco has modern houses with foundations built by the Incas as well as buildings constructed by the Spanish colonists. **(b)** Similarities: Both have had to adapt to living in the Altiplano, both have taken on some modern activities, such as playing soccer and learning about technology. The Uros live along a lake, while the Quechua live on the tundra. **(c)** Answers will vary. Students should support their opinions with facts from the section and from their personal knowledge.

Writing Activity
Use the *Rubric for Assessing a Writing Assignment* to evaluate students' letters to Modesto's friend.

📘 **Latin America Teaching Resources,** *Rubric for Assessing a Writing Assignment,* p. 349

Chile
Land of Contrasts

Prepare to Read

Objectives

In this section you will
1. Find out how the geography of Chile creates regions where people live very differently.
2. Learn how Chile's people live and what products they produce.
3. Find out how Chile restored democracy.

Taking Notes

As you read this section, look for the main ideas and details and how they relate to each other. Use the format below to create an outline of the section.

I. The geography of Chile
  A. The longest, narrowest country
    1. Only 100 miles wide
    2.

🎯 Target Reading Skill

Compare and Contrast One way to understand regions is to compare and contrast them, or identify similarities and differences. When you compare, you look at similarities between things. When you contrast, you look at differences. As you read this section, compare and contrast the geographic regions and lifestyles of Chile.

Key Terms

- **Ferdinand Magellan** (FUR duh nand muh JEL un) *n.* Portuguese explorer sailing for Spain, whose expedition first circumnavigated the globe
- **circumnavigate** (sur kum NAV ih gayt) *v.* to sail or fly all the way around something, such as Earth
- **glacier** (GLAY shur) *n.* a large, slow-moving mass of ice and snow
- **Augusto Pinochet Ugarte** (ah GOO stoh pea noh SHAY oo gahr TAY) *n.* military dictator of Chile from 1973 to 1988

W hen Ferdinand Magellan first saw the Pacific Ocean in 1520, tears ran down his cheeks. **Ferdinand Magellan** was a Portuguese explorer sailing for Spain. He was searching for a way around or through the Americas. Ever since Christopher Columbus had failed to find a westward sea route all the way to Asia, explorers had been looking for one. But the continents of North and South America were in the way.

Magellan sailed from Spain in 1519 and worked his way south along the coast of South America. Bad weather forced him to spend the winter on the stormy southern coast. His crew threatened to rebel, but Magellan kept exploring. Finally, he found a way through the islands at the "bottom" of South America. His ships sailed through this narrow, dangerous passage to the Pacific Ocean. Magellan wept when he realized his great accomplishment. He knew that now he could sail to Asia—and all the way around the world.

The passage that Magellan discovered is in present-day Chile. It allowed European sailors to explore the western coast of South America.

Magellan's ship nears the strait that bears his name.

Objectives

Social Studies
1. Find out how the geography of Chile creates regions where people live very differently.
2. Learn how Chile's people live and what products they produce.
3. Find out how Chile restored democracy.

Reading/Language Arts
Compare and contrast things to analyze and sort out information.

Prepare to Read

Build Background Knowledge　L2

In this section, students will learn about the vivid contrasts that exist in the geography and cultures of Chile. Ask students to preview the headings and visuals in the section with this question in mind: **What factors of geography have influenced the cultures of Chile?** Provide a few examples to get students started. Conduct an Idea Wave (TE, p. T35) to generate a list.

Set a Purpose for Reading　L2

- Preview the Objectives.
- Read each statement in the *Reading Readiness Guide* aloud. Ask students to mark the statements true or false.

  All in One Latin America Teaching Resources, *Reading Readiness Guide,* p. 324

- Have students discuss the statements in pairs or groups of four, then mark their worksheets again. Use the Numbered Heads participation structure (TE, p. T36) to call on students to share their group's perspectives.

Vocabulary Builder
Preview Key Terms　L2

Pronounce each Key Term, then ask students to say the word with you. Provide a simple explanation such as, "When a space shuttle circumnavigates the Earth, it flies all the way around it."

🎯 Target Reading Skill　L2

Compare and Contrast Point out the Target Reading Skill. Explain to students that you look for similarities when you compare things, and you look for differences when you contrast things. Tell them that comparing and contrasting can help them analyze information.

Model the skill by helping students identify the similarities and differences between northern and central Chile that are given on pp. 181–182. *(Similarity—Mining is important in both regions; Difference—Few plants can survive in the north while the central region has high grasses and dense forests.)*

Give students *Compare and Contrast.* Have them complete the activity in groups.

  All in One Latin America Teaching Resources, *Compare and Contrast,* p. 331

Guided Instruction   L2

Ask students to study the Country Profile on this page. Remind them to read the map key to understand what the different symbols on the map represent. Also encourage them to study the line graph carefully. As a class, answer the Map and Chart Skills questions. Allow students to briefly discuss their responses with a partner before sharing answers.

Independent Practice

Have students do an in-depth study on one of the following products and resources shown on the map of Chile: manufacturing, fish, or fruits. Ask students to do research to make a list of at least three types of fish that are caught, fruits that are grown, or manufactured items that are produced in Chile. Allow students to work in pairs to complete the activity.

Answers

Map and Chart Skills

1. Copper is found in northern Chile.

2. Fruits and fish

3. Agricultural and seafood exports make up 16 percent of Chile's total exports, while copper exports account for 25 percent.

4. Chile's economy improved at a faster rate than that of Latin America between 1990 and 2001.

5. Possible answer: Chile's economy has been steadily improving for over ten years, and none of its exports account for more than half of the total exports, so Chile has been able to create a stable, diversified economy.

Go Online
PHSchool.com Students can find more information about this topic in the DK World Desk Reference Online.

Chile

Chile produces more copper than any other country in the world. To avoid relying too much on one resource, however, the government of Chile has encouraged agriculture and new industry. The United States is Chile's largest trade partner. About 18 percent of Chile's exports are sold to the United States. Today, Chile's economy is seen as strong and stable. Study the map and charts. Think about how Chile's location and resources have affected its economy.

Chile: Products and Resources

KEY

- Copper
- Petroleum
- Manufacturing
- Fruits
- Fish
- —— National border
- ⊙ National capital
- • Other city

0 miles 800
0 kilometers 800
Lambert Azimuthal Equal Area

Average Annual Income per Citizen

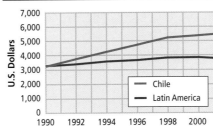

SOURCE: The World Bank Group

Chile's Exports

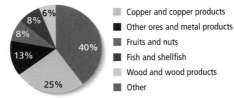

- Copper and copper products — 40%
- Other ores and metal products — 6%
- Fruits and nuts — 8%
- Fish and shellfish — 8%
- Wood and wood products — 13%
- Other — 25%

SOURCE: Government of Chile National Customs Service, 2002

Map and Chart Skills

1. **Locate** Where are Chile's mineral resources found?

2. **Identify** Which economic resources are found in most parts of the country?

3. **Compare** How do Chile's agricultural and seafood exports compare to its copper exports?

4. **Analyze Information** What do you learn about Chile's economy from the line graph?

5. **Draw Conclusions** Do you think Chile has been successful in using its resources to create a diversified economy? Explain your answer.

Use Web Code lfe-1613 for DK World Desk Reference Online.

Vocabulary Builder

Use the information below to teach students this section's high-use words.

High-Use Word	Definition and Sample Sentence
survive, p. 181	v. to continue to live after, or in spite of The plant did not **survive** because it did not get enough water.
regime, p. 185	n. a form of government or rule A new **regime** came to power after the votes were counted.
reject, p. 185	v. to refuse to take He **rejected** the idea of exchanging sandwiches because he didn't like peanut butter and jelly.

The Geography of Chile

The passage that Magellan discovered is now named after him. Find the Strait of Magellan on the map of Chile in the Country Profile. It is a major sea lane to this day. Although it is dangerous to sail through, the Strait of Magellan is safer than going all the way around Cape Horn to the south. Many ships have been lost in the Strait's stormy waters. While Magellan was lucky to get through the Strait, he was not lucky enough to return to Spain. He died during the voyage. Of the five ships that started Magellan's expedition, only one returned all the way to Spain. But it was the first ship to **circumnavigate,** or go all the way around, the globe.

The Longest, Narrowest Country Look at the map titled Physical Latin America on page 4. Find the Andes Mountains. They run down the whole length of Chile like a giant spine. Chile is narrow and shaped like a string bean. On average, it is only about 100 miles (161 kilometers) wide, but it is extremely long. It runs 2,650 miles (4,265 kilometers) down the Pacific Coast all the way to the tip of South America. It is the longest, narrowest country in the world.

The Driest Place in the World Chile contains an amazing variety of landforms and climates. In the north is the Atacama Desert, the driest region in the world. Not many plants or animals can survive there. But the desert is rich in copper, so the region is dotted with mines. Chile exports more copper than any country in the world.

Compare and Contrast How is sailing through the Strait of Magellan different from sailing around Cape Horn? How is it similar?

A man examines salt formations in the Atacama Desert (above). Magellanic penguins (left) sometimes come ashore near the Strait of Magellan.

Target Reading Skill L2

Compare and Contrast As a follow up, ask students to answer the Target Reading Skill question in the Student Edition. *(Both routes are dangerous to sail, but sailing through the Strait of Magellan is less dangerous and faster than sailing around Cape Horn.)*

Instruct

The Geography of Chile L2

Guided Instruction

- **Vocabulary Builder** Clarify the high-use word **survive** before reading.
- Read The Geography of Chile, using the Oral Cloze Reading technique (TE, p. T33).
- Discuss the features of northern and southern Chile. **Why do they make these regions undesirable places to live?** *(The northern third of Chile is a desert—the driest area in the world. Neither humans nor most plants and animals can live there well. The southern third of Chile is cold, wet, and stormy and thus also not an easy place to live.)*

Differentiated Instruction

For Advanced Readers L3

Have students complete the *Trade in a Global Economy* Internet activity. Then challenge them to do Internet or library research to create a circle graph that shows world exporters of copper and the percentage of the total world copper output for each.

Go Online PHSchool.com **For:** Environmental and Global Issues: *Trade in a Global Economy.*
Visit: PHSchool.com
Web Code: lfd-1606

Independent Practice

Ask students to create the Taking Notes graphic organizer on a blank piece of paper. Briefly model how to identify a main idea and its supporting details. Then have students fill in the supporting details they have just read.

Monitor Progress

As students fill in the graphic organizer, circulate and make sure individuals are choosing details that support the main idea. Provide assistance as needed.

Varied Landscapes Chile's long central valley has rolling hills, high grasses, and dense forests. This is the region where most of the people live and where the capital of Chile, Santiago, is located. Both farming and mining are important here. In the southern part of central Chile is the beautiful Lakes Region, with forests, waterfalls, and mountains topped by glaciers. **A glacier is a huge mass of slowly moving ice and snow.** Many of the mountains of this region are volcanoes, and volcanic eruptions and earthquakes occur often in Chile.

The southern third of Chile is cold and wet and often stormy. Far to the south, the Strait of Magellan separates the mainland of Chile from the islands of Tierra del Fuego (tee EHR uh del FWAY goh), which are divided between Chile and Argentina. Tierra del Fuego is Spanish for "Land of Fire." When Magellan sailed past these islands, he saw smoke from the fires of the indigenous people who lived there. Because of the smoke, he called the large island Tierra del Fuego. This region is only about 600 miles (970 kilometers) from Antarctica. Icebergs dot the sea, and penguins come ashore.

√ **Reading Check** Describe the central region of Chile.

Land of Contrasts
Icebergs float away from a glacier off Chile's southern coast (small photo). Below, a waterfall cascades in the central forest region. **Draw Conclusions** *What accounts for this difference in Chile's waterways?*

Answers

Draw Conclusions The climate is colder in southern Chile.

√ Reading Check The central region of Chile is a long valley with rolling hills, high grasses, and dense forests. The southern part of the region has lakes, forests, waterfalls, and mountains topped by glaciers. Some of the mountains are volcanoes. Most of Chile's population lives in the central region, and the capital city, Santiago, is located there. Farming and mining are important industries in the region.

Differentiated Instruction

For Less Proficient Readers L1
Partner Less Proficient Readers with more advanced readers. Have each pair create a simple table with three columns titled *Northern Chile, Central Chile, and Southern Chile*. As they read The Geography of Chile, they should list the geographic features mentioned in the text, in the correct column.

For Special Needs Students L1
Ask students to read The Geography of Chile as you play the recorded version on the Student Edition on Audio CD. Pause the CD after each paragraph and ask students to write down one key idea.

◉ Chapter 6, Section 3, **Student Edition on Audio CD**

Chile's People and Products

The lifestyles of Chileans vary from region to region. In the far south, sheep herders in heavy wool sweaters brave the strong winds. Farther north in the central valley, farmers grow wheat, potatoes, sugar beets, corn, tomatoes, and many fruits. In the cities, people in business suits hurry in and out of tall skyscrapers. Few people live in the Atacama Desert of the far north. While mining continues today, there are also ghost towns, or abandoned mining settlements, in the Atacama.

The People of Chile Chile's early Spanish settlers married Native Americans already living there. Today, mestizos make up more than 90 percent of the population. Only about 10 percent of Chileans are Native Americans.

Tonino Fuentes (toh NEE noh FWEN tays) lives in the countryside near Santiago. His family is mestizo. They work on a farm owned by a wealthy man of Spanish descent. Tonino's father trains horses that will appear in rodeos. He is teaching Tonino to be a rodeo rider. But Tonino has other things he must do. Every morning at sunrise, he and his mother milk their two cows. Then Tonino does his homework. That's because his school is in the afternoon, from 2:00 P.M. until 6:00 P.M. In the evening, Tonino often plays soccer with his friends.

Chile's Cities Today, more than 80 percent of Chile's people live in cities. Many rural Chileans have come to Santiago. In this capital city, old Spanish buildings stand near gleaming skyscrapers. The city is in the valley of the central plain, so the altitude is low enough to allow mild weather. The sea makes the air humid. Palm trees grow in the public parks. The snowcapped Andes lie to the east.

Unfortunately, the beautiful sights of Santiago are sometimes blocked by a thick layer of smog. The city is surrounded by mountains on three sides. The mountains trap exhaust from vehicles and smoke from factories in the valley. This is especially true in the winter, when there is not much wind. Pollution has become so bad that it makes many small children and elderly people sick. On a bad day, people wear surgical masks in order to breathe, or they press scarves to their faces.

The Spanish designed many of Chile's cities around a central square. Their buildings could not withstand Chile's earthquakes, however. Few colonial structures remain in Valparaiso, an important port. Chile's second-largest city, Concepción, was moved several miles inland in 1754 to protect it from tsunamis.

The "Real" Robinson Crusoe Many people have read the adventure story *Robinson Crusoe*, but few have visited the island named for this fictional character. The 1719 novel by Daniel Defoe is about a man named Robinson Crusoe who is stranded on a tropical island. It is based on the true story of Alexander Selkirk. In 1704, Selkirk, a Scottish sailor, quarreled with his captain and asked to be put ashore on one of the Juan Fernández Islands. He lived alone there until he was discovered by an English ship in 1709. Today, these islands are part of Chile. The largest island is named Robinson Crusoe and the second-largest is called Alexander Selkirk. An N. C. Wyeth illustration of the novel is shown below.

Chile's People and Products L2

Guided Instruction

- Read about the people who live in Chile and the goods they produce in Chile's People and Products. As students read, circulate and make sure individuals can answer the Reading Check question.

- Ask students to describe the ways people make a living in the different regions of Chile. (*In the north, people mine. In the south, many people herd sheep. In the central valley, some people farm while others work in business.*)

- Ask students to list the various mining and agricultural products of Chile. Then ask if students think these items represent enough diversification to keep Chile's economy healthy. (*Chilean products include wool, wheat, potatoes, sugar beets, corn, tomatoes, fruits, and copper. Some students may think the economy is diverse enough because there are so many different products. Other students may think that Chile needs to produce a wider variety of products, including products in technology and other modern businesses.*)

Independent Practice

Have students continue to fill in the graphic organizer by adding the information in this section to their outlines.

Monitor Progress

As students continue to fill in their outlines, circulate to make sure students are organizing the information correctly. Provide assistance as needed.

Links

Read the **Links to Language Arts** on this page. Have students find the Juan Fernández Island on the map at the beginning of this chapter. Ask students **What do you think living there would be like?** (*Answers will vary, but students should refer to the remoteness of these tiny islands that lie a good distance off the coast of Chile.*)

Differentiated Instruction

For Advanced Readers L3
Have students do research to answer at least two of the following questions: What is smog? How is it produced? What harm can it do? How can we prevent smog? Ask each student to present a brief oral report to the class on his or her findings.

For English Language Learners L1
Check for students' comprehension of terms on this page. If appropriate, have students read the section in the Spanish Reading and Vocabulary Study Guide to reinforce the concepts in this section.
Chapter 6, Section 3, **Latin America Spanish Reading and Vocabulary Study Guide,** pp. 49–50

Show students *Santiago, Chile: Between the Andes and the Sea.* Ask **Why do you think Santiago has become Chile's largest city?** (*It is a center of business and is located in a region where farming and mining are important.*)

Restoring Democracy L2

Guided Instruction

- **Vocabulary Builder** Clarify the high-use words **regime** and **reject** before reading.

- Ask students to read about Chile's struggle to maintain a democratic government in Restoring Democracy.

- Discuss the actions taken during Pinochet's control of Chile that were undemocratic. (*Under Pinochet's control, the Chilean congress could not meet, opposition political parties were banned, and people who spoke out against the regime were killed, imprisoned, or "disappeared"—all of these actions indicated a lack of democracy.*)

- Ask students **How was democracy restored?** (*In 1988, even though Pinochet's name was the only one on the election ballot, the people of Chile voted "no" and democracy was restored.*)

Independent Practice

Have students complete the graphic organizer by filling in the supporting details they identify in this section.

Monitor Progress

- Show *Section Reading Support Transparency LA 47* and ask students to check their graphic organizers individually. Go over key concepts and clarify key vocabulary as needed.

  Latin America Transparencies, *Section Reading Support Transparency LA 47*

- Tell students to fill in the last column of the *Reading Readiness Guide*. Probe for what they learned that confirms or invalidates each statement.

  All in One Latin America Teaching Resources, *Reading Readiness Guide,* p. 325

Answers

Identify Effects Farming creates jobs that involve shipping and processing farm products. People also have jobs making farming equipment.

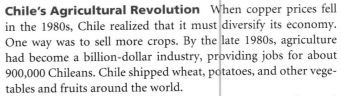

Explore Chile's capital, Santiago.

Farming Fuels the Economy
Grapes are harvested (below) and then shipped around the world from ports like this one in Valparaiso (bottom photo). **Identify Effects** *How does farming create jobs for people other than farm workers?*

184 Latin America

Chile's Agricultural Revolution When copper prices fell in the 1980s, Chile realized that it must diversify its economy. One way was to sell more crops. By the late 1980s, agriculture had become a billion-dollar industry, providing jobs for about 900,000 Chileans. Chile shipped wheat, potatoes, and other vegetables and fruits around the world.

The United States, Japan, and Europe are especially good markets for Chilean produce. From October through May, it is cold in the Northern Hemisphere but warm in the Southern Hemisphere. Chile provides fruits and vegetables to the United States during the months when American farmers cannot.

Another reason that Chilean produce is welcome in other countries is that Chile's fruits and vegetables are free of many common plant pests. Chile's farming regions are protected by the Andes Mountains, so some of the insect pests and animal diseases that plague other countries never reach Chile. The government wants to make sure that Chilean produce remains this way. Customs inspectors at Chile's airports search baggage carefully. They are checking that no plant or animal matter from foreign places is allowed into the country because it might bring disease to Chile's crops.

✓ **Reading Check** Why is Chilean produce free of many plant pests?

✓ **Reading Check** The Chilean produce is free of many plant pests because the Andes Mountains protect Chile's farming region, keeping out some of the pests that plague other countries. Officials at Chile's airports also help prevent pests from entering the country by checking bags to make sure that no plant or animal matter from a foreign place is allowed in.

Restoring Democracy

Today, Chile has a democratic government. But a dark cloud from its past still hangs over the country. In 1973, the armed forces took control of the government. They were led by General **Augusto Pinochet Ugarte** (ah GOO stoh pea noh SHAY oo gahr TAY), who became a brutal dictator. The Chilean congress could not meet during his rule. Opposition political parties were banned. People who spoke out against the military regime were killed, imprisoned, or "disappeared."

Nevertheless, there were national days of protest. The Catholic Church spoke out against the human rights abuses of the government. In the 1988 elections—even though Pinochet's name was the only one on the ballot—the people of Chile rejected him by voting "no." Democratic government was restored. Pinochet, however, remained an army general.

In 1998, at the age of 82, Pinochet went to London, England, for medical treatment. The government of Spain issued a warrant for his arrest for crimes against humanity. This caused an international crisis. Eventually, Pinochet was declared unfit for trial, and he returned to Chile. Some Chileans wanted him prosecuted; others did not. There is still controversy over bringing to trial those responsible for the abuses of the Pinochet regime.

Anti-Pinochet demonstrators gathered in London when the former dictator was there for medical treatment.

✔️ **Reading Check** How did Pinochet's rule end?

Section 3 Assessment

Key Terms
Review the key terms at the beginning of this section. Use each term in a sentence that explains its meaning.

🎯 Target Reading Skills
What are two ways that Tonino's life in the countryside is different from life in Santiago?

Comprehension and Critical Thinking
1. (a) Identify Describe Chile's geographic regions.

(b) Identify Cause and Effect How does Chile's geography contribute to its variety of climates and vegetation?
2. (a) Name What kinds of crops are grown in Chile?
(b) Identify Causes Why is Chilean produce so popular in foreign countries?
3. (a) Recall Describe life in Chile when Pinochet was in power.
(b) Evaluate Information Do you think Pinochet should be brought to trial? Explain.

Writing Activity
How do you think Magellan's crew must have felt during their exploration of Tierra del Fuego? Write a journal entry that one of the crew might have written about the experience.

Go Online
PHSchool.com
For: An activity on Chile
Visit: PHSchool.com
Web Code: lfd-1603

Chapter 6 Section 3 **185**

Assess and Reteach

Assess Progress L2
Have students complete the Section Assessment. Then administer the *Section Quiz*.

All in One **Latin America Teaching Resources,** *Section Quiz,* p. 326

Reteach L1
If students need more instruction, have them read this section in the Reading and Vocabulary Study Guide.

📖 Chapter 6, Section 3, **Latin America Reading and Vocabulary Study Guide,** pp. 68–70

Extend L3
Remind students that Pinochet was accused of committing crimes against humanity during his rule. Have students complete the *Analysis of Human Rights Violations* activity.

Go Online PHSchool.com **For:** Environmental and Global Issues: *Analysis of Human Rights Violations*
Visit: PHSchool.com
Web Code: lfd-1607

Answers

✔️ **Reading Check** Pinochet's rule ended when the Chilean people voted against his reelection.

Writing Activity
Use the *Rubric for Assessing a Journal Entry* to evaluate students' journal entries.

All in One **Latin America Teaching Resources,** *Rubric for Assessing a Journal Entry,* p. 350

Go Online PHSchool.com Typing in the web code when prompted will bring students directly to detailed instructions for this activity.

Section 3 Assessment

Key Terms
Students' sentences should reflect knowledge of each Key Term.

🎯 Target Reading Skill
Implied contrasts include: Tonino works on a farm; his school is from 2:00 P.M. to 6:00 P.M.; his father trains horses, all of which differs from life in a big city.

Comprehension and Critical Thinking
1. (a) Northern region: Atacama Desert, the driest region in the world; very few plants and animals; provides a lot of copper. Central valley: covered in hills, grasses, and forests; farming and mining take place there; and most of Chile's people live there. Southern region: cold, wet, and stormy. **(b)** Chile's long and thin shape, its nearness to the Pacific Ocean and South Pole, and the fact that the Andes run through it lead to a great variety in climate and vegetation

2. (a) wheat, potatoes, sugar beets, corn, tomatoes, and many fruits. **(b)** Chilean produce is free of many common plant pests.

3. (a) Congress was not allowed to meet, opposition political parties were not allowed to form, and many people were harshly punished or killed if they spoke out against the regime. **(b)** Students' opinions will vary.

Objective

Learn how to synthesize information.

Prepare to Read

Build Background Knowledge L2

Encourage students to think about instances in their own lives when they have to put together more than one type of information to understand something. Offer some examples such as museums where the exhibits involve visuals, texts, and audio recordings. Then ask students to provide their own examples.

Instruct

Synthesizing Information L2

Guided Instruction

- Read the steps to synthesize information as a class and write them on the board.

- Practice the skill by following the steps on p. 186 as a class. Model each step in the activity by choosing a photograph from Section 2 to analyze *(suspension bridge photograph on p. 178)*, identifying its main idea *(Peruvians have adapted to the deep gorges of the altiplano by building suspension bridges.)*, and identifying details that support the main ideas. *(The bridge shown is high up in the trees; no land below can be seen.)* Repeat these steps with the photograph of the Uros' reed islands on p. 173. *(The main idea is that the Uros adapted to their lake environment by building reed islands to live on. The supporting details are the lake and the huts on the island.)* Then ask students to list connections between the two main ideas *(Both reveal ways that people have adapted to their surroundings.)* and their conclusions. *(The people of Peru have found ways to live in many environments.)*

Skills for Life — Synthesizing Information

When Madelyn returned from Chile, she entertained the class with a wonderful presentation—a map of the route she had taken, a slide show of the Andes Mountains, and a videotape she had made of life in a small village. She had even managed to ask the villagers a couple of questions in Spanish.

When she finished, the class applauded. Her teacher beamed.

"Madelyn, the amount of information you have gathered is stunning," Mr. Rishell said. "Now perhaps you could synthesize all this material for us."

"Sure!" Madelyn replied. Then she paused. "Um . . . how do you synthesize something?"

When you synthesize information, you find the main ideas of several different sources and use them to draw a conclusion. This skill is particularly useful when you are doing research for a report.

Learn the Skill

To synthesize information, follow these steps.

1. **Identify the main idea of each of your sources.** Main ideas are broad, major ideas that are supported by details.

2. **Identify details that support each main idea.** Look in each source for supporting details. Jot them down or create a chart.

3. **Look for connections between pieces of information.** These connections may be similarities, differences, causes, effects, or examples.

4. **Draw conclusions based on the connections you found.** Be sure to use all of your sources.

186 Latin America

Independent Practice

Assign *Skills for Life* and have students complete it individually.

All in One **Latin America Teaching Resources,** *Skills for Life*, p. 336

Monitor Progress

The teacher should monitor the students doing the *Skills for Life* worksheet, checking to make sure they understand the skills steps.

Peru		
Main Ideas	**Supporting Details**	
1. Peru has three distinct geographic regions:	· Coastal Region—Desert and oases	
	· Sierra—Mountains	
	· Selva—Rain forest	
2. Peruvians speak different languages:	·	
	·	
	·	

Practice the Skill

Use the steps on page 186 to synthesize information about Peru. Use these sources: the text under the heading The Regions and People of Peru and the Country Profile of Peru on page 174. Make a table like the one started above.

1 Study the information about Peru in the text as well as in the map and charts in the Country Profile. Add at least two main ideas to the first column of the table.

2 Now write details that support each main idea. You may find details that support one idea in several different sources.

3 Do the main ideas show contrasts or similarities within Peru's geographic regions? Jot down connections.

4 Your main ideas should help you write a one- or two-sentence conclusion that answers a question such as, "What have I learned about the regions of Peru?"

Brasília, Brazil

Apply the Skill

Use the steps you have just practiced to synthesize information about Brazil. Select information from text, maps, photographs, captions, and other sources beginning on page 166. Do not try to summarize everything you read about Brazil, but choose a major topic, such as city life.

Chapter 6 **187**

Assess and Reteach

Assess Progress L2
Ask students to complete the Apply the Skill activity.

Reteach L1
If students are having trouble applying the skill steps, have them review the skill using the interactive Social Studies Skills Tutor CD-ROM.

⦿ *Synthesizing Information*, **Social Studies Skills Tutor CD-ROM**

Extend L3
■ To extend the lesson, ask students to use *Color Transparency LA 9: The World: Annual Precipitation* to locate a place with high annual precipitation. Have them then find a book in the library or in the classroom about that place. What activities do people participate in? How do they make a living? Then have them draw a conclusion as to whether or not high amounts of precipitation affect what kinds of activities people do and how they make a living.

📖 **Latin America Transparencies,** *Color Transparency LA 9: The World: Annual Precipitation*

■ Ask students to reread Section 3 and choose two or more pieces of information to synthesize using the steps they just learned. Have them create a chart like the one on page 187. (*Answers will vary, but be sure students have correctly completed the chart, choosing the appropriate main idea and supporting details for their pieces. Also, be sure they have drawn an appropriate conclusion.*)

Answers
Apply the Skill
Students' summaries should include accurate information drawn from more than one source.

Section 4
Step-by-Step Instruction

Objectives

Social Studies
1. Find out how Venezuela was made wealthy by oil.
2. Learn how the ups and downs of oil prices affected the economy and people of Venezuela.
3. Understand how Venezuela is changing.

Reading/Language Arts
Make comparisons to find out how two situations are alike.

Prepare to Read

Build Background Knowledge   L2
Tell students that in this section they will learn more about the economy of Venezuela. Have students preview the headings and visuals in this section with the following question in mind: **How has relying on one resource affected the economy and citizens of Venezuela?** Provide a few simple examples to get students started. Conduct an Idea Wave (TE, p. T35) to generate a list.

Set a Purpose for Reading   L2
- Preview the Objectives.
- Read each statement in the *Reading Readiness Guide* aloud. Ask students to mark the statements true or false.

  All in One **Latin America Teaching Resources,** *Reading Readiness Guide,* p.328

- Have students discuss the statements in pairs or groups of four, then mark their worksheets again. Use the Numbered Heads participation structure (TE, p. T36) to call on students to share their group's perspectives.

Vocabulary Builder
Preview Key Terms   L2
Pronounce each Key Term, then ask students to say the word with you. Provide a simple explanation such as, "When a group of people try to remove their country's government and take power themselves, they have attempted a coup."

Section 4

Venezuela
Oil Powers the Economy

Prepare to Read

Objectives
In this section you will
1. Find out how Venezuela was made wealthy by oil.
2. Learn how the ups and downs of oil prices affected the economy and people of Venezuela.
3. Understand how Venezuela is changing.

Taking Notes
As you read this section, look for ways that oil prices affect Venezuela. Copy the cause-and-effect chain below and record your findings in it. Add boxes as needed.

During the 1970s, world oil prices went up. → [ ] → [ ]

Target Reading Skill

Make Comparisons Comparing two or more situations enables you to see how they are alike. As you read this section, compare life in Venezuela before and after the oil boom. Consider the economy, the government, and the lives of ordinary people.

Key Terms
- **Caracas** (kuh RAH kus) *n.* the capital of Venezuela
- **boom** (boom) *n.* a period of business growth and prosperity
- **privatization** (pry vuh tih ZAY shun) *n.* the government's sale of land or industries it owns to private businesses or individuals
- **coup** (koo) *n.* the overthrow of a ruler or government by an organized group, which then takes power

Caracas, Venezuela

188 Latin America

Welcome to **Caracas** (kuh RAH kus), the capital and largest city of Venezuela. The view from a high-rise apartment building can be breathtaking. At night, thousands of lights dot the surrounding hills. Steep mountains rise in the distance. Now look down at street level. During the day, well-dressed people walk to their jobs in modern office buildings. Others may be going to a museum or to one of the city's public gardens. Later, they may stroll by on their way to dinner or the theater or a concert.

Outside, the air is balmy. It is also clean. Caracas is in a valley that runs from east to west. Winds blow through it. They sweep the exhaust of the city's many cars, buses, and taxis out of Caracas. The subway system also helps by transporting many people who would otherwise have to drive.

Of course, not everyone in Caracas is wealthy and well dressed. The city—and the whole nation of Venezuela—went through a period of rapid growth and prosperity. Then it suffered a decline. Today, the situation in Venezuela is uncertain. These changes have occurred in other countries too. Read on to see how Venezuela coped.

Target Reading Skill   L2

Make Comparisons Point out the Target Reading Skill. Explain that making comparisons can help students find the similarities between two situations

Model the skill by drawing students' attention to the first sentence on page 189. Ask students to identify a similarity between Venezuela and the Persian Gulf region. (*Both have some of the world's largest oil reserves.*)

Give students *Make Comparisons.* Have them complete the activity in groups.

All in One **Latin America Teaching Resources,** *Make Comparisons,* p. 333

A Land Made Wealthy by Oil

Except for the Persian Gulf region, Venezuela has the largest oil reserves in the world. The map of Venezuela in the Country Profile on page 190 shows where Venezuela's vast supplies of oil are located. Venezuela's oil has earned millions of dollars on the world market. In the 1970s, many Venezuelans migrated from the countryside to work for the oil companies. They helped maintain the giant oil rigs in Lake Maracaibo (mar uh KY boh). They also worked in oil refineries.

Both the government and private corporations own oil companies in Venezuela. They have grown rich pumping, processing, and selling oil. In the early 1980s, Venezuela was the richest country in Latin America. Much of the money went to Caracas, the economic center of Venezuela. At that time, there seemed to be no end to the money that could be made in the oil industry.

Ups and Downs of Oil Prices During the 1970s, the price of oil went up. An oil boom began. A **boom** is a period of business growth and prosperity. The standard of living of many Venezuelans went up, too. That is when the government started spending huge sums of money. Many people were hired to run government agencies and government-owned businesses. The government built expensive subways and high-quality roads. Then the government began to borrow money so that it could spend even more.

In the mid-1980s, the oil-producing countries of the world produced more oil than the world needed. The price of oil started to fall, but millions of people were still employed by the Venezuelan government. They ran the many government offices and worked in government industries. Finally, the government was spending much more than it could earn. As the price of oil continued to drop, many people lost their jobs.

■ Graph Skills

Oil pumped in Venezuela is important not only to that country but also to the United States. **Describe** According to the graph, what is the overall pattern of American imports of Venezuelan oil? **Predict** What do you think might happen to both countries if oil production were interrupted?

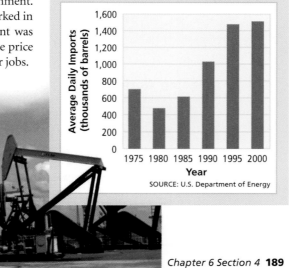

U.S. Petroleum Imports From Venezuela, 1975–2000

SOURCE: U.S. Department of Energy

Chapter 6 Section 4 **189**

┌ Vocabulary Builder

Use the information below to teach students this section's high-use words.

High-Use Word	Definition and Sample Sentence
policy, p. 192	*n.* a plan or course of action intended to influence and determine decisions or actions The government had a strict **policy** on importing fruits and vegetables.
occur, p. 192	*v.* to take place Halloween always **occurs** on October 31st.
individual, p. 192	*n.* a single human considered apart from a society or community Five **individuals** can fit comfortably in that car.

A Land Made Wealthy by Oil L2

Guided Instruction
- Read A Land Made Wealthy by Oil, using the Choral Reading technique (TE, p. T34).
- Ask students **How did oil help increase Venezuela's wealth?** *(Both the government and private corporations in Venezuela mined, processed, and sold the country's oil to countries around the world.)*
- Ask students **How did oil then lead to great poverty in Venezuela?** *(Venezuela and other oil-producing countries were producing more oil than the world needed. Prices dropped and Venezuela began making less and less money. Companies could not afford to keep all the workers they had hired. Many people lost their jobs and became poor.)*

Independent Practice
Ask students to create the Taking Notes graphic organizer on a blank piece of paper. Then have them fill in the boxes with the appropriate causes and their effects. Briefly model how to identify events that cause other events.

Monitor Progress
As students fill in the graphic organizer, circulate and make sure individuals are choosing events that cause or are caused by other events. Provide assistance as needed.

Answers

Graph Skills Describe Overall, the United States seems to be importing more oil from Venezuela every year. **Predict** Possible answer: Venezuela would lose money and the United States would export more oil from other oil producing countries.

Guided Instruction L2

Ask students to study the Country Profile on this page. Encourage them to study the map and the graphs on the page and think about the information each provides. As a class, answer the Map and Chart Skills questions. Allow students to briefly discuss their responses with a partner before sharing answers.

Independent Practice

Ask students to study the graphs, then reread the section's text. Have them write a paragraph using this topic sentence "Oil is extremely important in Venezuela." Allow students to brainstorm ideas in pairs.

Answers

Map and Chart Skills

1. World oil prices fluctuated between about $15 and $25 per barrel during this period. By 2000, prices were back to around $15 per barrel.

2. The bar graph shows that Venezuela is one of the world's leading oil exporters, which tells us that oil is important to its economy. The circle graph shows how much of Venezuela's earnings from exports are due to oil.

3. When oil prices are high, Venezuela's economy flourishes. When prices are low, the economy suffers and people in the oil industry may lose their jobs.

4. Most of Venezuela's oil is located in the north so the large number of people who work for the oil industry probably want to live nearby.

Go **Online** PHSchool.com **Students can find more information about this topic in the DK World Desk Reference Online.**

Venezuela

Venezuela's economy is dominated by oil. Much of this oil lies under Lake Maracaibo, but there are also large deposits in the northeastern part of the country and near the Orinoco River. Venezuela also has large amounts of coal, iron ore, and minerals. In addition, Venezuela has large areas of rain forest that have less economic value. As you examine the map and graphs, notice where Venezuela's resources are located. Think about how resources and their location can shape a nation's economy and culture.

Venezuela: Products and Resources

KEY
- Oil field
- Gold
- Petroleum
- Coffee
- Cocoa
- Fruit
- Tropical rain forest
- Tropical savanna
- Desert scrub
- National border
- National capital
- Other city

0 miles 400
0 kilometers 400
Lambert Azimuthal Equal Area

World Crude Oil Prices, 1970–2001

Price (dollars per barrel*)

* Figures are not adjusted for inflation.
SOURCE: U.S. Department of Energy, *EIA Annual Energy Review*

Venezuela: Earnings From Exports, 2002

Other 20%
Oil 80%

SOURCE: *CIA World Factbook*

Leading World Oil Exporters, 2001

Millions of Barrels per Day

Saudi Arabia	Russia	Norway	Iran	Venezuela
7380	4760	3220	2740	2600

SOURCE: U.S. Department of Energy, Energy Information Administration

Map and Chart Skills

1. **Describe** What is the pattern of the world price of oil from 1990 to 2000?
2. **Synthesize Information** How do two of the graphs show the importance of oil to Venezuela?
3. **Predict** In what ways could changes in the world price of oil affect Venezuela?
4. **Draw Conclusions** More than 80 percent of Venezuela's people live in cities. Use the information on the map and graphs to explain why Venezuela's cities are located in the north of the country.

Go **Online** PHSchool.com Use Web Code lfe-1614 for DK World Desk Reference Online.

190 Latin America

Background: Global Perspectives

World Oil Powers Venezuela was a founding member of the Organization of Petroleum Exporting Countries (OPEC), which formed in 1960. Members coordinate policies regarding the sale of oil and share economic aid with one another. In late 1973, OPEC twice raised oil prices. While at first OPEC profited greatly from the price increases, Western countries soon found other ways to access oil, forcing OPEC to bring its prices back down. Recent decades have seen more price fluctuations but never again to the extent of the 1970s. Today, OPEC membership includes Iran, Iraq, Kuwait, Libya, Saudi Arabia, Qatar, and the United Arab Emirates in Southwest Asia; Algeria and Nigeria in Africa; and Indonesia in Asia. Ecuador in South America and Gabon in Africa are former members.

The New Poverty   Poor people who had come from the countryside were hit the hardest by the drop in oil sales. They had come to Caracas and other cities to work in the growing industries. When the oil industries cut back, many of these people were left without jobs. They were surprised to find that they had traded poverty in the countryside for poverty in the cities.

✓ **Reading Check**   **Why did many people suddenly become poor in the 1980s?**

The Economy and the People

During the oil boom, Venezuela changed from a traditional culture based on agriculture to a modern urban country. Now more than 80 percent of the population lives in cities.

Venezuelans and the Oil Economy   This change can be seen in the story of Juan Varderi's family. Juan's grandfather raised sheep on a ranch east of Lake Maracaibo. He made a fairly good living selling wool and meat to people in Caracas. But Juan's father left the countryside and went to work on an oil rig that was owned by the government. By the time Juan was born, the family was living in Caracas in a small apartment. His father was making enough money for the family to have a television.

Juan loved living in the city, playing baseball in the street, and watching American television programs. "In the early 1980s, we thought we could live just like rich Americans seemed to live. We didn't understand it was only taking place on TV," Juan says. "We didn't know what was going to happen to us in just a few years."

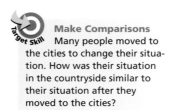
Make Comparisons
Many people moved to the cities to change their situation. How was their situation in the countryside similar to their situation after they moved to the cities?

Play Ball!
Boys enjoying a baseball game in Caracas **Infer** *Why do you think these boys are playing in this empty lot rather than on a baseball field?*

Differentiated Instruction

For Less Proficient Readers   L1
Pair less proficient readers with more advanced readers. Have them work together to write a short scene about one of the events in Juan Varderi's life described in the section. Then have pairs perform their scenes for the class.

For Special Needs Students   L1
Have students read the section with a partner. Then, to help with comprehension, ask students to write down as much of the story of Juan Varderi's experience as they can remember. When they have finished a draft, have them reread the section individually and add in any details that are missing.

Make Comparisons As a follow up, ask students to answer the Target Reading Skill question in the Student Edition. *(When the oil industry laid off workers, those that moved to the city to work in the oil industry experienced poverty similar to that which they suffered when they lived in rural areas.)*

The Economy and the People   L2

Guided Instruction
- **Vocabulary Builder** Clarify the high-use words **policy**, **occur**, and **individual** before reading.
- Read about the effect of oil prices on Venezuelans in The Economy and the People. As students read, circulate and make sure individuals can answer the Reading Check question.
- Ask students **How did the oil boom change the culture of Venezuela?** *(The oil boom changed Venezuela from a traditional culture based on agriculture into a modern urban culture in which 80 percent of the people live in cities.)*
- Discuss the ways life changed for many Venezuelans after the oil boom ended. *(Many Venezuelans lost their jobs and their homes. Once the oil industry became privatized, people did have the opportunity to get hired again, but they were paid lower salaries.)*

Answers

✓ **Reading Check** Many people became poor in the 1980s because they lost their jobs once the oil-producing countries of the world began producing more oil than was needed. This caused the price of oil to fall.

Infer Possible answer: The city may not have been able to afford to build a baseball field in this part of the city.

Independent Practice

Have students continue to fill in the boxes of their graphic organizers with the causes and effects of events discussed.

Monitor Progress

Circulate and check students' graphic organizers to make sure they are identifying all the events in Venezuela that fit into the cause-and-effect chain. Provide assistance to any students who need it.

When Juan turned 15, oil prices suddenly fell. Juan's father was one of the many who lost their jobs. And like many other Venezuelan families, Juan's family was in danger of losing their apartment. Things looked bleak for those who had depended on the oil industry for their living.

Government Businesses Go Public With many of its oil workers unemployed, the Venezuelan government took action. It started a new policy of privatization. **Privatization** (pry vuh tih ZAY shun) occurs when the government sells its industries to individuals or private companies. In the late 1980s and the 1990s, the government decided to sell some of its businesses to private corporations. It hoped that the corporations would make big profits. The profits would help the corporations to hire and pay workers. When the government turned over an oil refinery to a private company, Juan's father applied for a job there and was hired. Salaries in the private oil refinery were less than oil workers had earned when they were employed by the government, but they were enough for families to be able to keep their apartments.

✓ **Reading Check** How did salaries compare before and after privatization?

Disaster!
In 1999, flooding and landslides caused devastation around Caracas (left), and destroyed much of the town of Macuto (right). **Draw Conclusions** *Explain how a major disaster like this would probably affect a country's economy.*

Answers

Draw Conclusions A major disaster like this would probably devastate a country's economy. But, it might also create some new jobs related to rebuilding the city.

✓ Reading Check Salaries were lower after privatization.

Differentiated Instruction

For English Language Learners L2
Check students' comprehension of the term *privatization*. Tell students that *privatization* is the word *private* with two suffixes added. The suffixes are *–ize*, which means "to make," and *–ation*, which means "the act or process of." Write the word *private* on the board and go over the definition in a business context (*not official or public*). Walk through how the two suffixes, *–ize* and *–ation*, change the meaning of the word *private*.

Venezuela in Crisis

Although Venezuela had attempted to diversify its economy, at the end of the 1900s it was still very dependent on oil. The economy was so bad in 1989 that riots broke out when the government tried to save money by raising bus fares. Strikes and protests continued. There were even coup attempts in 1992. A **coup** (koo) is the overthrow of a ruler or government by an organized group, which then takes power. In 1998, the leader of one of the failed coups, Hugo Chavez, was elected president. He promised political reform and help for the poor. But the economy continued its downward slide.

Weather Plays a Role Venezuela's economic crisis grew in 1999 when floods and mudslides caused massive destruction and killed thousands of people. Unusually heavy rainstorms hit the northwest portion of the country. Rivers became raging torrents, and avalanches of mud, rocks, and water poured down mountainsides. The worst flooding was north of Caracas. There, shacks had been built on the mountainsides by people who could not afford other housing. Many of these shacks were swept away or buried in mud, and many of the people were killed or made homeless. Caracas, too, experienced severe flooding. Venezuela began rescue and disaster relief operations immediately, and other nations sent aid. The destruction was so great, however, that reconstruction and resettling of the homeless went on for years.

Learn about Simón Bolívar, the liberator of Venezuela.

Show students *The Liberator: Simón Bolívar.* Ask **Why was Bolívar known as the liberator of South America?** *(because he helped liberate the South American countries of Bolivia, Venezuela, Colombia, Panama, Ecuador, and Peru)*

Venezuela in Crisis L2

Guided Instruction
- Ask students to read about Venezuela's economic and political crises in Venezuela in Crisis.
- Discuss the effects of the economic crisis in Venezuela on the country's political situation. *(Riots broke out, leading to several coup attempts against the government. Even after reelecting Chavez in 2000, riots and strikes against the government continued.)*
- Ask students **How did Venezuela's political crisis affect the economy?** *(The strikes led to a crippling of oil production and the country nearly shut down.)*

Independent Practice
Have students complete the graphic organizer by filling in the final of the causes and effects they learned in this section.

Monitor Progress
- Show *Section Reading Support Transparency LA 48* and ask students to check their graphic organizers individually. Go over key concepts and clarify key vocabulary as needed

   Latin America Transparencies, *Section Reading Support Transparency LA 48*

- Tell students to fill in the last column of the *Reading Readiness Guide.* Probe for what they learned that confirms or invalidates each statement.

   All in One **Latin America Teaching Resources,** *Reading Readiness Guide,* p. 328

Differentiated Instruction

For Less Proficient Readers L1
Help students understand the ups and downs of Venezuela's economy by having pairs create a time line showing the changes. Use the *Rubric for Assessing a Timeline* to evaluate students' timelines.

   All in One **Latin America Teaching Resources,** *Rubric for Assessing a Timeline,* p. 351

For Special Needs Students L1
Have students read the section in the Reading and Vocabulary Study Guide. This version provides a summary of section content with interactive questions and activities to help students read.

   Chapter 6, Section 4, **Latin America Reading and Vocabulary Study Guide,** pp. 71–73

Some Venezuelans support Hugo Chavez (left), while others oppose his government (right).

Assess and Reteach

Assess Progress `L2`

Have students complete the Section Assessment. Then administer the *Section Quiz*.

All in One Latin America Teaching Resources, *Section Quiz*, p. 330

Reteach `L1`

If students need more instruction, have them read this section in the Reading and Vocabulary Study Guide.

 Chapter 6, Section 4, **Latin America Reading and Vocabulary Study Guide,** pp. 71–73

Extend `L3`

Ask students to write a persuasive essay arguing for or against the protests that occurred in Venezuela after the oil boom ended. Have them read *Writing to Persuade* and use the worksheet to guide their writing (disregarding its list of suggested topics.) Have students use the text and outside Internet and library research to support their arguments.

All in One Latin America Teaching Resources, *Writing to Persuade*, p. 346

Answer

✓ **Reading Check** The continued economic crisis and the way Chavez was increasing his power caused the riots and strikes.

Section 4 Assessment

Key Terms
Students' sentences should reflect knowledge of each Key Term.

◑ **Target Reading Skill**
Both crises caused an economic setback in Venezuela; both caused people to lose their homes; both hit the poor the hardest.

Comprehension and Critical Thinking
1. (a) The government responded by spending huge sums of money—by hiring many people to run government agencies and government-owned business and by building expensive subways and roads. (b) The country relied so heavily on that one industry.

2. (a) In the 1970s, many people from the countryside moved to the cities to get jobs in the growing oil industry. (b) The oil boom affected oil workers by allowing them to earn enough money to live comfortably. Privatization affected oil workers by giving them jobs

Political Crisis Chavez won reelection in 2000. But the continuing economic crisis and complaints about the way Chavez was increasing his power caused new riots and attempts to remove him from office. By the end of 2002, there was a general strike led by opponents of Chavez. It crippled oil production and almost shut down the country. Both the political and economic situation in Venezuela were deteriorating quickly. Even so, Chavez was still supported by the poor.

Whatever Venezuela's future is, one thing is certain. The oil boom brought Venezuela into the modern world. When televisions, cellular phones, and other conveniences came into people's homes, life in Venezuela changed permanently.

✓ **Reading Check** What caused riots and strikes in 2002?

Section 4 Assessment

Key Terms
Review the key terms at the beginning of this section. Use each term in a sentence that explains its meaning.

◑ **Target Reading Skills**
How were the effects of the fall of oil prices in the 1980s similar to the effects of the torrential rainstorms of 1999?

Comprehension and Critical Thinking
1. (a) **Describe** How did the government of Venezuela react to the oil boom?

(b) **Draw Conclusions** Why did the drop in oil prices affect Venezuela so much?
2. (a) **Recall** What brought many people from the countryside to the cities in the 1970s?
(b) **Identify Effects** How did the oil boom and then privatization affect oil workers?
3. (a) **Sequence** How did Hugo Chavez gain power?
(b) **Infer** Why do you think that people protesting the government wanted to shut down Venezuela's oil production?

Writing Activity
Juan Varderi learned about American families from television programs. Write the first scene of a television script about a Venezuelan family. First choose a time and place for your program, such as the 1970s in Caracas or today in the countryside. Then think about how a family would live in that setting.

Writing Tip List the setting and characters first. Then use the correct form to write dialogue and stage directions.

194 Latin America

after losing the government jobs, but with lower salaries.

3. (a) He was elected president after leading an unsuccessful coup against the government. (b) Answers will vary. Students might say that protesters knew it would hurt the government and hoped it would force them to make the changes they wanted.

Writing Activity
Use the *Rubric for Assessing a Writing Assignment* to evaluate students' scripts.

All in One Latin America Teaching Resources, *Rubric for Assessing a Writing Assignment*, p. 349

Review and Assessment

◆ Chapter Summary

Section 1: Brazil
- The geography of Brazil includes rain forests, plateaus, and savannas.
- Rain forests are important to Brazil and affect the whole world, but they face many dangers.
- Most Brazilians live in cities along the coast, but some live on farms and in the rain forest.

Section 2: Peru
- Most Peruvians live in the modern cities of the coastal plain.
- Many Native Americans still lead traditional lives in the mountain and forest regions.
- Old and new ways of life exist side by side in the Altiplano, the high plateau in the Andes Mountains.

Section 3: Chile
- The regions of Chile have distinct types of climate and geography, and people live very differently in each region.
- Although most of Chile's people live in cities, agriculture is very important to Chile's economy.
- Chileans voted out a dictator and replaced his brutal regime with a democratic government.

Section 4: Venezuela
- Oil production made Venezuela rich.
- A decrease in oil prices caused problems for Venezuela's economy and for ordinary people.
- Economic and political problems have led to a crisis in Venezuela.

Brazil

◆ Key Terms

Define each of the following terms.

1. Altiplano
2. sierra
3. oasis
4. boom
5. savanna
6. coup
7. canopy
8. Brasília
9. circumnavigate
10. privatization
11. Caracas
12. glacier
13. Rio de Janeiro
14. Amazon rain forest

Chapter 6 **195**

┌ Vocabulary Builder ┐

Revisit this chapter's high-use words:

occupy   foundation   reject
dense   adapt   policy
community   survive   occur
dwell   regime   individual

Ask students to review the definitions they recorded on their *Word Knowledge* worksheets.

All in One **Latin America Teaching Resources,** *Word Knowledge,* p. 334

Consider allowing students to earn extra credit if they use the words in their answers to the questions in the Chapter Review and Assessment. The words must be used correctly and in a natural context to win the extra points.

Review and Assessment

Review Chapter Content

- Review and revisit the major themes of this chapter by asking students to identify which Guiding Question each bulleted statement in the Chapter Summary answers. Have students write each statement down and work in groups to determine which statement applies to which Guiding Question. Refer to page 1 in the Student Edition for the text of Guiding Questions.

- Assign *Vocabulary Development* for students to review Key Terms.

  All in One **Latin America Teaching Resources,** *Vocabulary Development,* p. 347

Answers

Key Terms

1. The Altiplano is the high plateau in the Andes Mountains of Peru.
2. The sierra is the mountain region of Peru, which includes the altiplano and the Andes Mountains.
3. An oasis is a place in the desert that has water and is fertile.
4. A boom is a period of business growth and prosperity.
5. A savanna is a flat, grassy region, or plain.
6. A coup is the overthrow of a ruler or government by an organized group that then takes power.
7. The canopy is the dense mass of leaves at the top of the tree in a rain forest.
8. Brasília is Brazil's new capital city.
9. To circumnavigate something is to go all the way around it.
10. Privatization occurs when the government sells its industries to individuals or private companies.
11. Caracas is the capital of Venezuela.
12. A glacier is a huge mass of slowly moving ice and snow.
13. Rio de Janeiro is a large city located on Brazil's coast.
14. The Amazon rain forest is a large tropical rain forest occupying the Amazon Basin in northern South America.

Chapter 6 **195**

Comprehension and Critical Thinking

15. (a) A rain forest is hot, humid, and gets heavy rainfall. Plants grow abundantly and many different kinds of animals live there. **(b)** The Amazon rain forest helps produce about one third of the world's oxygen, it is home to millions of species of plants, animals, and insects, and many modern medicines have been made from plants there.

16. (a) along or near the coast and along rivers **(b)** to help the country use the resources of the rain forest to develop that region **(c)** Answers will vary slightly but should identify the areas along coasts and rivers as more accessible than the areas in the interior of the country. Also, the climate and terrain make it easier to live on the coast.

17. (a) The mountain region, or sierra, includes the Andes Mountains and the cold altiplano. Native Americans live and herd animals there. The coastal region is dry and dotted with oases. There are many cities in this region, which is the economic center of the country. The forested region, or selva, stretches from the base of the mountains to northeast Peru. It includes rain forest and is hot and humid. It has few roads to the other regions and little modern development. Some Native Americans live there. **(b)** Possible answer: They may begin to move away from some of their traditional ways of life and adopt more modern ways.

18. (a) Magellan discovered the strait when he was trying to find a way to sail around or through the Americas from Spain. The journey was difficult and Magellan did not make it back to Spain. **(b)** The mountains trap exhaust and smoke, creating pollution problems; Chile is in the Southern Hemisphere and can grow and sell produce when it is winter in the Northern Hemisphere; Chile's farming regions are protected by the Andes Mountains, which help keep out some insect pests and animal diseases that plague other countries. **(c)** Possible answer: There may be a great difference in culture between people in the north and people in the south because they are very far apart.

19. (a) Venezuela has one of the world's largest supplies of oil and has mined, processed, and sold it around the world. **(b)** Chile's and Venezuela's economic histories have been similar in that they each have had particular products they can sell worldwide—in Chile, their copper and produce,

◆ Comprehension and Critical Thinking

15. (a) Describe What are the characteristics of a rain forest?
(b) Apply Information Why is the Amazon rain forest important even to countries far from Brazil?

16. (a) Identify Where do most of Brazil's people live?
(b) Identify Causes Why did the Brazilian government want people to move to the interior of the country?
(c) Analyze Why do you think Brazil's population is distributed the way it is?

17. (a) Identify Describe the three geographical regions of Peru.
(b) Predict How do you think the coming of modern conveniences such as electricity will change life for the indigenous people of Peru? Explain.

18. (a) Summarize Describe Magellan's discovery of the strait that bears his name.
(b) Identify Effects How does Chile's geography contribute to both its pollution problem and its agricultural boom?
(c) Infer How might the fact that Chile is so long and narrow affect Chilean society?

19. (a) Describe How did Venezuela grow rich from oil?
(b) Compare and Contrast In what ways have Chile's and Venezuela's economic histories been similar? How have they been different?

◆ Skills Practice

Synthesizing Information In the Skills for Life activity in this chapter, you learned how to synthesize information from many sources. You also learned how to use what you found out to draw a conclusion about a particular topic.

Review the steps you followed to learn the skill. Then use those steps to synthesize information about Venezuela's economy from different sources within Section 4. Finally, draw a conclusion that pulls together what you learned.

◆ Writing Activity: Science

Suppose you are a science reporter for a local television station in Santiago, Chile. Santiago has been experiencing a week of very bad smog. Write a report explaining why the smog is so bad this week and suggesting how people might protect themselves from the pollution. Make sure your report can be read in two to three minutes.

Place Location For each place listed below, write the letter from the map that shows its location.
1. Peru
2. Brasília
3. Chile
4. Lake Titicaca
5. Tierra del Fuego
6. Venezuela
7. Rio de Janeiro

Go Online
PHSchool.com Use Web Code lfp-1301 for an **interactive map**.

and in Venezuela, their oil. Their economic histories have been different in that Chile has not gone through the tremendous economic downturn that Venezuela has.

Skills Practice
Students' answers will vary.

Possible conclusion Venezuela's economy has been negatively affected by relying heavily on one resource.

Writing Activity: Science
Students' answers will vary but should use the information provided in the section as well as information from other sources.

Use the Rubric for Assessing a Report to evaluate students' reports.

All in One **Latin America Teaching Resources,** *Rubric for Assessing a Report,* p. 352

Standardized Test Prep

MAP★MASTER
Skills Activity

1. C   2. B
3. F   4. E
5. A   6. D
7. G

Test-Taking Tips

Some questions on standardized tests ask you to analyze a reading selection to find the main ideas. Read the passage below. Then follow the tips to answer the sample question.

> Brazil is a major world coffee <u>grower</u>. Brazil's farms and plantations also <u>grow</u> soybeans, wheat, rice, corn, sugar cane, cacao, oranges, and lemons. The country's factories <u>make</u> many goods. Cars, iron, steel, shoes, textiles, and electrical equipment are all important industries.

This paragraph concerns which basic economic question?

A What goods does Brazil produce?

B What services does Brazil produce?

C How are goods and services produced in Brazil?

D Who will buy these goods and services?

TIP Read the whole passage to understand the main idea. Notice that it lists two kinds of goods from Brazil, those that grow and those made in factories.

Think It Through Notice that three of the answers contain the word *produce* or *produced*. You know that the main idea of the paragraph is that Brazil produces two kinds of goods—crops grown on farms and goods made in factories. The passage does not describe how the goods are produced (answer C) or who buys them (answer D). There is nothing in the paragraph about services (answer B). Therefore the answer is A.

TIP Look for key words in the passage and in the answer choices to help you answer the question. *Grow* and *make* both mean "produce."

Practice Questions

Choose the letter of the best answer.

1. Chilean produce has a large market in the United States from October through May because

   A Americans eat more produce over the winter.

   B less produce is grown in the United States during the winter than in the summer.

   C Chileans do not consume as much of their own produce during those months.

   D it is easiest to transport goods during those months.

2. What caused Venezuela's oil industry to decline in the mid-1980s?

   A The oil fields began to dry up.

   B People weren't driving cars as much.

   C The country began to focus on steel production.

   D World oil prices fell.

Read the passage below and answer the question that follows.

Peru has three distinct geographic regions: the cold, mountainous sierra; the dry coastal plain; and the warm, forested selva. The ways people live in these regions are very different. For example, many people on the coastal plain live in cities, while most people in the sierra live in small villages.

3. Which statement best expresses the main idea of the passage?

   A Peru's geography is varied.

   B Peru's sierra is mountainous and cold.

   C Peru's geography affects the lives of its people.

   D There are no cities in Peru's sierra region.

Go Online
PHSchool.com
Use Web Code lfa-1601
for a **Chapter 6 self-test.**

Chapter 6 **197**

Go Online
PHSchool.com Students may practice their map skills using the interactive online version of this map.

Standardized Test Prep

Answers

1. B

2. D

3. C

Go Online
PHSchool.com Students may use the Chapter 6 self-test on PHSchool.com to prepare for the Chapter Test.

Assessment Resources

Teaching Resources
Chapter Tests A and B, pp. 353–358
Final Exams A and B, pp. 363–368

Test Prep Workbook
Latin America Study Sheet, pp. 180–185
Latin America Practice Tests A, B, C, pp. 61–72

AYP Monitoring Assessments
Latin America Benchmark Test, pp. 101–104
Latin America Outcome Test, pp. 182–187

Technology
⊙ *ExamView Test Bank CD-ROM*

- Students can further explore the Guiding Questions by completing hands-on projects.

- Three pages of structured guidance in **All-in-One Latin America Teaching Resources** support each of the projects described on this page.

  All in One **Latin America Teaching Resources,** *Book Project: Latin America in the News,* pp. 76–78; *Book Project: A Latin American Concert,* pp. 79–81

- There are also two additional projects introduced, explained, and supported in the **All-in-One Latin America Teaching Resources.**

  All in One **Latin America Teaching Resources,** *Book Project: Visions of Latin America,* pp. 73–75; *Book Project: Explorer's Dictionary,* pp. 82–84

- Go over the four project suggestions with students.

- Ask each student to select one of the projects, or design his or her own. Work with students to create a project description and a schedule.

- Post project schedules and monitor student progress by asking for progress reports.

- Assess student projects using rubrics from the **All-in-One Latin America Teaching Resources.**

  All in One **Latin America Teaching Resources,** *Rubric for Assessing Student Performance on a Project,* p. 85; *Rubric for Assessing the Performance of an Entire Group,* p. 86; *Rubric for Assessing Individual Performance in a Group,* p. 87

Portfolio Activity Tell students they can add their completed Book Project as the final item in their portfolios. Assess student portfolios with *Rubric for Assessing a Student Portfolio.*

All in One **Latin America Teaching Resources,** *Rubric for Assessing a Student Portfolio,* p. 88

Projects

Create your own projects to learn more about Latin America. At the beginning of this book, you were introduced to the **Guiding Questions** for studying the chapters and special features. But you can also find answers to these questions by doing projects on your own or with a group. Use the questions to find topics you want to explore further. Then try the projects described on this page or create your own.

1 **Geography** What are the main physical features of Latin America?

2 **History** How has Latin America been shaped by its history?

3 **Culture** What factors have affected cultures in Latin America?

4 **Government** What types of government have existed in Latin America?

5 **Economics** How has geography influenced the ways in which Latin Americans make a living?

Project

CREATE A CLASS BULLETIN BOARD

Latin America in the News
As you read about Latin America, keep a class bulletin board display called Latin America in the News. Look in magazines and newspapers for articles about Latin American culture and current events. Print out articles from reliable online news sources. Choose a time, such as once a week, for the class to review and discuss the articles. You might have several students present the information to the class as a radio or television news report.

Project

RESEARCH LATIN AMERICAN MUSIC

A Latin American Concert
As you study Latin America, find out about the music of each region. Research the kinds of instruments people play and what they are made of. Learn how history and geography influenced the development of different kinds of music. Did you know, for example, that people in the Andes make a kind of rattle out of the hooves of llamas? That reggae developed as political protest? Find some examples of recorded Latin American music in the library, play them for your class, and report on what you learned about the music.

Reference

Table of Contents

Atlas 200
The World: Political 200
The World: Physical 202
North and South America: Political 204
North and South America: Physical 205
United States: Political 206
Europe: Political 208
Europe: Physical 209
Africa: Political 210
Africa: Physical 211
Asia: Political 212
Asia: Physical 213
Oceania 214
The Arctic 215
Antarctica 215

Glossary of Geographic Terms 216

Gazetteer 218

Glossary 220

Index 224
                                                232
Acknowledgments 233

The World: Political

0 miles _____ 2,000

0 kilometers _____ 2,000

Robinson

20° W | 0° | 20° E | 40° E | 60° E | 80° E | 100° E | 120° E | 140° E

SVALBARD
(Norway)

80° N

ICELAND

EUROPE AND SOUTHWEST ASIA
For detail, see maps Europe: Political
and Asia: Political.

RUSSIA

ASIA

Moscow ⊕

EUROPE

KAZAKHSTAN
Astana ⊕
UZBEKISTAN
Tashkent ⊕
Bishkek ⊕
KYRGYZSTAN
Dushanbe
TAJIKISTAN

Ulaanbaatar ⊕
MONGOLIA

NORTH
KOREA

Arctic Circle

Beijing ⊕
P'yŏngyang ⊕
JAPAN
Seoul ⊕
SOUTH
KOREA
Tokyo ⊕

40° N

Algiers Tunis
MADEIRA Rabat ⊕
(Portugal)
CANARY
ISLANDS
(Spain)
WESTERN
SAHARA
(Morocco)

TUNISIA
MOROCCO
Tripoli

TURKMENISTAN
Ashgabat ⊕
Tehran ⊕
IRAN
Kabul ⊕
AFGHANISTAN

Islamabad ⊕

CHINA
Thimphu ⊕
NEPAL
BHUTAN
Kathmandu ⊕

Taipei
TAIWAN

PACIFIC
OCEAN

Tropic of Cancer

ALGERIA
LIBYA
EGYPT
Cairo ⊕

AFRICA
WEST AFRICA
For detail, see map
Africa: Political.

Riyadh ⊕
SAUDI
ARABIA

Kuwait ⊕
KUWAIT
Manama BAHRAIN
Doha QATAR
Abu Dhabi U.A.E.
Muscat

PAKISTAN
New Delhi ⊕
BANGLADESH
INDIA
Dhaka ⊕

OMAN

MYANMAR
LAOS Hanoi ⊕
Yangon ⊕ Vientiane ⊕ VIETNAM
THAILAND CAMBODIA
Bangkok ⊕ Phnom Penh ⊕

PHILIPPINES
Manila ⊕

NORTHERN
MARIANA
ISLANDS
(U.S.)

20° N

NIGER
CHAD Khartoum ⊕
N'Djamena ⊕ SUDAN
NIGERIA Abuja ⊕
Asmara ⊕
ERITREA YEMEN
Sanaa ⊕
DJIBOUTI

SOCOTRA
(Yemen)

ANDAMAN
& NICOBAR
ISLANDS
(India)

Colombo
SRI LANKA

GUAM
(U.S.)

PALAU
Koror ⊕

Palikir ⊕

CENTRAL
CAMEROON AFRICAN
Yaoundé ⊕ REPUBLIC
Bangui ⊕
EQUATORIAL GUINEA
Malabo ⊕
São Tomé ⊕
SÃO TOMÉ & PRÍNCIPE
GABON
Libreville ⊕
CONGO
Brazzaville ⊕

Addis Ababa ⊕
Djibouti ⊕
ETHIOPIA
UGANDA
DEMOCRATIC
REPUBLIC
OF THE
CONGO
Kampala ⊕
Kigali ⊕
KENYA
RWANDA
Nairobi ⊕
Bujumbura ⊕ BURUNDI

SOMALIA

Mogadishu ⊕

Male ⊕
MALDIVES

Kuala Lumpur ⊕
Singapore ⊕

BRUNEI
Bandar Seri Begawan ⊕
MALAYSIA
SINGAPORE

FEDERATED STATES
OF MICRONESIA

Equator

0°

INDONESIA

PAPUA
NEW
GUINEA

CABINDA
(Angola)
Luanda ⊕
ANGOLA
Lusaka ⊕
NAMIBIA
Windhoek ⊕
Gaborone ⊕

Kinshasa ⊕
TANZANIA
Dodoma ⊕
Dar es Salaam ⊕
Lilongwe ⊕
MALAWI
COMOROS
Moroni ⊕
ZAMBIA
Harare ⊕
ZIMBABWE
BOTSWANA
Maputo ⊕

Victoria ⊕
SEYCHELLES

MADAGASCAR
Antananarivo ⊕
MAURITIUS
Port Louis ⊕
RÉUNION
(France)

Jakarta ⊕

Dili ⊕
EAST TIMOR

Port Moresby ⊕

AUSTRALIA

MOZAMBIQUE

20° S

ATLANTIC
OCEAN

Pretoria ⊕
Bloemfontein ⊕ Mbabane ⊕
SWAZILAND
Maseru ⊕
SOUTH LESOTHO
AFRICA
Cape Town ⊕

INDIAN
OCEAN

Tropic of Capricorn

AUSTRALIA

Canberra ⊕

40° S

60° S

SOUTHERN OCEAN

Antarctic Circle

ANTARCTICA

80° S

20° W | 0° | 20° E | 40° E | 60° E | 80° E | 100° E | 120° E | 140° E

KEY

——— National border

- - - Disputed border

⊛ National capital

The World: Physical

ARCTIC OCEAN
80° N
Beaufort Sea
Greenland
Baffin Island
Yukon R.
Bering Sea
Mackenzie R.
Hudson Bay
Labrador Sea
Aleutian Islands
ROCKY MOUNTAINS
NORTH AMERICA
CANADIAN SHIELD
Great Lakes
St. Lawrence R.
40° N
GREAT PLAINS
Missouri R.
APPALACHIAN MTS.
Mississippi R.
ATLANTIC OCEAN
Colorado R.
Tropic of Cancer
Rio Grande
Gulf of Mexico
20° N
Hawaiian Islands
West Indies
Caribbean Sea
MICRONESIA
Orinoco R.
GUIANA HIGHLANDS
Equator
0°
Galápagos Islands
Amazon R.
AMAZON BASIN
SOUTH AMERICA
N
W E
S
PACIFIC OCEAN
ANDES
BRAZILIAN HIGHLANDS
MELANESIA
POLYNESIA
20° S
Tropic of Capricorn
Tasman Sea
North Island
40° S
PAMPAS
Rio de La Plata
South Island
PATAGONIA
Cape Horn
60° S
SOUTHERN OCEAN
Drake Passage
ANTARCTIC PENINSULA
Antarctic Circle
Ross Sea
Weddell Sea
80° S
ANTARCTICA
180° 160° W 140° W 120° W 100° W 80° W 60° W 40° W 20° W

0 miles   2,000
0 kilometers   2,000
Robinson

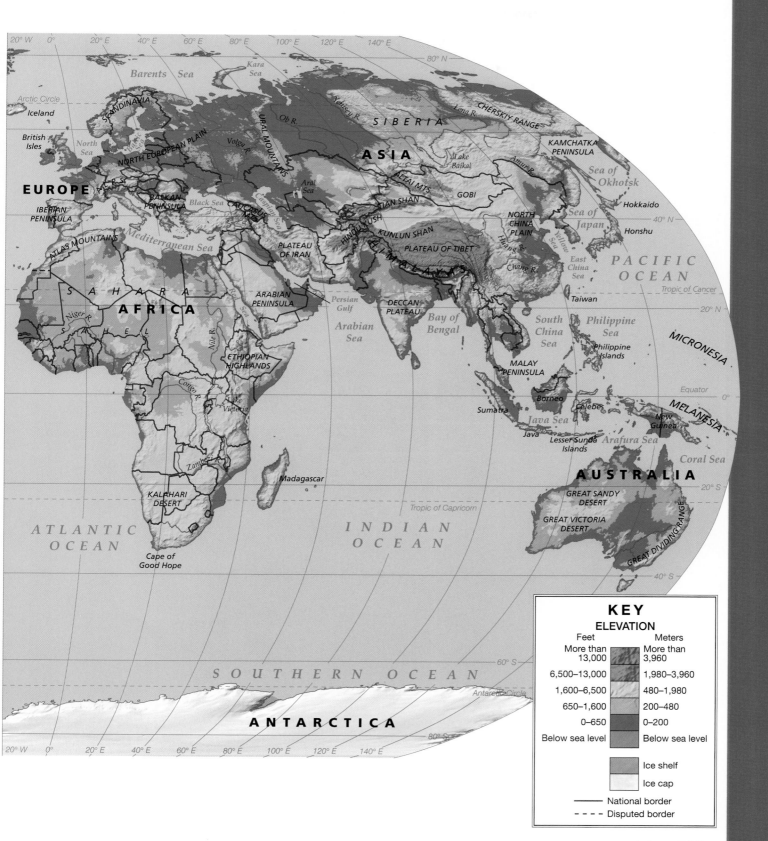

North and South America: Political

ASIA

ARCTIC OCEAN

180°
160° W
140° W
120° W
80° W
0°

Bering Strait

Beaufort Sea

Bering Sea

GREENLAND (Denmark)

40° W

ALASKA (U.S.)

Baffin Bay

EUROPE

60° N

Great Bear Lake

Great Slave Lake

Labrador Sea

Hudson Bay

C A N A D A

40° N

Lake Winnipeg

Great Lakes

Ottawa

ATLANTIC OCEAN

40°

New York City

U N I T E D
S T A T E S

Ohio R.

Washington, D.C.

Mississippi

Los Angeles

VIRGIN ISLANDS (U.S.)

Tropic of Cancer

Río Grande

DOMINICAN REPUBLIC

ST. KITTS & NEVIS

ANTIGUA & BARBUDA

20° N

Gulf of Mexico

BAHAMAS

PUERTO RICO (U.S.)

GUADELOUPE (France)

Tropic of Cancer

20° N

MEXICO

Havana   Nassau

DOMINICA

MARTINIQUE (France)

CUBA

HAITI

ST. LUCIA

PACIFIC OCEAN

Mexico City

Belmopan

JAMAICA

Santo Domingo

BARBADOS

BELIZE

Kingston

ST. VINCENT &
THE GRENADINES

GUATEMALA

HONDURAS

Port-au-Prince

Caribbean Sea

GRENADA

Guatemala

Tegucigalpa

San Salvador

NICARAGUA

TRINIDAD & TOBAGO

EL SALVADOR

Managua

Caracas Georgetown

San José

Panama

VENEZUELA

Paramaribo

COSTA RICA

Bogotá

GUYANA

Cayenne

PANAMA

COLOMBIA

SURINAME

FRENCH GUIANA (France)

0°

Equator

GALÁPAGOS
ISLANDS
(Ecuador)

Quito

Amazon R.

Equator

ECUADOR

PERU

BRAZIL

São Francisco R.

N

W   E

S

Lima

Brasília

La Paz

Lake Titicaca

BOLIVIA

20° S

Sucre

Paraná R.

Rio de Janeiro

Tropic of Capricorn

Tropic of Capricorn

PARAGUAY

São Paulo

CHILE

Asunción

KEY

——— National border

⊛ National capital

• Other city

URUGUAY

Santiago

Buenos Aires

Montevideo

ARGENTINA

Río de la Plata

40° S

0 miles   2,000

0 kilometers   2,000

Lambert Azimuthal Equal Area

ATLANTIC OCEAN

FALKLAND ISLANDS (U.K.)

Tierra del Fuego

Cape Horn

160° W   140° W   120° W   100° W   80° W   60° W   40° W   20° W   0°

North and South America: Physical

KEY

ELEVATION

Feet	Meters
More than 13,000	More than 3,960
6,500–13,000	1,980–3,960
1,600–6,500	480–1,980
650–1,600	200–480
0–650	0–200

Ice cap

National border

0 miles 2,000

0 kilometers 2,000

Lambert Azimuthal Equal Area

ASIA

ARCTIC OCEAN

EUROPE

Bering Strait

Beaufort Sea

Greenland

Bering Sea

Mt. McKinley 20,320 ft (6,194 m)

Baffin Bay

Aleutian Islands

Alaska Range

Gulf of Alaska

Mackenzie R.

Great Bear Lake

Great Slave Lake

Baffin Island

Davis Strait

Labrador Sea

Hudson Bay

CANADIAN SHIELD

Newfoundland

ROCKY MOUNTAINS

GREAT PLAINS

Lake Winnipeg

Great Lakes

Missouri R.

Mississippi R.

Ohio R.

Appalachian Mts.

ATLANTIC OCEAN

Tropic of Cancer

Colorado R.

Rio Grande

Tropic of Cancer

Baja California

Sierra Madre Occidental

Sierra Madre Oriental

Gulf of Mexico

Gulf of California

Yucatán Peninsula

Cuba

Hispaniola

Lesser Antilles

PACIFIC OCEAN

Greater Antilles

Caribbean Sea

Isthmus of Panama

Orinoco R.

Guiana Highlands

Galápagos Islands

Equator

Equator

AMAZON BASIN

Amazon R.

São Francisco R.

ANDES

Brazilian Highlands

Lake Titicaca

N
W E
S

Gran Chaco

Paraguay R.

Paraná R.

Tropic of Capricorn

Tropic of Capricorn

ANDES

Aconcagua 22,834 ft (6,960 m)

Pampas

Río de la Plata

Patagonia

ATLANTIC OCEAN

Falkland Islands

Tierra del Fuego

Cape Horn

United States: Political

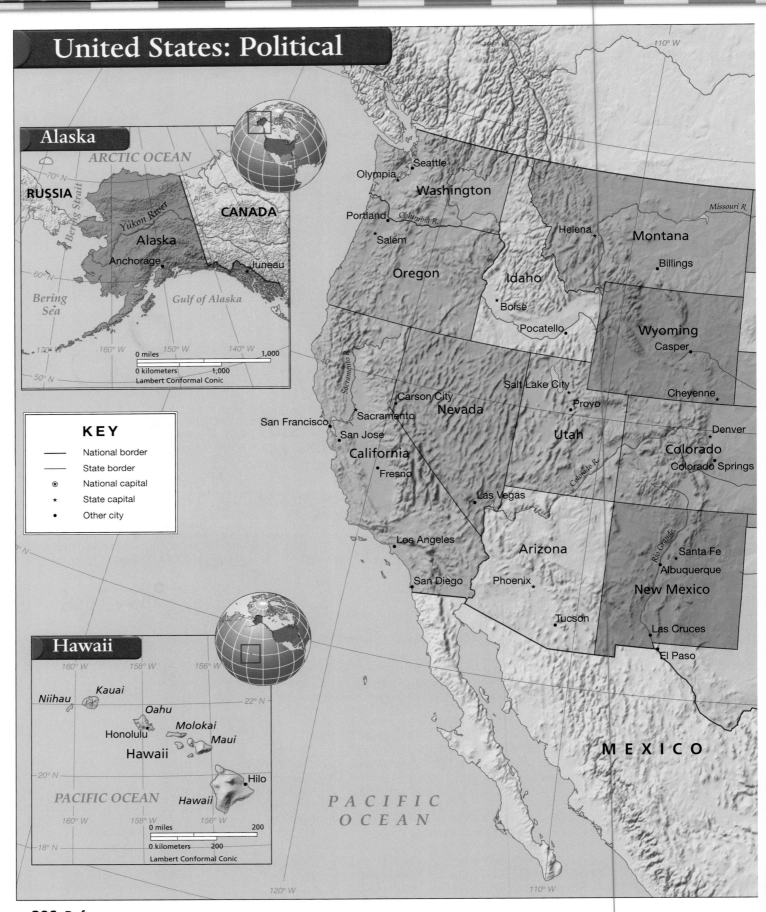

Alaska

ARCTIC OCEAN

RUSSIA

CANADA

Yukon River

Bering Strait

Arctic Circle

70° N

Alaska

Anchorage

Juneau

60° N

Bering Sea

Gulf of Alaska

170°

160° W

150° W

140° W

50° N

0 miles 1,000
0 kilometers 1,000

Lambert Conformal Conic

KEY

—— National border

—— State border

⊛ National capital

★ State capital

• Other city

Hawaii

160° W   158° W   156° W

Niihau

Kauai

Oahu

22° N

Honolulu

Molokai

Maui

Hawaii

20° N

PACIFIC OCEAN

Hawaii

Hilo

160° W   158° W   156° W

18° N

0 miles 200
0 kilometers 200

Lambert Conformal Conic

Seattle

Olympia

Washington

Portland

Columbia R.

Salem

Helena

Montana

Billings

Oregon

Idaho

Boise

Pocatello

Wyoming

Casper

Missouri R.

110° W

Sacramento R.

40° N

Carson City

Sacramento

Nevada

Salt Lake City

Provo

Cheyenne

San Francisco

San Jose

Utah

Denver

California

Fresno

Colorado R.

Colorado

Colorado Springs

Las Vegas

Los Angeles

Arizona

Rio Grande

Santa Fe

Albuquerque

San Diego

Phoenix

New Mexico

Tucson

Las Cruces

El Paso

MEXICO

PACIFIC OCEAN

120° W

110° W

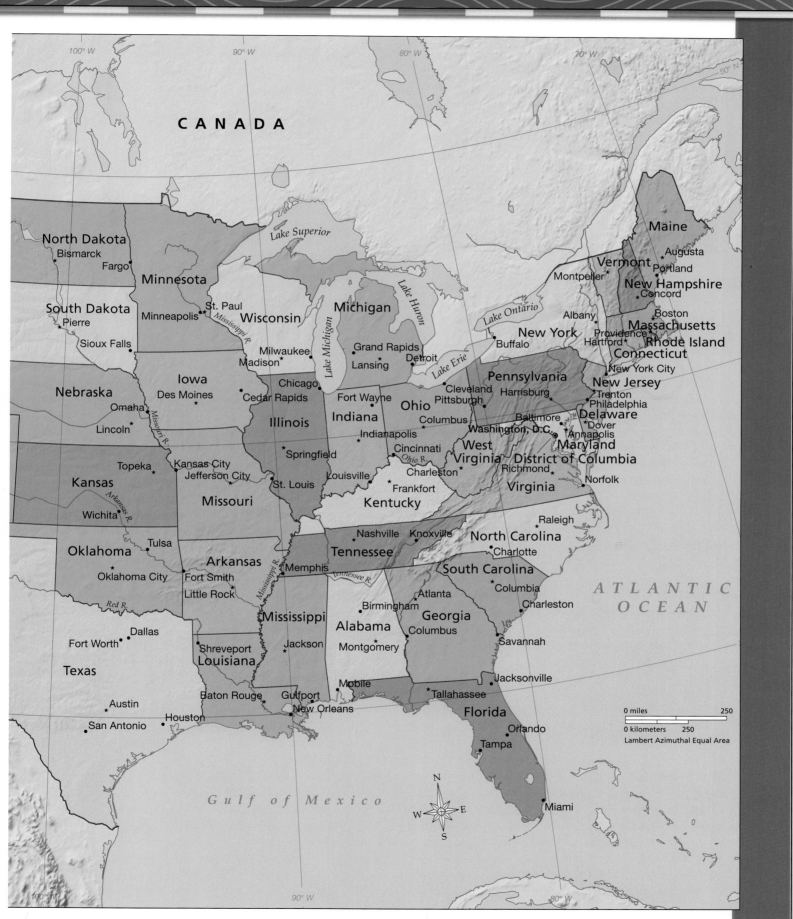

CANADA

North Dakota
  • Bismarck
    • Fargo

Minnesota

South Dakota
  • Pierre
    St. Paul ★
  Minneapolis •

  • Sioux Falls

Lake Superior

Wisconsin

Michigan

Lake Huron

Lake Michigan

  • Milwaukee
  Madison ★

  • Grand Rapids
    Lansing •
                • Detroit

Lake Ontario

Maine
  • Augusta
Vermont • Portland
Montpelier ★ New Hampshire
         ★ Concord

Albany •   • Boston
New York   Massachusetts
Providence •
Hartford ★ Rhode Island
            Connecticut

Nebraska
  • Omaha
  Lincoln ★

Iowa
Des Moines ★

  • Chicago

  Cedar Rapids •

Illinois

Fort Wayne •

Indiana

  Indianapolis ★

Ohio
  Columbus ★

  Cleveland •
Pittsburgh •

Pennsylvania
  Harrisburg ★

Buffalo •

New York City

New Jersey
  Trenton ★
    • Philadelphia
Delaware
  • Dover
Baltimore •
Washington, D.C. ★   ★ Annapolis
West   Maryland
Virginia   District of Columbia

Kansas
  Topeka ★
  Kansas City •
  Jefferson City ★
    • St. Louis

  Wichita •

  Springfield ★

Louisville •

Missouri

Cincinnati •
Ohio R.

Charleston ★

Frankfort ★

Kentucky

Richmond •

Virginia

Norfolk •

Oklahoma
  • Tulsa
  Oklahoma City ★

Arkansas
  Fort Smith •
  Little Rock •

Memphis •

Nashville • • Knoxville

Tennessee

Tennessee R.

North Carolina
    • Raleigh

  • Charlotte

South Carolina
  • Columbia

Texas

Fort Worth • • Dallas

  ★ Austin

  • San Antonio

Red R.

Shreveport •
Louisiana
  Baton Rouge •

Mississippi
  Jackson ★

Mississippi R.

  • Birmingham
Alabama
  Montgomery ★

• Mobile

Georgia
  • Atlanta
  Columbus •

  • Savannah

  Charleston •

ATLANTIC
OCEAN

Jacksonville •

Gulfport •
  New Orleans •

  ★ Tallahassee

Florida
    • Orlando

  • Tampa

Houston •

Gulf of Mexico

• Miami

N
W E
S

0 miles   250
0 kilometers   250
Lambert Azimuthal Equal Area

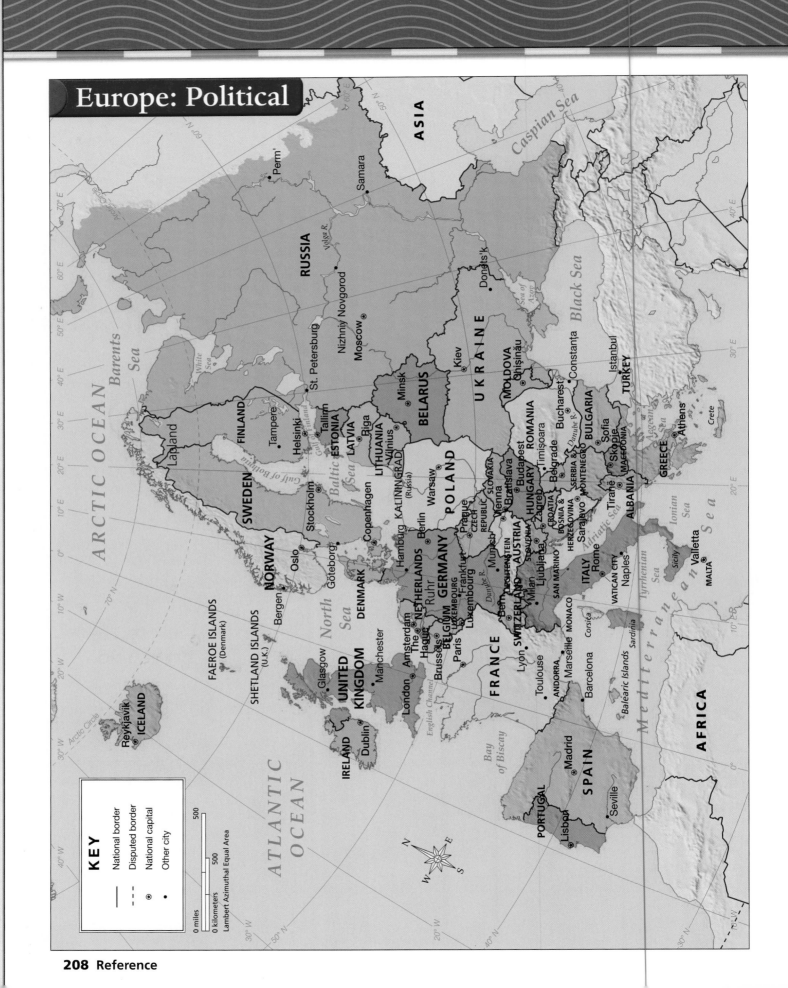

Europe: Political

KEY

——	National border
- - -	Disputed border
⊛	National capital
•	Other city

0 miles 500

0 kilometers 500

Lambert Azimuthal Equal Area

ASIA

RUSSIA

Caspian Sea

Perm'

Samara

Volga R.

Nizhniy Novgorod

Moscow ⊛

St. Petersburg

Donets'k

Sea of Azov

Black Sea

Barents Sea

White Sea

ARCTIC OCEAN

Arctic Ocean

FINLAND

Tampere

Helsinki ⊛

Gulf of Finland

Tallinn

ESTONIA

Riga ⊛

LATVIA

Minsk ⊛

BELARUS

Kiev ⊛

UKRAINE

MOLDOVA

Chişinău ⊛

Constanţa

Istanbul

TURKEY

Lapland

SWEDEN

Gulf of Bothnia

Stockholm ⊛

Baltic Sea

LITHUANIA

Vilnius ⊛

KALININGRAD (Russia)

Warsaw ⊛

POLAND

Bucharest ⊛

ROMANIA

Timişoara

Danube R.

BULGARIA

Sofia ⊛

Skopje ⊛

MACEDONIA

Tiranë ⊛

ALBANIA

Aegean Sea

GREECE

Athens ⊛

Crete

NORWAY

Oslo ⊛

Bergen

Göteborg

Copenhagen ⊛

DENMARK

Hamburg

Berlin ⊛

GERMANY

Prague ⊛

CZECH REPUBLIC

SLOVAKIA

Bratislava ⊛

Vienna ⊛

AUSTRIA

Budapest ⊛

HUNGARY

Zagreb ⊛

CROATIA

SLOVENIA

Ljubljana ⊛

Belgrade ⊛

SERBIA & MONTENEGRO

BOSNIA & HERZEGOVINA

Sarajevo ⊛

Adriatic Sea

Ionian Sea

FAEROE ISLANDS (Denmark)

SHETLAND ISLANDS (U.K.)

ICELAND

Reykjavík ⊛

Arctic Circle

North Sea

NETHERLANDS

Amsterdam ⊛

The Hague ⊛

Brussels ⊛

BELGIUM

LUXEMBOURG

Luxembourg ⊛

Ruhr

Frankfurt

Munich

LIECHTENSTEIN

SWITZERLAND

Bern ⊛

Milan

Ljubljana

SAN MARINO

ITALY

Rome ⊛

VATICAN CITY

Naples

MONACO

Corsica

Sardinia

Tyrrhenian Sea

Sicily

Valletta ⊛

MALTA

Mediterranean Sea

UNITED KINGDOM

Glasgow

Manchester

London ⊛

IRELAND

Dublin ⊛

English Channel

Bay of Biscay

FRANCE

Paris ⊛

Lyon

Toulouse

Marseille

ANDORRA

Barcelona

Balearic Islands

SPAIN

Madrid ⊛

Seville

PORTUGAL

Lisbon ⊛

ATLANTIC OCEAN

AFRICA

N E S W

208

Europe: Physical

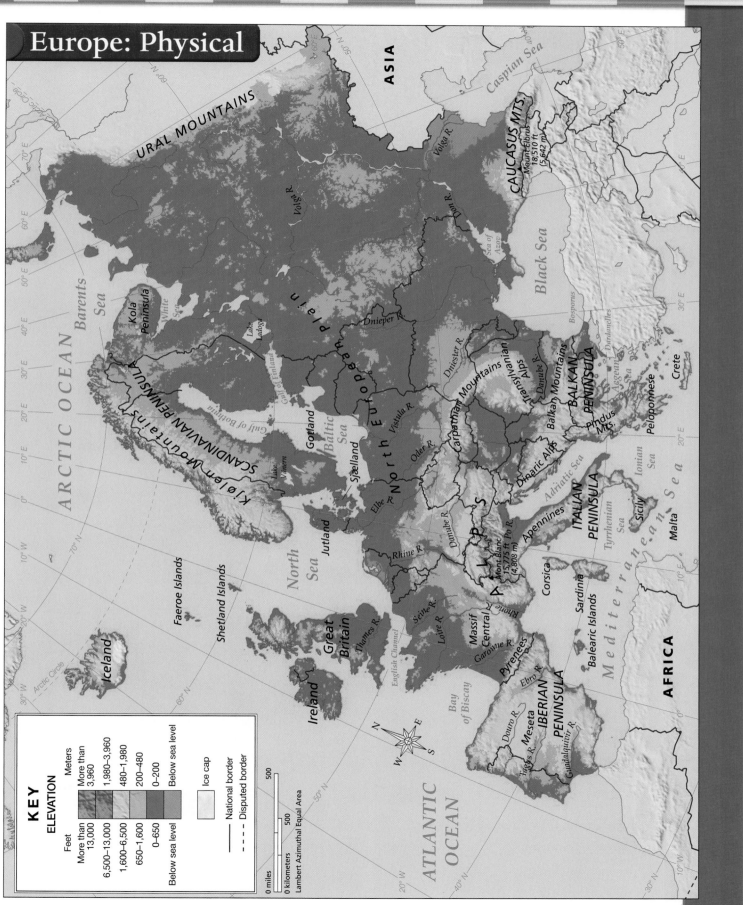

ASIA

URAL MOUNTAINS

Caspian Sea

CAUCASUS MTS.

Mount Elbrus
18,510 ft
(5,642 m)

Volga R.

Volga R.

Don R.

Sea of
Azov

Black Sea

ARCTIC OCEAN

Barents Sea

Kola Peninsula

White Sea

Lake Ladoga

North European Plain

Dnieper R.

Dniester R.

Bosporus

Dardanelles

SCANDINAVIAN PENINSULA

Kjölen Mountains

Gulf of Bothnia

Gulf of Finland

Baltic Sea

Gotland

Vistula R.

Carpathian Mountains

Transylvanian Alps

Danube R.

Balkan Mountains

BALKAN PENINSULA

Pindus Mts.

Aegean Sea

Crete

Lake Vänern

Sjælland

Oder R.

Dinaric Alps

Adriatic Sea

Peloponnese

Ionian Sea

North Sea

Jutland

Elbe R.

Danube R.

A L P S

Apennines

ITALIAN PENINSULA

Tyrrhenian Sea

Sicily

Malta

Mediterranean Sea

Rhine R.

Mont Blanc
15,775 ft (Po R.
4,808 m)

Corsica

Sardinia

Balearic Islands

Faeroe Islands

Shetland Islands

Great Britain

Thames R.

Seine R.

Loire R.

Massif Central

Garonne R.

English Channel

Rhône R.

Iceland

Arctic Circle

Ireland

Bay of Biscay

Pyrenees

Ebro R.

IBERIAN PENINSULA

Douro R.

Meseta

Tagus R.

Guadalquivir R.

ATLANTIC OCEAN

AFRICA

N
E
S
W

KEY

ELEVATION

Feet	Meters
More than 13,000	More than 3,960
6,500–13,000	1,980–3,960
1,600–6,500	480–1,980
650–1,600	200–480
0–650	0–200
Below sea level	Below sea level

Ice cap

—— National border
- - - Disputed border

0 miles 500
0 kilometers 500

Lambert Azimuthal Equal Area

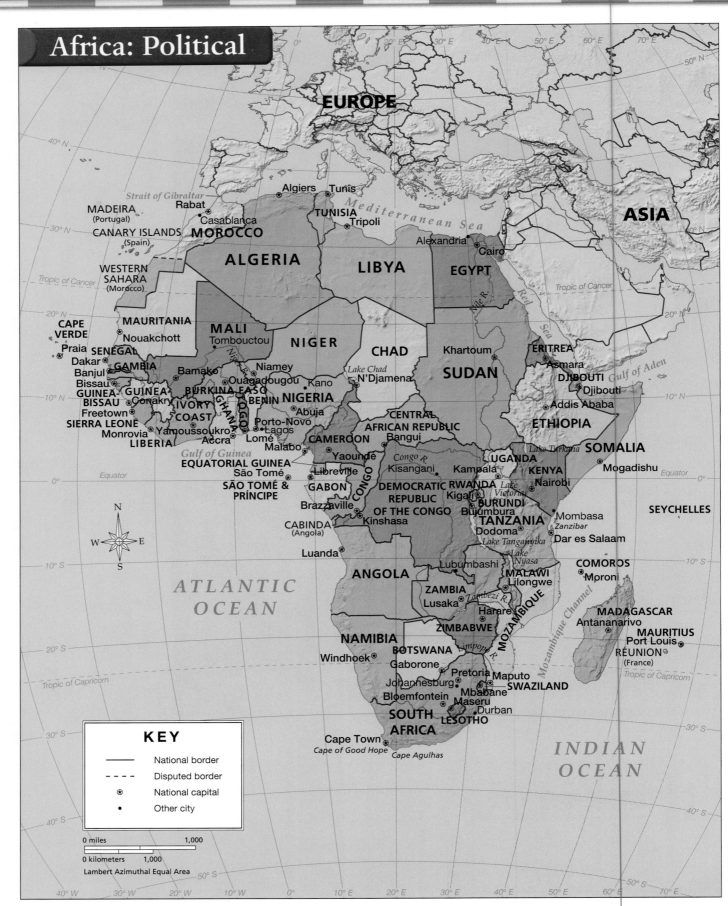

Africa: Political

EUROPE

ASIA

Strait of Gibraltar

MADEIRA
(Portugal)

CANARY ISLANDS
(Spain)

Rabat ⊛
Casablanca •
MOROCCO

Algiers ⊛   Tunis ⊛
TUNISIA • Tripoli
Mediterranean Sea

Alexandria •
⊛ Cairo
EGYPT

WESTERN
SAHARA
(Morocco)
Tropic of Cancer

ALGERIA

LIBYA

Nile R.

Red Sea

Tropic of Cancer

20° N

CAPE
VERDE
⊛ Praia

MAURITANIA
⊛ Nouakchott

MALI
Tombouctou •

NIGER

CHAD

Khartoum ⊛

ERITREA
⊛ Asmara

DJIBOUTI *Gulf of Aden*
• Djibouti

SENEGAL
Dakar ⊛
Banjul ⊛ GAMBIA
Bissau •
GUINEA- GUINEA
BISSAU ⊛ Conakry
Freetown •
SIERRA LEONE
Monrovia •
LIBERIA

Niger R.
Bamako ⊛
Niamey ⊛
Ouagadougou ⊛   Kano •
BURKINA FASO
IVORY GHANA
COAST TOGO BENIN NIGERIA
Yamoussoukro ⊛ Porto-Novo
Accra Lomé • Lagos
Abuja •

N'Djamena •

SUDAN

CENTRAL
AFRICAN REPUBLIC
Bangui •

ETHIOPIA
⊛ Addis Ababa

SOMALIA

Malabo •
CAMEROON

Gulf of Guinea
EQUATORIAL GUINEA
São Tomé •
SÃO TOMÉ &
PRÍNCIPE

GABON
Libreville ⊛
Yaoundé ⊛

Congo R.
Kisangani •

UGANDA
Kampala ⊛

Lake Turkana

KENYA
Nairobi ⊛

Mogadishu •

Equator

DEMOCRATIC
REPUBLIC
OF THE CONGO

RWANDA
⊛ Kigali
BURUNDI
Bujumbura ⊛

Lake Victoria

SEYCHELLES

Brazzaville ⊛
CONGO
CABINDA
(Angola)
Kinshasa

TANZANIA
Dodoma ⊛
Lake Tanganyika

Mombasa •
Zanzibar
Dar es Salaam •

Luanda ⊛

ANGOLA

Lubumbashi •

Lake Nyasa

MALAWI
Lilongwe ⊛

COMOROS
• Moroni

ATLANTIC
OCEAN

ZAMBIA
Lusaka ⊛

Zambezi R.

MOZAMBIQUE

MADAGASCAR
Antananarivo ⊛

MAURITIUS
Port Louis ⊛

NAMIBIA
Windhoek ⊛

BOTSWANA
Gaborone ⊛

Harare ⊛
ZIMBABWE
Limpopo R.

Mozambique Channel

RÉUNION
(France)

Tropic of Capricorn

Johannesburg •
Bloemfontein •

Pretoria ⊛ Maputo ⊛
SWAZILAND
Mbabane ⊛
Maseru ⊛ • Durban
LESOTHO

KEY

— National border

- - - Disputed border

⊛ National capital

• Other city

SOUTH
AFRICA

Cape Town •
Cape of Good Hope Cape Agulhas

INDIAN
OCEAN

0 miles   1,000

0 kilometers   1,000

Lambert Azimuthal Equal Area

Africa: Physical

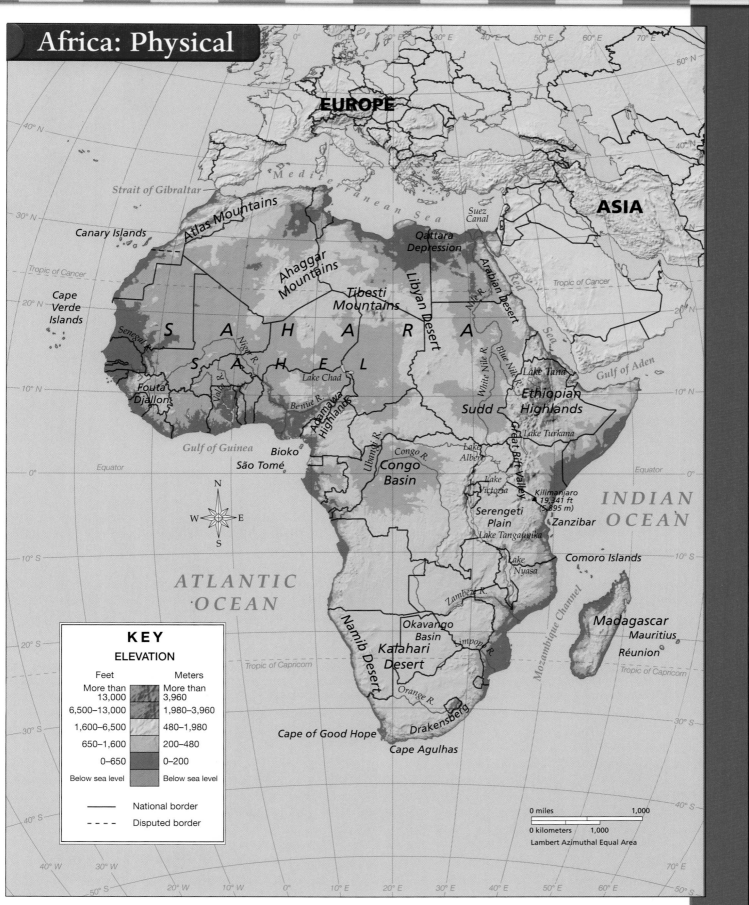

EUROPE

ASIA

Strait of Gibraltar

Canary Islands

Cape Verde Islands

Atlas Mountains

Tropic of Cancer

Mediterranean Sea

Suez Canal

Qattara Depression

Ahaggar Mountains

Tibesti Mountains

Libyan Desert

Arabian Desert

Nile R.

Tropic of Cancer

S A H A R A

S A H E L

Senegal R.

Niger R.

Fouta Djallon

Volta R.

Lake Chad

Benue R.

Adamawa Highlands

White Nile R.

Blue Nile R.

Lake Tana

Gulf of Aden

Ethiopian Highlands

Sudd

Red Sea

Gulf of Guinea

Bioko

São Tomé

Ubangi R.

Congo R.

Congo Basin

Lake Albert

Great Rift Valley

Lake Turkana

Equator

Equator

N

W   E

S

Lake Victoria

Kilimanjaro
19,341 ft
(5,895 m)

INDIAN OCEAN

Serengeti Plain

Zanzibar

Lake Tanganyika

ATLANTIC OCEAN

Lake Nyasa

Comoro Islands

Namib Desert

Okavango Basin

Zambezi R.

Mozambique Channel

Madagascar

Mauritius

Réunion

Kalahari Desert

Limpopo R.

Tropic of Capricorn

Tropic of Capricorn

Orange R.

Cape of Good Hope

Drakensberg

Cape Agulhas

KEY

ELEVATION

Feet		Meters
More than 13,000		More than 3,960
6,500–13,000		1,980–3,960
1,600–6,500		480–1,980
650–1,600		200–480
0–650		0–200
Below sea level		Below sea level

——— National border

– – – Disputed border

0 miles   1,000

0 kilometers   1,000

Lambert Azimuthal Equal Area

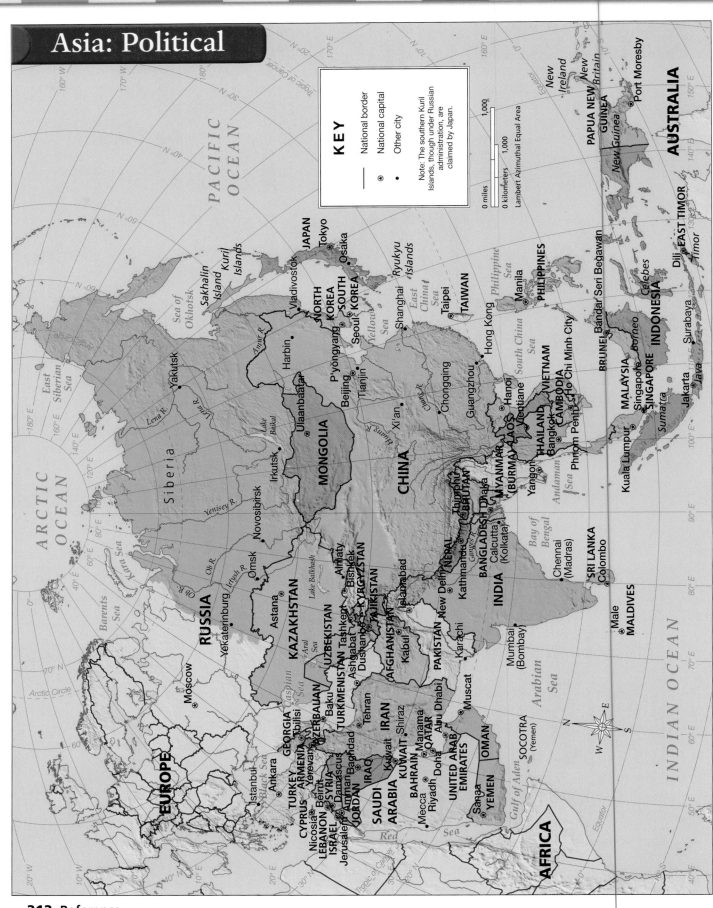

Asia: Political

KEY

— National border
⊛ National capital
• Other city

Note: The southern Kuril Islands, though under Russian administration, are claimed by Japan.

0 miles 1,000
0 kilometers 1,000

Lambert Azimuthal Equal Area

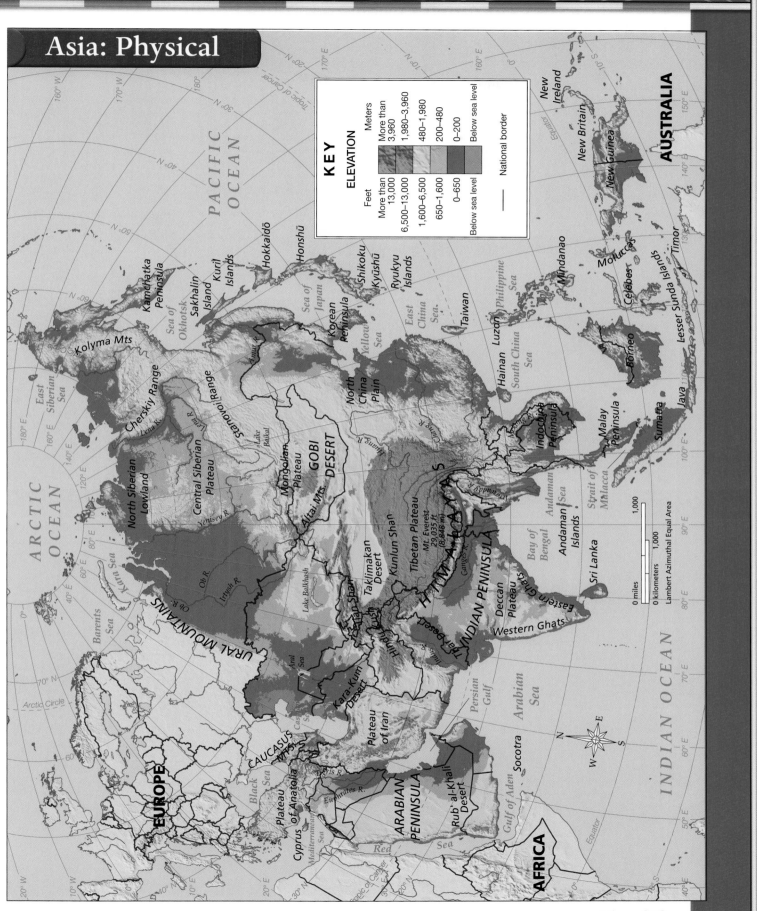

Asia: Physical

KEY

ELEVATION

Feet	Meters
More than 13,000	More than 3,960
6,500–13,000	1,980–3,960
1,600–6,500	480–1,980
650–1,600	200–480
0–650	0–200
Below sea level	Below sea level

National border

ARCTIC OCEAN

PACIFIC OCEAN

East Siberian Sea

Kara Sea

Barents Sea

Kolyma Mts

Kamchatka Peninsula

Sea of Okhotsk

Sakhalin Island

Kuril Islands

Hokkaidō

Honshū

Sea of Japan

Shikoku

Kyūshū

Ryukyu Islands

Korean Peninsula

Yellow Sea

East China Sea

Taiwan

Philippine Sea

Luzon

Mindanao

Moluccas

Celebes

New Ireland

New Britain

New Guinea

AUSTRALIA

South China Sea

Hainan

Borneo

Java

Sumatra

Malay Peninsula

Strait of Malacca

Lesser Sunda Islands

Timor

Cherskiy Range

Lena R.

Lena R.

Stanovoi Range

Amur R.

North Siberian Lowland

Central Siberian Plateau

Yenisey R.

Lake Baikal

Mongolian Plateau

GOBI DESERT

Altai Mts

North China Plain

Huang R.

Chang R.

Indochina Peninsula

Mekong R.

Andaman Islands

Andaman Sea

Ob R.

Irtysh R.

Ob R.

Lake Balkhash

Tian Shan

Taklimakan Desert

Kunlun Shan

Tibetan Plateau

Mt. Everest 29,035 ft (8,848 m)

HIMALAYAS

Ganges R.

INDIAN PENINSULA

Deccan Plateau

Eastern Ghats

Western Ghats

Sri Lanka

Bay of Bengal

Brahmaputra R.

Aral Sea

Kara-Kum Desert

Hindu Kush

Indus R.

URAL MOUNTAINS

EUROPE

Caspian Sea

CAUCASUS MTS.

Plateau of Anatolia

Cyprus

Mediterranean Sea

Black Sea

Plateau of Iran

Persian Gulf

Tigris R.

Euphrates R.

ARABIAN PENINSULA

Rub' al-Khali Desert

Gulf of Aden

Socotra

Arabian Sea

INDIAN OCEAN

Red Sea

AFRICA

Equator

Tropic of Cancer

Arctic Circle

Tropic of Cancer

0 miles 1,000

0 kilometers 1,000

Lambert Azimuthal Equal Area

N E S W

Oceania

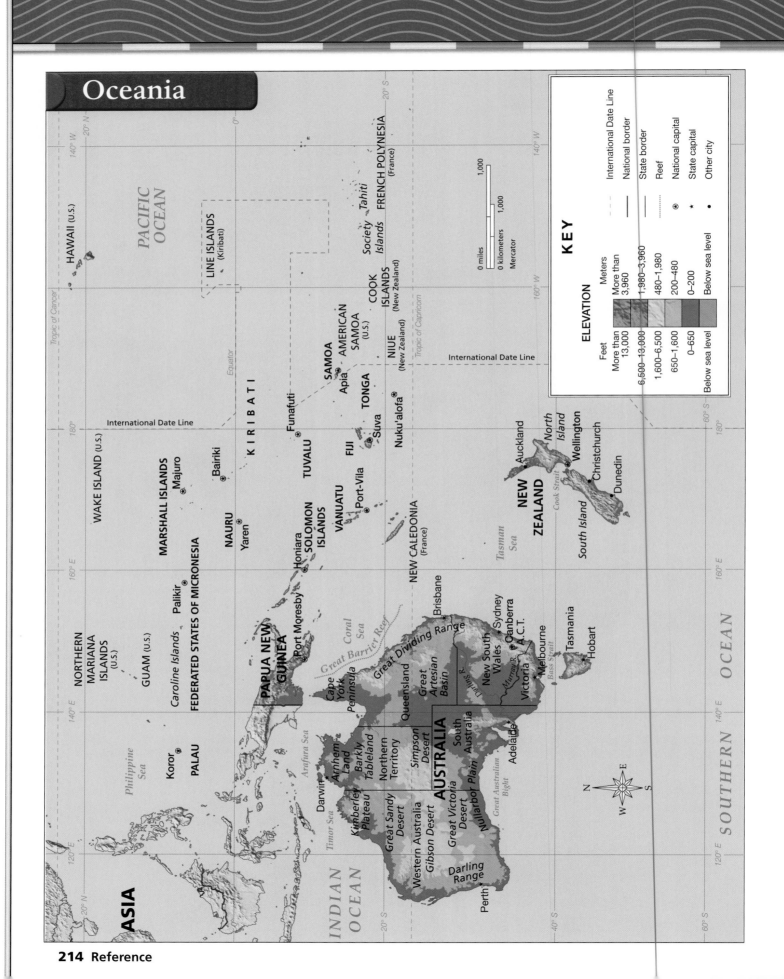

KEY

ELEVATION

Feet	Meters
More than 13,000	More than 3,960
6,500–13,000	1,980–3,960
1,600–6,500	480–1,980
650–1,600	200–480
0–650	0–200
Below sea level	Below sea level

- - - - - International Date Line
————— National border
——— State border
· · · · · · · Reef
⊛ National capital
★ State capital
• Other city

0 miles 1,000
0 kilometers 1,000
Mercator

PACIFIC OCEAN

HAWAII (U.S.)

LINE ISLANDS (Kiribati)

Tropic of Cancer

FRENCH POLYNESIA (France)

Society Islands   Tahiti

COOK ISLANDS (New Zealand)

SAMOA   AMERICAN SAMOA (U.S.)
Apia

NIUE (New Zealand)

TONGA
Nuku'alofa

Tropic of Capricorn

International Date Line

Equator

WAKE ISLAND (U.S.)

MARSHALL ISLANDS
Majuro

Bairiki

K I R I B A T I

Funafuti
TUVALU

FIJI
Suva

NAURU
Yaren

VANUATU
Port-Vila

NORTHERN MARIANA ISLANDS (U.S.)

GUAM (U.S.)

Caroline Islands   Palikir
FEDERATED STATES OF MICRONESIA

SOLOMON ISLANDS
Honiara

NEW CALEDONIA (France)

Auckland
North Island
Wellington
Christchurch
Dunedin
NEW ZEALAND
South Island
Cook Strait

Tasman Sea

Philippine Sea

Koror
PALAU

PAPUA NEW GUINEA
Port Moresby

Arafura Sea

Timor Sea

Great Coral Sea

Great Barrier Reef

Cape York Peninsula

Queensland

Great Dividing Range

Brisbane

Great Artesian Basin

New South Wales
Sydney
Canberra A.C.T.
Murray R.
Victoria
Melbourne

Bass Strait
Tasmania
Hobart

Darwin

Arnhem Land

Kimberley Plateau

Barkly Tableland

Northern Territory

Simpson Desert

AUSTRALIA

South Australia

Adelaide

Great Victoria Desert

Nullarbor Plain

Great Australian Bight

Western Australia

Great Sandy Desert

Gibson Desert

Darling Range

Perth

Darling R.

ASIA

INDIAN OCEAN

SOUTHERN OCEAN

N
W   E
S

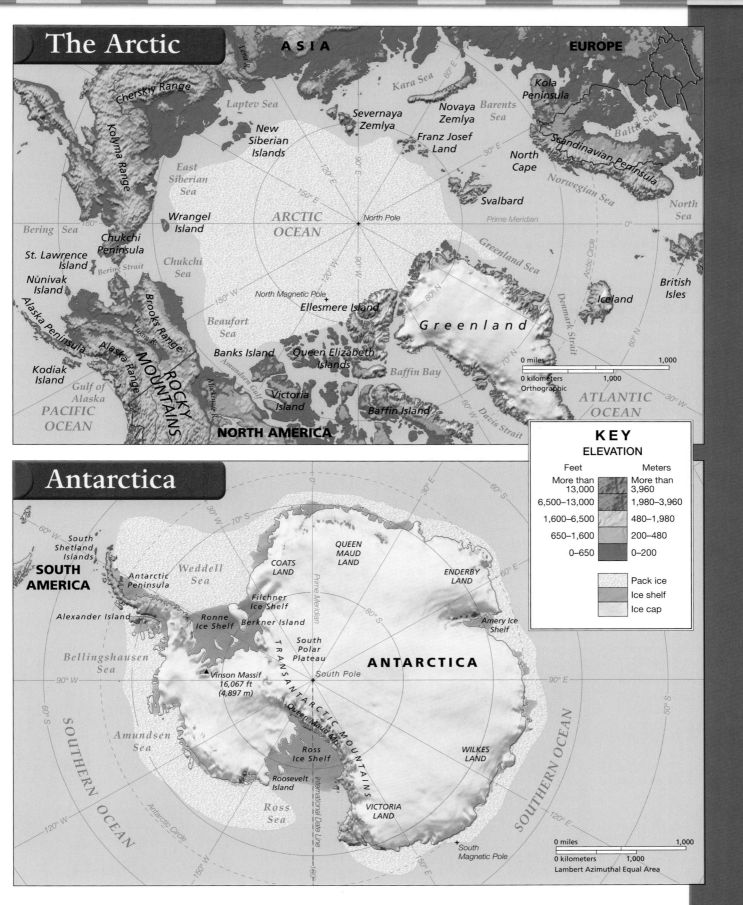

The Arctic

ASIA   EUROPE

Lena R.

Cherskiy Range

Kolyma Range

Laptev Sea

Kara Sea

Severnaya Zemlya

New Siberian Islands

Novaya Zemlya

Franz Josef Land

Barents Sea

Kola Peninsula

Baltic Sea

East Siberian Sea

150° E

120° E

90° E

60° E

30° E

North Cape

Scandinavian Peninsula

Norwegian Sea

Svalbard

Bering Sea

180°

Wrangel Island

ARCTIC OCEAN

North Pole

Prime Meridian

0°

North Sea

Chukchi Peninsula

St. Lawrence Island

Bering Strait

Chukchi Sea

Greenland Sea

Arctic Circle

Iceland

British Isles

Nunivak Island

150° W

North Magnetic Pole

Ellesmere Island

80° N

Denmark Strait

Alaska Peninsula

Brooks Range

Yukon R.

Beaufort Sea

Greenland

70° N

Kodiak Island

Alaska Range

ROCKY MOUNTAINS

Banks Island

Amundsen Gulf

Mackenzie R.

Queen Elizabeth Islands

Baffin Bay

0 miles   1,000

0 kilometers   1,000

Orthographic

Gulf of Alaska

PACIFIC OCEAN

Victoria Island

Baffin Island

60° N

Davis Strait

30° W

ATLANTIC OCEAN

NORTH AMERICA

Antarctica

SOUTH SHETLAND ISLANDS

SOUTH AMERICA

60° W

70° S

30° W

0°

Prime Meridian

30° E

QUEEN MAUD LAND

60° E

ENDERBY LAND

Antarctic Peninsula

Weddell Sea

COATS LAND

Filchner Ice Shelf

Ronne Ice Shelf

Berkner Island

80° S

Amery Ice Shelf

Alexander Island

South Polar Plateau

ANTARCTICA

Bellingshausen Sea

90° W

Vinson Massif 16,067 ft (4,897 m)

TRANSANTARCTIC MOUNTAINS

Queen Maud Mts.

South Pole

90° E

Amundsen Sea

60° S

WILKES LAND

Ross Ice Shelf

SOUTHERN OCEAN

Roosevelt Island

120° W

Ross Sea

VICTORIA LAND

120° E

International Date Line

Antarctic Circle

150° W

180°

South Magnetic Pole

50° S

0 miles   1,000

0 kilometers   1,000

Lambert Azimuthal Equal Area

KEY

ELEVATION

Feet	Meters
More than 13,000	More than 3,960
6,500–13,000	1,980–3,960
1,600–6,500	480–1,980
650–1,600	200–480
0–650	0–200

Pack ice

Ice shelf

Ice cap

Glossary of Geographic Terms

basin
an area that is lower than surrounding land areas; some basins are filled with water

bay
a body of water that is partly surrounded by land and that is connected to a larger body of water

butte
a small, high, flat-topped landform with cliff-like sides

▲ **butte**

canyon
a deep, narrow valley with steep sides; often with a stream flowing through it

cataract
a large waterfall or steep rapids

◀ **cataract**

delta
a plain at the mouth of a river, often triangular in shape, formed where sediment is deposited by flowing water

flood plain
a broad plain on either side of a river, formed where sediment settles during floods

glacier
a huge, slow-moving mass of snow and ice

hill
an area that rises above surrounding land and has a rounded top; lower and usually less steep than a mountain

island
an area of land completely surrounded by water

isthmus
a narrow strip of land that connects two larger areas of land

mesa
a high, flat-topped landform with cliff-like sides; larger than a butte

mountain
a landform that rises steeply at least 2,000 feet (610 meters) above surrounding land; usually wide at the bottom and rising to a narrow peak or ridge

▶ **glacier**

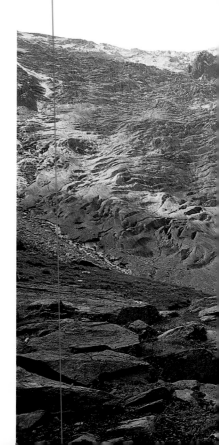

◀ **delta**

mountain pass
a gap between mountains

peninsula
an area of land almost completely surrounded by water but connected to the mainland

plain
a large area of flat or gently rolling land

plateau
a large, flat area that rises above the surrounding land; at least one side has a steep slope

river mouth
the point where a river enters a lake or sea

strait
a narrow stretch of water that connects two larger bodies of water

tributary
a river or stream that flows into a larger river

valley
a low stretch of land between mountains or hills; land that is drained by a river

volcano
an opening in Earth's surface through which molten rock, ashes, and gases escape from the interior

▶ **volcano**

Gazetteer

A

Amazon rain forest (0° S, 49° W) a large tropical rain forest in the drainage basin of the Amazon River in northern South America, p. 166

Amazon River (0° S, 49° W) the longest river in South America, flowing across Brazil into the Atlantic Ocean, p. 14

Andes Mountains (20° S, 67° W) a mountain system extending along the western coast of South America, p. 13

Argentina (34° S, 64° W) a country in South America, p. 160

Atacama Desert (25° S, 69° W) a desert in Chile, South America, p. 17

B

Bolivia (17° S, 65° W) a country in South America, p. 161

Brasília (15°47' S, 47°55' W) the capital city of Brazil, p. 167

Brazil (10° S, 55° W) the largest country in South America, p. 166

C

Canal Zone (9° N, 80° W) a 10-mile wide strip of land along the Panama Canal, stretching from the Atlantic Ocean to the Pacific Ocean, once governed by the United States, p. 120

Caracas (10°30' N, 66°56' W) the capital city of Venezuela, p.188

Caribbean Sea (15° N, 73° W) a sea bounded by the West Indies, Central America, and South America; part of the Atlantic Ocean, p. 12

Central America (11° N, 80° W) the part of Latin America south of Mexico and north of South America; it includes the seven republics of Guatemala, Honduras, El Salvador, Nicaragua, Costa Rica, Panama, and Belize, p. 12

Chile (30° S, 71° W) a country in South America, p. 179

Colombia (4° N, 72° W) a country in South America, p. 162

Cuba (21° N, 80° W) an island country, the largest of the Caribbean islands, p. 134

Cuzco (13°31' S, 71°59' W) a city in Peru; capital of the Incan empire, p. 46

E

El Salvador (13° N, 88° W) a country in Central America, p. 99

G

Guatemala (15° N, 90° W) a country in Central America, p. 109

H

Haiti (19° N, 72° W) a country in the Caribbean Sea, on the island of Hispaniola, p. 142

Hispaniola (19° N, 71° W) an island in the Caribbean Sea, divided between Haiti in the west and the Dominican Republic in the east, p. 84

I

Isthmus of Panama (9° N, 79° W) the narrow strip of land in Panama that separates the Atlantic Ocean and the Pacific Ocean, p. 116

J

Jamaica (18° N, 77° W) an island country in the Caribbean Sea, p. 131

L

Lake Titicaca (16° S, 69° W) the world's highest lake on which vessels can travel, located in the Andes Mountains in South America, p. 87

Lima (12°03' S, 77°03' W) the capital city of Peru, p. 175

M

Mexico (23° N, 102° W) a country in North America, south of the United States, p. 102

Mexico City (19°24' N, 99°09' W) the capital of and largest city in Mexico; one of the largest urban areas in the world, p. 105

Miami (25°46' N, 80°11' W) a city in south-eastern Florida, p. 138

Middle America (11° N, 80° W) another term for Mexico and Central America, p. 11

N

New York City (40°43' N, 74°01' W) a city in southeastern New York State, p. 150

P

Panama (9° N, 80° W) a country in Central America, p. 116

Panama Canal (9° N, 79° W) an important shipping canal across the Isthmus of Panama, linking the Caribbean Sea (and the Atlantic Ocean) to the Pacific Ocean, p. 117

Paraguay (23° S, 58° W) a country in South America, p. 163

Peru (10° S, 76° W) a country in South America, p. 173

Port-au-Prince (18°32' N, 72°20' W) the capital city and chief port of Haiti, p. 143

Puerto Rico (18° N, 64° W) an island commonwealth of the United States in the Caribbean Sea, p. 148

R

Rio de Janeiro (22°55' S, 43°30' W) a major city in Brazil, p. 167

S

San Juan (18°28' N, 66°07' W) the capital and largest city in Puerto Rico, p. 152

Santiago (33°27' S, 70°40' W) the capital city of Chile, p. 183

São Paulo (23°32' S, 46°37' W) the largest city in Brazil, p. 77

South America (15° S, 60° W) the world's fourth-largest continent, bounded by the Caribbean Sea, the Atlantic Ocean, and the Pacific Ocean, and linked to North America by the Isthmus of Panama, p. 13

Strait of Magellan (54° S, 71° W) a waterway separating mainland South America from the islands of Tierra del Fuego, at the southernmost tip of South America, p. 179

T

Tenochtitlán (19°24' N, 99°09' W) the capital of the Aztec empire, located where modern Mexico City now stands, p. 42

Tierra del Fuego (54° S, 67° W) an archipelago, or chain of islands, at the southernmost tip of South America, separated from the mainland by the Strait of Magellan, p. 180

Trinidad and Tobago (11° N, 61° W) a republic of the West Indies, on the two islands called Trinidad and Tobago, p. 133

V

Valley of Mexico (19° N, 99° W) the area in central Mexico where Mexico City is located and where most of the population lives, p. 42

Venezuela (8° N, 66° W) a country in South America, p. 188

W

West Indies (19° N, 70° W) the islands of the Caribbean, p. 82

Glossary

A

ally (AL eye) *n.* a country joined with another for a special purpose, p. 136

Altiplano (al tih PLAH noh) *n.* a high plateau in the Andes Mountains, p. 175

Amazon rain forest (AM uh zahn rayn FAWR ist) *n.* a large tropical rain forest occupying the Amazon Basin in northern South America, p. 166

Amazon River (AM uh zahn RIV ur) *n.* a long river in northern South America, p. 14

Andes Mountains (AN deez MOWN tunz) *n.* a mountain system extending along the western coast of South America, p. 13

aqueduct (AK wuh dukt) *n.* a pipe or channel used to carry water from a distant source, p. 48

Aristide, Jean-Bertrand (ah rees TEED, zhan behr TRAHN) *n.* former president of Haiti, first elected in 1990, p. 142

B

Bolívar, Simón (boh LEE vahr, see MOHN) *n.* a leader in the fight to free South America from Spanish rule, p. 59

boom (boom) *n.* a period of business growth and prosperity, p. 189

Brasília (bruh ZIL yuh) *n.* capital of Brazil, built in the 1950s to encourage people to move to the interior of the country, p. 167

C

campesino (kahm peh SEE noh) *n.* a poor Latin American farmer or farm worker, p. 74

Canal Zone (kuh NAL zohn) *n.* a 10-mile wide strip of land along the Panama Canal, once governed by the United States, p. 120

canopy (KAN uh pea) *n.* the dense mass of leaves and branches forming the top layer of a rain forest, p. 166

Caracas (kuh RAH kus) *n.* the capital of Venezuela, p. 188

Carnival (KAHR nuh vul) *n.* a lively annual celebration just before Lent in Latin America; similar to Mardi Gras in the United States, p. 85

cash crop (kash krahp) *n.* a crop grown mostly for sale rather than for a farmer's own needs, p. 91

Castro, Fidel (KAS troh, fih DEL), *n.* the leader of Cuba's government, p. 134

caudillo (kaw DEE yoh) *n.* a military officer who rules a country very strictly, p. 61

census (SEN sus) *n.* an official count of all the people in an area and how they make a living, p. 47

circumnavigate (sur kum NAV ih gayt) *v.* to sail or fly all the way around something, such as Earth, p. 181

citizen (SIT uh zun) *n.* a person with certain rights and responsibilities under a particular government, p. 149

Columbus, Christopher (kuh LUM bus, KRIS tuh fur) *n.* Italian explorer sponsored by Spain, who landed in the West Indies in 1492, p. 51

commonwealth (KAHM un welth) *n.* a self-governing political unit with strong ties to a particular country, p. 149

communism (KAHM yoo niz um) *n.* an economic system in which the government owns all large businesses and most of a country's land, p. 135

Carnival in Trinidad

A satellite photograph of El Niño

conquistador (kahn KEES tuh dawr) *n.* one of a group of conquerors who claimed and ruled land in the Americas for the Spanish government in the 1500s, p. 52

constitution (KAHN stuh TOO shun) *n.* a statement of a country's basic laws and values, p. 148

Cortés, Hernán (kohr TEZ, hur NAHN) *n.* conquistador who conquered the Aztecs, p. 52

coup (koo) *n.* short for coup d'état (koo day TAH), a French term meaning the overthrow of a ruler or government by an organized group which then takes power, p. 193

Creole (KREE ohl) *n.* a person of European and African descent, born in Haiti or other parts of the Americas, whose culture has strong French and African influence; a Haitian language based on French and African languages, p. 146

criollo (kree OH yoh) *n.* a person with Spanish parents who was born in the Spanish colonies in Latin America, p. 58

Cuzco (KOOS koh) *n.* the capital of the Incan empire; a city in modern Peru, p. 46

D

dictator (DIK tay tur) *n.* a ruler of a country with complete power, p. 65

diversify (duh VUR suh fy) *v.* to add variety, p. 30

diversity (duh VUR suh tee) *n.* variety, p. 74

E

economy (ih KAHN uh mee) *n.* the ways that goods and services are produced and made available to people, p. 21

ecotourism (ek oh TOOR iz um) *n.* travel to unspoiled areas in order to observe wildlife and learn about the environment, p. 122

elevation (el uh VAY shun) *n.* the height of land above sea level, p. 18

El Niño (el NEEN yoh) *n.* a warming of the ocean water along the western coast of South America; this current influences global weather patterns, p. 15

emigrate (EM ih grayt) *v.* to leave one country to settle in another, p. 79

encomienda (en koh mee EN dah) *n.* the right of Spanish colonists to demand taxes or labor from Native Americans, granted by the Spanish government, p. 56

ethnic group (ETH nik groop) *n.* a group of people who share the same ancestry, language, religion, or cultural traditions, p. 83

exile (EK syl) *n.* a person who leaves or is forced to leave his or her homeland for another country, often for political reasons, p. 137

export (eks PAWRT) *v.* to send products from one country to be sold in another country; (EKS pawrt) *n.* a product that is sold in another country, p. 65

F

foreign debt (FAWR in det) *n.* money owed by one country to another country or foreign financial institution, p. 66

G

gaucho (GOW choh) *n.* a cowboy of the pampas of South America, p. 89

glacier (GLAY shur) *n.* a large slow-moving mass of ice and snow, p. 182

H

hacienda (hah see EN dah) *n.* a large farm or plantation, often growing cash crops for export, p. 55

hieroglyphics (hy ur oh GLIF iks) *n.* a system of writing using signs and symbols, used by the Maya and other peoples, p. 41

hydroelectricity (hy droh ee lek TRIS ih tee) *n.* electrical power produced from rushing water, p. 26

I

illiterate (ih LIT ur ut) *n.* unable to read or write, p. 136

immigrant (IM uh grunt) *n.* a person who comes into a foreign country to make a new home, p. 79

import (im PAWRT) *v.* to bring products into one country from another; (IM pawrt) *n.* a product brought from another country to sell, p. 65

indigenous people (in DIJ uh nus PEA pul) *n.* people who are descended from the people who first lived in a region, p. 74

isthmus (IS mus) *n.* a narrow strip of land that has water on both sides and joins two larger bodies of land, p. 12

L

ladino (luh DEE noh) *n.* a mestizo, or person of mixed Spanish and Native American ancestry in Guatemala, p. 110

land reform (land ree FAWRM) *n.* the effort to distribute land more equally and fairly, p. 110

lock (lahk) *n.* a section of waterway in which ships are raised or lowered by adjusting the water level, p. 119

L'Ouverture, Toussaint (loo vehr TOOR, too SAN) *n.* a former slave who led the people of Haiti in their fight for independence, p. 57

M

Magellan, Ferdinand (muh JEL un, FUR duh nand) *n.* a Portuguese explorer sailing for Spain whose expedition was the first to circumnavigate the globe, p. 179

maize (mayz) *n.* corn, p. 41

maquiladora (mah kee luh DOHR ah) *n.* a factory that assembles imported parts to make products for export, often located in Mexico near the United States border, p. 77

The Aztec ruler Moctezuma

mestizo (meh STEE zoh) *n.* a person of mixed Spanish and Native American ancestry, p. 55

Mexico City (MEKS ih koh SIT ee) *n.* the capital and largest city of Mexico, p. 105

Middle America (MID ul uh MEHR ih kuh) *n.* Mexico and Central America, p. 11

migrant worker (MY grunt WUR kur) *n.* a laborer who travels from one area to another, picking crops that are in season, p. 102

Moctezuma (mahk tih ZOO muh) *n.* ruler of the Aztecs, p. 50

N

natural resources (NACH ur ul REE sawrs uz) *n.* things found in nature that people use to meet their needs, p. 24

O

oasis (oh AY sis) *n.* a fertile area in a desert that has a source of water, p. 175

one-resource economy (wun REE sawrs ih KAHN uh mee) *n.* a country's dependence largely on one resource or crop for income, p. 28

P

pampas (PAM puz) *n.* flat grassland regions in the southern part of South America; a region similar to the Great Plains in the United States, p. 13

Panama Canal (PAN uh mah kuh NAL) *n.* a shipping canal across the Isthmus of Panama, linking the Caribbean Sea (and the Atlantic Ocean) to the Pacific Ocean, p. 117

Pinochet Ugarte, Augusto (pea noh SHAY oo gahr TAY, ah GOO stoh) *n.* military dictator of Chile from 1973 to 1988, p. 185

Pizarro, Francesco (pea SAHR oh, frahn SEES koh) *n.* conquistador who conquered the Incas, p. 53

plateau (pla TOH) *n.* a large raised area of mostly level land, p. 12

plaza (PLAH zuh) *n.* a public square at the center of a village, a town, or a city, p. 103

political movement (puh LIT ih kul MOOV munt) *n.* a large group of people who work together for political change, p. 112

privatization (pry vuh tih ZAY shun) *n.* a government's sale of land or industries it owns to individuals or private companies, p. 192

Q

quipu (KEE poo) *n.* knotted strings on which the Incas recorded information, p. 47

R

rain forest (rayn FAWR ist) *n.* a dense evergreen forest that has abundant rainfall throughout the year, p. 13

refugee (ref yoo JEE) *n.* a person who leaves his or her homeland for personal safety or to escape persecution, p. 143

regime (ruh ZHEEM) *n.* a particular administration or government, p. 67

revolution (rev uh LOO shun) *n.* the overthrow of an existing government, with another government taking its place, p. 58

Rio de Janeiro (REE oh day zhuh NEHR oh) *n.* a large city in Brazil, p. 167

rural (ROOR ul) *adj.* having to do with the countryside, p. 77

S

San Martín, José de (sahn mahr TEEN, hoh SAY deh) *n.* a leader in the fight to free South America from Spanish rule, p. 60

savanna (suh VAN uh) *n.* a flat, grassy region, or open plain with scattered trees and thorny bushes, p. 167

sierra (see EHR uh) *n.* a range of mountains, such as the one that runs from northwest to southeast Peru, p. 175

squatter (SKWAHT ur) *n.* a person who settles on someone else's land without permission, p. 105

strike (stryk) *n.* a refusal to work until certain demands of workers are met, p. 113

subsistence farming (sub SIS tuns FAHR ming) *n.* growing only enough food to meet the needs of the farmer's family, p. 91

T

Tenochtitlán (teh nawch tee TLAHN) *n.* the capital of the Aztec empire, located where Mexico City now stands, p. 42

Topa Inca (TOH puh ING kuh) *n.* emperor of the Incas, who expanded their empire, p. 46

treaty (TREE tee) *n.* an agreement in writing made between two or more countries, p. 52

tributary (TRIB yoo tehr ee) *n.* a river or stream that flows into a larger river, p. 14

tundra (TUN druh) *n.* a treeless plain that supports only low-growing vegetation because the lower levels of the soil remain frozen all year; in mountains, the area above the tree line, p. 175

U

urban (UR bun) *adj.* having to do with cities, p. 77

W

West Indies (west IN deez) *n.* the Caribbean islands, p. 82

Rain forest in Brazil

Index

The *m*, *g*, or *p* following the number refers to maps *(m)*, charts, tables, or graphs *(g)* or pictures *(p)*.

Blue indicates Teacher's Edition entries.

A

Ada, Alma Flor, 34–37
Africa, 56, M10*m*, M11*m*
    independence, 60
African Americans, 64
agriculture, M16, 130. *See also* farming
Allende, Isabel, 90
ally, 136, 220
Altiplano, 161, 163, 175, 176, 220
Amazon Basin, 4, 4*m*, 166, 202*m*, 205*m*
Amazon rain forest, 161, 166, 218, 220
    importance of the, 168–169, 168*g*, 169*p*
    photosynthesis and, 167
    threats to the, 169
Amazon River, 8f, 14, 166, 218, 220
Americas, migration to, M14, M14*m*, M15*m*
Andes Mountains, 8f, 13, 89, 160, 163, 181, 184, 205*m*, 218, 220
Antigua and Barbuda, 128, 128*p*
aqueducts, 48, 220
Arawaks, 83
architecture, 48, 48*p*, 91–92, 92*p*. *See also* housing
Argentina, 159*m*, 160, 204*m*, 218
    beef industry, 89
    climate of, 17
    culture of, 89
    ethnic groups in, 160
    exports of, 160
    farming in, 91
    foreign debt of, 66*g*, 67
    gauchos in, 13*p*
    government of, 90, 90*p*, 160
    independence in, 59*m*
    landforms of, 13
    languages in, 160
    Mothers of Plaza de Mayo, 90, 90*p*
    natural resources in, 27, 27*p*
    population of, 160
    religion in, 160
    vegetation of, 19, 20*m*
    waterways in, 14
Aristide, Jean Bertrand, 142, 142*p*, 145, 220
art
    of Middle America, 75–76, 75*p*, 100*p*
    of Native Americans, 75, 76, 100*p*
    Pre-Colombian, 76
Aruba, 127*m*
astrolabe, 51*p*
Atacama Desert, 9*m*, 17, 19, 20*m*, 181, 181*p*, 183, 218
Aymara, 89, 177, 177*p*
Aztecs, 42–44, 42*p*, 43*p*, 44*p*, 46, 47*p*
    art of, 75
    Cortés and, 50*p*, 52–53
    farming and the, 43
    Spain and, 50*p*, 52–53
    See also Native Americans

B

Bahamas, 127*m*, 129, 204*m*
Baja California, 205*m*
Balboa, Vasco Nuñez de, 116, 116*p*
bammy, 86
bananas, 21, 25*m*, 26, 132
Barbados, 86, 127*m*, 129
baseball, 126f, 137, 138
Basseterre, 132
Batista, Fulgencio, 135, 135*p*
bauxite, 25*m*, 26, 27
Beaubrun, Bazelais, 143, 143*p*
Behaim, Martin, M4
Belize, 97*m*, 98, 204*m*
    cultural heritage of, 75
    languages of, 75
    Mayas in, 41
Belize City, 98
Belmopan, Belize, 98
Boiling Lake, 130
Bolívar, Simón, 59–60, 61, 62*p*, 193, 220
Bolivia, 4m, 161, 204*m*, 218
    culture of, 89
    economy of, 24, 24*p*
    ethnic groups in, 161
    exports of, 161
    foreign debt of, 66*g*
    government of, 161
    independence in, 59*m*
    population of, 161
    religion in, 161
Brasília, 92, 167, 168*g*, 218, 220
Brazil, 159*m*, 161, 204*m*, 218
    Carnival in, 168, 170
    cities of, 92, 92*p*
    climate of, 17, 166
    culture of, 89, 170, 170*g*
    economy of, 30, 66*g*, 197
    ethnic groups of, 161, 170*g*, 171, 171*p*
    exports of, 161, 172
    farming in, 171–172
    geography of, 167–170, 167*p*, 168*g*, 169*p*, 170*g*, 170*m*
    government of, 161
    hydroelectricity in, 5, 5*g*, 5*p*
    immigrants in, 171
    independence in, 59*m*, 61
    indigenous people in, 169, 170
    landforms of, 13
    languages of, 3*m*, 3*p*, 89, 161
    mining in, 169
    Native Americans in, 171, 171*p*
    natural resources in, 25*m*, 26*p*, 27
    population of, 161, 167, 170*m*
    Portugal and, 52
    rain forest in, 7, 7*m*, 7*p*, 158*g*, 166, 166*p*, 167, 167*p*
    religion in, 161
    revolution, 38h
    rivers in, 14*p*
    slavery in, 56, 161, 170, 171
Brazilian Highlands, 202*m*, 205*m*
bridges, 48, 178, 178*p*
Bridgetown, 129
British Honduras. *See* Belize
Buenos Aires, Argentina, 89, 89*p*, 91, 92*p*
buildings. *See* architecture

C

carbon dioxide, 169
cacao, 25*m*, 26
calendars, 41, 42, 42*p*
calypso music, 85, 86, 133
campesinos, 74, 102, 113, 220
Canada, 67
canals, 43, 43*p*, 48. *See also* Panama Canal
Canal Zone, 120, 218, 220. *See also* Panama Canal
canopy, 166, 220
Cape Horn, 9*m*, 180*m*, 181
capoeira, 171
Caracas, 188, 188*p*, 189, 193, 218, 220
Caribbean Islands, 127*m*, 128-133, 200*m*,
    Carnival in, 85, 85*p*
    climate of, 17, 18
    cultures of, 82–86, 82*p*, 83*p*, 84*p*, 85–86, 85*p*, 86*p*
    ethnic groups of, 83–84, 83*p*, 128–133
    exports of the, 128–133
    farming in, 84
    food of, 86, 86*p*
    government in the, 128–133
    immigrants in, 83

landforms of, 12
languages of, 84, 128–133
location of, 11, 11*m*, 156*m*
music of, 85, 86
natural resources of, 25*m*, 26, 26*p*
population of, 128–133
religion in the, 84, 128–133
See also individual countries
Caribbean Sea, 218
Carib Indians, 83, 130. *See also*
Native Americans
Carnival, 85, 85*p*, 168, 170, 220, 220*p*
Caroni Swamp, 133
Carrillo, Fermin, 79
Carter, Jimmy, 120
cash crops, 72f, 91, 138, 220
Castries, 132
Castro, Fidel, 129, 134, 135–136,
136p, 137, 139, 220
Catholic Church, 54, 76, 85, 85*p*
caudillos, 61, 220
census, 47, 220
Central America, 97*m*, 98-101, 200*m*,
218
early civilizations of, 39*m*, 40–44,
41*p*, 42*p*, 43*p*, 44*p*
ethnic groups in, 98–101
exports of, 98–101
landforms of, 12
languages of, 75, 98–101
location of, 11, 11*m*, 124*m*
natural resources of, 25*m*, 26
population of, 77, 98–101
religion in, 76, 76*p*, 98–101
vegetation of, 20*m*, 21
See also Middle America; individual
countries
**Central American Common
Market,** 99
Cerrado, 167
Chavez, Hugo, 193, 194
Chiapas, 100
Chichén Itzá, 41*p*
Chile, 7, 7*m*, 7*p*, 159*m*, 204*m*, 218
climate of, 17, 181
culture of, 89
economy of, 28, 180, 180*g*
ethnic groups of, 161
exports, 161, 180, 180*g*, 181, 184
farming in, 91, 183–184, 184*p*
foreign debt of, 66*g*
geography of, 181–182, 181*p*, 182*p*
government, 161, 185, 185*p*
human rights in, 185
independence in, 59*m*, 60
landforms of, 161, 181
languages of, 161
literature of, 90

Native Americans in, 19, 183
natural resources in, 28
population of, 161
religion of, 161
vegetation of, 19, 20*m*
Chinchorro, 19
chinampas, 43, 43*p*
Christianity, 54, 76
Clemente, Roberto, 126f
Ciboney, 83
circumnavigate, 181, 220
cities
population of, 77*g*, 78
of South America, 91–92, 92*p*
See also urbanization
citizen, 220
citizenship, 149
civilizations, early, 39*m*, 40–44, 41*p*,
42*p*, 43*p*, 44*p*, 46
civil war, 101, 112–113
climate, 15–21, 15*p*, 16*m*, 18*g*, 20*m*,
32, 32*m*, M1
of Brazil, 166, 168*g*
of Chile, 181
factors affecting, 18
of Peru, 174*g*
vegetation, 19–21, 19*p*, 20*m*, 21*p*
See also weather
climate maps, 22–23, 22*m*, 23*m*, 32,
32*p*, M12*m*
climate regions, 15*p*, 16*m*, 17–21,
18*g*, 20*m*, 23*m*, M1
coal, 5, 5*g*
coffee, 21, 25*m*, 26, 27, 28*g*, 111, 172
Cold War, 136
Colombia, 159*m*, 162, 204*m*, 218
culture of, 88
ethnic groups in, 162
exports of, 162
foreign debt of, 66*g*
government of, 162
independence in, 59*m*, 60
languages of, 162
literature of, 90
natural resources in, 25*m*, 27
Panama Canal and, 66, 119
population of, 162
religion in, 162
volcanoes in, 8f
Colón, 77, 101
colonization, 54–56, 54*m*, 55*g*
Columbian exchange, 55*g*
Columbus, Christopher, 51, 54*m*,
220, M14
Antigua and, 128
Native Americans and, 82, 83
Panama and, 116
San Salvador, 129

communications, 122
communism, 135, 220
Condado, 152
conquistadors, 52–53, 221
constitution, 148, 221
Copán, Honduras, 41
copper, 25*m*, 27, 180, 180*g*, 181
coral islands, 12
coral reefs, 132, 133
Cortés, Hernán, 50*p*, 52–53, 54*m*, 71,
221
Costa Rica, 75, 77, 97*m*, 99, 204*m*
cotton, 25*m*, 26
coup, 193, 221
Creoles, 146, 221
criollos, 58, 59, 64–65, 221
critical thinking
analyze, 32, 37, 61, 154, 172, 196
analyze cause and effect, 178
analyze images, 13, 43, 58, 78, 107,
110, 121, 139, 147
analyze information, 14, 28, 46, 61,
92
apply information, 21, 196
bar graphs, 165
categorize, 32, 86, 101, 133, 165
compare, 30, 56, 70, 156, 178, 191
compare and contrast, 27, 68, 92,
101, 133, 147, 165, 169, 181, 196
conclude, 44, 70, 94, 176
contrast, 32, 165
define, 32, 94, 122, 139, 147
describe, 28, 44, 49, 56, 94, 108,
113, 122, 139, 147, 154, 156, 178,
194, 196
draw conclusions, 18, 30, 49, 56, 68,
70, 77, 86, 88, 89, 94, 101, 119,
122, 124, 133, 150, 156, 165, 172,
182, 192, 194
draw inferences, 85, 175
evaluate information, 32, 37, 56,
108
explain, 70, 122, 154
find main idea, 139, 147, 156
generalize, 26, 32, 47, 70, 83, 124
identify, 14, 18, 21, 30, 32, 44, 46,
49, 55, 56, 61, 66, 70, 77, 79, 86,
92, 94, 113, 124, 149, 156, 172,
185, 196
identify cause, 32, 65, 70, 79, 86, 94,
108, 113, 124, 185, 196
identify cause and effect, 14, 30, 56,
66, 79, 92, 94, 122, 124, 147, 156,
185
identify effect, 32, 94, 124, 139, 156,
172, 184, 194, 196
infer, 14, 21, 32, 37, 41, 44, 49, 55,
61, 75, 76, 91, 92, 101, 103, 105,

117, 133, 135, 136, 143, 145, 149, 152, 172, 177, 191, 194, 196
list, 154, 156
locate, 51
make a reasonable judgment, 185
name, 14, 21, 70, 156, 172, 185
predict, 29, 79, 113, 139, 154, 178, 196
recall, 14, 21, 30, 32, 37, 49, 56, 61, 68, 70, 79, 86, 92, 94, 108, 113, 122, 124, 139, 156, 185, 194
respond, 37
sequence, 44, 49, 122, 147, 154, 156, 194
summarize, 32, 113, 124, 196
synthesize, 14, 21, 32, 108, 113, 124, 139, 146, 154, 171
transfer information, 153
Cry of Dolores, 58
cuatro, 152p
Cuba, 12, 127m, 129, 204m, 218
  baseball and, 137
  emigrants from, 134, 134p
  exiles from, 137–139, 138p
  government of, 134, 135–136, 137, 137g, 137m
  independence in, 60, 135
  literature of, 34–37, 34p, 35p, 36p
  natural resources of, 25m, 26
  Spain and, 60
  timeline of, 157
Cuban Missile Crisis, 136
culture, 1, M1
  Aztec, 42
  of Brazil, 170
  geography and, 178
  of Guatemala, 111
  of Middle America, 74–76, 74p, 75p, 76p
  migration and, M14–M15
  of Peru, 178
  Project Possibilities, 198
Cuzco, 46, 47, 53, 175, 176, 218, 221

D

Defoe, Daniel, 183
deforestation, 119
democracy, 185
dictators, 65, 221
Differentiated Instruction
  Advanced Readers, RW1, M, M5, M11, M14, 17, 27, 53, 59, 77, 106, 119, 129, 150, 162, 169, 176, 181, 183
  English Language Learners, RW5, M, M8, M12, M17, 7, 19, 53, 67, 91, 112, 145, 150, 161, 168, 183, 192
  Gifted and Talented, RW4, M6,

M12, 5, 20, 43, 47, 90, 112, 115, 144, 153, 164, 168, 175, 187
  Less Proficient Readers, RW3, M5, M8, M14, 26, 36, 59, 77, 81, 90, 100, 105, 119, 129, 136, 153, 161, 176, 182, 191, 193
  Special Needs Students, RW1, M3, M6, M11, 3, 23, 29, 63, 67, 81, 91, 100, 105, 115, 120, 136, 141, 145, 169, 182, 187, 191, 193
disease, 53, 56, 119–120, 169
diversify, 172, 183–184, 184p, 193, 221
diversity, 30, 100, 133, 221
Dominica, 83, 130
Dominican Republic, 127m, 130, 204m
  culture of, 84
  natural resources of, 25m, 26
Dom Pedro, 61
Dutch colonies, 83, 88, 163, 164
Duvalier, François, 145
Duvalier, Jean-Claude, 145

E

earth
  globes, M4–M5, M4
  movements of, M2–M3, M2
earthquakes, 12, 48, 99, 101, 107
economics/economic systems, 1, 221
  of Brazil, 197
  of Chile, 180, 180g
  climate and, 21
  diversifying the, 30, 100, 172, 183–184, 184p, 193, 221
  foreign debt, 66, 66g, 67–68
  of Guatemala, 111
  of Honduras, 100
  of Mexico, 104g, 104m
  natural resources and, 28–30, 28p, 29p, 30p
  one resource, 28, 29, 222
  Project Possibilities, 198
  of Puerto Rico, 131
  of Venezuela, 190, 190g, 190m, 191–192
  world, 29
ecotourism, 122, 122p, 221
Ecuador, 159m, 162, 162p, 204m
  culture of, 89
  ethnic groups in, 162
  exports of, 162
  factories in, 30p
  farming in, 91p, M16m, M16p
  foreign debt of, 66g
  government of, 162
  independence in, 59m, 60

  languages of, 162
  population of, 162
  oil in, 190
  religion in, 162
elevation, 4, 4, 4m, 18, 21, 221, M11
El Niño, 15, 15p, 29, 221, 221p
El Salvador, 97m, 99, 204m, 218
  economy of, 30
  Mayas in, 38h
  languages of, 75
emigration, 78p, 79, 134, 134p, 221
Empire of Gold, 55p
employment, in Mexico City, 105–106, 108
encomiendas, 56, 221
energy, 5, 5g
England, 54, 83, 88, 98, 129, 130, 132
environment
  climate and, 15–21
  earthquakes and, 12, 48, 99, 101
  human-environment interaction, 106m, M1
  importance of the rain forest to, 168–169, 168g, 169p
  photosynthesis and, 167
  smog and the, 183
  See also pollution
equal-area maps, M7
Equator, 2, 16m, 18, M2, M3, M4, M7
ethnic groups, 83–84, 83p, 221
  of Argentina, 160
  of Bolivia, 161
  of Brazil, 161, 170g, 171, 171p
  Caribbean, 128–133
  of Central America, 98–101
  of Chile, 161
  of Colombia, 162
  of Ecuador, 162
  of Guatemala, 109, 110, 111, 111g, 111m
  of Guyana, 163
  of Haiti, 146
  of Mexico, 100
  of Panama, 118g
  of Paraguay, 163
  of Peru, 163
  of South America, 160–165
  of Suriname, 164
  of Uruguay, 164
  of Venezuela, 165
exiles, 137–139, 138p, 221
exports, 65, 77, 91, 221
  of Argentina, 160
  of Bolivia, 161
  of Brazil, 161
  of the Caribbean, 128–133
  of Central America, 98–101
  of Chile, 161, 180, 180g, 181, 184
  of Colombia, 162

of Ecuador, 162
of Guyana, 163
of Mexico, 100, 104g, 104m
of Paraguay, 163
of Peru, 163
of South America, 160–165
of Suriname, 164
of Uruguay, 164
of Venezuela, 165, 190, 190g, 190m

F

factories, 30, 30p, 122, 171–172
Falkland Islands, 9m, 159m, 204m
farming, 29, M17p
    by the Aztecs, 42–43, 43p
    in Brazil, 171–172
    in the Caribbean, 25m, 26, 84
    in Chile, 182, 183–184, 184p
    in Ecuador, M16m, M16p
    in Guatemala, 110, 110p
    in Mexico, 103
    in South America, 27, 91
    subsistence, 49, 91, 162p, 223, M16
    in the United States, M16m, M16p
favelas, 92, 92p, 172
Ferdinand, Prince of Spain, 59, 60
fiber-optic networks, 122
fishing, 25m, 26, 27, 27p, 29
floating beds, 43, 43p
flooding, 192p, 193, 193p
flood plain, 216
food, 21, 25m, 26, 86, 86p, 132
foreign debt, 66, 66g, 67–68, 221
Fox, Vicente, 100, 108, 108p
France,
    colonization by, 54, 83, 88, 143
    Panama Canal and, 118
    revolution in, 58
French Guiana, culture of, 88
Fujimori, Alberto, 67

G

Galápagos Islands, 9m, 205m
Gatún Locks, 121, 121p
gauchos, 13p, 19, 89, 164p, 221
geography, 1
    of Brazil, 167–170, 167p, 168g,
        169p, 170g, 170m
    of Chile, 181–182, 181p, 182p
    culture and, 178
    of Latin America, 11m
    of Mexico City, 107, 107p
    of Panama, 116–120, 118, 118g,
        118m
    of Peru, 173, 173p, 174, 174g, 174m,
        175–178
    Project Possibilities, 198

themes of, M1–M2
    See also physical geography
glacier, 216, 216p, 221
gold, 25m, 27
gorges, 48
government, 1
    of Argentina, 90, 90p, 160
    of Bolivia, 161
    of Brazil, 161
    of the Caribbean, 128–133
    of Chile, 161, 185, 185p
    of Colombia, 162
    of Cuba, 134, 135–136, 137, 137g,
        137m
    of Ecuador, 162
    of Guyana, 163
    of Haiti, 142, 142p, 145
    Incan, 47
    of Mexico, 100
    oil boom and, 189, 192
    of Paraguay, 163
    of Peru, 163
    Project Possibilities, 198
    of Puerto Rico, 148, 151, 151g,
        151m
    in South America, 160–165
    of Suriname, 164
    of Uruguay, 164
    of Venezuela, 165, 193, 194, 194p
Gran Colombia, 59m, 61, 165
Grenada, 86p, 127m, 130
Guantánamo Bay, 129
Guaraní, 163
Guatemala, 97m, 99, 204m, 218
    civil war in, 96f, 112–113
    coffee from, 111
    culture of, 75, 111
    economy of, 111
    ethnic groups in, 109, 110, 111,
        111g, 111m
    farming in, 110, 110p
    land reform in, 110, 110p
    languages of, 75, 111m
    Mayas in, 41, 99, 99, 111, 111g,
        111m
    Native Americans in, 109, 110, 111,
        111g, 111m, 112
    political movements in, 112–113,
        112p
    population of, 125g
    weather in, 29p
    women in, 96p, 112
Guatemala City, 99
Guyana, 13, 88, 159m, 163, 204m

H

haciendas, 55, 56, 64, 221
Haiti, 57, 127m, 130, 131, 204m, 218

culture of, 84
ethnic diversity in, 146
government of, 142, 142p, 145
history of, 144, 144g, 144m
housing in, 146p
human rights in, 145
languages in, 146
poverty in, 146–147
slaves in, 6, 6p, 143
United States and, 143, 145
Havana, 129
Hawaii, M1
herding, 19, M17p
Hernandez, Orlando, 138
Hidalgo, Miguel, 58–59, 58p
hieroglyphics, 41, 42, 42, 221
Himalayas, 13
Hindi language, M13
Hinduism, 84
Hispaniola, 12, 84, 126f, 130, 131,
    143, 218
history, 1, 144, 144g, 144m
    Project Possibilities, 198
Honduras, 97m, 100, 204m
    cultural heritage of, 74p, 75
    economy of, 100
    Mayas in, 41
    vegetation of, 20m, 21
housing
    in Haiti, 146p
    in Mexico, 105–108, 105p, 106m,
        107p
    in Peru, 175, 175p
    See also architecture
human-environment interaction,
    106m, M1
human rights, 145, 185
humid subtropical climate, 17
hurricanes, 17, 17p, 100, 101
hydroelectricity, 5, 5m, 25m, 26, 221

I

illiterate, 222
immigration, 79, 83, 161, 171, 222
imports, 65, 222
Incas, 45–48, 45p, 46, 46p, 47p, 48p
    aquaduct, 48
    in Ecuador, 162p
    Machu Picchu, 176, 176p
    in Peru, 175, 178, 178p
    Pizarro and, 53
Indians, 51, 82. *See also* Native
    Americans
indigenous people, 74, 89, 163, 222
    in Brazil, 169, 170
    in Guatemala, 112
    in rain forest, 169, 170
    of Venezuela, 165

See also Native Americans
industrialization, 30, 30*p*, 122
inferences, making, 114–115, 114*p*, 115*p*, 124
injustice, 76
Instructional Strategies
  Applying New Words Outside the Classroom, 96f
  Author's Craft, 158g-158h
  Choral Reading, T34, 38h
  Encouraging Active Participation, 96f
  Give One, Get One, T37
  Idea Wave, T35
  Mapping Word Definitions, 72f
  Numbered Heads, T36, 158g
  Oral Cloze, T33
  Paragraph Shrinking, T34
  Pre-Teaching Vocabulary, 38h
  Previewing and Prereading, 8f
  Reciprocal Questioning (ReQuest), T35
  Questions and Answers, 158h
  Seeding Discussions, 126f
  Setting a Purpose for Reading, T32
  Summarizing, 72f, 126f
  Structured Silent Reading, T34
  Teaching High-Use Academic Words, T33, 8b, 38b, 72b, 96b, 126b, 158b
  Think-Write-Pair-Share, T36
Interdisciplinary
  language arts, 84, 183
  math, 41
  science, 17, 17p, 32, 48, 167
  time, 12
  world, 138
International Monetary Fund, 67
Inti, 48
iron ore, 25*m*, 27
Isabella, Queen of Spain, 51
island, 216
Isle of Spice, 130
isthmus, 12, 216, 222
Isthmus of Panama, 9*m*, 205*m*, 218
Itaipú Dam, 5, 5*p*
Iturbide, Agustín de, 59

J

Jamaica, 12, 127*m*, 131, 218
  farming in, 84
  music of, 86
  natural resources of, 25*m*, 26
jíbaros, 151
Judaism, 84

K

Kahlo, Frida, 75*p*
Kennedy, John F., 136
Kenya, Mount, M10
Khrushchev, Nikita, 136, 136*p*
Kingston, 131
Kilimanjaro, M10
Kingstown, 132
Kremer, Gerhard, M7

L

ladinos, 110, 111, 111*g*, 111*m*, 222
Lake Maracaibo, 14, 189
Lakes Region, 182
Lake Texcoco, 42
Lake Titicaca, 5, 5*p*, 14, 87, 87*p*, 173, 175, 218
landforms, 12–13, 12*p*, 13*p*, M1
  of Chile, 161, 181
  of Latin America, 4, 4*m*
land reform, 110, 110p, 222
landslides, 192*p*, 193, 193*p*
land use, 110, 110*p*, M16–M17. *See also* farming
language arts, 84, 183
languages, 73*m*, M1
  of Argentina, 160
  of Bolivia, 161
  of Brazil, 3*m*, 3*p*, 89, 161
  of Caribbean Islands, 84, 128–133
  of Central America, 75, 98–101
  of Chile, 161
  of Colombia, 162
  of Ecuador, 162
  of El Salvador, 75
  of Guatemala, 75, 99, 111*m*
  of Guyana, 163
  of Haiti, 144, 146
  Incan, 49
  Latin, 12
  of Latin America, 12, 49, 73*m*, 75, 84, 88, 89, 98–101
  maps of, M13*m*
  of Mexico, 100
  movement and, 3
  of Native Americans, 49
  of Panama, 75
  of Paraguay, 163
  of Peru, 163, 174*g*
  of Puerto Rico, 149
  of South America, 88, 158g, 160–165
  Spanglish, 150
  of Suriname, 164
  of Uruguay, 164
  of Venezuela, 165

La Paz, Bolivia, 10, 10*p*, 161
Las Casas, Bartolomé de, 55
Latin America, 2*m*, 3*m*, 4*m*, 6*m*
  climate of, 15–21, 15p, 16*m*, 18*g*, 20*m*
  foreign debt of, 66, 66*g*
  geographic features of, 11
  guiding questions, 1
  landforms of, 12–13, 12*p*, 13*p*
  languages of, 3, 12, 49, 73*m*, 75, 84, 88, 89, 98–101
  location of, 2*m*, 11, 11*m*, 32*m*, 70*m*, 94*m*
  migration to, M15*m*
  natural resources of, 24–30, 24*p*, 25*m*, 26*p*, 27*p*, 28*g*, 29*p*, 30*p*
  physical geography, 9*m*
  regions of, 11*m*
  United States and, 2
  waterways in, 14, 14*p*
  See also individual countries
Lent, 85, 85*p*
Lima, Peru, 55, 91, 163, 175, 175*p*, 218
Line of Demarcation, 52
literacy, 129, 136
literature
  of the Caribbean, 72f
  of Chile, 90
  of Colombia, 90
  of Cuba, 34–37, 34*p*, 35*p*, 36*p*
  of Trinidad, 84
Little Havana, 135, 138*p*
llamas, 6, 6*p*, 19, 88*p*
logging, 169, 169*p*
L'Ouverture, Toussaint, 57, 57*p*, 143, 145, 222
lowlands. *See* plains

M

Machu Picchu, 48, 176, 176*p*
Magellan, Ferdinand, 179, 179*p*, 181, 182, 222
maize, 41, 222
malaria, 96f, 119–120
Managua, Nicaragua, 101
maps
  of different scales, M9
  equal-area, M7
  how to use, M8–M9
  keys, M8, M9
  physical, 4, 4*m*, 202*m*–203*m*, 205*m*, 209*m*, 211*m*, 213*m*, 214*m*, 215*m*, M11
  political, 3*m*, 159*m*, 200*m*–201*m*, 204*m*, 206*m*–207*m*, 208*m*, 210*m*, 212*m*, M10

projections, M6–M7,
  Robinson, M7
  same-shape, M6
  special purpose, M12m, M13m,
    M16m
  titles, M8
  See also globes
map skills
  analyze, 174, 180
  applying information, 127m
  compare and contrast, 9m, 20m,
    180
  drawing conclusions, 16m, 25m,
    39m, 180, 190
  human-environment interaction,
    106m, M1
  identify, 174, 180
  identify effects, 159
  inferring, 11m, 174
  location, 2m, 16m, 20m, 32m, 70m,
    94m, 97m, 180, 196m
  movement, 25m, 54m, 117m
  place, 9m
  regions, 9m, 23m, 39m, 59m, 73m
maquiladoras, 77, 222
Márquez, Gabriel García, 90
Martí, José de San, 60
Martinique, 127m
Mayas, 40–41, 40p, 41p, 46, 46p, 99,
    111, 111g, 111m, M14
  art of, 75, 100p
  civil war and, 112–113
  village, 38h
  women, 109, 112
  writing system, 42
  See also Native Americans
medicine
  Aztec, 44
  from the rain forest, 168, 169
Mendes, Francisco "Chico," 158g
Mercator projection, M7
mestizos, 55, 64, 89, 176, 183, 222
  in Middle America, 74
  revolts led by, 58
Mexico, 6, 6p, 97m, 98, 100, 200m,
    204m, 206m, 218
  art of, 75–76, 75p, 100p
  climate of, 17
  cities of, 96f
  early civilizations of, 39m, 40–44,
    41p, 42p, 43p, 44p
  economy of, 104g, 104m
  ethnic groups in, 100
  exports of, 100, 104g, 104m
  farming in, 103
  foreign debt of, 66g, 67
  government in, 100
  independence in, 58–59, 58p
  landforms of, 12

  languages of, 75, 100
  location of, 2, 2p, 11, 11m, 124m
  Mayans in, 41, M14
  NAFTA and, 67, 108
  Native Americans in, 79p, 100
  natural hazards in, 106
  natural resources of, 25m, 26, 29
  population of, 72f, 77, 96f, 100,
    102, 106
  religion in, 76, 76p, 95g, 100
  vegetation of, 20m, 21
  volcanoes in, 4, 4p
  youth, 72f
Mexico City, 6, 6p, 55, 77, 106m, 219,
    222
  employment in, 105–106, 108
  geography of, 107, 107p
  housing in, 105–108, 105p, 106m,
    107p
  pollution in, 107, 107p
Miami, Florida, 135, 138p, 219
Middle America, 11, 219, 222
  art of, 75–76, 75p
  Aztecs in, 42–44, 42p, 43p, 44p
  cultures of, 74–76, 74p, 75p, 76p
  early civilizations of, 39m, 40–44,
    41p, 42p, 43p, 44p
  natural resources of, 25m, 26
  See also Central America; individual
    countries
migrant workers, 102, 222
migration, 77, 79, 83, M1, M14–M15,
    M14m, M15m
minerals, 25m, 26, 161
mining, 56, 169, 182
missionaries, 54
Mistral, Gabriela, 90
Mixtec people, 76
Moctezuma, 50, 50p, 52–53, 71, 222,
    222p
Montevideo, 164
mosquitoes, 120, 120p
Mothers of Plaza de Mayo, 90, 90p
mountain sickness, 10
mummies, 19
Munduruku Indian, 171
music, 85, 86, 198
  of the Caribbean, 130, 133
  of Puerto Rico, 152p
Muslims, 84

N

NAFTA. *See* North American Free
    Trade Agreement
Naipaul, V.S., 84
Nassau, 129
Native Americans
  in Andean countries, 89

  art of, 76
  in Bolivia, 24, 24p
  in Brazil, 171, 171p
  in Chile, 19, 183
  Columbus and, 51, 83
  diseases and, 53, 56, 169
  encomiendas, 56
  in El Salvador, 38h
  in Guatemala, 109, 110, 111, 111g,
    111m, 112
  languages of, 49
  llamas and, 19
  in Mexico, 79p, 100
  in Peru, 55, 175–176
  poverty and, 64
  rain forest and, 7, 7m, 7p
  religion of, 76
  revolts led by, 58
  totora reeds and, 87, 87p, 173, 173p
  See also Aztecs, indigenous people,
    Mayas
natural gas, 5, 5g, 25m, 26
natural resources, 24–30, 24p, 25m,
    26p, 27p, 28p, 29p, 30p
  economy and, 28–30, 28g, 29p, 30p
Neruda, Pablo, 90
New Spain, 55, 56, 106
New York City, 219
Nicaragua, 75, 97m, 101, 204m
Night of Fire, 57
North America, 51m, 58
North American Free Trade
    Agreement (NAFTA), 67, 108
Northern Hemisphere, 184, M3, M4
North Pole, 18, M2, M4, M5, M7
nuclear energy, 5, 5g
Nukuj Akpop, 112
number systems, 41

O

oasis, 175, 222
oil, 25m, 26, 27, 29, 190
  in Venezuela, 189, 189g, 189p,
    190g, 191–192
Olmecs, 76
one-resource economy, 28, 29, 222
Organization of Petroleum
    Exporting Countries (OPEC),
    190
Orinoco River, 14, 190, 190m
Orozco, José Clemente, 75

P

Pachacuti, 46
Pacific Ocean, 116, 179
pampas, 13, 19, 89, 89, 202m, 205m,
    222

Panama, 66, 97*m*, 101, 204*m*, 219
  Canal Zone, 120
  deforestation, 119
  ethnic groups of, 118*g*
  factories in, 122
  geography of, 116–120, 118, 118*g*,
    118*m*
  independence in, 60
  languages of, 75
  rain forest, 122, 122*p*
  vegetation of, 118*m*
Panama Canal, 66, 101, 219, 222
  building the, 117, 119–120, 119*p*
  shipping in the, 117, 117*p*, 121,
    121*p*
Panama City, 77, 101
Paraguay, 159*m*, 204*m*, 219
  climate of, 17
  culture of, 89
  ethnic groups of, 163
  exports of, 163
  foreign debt of, 66*g*
  government of, 163
  hydroelectricity in, 5, 5*g*, 5*p*
  independence in, 59*m*
  languages of, 163
  population of, 163
  religion in, 163
Paraguay River, 14, 163
Paraná River, 14
Patagonia, 13*p*, 17
Peru, 5, 5*p*, 45–48, 45*p*, 46*p*, 47*p*, 48*p*,
    55, 159*m*, 163, 204*m*, 219
  climate of, 174*g*
  culture of, 89
  economy of, 176
  ethnic groups in, 163
  exports of, 163
  foreign debt of, 66*g*
  geography of, 173, 173*p*, 174*g*,
    174*m*, 175–178
  government of, 163
  Incas in, 178, 178*p*
  independence in, 59m, 60
  languages of, 163, 174*g*
  llamas in, 6, 6*p*
  Native Americans in, 88*p*, 175–176
  population of, 163, 174*g*, 176
  reforms in, 67
  religion in, 163
  weather in, 29
petroleum resources, 5, 5*g*, 25*m*, 26
  in Venezuela, 189, 189*g*, 189*p*,
    190*g*, 191–192
photosynthesis, 167
physical geography, 9*m*. *See also*
  geography
physical maps, 202*m*–203*m*, 205*m*,
    209*m*, 211*m*, 213*m*, 214*m*, 215*m*,

M11
Pinochet Ugarte, Augusto, 185, 222
Pizarro, Francisco, 53, 54*m*, 55, 55*p*,
    163, 222
plains, 12, 19, 89, 217
plantations, 170, 172
plateau, 12, 217, 222
plaza, 78*p*, 103, 103*p*, 223
pok-ta-tok, 40, 41*p*
political maps, 200*m*–201*m*, 204*m*,
    206*m*–207*m*, 208*m*, 210*m*, 212*m*,
    M10
political movement, 223
political systems, 112–113, 112*p*
pollution, 107, 107*p*, 169, 183. *See*
    also environment
poncho, 49
Popocatépetl Volcano, 4, 4*p*
population
  of Argentina, 160
  of Bolivia, 161
  of Brazil, 161, 167, 170*m*
  of Caribbean Islands, 128–133
  of Central America, 77, 98–101
  of Chile, 161
  of cities, 77*g*, 78
  of Colombia, 162
  of Ecuador, 162
  of Guatemala, 125*g*
  of Guyana, 163
  in Mexico, 72f, 77, 100, 102, 106
  of Paraguay, 163
  of Peru, 163, 174*g*, 176
  of Puerto Rico, 151*m*
  of South America, 160–165
  of Suriname, 164
  of Uruguay, 164
  of Venezuela, 95*g*, 165
Port-au-Prince, 131, 143, 147, 219
Port-of-Spain, 133
Portugal,
  Brazil and, 3*m*, 3*p*, 52, 61, 161
  colonization by, 54–56, 179
  settlers from, 12
poverty, 64, 99, 161, 172
  in Haiti, 131, 146–147
  in South America, 92, 92*p*
  in Venezuela, 191
Pre-Columbian art, 76
privatization, 192, 223
Project Possibilities, 198
Puerto Rico, 12, 127*m*, 131, 204*m*,
    219
  commonwealth of, 149
  culture of, 152, 152*p*
  government of, 148, 151, 151*g*,
    151*m*
  independence question, 154, 154*p*

  languages of, 149
  music of, 152*p*
  population of, 151*m*
  Spain and, 60
  statehood question, 153, 153*p*
  timeline of, 157
  United States and, 148–150, 149*g*,
    149*p*, 151, 151*g*, 153–154, 153*p*,
    154*p*

Q

Quecha, 49, 89, 176, 177, 177*p*, 178
  language, 158g
Quetzalcoatl, 53, 53*p*
Quiché Maya, 99, 109
quipus, 45*p*, 47, 223

R

rain forest, 13, 122, 122*p*, 132, 223,
    223*p*
  in Brazil, 7, 7*m*, 7*p*, 166, 166*p*, 167,
    167*p*
  importance of the, 168–169, 168*g*,
    169*p*
  indigenous people in the, 170
  medicine from the, 168, 169
  of Peru, 174
  threats to the, 169
ranchos, 92
reading skills
  analyze author's purpose, RW1
  asking questions, 24
  clarifying meaning, 38
  comparing and contrasting, 158,
    166, 179
  distinguish between facts and
    opinions, RW1
  evaluate credibility, RW1
  identify contrasts, 173
  identify evidence, RW1
  identifying implied main ideas, 148
  identifying main ideas, 126, 134
  identifying supporting details, 142
  informational texts, RW1
  make comparisons, 188
  paraphrasing, 50, 54
  predicting, 15
  previewing, 10, 15, 24
  reading ahead, 45, 64
  recognizing multiple causes, 82
  rereading, 64
  setting a purpose, 10
  summarizing, 57
  understanding effects, 87
  using cause and effect, 72, 74
  using context, 96, 102, 109, 116
  using the reading process, 8
Redonda, 128

reforms, 67
refugees, 143, 223
reggae music, 86, 130, 198
regime, 67, 223
religion
    of Argentina, 160
    Aztec, 42
    of Bolivia, 161
    of Brazil, 161
    in Caribbean Islands, 84, 128–133
    in Central America, 76, 76p, 98–101
    of Chile, 161
    of Colombia, 162
    of Ecuador, 162
    of Guyana, 163
    Incan, 48
    of Mayas, 41, 41p
    in Mexico, 76, 76p, 95g, 100
    of Native Americans, 76
    of Paraguay, 163
    of Peru, 163
    in South America, 160–165
    of Suriname, 164
    of Uruguay, 164
    in Venezuela, 165
    See also individual religions
revolution, 57–58, 223
Rio de Janeiro, 3m, 3p, 64p, 167, 172, 172p, 219, 223
Río de la Plata, 8f, 14
Rivera, Diego, 75, 75p, 100p
River Platte, 164
Robinson Crusoe (Defoe), 183
Romero y Galdamez, Oscar Arnulfo, 76
Roosevelt, Theodore, 66, 119
Roseau, 130
rural, 223

S

Saint-Domingue, 57
Saint George's, 130
Saint John's, 128, 128p
St. Kitts and Nevis, 132
St. Lucia, 127m, 132
St. Vincent and the Grenadines, 127m, 132
Samuels, Dorothy, 84
San Geronimo Fortress, 152p
San José, Costa Rica, 77, 99
San Juan, 131, 152, 152p, 219
San Martin, José de, 223
San Salvador, 99, 129
Santiago, Chile, 161, 182, 183, 219
Santo Domingo, 130
São Paulo, Brazil, 7, 7m, 89, 89p, 219
savanna, 167, 223

science, 17, 17p, 32, 48, 124, 167. *See also* technology
Segovia Aqueduct, 48
Selkirk, Alexander, 183
selva, 174g, 175
shipping, 117, 117p, 121, 121p
sierra, 174, 175, 223
Siqueiros, David Alfaro, 75
Sisi, 171p
ska music, 86
Skills Mini Lesson
    analyzing graphic data, 66
    analyzing photographs, 18
    analyzing primary sources, 52
    decision making, 137
    identifying frame of reference, 177
    identifying main ideas, 84
    identifying point of view, 177
    making predictions, 78
    making valid generalizations, 12
    problem-solving, 111
    recognizing bias, 54
    summarizing, 84
    supporting a position, 146
    transferring information, 170
    using cartographer's tools, 104
    using reliable information, 118
Slave Coast, M15
slavery, 56, 57, 64, 64p
    African Americans and, 64
    in Brazil, 161, 170, 171
    in the Caribbean, 128
    in Haiti, 6, 6p, 143
    in Suriname, 164
smog, 107, 107p, 183
smuggling, 169
soccer, 171p
social classes, 55
Social Studies Skills
    analyzing climate maps, 22–23, 22m, 23m, 32, 32p
    comparing and contrasting, 140–141, 140p, 141p, 156
    distinguishing fact and opinion, 80–81, 81p, 94
    drawing inferences, 114–115, 114p, 115p, 124
    making timelines, 62–63, 62p, 70
    synthesizing information, 186–187, 186p, 187p, 196
Sonoran Desert, 17
Soufrière, 132
South America, 51m, 159m, 200m, 202m, 219
    agriculture, 72f
    cities of, 91–92, 92p
    cultural regions of, 88
    early civilizations of, 39m

    ethnic groups of, 160–165
    exports of, 160–165
    farming in, 91
    geography of, 160
    government in, 160–165
    independence in, 59–61, 59m, 60p
    landforms of, 13
    languages of, 88, 160–165
    literature of, 90
    location of, 11, 11m, 196m
    natural resources in, 25m, 27
    political map, 159m, 204m
    population of, 160–165
    religions in, 160–165
    women in, 90
    See also individual countries
Southern Hemisphere, 184, M3, M4
South Pole, 18, M2, M4, M5, M7
Soviet Union, 136, 139
Spain,
    Aztecs and, 50p, 52–53
    colonization by, 54–56, 88, 130, 148, 162, 165, 183
    conquistadors and, 52–53
    explorations by, 51–52
    Incans and, 49
    revolts against, 58–59, 58p
    settlers from, 12
Spanglish, 150
Spanish-American War, 126f, 135, 148
sports, 85
squatter, 105, 223
Standardized Test Prep
    analyze a reading selection, 125
    analyze graphs and charts, 95
    analyze point of view, 71
    find the main ideas, 197
    making mental maps, 33
    sequencing information, 157
steel drums, 86, 133
Strait of Magellan, 180m, 181, 182, 219
strike, 113, 223
subsistence farming, 49, 91, 162p, 223, M16
Suez Canal, 121
sugarcane, 21, 25m, 26, 132, 138
sulphur springs, 132
Suriname, 88, 159m, 164, 204m
***The Surveyor* (Ada),** 34–37
suspension bridge, 178, 178p

T

technology
    Aztec farming, 43, 43p
    learning with, xiii
    Panama Canal, 121, 121p

suspension bridge, 178, 178p
See also science
Tenochtitlán, 42, 43, 43p, 52–53, 106, 219, 223
Tierra del Fuego, 159m, 182, 219
Tikal, Guatemala, 41
timelines
of Cuba, 157
early civilizations, 46, 46p
of Haiti, 144
making, 62–63, 62p, 70
of Puerto Rico, 157
tin, 24, 24p, 25m, 27
Tobago, 85
Toco Indians, 88p
Topa Inca, 46, 223
totora reeds, 87, 87p, 173, 173p
tourism, 122, 122p
in the Caribbean, 128, 129, 130, 131, 132
in Cuba, 139, 139p
in Uruguay, 164
trade, 44, 55g, 65
transportation, 48
treaty, 52, 223
Treaty of Tordesillas, 52
Tribuna, 173
tributaries, 14, 217, 223
tribute, 42
Trinidad, 133
Carnival in, 85, 85p
literature of, 84
natural resources of, 25m, 26
Trinidad and Tobago, 127m, 133, 133p, 219
tropical rain forest, 19, 20m
tropical wet and dry climate, 17, M12
tropical wet climate, 17, M12
tundra, 175, 223
Twin Pitons, 132
Tzoc, Justina, 112

U

United States, 200m, 204m
Chile and, 180, 180g
compared to Latin America, 2
Cuba and, 129, 135, 136, 137–139, 138p
and economy of Latin America, 66, 66g
farming in, M16m, M16p
Haiti and, 143, 145
immigration to, 78p, 79
NAFTA and, 67
oil imports, 189g

Panama Canal and, 66, 118–120
political maps, 206m–207m
Puerto Rico and, 148–150, 149g, 149p, 151, 151g, 153–154, 153p, 154p
urbanization, 77, 77g, 78, 81, 91–92, 92p, 223. *See also* cities
Uros, 173, 175, 178
Uruguay, 159m, 164, 164p, 204m
climate of, 17
culture of, 89
farming in, 91
foreign debt of, 66g
independence in, 59m
landforms of, 13
vegetation of, 19, 20m
waterways in, 14
Uruguay River, 14

V

Valley of Mexico, 219
vegetation, 19–21, 19p, 20m, 21p, 118m
Venezuela, 59, 159m, 165, 165p, 204m, 219
culture of, 88
economy of, 30, 170, 170m, 190, 190g, 190m, 191–192
ethnic groups of, 165
exports of, 165, 190, 190g, 190g
foreign debt of, 66g
government of, 165, 193, 194, 194p
independence in, 59m, 60
landforms of, 13
languages of, 165
natural disasters in, 192p, 193, 193p
natural resources of, 25m, 27, 29
oil and, 189, 189g, 189p, 190g, 191–192
population of, 95g, 165
religion in, 165
tourism, 158h
waterways in, 14
vertical climate zones, 18, 18g, 21
Viaud, Louane, 145
Viracocha, 48
volcanoes, 4, 4p, 8f, 12, 99, 101, 132, 217, 217p

W

Walcott, Derek, 72f
weather, 29. *See also* climate
weaving, 49
West Indies, 219, 223. *See also* Caribbean Islands
wind patterns, 18

women
in Brazil, 171p
in Guatemala, 96p, 112
Mayan, 109, 112
in South America, 90
world
maps, 200m, 202m
physical maps, 202m–203m
political maps, 200m–201m
World Bank, 67
writing skills, 14, 21, 49, 68
compare and contrast, 86, 108, RW4
descriptive, 21, 56
editorial, 122
evaluating your writing, RW5
explain a process, RW4
explain cause and effect, RW4
expository essays, RW4
first person, 61
geography, 94
interviewing, 44
journal, 108, 154, 185
language arts, 70
letter writing, 139, 172, 178
math, 70, 156
narrative essays, RW2
newspaper, 92, 122, 147
paragraph, 49, 68
persuasive essay, 30, RW3
point of view, 56, 79, 139, 154
radio, 113
reporting, 113, 147
research papers, RW4–RW5
science, 32, 124, 196
short story, 37, 70
social studies, RW2–RW5
songs, 70
television script, 194
writing systems, 41

Y

Yanomami, 170, 171
yellow fever, 119–120
Yucatán Peninsula, 205m

Z

zero, concept of, 41

Acknowledgments

Cover Design

Pronk&Associates

Staff Credits

The people who made up *World Studies* ©05 team—representing design services, editorial, editorial services, educational technology, marketing, market research, photo research and art development, production services, project office, publishing processes, and rights & permissions—are listed below. Bold type denotes core team members.

Greg Abrom, Ernie Albanese, Rob Aleman, Susan Andariese, **Rachel Avenia-Prol,** Leann Davis Alspaugh, Penny Baker, Barbara Bertell, **Peter Brooks,** Rui Camarinha, John, Carle, **Lisa Del Gatto,** Paul Delsignore, Kathy Dempsey, Anne Drowns, Deborah Dukeshire, Marlies Dwyer, **Frederick Fellows,** Paula C. Foye, Lara Fox, Julia Gecha, **Mary Hanisco,** Salena Hastings, Lance Hatch, Kerri Hoar, **Beth Hyslip,** Katharine Ingram, Nancy Jones, John Kingston, Deborah Levheim, Constance J. McCarty, **Kathleen Mercandetti,** Art Mkrtchyan, Ken Myett, **Mark O'Malley,** Jen Paley, Ray Parenteau, **Gabriela Pérez Fiato,** Linda Punskovsky, Kirsten Richert, **Lynn Robbins,** Nancy Rogier, Bruce Rolff, Robin Samper, Mildred Schulte, **Malti Sharma,** Lisa Smith-Ruvalcaba, Roberta Warshaw, Sarah Yezzi

Additional Credits

Jonathan Ambar, Tom Benfatti, Lisa D. Ferrari, Paul Foster, Florrie Gadson, Phil Gagler, Ella Hanna, Jeffrey LaFountain, Karen Mancinelli, Michael McLaughlin, Meg Montgomery, Lesley Pierson, Debi Taffet, Linda Westerhoff

The DK Designs team who contributed to *World Studies* © 05 were as follows: Hilary Bird, Samantha Borland, Marian Broderick, Richard Czapnik, Nigel Duffield, Heather Dunleavy, Cynthia Frazer, James A. Hall, Lucy Heaver, Rose Horridge, Paul Jackson, Heather Jones, Ian Midson, Marie Ortu, Marie Osborn, Leyla Ostovar, Ralph Pitchford, Ilana Sallick, Pamela Shiels, Andrew Szudek, Amber Tokeley.

Maps

Maps and globes were created by **DK Cartography**. The team consisted of Tony Chambers, Damien Demaj, Julia Lunn, Ed Merritt, David Roberts, Ann Stephenson, Gail Townsley, Iorwerth Watkins.

Illustrations

Kenneth Batelman: 55, 141 t; Morgan Cain & Associates: 107; Jen Paley: 10, 15, 24, 28, 40, 45, 46–47, 50, 57, 64, 66, 74, 77, 80, 81, 82, 87, 95, 102, 104, 109, 111, 116, 118, 125, 131 b., 131 t., 134, 137, 140, 141 m, 142, 144, 148, 149, 151, 157, 161, 166, 168, 170, 173, 174, 179, 180, 186, 187, 188, 189, 190

Photos

Cover Photos

tl, W. Bertsch/Bruce Coleman Inc.; **tm,** Gianni Dagli Orti/Corbis/Magma; **tr,** Heatons/Firstlight.ca; **b,** Michael J P Scott/Getty Images, Inc.

Title Page

Michael J P Scott/Getty Images, Inc.

Table of Contents

T4–T5, Bruna Stude/Omni-Photo Communications, Inc.; **T5,** David Hiser/ PictureQuest; **T6,** Stuart Westmorland/Corbis; **T7,** Michel Zab/Dorling Kindersley; **T11,** National Geographic Image Collection

Professional Development

T35, Royalty-Free/Corbis; **T36,** PhotoDisc/Getty Images, Inc; **T37,** Comstock

Reading and Writing Handbook

RW, Michael Newman/PhotoEdit; **RW1,** Walter Hodges/Getty Images, Inc.; **RW2,** Digital Vision/Getty Images, Inc.; **RW3,** Will Hart/PhotoEdit; **RW5,** Jose Luis Pelaez, Inc./Corbis

MapMaster Skills Handbook

M, James Hall/DK Images; **M1,** Mertin Harvey/Gallo Images/Corbis; **M2-3 m,** NASA; **M2-3,** (globes) Planetary Visions: **M5 br,** Barnabas Kindersley/DK Images; **M6 tr,** Mike Dunning/DK Images; **M10 b,** Bernard and Catherine Desjeux/Corbis; **M11,** Hutchinson Library; **M12 b,** Pa Photos; **M13 r,** Panos Pictures; **M14 l,** Macduff Everton/Corbis; **M14 t,** MSCF/NASA; **M15 b,** Ariadne Van Zandbergen/Lonely Planet Images; **M16 l,** Bill Stormont/Corbis; **M16 b,** Pablo Corral/Corbis; **M17 t,** Stone Les/Sygma/Corbis; **M17 b,** W. Perry Conway/Corbis

Guiding Questions

1 t, Michel Zab/Dorling Kindersley; **1 b,** Travel Pix/Getty Images, Inc.

Regional Overview

2 l, Linda Whitwam/Dorling Kindersley; **3 tr,** Art Directors & TRIP; **4 tr,** Charles and Josette Lenars/Corbis; **5 t,** Getty Images; **5 b,** Hubert Stadler/Corbis; **6 b,** Galen Rowell/Corbis; **6 l,** Nik Wheeler/Corbis; **6 r,** Carol Halebian Photography; **7 t,** Owen Franken/Corbis; **7 b,** T. Bognar/Art Directors & TRIP

Chapter One

8f l, Royalty-Free/Corbis; **8f r,** PhotoDisc/Getty Images, Inc.; **8–9,** Darell Gulin/Getty Images, Inc.; **10,** Jimmy Dorantes/LatinFocus.com; **11,** Discovery Channel School; **12,** Jeff Hunter/Getty Images, Inc.; **13,** Corbis; **14,** Herve Collart/Corbis; **15,** R. B. Husar/NASA/SPL/Photo Researchers, Inc.; **17,** Prenas Nicaragua/Corbis Sygma; **18 t,** Bobby Model/Getty Images, Inc.; **18 b,** Ed Simpson/Getty Images, Inc.; **19,** Jonathan Blair/Corbis; **21,** Miguel Reyes/LatinFocus.com; **22,** Richard Haynes; **23,** Warren Morgan/Corbis; **24,** Fenno Jacobs/SuperStock, Inc.; **26 t,** Richard Bickel/Corbis; **26 b,** Jacques Jangoux/Peter Arnold, Inc.; **27 l,** Jonathan Smith; Cordaiy Photo/Corbis; **27 r,** Carlos Goldin/DDB Stock Photo; **28,** Sean Sprague/Stock Boston; **29,** AP/Wide World Photos/Jaime Puebla; **30,** Pablo Corral Vega/Corbis; **31 t,** Corbis; **31 m,** Miguel Reyes/LatinFocus.com; **31 b,** Jacques Jangoux/Peter Arnold, Inc.; **34,** Bryan Knox/Corbis; **35,** EyeWire Collection/Getty Images, Inc.; **36,** David Zimmerman/Corbis; **37,** Courtesy of Alma Flor Ada

Chapter Two

38h l, Royalty-Free/Corbis; **38h r,** PhotoDisc/Getty Images, Inc.; **38–39,** Macduff Everton/Corbis; **40-41 b,** Allen Prier/Panoramic Images; **41 t,** Private Collection/Bridgeman Art Library; **42,** Chip and Rosa Maria de la Cueva Peterson; **43 m,** DK Images, **43 t,** Mary Evans Picture Library; **43 b,** South American Pictures; **44,** David Hiser/PictureQuest; **45,** Werner Forman/Art Resource, New York; **46 t,** Chris Sharp/DDB Stock Photo; **46 b,** Bowers Museum of Cultural Art/Corbis; **47 t,** Charles & Josette Lenars/Corbis; **47 m,** Lee Boltin/Boltin Picture Library; **47 b,** Dorling Kindersley; **48,** Katie Attenborough/ Bridgeman Art Library; **49,** Larry Luxner/Luxner News; **50,** Bridgeman Art Library; **51 t,** Sebastian Munster/The New York Public Library/Art Resource, New York; **51 b,** The Granger Collection, New York; **52,** Gianni Dagli Orti/Corbis; **53,** Biblioteca Nacional Madrid, Spain/Bridgeman Art Library; **53 inset l,** Dave King/Dorling Kindersley; **53 inset m,** Michel Zab/Dorling Kindersley; **53 inset r,** Michel Zab/Dorling Kindersley; **53 inset b,** Dorling Kindersley; **55,** Discovery Channel School; **56,** The Granger Collection, New York; **57,** North Wind Picture Archives; **58,** Robert Frerck/Odyssey Productions; **60,** Rudi von Briel/PhotoEdit; **61,** AFP/Corbis; **62 t,** Werner Forman/Art Resource, New York; **62 b,** Bettmann/Corbis; **63,** Richard Haynes; **64,** Bibliothèque Nationale, Paris, France/Bridgeman Art Library; **65,** Underwood & Underwood/ Corbis; **66,** Brand X Pictures/Getty Images, Inc.; **67,** AP/Wide World Photos/ Natacha Pisarenko; **68,** D. Donne Bryant/DDB Stock Photo; **69,** Lee Boltin/ Boltin Picture Library

Chapter Three

72f l, Royalty-Free/Corbis; **72f r,** PhotoDisc/Getty Images, Inc.; **72–73,** Steve Simonsen/Lonely Planet Images; **74,** Sheryl Bjorkgren/ LatinFocus.com; **75 t,** CNAC/MNAM/Dist. Reunion des Musees Nationaux/Art Resource, New York; **75 b,** Philadelphia Museum of Art/Corbis; **76,** AP/Wide World Photos/Victor M. Camacho; **77,** Tibor Bognar/Corbis; **78,** Bill Aron/PhotoEdit; **79,** Joe Caveretta/LatinFocus.com; **82,** Michael Graham-Stewart/Bridgeman Art Library; **83,** Robert Fried Photography; **84 t,** MC Pherson Colin/Corbis Sygma; **84 b,** Doug Armand/Getty Images, Inc.;

85 t, Discovery Channel School; 85 b, Craig Duncan/DDB Stock Photo; 86, Bob Krist/Corbis; 87, Alex Irvin Photography; 88, A. Ramey/Woodfin Camp & Associates; 89, D. Donne Bryant/DDB Stock Photo; 89 inset, Larry Luxner/Luxner News; 90, Pelletier Micheline/Corbis Sygma; 91 t, Owen Franken/Corbis; 91 b, Bo Zaunders/Corbis; 92, Michael Brennan/Corbis; 93 t, Joe Caveretta/LatinFocus.com; 93 m, Robert Fried Photography; 93 b, Owen Franken/Corbis

Chapter Four

96f l, Royalty-Free/Corbis; 96f r, PhotoDisc/Getty Images, Inc.; 96–97, Sandy Ostroff/Index Stock Imagery, Inc.; 98 t, Discovery Channel School; 98 b, Frans Lanting/Minden Pictures; 100 t, National Geographic Image Collection; 100 b, Ben Blackwell/San Francisco Museum of Modern Art; 102, Jimmy Dorantes/LatinFocus.com; 103, Bob Krist/Corbis; 105 l, Mark Edwards/Peter Arnold, Inc.; 105 r, National Geographic Image Collection; 106 t, Discovery Channel School; 106 b, Keith Dannemiller/Corbis; 108, Cuartoscuro/Corbis Sygma; 109 t, Keith Gunnar/Bruce Coleman Inc.; 109 b, Michel Zab/Dorling Kindersley; 110, Suzanne Murphy-Larronde; 111, Discovery Channel School; 112, AP/Wide World Photos/Jaime Puebla; 113, Stone/Allstock/Getty Images Inc.; 114, GoodShoot/SuperStock, Inc.; 115 t, AP/Wide World Photos/Rodrigo Abd; 115 b, Wesley Bocxe/Photo Researchers, Inc.; 116, Jimmy Dorantes/LatinFocus.com; 117, Alex Farnsworth/The Image Works; 119 t, Discovery Channel School; 119 m, Panama Canal Museum; 119 b, Getty Images, Inc./Hulton Archive Photos; 120 t, C. W. Brown/Photo Researchers, Inc.; 120 b, J. Raga/Masterfile Corporation; 121 t, Corbis; 121 b, DK Images; 122, Danny Lehmann/Corbis; 123 t, Keith Dannemiller/Corbis; 123 m, Michel Zab/Dorling Kindersley; 123 b, Alex Farnsworth/The Image Works

Chapter Five

126f l, Royalty-Free/Corbis; 126f r, PhotoDisc/Getty Images, Inc.; 126–127, Philip Coblentz/Digital Vision/Getty Images, Inc.; 128 t, Discovery Channel School; 128 b, Bob Krist/Corbis; 130, Reinhard Eisele/Corbis; 131t, Jimmy Dorantes/LatinFocus.com; 131 b, Jimmy Dorantes/LatinFocus.com; 133, Konrad Wothe/Minden Pictures; 134, Najlah Feanny/Corbis; 135 t, Bettmann/Corbis; 135 b, Discovery Channel School; 136 l, AP/Wide World Photos; 136 r, 2002 Getty Images Inc.; 137, Discovery Channel School; 138 t, Peter Muhly/AFP/Corbis; 138 b, Robert Holmes/Corbis; 139, Angelo Cavalli/SuperStock Inc.; 140, Paul Thompson/Eye Ubiquitous/Corbis; 141, Jan Butchofsky-Houser/Corbis; 142, Reuters; 143 t, Carol Halebian Photography; 143 b, Discovery Channel School; 145, David Turnley/Corbis; 146 t, Wesley Bocxe/Photo Researchers, Inc.; 146 b, Philip Gould/Corbis; 147, Owen Franken/Corbis; 148, Robert Fried Photography; 149, Rudy Von Briel/PhotoEdit; 150 t, Benno Friedman; 150 b, Tom Bean/Corbis; 151, Discovery Channel School; 152 t, Stephanie Maze/Corbis; 152 b, Robert Frerck/Odyssey Productions Inc.; 153, AP/Wide World Photos; 154, Stephanie Maze/Corbis; 155, Angelo Cavalli/SuperStock Inc.

Chapter Six

158g l, Royalty-Free/Corbis; 158g r, PhotoDisc/Getty Images, Inc.; 158h l, GeoStock/Getty Images, Inc.; 158h ml, Comstock; 158h mr, PhotoDisc/Getty Images, Inc.; 158h r, SW Productions/Getty Images, Inc.; 158–159, Barbara Haynor/Index Stock Imagery, Inc.; 160 t, Discovery Channel School; 160 b, Paul A. Souders/Corbis; 162, Art Wolfe/Getty Images, Inc.; 164, Carlos Goldin/Focus/DDB Stock Photo; 165, Ulrike Welsch/PhotoEdit; 166, Wayne Lynch/DRK Photo; 167, Fabio Colombini/Animals Animals/Earth Scenes; 168 t, Discovery Channel School; 168 m, David Frazier/Image Works; 168 b, Larry Luxner/Luxner News; 169, Domingo Rodrigues/UNEP/Peter Arnold, Inc.; 170 l, AFP/Vanderlei Almeida/Corbis; 170 r, Joel W. Rogers/Corbis; 171 t, Greg Fiume/Corbis; 171 b, Cynthia Brito/DDB Stock Photo; 172, PhotoDisc/Getty Images, Inc.; 173, Roman Soumar/Corbis; 175 t, Inga Spence/DDB Stock Photo; 175 b, Alejandro Balaguer/Getty Images, Inc.; 176 t, Discovery Channel School; 176 b, Philippe Colombi/Getty Images, Inc.; 177 l, David Mangurian/Intern-American Development Bank; 177 r, David Mangurian/Intern-American Development Bank; 178, Stuart Westmorland/Corbis; 179, Gebbie & Co./Library of Congress; 181 l, Joseph Van Os/Getty Images, Inc.; 181 r, Charles

O'Rear/Corbis; 182 t, Zezmer Amos/Omni-Photo Communications, Inc.; 182 b, Ludovic Maisant/Corbis; 183, The Wilmington Library; 184 t, Discovery Channel School; 184 m, Jaime Villaseca/Getty Images, Inc.; 184 b, HIRB/Index Stock Imagery, Inc.; 185, AP/Wide World Photos/Alistair Grant; 186 lt, Hubert Stadler/Corbis; 186 lb, Hubert Stadler/Corbis; 186 rt, Jeremy Horner/Corbis; 186 rb, Frank Perkins/Index Stock Imagery, Inc.; 187, Yann Arthus-Bertrand/Corbis; 188, Larry Lee/Corbis; 189, AP/Wide World Photos/Jose Caruci; 191, Pablo Corral V/Corbis; 192, Kike Arnal/Corbis; 193 t, Discovery Channel School; 193 b, AFP/Corbis; 194 l, Reuters NewMedia Inc./Corbis; 194 r, AFP/Corbis; 195, Greg Fiume/Corbis

Projects

198 t, Travel Pix/Getty Images, Inc.; 198 m, C Squared Studios/Getty Images, Inc.; 198 b, Steve Cole/Getty Images, Inc.

Reference

199, Francesc Muntada/Corbis

Glossary of Geographic Terms

216 t, A & L Sinibaldi/Getty Images, Inc.; 216 b, John Beatty/Getty Images, Inc.; 216-217 b, Spencer Swanger/Tom Stack & Associates; 217 t, Hans Strand/Getty Images, Inc.; 217 m, Paul Chesley/Getty Images, Inc.

Glossary

220, Doug Armand/Getty Images, Inc.; 221, R.B.Husar/NASA/SPL/Photo Researchers, Inc.; 222, Bridgeman Art Library; 223, Fabio Colombini/Animals Animals/Earth Scenes

Text

Chapter One

Page 34, Exerpt from "The Surveyor," from *Where the Flame Trees Bloom* by Alma Flor Ada. Copyright © 1994 by Alma Flor Ada.

Note: Every effort has been made to locate the copyright owner of material used in this textbook. Omissions brought to our attention will be corrected in subsequent editions.

Turning
East

THE PROMISE AND PERIL
OF THE NEW ORIENTALISM

Harvey Cox

SIMON AND SCHUSTER
NEW YORK

This book is dedicated to my students at
The Seminario Bautista de Mexico
The Naropa Institute
Harvard Divinity School

Copyright © 1977 by Harvey Cox
All rights reserved
including the right of reproduction
in whole or in part in any form
Published by Simon and Schuster
A Division of Gulf & Western Corporation
Simon & Schuster Building
Rockefeller Center
1230 Avenue of the Americas
New York, New York 10020
Designed by Edith Fowler
Manufactured in the United States of America
1   2   3   4   5   6   7   8   9   10

Library of Congress Cataloging in Publication Data

Cox, Harvey Gallaher.
    Turning east.

    Bibliography: p.
    Includes index.
    1.   Cults—United States.   2.   United States
—Religion.   3.   Christianity and other religions.
4.   Cox, Harvey Gallaher.   5.   Spiritual life—
Baptist authors.   I.   Title.
BL2530.U6C69   200'.973   77-8600
ISBN 0-671-22851-X

Contents

1. Never the Twain   7

2. The Sound of One Hand:
    The Story of a Zen Drop-Out   22

3. The Flesh of the Gods:
    Turning On and Turning East   32

4. The Hag of Naropa   52

5. Meditation and Sabbath   63

6. The Pool of Narcissus:
    The Psychologizing of Meditation   74

7. Turning East   91

8. Buddhists and Benedictines:
    Christianity and the Turn East   111
        1. *Sangha* and Friendship
        2. Dharma and Gospel
        3. Jesus and the Guru

9. Enlightenment by Ticketron:
    American Society and the Turn East   129

10. The Myth of the Orient   146

11. Toward a Spirituality of the Secular   157

    Bibliography   177

    Index   181

1 Never the Twain

The idea for this book began on the day Harry, Denise and Michael knocked on my front door. It was a quiet Sunday afternoon, and when I opened the door, two young men and a young woman asked if they could come in and talk to me about Krishna. Both the men had shaved their heads, except for a small ponytail at the back. They wore bright saffron robes, simple bead necklaces and sandals. One wore a loose-fitting white shirt-blouse lined with intricate brown-and-blue patterning. Both carried tubular drums encased in woven baskets and ribbons and slung around their necks with broad sashes. The men had two white lines painted on their faces, beginning at the bridge on the nose and running up into their scalps. They told me later this was the sign of *tilaka*, a symbol of the dedication of their bodies to Krishna. All in all they might have looked downright menacing if they had not been smiling. The woman had blue eyes and wore a pale sari, a light shawl and sandals. Her hair was long. She carried finger cymbals and a shoulder pouch stuffed with books and pamphlets. Only later on did I learn that their names were Harry, Denise and Michael. They introduced themselves as Bhārgava dāsa, Krishna Kumari, and Caityaguru dāsa. They were all members of the International Society for Krishna Consciousness, better known as the Hare Krishna movement, and I asked them to come in.

"East is East and West is West," Rudyard Kipling once declared in an often quoted line, "and never the twain shall meet." But as I sat that day and listened to Harry (Bhārgava dāsa), Denise (Krishna Kumari), and Michael (Caityaguru dāsa), I wondered. Harry, it turned out, had been brought up in a liberal Protestant family in Orange, New Jersey. His family,

7

he said, attended church only episodically. They had, however, transmitted to him a "certain feeling for morality" but no very distinct idea of God. Denise had been born into a Jewish family in Brooklyn, had gone to Hebrew school and had recently returned home to attend a younger brother's bar mitzvah. Michael came from a Boston Irish Catholic family, had attended parochial schools for years and had once briefly considered becoming a priest. We talked for an hour, and as we did, my two younger children crept in, stared and then listened attentively as Bhārgava dāsa, Krishna Kumari and Caityaguru dāsa each told about the path that had brought them from the spiritual traditions of their families into the Hare Krishna Movement. As they spoke, Krishna Kumari took some *prasada*—cookies which have first been offered to Krishna—and handed them to the children, who munched them appreciatively. Later, as they arose to leave, the guests offered to give me (though a contribution would of course not be refused) a lushly illustrated English version of the Bhagavad Gita, the Song of God, one of the best known Hindu scriptures, as translated by the founder of their movement, A. C. Bhaktivedanta Swami Prabupada. I accepted, and as the visitors wended their way further down the street, drumming, clinking the cymbals and chanting "Hare Krishna," I noticed my children eagerly poring through the pages of the Bhagavad Gita and staring at the pictures of sky-blue Krishna and the dark-eyed cow-maidens of Vrindaban.

The unexpected Sunday visit puzzled me. Who were these strange visitors from so near and yet so far away? Were they purblind fanatics, confused adolescents, the brainwashed victims of some hypnotic cult leader? As we talked, they had not seemed like any of these. What were they, then? Was this the meeting of East and West that Kipling thought would not take place until both eventually stood at "God's great judgment seat"?

As a child I had scarcely heard of religions other than Christianity and Judaism. I had certainly never met any adherents of them. My initial encounter with the Bhagavad Gita came in a college sophomore comparative religion course. Now all that seemed to be changing. The Orient, or at least some of its Western representatives, was now literally knocking on my door, and the Gita lay open on the living-room floor. East and West were beginning to intersect in ways that neither Rudyard Kipling nor I had anticipated.

The Hare Krishna devotees themselves represented only a small group, but they are a part of something larger and much more significant—a wave of interest among Americans in Oriental spirituality whose scope and intensity is unprecedented in the history of American religion. True, a degree of fascination with the East has existed in America since at least the early nineteenth century. Ralph Waldo Emerson and Walt Whitman both read the Gita. Emerson published a Hindu-inspired poem called "Brahma," and his transcendentalist philosophy includes elements that sound distinctively Hindu, such as the idea of the "Oversoul." This early nineteenth-century wave of Indian thought not only influenced transcendentalists; it also created movements like Theosophy and the Unity School of Christianity. In the latter part of the century, a second wave of influence occurred. The famous Swami Vivekananda arrived in 1893 from India and founded the Vedanta Society, which still exists today. The influence of Oriental spirituality in the West is hardly something new.

But there is something new about the present situation. In previous decades, interest in Oriental philosophy was confined mostly to intellectuals and was centered largely on ideas, not on devotional practices. There is no evidence that Emerson ever sat in a full lotus. Today, on the other hand, not only are large numbers of people who are in no sense "intellectuals" involved, but they appear more interested in actual religious practices than in doctrinal ideas. The recent wave of interest in Oriental forms of spirituality seems both broader and deeper than the ones that preceded it.

As I began to look into this remarkable new development in American religious history, and to ask myself what it meant, I quickly noticed something else: the town I live in provides an extraordinarily fertile field for pursuing an inquiry into neo-Oriental religious movements. Cambridge, Massachusetts, was blessed by its English colonial founders with a name derived from their old university, and designed to suggest civility and higher learning. It is the home of Harvard, the oldest university in America. But in recent years Cambridge has also become something its Calvinistic founders could hardly have foreseen. It is one of the four or five most thriving American centers of the neo-Oriental religious surge. This should not be surprising, since Cambridge is full of just the kind of people to whom these movements appeal—mainly young, usually white, and almost always of middle-class background. An acquaintance of mine, recently returned from Benares, the Holy City of India, where millions come to bathe in the sacred waters of the Ganges, took a look around Cambridge last year and promptly rechristened it, "Benares-on-the-Charles."

The analogy is an apt one. Within twenty blocks of the intersection of Massachusetts Avenue and Boylston Street, forty or fifty different neo-Oriental religious movements thrive. A few blocks west stands the Zen center, furnished with black silk cushions, bells, an appropriately wizened and wise-looking resident master, and a visiting Zen swordplay instructor. In the other direction, in the basement of a hospitable Episcopal church, the Sufi dancers meet twice a week to twist and turn like the legendary whirling dervishes in a ritual circle dance, chanting verses from the Koran, the Muslim holy book, in atonal Arabic. A few blocks to the northeast is the Ananda Marga center, located in a large gray frame house on a maple-lined residential street, and specializing in a combination of meditation and community action. If one is ready for a deep plunge into imported odors and colors, one seeks out a few blocks to the south the headquarters of my Sunday visitors, the Hare Krishnas, officially known as the International Society for Krishna Consciousness. There the devotees hold a weekly feast of savory Indian food and a somewhat less piquant introductory lecture on the mysteries of the Krishna devotion. The clean-shaven followers of the young guru Maharaj Ji's Divine Light Mission have a meeting place ten blocks southeast, near Central Square. Recently a group of self-styled Sikhs, immaculately clad in white robes, turbans and wrist daggers, have opened a vegetarian restaurant near the shore of the Charles, called the Golden Temple of Conscious Cookery. One should not overlook the nearby International Student Meditation Center, founded several years ago by the Maharishi Mahesh Yoga, the best known of the swamis of the late sixties, where one can go to be initiated into the mysteries of TM. More recently, the followers of Sri Chinmoy, the former postal clerk guru who lives in Queens, have begun to be more in evidence. There is also Dharma House, eleven blocks north, founded recently by Chogyam Trungpa Rinpoche, the Tibetan Buddhist lama. And there are dozens of smaller, less stable groups, countless Yoga centers, Tai Chi exhibits and sitar concerts. When one adds them all together, the picture of Cambridge as an intellectually prim university town fades as the image of a hive of neo-Oriental religious fervor begins to take its place.

What has provoked this Oriental religious revival? Who are the people who find themselves caught up in it? Why have they left either some more conventional Christian or Jewish form of religious life—or no religious life at all—to become seekers or adherents in these new spiritual movements? What does it all mean for American culture and for Christianity?

When these questions began to puzzle me after the visit of the Krishna disciples, I decided to devote some of my own energy and to enlist my students into looking for the answers. Eventually, I thought, I might even write a book on the subject. Some of the students were already involved in one or another neo-Oriental practice and were eager to learn more. Most were just curious about what the movements meant to their adherents, why they had joined, what they were looking for. Consequently they were ready to visit, observe, participate in meetings and rituals, talk with devotees, and then pool their findings with the experiences of fellow students.

There was still a problem, however. I recognized that even though my home town provided a marvelous field of inquiry into the new Orientalism, and my students were eager to help, one very formidable obstacle remained. The obstacle was me. I could not afford to overlook the fact that, ever since my late teens, I have had a standing suspicion of excessively "inward" and socially passive religions. Especially since my college years, when I left a pietistic student religious organization because of its members' sanctimonious Toryism, I have steered clear of any religion that seemed to give people an excuse for withdrawing from the pain and confusion of the world. I had been intellectually converted from my own fundamentalism in my junior year in college by reading Reinhold Niebuhr's *Moral Man and Immoral Society* with its withering exposure of pietistic individualism. In my years of graduate study, I developed an admiration for Paul Tillich, who always considered himself a "religious socialist," and for Walter Rauschenbusch, the prophet of the American social gospel. Later I came to admire the Reverend Martin Luther King, Jr., and still later I became acquainted with the various schools of "liberation theology," including those emanating from the Catholic left of Latin America. This personal history made me very suspicious, at least initially, of the neo-Oriental wave, and I knew that, no matter how hard I tried to maintain scholarly objectivity, my inner distrust for all "opiates of the people," East or West, might continue to influence me, if mainly on the unconscious level. Even in my own judgment I did not seem to be the right person to carry out a fair and impartial study of something which many people saw as a massive retreat from the social activism of the previous decade.

After giving the problem of my own possible bias a lot of thought, I decided to do the study anyway. I was just too curious about the new movements to ignore them, and I desperately wanted to answer the questions they raised in my mind. Also, although my prejudice against some of the movements was undeniable, I was at least fully aware of it and could take it into consideration in any judgments I would make. Furthermore, as one colleague assured me when I asked for advice on this issue, anybody who is interested enough in anything to spend time learning about it inevitably has some feelings about it. Consequently, after I spent some preliminary weeks along with my students scouting out the turf, we screwed up our collective courage and plunged into our "field," the Benares-on-the-Charles.

During the first several weeks of the study we all had a marvelous time. Together and separately we attended dozens of meditation sessions, feasts, satsangs, introductory lectures, inquirers' meetings, worship services and study circles. We asked questions, read mounds of tracts and pamphlets, watched, listened and filled up countless tape cartridges. The students enjoyed the enterprise, and so did I. For once we were getting some things straight from the source instead of from the textbooks. And the groups we visited were invariably hospitable and open to our questions. What I would later refer to as Phase One, of three distinct phases of the study, was well under way.

As our work continued, we began to collate the answers people gave to our questions about why they had begun to participate in such movements. Many of the people we spoke with expressed a need for friendship or community, some antidote to loneliness. They seemed to have found in their fellow practitioners a degree of companionship they had not found elsewhere. Others told us they had wanted to learn a discipline or practice—chanting, meditating, bodily exercise—which they claimed had brought them into immediate touch with God or spiritual reality, or themselves, or something from which they had previously felt separated. Still others told us they had turned East because of their dissatisfaction with one or another aspect of Western religion, or because they simply needed a clear spiritual authority to make some sense out of their lives.

These answers were all interesting enough, but by the end of the semester I felt that something was lacking. I could understand the words people were saying to us, but somehow the key dimension seemed missing. Little by little, as the notebooks piled up, I began to wonder what it would feel like to be on the *inside* of one of the movements. Is such a feeling ever available to outsiders? No one can hope to know another person's God as she does, nor experience his faith as he does. As a Christian and a professional theologian, I realized I was neither a genuine Oriental pilgrim nor an authentic seeker. I was intrigued, curious, fascinated; but I was not a devotee. Still, I began to see that I would have to pursue some kind of "inside" knowing and feeling if I were going to understand the disciples I was studying. So I tried another method.

In this, Phase Two of my work, I tried to become as much of a participant as I could. I was still an investigator, but I no longer simply hovered on the edge of things. I did not merely observe the Sufi dancers, I whirled too. I did not just read about Zen, or visit centers; I "sat." I chanted with the Hare Krishnas. I stood on my head, stretched my torso and breathed deeply with the Yoga practitioners, and spent hours softly intoning a mantra to myself in a favorite form of Hindu devotional practice. I became a participant, not because I thought there was actually something in it for me, but because I wanted to nourish my capacity for empathy. I wanted to find out what I could about the lure of the East on the visceral level. This participant-observer phase of my inquiry, I should add, took me far away from Benares-on-the-Charles. It led me to spiritual centers in California, Texas and Vermont, and into long conversations with Zen abbots, Sufi drummers and Divine Light devotees. Eventually this second phase of my search brought me to Boulder, Colorado, where my investigation took a completely unexpected turn: Phase Two ended and Phase Three began.

I find it hard to characterize Phase Three. In the previous stages of participant-observation research, I had always continued to be more an observer than a participant. True, I had long since gone beyond simply reading descriptions and asking questions, but even in the dancing, the chanting and the breathing I retained a certain inner distance. It was all designed to make me a better observer and commentator. I was still asking what it all meant for other people, for the church, or for Western society. I was not asking what it meant for me, and I could not imagine myself as an East Turner.

Then something I had not anticipated happened. I discovered that when someone is studying beehives up close, regardless of how much inner distance is retained there is still a distinct possibility that the investigator can be stung. While trying to find out what it would feel like to be an East Turner, I found myself—contrary to all my expectations and prejudices—"turning East." While wondering what kind of personal void an Orientally derived spiritual discipline might fill in someone's life, I discovered something that filled a previously unnoticed void in my own. Almost without noticing what was happening, I slipped across the border between "them" and "us." Consequently, a book which had started out as sympathetic description became, at least in part, critical autobiography.

I did not become a convert. I have not shaved my head, adopted an exclusively brown-rice diet or taken up public chanting and drumming. In the course of my investigation, however, I became aware that many of the hopes and hungers that motivate people to turn toward the East were not just observable in others: they were also present in me. I believe, in fact, that nearly everyone in our society feels them in some measure. But I went a little further. I also discovered that at least one of the spiritual disciplines taught by one of the neo-Oriental movements—in my case it was the meditational practice taught by the Tibetan Buddhists in Colorado—met a deep, if previously unrecognized, need in my own life. Although I rejected nearly all the theological trappings the Buddhists have attached to meditation, the "shamatha" practice itself became an integral part of my life.

Now I had to cope with a difficult decision. Since the Turn East had become a personal rather than a merely professional consideration for me, I had to face the same problem I had struggled with earlier, this time from the other side. I considered the idea of discarding the book altogether. Since my study had unexpectedly come to mean so much to me personally, once again I had to ask how I could possibly be "objective." Even worse, would writing a book somehow undercut the subjective importance my quest had taken on? Troubled by both of these questions, I went back and reread all my notes. I was greatly relieved. I discovered as I went through the material again that, although I could now grasp the meaning of things that had eluded me before and could understand the whole Turn East much better, I was *not* more sympathetic. In fact, at certain points I was more suspicious. Contrary to what many social science theories insist, my being more or less "inside" the Turn East did not make me any less capable of sensing its dangers or noticing its foibles. To my great surprise, my own Turn East made me even more critical, and in rereading my earlier notes, I could now see why.

Before the change in my own perspective occurred, I had been going out of my way to see the best side of it all. Knowing my original anti-pietistic bias, I had been giving the benefit of every possible doubt to the Turn East, even to the point of repressing my hunches about impostors and humbug if the evidence was not unambiguously clear. I had been leaning over backward to be fair. After all, who wants to be accused of performing a hatchet job on someone else's religion? I had been a model of academic restraint and objectivity. Consequently, my conclusions had been tepid, commendably moderate, and above all, dull. After my involvement became personal, however, most of the scholarly restraint disappeared. I could give voice to my most troubling suspicions about many, indeed most, aspects of the Turn East, and I could express my anxieties about how badly Oriental teachings are misunderstood and misused in the West.

Furthermore, my other fear—that writing the book would endanger the personal reality of what I had found—also faded. Despite the popular belief that writing or talking about something invariably spoils it, I found that the attempt to describe my experience with the Turn East made it more real and more vivid. Without doubt there are mystical ascents and ecstatic visions that defy mere words, but my experience with the Tibetan practice of meditation had been nothing like that. In fact, it had been nearly the opposite—sane, clarifying, grounding, "ordinary." Furthermore, even though the inner essence of wordless meditation obviously cannot be described in words, one can say a lot about what the experience means for the rest of life. I have never liked the idea of *sacrificium intellectus*—that certain experiences, usually religious ones, require us to immolate our minds. Admittedly, language is an imperfect tool, but however imperfect it is, we must still use it to relate some parts of our lives to other parts and to share our experiences with our fellow human beings. I have found that writing about the spiritual discipline I learned has not eviscerated it, but has integrated it more fully into my life.

Not only did my experience with Buddhist meditation give me a clearer insight into both the perils and the possibilities of the new Orientalism; it also provided me with a central clue to the inner meaning of the whole phenomenon—something I had just not been able to find before. Now, as I look back, I can easily see why the clue had been so elusive. Indeed, how can anyone make sense out of the jumble of movements and the confusion of religious ideas and sentiments which I have lumped together under the phrase "the Turn East"? At first glance the problem of finding a focus seems nearly impossible. There are hundreds of neo-Oriental movements flourishing in America today, ranging in size from ambitious national networks down to tiny handfuls of disciples of this or that teacher. Here a quiet cabal gathers to listen to a tape of Ram Dass. There a study circle pores over the Lotus Sutra. Groups seem to appear and disappear overnight. Gurus come and go. Teachings and practices blend and overlap. Serious masters, parvenus and outright charlatans fly in and out. How can an inquirer sort through the confusion in an orderly way?

I began to study the Turn East as a confused, nearly bewildered, observer. I needed a map, and I tried two or three without hitting on one that satisfied me. Ordinarily I might have chalked up the failure of the first couple of maps to the initial difficulties one always encounters in trying to see patterns in what appears to be a hopelessly scrambled scene. But in this instance, I think, in retrospect, that my initial frustrations were helpful, because they eventually taught me something about the neo-Oriental movements themselves. The fact that they could not be adequately studied with the normal methods of religious research reveals a critical facet of their reality. New wine bursts old wineskins. Something is going on that the standard methods and categories cannot explain.

For example, it first seemed sensible to me to divide the movements into groups corresponding to the original religious traditions to which they claimed to be related. I called this the "great traditions" approach. But after I had sorted out dozens of groups and movements into the three categories of Hindu, Buddhist and Muslim, plus a special category for Sikhs, it was obvious that I did not understand the neo-Oriental phenomenon any better than I had before. The trouble was that what I had learned about Oriental religions in my previous years of reading their sacred texts and investigating their history seemed to have little connection with what was happening in Benares-on-the-Charles. People who claimed to be immersed in Hindu practices often seemed amazingly unfamiliar with the Hindu scriptures. Enthusiastic Zen disciples sometimes seemed to know very little about Buddhist philosophy. I talked with Sufi dancers who, though they could chant phrases from the Koran for hours, while twirling to staccato drums, had no inkling of what the words actually meant. One perspiring young dervish dancer, who told me she had been born Jewish, seemed a little nonplussed when I pointed out to her that the Arabic words she had been chanting all evening meant "There is no God but Allah, and Mohammed is his prophet."

The problem presented by trying to map neo-Oriental movements in relation to the classical traditions is that of radical adaptation. Adaptation takes place whenever a religious tradition travels to a new setting, but it seems to have reached new limits of elasticity in America. The fact is that most of the movements I looked into have altered the Oriental original so profoundly that little can be gained by viewing them in the light of classical ancestry. They are far more "neo-" than "Oriental." Their leaders have stirred in such generous portions of the occult, of Christian images and vocabulary, and of Western organizational patterns, that trying to understand them in relation to an older "mother tradition" can ultimately be quite misleading. By now most of them are Western movements and are best understood as such.

It took a real Asian to show me just how far this Americanizing of Oriental religions can go. The lesson came when a student from India, who is a Sikh, asked me for permission to write a research paper on a group of American young people who have organized the Boston branch of something called the 3 HO (Happy, Holy, Healthy Organization), which was started in America by a Sikh teacher named Yogi Bhajan. Sikhism is an independent Indian religious movement which was founded by Guru Nanak (A.D. 1469–1539), who was a vigorous opponent of ritualism and the caste system. It differs considerably from any form of Hinduism. Sikhs are easily recognizable because of their practice of not cutting their hair and of wearing large turbans and tiny wrist daggers. My turbaned Indian student spent several weeks getting to know these young American "Sikhs" well. He visited their commune, attended their services and talked with them at some length individually. Afterwards he wrote an informative and sympathetic paper on the group. He had learned to like them all very much. But he also concluded that their religious practice and ideas bore only the faintest resemblance to the Sikh teachings he had been reared on his whole life. Although the outward forms appeared similar —these young people also let their hair grow and wore turbans and wrist daggers—the meaning they attached to these practices turned out to be a mixture of astral metaphysics and esoteric lore completely unfamiliar to the young Indian, who wrote with good humor that his fellow Sikhs in India would be very surprised to learn that in the 3 HO movement the long hair is gathered on the forehead and covered by a turban to protect a particularly sensitive area of the brain from malignant cosmic rays. Obviously, studying this group in terms of classical Sikhism would cause more confusion than clarification.

So I junked the "great traditions" map of neo-Oriental religious movements. For a time my thinking seemed to lack any focus, and the task appeared impossible. Then I considered comparing the various movements in terms of *how much* they had adapted themselves to American culture. On one end of such a scale would stand those movements which almost seem to have been invented and distributed to appeal to the Western mind. Surely the Transcendental Meditation movement and the Divine Light Mission of the Maharaj Ji, which has its own Telex system and public-relations firm, would be located near this "high adaptation" border. These groups seem much more Western than Indian.

At the other edge one could place those movements which retain such a dense Oriental ethos that only a very small number of Westerners can find access to them. The Hare Krishna people, who not only wear distinctive costumes and try to learn Sanskrit, but also create a miniature Indian religious subculture, would belong at this nonadaptation end. Most groups range somewhere in the middle.

I soon discovered, however, that this degrees-of-adaptation scheme had its pitfalls, too. The problem is that there are various *kinds* of adaptation. Some movements conscientiously try to relate themselves to specifically Western modes of thought. Others seem to have been redesigned merely to increase their sales appeal. Some of the movements, the Zen Buddhist, for example, appear able to adapt very well in the realm of outside forms while retaining an impressive "inner" authenticity. Most of the movements are a hodgepodge of "authentic" and "adaptive" elements. So much for map number two.

It was not until after my own Turn East that I finally hit on an approach which seemed both faithful to the movements and helpful in interpreting them to other people. I had made my own Turn East for personal reasons. I had also made it with a host of internal reservations and for purposes that were quite different from the ones advanced by the teachers themselves. I was quite sure that mine was a most unusual case. I soon discovered, however, that it was not. Once I got to know them, it turned out that many of the people I met in these movements were there for personal reasons that often had little to do with the official teachings of their leaders. This was an astonishing and humbling discovery, but it did provide me with the clue I needed. I decided to avoid long descriptions of the movements or of the leaders or even of the ideas taught by the neo-Oriental groups. These are covered in other books anyway. I decided instead to focus on the people themselves. I decided to concentrate not on what the movements and their leaders claim to offer but on what the individuals who turn to them actually find. The two are often quite different. This approach finally seemed to make sense of my own experience. I had found something in one of the movements which was both relevant to my own life history and different from anything the literature had prepared me to find. I suspected the same was true for other people as well, and soon found that it was.

This book then is the record of a journey which began as a tour and turned into a pilgrimage. It describes what happened to an investigation that became a discovery. It recounts what took place as I moved from onlooker to actor, from describer to partaker. It concludes with a section on what it all taught me about the meaning of the Turn East for American society and for the American Christian churches in particular. Throughout the book I use the term "neo-Oriental" to indicate that I am not talking in these pages about the great Eastern traditions themselves, about Hinduism or Buddhism as they exist in their Asian settings. That would be another book. I am talking about the American versions of these traditions, which have begun, literally, to knock on our front doors, and about what they mean to the people who find something in them.

I have not seen Harry, Denise or Michael since the day they knocked at my door. I do not know if they still belong to the Hare Krishna group. They may not. In any case, I am grateful to them and I hope that wherever they now are in their pilgrimages, things are going well for them. They helped start me along a path which took a totally unexpected course. The journey I made, while helping me to appreciate more deeply what the East has to teach us today, also made me in some ways more Christian than I had been at the beginning. My guess is that the same thing, or something very similar, will happen to a lot of us before many more years go by.

2 The Sound of One Hand: Confessions of a Zen Drop-Out

My journey to the East began with a five-minute walk. When I moved into Phase Two of my inquiry and decided to explore the Turn East as a participant rather than simply as an observer, the next question was where, in the teeming Benares-on-the-Charles, to start. The easiest course was obviously to begin with the place closest to home. I did not have to go far. Two blocks from my doorstep, near the entrance to the A & P parking lot, stands a hulking gray frame house surrounded by high hedges. It shelters a group of very ordinary-looking young Americans—no shaved heads or saris—who are seriously engaged in the practice of Zen. I had already visited their center a few times in the first phase of the study, and they had always invited me to come back any time and "sit" with them; so one day I rang their doorbell and asked if I could join them in sitting. Phase Two was under way.

There are dozens of Zen centers in America, and they all look innocent enough. But beware of that first visit. The plainness, the lack of exotic decor, the friendliness of the residents could not be better designed to intrigue and frustrate the seeker. "What do you actually do during your sitting sessions?" I asked the young man who showed me in. "We sit," he said, "we just sit." He was right, as I soon learned for myself. One enters and is warmly welcomed by the residents (in this center, all Americans). One is given minimal instructions on how to sit cross-legged on a black silk cushion facing the wall, and then one sits and sits and sits some more, with short breaks only for silent meals. It is often boring and frustrating and—in terms of what our society deems useful—undeniably a total waste of time.

Then why do it? The answer is not what one "learns" from sitting: how it calms, focuses, centers or mellows people. The answer is no "answer" at all. Even to report what happened when I sat hour after hour, looking at a wall, hardly seems to be an answer. What happened is that my back began to hurt and my legs to ache. My mind wandered. I fidgeted. Fugitive thoughts somersaulted through my head, chased by my ineffective efforts to exclude them. Snatches of songs blew playfully into my ear. Things I had to do assumed pained faces in my mind and glanced conspicuously at their watches. I tried harder, and only very slowly, through many sessions of just sitting, did I find out that trying to exclude these cerebral intruders is just as useless and invalid as paying attention to them. Ever so slowly I learned how to let them scamper at will without either censoring them or surrendering to them, without interfering or identifying. Of all the writers about the Zen novice's ordeal, Claudio Naranjo puts it best:

In trying not to do anything, the first thing that the meditator will probably have to "do" is to stop trying. The issue will take him into paradoxical situations: thinking is a deviation from the assignment of non-doing, but so is any attempt to prevent the arising of thought. The way out, again, is not anything he can "do," but rather it is in the nature of a *realization*, a shift in point of view. It lies in the discovery that from the very beginning he has not done anything, and there is nothing he can do, however much he tries. . . . (Naranjo, 1972, p. 145)

Zen has sometimes been called an "asceticism of the mind," in contrast to the more familiar asceticisms of the bodily appetites. In one way this is true. Zen bears many of the marks of athletic training, and one Zen meditator who had run cross-country at college told me the two seem quite similar to him— that toward the end of a race he often became an observer watching his body stagger toward the finish, knowing somehow that if he fully entered that body and felt what it was feeling, he couldn't take another step. So with the Zen practitioner. He wants to limit the boisterous aspirations of consciousness, to school it in humility, to encourage it to watch its own processes, neither claiming them for its own nor disclaiming them. Yet in another way Zen meditation is not ascetic at all, at least not in the classical sense of a spirited wrestling match, an attempt to subdue and control. Quite the opposite—Zen seeks to allow all thoughts or none, neither embracing nor eschewing them. In "sitting," the hard part lies not, as many suppose, in *controlling* vagrant thoughts, but rather in seeking *not* to control them.

It is ironic that my first direct experience of the Turn East is also the most difficult to describe. Of all the movements I tried to learn about during this quest, the one that annoyed me and appealed to me most was Zen. No discipline came as close to persuading me of its validity; and, paradoxically, no other seemed as remote and unapproachable. The hours I spent in Zen meditation were both the most rewarding and the most frustrating, the most illuminating and the most unbearably boring. The "philosophy" of Zen, if that is what it can be called, seemed at the same time the most sensible and also the hardest to understand. This is why I find it so difficult to write *about* Zen. Even as the words appear on the page, I can hear the laughter of ten thousand masters and teachers echoing around me. The cascades of mirth arise from the Zen practitioner's sublime awareness that although Zen is one of the most fascinating of all the Oriental movements to "come West," no one has ever adequately described it in words.

Zen is a word shredder. It chews concepts to bits and spits out the fragments. But it is equally impossible to describe the "experience" of Zen. Unlike many other practices, Zen is not something one can describe as an "experience." The roshis, or masters, apply a simple, direct treatment to the innocents who come to Zen seeking "experience": they swat them with fans. Zen is not at all congenial to that avarice for experience which has begun to replace the old-style material gluttony in the West. Maybe that is why Zen attracts such an enormous number of curiosity seekers, and also why few novices stick with its rigorous disciplines very long.

One who comes to Zen with the desire to "experience" anything, including satori, or enlightenment, will eventually discover that Zen neither promises nor produces an experience of anything. Through its demanding disciplines one learns that all a person really needs to experience is the experience that one needs to experience nothing. Here then is a practical philosophy that manages to belittle both religious doctrine and religious experience, that provides no stated rituals, no heaven or hell, no God (and no "no-God"), and that offers no obvious ethic, since it sees such categories as "good" and "evil" as imposed and deceptive.

To the Western mind Zen seems to exemplify the mirror opposite of everything Western civilization affirms. It has no interest in results, finds such words as "aim" or "intention" misleading, undermines any sense of achievement or accomplishment and encourages an attitude in which even succeeding at Zen itself would be a kind of failure. "Success" and "failure" belong to the world of illusion. The books of Zen stories and sayings overflow with anecdotes about disciples who, just as they think they have succeeded in this or that Zen discipline, are tweaked on the nose or bashed on the back by the roshi—to remind them again that succeeding in Zen is not the way of Zen.

No wonder that by a curious twist of history this obscure Oriental sect called Zen has become a household word in America. It is the Dr. Jekyll of the West's Mr. Hyde, or, maybe, vice versa. Societies, like individuals, develop some traits at the expense of others. But the repressed elements never simply die. They lurk there in the psyche, seeking some means of expression. Consequently, every people harbors a fretful fascination for its polar opposite, its "shadow self." Zen Buddhism attracts and infuriates the Western spirit, seduces and rebuffs it at the same time. As the yin of the Western yang, its power to fascinate Western minds is infinite.

The word "Zen" itself is Japanese, derived from the Chinese "Ch'an," which refers to a particular form of meditation. Over the years, however, "Zen" has also come to signify the ultimate Void, the All-Mind or No-Mind that Buddhists believe is the basic reality. It also refers to the human awareness of this ultimate. Yet, desipte the word's ancient derivation, the Zen masters insist that Zen is not a form of meditation at all. Father Heinrich Dumoulin, a Jesuit scholar who has written *The History of Zen Buddhism*, calls it a "natural mysticism," but Zen practitioners would probably guffaw just as boisterously at this label as they do at all the others Westerners try to attach to Zen. Let us then simply say that Zen is a tradition of spiritual and psychological disciplines coming to us from China by way of Japan. For fifteen hundred years these disciplines have helped people to reach a form of consciousness which enables them to live serenely without withdrawing themselves from the everyday world of work, conflict and aggravation.

How does it happen? Although many Zen followers would stoutly deny it, and although one important school of Zen, the Soto school, does not use them at all, I believe the Zen sayings, or "Koans," remain the most helpful clue for Westerners to the method and mystery of Zen. A koan is a word, a riddle or a phrase that is generally given to a Zen initiate by the master as the focus for meditation. A koan has no answer or solution in any conventional meaning of those words. The most famous of these koans in the West is "What is the sound of one hand clapping?"—a question which either has an obvious, too obvious, answer or else has none at all. But for this very reason, the koan illustrates both the "Zen method" and the difficulty which all minds, not just Western ones, have with Zen. Here is a typical description given by Christmas Humphreys, a recognized Western authority on Zen, of his arduous and rattling encounter with the koan his master gave him.

The mind wraps itself round the given koan by night and day for weeks and months without end. First, the intellect tries to solve it and fails. Then, it is sucked dry of symbolism, analogy and metaphor. And so through endless methods the mind tries to solve the insoluble. Meanwhile the tension grows; the engine of thought is forced down a narrowing corridor with high walls on either side— only to face a high wall at the end. The pressure grows; the pupil sweats and is sleepless with effort, while the master watches, as a doctor over a woman in travail, helping where he can, controlling where he must.   (Humphreys, 1949)

Humphreys is so impressed with the lethal potency of the koan that he strongly warns against its use if there is no master present to preside over the travail. He urges us not simply to "have a go" at Zen without an experienced master at hand. Minds can snap, he reminds the reader, and some of the keenest have been known to fall apart in the struggle with the koan.

It seemed to me that Humphreys was exaggerating. Besides, who can resist the temptation to have at least a little bit of a "go" at a koan, especially after such a dire prediction? So, without any roshi's having given it to me, and without the immediate supervision of a master, I decided one day, after a month of occasionally sitting at the Zen center, to try to meditate for a few weeks on "What is the sound of one hand clapping?" Selecting that particular koan was doubtless a terrible choice, not just because I chose it myself rather than having it given me by a roshi, but also because it is so well known that it has almost become a cliché. Yet, I reasoned, if Zen is what it purports to be, then precisely the most banal and conventional koan was what I needed most. So I plunged in, finding a cushion, selecting a blank wall and meditating every day, sometimes at the Zen center and sometimes at home, on "What is the sound of one hand clapping?"

I could never record the numberless digressions and byways my mind traversed during those harrowing sessions. Nor my efforts first to exclude digressions and then not to exclude them. I was too sly to try to solve the riddle conceptually, and I started out by taking a certain pride in my shrewdness. On further reflection, however, I realized that the answer "This question has no answer" is itself an answer, and a resoundingly sensible one at that. So that response had to be discarded. As the days went on, I then turned to the meanings of "sound" and "one" and "hand" and "clapping." I spent a whole morning in meditation on "one" and nearly two on "hand." I waded through inversions and substitutions. Anagrams came to mind, reversals, varied intonations ("*What* is the sound . . . ?" "What *is* the sound . . . ?"). I rehearsed all the ways the question could be asked: analytically, angrily, desperately, factually, condescendingly. (For a long time I was sure it was condescendingly, even a little nastily: a way for my nonexistent roshi to cut me down to size.) As a recess relief, I played with the tone of the letters, the sibilance of the s's, the popping of the p's, the long way your lips travel to say "what." Then my renditions of the question became more desperate. Should I sing it, sob it, shriek it, chant it?

I began to marvel at the absurdity of the whole enterprise. I glowered inside at Christmas Humphreys, at Zen Buddhism, at the various masters of the koan-using Rinzai school of Zen, at pretentious anti-intellectual absurdities, and at myself for reaching such an impasse. Worst of all now, the koan, instead of being something I tried to meditate on while other thoughts knocked at the windows, became a persistent visitor who would not leave, even when invited, and who hovered around my head when I was in no mood to meditate. The koan became my own little surrogate of Martin Luther's pestiferous demon, leering at me impishly wherever I looked, bulging its eyes and thrusting out its tongue, inviting me to hurl an inkwell at it, as Luther did.

Finally, after several weeks of mounting fury and anxiety, I quit. I knew that I had gone far enough so that the next step would no longer be "having a go" at Zen, but "being had" by Zen. I remembered the Zen teaching that at some point the student *becomes* his or her koan, and I decided that at this point strategic retreat was the better part of spiritual valor. No doubt Humphreys is right. To pursue Zen any further I would need a master.

Let us set aside as entirely un-Zen any consideration of whether I "succeeded" or "failed" in my tiny venture into Zen koan meditation. Let us also set aside what Mr. Humphreys or any of the other tens of thousands of Westerns students of Zen would say about my exercise—namely, that it had nothing to do with Zen at all. For if what they say most of the time about Zen has any validity, then there is nothing in the world that has nothing to do with Zen. Also, although my description of my first tryst with a koan may sound flip and irreverent (both of which, however, are Zen virtues), it did give me a small sense of the enormous power the Zen masters are pointing to.

As a failed student of Zen, a drop-out from the school of the koan, what I admire and respect about Zen is that it is different. It represents the complete converse of the premises on which we proceed in the West. Unlike some other Oriental schools, especially those of Westernized Hindus, it does not claim to be "using different words for the same thing." It does not claim to incorporate all existing truths into a more all-embracing one. It picks us up and, often, throws us down because it cannot and will not be assimilated into our normal ways of thinking.

Because Zen is so different, it is a kind of giant koan itself. The thousands of little koans it uses, such as the one I meditated on, point beyond themselves to the ultimate koan. Zen itself is the sound of one hand clapping. This is why I resist well-intentioned Western efforts to explain or assimilate Zen. The late Thomas Merton made strenuous efforts, especially in the latter years of his life, to identify certain Zen words and practices with those of the Desert Fathers or other parts of the Western contemplative tradition. But the more Merton attempts to equate the Oriental *prajna* with the *logos* of the Greek fathers, or the *sunyata* of the Zen with the *todo y nada* of St. John of the Cross, the more unconvincing he becomes, especially when he concludes with the assertion that all Zen really needs to bring it to completion is "the Risen and Deathless Christ."

I'm afraid I hear the golden laughter again. Zen is not just an incomplete or culturally conditioned Oriental version of something Christianity teaches better or more comprehensively. Even though some Zen writers themselves try at times to minimize the differences, it is important *how* they do it. Zen writers do not proceed by examining the two traditions and noting alleged similarities, as Merton does. Rather, they minimize differences by denying, on the basis of Zen logic, that the whole idea of "difference" has any validity, no matter what it is applied to. Since ultimately nothing is different from anything else, why should Zen and Christianity differ? The ironic outcome of all this is that although some Christian and some Zen writers can agree that there are no important differences between the two traditions, they do so on the basis of premises which are so contradictory that they reveal the difference more starkly than ever.

The importance of Zen is that it cannot be accommodated to Western ways of thought and living. No matter how it is sliced or packaged, its singularity cannot be hidden. Despite what Zen teachers help their students to do in learning to glimpse an inclusive void or to realize a detached tranquility, Zen practice inevitably produces jarring differences and difficult choices. R. C. Zaehner, the great Catholic scholar of Oriental thought, has written that Zen is a spirituality for men and women "before the fall." He may be right. Zen resolutely holds to a vision which deals with pain, desire, choice, loss and tragedy in such a way that, while it does not deny their reality, it does not affirm it either ("neither affirming nor denying"). It equates work and play, doing and non-doing, rest and movement, being and non-being. It is a spirituality for saints and innocents, and insofar as all of us sinners maintain at least a memory or an intuition of that innocence, Zen will always have an appeal. The trouble is that most of us live "after the fall," and, if that is true, a mode of existence based on innocence can become both a temptation and a torture. Most of us need a religion for sinners.

By "fall" I do not mean an antediluvian transgression by some remote forefather; and by "sinners" I do not mean taboo breakers or even moral incompetents. To say we live in a "fallen world" means that we find ourselves in a cosmos where that primal unity that Zen allows us to glimpse is broken. It is broken, furthermore, not just because something is askew in our perception of it, but because something is askew in the thing itself. The whole creation "groans in travail," writhing and changing, heading either for a new black hole or an as yet unimagined new stage. Christianity postulates an integral link between the human phenomenon and the rest of the creation. It teaches that human beings are somehow both the victims and the perpetrators of this strange askewness. We suffer from the creation's brokenness and we often make it worse.

This underlying philosophical difference goes a long way toward explaining the messy unevenness of a lot of Christian art and liturgy, as contrasted with the striking balance, symmetry and order of Zen art. Zen has neither confessions nor Te Deum's, neither transgression nor transfiguration. Christianity is fascinated with hell and heaven. It plunges deeper and leaps higher. But at its heart, Christianity retains the hope that amidst death and suffering something is changing, not just in me but in reality itself. All this means that our liberation lies not just in altering our perception, as Zen would have it, but in opening ourselves to a cosmic energy which is overcoming desolation and pain.

Zen students sometimes claim that it is Zen which really goes deeper, since it sees beyond the *apparent* ups and downs to a common void beneath. They may be right. I am not arguing that the Christian vision is more accurate or even more credible —only that it is different. I came away from my joust with Zen bruised, humbled and, I hope, a little wiser. I also came away knowing that I had touched the outer edge of something *other* than anything I had ever known before. And Zen, despite my "failure," had taught me a lesson my further forays were to confirm—that once one starts down the road of "participation," almost anything can happen.

3 The Flesh of the Gods: Turning On and Turning East

During a visit in 1973 to San Francisco, another thriving neo-Oriental center, I noticed a curious sign outside the Hare Krishna temple there. It read: STAY HIGH ALL THE TIME! CHANT TO KRISHNA! I remembered that sign when two young followers of the Maharaj Ji told me with enthusiasm that since they had "received the knowledge" from one of his mahatmas, they no longer used any drugs at all. "We have something a thousand times better," they said.

Plainly, one issue I eventually had to face in my study of neo-Oriental movements was the question of whether the tide of Eastern spirituality in the 1970s was the successor of the psychedelic upsurge of the 1960s. Many of the young devotees I talked to in Cambridge thought it was, and offered their own experience as evidence. Some saw their movement from LSD to Eastern religion as a conversion from confusion and self-destruction to clarity and health. Others saw it as a natural progression from one level of discovery to another. In nearly every neo-Oriental movement I had studied, the use of drugs was strictly forbidden. What intrigued me in particular was the frequent assertion by people who had taken psychedelic drugs that their drug experience sharply undercut the credibility of any form of "Western" faith-vision and made some sort of "Eastern" religious world view the only credible one. Did the present "Turn East" of the seventies emerge from the turn-on of the sixties?

I was not experientially prepared for this part of my study, in part because my own relationships to psychedelic drugs had been strangely out of phase. I was a graduate student at Harvard during the years when Timothy Leary and Richard Alpert (who

32

later changed his name to Baba Ram Dass) were engaged there in their early, controversial research on the effects of ingesting psilocybin and LSD. Reports about their discoveries were whispered through Harvard Yard, but at that time there was little of the cultic or counterculture overtones that were later attached to the word "psychedelic." Still, there was excitement. I remember a scholarly senior professor of religion stopping me once on Kirkland Street in the midst of a pelting rain to describe his delight when he first listened to Bach's B Minor Mass after swallowing a small dose of a newly discovered substance he thought was called "LS-Something," administered by a young psychology teacher named Timothy Leary. As I felt the water seeping through my clothes, he went on to tell me that Leary was doing some promising research in the use of this drug at the Concord State Reformatory.

I was drenched but unimpressed. My first direct contact with Leary occurred a few weeks later. He had become puzzled by the religious images the prison inmates invariably used in describing an LSD trip. Looking for clues, he came to the Divinity School and asked me and some other doctoral students if we would like to try it. Leary argued, quite plausibly, that if scholars in the religious field could experience LSD, they might help him (at that time he described himself as "nonreligious") to understand why his prison subjects talked so frequently about "heaven and hell" or "seeing God" or "being born again" after taking the drug.

It sounded sensible, and it would certainly have been a change from sitting at a desk in the stacks at Widener Library. But I declined. I was eager to get out of school and preoccupied with completing my general examinations while trying to hold down a full-time job. Besides, I was suspicious of any kind of drug. I hesitated even to take aspirin or No-Doz, and I was reluctant to entrust my mind to some newly discovered pharmacological unguent. The Bach I listened to sounded pretty good already. Nor was my theological stance at the time particularly open to the exploration of ecstatic visions, religious or otherwise. I was a disciple of Dietrich Bonhoeffer's "religionless Christianity" and a strong believer in the Protestant neo-orthodox suspicion of all forms of "subjectivism"; so I doubted that Leary's special sugar cubes were going to contribute much to the ending of the Cold War, the abolition of segregation or the building of a nonacquisitive society.

Also, I was just plain scared. I had sometimes secretly wondered whether my toehold on sanity, already buffeted by years of graduate study, was as secure as it appeared to my friends; and I vaguely sensed that there were some remote closets of my inner self I would prefer not to open.

I became even more unwilling to take part in LSD experiments when my closest friend among the graduate students, a witty and imaginative man, became, temporarily at least, a kind of LSD convert and evangelist. Before his first "trip" we sometimes would sit for hours in Harvard Square cafés talking about everything from Greek mythology to modern philosophical ethics. Suddenly he wanted to talk about nothing but LSD: The *Magic Mountain* was a trip; the *Iliad* was a trip; *The Divine Comedy* was a trip. My incredulity bothered him and my reluctance to swallow the magic pill raised a barrier between us. The more he wheedled, the more I resisted, until gradually we began to avoid each other. I blamed Leary and acid for sabotaging a rare friendship.

I left Harvard soon after Leary was dismissed. Shortly after that, LSD became an international *cause célèbre*, and also much harder to obtain. This created a problem for me. Whenever it came out at dinner parties that I had actually been at Harvard during Leary's experimentation and had *not* taken acid, people looked at me as though I had muffed the opportunity of the epoch. Even those who were strongly against drugs seemed surprised that I had missed such an unusual chance. I became apologetic and embarrassed. I eventually decided that if the occasion ever presented itself in what appeared to be reassuring circumstances, I would ingest some LSD. Ironically, such an opportunity did not come until ten years later, and my experiences with LSD were neither frightening nor terribly significant. The real vertigo of a classical psychedelic experience did not come to me on the wings of an LSD cube at all. It came, rather, during a few days I spent in March 1974 with the Huichole Indians in San Luis Potosí State in the desert wilderness north of Mexico City, and it came through those small green-gray root growths called by the Huicholes "our little deer," by the Spanish *mescalina* and by most people "peyote."

Most writers on psychedelics stress what they designate as "set" and "setting." "Set" means the mental attitude or predisposition one brings to the experience: fear, curiosity, hope or skepticism. "Setting" refers to the physical and psychological environment within which one actually ingests the substance. When I went into the desert with the Huicholes, my set was curious and hopeful. The setting was magnificent. And something quite radiant occurred.

There are only about fifteen thousand Huicholes left in all of Mexico today. Always a somewhat obscure group, though they seem to be linguistically and culturally akin to the historically more prominent Aztecs, the Huicholes maintain traditions of religion and art that are worthy of extensive study. They weave bright red and yellow fabrics, shape their own pottery and construct a unique variety of sand painting. They coax maize and lentils from the soil with primitive tools. They keep largely to themselves, rarely participating in the growing industrial-consumer culture around them. Their religion is a synthesis of Catholic processions and pre-Columbian myths. It includes Lenten penance, fasts, dances and the annual ritual slaughter of a young bull. But what interests people most about the Huicholes is that they have used peyote in their rituals for many generations.

Once a year the Huicholes, who are scattered over three or four states in tiny isolated farming communities in the mountains, delegate a contingent of forty or fifty men and women, accompanied by a few children who have reached the age for puberty rites, to leave the villages and go out into the withering desert of San Luis Potosí State to bring home a year's supply of peyote. The hundred miles they have to traverse from the villages to the desert was once relatively free of human settlements. Now the same territory is crisscrossed by highways, power lines and railway tracks. Villages and small towns have appeared, so the reserved Huicholes—whose feathered bonnets and strange language make them objects of curiosity—have looked for more and more circuitous routes. The pilgrimage became increasingly arduous. Finally a colonel in the Mexican army who had been a patron and protector of the Huicholes offered to transport them in trucks over the most heavily inhabited parts of the route. The Indians reluctantly agreed, so now rubber tires and internal-combustion engines dispatch these pretechnological folks part of the way from their wood and stone shacks to the hiding place of the sacred cactus; they are screened from the mockery of the gawkers they would otherwise encounter along the road.

I first became acquainted with the Huicholes through a Mexican psychiatrist and public health physician named Salvador Roquet whom I met while I was teaching in Mexico in the spring of 1974. Roquet is highly regarded in Mexico for his advanced work in the psychotherapeutic use both of natural psychoactive substances such as peyote cactus, jimson weed and "magic mushrooms" and of synthetic substances such as LSD. Fifteen years ago, while working as a public health official, he became interested in the possible clinical uses of folk medicines and natural hallucinogens. Roquet has now successfully treated nearly a thousand patients in his clinic in Mexico City using his own bold combination of music therapy, psychodrama, group marathon and psychoactive drugs. Growing numbers of North American and Latin American doctors who have observed his work believe he may be on the edge of a clinical breakthrough in the treatment of people suffering from mild or severe depression and other neurotic conditions.

For a number of years Roquet worked both as a psychiatrist, seeing private patients and lecturing at the university medical school, and as a public health physician combating yellow fever. While working in remote areas of Mexico he became familiar with indigenous curing and healing rites but never thought much about their possible relevance for psychotherapy. In the late 1960's, when he was working in mountainous Oaxaca State of Southern Mexico, Roquet met a legendary old woman named Maria Sabina, a *curandera*, or healing woman. Her use of the *amanita muscaria* mushroom in healing ceremonies often seemed to help her clients, and it occurred to Roquet that some of his depressed patients back in Mexico City might profit from such a prescription. When he returned to his clinic he found five patients willing to give it a try. They all traveled to Oaxaca.

The wrinkled old woman chanted, prayed, fed the patients magic mushrooms and shepherded them through a pioneering venture into their own unconscious. Afterward, Roquet noticed that each of the five patients made a pronounced leap forward in therapy. From then on, with the guidance of Maria Sabina and of other indigenous practitioners of the curing arts, he began to use the natural hallucinogens in his own treatment of patients.

Roquet was not the first modern psychiatrist to make use of psychedelic drugs in therapy. He is probably the first, however, to do his work in such close contact with "primitive" practitioners. Several times each year Roquet travels either north to the Huichole desert country or south to the forested mountains of Oaxaca to renew his acquaintance with his Indian friends. During these trips he often gathers plants to use in his own practice, and he always takes along with him some of his staff and a few of his patients as a kind of ritual reenactment of that first curing liturgy in Maria Sabina's hut. Being invited to accompany him on one of these expeditions to the Huichole country enabled me to go where only a few white Westerners have ever gone and to taste the "flesh of the gods" in a setting prepared by a thousand years of prayer and practice.

Our sortie into the Huicholes' terrain bore few of the marks of a sober scientific enterprise. It looked more like an ill-prepared summer camping trip or a family outing. Staff members from the clinic haphazardly pushed portable hi-fi equipment, medical files, sleeping bags and coffeepots into an assortment of Fiats, VWs and one American compact. Roquet took along his wife, his ten-year-old son and his two youngest children, Roberto and Sarita, who were only four and five. There were nine patients and five staff members. One patient brought his girlfriend. I came as Roquet's personal guest. The Mexican army colonel met us along the way and accompanied us for the last leg of the journey, filling us in on Huichole character and mythology as we neared the desert. He also stayed with us during the visit as a kind of interlocutor between the Huicholes and ourselves.

It was not an easy journey. We traveled by car through the night, switched to a train in the morning, disembarked in the early afternoon and then choked and swayed the last hour in an open truck on a pitted path that billowed with gray dust. When we finally arrived at their campsite, sixteen sleepless hours after our departure from Mexico City, the Huicholes did not welcome us with songs and feasting. They watched us without expression as we jumped stiffly off the truck's tailgate, coughing and wheezing, piled our boxes and blankets on the sand and looked apprehensively at the desert. Was this where we would find wisdom, locked in the stares of the Huicholes and in the cactus bushes that stretched as far as we could see in all directions? My first thought, after trying unsuccessfully to brush the granulated dust particles from my tongue and lips with an even dustier handkerchief, was "Those Indians really don't want us here, and they're right." Just then the truck driver who had brought us noisily shifted gears, wheeled the vehicle around and headed back in the direction from which we had come, where I suspected he had a warm shower and a bed waiting.

We pitched our camp like the city folks we all were by piling dead cactus in a mound and tossing our sleeping bags down around it. At the colonel's suggestion we stationed ourselves about a hundred yards from the nearest Huichole campfire. The Huicholes had separated into three small groups strung out along a half mile of rocks, sand, cactus and (I was sure) scorpions, lizards and rattlesnakes. By the time our campsite was habitable the sun was setting, and for supper we had fresh apples which we had bought in a *mercado* on the way, cold tortillas and warm Coca-Cola. I ate sitting on my lumpy sleeping bag trying ineffectually to remove the thorns and needles that had implanted themselves in my pants, shirt, socks and various parts of my person. Mario, one of the clinic's staff, sauntered by where a group of us were crouched. Speaking casually, he warned us not to wander around in the dark too much because a four-inch needle had just penetrated his leather boot. I was wearing rubber-soled tennis sneakers and I didn't have a flashlight.

But the sunset changed my mood. The enormous blazing presence that had scorched our skins all afternoon was now a tiny red ball. As it teetered toward a world's edge serrated by the misshapen fingers of black cactus trunks, it seemed to compensate for its diminished size by reaching its shriveling purple arms all around the horizon. It was almost as though it wanted to hang on for a few extra minutes, or maybe it wanted to apologize to us for the blistering ordeal of the day and to demonstrate how much we were going to miss it. It seemed to cling for a long time to the edge. Everyone stopped talking and watched. Then quickly it sank. And we started to miss it, because the night got chilly, then cold, then raw. We snuggled into our bags, taking our thistles in with us. Most of us had not slept for nearly forty-eight hours.

But we were not allowed to sleep very long. The colonel had been talking with the Huicholes in their own language since we arrived. A few hours after sunset he roused us and told us that our Indian hosts had invited us—maybe "summoned us" puts it more clearly—to undergo a ritual purification without which we could not go near the peyote, or even stay in the desert. The colonel spoke calmly, translating what seemed to be the exact, subtle phrasing of the Huichole message into well-modulated Spanish. But he was quite insistent. Even the children were to be included. We all made our way over to the nearest Huichole fire.

The Huicholes eat some of the new peyote each night while they are gathering it. As we approached their fire they were chanting and playing reed flutes and small drums, and one of them—I blinked when I saw it—was teasing intervals from an old violin. We watched and listened, squatting just outside their circle. The inmost group seemed to be composed entirely of mature men who chanted, ate pieces of peyote, and occasionally called in other men or women from the larger circle to eat the plant or drink its juice from an earthen mug. The colonel was sitting with us, listening intently, and I noticed that he was softly translating the words of the chants into Spanish for those who were near him; so I crawled behind him and listened.

Some of the chants were traditional prayers and incantations to the high god of the tribe and to his coequal consort who is believed to be the generator of all life. Some prayers were addressed to the ancestors who, though gone in body, hover nearby and sometimes materialize themselves in pieces of white quartz (which sparks brilliantly when struck at night, a sure sign of

inherent life). But some of the chants were also original im-
provisations. These were especially interesting to me because
they indicated what a Huichole Indian who has been put more
directly in touch with his unconscious by the chemical effect of
the mescalin in the peyote ruminates about. I strained my ears
to catch the colonel's translation above the thump of the drums
and the rising and falling of the chant.

What the Huicholes were chanting about was rifles and
plastic water jars. They were troubled by what we would call
"technology" and the damage it could wreak on their way of
life. They know that technologies always exact a price, that they
carry with them new attitudes and values that dramatically alter
a culture. So the Huicholes wailed about metal tools and kero-
sene. They pleaded with the ancestors to try to understand that
in spite of the great danger these new inventions brought with
them, they did make life easier. They said they were sorry to
have to use modern implements. I edged near and asked the
colonel if they also seemed troubled about the truck that
brought them here. He said no.

After about two hours the tone of the ritual changed. The
confession seemed to be past. The Huicholes laughed and
moved about with more animation. The drumbeats became
more irregular and the flute music wilder. The violinist had
moved his fingers up the fingerboard so that the notes now
sounded more like pizzicato plucking, though he was still using
a bow. Also, our feathered hosts now seemed to notice us more
and gestured for us to come closer to the fire, which I did gladly,
since my buttocks and back were beginning to feel numb with
cold.

About midnight the music and chanting stopped. The fire
crackled for a while and then the Huichole spokesman asked
us, through the colonel, if we were now ready for the purification. We said we were. He walked to a woven bag and then
came back and gave us each a short strand of yellow rope. We
were instructed to sit quietly for a while and think of whatever
sins or transgressions might make us unworthy to join the search
for the magical little deer, the peyote. For each trespass we were
to make a small knot in the rope. Afterwards we would throw

our rope strands in the fire and our sins would be purged as the flames devoured the hemp.

I remember wondering at the time whether this part of the ritual had always been there or whether it had come in with the Dominicans and Franciscans during the Spanish *conquista*. Later I discovered not only that it had been there before the Spanish came but also that similar practices can be found among peoples who have never been touched by Christianity. Few cultures are without some ritual recognition that human beings can injure their appropriate relationship to a cosmic or social order and need some symbolic way of restoring it. This aspect of the Huichole ritual may come as a surprise to the sophisticated modern admirers of unspoiled primitive religion who somehow think Western faith alone contains a penitence-and-forgiveness axis.

My reflections on the sources of the ritual did not last long. With the other pilgrims from Mexico City I crouched on the sand, the jet-bright desert stars overhead, the sparks from the pyre sailing up to meet them, and thought hard about my life. I tied several knots, and when I threw the rope on the fire a little later it cheered me to see it devoured by the coals. The next day several of the people in our party told me they had felt silly at first but had found themselves swept along and cleansed by the tying and immolating. Even the children got the point and tied some knots in their smaller stringlets.

After we had thrown our transgressions into the fire, the shaman came by each of us individually, brushing us with a tuft of horsehairs and blessing us. Then we were dismissed. We were not given any peyote, since the Huicholes believed we should hunt and dig our own the next day. The ritual was over, but by now we all felt so purified and so wide-awake that we didn't want to crawl back into our bedrolls with the lizards and scorpions. Some of the staff and patients chatted and ate apples. Others of us cut through the darkness to the second Huichole campfire, where a similar ceremony was going on. We watched and listened, though without the benefit of translation.

Eventually we went to bed, but we didn't sleep long. Since the desert heat gets intolerable in the middle of the day, it is best to find the peyote in the early morning. We were awakened by the indomitable colonel and, after brief instructions by our Indian hosts, set out in small groups to find the little deer. The Huicholes had taught us how, when we found it, to intone a prayer of apology to its spirit, how to cut it carefully with special short-bladed knives so as to preserve the root, and how to dry and string it for later use.

Peyote is a root plant. It usually grows near the trunk of a larger cactus. Since only an inch or so of its top protrudes above the ground and it is never larger around than a small saucer, one of the early Spanish explorers was moved to praise it for its modesty and seemliness. But it was not hard to find, and after a few hours of searching, stopping now and then to gaze at a horizon totally clear of buildings, roads, power lines or any other evidence of human touch, we had assembled a sackful. We came back to our camp just as the sun, having lost again the soft color of the previous evening, began to simmer everything into a shiny white blur. We tried to sidle up to the larger cactus plants, close enough to be in the narrow strip of shade but far enough away to avoid the needles. Since the Coca-Cola was gone, we drank lukewarm Orange Crush, nibbled at the last of the apples, and wrapped some hard rolls around slices of sticky cheese. Some people even slept a little, but I stayed awake and thought.

As I lay on the sand, I remembered that I had not come here with any real intention of actually eating any peyote. I had come to the desert, I thought, to observe, not to participate. Perhaps I might pocket a mouthful or two of the little deer in my denim jacket pocket and gnaw on it discreetly while the patients were experiencing the divine madness. But I would not be in the inner circle.

A large desert hawk, a bird of prey, darted to a stop several hundred feet above where I lay and hovered motionless in the air. As I watched it I knew I would never be back here again, that this was a singular, perhaps unrepeatable opportunity. I turned my head and looked over toward the Huicholes. They had slung long strings of peyote cuttings on cords to dry and were lying in the cactus shade quietly talking with each other. My body, which should have been aching from sleeplessness, dust burn, thistle pricks and the bruises of a night spent sprawled on roots and pebbles, felt buoyant and fresh. I decided that if Roquet invited me, I would be a full participant in the peyote session. I looked up, and the hawk flew away. Satisfied, I balled up my jacket, placed it under my head, took a last swig of Orange Crush and went to sleep.

When I woke an hour later, the people in our group were gathering all the peyote we had cut into one batch to show our hosts. The Huicholes examined it closely and appeared to be blessing it, but I couldn't tell because the colonel didn't seem to want to translate. Then one of the high moments of the whole adventure took place. The Huicholes sat facing us, and one sensed they had become friendlier than they were when we arrived, although the outward expression on their faces was unchanged. One of them spoke.

We had come to the desert in search of the little deer, he told us. We had been purified, had sought out the magical fawn and were now ready. This little deer, he continued, had for a very long time helped his people to talk with their gods and their ancestors. (I thought I noticed that the words "god" and "ancestor" sounded similar in Huichole but I can't be sure.) He paused. They were grateful to the little deer, he said, for what it always did for them. Without it they could hardly live. But, he said suddenly furrowing his brown brow, "the gods and ancestors of the Huicholes are not your gods and ancestors." Now, he told us, we were on our own. The Huicholes could do nothing more for us. We should move our camp to a hill some two hundred yards away, and there, during the coming night and day, we should try, with the little deer's help, to talk with our own gods and our own forebears. He stopped, looked at each of us, and then turned and walked back with his companions to the fire that flickered only fifty yards away.

The new camp we created looked more like a temple than had our first one, which had resembled a bivouac of inept boy scouts. On the high ridge we dug a huge rectangular fire pit and arranged the bedding around it symmetrically. Some people dragged in piles of firewood while Roquet and his staff set up the portable hi-fi equipment through which the spirits of our gods and ancestors—Bach's B Minor Mass, Beethoven's Ninth

Symphony, Mozart's *Requiem*, Gregorian chants and a record called "The Flutes of Israel"—would sing to us all that night. As I dug and dragged and sweated, helping with the preparations, I became more and more eager not to miss my chance. Roquet noticed. "Do you want to participate," he asked me, "instead of just watching?" My answer came immediately: "*Cómo no?* Of course I do."

Seven patients, two staff members and I stayed up all that night around the fire, sang, laughed, cried and stared at the cosmic arch above us. And ate the flesh of the little deer. All the while we were carefully watched by the colonel and Dr. Roquet and his staff, who had portioned out the exact amount of peyote we each should have. The children slept in their ponchos by the fire, oblivious to the music. And from the darkness just outside our circle the Huicholes also watched us, silently, as we had watched them the night before.

The chemically active ingredient in peyote is mescalin, which is structurally related to psilocybin and LSD. Although some people call these substances "hallucinogens" (capable of triggering hallucinations) or even "psychotomimetics" (creating states of mind that seem psychotic), Roquet refuses to use this terminology, since few people really hallucinate when under the influence of these substances. They see and hear and feel what is actually there, only much more intensely. Roquet believes that the term most psychologists prefer, "psychedelic," has become relatively useless because of its sensational attachment to vivid poster art and fortissimo guitar music. In my experience, these substances suspend temporarily the feeling-inhibiting and perception-censoring mechanisms that operate in us during our "normal" hours. They do not add anything of their own. They are "tools" in the best sense of the word. They enable us to feel with full pungency the most deeply buried joys and fears our memories hold. They help us to see the starkness and complexity of what is around us, devoid of the gauze with which our manipulative minds usually cover them. They help us to remember past happinesses grown dim from time, present loves, bygone pains of separation and abandonment. But these substances are terribly potent. They are the psychological equivalent of nuclear energy, capable of doing enormous good and creating awesome destruction. No wonder the Huicholes wanted us to be purified before they let us touch peyote.

Peyote does not taste good. It has the stringy consistency of a turnip and the bitterness of a sour pickle. The first feeling I remember having a half hour after eating the initial slice was one of restlessness. I wanted to pace around the fire, move my arms, breathe quickly, wrinkle my nose, flex my leg muscles, perhaps trot a little. Maybe I was just cold, but it felt to me then more like impatience, a fidgety kind of wanderlust. So I walked around the fire several times, then sat.

Some of the participants gagged and retched on the pieces of peyote. But they didn't seem to mind. The Huicholes had said this might happen, that it wouldn't hurt. The little deer was cleaning us of our remaining impurities. Once one of the patients, a young Mexican film-maker named Felipe, put his arms around me and laughed hilariously because I, the sole gringo, was the only one who did not throw up. I told him not to give me too much credit too soon.

As the choral movement of the Ninth Symphony came onto our portable hi-fi, Caterina, one of the young woman patients, looked at the sky, now resplendent with a million stars, and told us she was about to give birth to the whole universe. At the time nothing seemed more sensible to me. She lay back, drew up her knees, and with the rest of us attending, grunted and moaned in travail until she had birthed all the spiral nebulae and the milky way. After the astral birth, exhausted and satisfied by her labor, Caterina told us she could now die happy. But she didn't. After a half-hour death on her bedroll she was up dancing to a Mozart *Kyrie*.

I sat by the fire, trembling, scared by the awful power of motherhood. Next to me sat a late-middle-aged patient named Maria. Who better for a mother? As my trembling continued I crawled over to her and nestled against her legs. Pulling myself into a fetal curve I pushed harder and harder between her knees, thighs and trunk. I became smaller, and though I knew I was by a fire in the central Mexican desert, I also knew I was back where I had come from, in the warm sustaining amniotic fluid that is sea and earth and mother.

Maria acted her part well. Roquet believes that in this form of therapy patients become therapists for each other, in mutual acting-out, and intense feeling expression. It is a therapeutic equivalent of the priesthood of all believers. Whether or not she was therapist or priest I don't know, but Maria was the perfect mother. She cradled her large prenate without smothering it (I am taller and heavier than she is). She crooned and soothed, but then, after several minutes, it was time to leave. I knew, and she knew too. The birth was easy, unresisted. She did not expel me, but she did not cling either. As I unwound, stood and stretched, she laughed and wordlessly rolled her head around.

Again I paced: Jason in search of the fleece, Odysseus on the high seas, the pilgrim, explorer, wanderer. The fire snapped and hissed. I listened. Flat on my stomach now, I watched it, felt its heat pulsations, listened to its flames oxydizing cactus branches. Suddenly I felt close to the animals: the snakes that live all the time on their bellies and see the whole world from this angle; the wolves and coyotes who fear the fire but creep close for warmth. I hissed, I crawled. I bared my teeth and stalked around the fire pit on all fours. I spat. I felt the warm sand around the pit against my face and the hard grains under my nails. Two of the clinic staff, always alert to the possibility of people hurting themselves, but never intrusive, got to their feet and stood behind me. The notion came to me that they thought I had flipped out and now they could be really useful psychiatric aides. I wanted to say to them, "It's OK, you can sit down again," but I was enjoying myself too much. Behind the aides I heard someone say, "It's anger!" and I wanted to snort. I had rarely been less angry.

Dr. Roquet had collected our watches before we started taking the peyote. He never likes his patients to be checking on the time because it distracts them from concentrating on what is going on inside them and around them. He removes all the props of normalcy so a patient descends into a period of temporary personality disorganization, a brief madness. The idea is that undergoing such dislocation, though it will be jarring and unsettling, reduces the obstacles to healing. A confrontation with repressed feelings occurs which might require years of treatment to reach by other techniques.

Since we had no watches, I had no idea what time it was

when one of the patients first noticed the morning star and pointed it out to us, glistening like a crown jewel over the eastern horizon. The other patients saw it and agreed it was beautiful, and then went back to whatever they were doing before. But I could not go back. In the church I belong to there is a group of young adults who like to sing selections from a nineteenth-century collection called *The Sacred Harp*, the oldest hymnbook still in use in America. They perform these old hymns with the same precision that other people devote to motets. One of the songs in this collection is a simple, stirring one entitled "Bright Morning Stars Are Rising." When I saw the morning star in the desert sky over San Luis Potosí State, I heard that hymn sung by a fifty-thousand-voice choir, or so it seemed. And it was all for me.

Strong feelings often center on one concrete object. That is what makes a symbol a symbol. It becomes the receptacle or conduit for something far more than itself. That night the morning star became for me the sign of a universe that throbbed with love—not just general beneficence, but personally focused love, pouring through real people. Watching the morning star I felt more intensely than I ever had before what I have nearly always believed, and had sensed on some previous occasions: that "God is love" is not just a pious hope but a factual statement about the character of the universe. The morning star and the song about it fused. The song was the star and the star was the song.

The feeling was too strong. At first I staggered out into the desert reaching toward the morning star. Then I fell, knelt, wept and cried, stood up, fell again. My knees shook and I trembled. Twice I tried to turn back toward the fire, away from the star. But each time its power turned me around and I was drawn toward it, only to stumble and fall again. I was deliriously happy. I thought of my family and my students, neighbors and friends—all the people whose love for me is a vehicle of the vital energy of the cosmos. Finally, exhausted from crying and weak with joy, I crept back to my colleagues around the fire and lay still.

The vision was not "pantheistic." The morning star was not the *object* of my veneration. It was, to use very traditional language, "an outward and visible sign of an inward and invisible grace," the standard textbook definition of a sacrament. Was it a "mystical experience"? I don't think so. I did not lose myself or merge with the star. I did not return as a drop of water to the great ocean or soar out of my body. I knew where I was and who I was at all times. What I felt was an Other moving toward me with a power of affirmation beyond anything I had ever imagined could exist. I was glad and grateful. No theory that what happened to me was "artificially induced" or psychotic or hallucinatory can erase its mark. "The bright morning stars are rising," as the old hymn puts it, "in my soul."

A short time later a gray line appeared all along the eastern horizon. Each of us noticed it, one by one fell silent, and walked toward the eastern edge of our camp. The sun was about to rise.

The sun, of course, rises every day. We all expect it; or rather, we rarely think about it. But somehow, on this particular morning in the desert, after births and deaths, tears and cries of gladness, the sun's possible arrival seemed like a miracle beyond the telling. As we watched, I thought of the Aztecs, those ancient kinsmen of our Huichole hosts, who were so afraid the sun would not rise some day that they made a sacrifice by cutting out living human hearts every year to make sure it did. We watched quietly. The gray line widened and became lighter. Then it came, a tiny bright yellow crescent, then a half-circle: the sun, our old tormentor and friend. We cheered briefly, weakly, and then collapsed. Our night with our gods and ancestors was over. Across the ravine the Huicholes were preparing breakfast. At our fireside Roberto and Sarita sat up and scurried to the edge of the camp to urinate. Somewhere, a few hills away, a burro whinnied. Sitting on her wrinkled sleeping bag, Maria was carefully applying her mascara. A new day had begun.

During the morning we sat around the fire, smaller now and by daylight less fearsome when compared to its blazing prototype in the sky. And we talked about the night. Dr. Roquet believes that the peyote vision is not complete until each person has talked through what he or she felt, has heard the responses of the others, and has had a chance to integrate it all into the ongoing reality of quotidian life. Peyote is not magic, and if the insight it gives us remains isolated in the demiworld of a "trip," it can do more harm than good. So we talked. We spoke of Hernando's fear, of Caterina's becoming *la madre del universo*, of Maria's maternal serenity and my fetal restlessness. I tried to talk about the morning star, but it was hard to do, especially in a language that was not my own.

After lunch we said goodbye to the Huicholes and retraced our path to Mexico City. We traveled all night, and when we arrived it was Sunday morning, but the traffic was brisk, so we said awkward *Hasta luego's* as we dropped weary people at street corners and bus stops. I returned to my room in the San Angel district, and even before I had showered I sat at my tape recorder and described as much as I could of what had happened. My precautions were not all that necessary. Months later, my memory of those days and nights in the desert was as clear as ever.

My visit with the Huicholes reminded me again that the old saying, "One man's food is another's poison," still holds. For the North American counterculture of the 1960's, swept along in the compulsive quest for some experience one could truly *feel*, the psychedelics became a new thing one had to do, a stimulus for jaded senses, a "trip." For the Huicholes they are none of these. Rather, they are an essential link with ancestors and gods, a sacrament. The hippies used them to escape their culture; the Huicholes use them to enter deeper into theirs.

So there is indeed some connection between the Turn On of the sixties and the Turn East of the seventies. Both are a scream of longing for what a consumer culture cannot provide—a community of love and the capacity to experience things intensely. Both may supply temporary, short-term relief. Neither can remedy the situation very deeply or for very long. It is pointless and irrelevant to bicker either with those who need to rely on drugs or with those who find solace in neo-Oriental spirituality. Both have found something—which is always better than nothing. But neither has the answer we need so badly ourselves.

What the Huicholes have that we do not have is *not* peyote. We have it, or its rough chemical equivalents, so that is not the issue. What they have is a society which honors its own past, which does not set person against person in a ruthless race for gold, which honors sharing and nurturing, which has no interest in accumulating more than it needs.

We cannot copy the Huichole culture. But if we want to have a society in which plants and foods and trances and songs can be used for joyous human purposes, rather than as desperate getaways, then sooner or later we must lance the pustule that is poisoning everything else, the system of greed and gain that makes us all gluttons whether we want to be or not.

What did my visit with the Huicholes do to answer my original question about a possible link between psychedelic states and Oriental mysticism? It led me to suspect that the peculiar sociology of the "drug culture" of the 1960's gave it a predictable countercultural flavor, and that its "setting," not the chemical catalysts themselves, pushed its religious language in such an "Oriental" direction. The "set" of the people who used these substances was already upper bohemian, romantic and anti-Western, and this stance led them to use the most esoteric symbols available to codify their experiences. I doubt that there is anything essentially Oriental about the psychedelics. My experience with peyote was not "Oriental" in any sense, and may not even have been mystical. Rather, my vision involved creation stories, second births, and a star in the east signaling grace to people on earth—all very biblical, perhaps even "Christian."

A few weeks after the visit with the Huicholes I met a young anthropologist at a dinner party in a suburb of Mexico City. At my host's urging I told the anthropologist something about my visit with the Huicholes. He seemed interested, but informed me at once that I had made a serious mistake when I actually ate the peyote. Some anthropologists have tried for years to see what I saw, he said. If I had remained an observer throughout, I might have written a publishable article on the subject. But since I had not been myself all that night, what I wrote now would naturally be read with considerable suspicion.

After the anthropologist and I had parted, I thought of Dr. Roquet's question to me on the night we feasted on the little deer. Did I want to watch or to take part? I knew that the

Huicholes had brought me to the end of Phase Two of my work. I was now ready for a new level of participation in the movements I had been studying. A few weeks later I packed and left Mexico to go to the Naropa Institute in Boulder, Colorado. It was there that Phase Three really began.

4 The Hag of Naropa

The red-and-orange cushion under me felt harder than it had an hour before. The room was hot, and outside the large windows of the Karma Dzong meditation hall the increasingly loud grinding of gears and bleep of horns reminded me that Boulder's late-afternoon traffic was already in the streets. Across from me and beside me sat long rows of fellow meditators, legs crossed, eyes looking straight ahead. Some of the men had removed their shirts, but most people were dressed in jeans and tank tops or T-shirts. A lazy August fly buzzed past my nose but decided not to land. Inside me a parade of images and memories marched by, but as I noticed them I kept returning to take note of my departing breath, as the instructor had told me. I was serene and unhurried even though I had a supper engagement and the traffic noises were telling me it was time to go.

Now the horns and engines grew more insistent. I shifted my weight on the cushion and felt the familiar tiny abdominal quiver which, like a doctor's pocket bleeper, dependably reminds one of an impending obligation to be met. Instinctively I started to glance at my watch, to check on whether it was indeed time now to leave the meditation hall and join my friends for dinner. But for some reason, I did not move. I did not turn my watch toward me. I did not move my eyes toward its dial. I sat still, and slowly noticed a slight—an ever so slight—shift in my perspective. The shift was both tiny and tremendous, like the split second just before and just after midnight on New Year's Eve. At the moment when I did not look at my watch, I became aware that whether I got to supper late, or at all, was significant, but not urgent. I would go when I was ready. The choice of when and whether to go was mine. To anyone else, such a realization might seem utterly commonplace. But to me the change it signaled—not just in my attitude toward the meditation I had been trying so hard to learn, but also in my attitude toward many other things—was immeasurable. Slowly, still without looking at the watch, I slipped it off my wrist and into my pocket.

After a few minutes I glanced around at the other meditators and felt another change. They all looked the same, but somehow they also looked completely different. What had changed was that now my status was different. I was no longer merely a visitor—or a sympathetic observer or a friendly outsider. Although I did not know the names of most of the people in the hall, I felt closer to them, at least at that moment, than I did to the people outside the window scurrying to their supper-hour engagements.

The feeling left as quickly as it came. Then I did consult my watch, put my sandals on, puffed up my cushion for the next user and made my way out of the hall. On the street, too, surprisingly, I was also at home. I looked forward to supper, to seeing my friends, to conversation. I did not feel that I had been interrupted. As I walked toward the bus stop, however, I knew that on this day the meditation I had been learning for the past three weeks was no longer merely an option or a luxury. I was now a practitioner of meditation, not merely an observer. Noiselessly, almost without noticing it, I had taken another step in my journey to the East. Without being converted or changing my theology or joining anything, I had become something of an East Turner myself. Phase Three was beginning.

Perhaps, in retrospect, there was no reason to be surprised. My sympathetic trek through America's neo-Oriental county fair had been proceeding on schedule and I had been savoring all the sights. I had met fascinating people, sampled varieties of cotton fluff and candied apples, peered into the dark sideshows and listened to the spiels of the barkers. My notebooks were crammed and my collection of tapes was piling up. I knew there was a book to be written on this. Then, on this summer day in Boulder, in the middle of the midway, something I should have anticipated happened. I became a part of what I was studying.

The tourist-pilgrim had become more pilgrim than tourist. The East Turners became "us" instead of "them." The subtle line between writing about other people, with whose search I could often identify, versus writing about myself as one of the seekers, had been crossed. I was now writing about a phenomenon I was part of, and my evaluations and criticisms would now be judgments about myself.

This unexpected role reversal did not make me any less critical of many facets of the Turn East. In fact, if anything, it sharpened my awareness of the overlaid tiers of phoniness and gimmickry, of desperate need and cheap comfort which can be found in so much of the neo-Oriental mystique. But I could see the other side more clearly, too. I could detect the sources of the Turn East—the search for friends, the thirst for immediacy, in myself as well as in others. I could taste the lure of the exotic and sense the strong appeal of a teacher who knew something I wanted to know. I did not renounce any previous memberships, undergo any initiation rites or subscribe to any neo-Oriental mythology. But I did discover a *practice* which had become important, not for my study but for me. So I had to admit that, even according to my own categories, I was an East Turner myself.

It all started innocently enough. I had come to Boulder from Mexico in response to what seemed a golden opportunity to gather more impressions for my book. The opportunity came in the form of an invitation to teach a course in Christianity at the Naropa Institute, a Buddhist study center (now a college) in Boulder, which had been founded a year or two before by Chogyam Trungpa Rinpoche, who, besides being a meditation teacher, is also a scholar of Western and Buddhist art. Trungpa (the "Rinpoche" is a traditional title applied to lamas) and thousands of other Tibetans had been forced to leave Tibet in 1961 when the Chinese invaded and closed the monasteries. He first stayed in India, where many of the refugee Tibetans still live, then moved to England, studied at Oxford University, and later organized a Buddhist meditation center in Scotland. Trungpa came to the United States in 1970 and founded a meditation center called Karmê Chöling (formerly Tail of the

Tiger) in Barnet, Vermont. Then, in 1973, he started a study institute in Boulder and named it Naropa after a revered eleventh-century Buddhist teacher. In keeping with the ancient Buddhist monastic practice of welcoming visitors from the other great traditions, and also because he wants Naropa to become a genuine East-West exchange center, Trungpa invited me to teach a course on the life and teachings of Jesus there during the summer session.

It is not hard to see why a refugee lama from Tibet might settle in Colorado. The foothills of the Rocky Mountains begin at Boulder and the peaks themselves can be seen from the streets. Snow-patched cliffs and cold glens alternate with carpets of sturdy grass and mountain laurel. Steep trails and narrow valley roads climb and intersect. The air is clean and clear. The scenery probably comes closer to the Tibetan Himalayas than anything else America offers.

When I arrived at Naropa to teach my course on the New Testament, nothing in the environment surprised me. Boulder is the home of the University of Colorado. It is full of bookstores, natural-food restaurants, denim cut-offs and shoulder bags. I was at home. Also, I had taught at summer institutes before, and this one seemed familiar. There were nearly a thousand students and a faculty of forty offering almost a hundred courses. There was the usual gossip about which teachers and seminars were worth taking, where to eat, what mountain roads to explore, where the action was. Yet under the frivolity and humor and sunbathing at the pools I sensed a serious, at times frighteningly serious, commitment to the "practice," the word the Naropa students invariably applied to sitting in meditation in a regular, disciplined way. Nearly all the faculty and most of the students engaged in this "sitting" one or two hours every day, either in their own rooms or in one of the group meditation halls. And every other week many of them participated in the Sunday *nyinthun*—twelve hours of consecutive sitting with breaks only for short meals and even shorter periods of "walking meditation" around the inside of the hall. I got the message. If I was going to learn anything at Naropa I would have to "sit," and sit a lot. Furthermore, I

decided I would not use a do-it-yourself approach as I had with
Zen, but would take advantage of the instruction in meditation
that Naropa offered.

The Tibetan method of meditating is so simple that it sounds
trite. There is little emphasis on correct posture or hand position. No special clothing or setting is needed (though I found
it better to wear loose clothes and to meditate in the same room
with other meditators). No koans or mantras are used, at least
in the early stages. No master ever hits a student with a fan.
What is emphasized, however, is sitting frequently, sitting
regularly, and sitting for long periods. Although many Zen instructors start their students out on short sittings and do not
encourage day-long periods of meditation until the novice has
learned the basics well, Trungpa seems to have enormous confidence in what sitting itself can do for those who will simply
plunge in, with periodic help from an instructor. He believes
that no amount of reading about Buddhist teaching will make
any sense at all unless the student is engaged in sitting meditation. One night at a public lecture he shocked some experienced
sitters by inviting, even urging, all eight hundred people present,
many of whom were visitors who had never sat for even an
hour, to participate in an upcoming twelve-hour *nyinthun.*
"You can do it," he assured them, and many did.

In my own desultory attempt to learn meditation, I had already sparred with a form of Zen, using a koan—and had lost.
Later I had evolved my own hybrid brand of meditation and
practiced it sporadically, always realizing that something was
missing when I neglected it. But I was always too busy and too
undisciplined to sit regularly. At Naropa, however, I found myself in an atmosphere where sitting was somehow expected. So
I picked out a red-and-orange cushion at the Pearl Street Karma
Dzong in Boulder, the local branch of Trungpa's growing network of Dharmadatus (teaching and meditation centers). There
I sat an hour every day, sometimes twice a day, in a sunny room
with a varnished floor where from eight to eighty other meditators might gather. Most important of all, I had an instructor.

At first the only thing my instructor in the Tibetan form of
meditation showed me was how to be aware of my exhaling, to
"follow my breath" out into the world, identifying as far as

possible with breathing out and letting go, not thinking at all about breathing in. Surprisingly I found that within a few days I had mastered the basics. Thoughts of all kinds do occur, of course, but the meditator, as in Zen, makes no effort to sort, censor or exclude. One merely returns again and again to the departing breath as a kind of home plate or ground zero. Squatting on a cushion, hands resting lightly on one's knees, eyes open but slightly lidded and not focused on anything in particular, the meditator gradually discovers a perspective on the endless rush of mental processes. It feels a bit like standing on a bridge and watching the leaves and twigs float by on the stream passing underneath. Sometimes the mind does follow one of these bits of flotsam, frequently even becoming absorbed or agitated by it. But when the meditator notices that this has happened, he or she simply returns to the departing breath again. The stream rolls on and the flotsam slowly drifts around the bend as more appears upstream.

Before I arrived at Naropa I decided I would enroll in some formal courses in Buddhism, since my previous exposure to Buddhist thought had been minimal. The catalog was crammed with intriguing seminars on the Bardo Thodol, Vajrayana literature and Theravadan theory and practice. However, since as a concept-oriented person I would be inclined to burrow in a library and read all the texts and monographs I could find on the subject, I decided—as a corrective—that this time I would approach things differently. I would go the *visual* route. So, in addition to the daily meditation with the instructor's guidance, I signed up for two courses in the history and significance of Buddhist art, one offered by Trungpa himself. I laid aside words for pictures and postures.

As the days and weeks went by, I found that although I was fascinated by the art history of Buddhism, it remained somewhat exotic and merely "interesting" for me. The meditation, however, was something else. From the very outset, from the first hour-long sitting, I sensed that something unusual was happening to me. My level of internal chatter went down. I did not invest situations with so many false hopes and fantasies. I walked away from the sitting feeling unruffled and clear-headed. I could teach with more precision and listen to people more attentively. Soon the hour or two of sitting was not a chore but something I looked forward to. I began to sense in myself something many East Turners had told me about in words I had not comprehended. Even the excited testimonies of the Divine Light people and the practitioners of Transcendental Meditation now seemed a little more credible.

Ironically, the more I meditated, following my Buddhist instructor's advice, the more my assigned role as resident Christian theologian at Naropa seemed eminently sensible and right. I even noticed certain "buddhistic" elements in Jesus that I had never seen so clearly before, especially his refusal to be what people expected him to be, his unwillingness to be drawn into abstract discussions, and his constant insistence that if people would only look closely at what was going on in their midst they would see that the Kingdom of God was already coming to them. Paradoxically my plunge into Buddhism at Naropa had made me feel more "Christian" than I had felt when I arrived there.

I found Chogyam Trungpa Rinpoche, the founder of Naropa, a likeable and approachable figure, not at all the costumed sadhu so many East Turners yearn for. He dresses in conventional Western style, with jacket and tie, forgoing all the flim-flam of Guru-dom. Though many of his students want to press him into the holy man role, Trungpa constantly warns them against it. In his public lectures he pokes fun at those who are seduced by brocades and incense and exotic music. "My lineage is really quite dull," he insists. His book *Cutting Through Spiritual Materialism* sounds the same cautionary note again and again. He once warned an audience of eager listeners they should not look to him or Tibet or Buddhism for answers, that all would come clear if they could once really see the mountains outside Boulder.

Dull lineage or not, Chogyam Trungpa, in his public lectures given every Tuesday and Thursday evening, provided the big occasions of the week for everyone at Naropa. Scheduled for eight o'clock, the lectures rarely began before nine thirty, sometimes not until ten or ten thirty. Although people complained at first, they quickly learned to accept and even appreciate the teacher's tardiness. Part of the ease of adjustment was due to the physical setting. The lectures were held in the rented gymnasium of a local parochial school. The gym floor had been temporarily covered with a huge segmented rug. There were no chairs; the audience had to lie or sit on the floor. Consequently the atmosphere between eight and ten resembled a friendly beach scene. People lounged on blankets and cushions, read, chatted in small groups, snoozed, and circulated to check on friends and to gossip. No one ever seemed bored. It occurred to me that in arriving two hours late, Trungpa, who constantly criticizes the frantic pace and needless hurry of American life, had cleverly created a small oasis in time. It was a social hour without agenda, an open clearing for quiet conversation and relaxed camaraderie.

The lectures themselves were puzzling to me, at least at first. A small unimpressive brown-skinned man with a slight limp, Trungpa talks in a flat, husky voice and is often repetitious. He sits as he speaks, sips sake from a glass, indulges in long pauses, and appears to use no notes at all. At first I simply could not understand why eight hundred people would wait two hours to listen to his often tedious utterances. But as I returned each time and let his remarks connect with the realization that was slowly dawning on me while "sitting," I began to appreciate what was going on: he was using the lecture to help us grasp what was happening to us in our meditation. The lectures were a massive, if subtle, attempt to help us deal with the self-confrontation "sitting" inevitably produces.

Trungpa is a different kind of teacher from those most of us have met. Some teachers write so well one doesn't need to know them personally at all. Their printed words speak for themselves. Others teach by communicating some elusive aspect of their own person: eye contact and body movement say all. Their words mean nothing on a printed page, and little even on a tape. Still others communicate only if both teacher and student are sharing in some common enterprise. This is the way masters work with apprentices in many of the arts and crafts. Trungpa's teaching falls in the third category. His books, though interesting, are hardly commanding. When he lectures to ordinary audiences he may or may not impress his hearers, depending largely on the circumstances. But in a master-apprentice setting, where nearly everyone is working at the development of a personally adequate spiritual discipline, and where everyone knows that Trungpa, whatever his weakness, is an acknowledged master of just such a discipline, intense and genuine learning occurs. I know because I learned.

I learned so quickly at Naropa that it raised questions in my mind about the virtual disappearance of the master-apprentice axis in American higher education. Even in religious studies we generally think of fields and areas of competence. We blithely accept the divorce between a student's mastery of the subject matter and his or her personal growth and maturation. We sometimes even purposely arrange curricula to minimize the chances of a student's working too closely with any one teacher, and we tend to discourage anyone's having "disciples." While this educational strategy may facilitate the student's achieving a certain abstract competence, it perpetuates a chasm between knowing and doing, information and growth. This hiatus is not only debilitating to the student, it actually falsifies what most religious traditions teach: that mere data gathering undermines the life of faith. What happened to me at Naropa occurred not because I had learned something *about* Buddhism, but because Trungpa and his students had taught me *how* to meditate.

For me, meditation is not a mystical experience. It is almost the opposite. It forces me to pare back daydreams, cut through rosy expectations and look carefully, often even painfully, at what is actually there in front of me and inside me. There are hundreds of ways to meditate, and endless theories about what it does or doesn't do, and why. Researchers have measured the pulse, skin temperature, brain waves, and breathing rates of various people doing different kinds of meditation. They know the effects are not just mental. Many doctors, including my Harvard colleague Dr. Herbert Bensen, a cardiologist, believe, with excellent evidence, that meditation can help patients with chronic heart problems.

My own experience, mainly gained from the type of meditation I learned from Trungpa and his students, is that, far from luring me away from active participation in the world (as some critics claim it does), it enables me to think and act more decisively, to see things and people in sharper focus, and to suffer fewer regrets and recriminations. I came away from Naropa convinced that a sitting-type meditation is perfectly compatible with Christian life. Eventually it might even provide a modern equivalent of something we have lost from our heritage, the idea of a Sabbath or a stated time to cease, to do nothing, to allow what is to be. I will return to the idea in the next chapter.

Despite the fact that Naropa produced a role change in my study of the Turn East, it did not in any way lessen my doubts and suspicions about the neo-Oriental wave. It confirmed all my worst fears about how even the most valuable teaching, including the art of meditation, can be misused, often unconsciously. New adepts strode about the streets of Boulder wearing imported "meditation pants" and ostentatiously lugging their sitting cushions under their arms. Peddlers hawked vaguely Tibetan-looking bracelets and ornaments. The question of how long one had been "sitting"—and even how long one could sit at a stretch—sometimes became the arena for a sort of spiritual one-upmanship, reminding me of the way young civil rights workers used to compare the length of their jail terms in the sixties. Worst of all, I found people leaping into the labyrinth of Buddhist concepts and ill-digested Sanskrit or Tibetan terms in what often sounded like an unintended caricature of serious discipleship. Phrases like "bad karma" and "more evolved person" swirled like incense smoke screens over meals and conversations. I am sure it all made the Buddha chuckle.

My principal reservation about the Buddhist teaching I heard at Naropa, as opposed to the sitting practice itself, is that despite its explicit emphasis on not trying too hard, it seems to lay out a very long path. One hears a lot about "cessation," but there hovers in the background the specter of a stupendous mountain the seeker must eventually climb in order to become enlightened. The "path" has many stages. And to an outsider it appears cluttered with snares and laden with possibilities for backsliding and frustration. More "advanced" students hinted seductively about what lay ahead for beginners, especially in the sexual imagery of Tantra. Others talked evasively about the "hundred thousand prostrations" one must do at a certain stage, and of complex forms of visual meditation and internal chanting and the rest. Novices listened, wide-eyed, while veteran meditators smiled at their enthusiasm and looked at each other knowingly.

When I noticed all this I shuddered. It called to mind the story of the pious young Martin Luther crawling up the stairs of St. Peter's on his knees, or the practice of adding up "Hail Mary's" and "Our Father's" which eventually enraged so many Catholics. I detected in this excessive elaboration that Buddhism, like every other spiritual tradition, has an uncanny capacity to complicate the simple, to escalate an elemental insight into a colossal caricature of itself.

But the sitting meditation remains the core. No teaching should be discarded either because of the excesses of its students or the pretentiousness of its interpreters. Learning to meditate does not entail ingesting the entire corpus of Buddhist ideology, doctrine and world view—or any of it. In fact, I believe there is no reason why it cannot become an integral part of Christian discipleship. I returned from Naropa convinced that it would be a part of mine.

On the night before I left Boulder some students and faculty colleagues gave me a farewell party. During the festivities someone pressed into my hand a small book describing the life of the original Naropa, the eleventh-century sage after whom the institute had been named. On the plane the next day I pulled it out of my pocket and thumbed through the story. Naropa, it seems, was a famous Indian teacher who, by the time he had reached middle age, was the acknowledged authority in the Buddhist scriptures. In all the world he had no equal in his scholarly acumen, and students came in from far and wide to sit at his feet. One day, however, there appeared at his hut a blemished and crotchety old hag who began to berate and insult him. As he tried to study she continually taunted him and asked him about the meaning of passages in the sacred texts. Whenever he answered she merely cackled. Sometimes she would sneak up close and poke him with a stick. Finally, in a fury, Naropa shouted at her to go away and reminded her that in the entire world there was no one who was more versed in explaining the sense of the texts. The hag laughed uproariously. "Yes, you know the sense," she croaked, "you know the sense. But do you know the *meaning*?" She disappeared. And Naropa left his desk, went to the forest and apprenticed himself to a teacher. Having spent his life mastering the texts, he now wanted to learn what they meant for Naropa.

5 Meditation and Sabbath

Even before I left Tibet-in-the-Rockies for Benares-on-the-Charles, I began to wrestle with what it means to be a Christian who practices a "Buddhist" form of meditation. For many people this would not pose any problems, because mixing assorted tidbits from different religious traditions comes easily to some. But it does not come easily to me. Others would simply sever previous affiliations, but I had not done that, either. I was not a convert, and had no intention of becoming one. So the question remained: What role can meditation play in the life of a person who is neither a Buddhist nor a syncretist, but remains a Jew or a Christian?

For the past several years, Eastern meditation has been finding a larger and larger place in Christian practice. In monasteries from Maine to New Mexico, Roman Catholic contemplative orders have begun to integrate one or another form of sitting into their daily liturgical schedule. The Benedictine monks I visited in Vermont last winter began the day by "sitting" at 4:30 A.M., two hours before dawn, using cushions and postures similar to the ones I had encountered at Naropa. And in many churches, basic meditation techniques are taught to Christians, most of whom have no interest in becoming Hindus or Buddhists.

It should come as no surprise that certain Oriental spiritual disciplines are finding a resonance in the modern West. Christianity has its own contemplative tradition, much of which is highly reminiscent of such Oriental practices as sitting, breath concentration and mantra chanting. According to the New Testament, Jesus himself, despite his turbulent life, often took out times to withdraw and be alone. The early desert fathers developed a wide range of contemplative techniques. In the Eastern Christian church, a practice known as "Hesychasm," the attempt to achieve "divine quietness"—for which the Greek word is *hesychia*—emerged. One of its early proponents, St. John Climacus, taught his followers to concentrate on each breath they took, using the name of Jesus as a kind of mantra to accompany this breathing. A later Hesychast, St. Nicephorus, instructed his disciples to attach a prayer to each breath and to focus their attention on the centers of their own bodies while meditating. Later Hesychasts believed that while in such a state of prayerful contemplation people could see the inner light of the Transfiguration. This will all sound familiar to any Westerner who has recently had instruction in a form of Oriental meditation in which breath concentration, chanting or an inner light play an important role.

Christian contemplative practices in the West developed in a somewhat more intellectual and moralistic direction. St. Ignatius Loyola, the founder of the Jesuit order, prescribed a rigorous form of spiritual discipline suitable for a soldier in Christ's army. Yet even the Ignatian *Spiritual Exercises* outline methods of introspection and patterned imagining which would seem familiar to practitioners of Oriental forms. Among Protestants, the practice of daily prayer and Bible reading was once held to be indispensable to Christian life. But the failure of most churches actually to teach people how to pray and the difficulties involved in learning the difference between reading, studying and meditation on a text have produced a generation of Protestants who live with practically no spiritual discipline at all.

Still, despite similarities with Western practices, a vague uneasiness often bothers many Christians and Jews who meditate. Some feel uneasy because they seem to be filching someone else's spiritual inheritance. They suspect that to use the technique without the religious world view that comes with it is somehow dishonest, that it shows a disrespect for the whole philosophical structure within which meditational practices have come to the West. I respect the reservations these people have, and their reluctance. They are rightly suspicious of the groups that have cut meditation out of its metaphysical setting and reduced it to a mere psychological gimmick. They can not accept the world view within which meditation has been integrated in Buddhism. Yet they have found that the practice of meditation undeniably resonates with something within them. What can they do?

I have come to believe that the answer to this question lies neither in swallowing the entire corpus of Buddhist philosophy nor in reducing meditation to a psychological self-help device. Rather, a third possibility presents itself. It consists in combining the serious practice of meditation with a patient rethinking of the biblical tradition and the history of Jewish and Christian spirituality—uncovering those points in our own spiritual tradition where the functional equivalents of meditation appear. I think there are many such points—that meditation need not be viewed as an exotic import, but as something with roots in our own tradition.

I did not come to this conclusion easily, and as usual the basic insight—that Judeo-Christian spirituality has its own equivalent of the meditational practice—came to me first not from a book but through an experience that altered my way of thinking out the issue.

A few days before I was scheduled to leave Naropa, a rabbi who lives in a small town near Boulder invited me to join him and his tiny congregation in celebrating the weekly Sabbath— not just the religious service that took place in his back yard, but a genuine, old-fashioned Shabbat, a whole day of doing very little, enjoying the creation as it is, appreciating the world rather than fixing it up. I accepted the invitation and joined in the relaxed Sabbath, which lasted, as tradition dictates, from Friday sundown until sundown on Saturday. During those luminous hours, as we talked quietly, slept, ate, repeated the ancient Hebrew prayers and savored just being, rather than doing, it occurred to me that meditation is in essence a kind of miniature Sabbath. For twentieth-century Christians, and for many Jews as well, it provides a modern equivalent of what the observance of Sabbath once did, but does no more.

The Jews did not invent the idea of Sabbath. Though its origins remain obscure, it undoubtedly had antecedents in the religious milieu of the ancient Near East. It is not impossible that the core insight from which Sabbath developed is identical with the one which, under different historical circumstances, eventually produced the practice of meditation. Both prescribe a regular time when human beings *do nothing*. This connection becomes even more evident when we realize that the word for Sabbath in Hebrew comes from a root meaning "to desist." Sabbath originally meant a time that was designated for ceasing all activity and simply acknowledging the goodness of creation. It was not, at first, a day for cultic acts or long worship services. It was a time set aside for affirming what is.

But meditation and Sabbath also differ, at least when we compare Sabbath with the theories of meditation as they are now frequently taught by neo-Oriental masters. Meditation, though it begins as something one does at a particular stated time, is also often interpreted as the key to a total way of life. Sabbath, on the other hand, is one day out of seven. It never becomes a complete way of life. It represents the Israelites' recognition that although human beings can catch a glimpse of the pure realm of unity and innocence, they also live in the fractured world of division, greed and sorrow. Sabbath is Israel's ingenious attempt to live both in history and beyond it, both in time and eternity.

In the earliest recorded expression of the idea of Sabbath, in the Fourth Commandment of Moses, one day in every seven is set aside.

Six days shalt thou labor and do all thy work; but the seventh is the Sabbath of Yahweh: in it thou shalt not do any work, thou, nor thy son, nor thy daughter, thy manservant nor thy maidservant, nor thy cattle, nor thy stranger that is within thy gates; for in six days Yahweh made heaven and earth, the sea and all that in them is, and rested the seventh day; wherefore Yahweh blessed the sabbath day and hallowed it.

At first reading, the suggestion that God "rested" after the toil of creation—the image is of a craftsman sitting down and wiping his brow—sounds quaintly anthropomorphic. The word "rest" literally means "to catch one's breath." God, like us, gets tired and has to restore himself. The passage may indeed depict a less exalted view of God than later emerges in Jewish faith. On further reflection, however, and with the anthropomorphic symbol somewhat decoded, a deeper truth appears, and with it a possible link with the tradition of sitting meditation.

The first thing to notice about God's activity on the Sabbath is that it focuses on breathing. We all stop to draw breath after we have been exerting ourselves, and the passage may mean no more than this. But to depict God himself as one who ceases work and does nothing but breathe could suggest a deeper and older stratum of spiritual consciousness which lies behind the passage itself. Breath is a source of renewal, and God, like human beings, returns periodically to the source.

The second facet of this ancient passage is even more telling. Sabbath is the Jewish answer to the profound question all religions face about the relationship between doing and being, between what Indian mystics call *sat* (perfect being) and *prana* (spirit and energy). All religions must cope with the apparent contradiction between a vision of reality as ultimately changeless and one that contains contrast, opposition and change. In the Bible the key terms are not "being" and "energy" but "creation" and "rest." Viewed in this light, the idea of Sabbath is not naïve or primitive at all. It is a highly sophisticated philosophical notion. It postulates an ultimate force in the universe which is not just passive and changeless but which acts and is acted upon. Yet it affirms what most religions also say about the ultimate: it is eternal and perfect. Sabbath links God and world and human beings in a dialectic of action and rest, of purposeful doing and "just sitting." The seventh day is holy to Yahweh, and one keeps it holy not by *doing* things for God or even for one's fellow human beings. One keeps it holy by doing nothing.

I think Hui-neng, the legendary sixth Zen patriarch, whose teaching constantly returned to learning how to do nothing, would understand Sabbath. I can almost see him, magically transported into a nineteenth-century Hasidic *shtetl* or into an ancient Jewish village on the seventh day, smiling appreciatively: these barbarians certainly had an inkling of the truth one day of the week at least. But what would disturb Hui-neng is that after sundown on the Sabbath, the Jews do begin again to live as though work and effort and time are real, as though action does make a difference and salvation has not yet come in its fullness. Maybe Hui-neng would swat a few behinds with his fan, or pull a few beards. But his efforts would be useless, because his reality and the reality of Moses are not the same. The difference is that Hui-neng views the world either as total transience or total stillness, and for him there is no real difference between the two. The Hebrew vision sees both acting and being, doing and nondoing, as equally real and equally important. By observing the rhythmic return of Sabbath, human beings reflect the divine reality itself.

Pre-Israelite versions of Sabbath did not extend the provisions for rest to domestic animals, or to strangers and sojourners temporarily resident in someone's house. They probably did not apply to women either. The Hebrew Sabbath ordinance, on the other hand, is universal. Everyone, including animals, slaves and guests, must stop work. There is no elitism. In the Orient, on the other hand, meditation is practiced mostly by a privileged, partially leisured class. The vast majority of Buddhists in the world do not meditate. They pray or chant on occasion. Meditation is left mostly to the monks. In fact, in most cultures, East and West, prayer and meditation are turned over to a special elite. But this approach presupposes a society where some people work while others meditate—not a very democratic form of spiritual discipline. Such elitism has also dogged the history of Western monasticism, which is Christianity's way of coping with the clash between the *via activa* and the *via contemplativa*. Some people worked while others prayed. For the Jews, however, there was no such spiritual elite. On the Sabbath everyone stopped and just sat.

Sabbath differs from meditation in another way. Not only is it universal, rather than elitist, it is also ethical. For Zen disciples, "just sitting" has no ethical significance whatever, at least not from a Western perspective in which distinguishing good, less good, and evil possibilities is important. In the Sabbath practice, on the other hand, the loftiest of all realities, God himself, is linked to the human needs of the lowest bonded servant. The link is a rare Hebrew verb ("to rest") found only twice in the entire Bible. It means, as we have seen, "to draw one's breath." Both Yahweh and the exhausted slave need to stop and catch their breath, to look up from the task at hand. As the sovereign of the universe, Yahweh can presumably pause whenever he chooses. But the kitchen slave and the grape picker must be protected by divine law from the greed and insensitivity of the rich. The Sabbath discipline is not just an option. It is a legal mandate in order to insure the extension of its full benefits to the poor and the powerless. One ancient version of the Sabbath rule underlines its seriousness by imposing the death penalty on anyone who works or who *makes someone else work* on Sabbath.

Few Jewish practices are more misunderstood by Christians than the Sabbath. One reason for this misunderstanding is that several of the stories of Jesus in the Gospels depict him as deliberately breaking Sabbath rules, especially by healing people. Because of the way these stories are often interpreted in sermons and church-school lessons, many Christians grow up with an image of the Jewish Sabbath as an unsparingly legalistic straitjacket or an empty attempt to observe meaningless ritual rules. No doubt there were abuses of the spirit of the Sabbath in Jesus' time. But most Christian educational material fails utterly to point out why the Sabbath was instituted or to describe its ingenious blending of contemplative and ethical purposes. Its importance has been further obscured where Jews have changed it from an ethical-universal discipline into a badge of ethnic and religious identity, and where zealous Christian "sabbatarians" have tried to enforce blue laws against Sunday sports entertainment and closing hours, conveying the impression that a Sabbath (now a Sunday) is perversely designed to prevent anyone from enjoying anything.

The spirit of Sabbath is a biblical equivalent of meditation. It nurtures the same kind of awareness that meditation nurtures, for Sabbath is not just a day for doing nothing. It is a particular form of consciousness, a way of thinking and being that strongly resembles what the Buddhists call "mindfulness." In the Hasidic tradition, where it reached its clearest expression, Sabbath not only excludes our ordinary forms of intervening and ordering, it also excludes manipulative ways of thinking about the world. Abraham Heschel repeats a story that exemplifies this point well. A certain rabbi, it seems, who was renowned for his wisdom and piety, and especially for his zeal in keeping Sabbath, once took a leisurely walk in his garden on the Sabbath day—an activity which even the severest interpreters allowed. Strolling in the shade of the branches the rabbi noticed that one of the apple trees badly needed pruning. Recognizing that, of course, such a thing could not be done on the seventh day, the rabbi nonetheless made a mental note to himself that he would see to the pruning early the next week. The Sabbath passed. But when the rabbi went out to the tree a few days later with ladder and clippers, he found it shriveled and lifeless. God had destroyed the apple tree to teach the rabbi that even *thinking* about work on the Sabbath is a violation of the commandment and of the true spirit of the Holy Day.

It is a matter of consciousness. When we plan to prune a tree, we perceive it differently than we do when we are simply aware of it, allowing it—for the moment at least—simply to be as it is. The Buddhist scriptures make this same point in a distinction they frequently draw between two forms of consciousness, which are often confused with each other. The first they call *sati*, usually translated with the English word "mindfulness." This is the "bare awareness" which is strengthened by the practice of meditation. It is being aware, fully aware of the apple tree, but having no judgments, plans or prospects for it. This *sati* is then often contrasted in the Buddhist texts with *sampajanna*, a form of consciousness which is sometimes translated as "clear comprehension." It refers to the attitude appropriate to doing something. *Sati* is receptive, open, passive. *Sampajanna* comes into play when action is required. According to the Buddhist notion, the two must be carefully distinguished and separately nourished before they can be correctly combined into what the texts call *satipatthana*, or "right mindfulness." Meditation is the cultivation of the first, receptive state of awareness, *sati*. Its purpose thus seems nearly identical with that of Sabbath.

Can we ever regain the glorious vision of Sabbath as a radiant queen, a jeweled sovereign who comes to visit bringing warmth and joy in her train? The poor and often inept Hasidic Jews in the stories of Isaac Bashevis Singer may bicker and complain, and they surely suffer, but when the sun goes down and the lamps begin to flicker on Friday evening, a kind of magic touches their world. Special cakes have been baked, and now the sacred candles are lighted. Sabbath is eternity in time, as Abraham Heschel says; it is a cathedral made not with stones and glass but with hours and minutes. It is a sacred symbol that no one can tear down or destroy. It comes every week, inviting human beings not to strive and succeed, not even to pray very much, but to taste and know that God is good, that the earth and the flesh are there to be shared and enjoyed.

To rediscover in our time this underlying human meaning of the Sabbath should make Jewish young people think twice about whether they want to follow in the footsteps of "enlightened" parents who have shied away from Sabbath observance as an embarrassment. And it should cause Christians to wonder how some of the seventh-day spell, so spoiled by misguided Puritan opposition to enjoying its freedom, can be found again.

It is foolish, however, to imagine that a general observance of Sabbath can be reinstituted in our time. Bringing back an old-fashioned Sabbath would require either a religiously unified culture—which we obviously do not have—or a tight and self-conscious subculture, which Jews once had but do not have any longer. We already have empty time, and major industries devoted to filling that time for us. Empty time is neither Sabbath nor meditation. What we need is a form of Sabbath observance which can be practiced in the modern, pluralistic world, which can function on an individual or a small group basis, but which restores the lost dialectic of action and repose, of intervention and letting be.

Meditation could become a modern equivalent of Sabbath. Sabbath is the key to a biblical understanding of meditation. True, meditation does not take the place of the gathered congregation, of celebrating and breaking bread. But it can restore the Sabbath insight that despite all the things that *must* be done in the world—to feed and liberate and heal—even God occasionally pauses to draw breath. Sabbath is a reminder that there will again be a time, as there once was a time, when toil and pain will cease, when play and song and just sitting will fill out the hours and days, when we will no longer require the rhythm of work and repose because there will be no real difference between them. Sabbath reminds us that that day will come, but it also reminds us that that day is not yet here. We need both reminders.

Our problem is that we need Sabbath but we live in a society whose pluralism militates against a particular day, shared by all, in which being replaces doing, and affirming takes precedence over accumulating. It seems unlikely that a common Sabbath can be recovered. For the time being we will have to get along on a somewhat more personal version of the Sabbath. The person whose vision of the world is derived from biblical faith rather than from the wisdom of the Orient can incorporate meditation as a part of a daily dialectic of withdrawal and involvement, of clarification and action. For inevitably, on this earth and in our history, we cannot live in an eternal Sabbath. We always have to go back again to those other six days, days which, though suffused with the memory and anticipation of Sabbath, are still days when action makes a difference.

The greed of an acquisitive society, the pace of industrial production—signaled by lights that never go out and belts that move day and night, all week and all year—the historic Christian contempt for the Jewish religious vision, the compulsive rationalism of a truncated form of science, all these have conspired to create a mindset in the modern West for which the wisdom of the East, the inevitable shadow of self, is bound to hold an immense appeal. But the Eastern path, as its wisest interpreters know full well, will never accommodate more than a few converts. Its ultimate answer, or non-answer, if it ever triumphed in the West, would do so at the cost of much that is valuable in the Western ethical and religious tradition. The wisest of the Zen masters will eventually inform us to look more closely at the land from which we have ridden off to seek enlightenment. If we do, we may discover that meditation can restore a lost treasure, the Fourth Commandment. It may be tarnished and twisted out of shape, but it still belongs to us; and as creatures who must live amid the contradictions and dislocations of history, the mini-Sabbath of meditation can be the gift of life itself.

I arrived back in Cambridge-Benares from the American Tibet not only having learned how to meditate, but also with the beginnings of a way to integrate my meditational practice into my own religious tradition. This had come about because a wise rabbi had not abandoned God's gift of Sabbath. I had learned what it means to be a Christian who practices a "Buddhist" form of meditation—from the Jews.

6 The Pool of Narcissus: The Psychologizing of Meditation

The descent from the moutain is never easy. My return from Naropa was made even more difficult by the fact that I had a hard time finding people to talk to about what had happened there. It was still summer, so most of my students were not around. Also, the people I most wanted to talk with seemed uninterested—and those who were willing to listen seemed to be interested for the wrong reasons. The fact is that the ministers and theologians I sought out were polite but evasive. The people who pressed me most avidly were mainly practicing psychologists and psychotherapists—or aspiring ones. Eastern spirituality seemed to bore the priests and fascinate the shrinks.

Part of the reason for this curious phenomenon is that some of the Eastern teachers have consciously chosen to present their ideas in Western psychological language. Trungpa himself, for example, often prefers to describe the human problem as "psychological pollution" and his goal as "sanity" (rather than "enlightenment"). Other gurus talk a lot about tranquility, inner peace and serenity. The other reason for the psychologist's fascination with the East, however, is that Western psychology itself is now floundering badly and many psychologists are eagerly turning to Eastern teaching as a possible means of deliverance.

One can understand why the psychotherapists are flocking to the gurus—some psychologists, like Baba Ram Dass, actually becoming gurus. Psychology, after all, is supposed to be the "science of the soul." But most Western psychologies, and the therapies that grow from them, premised as they are on the assumptions of modern science, find it burdensome to deal with "soul" at all. The reason for the difficulty is not hard to uncover. "Soul" and "psyche" are stubbornly religious words, and have been for most of their histories. But modern psychology tries to comprehend the psyche without reference to the vaster and more encompassing whole to which the teachings of all the great religions point. All psychologists today are in part children of the Enlightenment and of its condescending attitude toward superstition and spirituality. They are alienated by the history of their discipline from most of their own Western religious tradition. Consequently, when they begin to look for a new basis for the science of the soul, they usually turn toward the East.

It is not a new impulse. From the earliest decades of the nineteenth century, whenever Western intellectuals begin to feel disillusioned with the limits of science or the Enlightenment, they have almost always looked to the Orient for a fresh transfusion of magic or mysticism. Students of intellectual history have a name for this recurrent Western tendency. They call it "Orientalism." It should come as no surprise, therefore, to discover that Western psychology today is reenacting the same trope. The problem is that previous episodes of Orientalism have not restored the spiritual dimension to Western science but, on the contrary, have deepened the split between science and religion, thus rendering science more rigid and religion less self-critical. Western psychology's present love affair with the Orient seems to me just as unpromising and possibly even dangerous. The danger lies in the enormous power psychological ways of thinking now wield in our culture, a power so vast that the current psychologizing of Eastern contemplative disciplines—unless it is preceded by a thorough revolution in Western psychology itself—could rob these disciplines of their spiritual substance. It could pervert them into Western mental-health gimmicks and thereby prevent them from introducing the sharply alternative vision of life they are capable of bringing to us. In short, the merger of Western psychology and Eastern spirituality would resemble the marriage of an elephant and a flea. It would not be a merger but an absorption. It would not cure the soullessness of psychology but would distort the Oriental teachings into something they are not. The elephant today is just too big and too powerful—and too clumsy—for the flea. If the marriage is ever to occur, it can only be when the two parties approach each other more as equals than is possible —at least on Western intellectual soil—today.

Why are we in danger that Western psychology will spoil the meaning Eastern spirituality could have for us unless or until Western psychology undergoes its own reformation first? The reason is that Western psychology—despite occasional claims to the contrary—still continues to concentrate on the *self*. Its focus remains the ego, the id, the psyche, the secret-me-inside— with only peripheral interest directed toward the integral en- meshment of the self in its society, its cosmos and the other immense traceries within which it lives. Psychology has accepted too readily the specialized function modern science has assigned it. It has backed away from cosmology, metaphysics and theology —the rich matrix from which it first emerged—and has accepted a reduced and even trivialized role for itself. The result is that some psychologists, including a growing number of clinicians, are beginning to feel that they have reached a dead end. Their effort to understand the psyche without reference to the psyche's relationship to other realms of being has resulted in shallowness and aridity.

But there is something in every self that balks at this re- duced status, a divine spark that senses more ample settings. Psychologists know this too. Consequently a revolt is under way in psychology—or rather, several revolts are going on at the same time. Psychotherapy is now under siege from within by a whole new set of psychological romantics. The followers of Freud and of various schools of behaviorism find themselves attacked by one or another of the celebrants of madness epitomized by R. D. Laing. But this battle has no winners. While one side eulogizes the benefits of reason and control and the other extols the beauty of insanity, both parties isolate the self from any larger spiritual cosmos. Sane or mad, the soul remains miniaturized. Even C. G. Jung and his interpreters, who want to call the gods, devils and angels back into the picture, usually do so by packing them all into an expanded self. Western psychology, like Narcissus, finds itself frozen at the edge of an eternal reflecting pond, staring into its own likeness.

Into this troubled situation come the new Oriental teachings such as sitting meditation. Not surprisingly, meditation has already been seized upon, both by psychologists and neo-Oriental teachers, as yet another device for delving into the bottomless recesses of the self. The Western proclivity for narcissism has been given a new baptism. It has been sanctified not only as a therapeutic technique but now also as a sacramental procedure, a means of grace. Self had already been made ultimate, and now the quest for the true self becomes the path to the Kingdom.

This congenital narcissism, pervading as it does a culture in which the search for the true self has taken on all the marks of a religious quest, makes it virtually certain that meditation—divorced from an ethical vision—will be grossly misunderstood and misused. Neither in Buddhism nor in Christianity is meditation a method for self-discovery or self-actualization. In the Orient it is a step toward escaping illusion and ego, and toward seeing the world of impermanence and suffering for what it is. In Christianity meditation is one pole in the dialectic of action and repose, being and doing. Both religions reject the idea of meditation merely as inquiry into the self: Buddhism because it sees selfhood as an artificial construct, and Christianity because it sees the self only in relation to other selves, to God, and to a world abounding in death-dealing and life-giving powers.

As it becomes psychologized, meditation loses its capacity to move us away from our narcissism. Instead, it turns into an excuse to keep Narcissus poised by the side of the reflecting pool, to persuade him that if he just keeps on staring he will eventually discover something. The danger posed by this impoverishment of spiritual discipline has already been noticed by some psychologists. James Hillman, who began as a follower of Jung but has attempted in his most recent work, *Revisioning Psychology*, to move on to a more independent stand, is one. Hillman bases his work on the premise that all human life inevitably includes a certain amount of pain, distress, confusion and depression. He understands this "pathos," however, not as something to be avoided, but as a potential source of growth and change. He fears, however, that appropriating Eastern spirituality will obscure the place of this "pathos," and that our preoccupation with finding a self freed from terror and uncertainty, impervious to the cackles of demons or the songs of sirens, will reduce the Eastern disciplines into caricatures of themselves. Hillman regrets that because of the way many of the Eastern techniques and philosophies are taught in the West, the necessary pain and hurt of human existence come to be seen as " . . . but part of the ten thousand illusions to be encountered on the path of life, a piece of appearance . . . or even a load of karma to which one pays duty . . . evidence of the lower, unactualized rungs of the ladder." Hillman fears Westernized versions of Eastern disciplines will encourage us to " . . . meditate, contemplate, exercise through and away from them," but will not teach us to see these hard moments as occasions for valuable insight.

Hillman does not want psychology to become an accomplice in this denial. He sees the hard experiences of life not merely as illusions to be risen above or sickness to be cured, but as the very moments when "the soul's divinity" expresses itself most clearly. But when Western definitions lay hold on them, Oriental approaches become forms of denial, tricking us into thinking that divinity is always found at the peaks of experience, not in the disappointments and never " . . . in the sludge of depression and anxiety, the depths to which actual life regularly returns."

Hillman is aware that what he is criticizing is not the Oriental path itself, but the way it is adapted by Westerners. "In the East the spirit is rooted in the thick yellow loam of richly pathologized imagery—" he writes—"demons, monsters, grotesque goddesses, tortures and obscenities. . . . But once uprooted and imported to the West it arrives debrided of its imaginal ground, dirt-free and smelling of sandalwood . . . Eastern doctrines as experienced through the archetypal structures of the Western psyche become a major and systematic denial of pathologizing." (Hillman, 1975) His disquietude about abuses of meditation and of other Oriental disciplines is based on his expansive vision of what the "soul" should include. He believes the soul should be an ample arena in which conflicting forces swirl and contend, and that therefore the present Western quest for freedom from depression and for instant serenity (reflected in the claims, for example, of Transcendental Meditation) excludes whole ranges of human experience. He detects behind the farfetched promises of some of the gurus an anodyzing of experience. He opts for more chaos and jaggedness in the realm of the psyche, a willingness to court dimensions of reality that many Western understandings of the self would gladly eliminate.

I believe Hillman is right, that meditation and the other Oriental disciplines should not be thought of as methods for eliminating psychic turmoil. But what about the widely discussed "quest for identity"? Can meditation be used to facilitate it? Again, I think the answer must be no. The "quest for identity" is the current code phrase for the search for self. It is still a symptom of narcissism, but because of its scientific-psychological ring, "identity quest" sounds more acceptable to people who might find engaging in a lifelong search for "self" futile or frivolous. But the result is the same, and just as neither Christian nor Buddhist forms of meditation can be used for purposes of self-discovery without doing violence to their intent, they should also not be twisted into tools for an identity quest. Although biblical thought and Buddhist philosophy oppose the notion of a quest for identity for different reasons, both would reject it as a valid goal.

The tension between biblical spirituality and the "quest for identity" arises in part from the fact that finding one's identity for most people today has to do in large measure with coming to terms with one's place in the life cycle. Erik Erikson's famous monograph, "Identity and the Life Cycle," is a good example of how closely these ideas are related in most psychological thought. In the biblical version, on the other hand, the life cycle is just not seen as a dependable source of clues to the question posed today as the "problem of identity."

On the surface, the idea of a universal life cycle through which all persons pass, and which can help individuals answer questions about the meaning of their own lives, is a very attractive one. After all, everyone has a life cycle. It begins with the adjustment infants must make to the physical reality of being born, having parents and perhaps siblings, of having to eat and sleep and defecate and be warmed and protected. The cycle goes on to speech, sexual maturation, mating, work, child-rearing, and eventually old age. In some way, the theory claims, all human beings pass through this cycle, touching most of its points, until they die.

So far, so good. Nor do problems arise when psychologists go on to claim that they can observe, in various cultures, normal or healthy ways of living within each stage of the cycle. The problems begin when the psychological *descriptions* subtly turn into moral *prescriptions*. Soon that unlucky individual who lingers too long at one stage or whose eccentric way of being adolescent or elderly differs markedly from the way most others do it may be regarded as retarded or neurotic. A quirky individualist may be seen as having an "identity crisis." And that can only be resolved by finding again the lost place in the life cycle.

All psychotherapies, of course, need some working definition of health, and such definitions are derived from the cultures within which the therapies function. Once a culture's norms for what constitutes healthy development are set, individuals who fail to mature in the culture's terms can be desperately unhappy. Therapists and educators are often expected to help get such people back on the track. The theological problem arises when, either consciously or not, therapists start to equate this getting on the track with salvation, or when they confuse the social function of ritual or meditation with their spiritual purposes. When this happens, therapists begin to think that the goal of religion is helping people discover their identities. For biblical faith, however, and for many other religious expressions as well, this functionalism misses the point. Biblical spirituality with its version of a God beyond the social order is not just an integrating force. It can be disruptive and subversive. The Jewish boy who solemnly lights the candles and recites the Hebrew cadences in the ritual of *bar mitzvah* is undoubtedly being helped, psychologists would say, to make personal sense out of adolescence. This is fine as far as it goes. What is lost in such a statement is that the boy, in some region of his being, should be dedicating himself to God; and seriously following the God of Israel can play havoc with social roles. It can bring suffering and unhappiness. It can even undermine expectations of appropriate "identity" in a given stage of the life cycle. Sarah, the dried-out octogenarian wife of Abraham, discovered this when she found herself expecting a child. So did downy David when he was told to take an adult warrior's role before he had had his first shave.

The Bible is not a useful source for life-cycle identity models. It is full of "dirty old men" and precocious kids. Noah slips into inebriation and illicit sex when he should be exhibiting composure and dignity. God's call comes to Moses too early and to Sarah too late, at least for normal expectations. Jesus is confounding the elders when he should be working through the trauma of voice change. The biblical God seems to be no respecter of the life cycles of men and women.

This is more than a random set of counter-examples. The underlying theological problem is that "identity" can become little more than a cluster of traits which the individual learns from the culture and internalizes, the end product of a tough series of negotiations between that surging little id, which detests any form of control, and the social roles a society's institutions prescribe for folks at that stage. "Identities" constitute a society's self-understanding. They are created and perpetuated by its privileged groups and reside in the heads of its people. But they reside there precariously. One of the reasons for the unexpected popularity of the movie *Harold and Maud* is that in depicting a love affair between a teen-age boy and an eighty-four-year-old woman, the movie lampoons the alleged regularity of life-cycle identities and appeals to the secret scorn many people feel toward them.

A theology based on the "quest for identity" is bound to be conservative. It lacks that element of the ridiculous, the unprecedented, the custom-shattering which comes from the transcendent realm. The "God" to whom faith points is not the protector of the social hierarchies but the One who sometimes breaks down and overturns them. For the prophets of Israel and their successors, from Jesus of Nazareth to Baal Shem Tov, finding one's identity within any society on earth may not be salvation at all, but bondage.

Underlying the difference between biblical faith and the quest for identity is a profound disparity between two basic views of what the "self" is. For the identity seeker, self appears as some sort of inner essence. It is a core which, though it can grow, never does more than actualize a potential which is already there. The essential self may be covered by layers of en-crustation or coiled in compact possibility; nonetheless, it is there. It can be realized, laid bare, if one's search is persistent enough. It is the psychologized diminutive of the timeless un-created soul of Neoplatonic philosophy. We may be unable to see it now, so the teaching goes, because of the weight of the flesh, the darkness of the material world, or the blindness of childhood repression. But that inner essence is there, we are assured: the real you, waiting to be pursued until its now-hidden light is sufficiently uncovered to allow its glow to illuminate the darkness.

It is important to understand that this modern psychological view of the self as something to be searched for, an essence to be uncovered or developed, not only runs against the grain of bibli-cal spirituality; it also has nothing to do with the self-as-illusion idea taught by most Buddhist schools. Buddhist practitioners would be shocked to learn that meditation might be used in the pursuit of something as phantasmagoreal as the "self." When meditation is interpreted in a Buddhist light, it is seen as a way to help us escape the misleading notion that there is any self at all to be discovered.

The quest for identity is neither Buddhist nor biblical. It is the impoverished modern heir to a tradition going back to Plato and beyond, which sees the soul as part of the changeless stuff of the universe. It is impoverished, however, because the characteristics which were once attributed to the universe itself are now packed into the individual soul. Thus the self/soul may unfold and flower, but it only actualizes an original potential. Its development can be foreseen and facilitated. Nothing totally unanticipated or surprising ever occurs. This self/soul exhibits all of the qualities of a "surprise-free" phenomenon. It is the microscopic replication of a universe modern scientists would describe as "entropic," in which fruition within a form might be expected, but nothing unprecedented ever occurs.

For the individual person, the trouble with basing one's life on the quest for an essential self is that it results in a mode of living that might be called "concentric." The self, instead of enlarging and deepening its capacities, becomes more and more like itself. Gestures become posture. If the "real self" I am uncovering progressively becomes the determinant of my behavior, rigidity and sclerosis set in early. My actions become predictable and my perception of alternative modes of life narrows. I lose my vulnerability, my capacity to be shattered, or even to catch myself by surprise. I fall prey to the spiritual equivalent of "premature senility" (Rubert de Ventos, 1971).

There is, however, another way of looking at the world and the self. To oppose it to "concentric," let us call it "ec-centric," not in the sense of "peculiar," but following the more literal meaning of eccentric: centered outside of itself. This eccentric view of the self comes to us from the Hebrews, and informs those schools of theology and psychology which stress *novum*— unprecedented emergence and novelty. The opposite of the "surprise-free" universe, its world is characterized by singular, unanticipated events and unique persons. It sees sickness in the average, and health in the uncommon. It is the world touched by what Christian theology calls "grace."

In the biblical universe of grace and surprise, the human self is not a timeless essence. It is an open, physico-spiritual field that is both the product and the producer of real change. As St. John says, "It doth not yet appear what we shall be." For the "concentric" view, time is a circle in which all things, despite their appearance of originality, ultimately return to an entropic *status quo ante* (a pattern betrayed by the word "cycle" in "life cycle"). For the "eccentric," time is an arrow in uncertain flight, and the self is not an inner essence to be discovered and developed but an unfinished and unfinishable poem, a unique statement for which no archetypal pattern exists. In this biblical universe, concrete selves meet each other as combatants and companions, not as separated particles of One Cosmic Self. They are centers of being who grapple, love and hate. This irreducible otherness of the other defines the biblical view of the self. It also provides the only view of the self or psyche on which modern psychology can build a new and liberating science of the soul.

Although biblical spirituality and Buddhist philosophy agree in their common rejection of the idea of the "self" on which much of modern psychology and the popular search for identity are based, their agreement on this issue should not be allowed to obscure the important differences between them. If modern psychology needs to go through a revolution and to reincorporate its lost "theological" dimensions—as I believe it must— these differences between Eastern and Western views of the psyche are of critical significance. The truth is that the biblical understanding of the self as a center of decision and will, a free agent capable of choice, is the source of both our grandeur and our misery. When this personal self is located in a world of other selves and in a universe which is touched on by Another Self, then the richest possibilities of friendship and mutuality—as well as their awful opposites—emerge. It is a high-risk situation.

Oriental thinking, typified by classical Buddhist thinking, moves in a different direction. By eliminating the whole idea of selves, it frees human beings from the trauma of relationships, but at the same time it precludes the possibility of love, too. Thus Buddhism presents us with a totally unsentimental, fully unblinking way of living in a transient world where deep relationships with things and people lead only to pain and loss. It is appropriate that the word "detachment" should have come to occupy such a central place in Buddhist teaching. As people grow older and experience the sting of impermanence, the loss of friends and relatives, the ebbing of physical and mental powers, this venerable tradition commends itself more and more. The problem is, however, that in a culture like ours, already steeped in the philosophy of "You do your thing and I'll do mine," the lofty Buddhist idea of nonattachment can hardly escape distortion. Westerners will not be able to practice the Oriental posture of nonattachment until they move not just beyond attachments, but also beyond an "I" which does "my thing." Real nonattachment will become possible only when self slips away too. But this is something most Westerners either cannot or will not concede.

What is the alternative? We live in a period which, because of its continuing preoccupation with self-realization, has found any form of other-relatedness increasingly difficult. This difficulty contaminates not only love and friendship but also anger and other "negative" feelings toward others. The alternative to both the Oriental idea of selflessness and the modern psychological notion of concentric self-centeredness is the biblical view that there is a self which, though capable of fear and hatred of other selves, is also capable of concern and friendship. In fact, this biblical tradition teaches that without such high-risk involvements with other selves, the self shrivels into a brittle shard.

Love is the central theme in the biblical view of life. The opposite of love, however, is not hatred. It is possessiveness, the deep-set human drive to control and own the other. Biblical faith is not naive about this human inclination. It recognizes that possessiveness cannot be overcome by self-improvement programs. One quasi-religious movement, the Erhard Training Seminars (EST) already dishes up a combination of encounter-group techniques, behavior modification methods and Westernized Orientalism designed quite specifically to enable people—for a price—to learn how to calculate their own self-interest more efficiently and consistently. EST represents a particularly vivid example of what happens to Oriental insights when they are grafted onto a program of ego expansion and self-gratification. EST is a crossbreed of psychological and religious ideas and practices all brought to the service of self-realization and narcissism. Needless to say, the distortion of the Oriental insight is virtually complete, and the trouble lies in our modern readiness to use anything to help us cling to ego.

Jesus taught that the power to overcome our compulsion to control comes from a source outside ourselves. It originates in the marrow of the universe itself, in the heart of God, and reaches us through other imperfect human beings. This is what St. John meant by the now so banalized teaching that "God loves the world." The word "love," however emptied it may be, is crucial here because love can exist only in a world where there are genuinely different selves. When Jesus and the prophets teach that I should love my neighbor as myself, they do not mean to say that my neighbor *is* myself. Love is made both necessary and possible because my neighbor is not me.

Eastern philosophies stress compassion or detachment or unification. But the best-informed representatives of the Oriental traditions rightly refer to Christianity as the "religion of love." To say "God loves the world" is different from saying "God is the world," or God "is" and the world is not, or vice versa. In Christianity and Judaism, God and the world are equally real, but different. And the relationship between them is, or should be, one of love.

The psychological consequences of this world view are considerable, and few psychological systems, East or West, have fully grasped the implications of a universe held together by love between genuinely different entities. Eastern psychologies, in their manifold variety, serve mainly to present the picture of how life can be lived if what we think are differences are actually illusory. Since there is no real difference, love is redundant. Despite claims to the contrary, many Western philosophies arrive at the same point, though by a different route. They see "the other" not in its full otherness but as an occasion for one's own self-discovery or self-realization. Immanuel Kant, contrary to what one usually learns about him in philosophy courses, also failed to escape this trap. Kant set out to fashion an ethic based on an individual's obligation to fulfill his or her duty with regard to the other person. This other person was under no circumstances to be regarded as a "means." But even Kant's attempt finally failed. His "categorical imperative" to obey the inner call of duty ironically results in one's viewing the other not as a real other but as that entity to whom I am now fulfilling an obligation, thus contributing to my self-development as a duty-doing creature. Aristotle was at least honest in his defense of the exercise of reason as contributing to one's own self-realization. Modern writers, such as Norman Brown, who define human beings in terms of their capacity for erotic feeling do not succeed either. The other person is reduced to the occasion for my experience of ecstasy.

In short, despite centuries of effort, most, if not all, Western philosophies fall short of an ethic of love. They invariably make other people into valuable investments which will pay off eventually in the dividends of one's own self-realization. As one of my favorite teachers, the late Harvard philosopher John Wild, once said, after a lifetime of reading and teaching in the field of ethics, "In fact every influential ethic that has been formulated in our intellectual history is some version of self-realization." Wild began his career in the Harvard philosophy department while such great teachers as George Santayana and Josiah Royce were still present. He started out as an enthusiastic disciple and interpreter of Aristotle. But as he grew older he did not, as some teachers do, become more set in his ways. He changed his mind, finally discarding much of his Aristotelianism and becoming more convinced that the Christian concept of "sacrifice" made more sense than "development," "actualization," or "self-realization." (Wild, 1959)

The idea of sacrifice as it appears in many traditions, but especially as it is used in Christianity, presents a clear alternative to Narcissus. It is something different from either the non-self of Oriental philosophy or from the self-realization ethic of modern Western thought. Sacrifice does not mean withdrawing from the other or using the other, but giving oneself to the other. The use of the word "sacrifice" as the pivotal point of Christian ethics as opposed to "self-realization" ethics is obviously not a strategy designed to win converts today. Self-realization is our reigning philosophy, and many liberal Christians, especially those practicing various forms of counseling, interpret Christianity as one more form of self-realization. From such a perspective, meditation can easily be prescribed as yet another aid to the realization of the self.

The trouble is that Christianity is not a form of self-realization. Jesus was no Narcissus. The Gospel is premised on my turning away from a concern about my own self, what Luther called the heart's *incurvatus in se*, and *toward* the possibilities inherent in reorienting myself toward something outside. It is not concentric, but eccentric. Self-realization views the self as growing and developing within a fixed structure: growth brings to actuality what is already there in potentiality. The term "sacrifice," on the other hand, indicates that the new must come with a radical departure from the old: real change comes by a process so jarring and traumatic that it is like starting all over again ("Ye must be born anew"). Also, the person not only effects changes in the standard pattern; the pattern itself can be altered. Sacrifice has nothing to do with self-effacement or servility. It signifies a style of existence in which we let go not just of what is no longer serviceable, but of what could still be useful and good in order to claim the promise of the future.

I have said that all the dominant Western psychological theories turn out, on close examination, to be based on self-realization. But perhaps it is naive to expect any more. Like most creations of any given social system, psychological theories are meant to order and stabilize. They rarely try to incorporate into themselves the radical Christian notion that love for the genuinely different is the key to the whole evolutionary process. So a necessary tension always exists between Christianity and even the most carefully constructed psychological theory. If our current psychological language bears the unmistakable mark of being a product of a profit-oriented culture—as the use of terms such as "investment" in persons and psychic "dividends" indicates—that should not be surprising. There is even evidence that the search for identity is a useful activity for dominant groups to encourage. People engaged in an incessant identity quest will not have time to ask questions about cartels and juntas.

Love and sacrifice are two old and worn terms, but together they provide the only promising foundation I know for a new psychology, or for a new politics. Love means affirming what is genuinely and radically "not-me." It also entails sacrifice. In Christian theology, God affirms the human world in the most decisive manner imaginable—by putting himself within it, allowing himself to be touched by it, becoming vulnerable in its hands. This is the meaning of the incarnation of God in the man Jesus. But even before Christ's coming, so the Patristic Fathers speculated, God's reality itself contained the affirmation of otherness in its inner life. The doctrine of the Trinity, so quaint and comical to the modern mind, is the symbolic attempt of those early thinkers to say that in God himself, that is, at the core of cosmic reality, there is real difference and real love. The three-equals-one idea of the Trinity may sound bizarre to contemporary ears. But when one contrasts it to most Oriental views of reality, its significance becomes clear. For most Eastern thought, unity is real, but diversity and difference are lower, illusory or less real. They are eventually swallowed in what philosophers call an "ultimate monism." Not so for the Patristic

Christian philosophers. They wanted to describe a God who not only loved what was externally different, but also contained genuine love and real opposition within himself. If the Trinitarian doctrine, because it has been confused with some sort of numerical magic, succeeds mainly in obscuring this insight, we should remember that the Trinity has nothing to do with numbers. It has to do with the one and the many, with stability and change, and with the relationship between dynamic centers of freely deciding action.

The key term in Hebrew scripture for describing the relation of God to the world is 'ezer, usually translated by the English term "helper." But the lackluster word "help" fails to describe the kind of action the holy 'ezrah brings or the difference it makes. This 'ezrah is not first aid or dishwashing assistance. It has nothing to do with crutches and braces. The holy one helps humankind by entering so thoroughly into the human situation that it is broken and transformed. God "helps" and the mountains melt, springs appear in the wilderness, and thrones topple. God helps human beings by liberating them from whatever prevents them from loving and receiving love.

Only when the revolutionary form of God's love is made clear can we then properly understand those well-known biblical passages which describe God as one who takes the form of a servant and who tells his people to become a servant nation. The purpose of this servanthood, as Isaiah puts it in chapter 42:1 is not to bow and scrape but "to bring forth justice to the nations." The servant or helper is not placed in a position of social subordination. Rather he or she brings to the relationship the power of love, which originates in the heart of the universe itself. These servant-helpers are ambassadors or agents, to use St. Paul's terms, of a cosmic energy that comes in weakness but eventually erodes all opposition.

In the decades to come Christianity will find itself engaged in spirited intellectual exchange with a number of differing psychological views of what constitutes the human self, the person, and the relation of a person to others and to the universe. All of these views will have important political and ethical implication. Some views, like the black-box behaviorism of B. F. Skinner, are so far from any religious definition of the self that the argument can proceed with some clarity. On two other fronts, however, the lines may become fuzzy, and both psychologists and theologians must make a continuous effort not to blur distinctions. From the many neo-Oriental movements we will hear more and more about "egolessness" and the "illusion of selfhood" and the value of nonattachment. In its classical Oriental expressions this philosophy merits attention and respect. But when it is watered down in such a way that Oriental detachment is simply added to Western ego, then we have the worst of all possible worlds: people using each other but avoiding entangling alliances. I expect this Westernized pseudo-Oriental pastiche to spread, and even at points to label itself religious or Christian. At the same time I think we can expect to see the growing use of meditation, and eventually of any religious discipline available—prayer, contemplation, fasting —to enhance the exploration and realization of the insatiable Western self. This will also no doubt be called "Christianity" even though it completely reverses the spirit of the prophets and Jesus.

I think both of these distortions of biblical faith should be unmasked, not to preserve pure doctrine but to enhance human options, to help at least a few people see that in addition to the way of pseudodetachment and the way of self-realization, there is also a third way—of sacrifice, love and risk.

7 Turning East

A few weeks after I returned from Naropa I went to my desk and pulled out the notes on neo-Oriental religious movements. The information was still there on the cards and scraps of paper, so I reread the interviews with devotees and the descriptions of satsangs. Although the handwriting was mine, the notes seemed to have been written by another person, an outsider. It was then that I began to consider chucking the whole idea of a book, not because I might be too critical of or too lenient with these movements, but because my own involvement with one of the disciplines had become sufficiently important to me that I did not want to bury it in a sea of descriptions. What if I wrote about myself with the same curiosity and tolerance with which I had written about other people: attentive but dispassionate, concerned but cool? It did not seem worth it.

As I read more notes and listened again to taped conversations, however, the temptation to abandon the book faded, and the clue I had previously sought in vain began to emerge in my mind. I had not become a convert. I had accepted and begun to practice a spiritual discipline for reasons of my own that sounded very different from the ideas of the individual who had taught me. I had felt like an East Turner manqué, a doubtful case, an exception. But as I listened again to the interviews, I heard many of the people I had talked to saying exactly the same thing. Each had turned East, in some measure or another, for reasons that each perceived to be unique to himself or herself. Although I had viewed them all as parts of a trend or movement, I did not see myself as simply part of a trend. And neither did they. All of a sudden I had found my focus. I would write about the Turn East as it looks from the viewpoint of an East Turner—not "the" East Turner, since they were all different, but from the various perspectives of various people who had turned that way. This would include myself. Now my criticisms would come not from outside, but from a critical "insider."

Who then are the "East Turners"? The people I am talking about here have not moved to India to live in an ashram. They have not left home to go to the Orient to dwell in a Tibetan temple or a Zen monastery, at least not permanently. They still live in Texas or Ohio or New York or somewhere else in the U.S.A. They have not gone East, they have *turned.* The term refers to those thousands of Americans who find themselves attracted today to groups, practices and ideas derived from one or another of the great traditions of Oriental spiritual wisdom. Their interest comes in widely varying degrees of seriousness and persistence. It extends from those who sneak a glance at a paperback edition of the *I Ching* or try some yoga postures to those who find as I did that one of the Eastern practices becomes important to them and to those who leave everything behind and sleep on mats in an American Hare Krishna temple. It includes serious seekers and frivolous dilettantes, converts and fellow travelers. But the fact is that large numbers of people are involved, not just a fringe group, and the extent of the interest has no precedent in American religious history.

How many are there? It is hard to say. The followers of the Maharaj Ji have sometimes claimed hundreds of thousands for his Divine Light Mission. The organization has two hundred local branches plus a string of food stores and filling stations. Although the spectacular failure of its well-publicized 1973 rally in the Houston Astrodome to attract as many people as expected casts some doubt on the figures supplied by the movement leaders themselves, and the public tiffs between the guru and his family have probably cost members as well as caused severe embarrassment, still, the movement has enlisted large numbers of devotees. The Tibetan Buddhists have attracted thousands of people, many of them artists, poets, psychotherapists and film makers, to Naropa and to their meditation-and-study centers in other parts of the country. Practitioners of TM (Transcendental Meditation) have organized meditation groups all over America and have started a university, the Maharishi University, in Goleta, near Los Angeles. The university's catalog runs to over 400 pages, listing hundreds of courses and institutes in a wide variety of subjects and featuring full-color photos of scores of faculty persons. Add to this the people who practice, regularly or sporadically, one or another form of Oriental meditation, or whose practice of karate goes beyond self-defense to its underlying Buddhist philosophy, and the numbers become significant. Although overall estimates vary widely, my own guess is that by now several million Americans have been touched in one way or another by some form of neo-Oriental thought or devotional practice.

Who are the people who are drawn to neo-Oriental movements? One way to answer this question would be to register the standard sociological data about the class, age, race, sex, regional residence, amount of education and ethnic background of the devotees of various groups. It is not difficult to answer this way, and such studies have been done. But this leaves much unsaid. We found that the participants tended to be young, in their late teens, twenties or early thirties. There are exceptions, of course. I met many people in their forties and fifties at Naropa. One of my most enthusiastic informants about the Hare Krishna movement was a fifty-five-year-old woman who had found some help among the devotees in dealing with her alcoholic husband. Although some early teen-agers learn how to do yoga or read a little Eastern philosophy, few become seriously involved until late adolescence. The twenties are the prime turning time.

In class and race, it is easy to see that the neo-Oriental movements are made up almost exclusively of white, educated, middle- and upper-middle-class young people. Most of the East Turners come from families that are comfortably fixed and have themselves at least begun to attend college—although some have dropped out after a year or two. Whether they intend to return to college largely depends on whether they belong to a group with a high degree of opposition to Western culture such as the Hare Krishnas or one that allows for or encourages compromise, such as the Divine Light Mission. Except for the Black Muslim organization, there are very few black young people in any of these movements, far fewer than the proportion of blacks in the population at large.

Women and men seem to participate in fairly equal numbers in all the movements, but men control the leadership posts. There is little evidence of the predominance of any particular regional background, although more devotees seem to come from urban than from rural areas—which is understandable, since one has at least to hear about the movement before one thinks of joining, and this is more likely in Chicago or Seattle than it is in a small town.

As a theologian I was interested in the religious backgrounds of the people we met. What kind of training or nurture, or lack of either, I wondered, would one discover among people who had made what appeared to be such a sharp break with their religious pasts? We did not always ask the people we talked with about their religious backgrounds, since this is often a delicate matter; and sometimes when we did ask they were not eager to talk about it. Some statistics are available, however. In his excellent study of the Hare Krishna Movement, J. Stillson Judah found that about 70 percent of the parents of the Krishna devotees he interviewed were members of a church or synagogue and that almost two-thirds of the devotees themselves had once attended their parents' churches regularly. Here are the affiliations of the parents of the devotees:

Roman Catholic	18.0%
Methodist	13.0%
Presbyterian	7.0%
Episcopalian	5.5%
Congregational	4.0%
Mormon	2.0%
Jewish	14.5%
Jehovah's Witnesses	3.5%
Other	7.0%
None	25.0%

Judah correctly observes that ". . . the large liberal Protestant churches whose church school attendance declined even more during the 1960s than their adult membership, contribute most to the membership of the Hare Krishna Movement." This is obviously true, but what strikes me in examining these backgrounds is the much higher proportion of devotees from a Jewish background (14.5 percent) than one might have expected in view of the fact that Jews constitute only about 3 percent of the American population. (Judah, 1974)

When all these statistics and categories have been reported, however, how much do we know about the actual human beings who have made this decisive choice? Not very much. This is why my students and I took another step in our effort to find out something about inner motivation from the East Turners themselves. Without using interview schedules, questionnaires or elaborate survey instruments, we simply went to the people themselves and asked them to tell us in their own words what they found in the groups they belonged to and why they continued to be a part of them. The answers they gave us varied in length, content and emotional tone, but as we sorted through them, despite the fact that every person had turned East for personal reasons, certain common patterns did emerge. There seemed to be roughly six clusters.

1. One thing people seem to be looking for in the neo-Oriental movements is simple human *friendship*. The reply we heard most, coming especially from people who actually resided in a religious commune or ashram, told a story of loneliness, isolation and the search for a supportive community. These accounts ran something like this:

They seem to care for me here. I was bummed out, confused, just wandering around. When I first came here I didn't know what they were talking about. They all seemed crazy, and I told them so. But that didn't seem to bother them. They took me in. They made me feel at home. Now I feel like I'm a part of it, an important part too. I belong here. It's where I was meant to be.

We noticed that the shorter the time people had been involved in a given movement, the more often this reply came. After a few months or even a few weeks, however, the novices seem to begin to learn a more theologically "proper" answer such as "Krishna called me here" or "It was my karma." Many seekers who drift into such movements looking for intimacy quickly learn to express their reasons in the in-group argot. But clearly, the need for just plain friendship is the chief motiva-

tion for many of the East Turners. They are looking for
warmth, affection and close ties of feeling. They don't find
them at work, at school, in churches they attend or even at
home. But they do seem to find all these and more, at least for
a while, in the community of devotees.

This quest for a feeling-founded association is articulated
most openly by the followers of the late Indian teacher Meher
Baba. They like to call themselves "Baba Lovers," in part because the phrase itself contains a nice *double-entendre*. They
love Baba, but they are also inspired by his teaching to *be*
"lovers," that is, to welcome more affective and expressive relationships than are normally encouraged by outside society. Although few of the movements we studied made this warmth
element as explicit as the Baba Lovers do, it was always there.
Friendship is a scarce resource in modern society. The groups
we visited provide an island of companionship in what the
adherents feel is a world devoid of fraternity.

2. The East Turners are also looking for a way to experience
life directly, without the intervention of ideas and concepts.
Many told us they were looking for a kind of *immediacy* they
had not been able to find elsewhere. I do not refer here to those
who were looking for experience merely for its own sake, for
another kick or another "trip" to add to their collection. That
represents a pathological distortion of the quest, which I will
discuss later. Here I refer to those persons who seemed to want
a real personal encounter with God or the Holy, or simply
with life, nature and other people. It also includes those who
needed to find a kind of inner peace and had not found it anywhere else. Again, paraphrasing a large number of replies, the
responses ran something like this:

All I got at any church I ever went to were sermons or homilies
about God, *about* "the peace that passes understanding." Words,
words, words. It was all up here [pointing to the head]. I never
really *felt* it. It was all abstract, never direct, always somebody else's
account of it. It was dull, boring, cold coffee. I'd sit or kneel or
stand. I'd listen or read prayers. But it seemed lifeless. It was like
reading the label instead of eating the contents. But here it happened to *me*. I experienced it myself. I don't have to take someone

else's word for it because it happened to me. It's still happening. It was direct. I can never deny it.

This testimony of direct experience versus mediated teaching became more understandable when we noticed that almost all the neo-Oriental movements include instruction in some form of spiritual discipline. Leaders in the neo-Oriental movements show initiates the primary techniques of prayer, contemplation or meditation. Inquirers learn to breathe or dance or chant. They use archery or swordplay or acupuncture or massage. Teachers do not rely entirely on words but move inquirers quickly into the actual techniques—either quite simple, as in Transcendental Meditation, or very complex, as in Zen—for inducing the desired forms of consciousness. Unlike many of the currently available Western religious options, which stress beliefs or codes of ethics sometimes at the expense of a primary encounter of the person with reality, most of the neo-Oriental groups begin right away at the level of practice.

The most vivid example I found of this tendency to thrust the inquirer into practice, and to refuse to deal in ideas about it, came at the local Zen center. The teachers there not only sit you down immediately to face a blank wall, they also smilingly refuse to answer all but the most elementary questions until you have taken the practical step of trying to meditate. Even after that, they keep the ideas to a minimum. Practice and direct exposure are the keys to the kingdom, and if the responses of many of the people among the East Turners are to be trusted, this is one important facet of Zen's appeal.

3. Some East Turners are looking for *authority.* A third group of our respondents differed quite markedly from the second group. They told us, in one way or another, that they had turned East to find truth, to lay hold on a message or teaching they could believe and trust. They found themselves in these groups as refugees from uncertainty and doubt. Very often the people who gave this answer put a major emphasis on the role of the particular swami or guru whose wisdom or charismatic power had resulted in such a change in their lives. They gave answers like this:

I tried everything. I read all the books, went to lectures, listened to different teachers. But all that happened was that I got all the more confused and baffled. I couldn't think straight anymore. I wandered around in a daze. I couldn't get myself together or make any decisions. Then I met [heard, saw, read] him [The name of the teacher varies, but the testimony is nearly identical] and what he said finally *made sense*. Everything finally clicked. I knew he was for real, that if anyone had the answer he certainly did. Besides, I could tell just from the way he spoke [the way he looked at me, etc.] that he knew what he was talking about. Now my confusion is over.

I call this reason for the Turn East the "quest for authority." It results from a wide range of factors that dozens of sociologists have documented: the dissolution of conventional moral codes, the erosion of traditional authorities, the emergence of what Alvin Toffler once called "overchoice." Although it could be cogently argued that we may have fewer real choices to make today (since the decision between Brand X and Brand Y is actually only an illusory choice), still the appearance of more choices is there, and it takes its toll. As a result, large numbers of people begin to suffer a kind of choice-fatigue. They hunger for an authority that will simplify, straighten out, assure—something or somebody that will make their choices fewer and less arduous. For some people the Teacher of Wisdom, touched by that mantle of light which the East seems to carry, brings an answer. The search for authority ends at the swami's feet.

4. A smaller number of people, though enough to notice, told us in one way or another that they had turned to the East because somehow it seemed more *"natural."* These people also appear to have changed their faith orientation more self-consciously than others and with deliberate rejection of what they believed was the effete, corrupt or outworn religious tradition of the West. They saw in Eastern spirituality a kind of unspoiled purity. In contrast to Western faith, to them the East seemed artless, simple and fresh. Significantly these people could often tell us why they had turned *from* some Western religion more clearly than they could say why they had turned *toward* the East. Although they said it in a number of ways, it came out something like this:

Western civilization is shot. It is nothing but technology and power and rationalization. A bloody record of war and pogroms and crusades. A monster: corrupted to its core by power and money. No contact with nature, feeling, spontaneity; and at its very heart is the Christian tradition which has probably made it worse. What we need to do now is learn from the Oriental peoples who have never been ruined by machines and science, who have kept close to their ancestors' simplicity, their inner feelings and the given rhythms of nature and the cosmos. Western religion has invalidated itself. Now only the East is possible.

The people who talked to us in this vein were often the most widely read and best educated of the East Turners. Many had read the Zen-and-nature poetry of Gary Snyder or the anti-Christian polemics of Alan Watts. They could cite evidence more specifically and phrase their arguments more clearly than some of the others. Though they did not put it this way themselves, to me their choice to turn East often seemed to have some of the quality of a purification ritual. They were having a Western equivalent of a bath in the Ganges, shedding the tainted and the impure, choosing the pure and the innocent.

5. A relatively small number of people, mainly women, but some men, told us they had become involved in Eastern spirituality to get away from the seemingly total *male domination* of the Western faiths. They saw this oppressive patriarchy in both the doctrines and symbols of Western religious groups and in their patterns of leadership and practice. They looked to the East to find a better balance.

A male god creates a man who is supposedly led astray by a woman. There are male patriarchs and prophets, a male Christ and twelve male apostles. Male popes and bishops. Women are either virgins or witches or whores or grateful child-bearers. There is obviously no place in this religion for a woman. Now take the Hindus, they have Kali . . .

Significantly, the people who gave this answer were involved in one of the East-Turning groups mainly at an intellectual rather than a devotional level. Usually they were not very deeply involved at that. Though the inherited male-chauvinist structures of Christianity and Judaism obviously enrage many people, only a very few make it their reason for a serious turn to the East, for reasons that become obvious once one finds out that most other spiritual traditions have their own versions of male chauvinism, some of it even worse.

6. Finally, an interesting scattering of people told us they had turned to some version of an Eastern tradition as the result of a concern for health, ecology and the conservation of the planet's dwindling resources. Many of these East Turners also follow a macrobiotic or vegetarian diet or display a more than average amount of interest in the subtle but important relationship between the foods we eat and the condition of the spirit. Their argument runs something like this:

Western religion has no real reverence for the sacred quality of the earth, the water, the trees. Since its God transcends nature and the Bible makes man have dominion over it, the result is that nature is misused and wasted and poisoned. Western faith is external and manipulative. Eastern spirituality sees the holy in nature and encourages a calm, noninterventionist attitude toward it. Unless we adopt the Eastern view and see that man has no more inherent rights than any other part of nature, we will destroy our planet.

The people who give this kind of answer may also hold up the American Indians or the Eskimos or some other group as having a more exemplary relationship to nature. But they usually claim that in one way or another the biblical view of human beings' relationship to nature contributed to the ecological crisis.

These then are the answers the East Turners themselves give most often when asked about the reasons for their turn. They are looking first of all for friendship and second for a directly felt experience of God and the world. In addition they seem to be seeking a way out of intellectual and moral confusion, a kind of innocence, or a way of life unmarred by sex stereotypes or technological overkill. When one examines this list of goals, it quickly becomes evident that the East Turners are not really very different from anyone else. They are looking for exactly what most people in America are looking for today. They have chosen a more visible and dramatic way of looking. The question, of course, is, Will they find it, there or anywhere else?

I believe that to respond to this question adequately, one must probe deeper than these actual replies to the underlying, often unconscious or unarticulated theological basis for the Turn East. When one does so, and notices that the Turn East is a part of a larger cultural malaise, the most ironic aspect of the whole thing is that it is occurring just as many millions of Asians are involved in an epochal "Turn West"—toward science and technology, Western political systems and occidental cultural forms. It is also clear in this otherwise confused situation, that East and West have much more than a merely geographical significance. Later on I will say more about the Western "myth of the Orient." Here it is mainly important to remember that, in the West, "Eastern" has always meant a certain cautious reserve about human initiative. For the Western mind the Eastern spiritual traditions have for centuries epitomized the archetypal image which Mircea Eliade identifies with "archaic man," while Christianity and Western culture have represented activism. Today, however, vast sections of Asia have moved out of the archaic pattern into a vigorous period of "making" their own history. And as they have, the religious traditions of those areas have become more activist, often drawing on strands that were there from their beginnings, unnoticed in the West, and sometimes borrowing insights from biblical faith. Just as this great awakening to history has begun to occur in the real Asia, millions of Americans have fallen in love with an Asia that is disappearing, or maybe never existed: the "mysterious Orient" of the old Western myth. Consequently it is misleading to see the East Turners opting for an outlook grounded in the contemporary Orient. The actual Asian outlook, as well as the Oriental faiths, is becoming more activist and more "historical," as Gandhi and Thich Nhat Hanh, a leader of the Vietnamese Buddhist antiwar movement, demonstrate. In fact, those who yearn for what they call an "Oriental" approach today are really opting for an "archaic" rather than for a "historical" way of life. They may be "turning back" instead of Turning East.

And they are in good company. The work of many of our most influential Western writers—T.S. Eliot and James Joyce, for example—is, as Mircea Eliade has written, "saturated in nostalgia for the myth of eternal repetition and in the last analysis, for the abolition of time." (Eliade, 1954) It is possible that in the current Turn East, what was once a hankering among artists and intellectuals has now reached the popular level. Below the surface of the quest for companionship and felt experience, and in addition to the other pressures that motivated them, it is possible that some of the East Turners of today are simply doubtful about the prospect of "making history," and prefer to sit it out. If this is true, and I believe it is, then it puts the challenge of the Turn East on a profound theological level. Why, given the calamitous history of this century, should we not be skeptical about the prospect of making history? Why not simply let things be? Surely the result could not be much worse than the result of centuries of Western history making.

Or could it? I believe the current wave of skepticism about the human prospect and about our capacity to influence history is mainly the result of the modern assumption that human beings are fully responsible for everything that happens, that there is no higher intelligence or grander purpose at work in cosmic evolution and human history. The Turn East is the logical outcome of the death of God. This represents a curious twist in intellectual history. It was once argued by secular humanists that positing the existence of a deity makes human beings lazy, that they will merely sit back and let God do it. The other side of that coin, however, is that when the tasks become enormous and the challenges nearly overwhelming, it is not the presence of a cosmic ally but the lack of one that drives people to despair.

This seems to be where many people who were once confident they could make a difference find themselves recently. The impact of biblical religion brought the idea of history and human responsibility for it into existence. But in its original version, this responsibility was to be exercised under the judgment and promise of God. In the modern and secular form of historical faith, God disappeared from the picture. Humankind was left with history to make but without cosmic support or any final source of accountability. Profit and power became the goals. The current feeling of powerlessness and the inability to do anything to avert famine or planetary pollution is the result. No wonder some people simply want to resign. In contrast to what Ivan Karamazov believed, without God now nothing seems possible.

The East Turners do not represent a way out of our Western spiritual crises. But they do help us understand it much better, in part because they embody it so clearly and often so attractively. In doing so they help us to understand and confront that part of ourselves which would like to abdicate history-making and let nature take its course. This temptation to dignified resignation has always been a part, though a repressed one, of the Western soul. It is especially evident now among many people —and I include myself in this group—who were passionately involved in the upheavals of the 1960s and whose hopes for genuine change were often disappointed. Eliade seemed to foresee the emergence of this mood of resignation when he wrote, just after World War II:

It is not inadmissible to think of an epoch, and an epoch not too far distant, when humanity, to ensure its survival, will find itself reduced to desisting from any further "making" of history . . . [and] will confine itself to repeating prescribed archetypal gestures, and will strive to forget, as meaningless and dangerous, any spontaneous gesture which might entail "historical" consequences. It would even be interesting to compare the anhistorical solution of future societies with the paradisical or eschatological myths of the golden age of the beginning or the end of the world.   (Eliade, 1949)

It may well be that Eliade's delphic prediction is now beginning to come true. For the "Western" spirit, inspired by biblical faith and now found in all parts of the world, not just the West, history is a challenge and a task. It is fraught with peril and promise, but it is an open process in which human beings have the responsibility and the freedom to make a new future. In our time, the burden of history and the enormity of the tasks we face have begun to make even the youngest and most energetic skeptical. Like the "archaic man" Eliade describes, we are tempted to step back from taking responsibility and to choose a world view that simply lets it all be. When I began to think about the various replies the East Turners gave to our questions—in the light both of Eliade's prediction and of my own experience—they began to make much more sense. What the East Turners told us were not prescriptions for a general cure. They were indications of a malaise with which we must all contend.

Take, for example, the replies that indicated a terrible hunger for fraternity and a search for a direct exposure to the real. These reasons for Turning East point to two tubercles in the body politic which debilitate both our churches and our culture —the erosion of human community and the evaporation of genuine experience. The first problem, the attenuation of bonds of friendship, has been discussed and deplored by sociologists and writers ever since the impact of the industrial revolution began to weaken traditional ties, and capitalism began to substitute relationships built on profit. Although the second illness, the substitution of abstraction for direct experience, has come to notice more recently, I believe it stems from the same sources. A way of life based on money, as ours is, ultimately undercuts both genuine community and real experience. It ingrains in us a way of perceiving both people and things as possible means to profitable ends. Even when we do not think about it consciously, our ability to befriend people is decimated, and our faculty for feeling deeply is corroded.

How are friendship and feeling made difficult in a society based on profits? Sometimes both the symptom and the sickness in any society can be illuminated by focusing on one phenomenon in that society in which they interact. In our society, prostitution as a business provides this focus. It is the most cogent paradigm of how both intimacy and feeling suffer when the market mentality takes over. There have always been prostitutes, at least as long as there has been someone to pay them. Ever since men have dominated women, which is probably since the beginning, there have been fertility priestesses, courtesans and concubines. The difference in our time is that cash payment relationships are not merely one type among others, they dominate nearly everything else, not just in prostitution but in education, art and politics too. Consequently sexuality, which is the place where intimacy and experience intersect, is bound to become distorted. In a sense, prostitution is an explicit example of what obtains in less explicit ways in all our relationships. We pay for what should be an exchange of gifts. We try to buy what ultimately cannot be bought. We use the money to purchase something—affection or experience —that can only be obtained by an investment of ourselves. The very possibility of human bonding disappears.

But the ability to feel deeply—about anything—also disappears in a market/money world. Since both people and things exist to be utilized for profit, one simply cannot get attached to them. The ability of prostitutes to avoid any emotional rapport with their clients is so accepted that the exceptions become famous. What is not noticed so often is that a cash-based culture teaches us to fear such rapport anywhere. But making oneself incapable of such involvements also systematically destroys one's capacity to experience anything else either. Anthropologists who have studied pre-literate religions rightly point out that capitalist countries display a kind of fetishism. They endow the symbols of things with more energy than the things themselves. Money itself is the principal fetish. Soon one does begin to "eat the label and disregard the goods." Not only is the capacity for experience gone, but the victim doesn't even know it. Christianity in a capitalist culture inevitably falls into fetishism and label-eating. Teachings *about* God and words *about* Christ and phrases *about* the Kingdom begin to replace the real thing. So the East Turners who recoil from the society around them in a desperate effort to find friendship and experience of the real have put their finger on something. They are right in their diagnosis. But are they right in their remedy?

Religious remedies for the ills of a culture take two basic forms. One is to try to get at the underlying causes of the malady. The other is to provide a way for people to live in spite of the illness, usually by providing them with an alternate mini-world, sufficiently removed from the big one outside so that its perils are kept away from the gate. The East Turners have almost all chosen the second form. The only solution they offer to other people is to join them in their mini-world. But if we all did, it would soon be a maxi-world with all the problems back again. Part of its answer is that it cannot be the answer for everyone. Some East Turners have found a haven from the impersonality and vacuousness of the larger society and, they would say, of its churches. They have rightly located two of the most severe symptoms of our ailing era, but their solution, though it may work for them individually, at least for a while, is ultimately no solution for the rest of us.

It would also be no solution, however, if we merely made our churches over into places where intimacy and direct experience are encouraged. This renovation is already going on in many churches and takes the form of everything from encounter-group liturgies, which purportedly facilitate intimacy, to pentecostal speaking in tongues which celebrates immediate experience. But the solution remains partial and stopgap unless the underlying cause, the organization of a whole civilization around greed, is changed. So the turn toward the East, like the candid mirror of prostitution, does point to a real deficiency in our way of life, not just an imaginary one.

Less cogent are two other reasons people gave us for their participation in neo-Oriental movements. Although the impulses they express seem legitimate enough, the pilgrims' hopes of finding any real succor in Oriental movements—at least for very long—appears remote. Included here are those people who yearn for a spirituality that balances masculine and feminine components better, or at least does not perpetuate male domination. I also include here the Zen macrobiotic dieters and religious vegetarians (as opposed to those whose non-meat-eating stems mainly from ethical and political grounds), those who seek a world view that endows nature with a more sacred significance than technical civilization does, and those who believe some form of Eastern spirituality can help us avoid an ecological collapse.

Although to these East Turners themselves such reasons seem compelling, I do not believe they raise questions that are as crucial as the search for experience and friendship. René Dubos, in his book *The God Within*, has already shattered the myth that only Christian cultures suffer from an ecological crisis by showing how pre-Christian Greeks and ancient Chinese also ruined environments. You don't have to be Christian to abuse nature. But Turning East for an ecological solution seems mistaken to me for a more obvious reason. The ecological mess we face is a macrostructural one. Unlike the other problems the East Turners are trying to solve, it is difficult to see how a merely personal way out is viable, even for a short time. The solution to this challenge must obviously be large-scale. The depletion of resources cannot be corrected by even the most stringent application of individual and small-group disciplines. While loneliness and feelinglessness are apparently solvable at this level, pollution simply is not. Even residents of macrobiotic communes must breathe the air and will die if the stratosphere is punctured (due to jet travel) or the polar ice cap melts (due to heat pollution). Again, if the only solution is for entire civilizations to convert to a new religion, for example Buddhism (which in any case has not prevented similar problems from emerging in Japan), that is no solution at all.

The people who Turn East to escape Western religious male chauvinism will also be disillusioned very quickly. They discover that patriarchy is not a Hebrew plot. If anything, the degree and scope of male domination in the neo-Oriental movements is even more pronounced than it is in most Christian denominations. My own belief is that both our abuse of nature and the perpetuation of male domination, however it started, is now integrally linked with the same profit-oriented mindset that deprives us of intimacy and real experience. Like the seekers previously discussed, those who look to the new Oriental movements to deliver us from our destruction of nature and the debasement of women serve us best by calling attention to a problem. But the way out they offer seems even less plausible than it did for the community-and-experience seekers.

Finally, in addition to replies from East Turners that are authentically challenging and others that are a little more ambiguous, there are also two kinds that are disturbing for another reason. These are the replies that reveal a quest that will lead not just to disillusionment but to frustration and bitterness. These include the replies that came to us from those people who turn to the East to try to regain a lost innocence—a world free of complications and shades-of-gray choices. One can sympathize with the yearning such seekers display. But one hopes people will eventually find out that since no such world will ever be found, religious maturity means learning to live in a complex, shades-of-gray world.

Also, the same qualms arise about the people whose talks with us showed that they longed deeply for an authority so unquestionable and total that they would not have to make hard decisions or chew through choices on their own. When it comes to quests for innocence and absolute answers, it is not the biblical faith or even its current expression that is deficient. It is the search itself that is ill-advised. In this regard the East Turners are right when they say they have not found what they are looking for in Christianity. There is no real Christian equivalent to the restored innocence promised, implicitly or explicitly, by some versions of Eastern piety. The spirituality of both the Old and the New Testaments teaches that men and women have indeed lost their innocence, and there is no immediate way to get it back—that in fact those who consider themselves most innocent are often the ones to watch out for most. "Beware of the children of light!" Often, at least for a while, converts to neo-Oriental movements do seem to find a kind of new innocence. They are "blissed out" and have a hassle-free life. The emphasis many of these movements place on the inner life, plus their relegation of secular society to an inferior form of reality, means that adhering to their teachings, even quite devotedly, will not create uncomfortable tensions at work or with the landlord. Since money and power and in some cases even the capacity to make choices are viewed as illusory or insignificant in some neo-Oriental movements, the causes of most political tussles disappear. The problem is that the nasty issues of work, politics and the rest do not *really* disappear. Eventually even East Turners have to grapple with them. But they must now do so with a world view that gives them little help, because it refuses to recognize that the problems even exist.

As regards the pursuit of an absolute religious and moral authority that will relieve human beings of the discomfort of making decisions, it is obvious that Christianity has all too often succumbed to the temptation of trying to provide it, as Dostoyevsky shows in his chapter on the Grand Inquisitor in *The Brothers Karamazov*. In that story the Inquisitor scolds Christ for expecting humans to become mature and insists the church must think and decide for them. But these lapses have been temporary detours. The central core of biblical faith points away from the infallible pope and the inerrant page. It requires a movement toward maturity among ordinary people, more personal choice and less dependency on higher-ups. This same direction can also be found in the cores of the great Oriental traditions, especially of Buddhism. But here we are not dealing with either the Bible or the Oriental traditions themselves. We are concerned with the way they have been used, or maybe even misused, to keep people immature. Nor does this entail any blaming of the particular individuals who in their pain and confusion reach out for some authority. People who hunger for this kind of authority over them suffer from the wounds dealt out by parents and schools and jobs where they have never been encouraged to flex their decision-making capacities. But in order to mature, the last thing they need is one more perfect master to solve their problems for them. They need friends and families and larger settings in which their confidence in their own capacities will be strengthened. Ultimately this, too, points toward the need for a whole society in which the making of decisions, instead of being concentrated in the hands of a few at the top, is diffused among those whose lives such decisions touch and shape.

After months of talking with those I have called the East Turners, and more months of reflecting on what I learned, I became increasingly grateful for what they taught me. Their often costly decisions to leave behind the values and beliefs of a system they found hollow moved me more than once. It reminded me again just how much people are willing to sacrifice for the nonmaterial needs of the spirit. Practically, the dozens of masters and gurus I talked with taught me some basic tools for psychic survival. I learned a meditation practice that I will always follow. But most importantly, they all showed me how urgent it is that Christianity break off its debilitating alliance with the spirit of profit, the demon which must be exorcised before it destroys us all.

I do not believe that the mere abolition of cash culture will solve all the hurts that pushed the people I talked with toward neo-Oriental paths. But neither do I believe we can take even a few steps toward eradicating the deepset evils that underlie the pain they are escaping as long as we retain a way of life explicitly constructed on accumulating and competing. Jesus might not have smashed the money-changers' tables if they had not taken over the temple. The market has a place in every society. It is when it becomes our faith, gold our fetish, and financial security our goal in life, that the confrontation must occur.

Jacob Needleman in his excellent book *The New Religions* concludes by suggesting that in the long run what the new Orientalism will do is to stimulate in the West a new appreciation for its own heritage. I agree with Needleman, except that he means mainly the mystical and esoteric heritage of the West; I mean something more. In the short run we can learn to appreciate those contemplative and communal aspects of our faith that have been hidden or denied or have atrophied through misuse. In the long run, however, we must see that a merely religious answer will not suffice. Only a profound change in the way we work and own and love will do that, and this will require Christianity to challenge deep-seated values and powerful interests. Unless that happens, the passionate quest for the human, so eloquently displayed by the East Turners, but felt by all of us, will surely fail.

One must begin somewhere, though, and here Needleman is right. My response to what the East Turners had taught me and to the questions raised by my experience at Naropa was to start looking for those ingredients of Christian tradition which my Protestant upbringing had hidden from me, but which I had long suspected were there. This began with a visit to a Benedictine monastery—Weston Priory in Vermont—and an unforgettable taste of the Christian contemplative tradition.

8 Buddhists and Benedictines: Christianity and the Turn East

The bell began ringing in my dream, a sweet unintrusive peal-ing, distant and melodious. But as the dream faded I knew the bell was sounding just outside my window, that Brother Richard in his plaid jacket and Levi's was pulling the cord, and that in ten minutes, at 4:30 A.M., the monks would be gathering for matins.

> O sing unto the Lord a new song:
> Sing unto the Lord, all the earth.
> Sing unto the Lord, bless his name;
> Show forth his salvation from day to day.

Without allowing myself the time to decide whether I wanted to get up or not, I rolled out of bed, sloshed cold water from the basin on my face, and pulled on my clothes. My visi-tor's cell in the Weston priory, following the explicit directions of St. Benedict's Rule itself, was scantily but adequately fur-nished with a cot, chair, table, lamp, closet, sink and crucifix. Little to distract. It was February in Vermont, and cold. I put on heavy socks and a wool sweater and picked my way down-stairs to the simple common room where the earliest prayers of the day would be sung.

When I got to the room, most of the tiny monastery's six-teen monks were already there, sitting quietly on cushions in a semicircle near the huge picture window. Along the edge of the darkened hills across a valley, the gray light of the new day was just beginning to appear. Now one monk struck a chord on his guitar. Together they all sang, in perfect harmony, to a modern tune.

111

Calm is the night, O Lord
as we wait for you.
All the stars are laughing
at our wonder.

For a moment I felt utterly at home—with myself, with the monks and with the universe. For a millennium and a half, Benedictine monks have been greeting the morning with songs of praise. Here a steel-string guitar, Zen-type cushions and a melody reminiscent of Judy Collins had been added to an ancient ritual with no apparent incongruence. After the prayers and psalms we returned to our cells for a period of individual prayer, then gathered for a silent breakfast, then proceeded to the work of the day. Underfoot the snow squeaked in the 20-below temperature.

I was visiting a Benedictine monastery because, as is the case with many people, my encounter with Oriental spirituality had aroused my interest in part of my own tradition I had previously overlooked. Odd to have visited a Buddhist monastery before I ever visited a Christian one. But it was no accident that I had chosen this kind of Christian monastery. The Tibetans are, in some sense, the Benedictines of Buddhism. Although serious in their monastic life, the Tibetans have not shunned the world as many Theravada Buddhists and some Trappists and Carthusians have. Their monasteries performed in Tibet the same civilizing function the Benedictines performed in Barbarian Europe. Although both Tibetan (Vajrayana) Buddhists and Benedictines recognize that not everyone can or should be a monk, their communal discipline is a way to live together in the world, not a way to abandon it.

Among the reasons why people Turn East today, as our interviews and visits showed, is that they are looking for friendship, for experience, and for a teacher and a teaching that seem true. In Buddhist language, they are looking for a *sangha* (a group of serious colleagues), a guru (teacher) and a dharma (an authoritative teaching). The question that inevitably presented itself to my mind when I returned from Naropa was whether any or all of these might be found in Christianity itself. As I lived among the monks during those days in Vermont, I thought a lot about *sangha*, guru and dharma—and about their possible counterparts in my own tradition.

At first glance, parallels seem all too obvious. The search for *sangha* recalls the biblical idea of the covenant people, the congregation or the *ecclesia*. Dharma suggests a comparison with the Gospel. The place of Jesus, at first, seems similar to that of a guru. The question remains, however, whether or not there is real similarity below the surface.

1. SANGHA AND FRIENDSHIP

Biblical faith recognizes the universal human need for friendship. In the Genesis narrative, God creates men and women to live in friendship and mutuality, not in isolation. But fear and possessiveness lead to betrayal, fratricide and exile. The Adam and Eve and the Cain and Abel in each of us destroy mutuality through jealousy and hunger for power: the result is loneliness and suspicion. But it does not end there. In the biblical saga, "God" is that nameless energy which pulls isolated people out of loneliness and oppression into a new form of human solidarity. God discloses himself primarily as the one who creates a nation out of scattered tribes, makes a covenant (*berith*) with them, and promises that eventually the covenant will include all the peoples of the earth.

The most significant feature of the new community that God initiates among the separated tribes is that it not only binds people to each other but binds them at the same time to God. The importance of this idea of covenant should not be lost sight of just because it is cast in mythological language. The inner meaning of "covenant" is that the most basic power of the universe is itself a source of, and a participant in, human friendship. Friendship is not something human beings must eke out of the wilderness themselves. Friendship includes the constellations and the oceans, and the source from which they all arise. *Berith* is no mere social contract. God enters into friendship with the world and with humanity. The covenant is not an incidental aspect of God. It expresses the divine essence. God *is* that which makes friendship possible in human life.

The concept of *berith* gives the idea of friendship a centrality in biblical faith which goes beyond even the notion of *sangha*. Since the inner mystery of the cosmos is both the originator of and a partner in the covenant, the divine presence within each person becomes the basis for friendship. This community is not based on mere consensus or shared aspiration. Nor is it hierarchical. Since all human rank and station shrink to insignificance before God, all members of the covenant are essentially equal. Leadership and authority are intended only to serve the community. Moreover, the basis of human participation in the community is affected by the nature of *berith*. People can accept and live in the community freely because they have not created it themselves. It is not some awkward arrangement which constantly needs to be mended or pumped up. In a community with such a grounding, people can let each other be. Since everyone in the community enjoys the same status, there is a quality of freedom that no mutual-interest society can have.

This all sounds good theologically, but it does not answer the question of why Westerners are looking for friendship in Oriental forms. What has happened to covenant community in the West? Like any expression of friendship, the reality of the covenant has been damaged by the acids of the modern industrial world. Eventually these corrosions will surely take their toll of neo-Oriental *sanghas* as well. But there were flaws in the way the covenant worked even before it was attacked by industrial values. In actual practice the covenant community, despite its cosmic grounding, never fully broke out of its ethnic definition. Although here and there in Jewish theology the idea of an inclusive human community is expressed, it is usually in visionary or utopian terms. In reality the covenant was mostly for Israelites.

The problem was not solved by the advent of Christianity. At first the Christian movement gave the covenant a universal quality, at least theoretically. In the great debate at the Council of Jerusalem it was decided that uncircumcised gentiles could also be full members of the *ecclesia*, the new community founded by Christ, and intended to appeal to everyone regardless of lineage. Christianity began as a movement of hundreds of tiny "societies of friends" spread around the shores of the

Mediterranean and tied to each other at first only through visiting teachers and the exchange of letters and gifts. But it soon became hierarchical and exclusive. Finally, when Emperor Constantine made the new faith the ideology of his empire and entire Visigoth tribes were baptized en masse, being a Christian meant joining an organization and adhering to a prescribed creed. The societies of friends soon virtually disappeared.

The early Benedictines made one response to this disappearance. It is often said that the monastic movement began in the West because thousands of individuals became disgusted with the church's subservience to the empire, and with the widespread corruption that accompanied its legal establishment. One may argue, however, that people abandoned imperial religion and lived in monastic settlements to reestablish a measure of communalism. They fled to the desert not to escape the despoiling of doctrine but to get away from the destruction of circles of friends and their replacement by a hierarchically ordered imperium. Christianity seems to have introduced the dream of a network of local communities united in a universal covenant—only to have lost it almost immediately.

But the idea of a covenant community was never entirely lost. Parallel to the official history of the church from Constantine on, there is another history of the restless search for a viable form of community where friendship could flourish. Bands of hermits, roving groups of monks, heretical movements and religious orders kept appearing. In almost every one of them the idea of spiritual friendship and sharing was central. It was the heart of the teaching of St. Benedict, who lived in the early sixth century. People took great risks and endured awful deprivation in these movements. During the five-hundred-year period from A.D. 1200 until A.D. 1700 in which the events we call the Reformation took place, thousands of efforts were made, most of them short-lived, to reconstitute the *ecclesia* on a more communal, less hierarchical basis. It would be tempting to reread the tempestuous history of Christianity not so much as strife over doctrines but as a series of attempts to establish an authentic community. The labels used by the various parties during the Reformation help to show what was at stake: "Papist," "Congregationalist," and "Presbyterian" refer to different theories of how a community is best organized, nurtured and governed. Christians, too, have spent a lot of energy in the search for *sangha*.

After 1600 the American wilderness received thousands of settlers who crossed the seas determined to found religious communities where fraternity and sorority would flourish. They often failed, but throughout the nineteenth century the United States was dotted with religious communes and spiritual utopias —in Ephrata, Oneida, New Harmony, the Shaker villages, to name only some of the better-known examples. I believe we can see in the current search for *sangha*, which has brought thousands of Americans to the doors of neo-Oriental groups, a continuing expression of a quest which began millennia ago and which has had an especially lively history in America.

2. DHARMA AND GOSPEL

With respect to dharma, or teaching, the East Turners, as I have already noted, are searching for a discipline that will enable them to meet both the sacred and the secular aspects of life with a directness not gutted by abstraction or sullied by analysis. Their quest represents the revolt of heart against head, which is also familiar to students of revivalism in Christianity. It is important to repeat, however, that for East Turners this quest for immediacy is not directed only at the experience of God. It is a search for an unaffected and honest encounter with all one meets—with nature, other people, and the self. Although some Eastern movements claim the techniques they teach can produce a direct relationship with the holy, others explicitly deny they can do any such thing. What such disciplines do make possible for many people is a way of coming into touch with persons and things without having to see them through a fuzzy screen of cerebral overlay.

Where does the screen come from? Here Christian and Oriental answers differ. I heard Ram Dass, the psychologist-turned-guru, articulate a typical Eastern answer to a large audience of enthusiastic listeners some months ago. Like many other neo-Oriental teachers, Ram Dass located the distorting screen in the phenomenon of language. He told of the problem he had eating pizza, an activity sure to bridge the gap to his youthful audience. Ram Dass said that in times past, just as he was about to bite into a large onion-mushroom-and-cheese pizza, he heard a voice within him say, "Eating pizza." The voice was not judgmental or mocking, just observing. Yet, putting the experience of eating pizza into words while it was happening detracted from the sheer taste of the pungent ingredients.

So far, I can agree completely with the diagnosis. All of us seem to have as a constant companion this loquacious little interior commentator, editorialist and observer. His running chatter constantly distracts us from the pure taste and smell and feel of whatever it is we are doing. Reality becomes increasingly hidden behind its labels. Chatter is distracting, which is why the Benedictines eat their meals in silence and the Trappists discourage any idle talk. How do we get beyond labels?

In Buddhist thought the word *dharmakaya* is sometimes used to designate the raw experience of being. It stands for the sheer "thatness" of reality, what is there before we name it or classify it. It is the pizza in the mouth at the moment when tongue and saliva and onions and hot tomato sauce seem indistinguishable from each other. *Dharmakaya* might also be described as the way of touching and seeing that the discipline of sitting meditation exemplifies. When one is simply watching one's own breath, no words or concepts are needed. But not all experiences are as pleasant as eating pizza, so meditation should not be presented as a technique to make life happier. Only a saccharinish form of meditation would produce exclusively enjoyable results. One who can taste pizza directly will inevitably go on to be able to taste anger, fear and pain more keenly also. That is why the experience of *dharmakaya* needs to be placed in a more inclusive vision of the world. It requires both a community of support, which in some forms of Buddhism is provided by the *sangha*, and an ethical framework, which Mahayana Buddhism supplies for many people in the ideal of *bodhisattva* (the notion that one does not accept the fullness of human liberation oneself until all sentient creatures share it).

In order to understand how the message of Jesus compares with the idea of *dharmakaya,* one must begin by noting that the Gospel is not a "message" in the usual sense at all. Jesus himself is the message. The Gospel is neither a dogma about him nor even a compilation of his own teachings. The reason the Jesus dharma centers in the life of a concrete historical person rather than in a body of verbal teachings derives from an insight which is not altogether unlike the notion of *dharmakaya.* The reason goes back to the ancient Hebrew recognition that no one can adequately represent either God or human beings in words or pictures. According to the Second Commandment, one should never use any image to depict either God or human beings or animals, and according to ancient Hebrew custom the name of God should never be uttered by human lips. All these proscriptions express the belief that since God is not just a transcendent being, but the essential constituent in the being of everything, there is something in every person and thing that resists labels. We err badly, this teaching insists, if we believe that what is real in the world around us can be grasped by words and concepts. We are commanded to make no images, not because it would be disrespectful, but because no image, no matter how carefully wrought, can possibly do justice to that which it is supposed to depict. All such constructs inevitably mislead and distort.

There are differences, however, between the Buddhist idea of *dharmakaya,* with its suspicion of words, and the biblical idea of the Holy, with its suspicion of trying to depict either God or human beings in any way. The difference is that where in most Buddhist schools of thought it is the words themselves that distort, in biblical faith it is not the words but our human inclination to use words to twist reality in our direction. Words themselves, and even pictures, are not, in the biblical view, essentially evil or misleading. But because we live as human persons in a world infected by possessiveness and hostility, we inevitably tend to use even the most valuable gifts in destructive ways. The problem is not language or concepts as such, but our misuse of them. Adam and Eve spoke with each other in the innocence of Eden. We lose our capacity for *dharmakaya* or direct experience (symbolized by the Garden of Eden) not because we use concepts and language, but because we try to control and dominate, seize and grasp. It is not the use of words that poisons our interaction with life; rather, our prior poisoning of life in turn poisons our words and concepts.

Since the Buddhist and biblical views of the locus of the infection differ, naturally their prescriptions for recovery vary too. Since in the biblical view our basic dislocation is a fractured relationship to the people and things around us, only the healing of these relationships will allow us to begin to use words to affirm people rather than to control them. The biblical faith teaches that this healing and restoring energy is available, and that as we are touched by it our thinking and speaking become less despoiling. For Buddhists, one slowly learns to realize that all the words and categories we use are illusory constructs, and this insight is itself liberating. In the Buddhist view we learn to use words sparingly because there is no way words can avoid distorting: "Words are liars." In the biblical view we allow ourselves to be weaned away from our need to grasp and clutch at those around us, and we find that this allows us to see and speak with less distortion—even to say, "I love you," not to control someone but because we mean it.

Both Buddhism and biblical faith recognize the validity of the human need for a direct encounter with the real stuff of life. Buddhism locates our alienation from reality in ignorance, wishful thinking, abstracting, concept-pandering. It has elaborated a sophisticated range of techniques and teachings for helping people to rise above this ignorance and face reality as it is. Biblical faith attributes our dilemma not to ignorance but to fear and lovelessness, our anxious need either to dominate the people around us or to keep them at a safe distance. Therefore the Buddhist path emphasizes overcoming ignorance, the biblical course concentrates on the restoration of mutuality.

Both the overlapping and the distinction between these two interpretations of a universal malady come to focus in the practice of meditation. Some Buddhists claim that the more they meditate the surer they become of the illusory quality of relationships. In my own experience of meditation quite the opposite occurs: I become increasingly aware that my life is constituted by relationships and that the health of those relationships is largely a matter of how much I am falling into controlling and allowing myself to be controlled by the people around me. When I return time and again to my departing breath, it is like taking a step away from the need to master or to be mastered, and a step toward the kind of mutuality which is possible when the liberating ingredients of any relationship are permitted to surface. When I get up from the cushion, my feeling toward other people is both more independent and more interdependent, closer and not as cloying, more integral and less entangling.

I agree with the Buddhist teaching that meditation helps people to respond to "what is really there." But included in what is really there is something that moves toward me from others, an energy that enables human beings to take a step beyond gamesmanship, toward meeting. This energy has its source not just in human beings themselves, but in something embedded in the structure of the cosmos. If I had to call it something I would use the word "grace." It is the mystery of grace which has the power to soften our hearts, still our fears, and restore us to each other. As this process begins, the poison level in our language goes down, concepts begin to function as bridges instead of walls, and one can accept people as God accepts them—not for what they can or cannot do for us but for what they are. A kind of *dharmakaya* occurs. Finally, we may be able to nibble a pizza without a troublesome little internal commentator whispering in our ear.

The Christian Gospel is a kind of dharma, a teaching. What it says, however, is that a direct encounter, a *dharmakaya*, not only with God but with our fellow earthlings, with nature and with our own deepest selves *is* in fact possible. The "message" comes, however, not as advice or exhortation. It comes in the only way it is credible, in a human person, Jesus, who actually did all these things and who points us toward other human beings as the indispensable clue to the discovery of the daily *dharmakaya* in our midst.

3. JESUS AND THE GURU

Jesus himself is the centerpiece of the Christian dharma. Was he then also a guru? Ever since he first appeared preaching and healing in the remote province of Galilee, people have tried to find the right word for Jesus, a credible way of grasping what he was about. In the pages of the New Testament alone, dozens of attempts to name and classify him appear. One group of followers, fired by a passion for the liberation of Judea from Rome, wanted him to be King of the Judeans, or the "Son of David," the one who would restore the storied empire of King David. Others wanted him to bring back religious purity to the Jews, to cleanse and purge and sanctify the nation. To these spiritual revivalists, Jesus seemed anointed by God in much the same way the great prophets and John the Baptist had been. Still others hoped this unlikely Galilean would actually become the legendary Son of Man mentioned widely in the popular piety of the day, a cosmic hero who would close the present world age with a crash and introduce a universal epoch of justice and peace, punishing the wicked and rewarding the righteous.

Jesus disappointed all of them. Occasionally he seemed to lend hope to the national-liberation enthusiasts. They must have been sparked with anticipation, for example, when he entered Jerusalem in a kind of caricature of the great Roman triumphal marches, riding a colt, with the crowds strewing branches before him. Still, he led no attack on the occupation forces and discouraged his followers from carrying weapons. Although he was finally executed in a manner clearly reserved for insurrectionaries, this happened because the local Judean leadership clique was obviously upset by his presence and succeeded in persuading the Romans that he was a menace.

But Jesus burst the hopes of the other groups, too. Those who looked for a great revival and a restoration of religious purity were enraged by his violation of ritual taboos. He would not engage in ceremonial hand washing, and he healed people on the Sabbath, which though condoned by other rabbis of his time, infuriated the stricter interpreters of seventh-day propriety. As if this were not enough, he completely dashed the hopes of the religious-revival party by associating with the ritually unclean—lepers and Gentiles—and by insisting that such pariahs would actually precede the righteous people into the Kingdom of God. He especially confused and disillusioned the people who wanted to apply to him the title Son of Man, which was the name attached to the coming hero of the popular folk religion of his day. He did this first by accepting the title, then allowing himself to be defeated, humiliated and killed, the exact opposite of the Son of Man scenario.

Jesus seemed determined to smash every expectation, label and title anyone tried to affix to him. He destroyed some by refusing the title in the first place. He destroyed others by accepting the title (Messiah, Son of Man, maybe even King of the Judeans) and then acting in a way that exploded what the title meant to those who used it.

Jesus would not be what anyone wanted him to be or do what they wanted him to do. Although he healed and taught and even fed people at times, he was not really a healer or teacher in the usual sense. When he cured people, it was to demonstrate the healing powers of the new epoch he claimed was dawning. When he taught, it was not to convey a tradition or pass on some kind of wisdom. Rather than teaching in the normal sense of the word, Jesus *announced* something. He pointed people to a spiritual reality he called the reign of God, which he insisted was now accessible to everyone and did not have to be awaited or anticipated in some near or remote future.

Jesus left behind him a trail of shattered illusions and wrecked expectations. When we say today that Jesus was in some way a key clue to the nature of God, this expectation-destroying quality of his life suggests what such a claim means. The God Jesus discloses will not be the God anyone wants. This God will not be a mere extension of human programs and aspirations. Divine "transcendence" therefore is not a matter of spatial distance or mystic fuzziness. It refers to the continuous power of the Holy to break through all concepts, doctrines, mental sets and cultural patterns. Jesus reveals God exactly because he was not what anybody expected or wanted. He refused to be classified, and he constantly forced people to deal directly with him rather than with their ideas about him. In doing so, Jesus exemplified in his life something Buddhist teachers constantly emphasize—that reality is always different from even our best ways of talking and thinking about it.

People's efforts to cast Jesus in a role that would serve their own purposes continued after his death. Even the pages of the New Testament are not entirely free of this redrawing of Jesus's portrait. Within a few years he was depicted as a dying and rising nature god in the style of Mithras. Later he became a frowning and all-powerful Byzantine emperor, the Pantocrator; still later a gentle teacher of virtue and charity, as the nineteenth-century liberals saw him. It is understandable that people over the centuries have tried to grasp the meaning of Jesus in categories familiar to them. Since Jesus cannot be entirely defined by any single role, this process will always go on. Each attempt has its own strengths and its own dangers. So today we find Jesus pictured as a circus clown, a national liberation rebel, a teacher of mystical wisdom, a preacher of feminism, an impulsive superstar or, as Kazantzakis portrays him, as a hot-blooded romantic hero. But because the spirit of Christ is still alive, the same refusal to be pigeonholed goes on today. No one of these costumes ever quite fits. Jesus still continues to shatter expectations and smear the pictures people paint of him.

Today, as the Turn East proceeds apace, there are two titles drawn from Eastern thought that some people are eager to press on Jesus. Both carry with them a considerable weight of Oriental metaphysics and theology, but once again, neither quite fits the one to whom they wish to attach it. One of these titles is "avatar." The other is "guru."

An avatar, the conception of which originated in Hindu spirituality, is one among many embodiments of the ultimate. Ideas of what an avatar is vary widely, but one current theory teaches that in each age there is an avatar on the earth somewhere—that Confucius, Moses, Jesus, the Buddha, St. Francis, Mohamet, Lao Tzu and many others were such embodiments of the divine. After these familiar names, the list of candidates begins to vary, depending on who makes the list, but the idea is clear: there is always a divine incarnation walking around on earth somewhere, and if we are tuned in properly we can locate him or her.

Although Jesus was probably not familiar with the avatar theory in this form, paradoxically he both abolished it and accepted it at the same time. He abolished the avatar idea, ironically, by accepting it so radically and so universally that it no longer made sense. He did this by allowing himself to be called Christ (or Messiah, which is the same word). In his time the

title meant one who is anointed by God, a special representative of God among others—an idea not unlike that of avatar.
However, Jesus went on to insist that henceforth God could be
found not just in prophets, wise men or holy teachers but in all
human beings. He emphasized the sweeping inclusiveness of
"all" by especially singling out the poor, prisoners, sick and dis-
reputable people, the ritually impure and the racially excluded
as the ones in whom the presence of the Holy now dwelled.
Jesus was the avatar to end all avatars. If we take his life message seriously, we need not rack our brains to figure out which
of the current contenders is an avatar of the divine. All are, and
none is; and the avatar we are seeking is already in the midst of
us, in us and in those closest to us and farthest away.

If Jesus does not quite fit the classical role of avatar, then can
he be understood as a guru? The term "guru" is also not one
about which there is complete agreement. According to the informative section on the guru-disciple relationship in Herbert
V. Guenther's and Chogyam Trungpa's *The Dawn of Tantra*:

The term *guru* is an Indian word, which has now almost become
part of the English language. Properly used, this term does not
refer so much to a human person as to the object of a shift in
attention which takes place from the human person who imparts
the teaching to the teaching itself. The human person might more
properly be called the *kalyanamitra* or spiritual friend . . . one
who is able to impart spiritual guidance because he has been
through the process himself.   (Guenther and Trungpa, 1975)

The writers go on to say that although at a certain stage in
the teaching process the guru may be identified with the *kalyanamitra*, this should not become a matter of personality cult.
Eventually the teaching eclipses the teacher. Finally the world
itself, as it unfolds from moment to moment, becomes the guru.

Can we see Jesus either as a guru or as a *kalyanamitra?* Soon
after the death of Jesus a movement began among the first-century Greek-speaking followers of the new Christian movement
which understood him as what scholars now call a *theios aner*
(divine man). These early Hellenistic Christians saw Jesus as a
superhuman figure, endowed with near-magical powers, the

possessor of a kind of supernatural knowledge that " . . . he selectively reveals as divine revelation to those of his own choosing." (Weeden, 1971, p. 55) The majority of early Christians, however, rejected the divine man theology. It seems clear that one of the main purposes St. Mark had in mind when he wrote his account of the life of Jesus, the earliest Gospel we have, was to fight this first-century effort to make Jesus into the equivalent of a guru in our present popular sense.

According to St. Mark and the other synoptic Gospel writers, Jesus was decidedly not a teacher of divine wisdom who selectively imparted a secret teaching to a specially chosen few. He healed the sick and was reported to have worked other miracles. But nothing he did of this nature was calculated to dazzle audiences. On the contrary, rather than using his gifts to attract attention, Jesus often warned people not to make too much of the healings themselves. Above all, Jesus did not hand down clandestine lore. When he spoke, he addressed crowds in the open fields and in the synagogues. His whole life was devoted to warning people against teachings which were reserved for the select few or which required some rare gift of spiritual receptivity. He claimed that even the despised collectors of the Roman taxes could understand, and he seemed to go out of his way to consort with those he called the "poor in spirit," the religiously inept and the morally retarded. If we think of the title "guru" not in the elevated sense in which Trungpa and Guenther define it, but in its current popular usage as designating a superlatively holy person, perhaps capable of breathtaking feats, who secretly passes on some supreme wisdom to a selected coterie, then Jesus was no guru.

But can we understand Jesus as a guru in the more refined sense, or possibly as a *kalyanamitra*, an experienced spiritual friend? Certainly if the term "guru" entails a shift of attention from the person to the teaching, Jesus does not qualify. In what still appears to many people as patent arrogance, Jesus insisted that he himself exemplified his own teachings, that the two were inseparable. People eventually had to deal with *him*, not with what he said or with what was said about him.

Is this arrogance? I think not. It is simply Jesus' way of forcing us to deal directly with people rather than with ideas or conceptualizations. This is why Christianity has been correct in emphasizing that the Gospel points to a person, not to a system of thought or an ethical code. Jesus is a "spiritual friend" only insofar as he does what only a very close friend can do: he refuses to allow us to use him to reinforce our habitual patterns and our tendency to throw off the responsibility for our own lives onto other people. He did not permit himself to become the occasion for illusory hopes or passing the buck. He showed the anti-Roman guerrillas that if they believed God would cast off the Roman yoke they were deluding themselves. They would have to bring down the tyrant themselves. Jesus would not cater to the religious hopes of the people who yearned for a spiritual renaissance. He would not allow anyone to cope with him by using platitudes, conventional formulations or any existing *modus operandi*. Jesus was a unique person and as such he enables us to see the uniqueness of all persons.

Jesus is the person par excellence. In him we meet what we then realize is equally true for all persons: they are singular and unrepeatable centers of creativity and decision. They are not merely the occasions for perpetuating our own schemes or illustrations of our ideas or facilities for advancing our programs. Christian theology has correctly insisted that Jesus was both "true God and true man," not some well-blended admixture. He was fully divine and fully human. But in its one-sided reiteration of the "true God" part of this teaching, theology has frequently neglected to say that Jesus also shows us what a true human being is. This side is not only equally important; it is also integral to the "true God" part. No one knows what the "true God" side means unless he knows what the "true person" side means. Jesus is divine *because* he was fully human, and that which is most human in anyone is at the same time the *imago dei*, that which is most divine.

Jesus's final confrontation with the effort of his contemporaries to cast him in the role of guru or *kalyanamitra* came with his decision to allow himself to be identified with God—and then to be crucified. This was the ultimate overturning of dogmas and expectations. Whatever else gods do, they do not allow themselves to be cornered, railroaded, disgraced and lynched. Jesus had a clear choice. He could have refused the divine title, in which case his crucifixion would have offended no one. Rebels and rabble-rousers of his time frequently met such an end. Or Jesus could have accepted the title and then done what everyone expected God to do: destroy the oppressors, purify the nation, bring in an era of kindness and goodwill. Either of these courses would have made sense to his contemporaries.

Instead, Jesus chose a third course. He accepted the divine title *and* he allowed himself to be tracked down, tried and executed. The final destruction of everybody's fondest religious ideas occurred: God on a cross. In this denouement, Jesus put an end to any notion of God as the great guru in the skies, the magical *deus ex machina* or the omnipotent Big Brother. As Dietrich Bonhoeffer puts it in one of his most eloquent passages, "The only God who can help us is the one who cannot help."

After nearly two thousand years, the truth about Jesus has still hardly sunk in. Right after his death, stories began to circulate that he had escaped the gibbet, that a look-alike had been substituted, that while the crucifixion occurred he was standing on a nearby hill chuckling. Since then other people have tried to use the resurrection appearances of Jesus to reinstate the idea of a Big Daddy God who solves our problems for us and keeps us in eternal early adolescence. But the resurrection stories depict a crucified figure who still bears the wounds of the nails, and who gets hungry and must be fed. True, some current theologians object to this interpretation and argue that a crucified God cannot bring hope to the downtrodden and disenfranchised. Only an omnipotent God, they say, can buoy up the powerless. But Jesus knew better. To the landless peons of his day his life had an unmistakable message: God does not support the rich and the powerful, but neither does he intercede with magic arrows or well-aimed thunderbolts to remove an oppressor from the palace. God liberates the oppressed by enabling them to liberate themselves. This, I believe, is the only credible "liberation theology." Anything else feeds the kind of millennial fantasies which have kept the poor in bondage for centuries.

Was Jesus a guru? Is he a guru? The answer is that whatever

kind of guru one is looking for is the one Jesus refuses to be.
He is an elusive figure, the saboteur of prefabrications, the true
kalyanamitra who deftly places the ball back in our court. He is
not the guru we want, but he is the guru whom, whether we
know it or not, we need.

The monks at Weston Priory go to bed early. Since the day
begins at 4:30 A.M. with Brother Richard pulling the bell cord,
they need to. Also, the February nights in Vermont are dark
and cold. Despite the arctic temperature, I took a walk the
night before I left. The frosted air burned my nostrils and even
the stars seemed to shiver. The monastery's dogs barked briefly
as I crunched by, but then quickly crept back into their boxes.
I felt cold, but comfortable. I was not a Benedictine or even a
Catholic, but I felt that through the lens of these men's life
together I had been able to catch a glimpse of something that
was mine, something which in its own way could meet the need
for *sangha*, dharma and guru that I had found not only in other
people but in myself. I could see that, at least for me,
Christian faith, despite the distortions which have marred it,
can still answer the universal human yearning for friendship,
authentic experience and even for trustworthy authority. But I
also realized that it would be idle to urge the present East
Turners to forgo their quest and return to their ancestral tradition. They have not found what they were looking for where it
was supposed to be, and they have gone to look elsewhere. The
only problem is that the same forces which have conspired to
decimate the power of the biblical faith in the modern West
will also inevitably work their spell on the Oriental traditions
that reach our shores. The difficulty lies not so much with the
traditions, Eastern or Western, as it does with the stony and
unpromising soil on which the seed is scattered. To understand
the chemistry of this stony soil, we will need to move on now
to a spiritual assay of our own society in the closing decades of
the twentieth century.

9 Enlightenment by Ticketron: American Society and the Turn East

On my desk lies a handsomely designed folder inviting me to an international conference on yoga and meditation. Sponsored by an organization in Glenview, Illinois, it is scheduled for the Palmer House in Chicago. When unfolded, the pamphlet displays the pictures and the credentials of no fewer than forty-eight swamis, gurus, psychological specialists on alternative states of consciousness, and practitioners of biofeedback and Oriental medicine. Featured prominently at the top of the first page, over the photograph of Swami Rama, who seems to be a central figure in the proceedings, stands the overall theme of the gathering: "Come Enlighten Yourself" . . . "Love all and exclude none—that is the way to enlightenment." The flyer indicates that in addition to thirty-five scheduled sessions, there will also be displays of art, sculpture and craft, " . . . each depicting in its own way, a message of yoga and meditation," exhibits of response-monitoring machinery, presentations of "the cultural and entertainment pastimes of East and West," and a widely varied selection of printed literature. A further note promises that "conference technicians will be capturing each seminar on film and tape" using either sound film or on stereophonic cassette tapes. The cost for the "total package" plan is seventy-five dollars, which does not, however, include lodging, meals or other costs. Tickets can also be obtained through Ticketron.

The business of America is business, and that includes the religion business. The greatest irony of the neo-Oriental religious movements is that in their effort to present an alternative to the Western way of life most have succeeded in adding only one more line of spiritual products to the American religious marketplace. They have become a part of the "consumer culture" they set out to call in question.

Maybe this accelerated consumerization of the new religious movements should not surprise us. After all, the genius of any consumer society is its capacity for changing anything, including its critics, into items for distribution and sale. Religious teachings and disciplines, Eastern or Western, can be transformed into commodities, assigned prices, packaged attractively and made available to prospective buyers. A popular mass-circulation magazine recently published an article entitled "A Consumer's Guide to Mysticism."

American history has recently entered a phase that might have surprised Thorstein Veblen, best known for his famous essay on conspicuous consumption. In our time, consumption of most things is expected to be *in*conspicuous. Except for a few hardy clotheshorses and jewelry displayers, the affluent of today are noted not for how elaborately they dress but for how casually. Patched and faded jeans actually sell for higher prices than those that look new. Big shiny new cars are bought only by well-intentioned but gauche social climbers who are still imitating Grandpa's climb to success. The children of the rich want outdated old cars with faded upholstery and failing mufflers. The unkempt young people who hitchhike across Europe generally come from families who could well afford the train, perhaps even the jet.

Conspicuous consumption is no longer a mark of distinction; what we have in its place is something I call the new gluttony. Gluttony is not a nice word. Many will confess without much shame to offenses of lust or pride. Few persons, however, would like to be described as gluttons. Yet I believe the idea of gluttony may help us understand our situation, including the flurry of interest in the Orient. Gluttony is the characteristic vice of consumer society, just as greed was the vice of early capitalist society. In classical theology, gluttony is one of the seven deadly sins, falling in most lists, significantly, just after envy and just before anger. Although the term has sometimes been reduced to mean overeating, gluttony actually refers to taking in or accumulating more than one needs or can use. In different historical periods the glutton directs his insatiable appetite to different objects. Today only the old-fashioned glutton still stuffs his mouth with too many entrees. Rather, he craves experiences—in quantity and variety, more and better, increasingly exotic; even spiritual experience is the object of the new gluttony.

The "poor little rich girl" in Shirley Temple movies sat at a gilded table in a palatial mansion, waited on by liveried retainers carrying silver goblets. She possessed everything a Depression population thought they wanted, and since they did not have what Shirley had, they were comforted to see that wealth did not make her happy. Shirley's counterpart now wears denim cut-offs and eats pizza, but she is accumulating experiences at a rate that would have dizzied the little heiress. Today's money is not chasing houses, cars and clothes, but travel, drugs, unusual sights and sounds, exotic tastes, therapies, and new emotional states. If disgrace haunts the new glutton, it is not for failing to *have* something but rather for failing to have *tried* something. Wardrobes and jewelry boxes may not bulge as much, but memory books are jammed. The very thought that out there somewhere lurks an experience one has not had now sends the affluent into more panic than their grandfathers felt when they discovered that another family in the club had commissioned a longer yacht. The affluent elite *look* outwardly very much like everyone else, but the chances are that they have been to more places and done more things and still look depressed, so the deprived viewers remain comforted.

The new gluttony transforms the entire range of human ideas and emotions into a well-stocked pantry. All that human beings have ever done or thought is stored there now, wrapped in foil and kept at the proper temperature, ready to be dished up when the experienced gourmet's appetite begins to lose its edge. Hermann Hesse may have foreseen something like the new gluttony when he described the "glass bead game" in his last and most mature novel, *Magister Ludi*. But in that story the residents of the fabled province of Castalia at least played imaginatively with the chits that represented all previous art, literature, religion and humanism. In our consumer-Castalia, the pieces are merely collected and devoured. The process is only cumulative. Nothing new emerges because it is of the essence of the glutton that he must hurry from one dish to the next lest he miss some fleeting taste or tantalizing flavor. He cannot really savor experience. He gobbles it up and goes on, letting the bones and pits pile up under the table.

No doubt economists as well as theologians could advance explanations for why we are moving from a greed-for-things to a gluttony-of-experience. In a system based on encouraging greed, people eventually become sated. It is hard to sell another radio to the family which already has one in every room, one in each car, and two portables for the beach. Of course, styles can be changed endlessly for common products, and they can be designed to wear out quickly and to be difficult to repair. Still, there is a limit to what most people can stack up.

With respect to experiences, however, there seems to be no such limit, and the experience merchants do not need to plan obsolescence or invent style changes. Their product self-destructs immediately, except for one's memory, and last year's model is unusable not for any reason so trivial as changing hemlines or fads in chrome trimming, but because it is gone. Economists can explain the new gluttony in the classical terms of a movement from goods to services. It is the old story of expanding markets, finding new resources and developing novel products. But now the product is an experience that can be sold and delivered to a customer. The resources are virtually infinite for the imaginative entrepreneur, and the market is that growing group of people whose hunger for accumulating mere things has begun to slow down.

Not all new gluttons were once old ones. They do not own piles of material possessions. But they have lived in a society surrounded by many old-fashioned acquirers. Having witnessed the futility of old-fashioned accumulating, they often lose interest in the race to acquire things before the starting gun goes off. But the gluttony remains. They simply choose a new set of goodies.

Theologians would not disagree with economists on the sources of the new gluttony, but they surely add another dimension to the discussion. Theology teaches that the most dangerous sins are those of the spirit, not those of the body. As persons and societies mature, their faults become more subtle and refined, less gross and obvious. Christianity teaches that the refined and subtle sins are the most dangerous, because they are the most destructive to oneself and to others. Jesus scorned the self-righteousness of the ministers and lawyers, but was so forgiving of those guilty of fleshly vices that he became the subject of whispers and complaints among the more conventional citizenry. Normally, as one's sins slide along the scale from flesh to spirit, one becomes increasingly subject to worse offenses, especially arrogance and self-righteousness. At the same time an even more lethal process sets in. All of one's venalities grow more ethereal. Lust moves from the loins to the heart. Anger poses as patience and martyred condescension. Even pride no longer delights in its own possessions but in its humility; and gluttony, as we have seen, does its own metamorphosis. If there is anything more unattractive than a self-righteous Pharisee boasting to God about his piety it is a self-righteously humble publican parading his lack of it.

It was the Spanish mystics who thought most deeply about the spiritualization of sin. St. John of the Cross warned his readers against what he called spiritual avarice, the focusing of covetousness and unseemly desire on the realm of the spirit. Here, also, he warned, there is danger in excess, and restraint should rule. One Carmelite novice master was in the habit of giving his charges only half a communion wafer at mass, to teach them to get along on less in the realm of the spirit as well as in earthly things. The consensus of the theological tradition seems to be that gluttony of the spirit is not only no improvement over its coarser cousin, but is even more dangerous to the soul.

Is there an element of spiritual gluttony in the current fascination with Oriental spirituality? I think there is. It must be quickly added that this is not to be laid at the feet of the Oriental traditions themselves, most of which are highly sensitive to the pitfalls of spiritual pride; awareness of this peril, for example, permeates the Zen tradition. Nor can we blame the often anguished people who are driven by forces they can neither control nor understand toward searching out more and more exhilarating "spiritual experiences." We have called gluttony a sin, and so it is. However, it is important to recall that in classical theology "sin" is not to be understood as a fault for which someone must be blamed. Sin is a bondage from which captives can be liberated. Jesus himself refused to be drawn into his disciples' bickering about who was to be faulted for this or that. He was principally interested in helping people to get disentangled from the grip of whatever was crippling or controlling them.

If there is any fault to be allocated, it lies not with the victims but with the buyer-seller nexus within which the new Oriental religious wave is marketed. Despite what may be good intentions all around, the consumer mentality can rot the fragile fruits of Eastern spirituality as soon as they are unpacked. The process is both ironic and pathetic. What begins in Benares at a protest against possessiveness ends up in Boston as still another possession. Dark Kali, the great and terrible destroyer, whose very glance can melt the flesh of the strongest warrior, whose slightest breath can stop the pulse and paralyze the soul, finds herself dangling from bracelets with all the other charms.

No deity however terrible, no devotion however deep, no ritual however splendid is exempt from the voracious process of trivialization. The smiling Buddha himself and the worldly-wise Krishna can be transformed by the new gluttony into collectors' trinkets. It was bad enough for King Midas that everything he touched turned to gold; the acquisition-accumulation pattern of the new gluttony does even more. Reversing the alchemist's course, it transforms rubies and emeralds into plastic, the sacred into the silly, the holy into the hokey.

The process of changing the gods into consumer software bears a certain similarity to the alchemy described by Karl Marx by which early capitalism transforms everything into what he called a "commodity." Persons and things subjected to this treatment cease to be looked at for what they are and begin to be viewed solely for their cash value. For Marx, there was something uncanny about this process. The commodity became a kind of astral body floating over the real thing, diverting our attention. Like the mad Pythagoreans of old, the stunned victims of consumer culture look at the heavens and instead of seeing stars, see price tags and numbers.

This process reaches its nadir, Marx wrote, when the human

being begins to see himself or herself as just another commodity devoid of genuine subjective experience. This disappearance of real things and persons cannot be corrected, he asserted, just by thinking about it. As long as the market defines value, and market value defines worth, we will all continue to wander like sleepwalkers through a nightmare world of insubstantial shadows, with even our own minds and bodies becoming the quotients of what someone somewhere will pay for them.

Whatever one may think now of Marx's predictions and prescriptions for escaping the ghostly world of commodities, there can be little doubt that his description of its strangeness still rings true. He saw that we live in a world where things and persons do not come to us with some inherent meaning but with a meaning infused into them by our particular culture. What Marx did not see is that the gods themselves are also subject to this awful metamorphosis. The gods of the Orient mean one thing there and something quite different here, and this is not to be blamed either on the gods themselves or on their original devotees or on their new seekers. It happens because when the gods migrate, or are transported, to a civilization where everything is to some extent a commodity, they become commodities too.

The cultural barrier which a commodity culture erects against the possibility of genuine interreligious exchange is thus a formidable one. It raises the question of whether we in the West can ever hear the voice of the East, can ever learn about the Buddhist or Hindu paths without corrupting them in the process. At its worst, the issue expresses itself in the paradoxical fact that although America today *seems* uncommonly receptive to spiritual ideas and practices from the East, the truth is that we are not really receptive to them at all. True, no stone walls have been erected to keep the pagans out. No Orders of Knights Templar have ridden forth to hurl back the infidels. The gates are open and the citizens seem ready to listen. No wonder many Eastern teachers view America as white unto harvest or a fertile ground in which to sow their seeds.

But curiously, it is precisely America's receptivity, its eagerness to hear, explore and experience, which creates the most difficult barrier to our actually learning from Eastern spirituality.

The very insatiable hunger for novelty, for intimacy, even for a kind of spirituality, which motivates so many Americans to turn toward the East also virtually guarantees that the turn will ultimately fail. It is the story of the Trojan horse, only this time in reverse. Oriental teachers need not sneak into America in disguise. Americans rush out to meet them, shower them with gifts, overwhelm them with attention. They are borne into the city as saviors. Only later do the teachers from afar discover that the precepts they have imparted have been heard and absorbed in such a way that the teacher would hardly recognize the results. Alfred Loisey once remarked that Jesus came preaching the Kingdom of God but what happened was the church. It could be said similarly of many of the current Eastern masters that they came teaching enlightenment but what happened was yet another spate of American self-improvement sects.

The problem with introducing Oriental spirituality into America today is that the cultural barrier which the light from the East must pass through functions as a thick prism. The prism consists of American consumer culture and psychological individualism. What emerges from the filtration process is something which has neither the impact of a genuine alternative vision nor the critical potential of biblical faith. Robbed by the prism of its color and sharpness, the now-refracted Oriental light serves as one more support for the structure its original teachers had most hoped it would undermine: the isolated, Western competitive ego. The effort to introduce Vajrayana (Tibetan) Buddhism into America, although it is only one example of the process of distortion, is a particularly vivid one and sheds some light on how the same thing happens to other traditions.

The two central tenets of this form of Buddhist teaching—something it shares with several other varieties of Buddhism—are the ideas of *detachment* and of *egolessness*. Few Buddhists would deny that "transience"—the fact that everything is always changing—is the main basis for suffering in the world, and that the Way of the Buddha is designed to overcome suffering. Therefore ego and attachment are the two main obstacles to tranquility and enlightenment. We suffer because we develop attachments, within and without, to something which by its very nature will inevitably disappoint and disillusion us. In fact,

Buddhists would say that the mistaken notion that we even have an ego, or that attachment is even possible, are the real sources of pain. The path of the Buddha is laid out for us, not, as is often supposed, to help us overcome ego and attachment. Rather it is there to help us to realize that, since everything within us and outside of us is always changing anyway, ego is illusory and attachment is impossible. We come to this awareness, however—so the teaching goes—not by understanding the ideas but by discovering this truth for ourselves in the process of meditation and spiritual discipline. Thus we eventually come to egolessness and detachment not as ideals to strive for but as accurate descriptions of a reality we had been refusing to recognize.

I find this central Buddhist teaching a challenging vision that, if taken at all seriously, would surely transform completely the way we Americans live and work and organize our society. I am not saying that I agree with this vision. It is not, in any case, a theory with which one can agree or disagree—and Buddhists generally refuse to enter into debates about it. Still, I think it can be maintained that egolessness and detachment lie close to the heart of the teaching. But prisms can turn blue into red, and it is dismaying to see how this truly alternative world view is so fragmented and recombined by the Western prism that what results is something far different from what went in, so different that it appears to be nearly its opposite.

The prism problem begins with the fact that contemporary Americans already experience a kind of "detachment," albeit very different from what the Buddhists have in mind. Our detachment comes from our living in a mobile, throwaway civilization in which we are schooled by the media not to get too attached to anything—or anybody—because we will soon have to discard it (or him or her) when an improved model appears. Our American form of detachment comes not from the spiritual insight that all things are moving toward nothingness, but from planned obsolescence, fashion changes and the constant introduction of new products to replace the ones we have. Our form of "detachment" is a kind of alienation that also infects relationships to persons, not just to things. It is the result of a Kleenex, paper-plate and styrofoam-cup way of life—itself the result of our economy's unending need to sell new products. The outcome of all this is that many Americans, especially from the most affluent groups, already suffer an amorphous sense of "detachment," an inability to form lasting and significant relationships with either persons or things. The rising divorce rate and the insoluble problem of where to pile our mountainous rubbish both give witness to our inability to care deeply about what is already there.

It must be said at once that this alienated form of consumer detachment is not what the Buddhists teach. They would see it as a pathological form of attachment; not detachment at all but a kind of insatiable grasping after something that cannot be grasped. Consumer "detachment" is not a part of Buddhist teaching. But it is a part of the Western prism through which that teaching must pass, and therein lies the difficulty. Many of the earnest seekers and serious practitioners I met at Naropa turned out to be very "detached" people whose lives had made them wary of the pain that can result from forming deep attachments to others. Many were divorced, single and adrift, or unhappily married. Many had moved in and out of careers or colleges, none of which had been particularly satisfying to them. Several had dabbled in other spiritual movements or in drugs or politics. They all seemed open, likable and friendly. But somehow I got the impression that they had no real turf, little sense of home or hearth, no person or purpose to which they were willing to bind themselves very deeply or for very long. Even those who were most wrapped up with Chogyam Trungpa, the founder and resident master of Naropa, seemed to appreciate the fact that he discouraged enthusiastic attachment either to himself or to his movement. They were people who had come to terms with the built-in transience of consumer society and who had found in Buddhism a philosophy that allowed them to live without guilt and without too many regrets.

Up to this point the prism effect, the distortion of Oriental teaching by occidental expectation, had probably not corrupted the core idea of "detachment" too badly. Although the two forms of detachment, Buddhist and American, are very different, even the distorted idea gave these people a certain amount of inner peace and personal support. The real problem enters, however, with the idea of egolessness and its prismatic distortion in the West.

There is no basis whatever in our Western experience for understanding what the Buddhists mean by egolessness. Here even the most eloquent Oriental teachers come to a dead end. I have heard learned and articulate Buddhists try every device they know to get the idea of egolessness across to receptive, attentive Western audiences—never with any success. Westerners listen, ponder, puzzle and listen again, but almost never understand. Worse still, they sometimes believe they have grasped what the Buddhists mean when they say "ego is illusion," when the truth is they have not grasped it at all. Except for the very rare mystic, or the person who has lived through a period of psychotic personality disintegration to which he probably does not wish to return, there is hardly anything in ordinary Western experiences (even, I think, after long periods of meditation) that even remotely connects with the key Oriental idea of egolessness. Here the prism becomes opaque. Not even a faint glimmer of light gets through.

The result of the failure of even serious Western seekers to catch on to the Buddhist idea of "ego is illusion" is that this part of the teaching remains a more or less dead letter. Though Western practitioners may talk about it, using the correct Buddhist language, one inevitably gains the impression that they are not really describing their own experience but are repeating a credo. At another level, beginners on the Buddhist path, stumped by the idea of egolessness, end up identifying it with something like the opposite of egoism, or with not being "egotistical." To them it sounds like the familiar moral injunctions against selfishness they have heard since childhood. Few realize the utter radicalness and frightening profundity of egolessness in its naked reality. This teaching just does not make it through the prism.

The end result of the Western prismatic refraction of the light from the East is a wholly new pattern. This new pattern combines the Western ego—only slightly curbed by warnings against selfishness—with an idea of detachment already distorted by consumer living. The product is in some ways a combination of the worst elements of both cultures. Western religion tends to accept the ego but teaches that love as a positive form of attachment can replace possessiveness and manipulation. Eastern spirituality does not give love such a central place, but teaches that ego is unreal, and that all forms of attachment lead to suffering. The prism-distorted Western version of Buddhism combines loveless ego with psychological "detachment." What comes out looks much like irresponsibility with a spiritual cover, a metaphysical license to avoid risky, demanding relationships, a mystical permit to skip from one person, bed, cause or program to another without ever taking the plunge.

Does this mean that the spiritual wisdom of the Orient, the light from the East, is fated always to be deflected—that it can never reach us except in a grossly distorted form? At first the outlook appears grim. Obviously, merely increasing the intensity of the light will accomplish nothing. A stronger light from the East passing through the same prism will only produce an even more grotesque monstrosity. Can anything be done?

I have occasionally met individuals who know how integral religion and culture are, and who have made a serious effort to avoid the prism by becoming deeply involved in a wholly different culture. Some have spent years in Japanese monasteries or Indian temples, adapting themselves to new clothes and diet and language as well as to unfamiliar techniques of prayer and meditation. Without fail, each of these bold spirits told me that as the months and years went on they became aware of what a nearly impossible task they had set for themselves. One man said that after his first two years in a Zen monastery in Kyoto he believed he was making real progress, but that at the end of five years he felt further from his goal than he had felt on the first day he shaved his head and sat down cross-legged with his face to the paper-and-bamboo wall. When I compare such patient and ruthlessly honest pilgrims with the enthusiastic converts who tell me that everything changed on that wonderful day when they memorized their mantra or opened their third eye, I cannot help wondering, in the latter cases, how deep a change has actually taken place. Is there any hope then that the new Orientalism can ever help us escape our captivity to commodities?

I believe there is a basis for hope and that the Turn East can eventually help us. Although it is easy to single out a spiritual cafeteria held at a luxury hotel in Chicago and to show, as I have done, how far it has abandoned the spirit of the Vedas or the wisdom of the ancient masters, there is another side. Any movement, religious or otherwise, which wants to reach people in America will eventually have to confront in one way or another the business culture. So far, however, the neo-Oriental movements have done so only at the individual level, and this is not enough. I do not condemn the eager spiritual seekers who flock to such conferences. They did not invent spiritual gluttony, nor did they create the acquisitive system which transforms their most idealistic quest into a need which can be located in a market survey and transformed into a sales possibility. They are as much victims as malefactors.

What is the proper response of the churches and synagogues of America to the new influx of consumerized neo-Oriental spirituality? Surely it is not the panicky utilization of the so-called "deprogramming" methods popularized by Ted Patrick's sensational book *Let Our Children Go*. When used on minors who have been kidnapped with parental approval, these techniques are nothing more than a debasing form of behavior modification that should be rejected out of hand by any religiously sensitive person. When used on adults, deprogramming is also plainly illegal and unconstitutional. It is frightening to me to see people who are otherwise alert guardians of the First Amendment's guarantee of freedom of religious expression condoning the deprogrammers when we are all aware that such methods could also be used—and have been used—on Catholics, members of Christian sects and followers of other religious movements. Some psychiatrists have even been known to lend support to the incarceration of the devotees of the Krishna Consciousness movement, for example, because they think that anyone who chooses a life of prayer and worship instead of a career must obviously be mentally disturbed. One wonders what these zealous defenders of psychological orthodoxy would have done with Jesus—whose parents considered him demented—or with Saint Francis or the Baal Shem Tov.

The most famous incident of deprogramming in religious history involves St. Thomas Aquinas, whose parents tried every device they knew to get him to renounce his religious vows. It is also pertinent to observe that the most assiduous efforts of the deprogrammers are directed not to the customers of Ticketron enlightenment but to those who, like the Hare Krishna devotees, exhibit a life style which is at radical variance with a society caught up in success and self-expression. I believe the religious institutions of the West should not rely on psychological deprogrammers to meet the challenge of the East but should do what they can, first to insure the freedom of all religious groups, second to expose the sources of the consumerization that affects all religions, including our own, and third to respond to the challenge at a genuinely theological level.

A proper theological response to the consumerization of Oriental spirituality should be directed not at its victims but at the underlying system which makes such a trivialization all but inevitable. In recent years Christianity has either ignored the sin of acquisitiveness or has also directed its criticism mainly against individuals. But this has not always been the case. At times, though not frequently, Christianity has transcended mere individualism and has brought the weight of its moral vision to bear against the gross injustice and dehumanizing effects of corporate systems. In the history of American Christianity, for example, Walter Rauschenbusch, the Niebuhrs, Washington Gladden and many others have reminded us that the acquisitive society is an enemy of the soul and that we cannot ultimately serve both God and profit. We need to hear this message again today.

The irony of the Turn East is that in seeking to oppose the system, it seems to reinforce it; in fleeing it, it extends its perimeters. Its tragic failure to make any significant impact at the inner core of our culture could, however, have at least one positive effect. It could help us to become more aware of our own shortcomings. It could make us see more clearly how badly Christianity has also failed in this respect. If this realization then stimulated a rebirth of the biblical social vision during a period when it seems to have fallen on hard times, then the Turn East may have contributed to our healing after all.

The American philosopher Jacob Needleman has eloquently addressed himself in some of his recent books to the issue of whether Americans can ever hear the message of the East. Needleman is concerned about the fact that sacred teachings, especially those emanating from the East, were originally transmitted only to persons who were seriously committed to the demanding disciplines of a *path*. The master conveyed the teaching to the disciple only when he was sure the disciple had made himself ready. Now, Needleman fears, these "esoteric" ideas (esoteric only in the sense that they are communicated in the closed context of a shared trust) have been made "exoteric." They have been placed on the market. Needleman puts it very strongly. We must understand, he says, " . . . the deviation that takes place when the formulations of esoteric ideas are 'stolen' from the personal disciplines of the *path* to be organized and promoted by individuals who are themselves in the condition of unconscious psychological fragmentation." (Needleman, 1975, p. 163) Under such conditions, Needleman fears, even the subtlest and most profound teachings are fated to become mere concepts, to contribute willy-nilly to the further reinforcement of ego. He does not seem at all hopeful that we can escape this awful impasse, since the "guardians" who once stood at the gates preventing easy access to the treasures now seem to have vanished. (Needleman, 1975, p. 170)

Although I share something of Needleman's grave outlook, I am not quite as pessimistic as he seems to be. Obviously, as he shows, spiritual ideas coming in from the Orient have begun to serve purposes that are often nearly the opposite of their original ones. For Needleman, the problem lies in the split between idea and experience, between personal discipline and truth, and the result is that teachings that were meant to undermine the whole idea of ego end up being part of ego's armament. Although I agree in part with Needleman's diagnosis, I see this split not just as an individual shortcoming but as the product of a centuries-long social development in the West—a development which is both economic and cultural—which has created in our time a characteristic personality: the competitive consumer of ideas, the compulsive devourer of experiences. When Needleman describes current Western man as one who "steals" the esoteric ideas to bolster his conceptual schemas, this is what he may have in mind.

The reason why I still hope, where Needleman seems almost to despair, is that I can never give up the conviction that change, even profound change, in a person or in a society, is possible. In its most original formulation, Christianity not only *requires* "repentance" in order to participate in the Kingdom of God; it also insists on something that is more difficult to believe, namely that repentance is *possible*. The possibility of repentance is postulated on an "open" universe in which neither persons nor nations need stumble in perpetuity, eternally trapped in their current outlooks, habits or perceptual prisms. The spiritual power at the core of reality makes new life chances possible. This is where the recently widely discussed "theology of hope" meets the core dilemma of the Turn East. As presented by its most eloquent interpreters, the theology of hope is not a fuzzy brand of religious utopianism. Nor is it a blind belief that some extraterrestrial being will intervene on humankind's behalf like a magic genie. Rather, theology of hope is based on the confidence that real change, genuine novelty and unprecedented newness can appear in human life, that indeed the cosmos itself is supportive of such change. Based on this foundational faith, I do not believe Americans are sentenced to grope forever in the grotesque light patterns emitted by the prism. People can begin again. Even "new birth" is possible.

The answer to the riddle of the distorting prism is not a stronger light—it is the dismantling of the prism. This will not be easy, because the prism of the competitive-consumer way of life is part of a larger edifice of social patterns and economic practices. It is the result of our allowing those institutions that live by profit, expansion and cash value to assume the seats of power and to dictate their modes of thought to everyone else. Jesus told the rich young inquirer he had to sell all his goods and give the money to the poor before he could even set foot on the path to the Kingdom of God. We should be careful not to universalize this command too glibly—yet surely there is a direct connection between our inability really to hear the Eastern teachings and our unwillingness to give up our personal and national quest for economic supremacy and military invulnerability. As a society, and often as individuals, we want to set our feet unswervingly toward enlightenment, but to keep a firm toehold on the securities of whatever privileges we have been able to garner. The contradiction is an impossible one. Although America seems receptive to Eastern spiritual teachings, it is receptive only up to a point. Just as repentance must *precede* entrance into the Kingdom, so the willingness to alter the very basis of our common life must precede our ability to hear, really to hear, what the East has to teach us. We will not hear until we change.

It may seem ironic, even contradictory, that I base my confidence on the eventual possibility of our hearing and learning from the East on what many will identify as a "Western" theological premise: the capacity of human beings, and even of human societies, to change. But I do not believe this need be contradictory. If the biblical belief that grace makes change possible is true at all, then it must surely include the possibility that Western people will be able to sacrifice their current confidence in production and performance and thus be inwardly prepared to hear what the East has to teach. For the truth is that just as, in the Buddhist teaching, egolessness and detachment are not merely ideas to be discussed, but discoveries, so the genuine possibility of seemingly impossible change (called "grace" by theologians) is not simply an article of belief, but something that must be experienced. It can be experienced, however, only by those who let go of their current survival tactics and open themselves to just that impossible possibility.

There is no contradiction in my idea that only the reality of grace can open the West to the East, because ultimately the "meeting of East and West" is not a matter of ideas at all. When it occurs at the level of ideas, the result is always either polemic and proselytizing or—what we now seem to have— premature synthesizing and superficial equating. We have now come to a time when the meeting must take place not in the realm of ideas but in the lives of actual persons living in real societies—that is, in the flesh. When that begins to happen, as I believe it can, then eventually the ideas will follow. "He that doeth the will of God shall know the doctrine."

10 The Myth of the Orient

During the summer of 1976 I returned to Naropa, again to offer a course on the "Life and Teachings of Jesus"—and to learn more about the Buddhist path. As soon as I arrived I began to notice changes, both in Naropa and in myself. At the opening faculty reception, Chogyam Trungpa shook my hand and asked, "How long can you stay with us this summer?" It was a perfectly hospitable welcome, but I also caught an intonation which I had not detected before: "you" and "us." Naropa was becoming more explicitly "Buddhist." I was an honored guest, as I had been the year before, but despite my year-old meditational practice, I was no more than a guest. Just as I had needed to adjust to being a practitioner of shamatha meditation who was, however, not a Buddhist, so the Buddhists had learned not to regard me as a prospective convert. The lines had become clearer all around.

I was not the only one who noticed the difference. The evidence of the clarification process was everywhere. Naropa was now administered by people who had all lived through years of Buddhist training and practice. Some had been sent by Chogyam Trungpa from Karmê Chöling, the study and meditation center which an acquaintance of mine had once dubbed "Buddhist bootcamp." It was clear that the process had been Trungpa's own decision. "We are not concerned with adapting . . ." he had told an interviewer a few months earlier, "but with handling the teaching here in a skillful way."

When Tibetans began to present Buddhism in this country, we did it in keeping with the people's mentality and language. As people understand it more and more, it begins to take a real traditional

146

form. If we were to present all the heavy traditional stuff at the beginning, then all sorts of fascination with Tibetan culture and enlightenment would take place, and the basic message would be lost. So it is good to start with a somewhat free form and slowly tighten it up. (Trungpa, 1976)

It is significant that, according to this quotation, Trungpa had chosen this free form—followed by tightening up—approach not because he was afraid that beginning with the "heavy traditional stuff" would scare people away. Just the opposite. He did not want to fascinate people with Tibetan exotica and have them lose the basic message.

Whatever the reason, the most dramatic sign of the tightening up was the change in the format of Trungpa's two weekly lecture sessions. The "open space" I had enjoyed so much the year before, the two hours of informal conversation and idleness in the gym before lectures began, was now no more. Although Trungpa continued to appear two hours late, now the waiting period had been transformed into another sitting meditation session. Instead of the disorganized "beach scene" of the previous summer, now hundreds of students sat silently on black or yellow-and-orange *zafus* and meditated until the teacher appeared.

No doubt about it, Trungpa was tightening up. One rumor had it that the new toughness had been a result of the visit a few months earlier of His Holiness Gyalwa Karmapa, Trungpa's superior in the Kagyupa Order of Tibetan Buddhism, who had reportedly advised Trungpa to sharpen up the Buddhist identity of his Naropa operation. Other people denied the rumor, claimed that the Karmapa had been very pleased with Trungpa's work and insisted that Naropa's clearer Buddhist profile was a natural expression of Trungpa's own strategy for introducing Buddhism to America.

Whatever the reasons for the changes, I found that I appreciated them. The more explicit Buddhist atmosphere helped make the differences between the Buddhist and the Christian paths even plainer. It sharpened the dialogue. This in turn pressed me further along in the reappropriation of neglected aspects of my own tradition, a process which had begun with my first visit to Naropa. But the new particularity did not suit everyone. One young man who had spent two years studying with Trungpa and had considered himself well along the first stages of the Buddhist path confessed to me that he had been shocked and bewildered by the Karmapa's visit. After studying with Trungpa, who wears a sports coat and loves to use words like "terrific," "fantastic," and "bullshit," meeting the Karmapa, who speaks no English, wears traditional Tibetan garb, and puts much more emphasis on the ceremonial aspect of Buddhism than Trungpa himself does, was terribly disquieting. Indeed, while in America, the Karmapa staged the ancient Tibetan Black Crown ceremony, which features Tibetan horn and drum music, brocaded fabrics heaped on the Karmapa's throne and the displaying of a centuries-old Black Crown that is said to have the power of liberating people on sight. In the hours-long ceremony, the Karmapa places the crown on his own head and goes into a state of deep meditation called *samadhi*, after which he blesses some people, initiates others and gives out mantras and sacred words to devotees.

The Karmapa is unapologetically ritualistic in his approach. "In order to cleanse the sins and impurities of the body," he says through his British-born interpreter, "we use the yogic prostration practice. In order to cleanse the sins of the voice . . . we take the refuge of the Triple Gem and recite the one-hundred-syllable mantra of the Vajra Sattva. In order to cleanse the sins and impurities of the mind, tendencies which have been collected through countless lives and endless *kalpas* of time, we say mantras and bow to the Buddhas with a heartrending feeling of penitence for all the suffering we knowingly or unknowingly have caused others or inflicted on them." (Karmapa, 1976) One of his disciples put her attitude toward Karmapa as succinctly as it could be put. "To us," she said, "he *is* Buddha."

It is not surprising that some of Trungpa's fledgling followers were upset by their encounter with the Karmapa and the Black Crown ceremony. After listening for months to Trungpa's colloquial and often derisively antiritualistic lectures, meeting his superior must have come as something of a surprise. Some, of course, were fascinated and drawn deeper into the Vajrayana

Buddhist tradition. Some began to wonder if they had not made a mistake to embark on a path that now seemed to lead toward elaborate penitential rituals, prostrations and magic crowns. But I am sure Trungpa's strategy was correct and that the Karmapa's visit was well timed. Eventually those attracted to this version of the Buddhist path should understand clearly just how demanding and elaborate, in a sense, how "foreign," it is. This will separate the dilettantes from the disciples. It will prevent premature synthesizing and make it more possible for Buddhism to be presented in America as a genuinely *different* option, not as one more candidate for cultural cooptation.

Just before I left Naropa for the second time I was invited by the faculty to give a kind of farewell lecture. Speaking from the same stage from which Trungpa ordinarily lectures, I gave some reflections—as a Christian theologian—on what I had come to know of the Buddhist path. I welcomed the Buddhist teachers to America and wished them well in their efforts to introduce this venerable tradition here. But I warned them about the problem of the cultural prism, the pseudodetachment we already have, the danger that what appears to be a genuine receptivity to their ideas may be just the opposite. And I ended by warning them that Americans will never be able to hear the message the real Orient has for us so long as we keep a mythical Orient in our heads.

This last problem seems to me the most difficult one, the one that continues to make the new Orientalism more a peril than a promise. It is the fact that there are actually two "Orients." One is made of real people and real earth. The other is a myth that resides in the head of Westerners. One is an actual cultural area, stretching from India to Japan and from Mongolia to Singapore. The other is a convenient screen on which the West projects reverse images of its own deficiencies. This mythical Orient once consisted almost entirely of sages and fakirs, magical talismans and esoteric lore, serpents weaving to nasal flutes, infinite holiness, wisdom and inner peace. Recently this Western dream of an Eastern Xanadu has soured somewhat. It now includes some nightmare qualities: elusive guerrilla bands, teeming pools of population, swarming yellow hordes waving little red books and hypnotic cult leaders bent on brainwashing idealistic youngsters. The West's inner Orient accommodates both our fondest fantasies and our most gruesome fears. The Orient symbolizes both threat and promise in the imagination of the West, and the two elements feed on each other, like paradise and perdition.

Psychologists and theologians both know the myth-making inclinations of human beings, their tendency to invent a Beulah Land of perfection over the rainbow or beyond the blue horizon. In the Western psyche "the Indies" has always had more of a mythical than a geographical meaning. In Columbus' time the Indies meant not only India and Cathay (as China was called then); it also signified whatever it was that Europe lacked and sought. Was the West poor? To the East lay El Dorado, the landscape tiered with cities of gold. Was the West aging, failing in vigor? Somewhere in the East bubbled the miraculous fountain of youth. Was our religion corrupt and repressive? There, unspoiled natives dwelt in naked innocence, enjoying childlike pleasures and recognizing only the benevolent creator whose sacred writ was the ebb and flow of nature itself. Were our rulers stupid and arrogant? There, one could find the great Khan who always governed wisely and well, or the righteous realm of Prester John, the perfect priest king.

Why was it that Europe pushed eastward until it met itself on the other side? Undoubtedly commerce had much to do with it, and it surely is no coincidence that the European expansion into the Orient happened just as the early signs of capitalism were showing. But it was more than that. As J. W. Parry says in *The European Reconnaissance*, "If the search for India had been only a matter of balancing possible profit against financial and maritime risk, the decision to attempt it might have been still longer delayed; but the pull which India exerted on the European imagination was not commercial only." (Parry, 1968)

The "pull" of which Parry speaks may be the other side of an inner push, that restlessness which Augustine found in himself and which some theologians see in all souls, but which is probably more Western than universal. Parry himself says that the explorers of the Renaissance period were motivated not only by practical ends but also by "a search for Christian perfection." Though fifteenth-century Europe was assured, as he says, "of its possession of Christian revelation," it had reason to doubt whether its way of life was a very exemplary embodiment of that revelation. "For some, at least, of its spiritual and intellectual leaders," he continues, "perfection was not here, not now; it had existed long ago in time; it might be found again surviving far away in space."

The East, first as the "New World," then as the "Far East," is where Westerners have gone to convert, to conquer, to colonize, always driven by an inner disquietude. As Hernando Cortez said to the Aztecs when he landed, "We have a sickness of the soul for which gold is the only cure." But gold was obviously not the cure; why then has the search continued when, despite shiploads of bullion, no answer has been found to the soul sickness of the searcher? The question can never be answered satisfactorily, because myths cannot be refuted by facts, and human beings stubbornly persist in finding what they are looking for. Columbus died firm in the belief that the sandy Caribbean islands he had discovered were the outlying islands of India or Japan.

Throughout Western history this mythical Orient has had its cartographers and explorers just as the real Orient has. The human proclivity to see what one has been looking for is so strong that many travelers and traders who journeyed to the Orient also became elaborators of its myth. After Marco Polo and his brothers did actually visit China, they helped to perpetuate and embellish the Western legends about the East. Columbus, a good sailor, kept the myth of the Indies alive even when the facts were not very supportive. Cortez and Pizarro immortalized the fables of Mexico and Peru before destroying them. Any contemporary traveler to the Orient is so programmed by hundreds of years of image-making that his capacity to see what is actually there is much diminished.

Enterprising Orientals have learned, of course, how to show us what we want to see. Perceptive entrepreneurs, East and West, can now supply the pilgrim or tourist (the distinction between the two is seldom clear) with precisely the Orient he or she sets out to see. This same process happens everywhere. It is the "prepared environment syndrome." In parts of Africa guides have become skilled in leading inexperienced hunters on a safari that actually moves in a large circle and ends, after a few days, at a location where the guides knew there were some aging lions even before the trek began. Latin America inn-keepers, realizing that most travelers long to return home and report that they avoided tourist traps and got close to the local people, have now constructed shelters that specifically cater to this anti-tourist taste. On the Rue Pigalle in Paris there stands a nightclub called Les Naturistes whose builders intentionally designed it and decorated it so that it would look exactly like a Hollywood movie version of a French nightclub. They did so because they had noticed that many Americans, their ex-pectations shaped by films, tended to be disappointed by the genuine *boites de nuit*. Les Naturistes does a splendid business, not only with Americans but with Europeans whose introduc-tion to what a nightclub looks like came first from a movie. It would be naïve indeed to suppose that the same prepared environment syndrome does not apply to the Oriental pagodas and ashrams Westerners visit. It applies especially to Oriental movements that set out to cultivate an American clientele. Reality imitates art, and institutions of religion are often shaped around images of what they are believed and hoped to be.

Who actually forges our images of the "mysterious East"? The truth is that they are not simply forged. They arise from deep needs in the Western psyche and are then polished, re-fined and distributed by writers, film-makers, and inventors of advertising copy. Rudyard Kipling, the Victorian poet, is per-haps the best example of the influential Oriental image polisher. Kipling wrote his poems and stories at the height of the power of the British Empire, and he left impressions and characters that still affect us. There was a time when nearly every English schoolboy, and many Americans as well, could recite at least a part of "Gunga Din"; that loyal water carrier who died taking a canteen to a British grenadier under fire was, according to one critic, the best known Indian in the West until Gandhi came on the scene.

Kipling is long since dead, the Empire in retreat, and the Victorian ethos dethroned. But songs reverberate after the sing-ing is done and images linger when the stimulus is past. Kipling's India still retains a grip on the imagination of the West. This is not just because his plots and characters have appeared in all manner of films—*Gunga Din* alone was filmed three times in Hollywood—but also because Kipling captured the imaginary India that survives in the fantasy life of Westerners. Never a reliable guide to the real India, Kipling is the conjurer par excellence of that bundle of impressions the Western mind calls "India." These strange Orientals in Kipling's lines have something we lack. Ignorant, wily, elusive, intransigent they may be—perhaps even ungrateful and ferocious at times—but underneath they possess a purity we lack. The quest for perfection which J. H. Parry sees as the spark of Western colonialism remains alive in Kipling's attitude toward Her Majesty's heathen subjects. The myth says there is a place of perfection and it lies Somewhere Else. It is a myth that springs from hope.

Another part of the myth springs from fear. Orientals possess strange powers they could use against us. They are wily and malevolent, like another movie favorite, Dr. Fu Man-Chu. Of the two stereotypes, we strongly prefer Gunga Din. Him we can trust. After all, he earned the right to be praised as "a better man than I am" by dying in the service of the Queen of England. We like him ever so much more than Dr. Fu Man-Chu. Still it is not hard to see behind the Gunga Din image of the gentle, spiritually pristine Oriental a certain wishful thinking on the part of the English colonizer. Better a servile water carrier with a soul of gold than an angry Sepoy rebel with a black heart. Better a smiling meditator than a frowning Maoist.

What happens when history threatens to shatter the myth we hold of the Orient? How do our perceptions change when the Orient asserts an identity that does not conform to our image? The answer is that when reality threatens to engulf the myth, we cling to the myth more fiercely. Even Kipling knew that empires do not last forever. After singing about holding "dominion over palm and pine," he could remind us of the inevitable day when "all the pomp of yesterday" would be "One with Nineveh and Tyre." In decline as well as glory, empires retain a mythical attitude toward the colonial. As facts undermine the myth a painful ambivalence sets in. Tommy Atkins grudgingly respects Gunga Din while shooting at the latter's countrymen; and the Anglican missionary vaguely suspects that the Hindus may have valuable wisdom of their own even as he passes out Malayalam translations of the Book of Common Prayer. My point here is that Americans have inherited the same myth and are experiencing the same ambivalence, and we cannot understand the current massive interest in the spirituality of Asia unless we see it within the context of America's shrinking Asian "empire." Whatever their intentions, visiting gurus will be cast as religious versions of Dr. Fu Man-Chu or Gunga Din. They embody our fantasies of what Orientals *should* be like.

Empires must always deal with the religions of those societies they dominate. Sometimes they simply destroy them. Christians and Muslims seem to have favored this strategy. Sometimes they use the religions of their satraps for the purpose of dividing and dominating, as England did so adroitly for so long in India, or they may try to emulate as the Romans did the Greeks. Always they distort indigenous faiths in one way or another. Eventually the colonizers begin to realize the enormity of what they have done, and the guilt begins to tincture hope and engender fear.

The Aztecs of Mexico never quite forgave themselves for their ruthless suppression of the Toltecs, and they were always a little frightened at the prospect of a Toltec uprising. They admired Toltec culture, added Toltec ancestors to their elaborate family genealogies, and integrated Toltec deities into their own pantheon as smoothly as the Romans once appropriated the Greek pantheon shortly after conquering the Greek states. Still, the Aztecs always feared that the legendary Toltec god-king Quetzalcoatl would return one day to take vengeance and reestablish his throne. This fear, incidentally, made them extremely vulnerable to the Spanish conquistadores who were first mistakenly seen as the exiled god's avatars, and who were more than willing to sit in for Quetzalcoatl if it would help them defeat the Aztecs.

In view of these distinguished precedents it seems less than surprising that the American fascination with Eastern spirituality should have begun in the nineteenth century just as our belief in manifest destiny began to reach out toward the Pacific —and has culminated just as our country's power has crested and begun to recede in Asia. The dominator gets rid of his guilt by making the dominated holier, wiser or more virtuous than himself.

Our current admiration for what we think are Oriental religions, whatever else it may be, is one way of coping with a bad conscience. Unable to slow down the swift Westernization of some parts of Asia, bewildered by the power and independence of other parts, we try to console ourselves with thoughts of how simple and virtuous the Asians really are. Two centuries ago Marie Antoinette and her court attributed the same virtues to unlettered shepherds. She wore a peasant's cap and bade her courtiers dress in silks cut to give a pastoral impression. She distributed shepherds' crooks to the court and ordered everyone to sing country ditties while lounging around carefully built replicas of rustic cottages. Our interest in the Orient today has something of the same quality. While inundating the East with American products, yet sensing vaguely that we can no longer dominate parts of Asia, we begin to dress in their costumes and help ourselves to their religions—conveniently packaged for Western consumption.

The final paradox is that few Easterners ever claim to be able to save the West. Frequently they deny having any interest in doing so even if they could. They rarely send missionaries here and they accept Western novices with reluctance. Although the Westernized versions of Eastern faiths do often claim to bring salvation to the West, at this point they betray the spirit of their sources and actually worsen the Western dilemma by advertising more than they can deliver. The spiritual crisis of the West will not be resolved by spiritual importations or individual salvation. It is the crisis of a whole civilization, and one of its major symptoms is the belief that the answer must come from Elsewhere. Thus the crisis can be met only when the West sets aside myths of the Orient and returns to its own primal roots.

An old Zen story tells of a pilgrim who mounted his horse and crossed formidable mountains and swift rivers seeking a famous roshi in order to ask him how to find true enlightenment. After months of searching, the pilgrim located the teacher in a cave. The roshi listened to the question and said nothing. The seeker waited. Finally after hours of silence, the roshi looked at the steed on which the pilgrim had arrived and asked the pilgrim why he was not looking for a horse instead of enlightenment. The pilgrim responded that obviously he already had a horse. The roshi smiled and retreated to his cave.

Eventually the spiritual disciplines of the Orient will make a profound contribution to our consciousness and our way of life. Some day, somewhere, we will hear the message the East has for us. But we can only begin to know the real Orient when we are willing to let go of the mythical one. And we can only begin to hear the message of the Oriental religious traditions when we are willing to confront the inner dislocations in our own civilizations which caused us to invent the myth of the East in the first place; and when we are willing to do that, we may realize that what we are seeking so frantically elsewhere may turn out to be the horse we have been riding all along.

11 Toward a Spirituality of the Secular

We need an authentic contemporary form of spirituality. We must find it, I believe, in our own tradition, not somewhere else. But where do we begin to look for it? In the Buddhist spiritual path the whole lineage of masters through whom the dharma has been conveyed is honored, but the most important masters are the founders of the line at one end and one's own master at the other—the classical source and the living teacher through whom the dharma comes to me. In the meditation hall of the Boston Dharmadatu, for example, where I sometimes go to meditate, there are four prominently displayed pictures. One is of the Buddha. One is of Avilokitsvara, the founder of the lineage. Another is the master of the current teacher; and the last is of the current master himself. I believe this same principle of geneological selectivity also applies in Christianity. Next to Jesus and the first Christians, it is our direct mentors in the faith who play the most significant role. We should honor these godfathers and godmothers more than we usually do. Not only honor them but, in a sense, become their disciples. They constitute the critical link between ourselves and our past. Thus I believe that as late twentieth-century Christians trying to work out a viable spirituality, there are two principal historical sources to which we should look. They are the earliest period of our history and the most recent, the first Christian generations and the generation just before us.

I believe we should look principally to the primal sources and to the Christians nearest us, because the ransacking of other periods for help in working out a contemporary spirituality soon becomes either antiquarian or downright misleading. The

157

Catholic nostalgia for medieval culture—shorn of pogroms and plagues, of course—seems to be fading now. So does the Protestant idealization of an allegedly more godly small-town Currier and Ives America. It is just as well. We cannot recycle either of these highly mythicized eons for our own spirituality today. When we try, we soon recognize that the saints of those and other in-between eras were different from us in ways that make it virtually impossible to turn to them as models. They were saints, in fact, because they successfully shaped a mode of religious existence that reverberated with *their* cultures as ours must with ours.

When we study the first few generations of Christians, however, we feel a strange shock of recognition. They are different from us too, but to our surprise we find we have more in common with them than we expected. The first practitioners of the Christ dharma, for example, lived in a pre-Christian culture. We live in a post-Christian culture. They had little to go on except the Law and the Prophets and their own experience of Jesus and the Spirit. They did not even have the New Testament, since they were, in fact, creating it. We are also feeling our way with few available guidelines. Since no one else has ever had to live out the Christian vision in a culture that was once allegedly "Christian" and no longer is, we must rely mainly on the same sources they did. They constituted the first generations after Christ. We are the first generations after Christendom. They were a tiny minority in a none-too-hospitable world. We are swiftly attaining the same status. They had to hammer out what they believed in the face of a cascade of varying religious world views that swirled not just around their congregations but through them. So must we. They worked on the task of defining the Christ dharma with what appears in retrospect to have been amazing skill and subtlety. They boldly absorbed religious practices and ideas—eucharist, baptism, logos philosophy—from their environment with what many theologians today would reject as blatant syncretism. We are free to be equally bold. They also drew lines and made distinctions that others recoil from today as arrogant, but they did so because they wanted their bewildered contemporaries to hear the Christ dharma with unmistakable clarity. They were

convinced it was "good news," the best news, in fact, that anyone could possibly hear. We have the same responsibility—to
make sure that what people hear is the gospel and not a culturally disfigured caricature. At no time in the nineteen centuries since Jesus has the Christian movement had more to
learn than we do from the early formative years. Those waver-
ing backsliders and ecstatic dreamers of Corinth, Rome, and
Philippi are our brothers and sisters in a more important sense
than are all the popes and preachers in between. Any authentic
post-modern spirituality must begin by going back to the
sources.

This does not mean we can neglect the long and variegated
history of Christianity that stretches from the age of the
Apostles and their followers to the beginning of our time. We
need to know this period. But I think we should read it more
as a cautionary tale than as a treasure house of available inspiration. We Christians today need to understand our history
much as a compulsive neurotic needs to understand his—in
order to see where we veered off, lost genuine options, glimpsed
something we were afraid to pursue, or denied who we really
are. Indeed, the most therapeutic accounts of our history for
us today may not be the official ones, which sound defensive
and self-serving, and often read like the religious equivalents
of campaign biographies. What we need more are the neglected
and repressed histories of what happened to the Montanists
and the Cathari, to the Hussites and the Waldensians, to those
who were branded as witches, heretics and schismatics. We
need to reabsorb these people into our history today much as a
neurotic person needs to reclaim parts of the self that have
been denied or projected onto others. The outcasts of our history were burned or banished—at the time the social equivalent
to repressing and projecting—but they have more to teach us
now than their orthodox judges do. Their vision may have been
too early for their time, but it is not too early for ours.

A trite adage avers that we must learn from history or suffer
the pain of repeating it. The fact is that religious people often
seem to read their history fired by a blind determination to repeat it at all costs. But it need not be so. We should study our
Christian history not to suffuse it with sanctity but to discover

how much of it has been excrescence and grotesquerie, to realize that we—like those earliest People of the Way—have got to start all over, or almost. If we are going to have a spirituality for our time, then we cannot borrow it from the East or resuscitate it from the past. We will have to forge it ourselves with the materials at hand, just as they did.

To some, the challenge to shape a spirituality that is at once biblical and contemporary will sound impossible of attainment, a herculean task in an age without heroes. But the nub of what I have just said about starting over is not so much that we *must* as that we *can*. Imagine a contemporary Christian spirituality rooted in the Hebrew prophets, the Christ dharma and the creativity of the early Christians. How much spurious encumbrance and religious nostalgia it could cut through. If we need not stagger into the twenty-first century dragging the full impedimenta of nineteen previous centuries, all things become possible. Then we can look to St. Thomas Aquinas (whose books, after all, were publicly burned by his contemporaries), St. Francis (who was nearly excommunicated), Martin Luther (who was), more as explorers who went ahead by first returning to the sources. We honor them today not by mimicking Franciscan piety or perpetuating Thomist or Lutheran theology, but by returning to the same sources and risking the same willingness to innovate. We should be careful, above all, not to sanctify this or that allegedly golden period of the Christian past into another storied realm of Prester John, removed from us not by space but by time. For Christians, just as the Kingdom of God never was situated somewhere else in space, it also never lies in some bygone era in time. It is coming, and in the midst of us, or it is nowhere at all.

I have said that in order to work out a spirituality for our post-modern times we need to come to grips with two generations of Christians, the first one and our own. Both are crucial. From the first Christians we can learn how to be born again, how to flourish as a fringe group, how to use whatever is at hand to celebrate the Spirit, feed the widows, and make known the Christ. But beyond that, the early Christians cannot teach us very much else. As we avoid mythicizing other periods of history, we should also spare the first Christians this fate. We have little to learn from them, for example, about dislodging ensconced power, taming the atom, preventing the poisoning of the sea, or how to talk with life on other galaxies. They have less than nothing to teach us, it would seem, about the proper role of women, the place of slaves, and some other matters. Like us, they were fallible and finite. They made mistakes we need not repeat. But, unlike anyone else, they were there when it started; so it is to them we must go in order to start again. They teach us not by *what* they did but by *how* they did it—with serenity and the zestful conviction that they could risk untried stratagems because God would survive their mistakes. The Christians of the New Testament period remind us that we have the freedom to create an authentic contemporary form of spirituality. For the concrete shape of that spirituality, however, we must turn to each other and to our immediate predecessors in this first post-Christian century, the earliest post-Christendom Christians. Who are they?

For each of us, the list of near-contemporaries who have nourished our spirituality will be different. But I believe there is a growing consensus about a few figures to whom all, or nearly all, of us are drawn as our own gurus, as the first generation of post-modern Christians, whose exemplary lives and teachings help us eke out our own way of being. When I returned from Naropa for the last time, grateful for what I had learned but certain that my journey would now wend westward, I found myself turning to some of these gurus, or at least to their books, since some of them are already dead.

The first contemporary I turned to in my own attempt to construct a workable spirituality was Dietrich Bonhoeffer. This may come as no surprise, since Bonhoeffer, like myself, was a pastor and a theological writer. But there are others who fill this description. Why Bonhoeffer in particular? Maybe because he was a twentieth-century man par excellence, and yet a man of deep faith. The elegant, brilliant—perhaps even somewhat conceited—scion of a notable aristocratic family in Berlin, Bonhoeffer was a world traveler, a lover of the arts, a connoisseur of vintage wines and string quartets. An admirer of Gandhi, he nevertheless was able to sacrifice his philosophical pacifism in order to join the plot to assassinate Hitler, an act for which he was hanged in Flossenbürg concentration camp in April 1945, hours before the camp was liberated by the advancing American army.

Bonhoeffer speaks to my search for a contemporary spirituality because he too returned to the sources, the New Testament itself, and came to read it as an invitation to begin again. His *Letters and Papers from Prison* sketch in barest outline the dream of a Gospel freed at last from the remnants of obsolete metaphysics and constrictive pietism. Bonhoeffer tried until his dying day, although never successfully, to find a spirituality that would enable him to live in a world in which, as he put it, God had allowed himself to be edged out, but Christ could be met "at the center" where earthy life is thickest and most worldly. Bonhoeffer is an indispensable guru for those of us who, as he said, need to "live before God as though God did not exist"—which is what it must mean in part to be a Christian in the late twentieth century. His ideas of "anonymous Christianity" and "secret discipline," his reliance on a cadre of compatriots and his adamant refusal to let God be used to make up for human weakness or ignorance—all provide us with the building blocks we need to assemble the spirituality he never lived to develop himself.

Along with Bonhoeffer, the second guru I have turned to most often is that stubbornly indigestible Frenchwoman, Simone Weil. Roughly the contemporary of Bonhoeffer, Weil grew up in an educated if not a privileged family. Like him she was also raised on the classics but came later to yearn for nothing more than to serve God among the godless. As it happened, Weil's entry into the "godless world" was different from Bonhoeffer's and took her to a different kind of prison—the Renault automobile factory. But while working there she learned, as he did in the cellblock at Tegel, about affliction, courage and cowardice, and the tiny but infinitely valuable joys fellow prisoners and co-workers can share with one another. Like Bonhoeffer, Simone Weil hated the boundary the church had erected between believers and nonbelievers. Bonhoeffer dismantled the wall by insisting that the "true church" is nothing else than the world, claimed by God and inhabited by Christ. But Simone was born Jewish, raised a pagan and became a quasi-Marxist. She did not really have to go anywhere to be in the godless world; she was already there. Consequently, for Simone Weil, it was her refusal to be baptized into the church she believed in which signified her conviction that the Christ she loved dwelt also among scoffers and sinners.

It seems that all our post-modern gurus hold in common a firm conviction that to encounter the holy today one must move deeper *into* the "godless" world, not away from it. For all of them the narrow road to the Kingdom of God leads through the terrestrial city. No one has thought out this dimension of modern spirituality better than Amos Wilder in his essay on the "lay mystery" in which he says:

Is it not true that Christianity has a need of recurrent baptism in the secular, in the human, to renew itself . . . to be saved over and over again from a spurious and phantom Christ? . . . Theology and witness today will be impoverished unless they take account of the secular man in all his dynamics; of the lay mystery that gives evidence of itself precisely in a desacralized world. (Wilder, 1969)

Dietrich Bonhoeffer and Simone Weil died within a year of each other. Neither ever read Wilder's words. But both dramatize how right he is. Both represent the rebaptism of the holy in the secular, a dawning awareness of the mystery that evidences itself in the desacralized world. Their paths into that mystery were different. Bonhoeffer's took him into the dark demiworld of conspiracy and espionage, and eventually to the gallows. Weil's took her into the often petty and acrimonious world of French intellectualism, and then to an early death in England caused in part by her refusal, though she was ill, to eat more than was permitted to her countrymen in occupied France. Both, however, died determined to share fully in whatever it means to embrace life in a century that believes it has left God behind, yet feels a hunger for a holiness that no churchly provision seems to feed. Both, from different sides, refused to allow the church wall to cut them off from a world where they believed Christ is present among the least likely.

There are other immediate forerunners of our own generation. My own hagiography includes one doughty octogenarian, Dorothy Day, the founder of the Catholic Worker movement, herself a pacifist and anarchist. Dorothy started her adult life by purposely getting arrested in New York City on Saturday nights so that she could share the tank with the prostitutes. She got herself in jail again about twenty years ago by calmly refusing to crawl into an air-raid shelter during a test alert. Her most recent brush with the authorities came when she sat serenely on a picket line with Mexican-American farmworkers in California and sweetly refused to move when ordered. On the other side of the violence/nonviolence spectrum, my calendar of saints includes Father Camilo Torres-Restrepo. Torres is the Colombian priest-sociologist who tried to organize a united people's political movement in his country in the 1960s, failed, and finally abandoned the effort to join a band of armed guerrillas in the hills. He was killed a few weeks afterward in a skirmish with the army. His body was never recovered. The authorities no doubt wanted to prevent a cult from growing up around his remains. Their caution was probably justified, for already a popular Latin American song declares that "where Camilo Torres fell, there sprung up a cross, not of wood but of light."

It might seem strange at first to include both Dorothy Day the pacifist and Camilo Torres the guerrilla in a single list of exemplars of present-day spirituality. But it should not be. What Dorothy and Camilo share, in addition to a certain personal quality of intensity modulated by irony, is the recognition that the world has taken the place of the Wilderness as the classical place for testing and purification. Though they might not have approved of each other's methods, and though they came from different social strata (Torres-Restrepo remains one of Colombia's most aristocratic families), still I suspect Dorothy and Camilo would have sensed a strong cord between them. Both had a commitment to the struggle for bread, spiced by a winning tolerance for the weaknesses of the flesh, even in themselves. Dorothy Day bore a child out of wedlock. Camilo is said to have enjoyed the companionship of women in a manner that did not seem commensurate with his vows of celibacy, at least to some of his acquaintances. In other words, both Dorothy Day and Camilo Torres broke from the cloying custom of identifying piety with moralism. They both felt that personal holiness is a wrestling match with the powers of evil in high places, and that this duel must be fought today eye to eye with monstrous corporate forces. Here is the indispensable insight any genuine contemporary spirituality must incorporate. It is the lay mystery.

I could add more names to my list of contemporary gurus. Martin Luther King has been idolized too soon by many (his birthday is already a legal holiday in some states) and discredited too quickly by others. But those who were stirred by his preaching and followed him willingly through the streets and into the jails know that he had begun to represent an engaging example of being fully Christian and fully immersed in both the joy and the pain of the urban world. Other politically committed Christians come to mind, such as Chief Albert Luthuli and Bishop Helder Câmara. But for most Americans—black or white—King still seems closer and more credible. And his assassination at the age of thirty-nine reminds everyone that modern discipleship still exacts its price.

Sometimes as I immerse myself in the lives and writings of these recent Christian voyagers I think about those writers on "spirituality" who are constantly exhorting us to cultivate the habit of reading devotional literature. They may be right, but the problem is that material published for such purposes today is almost universally admitted to be indescribably bad. Maybe these men and women I have just been discussing are in fact the ones whose lives and words should become our "devotional reading" today. There is an essential link between a style of spirituality and the kind of literature that feeds that style. The trouble is that most allegedly "devotional" literature today is actually a kind of religious pornography. This is true in a very literal sense. The pornography of sex and violence qualifies as pornography because it presents sex and violence unrelated to the concrete lives and circumstances of recognizable human beings. It is faceless. But so is much of the ostensibly pious literature of our day. Here, as elsewhere, we would do well to avoid the pornography (which like all porn eventually becomes tiresome) and steep ourselves instead in the "Lives of the Saints"—our own saints.

The Kings and Weils and Bonhoeffers and Days feed us today for more than one reason. First of all they are not simple shepherds, fisherfolk or unlettered peasants. They are urban, post-modern people like us. They know about Darwin, Freud, Marx, contraception, imperialism and ennui. Their lives span not some idealized past, but our own fractured times. They carry all the alleged handicaps to belief that we do, yet they still manage to be Christians. Not only does the Christ dharma come to us through them, but the temporal proximity of their lives to ours makes the gospel more credible. Watching them, we realize that we must now find a way to live faithfully in a world that is already in some measure different from theirs, in which another generation will look to us for credible models of Christian existence.

It is important to realize that to learn from our forerunners we need not always agree with them. I cannot accept whole sections in some of their writings. Bonhoeffer, for example, often seems to me never to have shed his aristocratic hauteur, even in prison. Simone Weil occasionally let her spirited criticisms of the history of Israel cross the border into something close to antisemitism. I have other difficulties with Dorothy Day and Martin Luther King. But our disagreements with our godparents need not prevent us from learning from them. Also, we ought to remember that each of these twentieth-century disciples had a singular style. We learn from each of them individually, not as mere representatives of a vague construct such as "contemporary spirituality." Still, when one examines their lives and writings with care, some common threads do emerge, and these also help us in our quest. For example, of the exemplary figures I have mentioned probably only Simone Weil would have been conversant with the Buddhist belief that the essential pillars of any spiritual path must include dharma (teaching), sangha (community), and Buddha or guru (the teacher or model). But the more I learn about the people I have named above, the more the presence of these three pillars becomes evident. It is here that my own search for a viable spirituality intersects with theirs. I know that I, like them, need a clear teaching I can believe with both head and heart, a dharma. Also I, like them, need a company of trusted comrades who will chasten, criticize and support me, be there when I need them, go away when I don't want them, and expect the same from me. This is what the Buddhists call the *sangha*. And, as is evident from this chapter, I need *provisional* gurus, partial exemplars, models not so much to emulate as to argue with, learn from and—eventually—discard.

Does everyone need all three components? Some people may be able to get along today without one or more of the three. There are some, for example, who seem to thrive on dharma alone. They read Auden or Eliot, or Tillich or C. S. Lewis, depending on their tastes, and seem to need *sanghas* or gurus only in very minor ways. Their worship is often confined to Christmas Eve and Easter Sunday plus periodic feast days and *rites de passage*. These Christian intellectuals are an imposing breed, but their spirituality seems a little airy to me. Personally, I cannot survive as a Christian on pure dharma alone.

Another species of contemporary Christian relies mainly on the liturgy or congregation but seems generally untroubled by the question of what message this medium is conveying. Like the Sufi dancers I mentioned earlier, who did not know—or care much about—the meanings of the Arabic words they were chanting, there are *sangha* Christians who seem genuinely uninterested in the content of the dharma except in the most conventional terms. These are the people who can lose themselves in the mass, soar with real fervor into Bach anthems or traditional prayers, or give of themselves unsparingly in social-action projects, but whose eyes assume a glazed quality when asked to tell anyone why. Again, I am not denigrating this communal-liturgical mode of spirituality. There are times in the history of any religion—and this may be such a time—when the dharma may seem confused and opaque but the community of concern goes on, sharing the uncertainty but sharing nonetheless. *Sangha* spirituality should not be viewed with contempt by the more content-oriented. In our lonely era especially, when so many people are so starved for friendship, *sangha* without dharma must be expected. But for me, as indispensable as a liturgical community is, it is not enough.

Finally, there is a form of spirituality that survives without either *sangha* or dharma but relies entirely on the one-to-one dyad. Let us call it "guru spirituality." It is less familiar than the other two because it has, by its very nature, become ever less institutionalized and therefore less visible. It consists in the spiritual direction given by one person to another in relationships ranging from single counseling sessions to extended psychoanalysis. For some people it is all they ever get by way of spiritual direction and nurture. We often hear today about the similarity between what a good guru and a skilled therapist can do for a person. There is much truth in the comparison. But there is much that is misleading in it too. In our culture the therapist operates, at least ostensibly, without either a dharma or a *sangha*. Even if his clients constitute a group, as they do in some forms of counseling, the group usually has few other characteristics of a *sangha*; and if there is a teaching it is some mixture of psychological theory and popular humanism that the best practitioners concede will just not do as real dharma.

Once more, it is important for dharma and *sangha* Christians not to be too severe with those who rely on some westernized kind of guru in the person of a counselor or analyst. Since our own religious tradition, apart from a few scattered novice masters, is so deficient in providing spiritual directors, it is not surprising that hundreds of thousands of people have turned, often at great personal expense and sacrifice, to their secular equivalents.

But again, it is just not enough—at least for me, and I suspect for most people. All the most effective counselors or analysts can do is to help their clients to be able to make decisions on their own. They help bring about a condition in which the unconscious underbrush is hacked away and the person is ready to start making choices unimpeded by invisible encumbrances. But this is just the moment when both the Word and the Sacramental Community have their greatest importance. A spirituality reduced to the master-disciple or therapist-client scale is surely better than nothing at all. But because it lacks both dharma and *sangha*, it cannot suffice, not in the long run.

What, then, can our near contemporary spiritual masters teach us about *sangha*, dharma, and guru, the three pillars of any spirituality? To answer this question we have to probe their lives as well as their writings, for none of them dealt with this question in just these terms. But even a cursory examination of how they lived will quickly reveal the pillars.

Sangha: No one who reads Dorothy Day's column "On Pilgrimage" can possibly miss noticing that it reads almost like a travel diary and address book:

It is a beautiful, sunny day, midwinter in Tivoli. No wind to chill the bones, and the children, those who are not napping, are out playing on the lawn. Only Tanya goes to school and she will be home soon.

The men are hauling wood down from the hillside, clearing out dead trees, and Chuck Matthei and Charles Goodding have brought loads of driftwood from the Hudson. . . . There is no ice yet, but I just saw a wagon load of driftwood, tree trunks and logs go by the window towed by John Filliger's tractor. . . . The repairs of the ceiling were accomplished by two students from Iowa, who spent their strength and the three hundred dollars donated by their friends and by Jean's parents, Al and Monica Hagan. . . . (Day, 1976)

The rest of this column is studded, as are all her books and columns, with the names of people, living and dead, and places, near and far. For Dorothy Day the mystical body of Christ is not very mystical at all. It is not even "The Catholic Worker" as an organization. It is the Joe's and Marcia's and Gordon's she visits, eats with, travels with, and prays for. Dorothy Day's spirituality is utterly dependent on a *sangha*. Without it, her life and witness would be unimaginable.

The same centrality of the *sangha* principle holds for Bonhoeffer. During the early Hitler years, Bonhoeffer was deprived by the Nazis of any opportunity to teach or preach legally; so he organized an underground seminary. But, unlike a university theological school, Bonhoeffer's seminary-in-exile in Finkenwalde was a closely knit household where students and professors lived together and shared everything, including the constant danger of a Gestapo raid (which eventually came, causing the closing of the school). After the dispersal of the Finkenwalde brotherhood, Bonhoeffer expended long hours composing letters by the dozens to the students and colleagues who had been drafted into the army. But he did not find such companionship again until his brother-in-law, Hans von Dohnanyi, initiated him into the secret cabal that was planning to kill Adolf Hitler. Bonhoeffer's arrest on another charge in April 1943 deprived him of these friends too. It was then that, much to his own surprise, he began to discover a *sangha* among both the political prisoners and the common offenders with whom he shared the gray routine of incarceration. In his *Life Together*, based on the Finkenwalde years, Bonhoeffer writes explicitly about the indispensability of a disciplined supportive circle. Though he is sometimes seen as a lonely and isolated man— which he often was—I still believe Bonhoeffer's spirituality could have emerged only from his *sangha*.

In the individualistic religious climate of our time we have something to learn from the fact that all the godparents I have mentioned attached a great importance to *sangha*. Martin Luther King's Southern Christian Leadership Conference multiplied local branches during the 1960s and provided a web of confidantes and phone numbers for hundreds of civil-rights activists at a time when official church bodies often looked askance at pickets and demonstrators. And it supplied a *sangha* for King himself. Only Simone Weil, among our godparents, seems to be the exception. Although attracted by the Catholic Church, she never joined it. In fact she resisted joining anything. My own conviction is, however, that this resistance to organizations is not an expression of Weil's rejection of the idea of *sangha* but rather a mark of the earnestness with which she sought it. In her little book *The Mysticism of Simone Weil*, Marie-Magdeleine Davy attributes the striking lack of any corporate quality in Weil's spirituality to her sometimes overly zealous pursuit of self-denial and solitude. Weil often consciously deprived herself of just what she wanted most, not to gain some other goal but in order to share in the historic suffering of humankind. Her rejection of organizations was both a self-discipline and a criticism of the artificiality of the solidarity proffered. "She rejected [the collective]," Davy writes, "with a violence which is only explicable through the purity and intransigence of her search for the holy. . . ." She was such a perfectionist that she never found the friendship she so obviously longed for. (Day, 1951)

Dharma: The most striking thing to me about our godparents' understanding of the Teaching is that no one of them is a "liberal." They all have more or less orthodox theologies, so much so, in fact, that this makes them appear radical in light of the dominant interest of modern theology in modernizing and accommodating.

Bonhoeffer, for example, was often considered a maverick by his scholarly colleagues. Like Karl Barth, the leading "neo-orthodox" theologian of his time, whom Bonhoeffer admired—though with reservations—he rejected most of the liberal German theologians' efforts to accommodate Christianity to modern culture. Thus, in one of his better-known letters, Bonhoeffer sharply criticized Rudolf Bultmann, a fellow theologian, for the "typical liberal reduction process," he used in interpreting the New Testament. Bonhoeffer asserted that he was of the view that " . . . the full content, including the mythological concepts, must be maintained." The New Testament "is not a mythological garbing of the universal truth; this mythology (resurrection and so on) is the thing itself—but the concepts must be interpreted in such a way as not to make religion a precondition of faith. . . . Not until that is achieved," Bonhoeffer concludes, "will, in my opinion, liberal theology be overcome." (Bonhoeffer, 1967)

Although Bonhoeffer often seems to be criticizing his colleagues for being too timid, what he really was striving for was a devastating rejection of all conventional Christianity, a rejection based on a bold reappropriation of the most thoroughgoing reading of the Incarnation. His point was that since God had already joined the human race irrevocably in Christ, no further accommodation was needed. The ultimate accommodation, so to speak, had already taken place. Bonhoeffer's ultra-orthodoxy made him a radical among the liberals.

Exactly the same can be said, in their own ways, for both

Dorothy Day and Simone Weil. Dorothy Day's discomfort
with some aspects of the Vatican Two "*aggiornamento*" is
well known. She has never advocated women priests, a vernacu-
lar Mass, or even a rethinking of infallibility. It is said that she
once scolded Father Daniel Berrigan for not treating the host
with sufficient deference during a war-protest Mass. She describes herself as an angry but loyal daughter of the church,
and she has been able to coax so many people toward a more
radical social stance in part because she has remained so conservative in other respects. Like Bonhoeffer and Simone Weil,
who was also no modernist, Dorothy Day demonstrates how a
genuinely orthodox dharma can provide a more cutting, critical
perspective on the world than a grossly accommodated one.
Our other godparents have discovered the same thing. Even
Martin Luther King, who came closer to being a liberal theologian in some of his writings than the others do, was at his best
when his preaching and protest were grounded in the Hebrew
prophets and the spiritual tradition of the Black Baptist church.

Guru: Finally, all our immediate forerunners had a strong
sense of the role of the spiritual friend, the Christian *kalyanamitra*. Dorothy Day hardly writes a paragraph without
mentioning the name of Peter Maurin, her own teacher and
example. She not only looked to him for guidance and inspiration while he was alive, but returns to his *Easy Essays* and his
memory now that he is dead. Simone Weil carried on a lifelong correspondence with the people she met whom she considered her spiritual guides. Bonhoeffer's most memorable book
is not a book at all but a posthumous collection of the letters
he sent from prison, many of them to his lifelong friend and
colleague Eberhard Bethge.

Throughout the *Letters and Papers from Prison* Bonhoeffer
reveals the trust and confidence he feels for Bethge. "They keep
on telling me," he writes from his cell on April 30, 1944, "that
I am 'radiating so much peace around me,' and that I am 'ever
so cheerful.' Very flattering, no doubt, but I'm afraid I don't
always feel like that myself. You would be surprised and perhaps
disturbed if you knew how my ideas on theology are taking
shape. This is where I miss you most of all, for there is no one
else who could help me so much to clarify my own mind." On

June 5 he writes, "I don't see any point in my not telling you I have occasionally felt the urge to write poetry. You are the first person I have mentioned it to. So I'm sending you a sample, because I think it's silly to have any secrets from you. . . ." Other similar passages appear in letter after letter. Bethge was Bonhoeffer's *kalyanamitra*, though neither man knew the word.

Simone seems to have placed the same kind of confidence, at least for a while, in her adviser and correspondent Father Perrin. "I owe you an immense debt of gratitude. Sometimes, through my friendship, I have given some human beings an easy opportunity of wounding me. Some have taken advantage of it, either frequently or infrequently, some consciously, some unconsciously, but all have done it at one time or another. But you never."

Martin Luther King, Jr., was more fortunate than most. He grew up in a tradition in which the role of spiritual master still obtains, at least for preachers. It continues in the apprenticeship practice of the black churches, the custom by which aspiring young pastors work closely with an older pastor, not just learning how to preach but also being schooled in a religious way of life. All of our predecessors in the faith had their gurus or, more importantly, they knew how to discover the *kalyanamitra* in friends and co-workers, how to seek personal guidance and criticism not only from books, but also from loving persons. We need to do the same.

Where does this leave me in my personal quest for a spiritual path and discipline today? My goal is summed up in a quotation from one of my oldest teachers, Professor Emeritus Amos Wilder. "If we are to have any transcendence today," writes Wilder, in the essay on the lay mystery to which I alluded earlier, " . . . it must be in and through the secular. . . . If we are to find any grace it is to be found in the world and not overhead. . . . " I think Wilder is right and that to uncover this "lay mystery" I need a "worldly" form of spirituality—one that includes a *group* of actual flesh-and-blood human beings who will nourish me without extricating me from society. I need a *gospel* that makes sense not of some special religious realm but of the actual day-to-day world I live in. And I need guides, *kalyanamitras*—both living and dead—to whom

I can apprentice myself. In my case the *sangha* is a struggling little church in my neighborhood, a place where I must contend with younger and older people some of whose views I appreciate and others of whose ideas I find intolerable. The music is often stirring, sometimes off key. The preaching is uneven. There is never enough money for the oil, despite numerous potluck suppers. How often I have been tempted to jettison this all-too-human little freckle on the Body of Christ and stay home on Sunday with better music (on the hi-fi) and better theology (from the bookshelf). But I do not. A voice within me keeps reminding me that I need these fallible human confreres, whose petty complaints never quite overshadow the love and concern underneath. This precarious little local church may not be the ideal Christian *sangha* for our time, though it has done more to become one than many other parishes have. Still, it exists. It is where Word becomes flesh, and it offers something of what a *sangha* should. I do not believe any modern Christian, whether a returnee from the East or not, can survive without some such grounding in a local congregation. Although this may require vast patience and tenacity, I see no other way it can be done. "One Christian," as Péguy said, "is no Christian."

As for the Christian dharma today, I have already indicated my decision to focus on the biblical roots. This is just what I do. When I was invited to teach the one course on Christianity at the Naropa Institute, I consciously decided to make it a course on Jesus and the beginnings of Christianity. I chose this topic as much for myself as for my students. I still believe there is no "spiritual reading" that can compare with Isaiah, Amos, Mark, and John, especially when they are read in tandem with the diaries of our contemporary saints. Admittedly, in concentrating on the biblical dharma as normative, there are serious problems today. One is residual American fundamentalism, which distorts the Bible into a magical oracle. The other is a kind of arid scholarship that details every critical theory about a text but never asks what it would mean to live by it. My struggle with the dharma will continue to concentrate on the sources themselves and on their most recent appropriations. I strongly suspect that people who are looking elsewhere will eventually come to this view too.

Finally, in my search for gurus, for Christian versions of the *kalyanamitra*, I turn to whoever can help: to the books of the "saints" I have discussed earlier in this chapter; to the brothers at the Benedictine monastery where I make a retreat twice a year; to the Buddhist meditation instructors who still patiently help me with my laggardly sitting practice, even though they know I will never become one of them; to a psychoanalytic counselor who mixes Freud with Buber and episodically but firmly prevents me from deceiving myself too spectacularly; to Nancy, my wife of nineteen years, who knows me better than anyone in the world and is the best *kalyanamitra* I could have; to numerous friends who would be surprised or embarrassed to find themselves so listed.

Admittedly, the resources I have catalogued here for constructing a post-modern spiritual discipline sound unpromising —the shards and clinkers of a disintegrating culture, the remnants of previously taken paths, the often preoccupied and theologically unsophisticated people around me. But it is all I have. And it is all anyone has today. If we look for something else, or somewhere else, we will look, I fear, in vain. But I hope that does not discourage us. As a first-century *kalyanamitra* once wrote to a confused little urban *sangha* that was trying to understand a dharma that had recently come from the East, " . . . the divine weakness is stronger than man's strength. To shame the wise, God has chosen what the world counts weakness. He has chosen things low and contemptible, mere nothings, to overthrow the existing order." (I Corinthians 1:26–28)

Bibliography

Anderson, Niels-Erik A., *The Old Testament Sabbath: A Traditional-Historical Investigation*. Dissertation Series #7, for Form Criticism Seminar (Missoula, Montana: Society of Biblical Literature, 1972)

Baba, Pagal, *Temple of the Phallic King, The Mind of India: Yogis, Swamis, Saints and Avatars* (New York: Simon and Schuster, 1973)

Benson, Herbert, *The Relaxation Response* (New York: William Morrow and Co., Inc., 1975)

Berrigan, Daniel and Thich Nhat Hanh, *The Raft Is Not the Shore: Conversations Toward A Buddhist/Christian Awareness* (Boston: Beacon Press, 1975)

Biersdorf, John E., *Hunger for Experience* (New York: Seabury Press, 1975)

Blofeld, John, *The Tantric Mysticism of Tibet* (New York: E. P. Dutton and Co., Inc., 1970)

Bonhoeffer, Dietrich, *Letters and Papers from Prison* (New York: Macmillan, 1967)

Cohen, Daniel, *The New Believers, Young Religion in America* (New York: Evans and Co., 1975)

Corwin, Charles, *East to Eden, Religion and the Dynamics of Social Change* (Grand Rapids: William Eerdmans Publishing Co., 1972)

Danto, Arthur C., *Mysticism and Morality, Oriental Thought and Moral Philosophy* (New York: Basic Books, 1972)

Davy, Marie-Magdeleine, *The Mysticism of Simone Weil* (London: Rockliff, 1951)

Day, Dorothy, "On Pilgrimage" in *The Catholic Worker*, Vol. XLII, No. 9, December 1976

Dubos, Rene, *A God Within* (New York: Charles Scribner's Sons, 1972)

Dumoulin, Heinrich, *A History of Zen Buddhism*. Translated from the German by Paul Peachey (New York: Pantheon Books, 1963)

Eliade, Mircea, *Cosmos and History, The Myth of the Eternal Return.* Translated from the French by W. R. Trask (New York: Harper and Row, 1954)

Ellwood, Robert S., Jr., *Religious and Spiritual Groups in Modern America* (New Jersey: Prentice-Hall, Inc., 1973)

Erikson, Erik, *Identity and the Life Cycle:* Selected Papers, *Psychological Issues,* Monograph #1, Vol. 1, No. 1 (New York: International University Press, 1967)

Guenther, Herbert and Chogyam Trungpa, *The Dawn of Tantra* (Berkeley: Shambala; New York: Random House, distributor, 1975)

Hendin, Herbert, *The Age of Sensation* (New York: Norton, 1975)

Heschel, Abraham Joshua, *The Sabbath,* from *The Earth Is the Lord's* and *The Sabbath* (New York: Harper Torchbook, 1966)

Hillman, James, *Re-Visioning Psychology* (New York: Harper and Row, 1975)

Homans, Peter, "Psychology and Hermeneutics: An exploration of Basic Issues and Resources," from *Journal of Religion,* Vol. 55, No. 3, July 1975, pp. 327–347.

Humphreys, Christmas, *Zen Buddhism* (New York: Macmillan, 1949)

Hyers, M. Conrad, *Zen and the Comic Spirit* (London: Rider and Co., 1973)

Johnston, William, *Christian Zen* (New York: Harper and Row, 1971)

————, *Silent Music: The Science of Meditation* (New York: Harper and Row, 1974)

Judah, J. Stillson, *Hare Krishna and the Counterculture* (New York: John Wiley and Sons, 1974)

Kelley, Dean M., *Why Conservative Churches Are Growing* (New York: Harper and Row, 1972)

Knowles, David, *Christian Monasticism* (London: World University Library, 1969)

MacCormick, Chalmers, "The Zen Catholicism of Thomas Merton," in *Journal of Ecumenical Studies,* Fall 1972, Vol. 9, No. 4.

Maharishi International University, *Science of Creative Intelligence for Secondary Education* (Goleta, California: MIU Press Publication No. G1-184-875, 1975)

Masters, R. E. L., and Jean Houston, *The Varieties of Psychedelic Experience* (New York: Dell Publishing Co., Inc., 1966)

Merton, Thomas, *Mystics and Zen Masters* (New York: Dell Publishing Co., 1961)

————, *Raids on the Unspeakable* (New York: New Directions, 1964)

Myerhoff, Barbara, "The Huichole and the Quest for Paradise," in *Parabola*, Winter, 1976, Vol. 1, Issue 1, pp. 22–29.

————, *Peyote Hunt: The Sacred Journey of the Huichole Indians* (Ithaca: Cornell University Press, 1974)

Naranjo, Claudio, *The One Quest* (New York: Viking Press, 1972)

Naranjo, Claudio and Robert Arnstein, *On the Psychology of Meditation* (New York: Viking Press, 1971)

Needleman, Jacob, *The New Religions* (New York: Doubleday, 1970)

————, *A Sense of the Cosmos: The Encounter of Modern Science and Ancient Truth* (New York: Doubleday, 1975)

Northrop, F. S. C., *The Meeting of East and West: An Inquiry Concerning World Understanding* (New York: Macmillan, 1960)

Parry, J. H., *The European Reconnaissance* (New York: Walker and Co., 1968)

Pope, Harrison, Jr., *The Road East: America's New Discovery of Eastern Wisdom* (Boston: Beacon Press, 1974)

Raskin, Jonah, *The Mythology of Imperialism* (New York: Random House, 1971)

Rupp, George, *Christologies and Cultures: Toward a Typology of Religious Worldviews* (The Hague: Mouton and Co., 1974)

Schleiffer, Hedwig, *Sacred Narcotic Plants of the New World Indians: An Anthology of Texts from the Sixteenth Century to Date* (New York: Macmillan and Co., 1973)

Schneider, Michael, *Neurose und Klassenkampf* (Towohlt, Germany, 1973)

Segundo, Juan Luis, *Our Idea of God*, Vol. 3; Translated by John Drury (Maryknoll, New York: Orbis Books, 1974)

Singer, Isaac Bashevis, *Short Friday and Other Stories* (New York: Farrar, Straus and Giroux, 1961; Signet Books, 1965)

Singer, Milton, *When a Great Tradition Modernizes* (London: Pall Mall Press, 1972)

Snyder, Gary, *Earth House Hold* (New York: New Directions Book, 1957; 1969)

Soelle, Dorothee, *Political Theology*, translated by John Shelley (Philadelphia, Fortress Press, 1974)

Starr, Susan Leigh, "The Politics of Wholeness: A Feminist Critique of the New Spirituality," in *Sinister Wisdom*, Vol. 1, No. 2

Suzuki, Shunryu, *Zen Mind, Beginner's Mind* (New York and Tokyo: Weatherhill, 1973)

Trungpa, Chogyam, *Born in Tibet* (Hammondsworth, Middlesex, England: Penguin Books, 1971)

————, *Cutting Through Spiritual Materialism* (Berkeley: Shambala, 1973)

————, *The Myth of Freedom and the Way of Meditation* (Berkeley and London: Shambala, 1976)

————, in an interview, "Things Get Very Clear When You're Cornered," in *The Laughing Man*, No. 2, 1976, p. 56 (San Francisco: *The Laughing Man*, 1976)

Underhill, Evelyn, *The Mystics of the Church* (New York: Schocken, 1964)

Veblen, Thorstein, *The Theory of the Leisure Class*. Introduction by C. Wright Mills (New York: Mentor Books, New American Library, 1953)

de Ventos, Xavier Rubert, *Self-Defeated Man: Personal Identity and Beyond* (New York: Harper and Row, 1975). Originally published in Spain as *Moral y Nueva Cultura* (Alianza Editorial, 1971)

Weeden, Theodore J., *Mark—Traditions in Conflict* (Philadelphia: Fortress Press, 1971)

Weil, Simone, *Waiting for God* (New York: Harper and Row, 1973)

Wheelis, Allen, *The Quest for Modernity* (New York: W. W. Norton, 1958)

Whitworth, John McK., *God's Blueprints: A Sociological Study of Three Utopian Sects*

Wild, John, *Human Freedom and Social Order* (Durham: University of North Carolina Press, 1959)

Wilder, Amos, *The New Voice* (New York: Harper and Herder, 1969)

Zaehner, R. C., *Our Savage God—The Perverse Use of Eastern Thought* (Mission, Kansas: Sheed and Ward, 1975)

Index

Abraham, 81
"Actualization," see "Self-reali-
    zation"
Acupuncture, 97
Adam and Eve, 113, 118
"Aggiornamento," 172
All-Mind (No-Mind), 25
Alpert, Richard, see Ram Dass,
    Baba
Amanita muscaria, 36
Amos, 174
Ananda Marga center, 10
Apostles, 159
Aquinas, St. Thomas, 141–42,
    160
"Archaic man," 101
Archery, 97
Aristotle, 86–87
Art
    in Yoga, 129
    in Zen and Christianity, 30
Asceticism, 23–24
Ashrams, 152
Asia, see specific countries
Auden, W. H., 167
Authority, 128
    in Bible, 108–9
    "overchoice" and, 98
    to serving community, 114
    spiritual need of, 13
Avatars, 123–24
Avilokitsvara, 157
Aztecs, 151, 154

Baal Shem Tov, 81, 141

Baba, Meher, 96
Bach, Johann Sebastian,
    B Minor Mass of, 33, 43
Baptism, 158
Bardo Thodol, 57
Bar mitzvah, 80
Barnet (Vt.), 154–55
Barth, Karl, 171
Beethoven, Ninth Symphony
    of, 43–44
"Being," 67, 117
    See also: Dharmakaya
Benares (India), 10, 134
"Benares-on-the-Charles,"   10,
    12, 14, 17, 22, 63, 73
Benedict, St.
    Rule of, 111
    teachings of, 115
Benedictines, 110–17, 128
    community of, 115–16
    meals of, 117
    meditation of, 63
    praise songs of, 111–12
    Weston Priory monastery of,
        110–13, 128, 175
Bensen, Herbert, 60
Berith, 113–14
Berlin (Germany), 16
Berrigan, Daniel, 172
Bethge Eberhard, 172
Beulah Land, 150
Bhagavad Gita (Song of God),
    8–9
Bhajan, Togi, 81

Bible
  authority in, 109
  domination over nature in,
    100
Biofeedback, 129
Black Baptists, 172
Black Muslims, 93
Bodhisattva, 117; *see also* Bud-
    dhism
Bodily exercise, 13
Body of Christ, 174; *see also*
    Christ, mystical body of
Bonhoeffer, Dietrich, 33, 161–
    163, 166, 169
  quoted, 127, 170–73
Book of Common Prayer, Ma-
    layalam translation of,
    154
Boston (Mass.), 134, 157
Boulder (Colo.), 14–15, 51–55,
    58, 61, 65
"Brahma" (poem), 9
British empire, 152–54
Brothers Karamazov, The (Dos-
    toevski), Grand Inquisi-
    tor in, 109
Brown, Norman O., 86
Buber, Martin, 175
Buddha, 123, 134, 157
  Karmapa as, 148
  path of, 137, 143, 147
  See also Guru
Buddhism, 61–62
  All-Mind (No-Mind or Void)
    in, 25
  authority in, 109
  Benedictines of, 112
  consciousness in, 70
  conversion to, 107
  detachment in, 136–40
  dharma in, 112–20, 157, 166
  dharmakaya in, 118–20
  egolessness in, 136–40
  "great traditions of," 17–18
  guru in, 112–13, 123–24
  Kalyanamitra, 124–25
  meditation in, 77, 52–62, 93,
    119–20, 137, 146, 175

  mentors of, 157
  nonattachment in, 84–85
  quest for identity in, 79, 82–
    84
  reality in, 117, 119–20
  sangha in, 112–14
  self-as-illusion in, 82
  Theravada sect of, 112
  Vajrayama, *see* Tibetan Bud-
    dhism
  in Vietnam, 101
  See also Tibetan Buddhism
Bultmann, Rudolf, quoted, 171

California, 164
Câmara, Helder (Bishop), 165
Cambridge (Mass.), neo-Orien-
    talism in, 9–14, 32
Carmelites, 133
Carthusians, 112
Castalia (fabled province), 131
"Categorical imperative," 86
Cathari, 159
Cathay, 150
Catholicism, see Roman Cathol-
    icism
"Catholic Worker, The," 169
"Cessation," 61
Chanting, 13, 18, 97
Charisma, 97
Chicago (Ill.), 141
Chinmoy, Sri, 11
Christ
  community of, 114
  dharma of, 158, 166
  as male chauvinist, 99, 100
  mystical body of, 169, 171
Christianity
  activism in, 101
  community and covenant in,
    114–15
  Cox's course in, 54–55
  divine man in, 124–27
  domination by, 154
  fetishism of, 105
  hell and heaven in, 30
  Hellenism in, 124–25
  liturgy and art of, 30

love in, 85–86, 88
male chauvinism of, 99–100
meditation in, 63–65, 77,
110–28
mentors of, 157–58, 160
pre- and post-, 158–60
rejection of, 171
"religionless of," 33
revivalism in, 116
sacrifice in, 87–88
sin in, 133–34, 142
and the spirit of profit, 109–
110
tradition of, 99
Zen and, 29–31
Christmas, worship of, 167
Climacus, St. John, 64
Colombia, 164
Colorado, 14–15, 15–55, 58–61,
65
Columbus, Christopher, 150–51
Commandments
Fourth, 66, 72
Second, 118
Commoditization of Eastern
spirituality, 130, 134–35,
140–41, 155
"Commodity," value of, 134–35
Communion, 133
Communities in the United
States, 116
Community, 13, 112–17
of concern, 167–68
covenant and, 113–14
of support, 117
See also Sangha
Concord State Reformatory
(Mass.), 33
Confucius, 123
Congregationalists, 115–16
Consciousness, Buddhist con-
cepts of, 70–71
Conspicuous consumption, 130
Constantine (Emperor), 115
Consumerism, 130–36, 142–44
Contemplation, see Meditation
Contraception, 166
Corinth (Greece), 159

I Corinthians, quoted, 175
Cortez, Hernando, 151
Covenant, 113–14; see also
Community; Sangha
Cox, Nancy, 175
Creation, 67
*Cutting Through Spiritual Ma-
terialism* (Trungpa), 58

Dance, 97
Darwin, Charles, 166
David, Ing, 81, 121
Davy, Marie-Magdeleine, 170
Dawn of Tantra, The (Trungpa),
quoted, 124
Day, Dorothy, 65–66, 164, 168,
172
Death of God, 102
Denim, 130–31
Depression, 1930s, 131
Deprogramming, 141–42
Desert Fathers, 29
Detachment, 136–40, 145
De Ventos, X. Rubert, 83
Dharma, 112–13, 116–20
in contemporary spirituality,
166–69, 171–72, 174–75
conveyance of, 157
Jesus and, 120–21, 158
See also Guru; *Kalyamitra*;
Teaching
Dharmadatus, 56, 153
Dharma House (Cambridge,
Mass.), 11
Dharmakaya, 117–18, 120; see
also "Being"
Divine Comedy, The (poem),
34
Divine Light Mission, 10, 14,
17, 58, 92–93; see also
Maharaj Ji
Divine man, 124–27
Dohnanyi, Hans von, 170
Domination by males, 99–100,
104, 106–7
Dominicans, 41
Dostoevsky, Feodor, 109
Dubos, René, 106–7

Dumoulin, Heinrich, 25

East
  images of the, 153–54
  mythos of the, 149–53, 155–156
  and West, 98–99, 101, 103, 128–30, 135, 145
Easter, worship of, 167
"East Turners," 53–54, 58, 91–92
  background of
    sociological, 93–94
    religious, 94–95
  ecological solution of, 106–7
  in making history, 95–96, 102–3, 159–60
  mini-world of, 105–6
  point of view of, 96
  quest by
    for authority, 97–98
    for friendship, 105, 112, 114–16
    for health, 100
    for the human, 110
    for immediacy, 116
    for innocence, 107–8
    for teaching, 116–20
  See also Neo-Orientalism; "Turn East"
East-West
  entrepreneurs of, 151–52
  influence between, 155–56
  "meeting of," 7–9, 145
Easy Essays (Day), 172
Ecclesia, 113, 115
Eden, Garden of, 118–19
Ego, 136–37, 139–40, 143
  expansion training of, 85
  "is illusion," 139
Egolessness, 136, 138–40, 145
El Dorado, 150
Eliade, Mircea, 101–4
Eliot, T. S., 102, 167
Emerson, Ralph Waldo, 9
Encounter groups, 105
"Energy," 67

England, domination of India by, 152–54
Enlightenment, Zen tale of, 155–56
Ennui, 166
Ephrata community, 116
Episcopalians, 94
Erhard Training Seminars (EST), 85
Erikson, Erik, 79
Ethics
  of love, 85–89
  of sacrifice, 87–88
Eucharist, 158
European Reconnaissance, The (Parry), quoted, 150–51
Experience, gluttony of, 130–134, 143
'Ezrah, 89

Fillinger, John, 169
Finkenwalde (German seminary), 169–70
First Amendment, 141
Flossenbürg (German concentration camp), 162
"Flutes of Israel, The" (recording), 44
Francis, St., 123, 141, 160
Franciscans, 41, 160
Freud, Sigmund, 166, 175
Friendship, 95–96, 105, 112–116, 128; see also *Sangha*
Fu Man-Chu, Dr. (fictional character), 153–54
Fundamentalism in America, 174

Galilee, 121–22
Gandhi, Mohandas K., 101, 152, 161
Ganges, 99
Garden of Eden, 118–19
Genesis, 113, 118
Gestapo, 170
Gladden, Washington, 142
Glenview (Ill.), 129

Gluttony of experience, 130–134, 143
God
  covenant of, 113–14
  death of, 102
  "great judgement seat" of, 8
  idea of, 8, 25, 105
  love of, 86, 88–89
God Within, The (Dubos), 106–7
Golden Temple of Conscious Cookery, 10
Goleta (Calif.), 93
Goodding, Charles, 169
Gospel
  defined, 118
  author's definition of, 173–74
  Dharma and, 112, 116–20, 158–59
  Bonhoeffer's dream of, 162
Grace, 120
Grand Inquisitor, 109
"Great traditions of Oriental religion," 17–19
Greeks conquered by Rome, 154
Gregorian chants, 44
Guenther, Herbert V., quoted, 124–25
"Gunga Din" (Kipling), 152–154
Gunga Din (film), 153
Guru, 112–13
  in contemporary spirituality, 166–69, 172–73, 175
  Jesus as, 120–28
  See also Dharma; Kalyanamitra
"Guru spirituality," 168

Hallucinogens, 44
Hanh, Thich Nhat, 101
"Hare Krishna" (chant), 8
Hare Krishnas, 7–10, 13, 14, 21, 92–93, 142
  background of, 94–95
Harold and Maud (film), 81

Harvard University, 9–10
  Divinity School of, 33–34
Hasidic Jews, 67, 69, 70–71
Hebrew language, prayers in, 65
Hebrews
  prophets of, 160, 170
  proscriptions of, 118
Hellenism, 124–25
Heresy, 159
Heschel, Abraham, 69, 71
Hesse, Hermann, 131
Hesychasts, 64
Hillman, James, 77–79
Himalayas, 55
Hinduism
  Anglican missionaries and, 154
  "great traditions of," 17–18
History, making of, 102–3, 159–60
History of Zen Buddhism, The (Dumoulin), 25
Hitler, Adolf, 161, 169–70
Houston Astrodome, Maharaj Ji at, 92
Hudson River, 169
Huichole Indians, 34–51
  purification rites of, 40–41
Hui-neng, 67–68
Humphreys, Christmas, 26–28
Hussites, 159

I Ching, 92
Identity
  crisis of, 80
  life cycle and, 79–81
  quest for, 79–82, 88
  See also "Self"
"Identity and the Life Cycle" (Erikson), 79
Iliad, 34
Images, *dharmakaya* and, 118–20
Imperialism, 166
Incarnation, 171
India, 149–151, 153
  colonialism in, 152–54

India (*continued*)
  Tibetans in, 54
Indies, The, 150
International Student Medita-
    tion Center (Cambridge,
    Mass.), 10
Isaiah, 89, 174
Israel, ancient
  criticisms of the history of,
    166
  prophets of, 81

Japan, 151
Jehovah's Witnesses, 94
Jerusalem, Jesus' entry into, 121
Jesuits, 64
Jesus, 81
  as avatar, 123–24
  "Buddhistic" elements in, 55
  contemplation by, 63
  considered demented, 141
  dharma of, 120–21, 158
  dharmakaya, 117–118
  as divine man, 124
  God revealed in, 122–24
  as Guru, 113, 120
  as *Kalyanamitra*, 124–26, 128
  and Kingdom of God, 136
  love taught by, 85
  as mentor, 157
  as Messiah, 122–24
  and the money-changers, 110
  as Pantocrator, 123
  realization and, 87
  St. Mark's gospel of, 125
  on self-righteousness, 133–34
  as Son of David, 121
  as Son of Man, 121–22
  teachings of by author, 54–
    55, 146, 149, 161
Jews
  community and covenant
    (*berith*) of, 113–14
  among "East Turners," 94
  as Hare Krishnas, 94–95
  Hasidic Sabbath of, 70–71
  Shabbat among, 63–73

want Jesus, 121–22
John, St. (apostle), 174
John the Baptist, 121
John of the Cross, St., 29, 133
Joyce, James, 102
Judah, J. Stillson, 94–95
Judea, 121
Jung, Carl Gustav, 76

Kagyupa Order, 147
Kali, 134
Kalpas, 148
Kalyanamitra, 124–26, 128, 173,
    175; see also Dharma;
    Guru
Kant, Immanuel, 86
Karate, 97
Karma, bad, 61
Karma Dzong meditation hall
    (Naropa Institute), 52
Karmapa Gyalwa, quoted, 147–
    149
Karmê Chöling (Vt.), 54–55,
    146
Kazantzakis, Nikos, 123
Khan, the great, 150
King, Martin Luther, Jr., 12,
    165–66, 170–73
Kingdom of God, 58, 121, 136,
    144–45, 160, 163
Kipling, Rudyard, 7–9, 152–53
Knights Templar, Order of, 135
Koans, 26–29
  used in meditation, 56
Koran, 10, 17–18
Krishna, 7, 10, 95, 134
Krishna Consciousness, The In-
    ternational Society for,
    7–11, 141
Kyoto (Japan), 140

Lao Tzu, 123
Laing, R. D., 76
Latin America, 152, 164
Leary, Timothy, 32–34
Les Naturistes (Paris), 152

Let Our Children Go (Patrick), 141

Letters and Papers From Prison (Bonhoeffer), 162, 172–173

Lewis, C. S., 167

Liberation theology, 12, 127; *see also* Bodhisattva

Life Together (Bonhoeffer), 170

Liturgy
  spirituality of, 167–68
  Zen and Christianity, 167–68

Logos philosophy, 158

Loisey, Alfred, 136

Lotus Sutra, 17

Love
  in Christianity, 84–86, 88
  ego and, 139–40
  ethics of, 85–89
  friendship and, 84–85
  psychological basis of, 88
  sacrifice and, 87–88

Loyola, St. Ignatius, 64

LSD, 32–34, 36, 44

Luther, Martin, 28, 61–62, 160

Luthuli, Chief Albert, 165

Macrobiotic diet, 100, 106–7

Magic Mountain, The (Mann), 34

"Magic mushrooms," 36–37

Magister Ludi (Hesse), 131

Maharaj Ji, 10, 19, 92–93; *see also* Divine Light Mission

Maharishi Mahesh Yoga, 10–11; *see also* Transcendental Meditation

Maharishi University, 93

Malayalam translation of the Book of Common Prayer, 154

Mantras, 14, 56, 63–64, 140, 148

Maoists, 153

Marie Antoinette (Queen of France), 155

Mark, St., 125, 174

Marx, Karl, 134–35, 167

Marxism, 163

Massage, 97

Matthei, Chuck, 169

Maurin, Peter, 172

Meditation, 10, 13, 15–16, 19, 117, 129
  by author, 24–31, 52–62, 109, 157
  by Benedictines, 63, 110–28
  in Buddhism, 55–62, 77, 93, 119–20, 137, 146
  by Catholics, 63–65
  as discipline, 97
  elitism in, 68
  exhaling in, 56–57
  by Jews, 63–73
  at Naropa, 146
  "pathos" and, 77–79
  by Protestants, 64
  psychologizing of, 74–90
  in Tibetan Buddhism, 50–63
  in Transcendental Meditation, 92–93
  in Zen, 24–31

Mediterranean Sea, 115

Merton, Thomas, 29

Mescalin, 44

Methodists, 94

Mexican-Americans, 164

Mexico, 34–51
  Conquest of, 41, 151, 154

Mexico City, 36, 38, 41, 50

Midas, King, 134

Mithras, 123

Mohamet (prophet), 123

Montanists, 159

Moral Man and Immoral Society (R. Niebuhr), 12

Mormons, 94

Moses
  as avatar, 123
  Fourth Commandment of, 66, 72

Moses (*continued*)
   God and, 81
   reality of, 68
   Second Commandment of,
      118
Mozart, Wolfgang Amadeus,
      Requiem of, 44, 45
Muslims
   domination by, 154
   "great traditions" of, 17–18
Mutuality, 119–20
Mysticism, 75
   in Zen, 25–26
Mysticism of Simone Weil, The
      (Davy), 170

Nanak, Guru, 18
Naranjo, Claudio, 23
Narcissism
   as sacrament, 77
   and self-realization, 87
Narcissus, 76–77, 87
Naropa (11th-century sage), 55
   story of hag and, 62
Naropa   Institute   (Boulder,
      Colo.),   50–62,   65,   74,
      91–93, 110, 112
   detachment taught at, 138
   Karmapa at, 147–49
   lectures at, 58–62, 147
      by   author,   54–55,   146,
         149, 161, 174
   meditation at, 52–62, 77, 92,
      146
   namesake of, 55, 62
   superior visits, 147–49
Nazis, 169–70
Needleman, Jacob, 110
   quoted, 142–44
Neo-Orientalism
   alternatives presented by, 129
   balance of sexes in, 106
   in Cambridge, Mass., 9–14,
      32
   collecting material on, 91
   commoditization   of,   130,
      134–35, 140–41

cultural barrier/prism effect
      in, 136–40, 144–45
   deprogramming of, 141–42
   described, 9–21, 54
   discipline in, 97
   discovered by author, 11–22
   ego in, 140
   and heritage of the West,
      110, 116
   immediacy of, 116–17
   leadership in, 94
   a natural choice, 98–99
   prayer in, 97
   psychedelics and, 50
   psychologizing of, 74–90
   quest for friendship in, 95–96
   religious vegetarianism in, 106
   See also "Orientalism"
Neoplatonism, "self" in, 82
New Harmony community, 116
New Religions, The (Needle-
      man), 110
New Testament
   Jesus recast in, 122–23
   mythology of, 170
   names of Jesus in, 121
   reference in, 63–64
   St. Mark in, 125
   taught at Naropa Institute,
      54–55
New York City, 164
Nicephorus, St., 64
Niebuhr, H. Richard, 142
Niebuhr, Reinhold, 12, 142
No-Mind (All-Mind), 25
Nonattachment, value of, 90
Novum, 83
Nyinthum, 55–56; *see also*
      Meditation

Oaxaca (Mexico), 36–37
"Occidentalism," *see* "Turn
      West"
"On Pilgrimage" (Day),
      quoted, 169
One Cosmic Self, 83
Oneida community, 116

Orange (N.J.), 7
Orient, Western myth of, 101, 149–53, 155–56
Oriental medicine, 129
"Orientalism," 11, 75, 149, 155–56; *see also* Orient
Orientalism, new, *see* Neo-Orientalism
"Overchoice," 98
Oversoul, 9
Oxford University, 54

Palmer House (Chicago), 192
Papists, 115–16
Paris, Rue Pigalle in, 152
Parry, J. W., 150–51, 154
Patriarchy, 107; *see also* Domination by males
Patrick, Ted, 141
Paul, St., 89
Péguy, Charles Pierce, 174
Pentecostalism, 105
Peru, 151
Peyote, 34–50
    effects of, 45–50
    ingested by author, 34–51
Pharisees, 133
Philippi (ancient Greece), 159
Pizarro, Francisco, 151
Pizza, 117, 120
Pluralism, 71–72
Polo, Marco, 151
Pornography of devotional material, 165–66
Prabupada, A. C. Bhaktivedanta Swami, 8
Prajna, 29
Prana, 67
Prasada, 8
Prayer in Neo-Orientalism, 97
Presbyterians, 94, 115–16
Prester John, 150, 160
Prophets, 158
Protestantism
    anti-subjectivism of neo-orthodox, 33

Hare Krishnas defecting from, 94–95
    small-town ideal in, 157
    spiritual discipline in, 64
Psilocybin, 44
Psychedelic drugs, 44
    at Harvard, 33–34
    set and setting of, 35, 50
    use in neo-Orientalism, 32, 50
Psychoactive substances, for treating depression, 36
Psychoanalysis, 168; *see also* Psychotherapy
Psychology
    focus of, 76
    moral prescriptions in, 80
    new basis for, 88
    theory of, 168
    of universal love, 86
    view of "self" in, 82
    of the West
        and Eastern religions, 74
        limits of, 74–76
Psychotherapy, 74, 76, 80, 168–169
Psychotomimetics, 44

Rama, Swami, 129
Ram Dass, Baba (Richard Alpert), 17, 33, 73, 116–117
Rauchenbusch, Walter, 12, 142
Reformation, 115–16
Religion
    culture and, 140
    of love, 86
    psychology and, 74
    science and, 75
Renaissance, 150–55
Renault factory, 162
"Rest," 67, 71
Revisioning Psychology (Hillman), 77–79
Richard, Brother, 111, 128
Rites de passage, spirituality of, 167

Rocky Mountains in Colorado, 55

Roman Catholicism, 94, 128, 170
  Catholic left of Latin America, 12
  meditation in, 63–65, 110–28

Rome (ancient), 159
  Jerusalem and, 121, 126
  tax collectors of, 125

Roquet, Salvador, 36–50

Royce, Josiah, 87

Sabbatarians, 69

Sabbath, 63–73, 121

Sabina, Maria, 36–37

Sacramental Community, 168

Sacred Harp, The (hymnbook), 47

Sacrifice
  love and, 88–90
  psychological basis of, 88
  self-realization and, 87–88

Sacrificium intellectus, 16

Saints
  as spiritual models, 158
  See also names of specific saints

"Saints," books of, 175

Samadhi, 148

Sampajanna, 70

Sangha, 112–17, 128
  spirituality of, 166–71, 174–175
  See also Community; Covenant; Friendship

San Luis Potosí (Mexico), 34–35, 47

Sanskrit, 19, 61

Santayana, George, 87

Sarah, 81

Sati, 76

Satipatthana, 70

Satori, 24

Scotland, Tibetan Buddhism in, 54

Secular, the, 146–75

"Self," 76–77
  biblical view of, 83–84
  identity and, 81–84
  quest for, 77, 159
    modes of living in the, 82–83, 85
  views of, 81–82
  See also Identity

Self-discovery, 79

"Self-realization," 87–88, 90

Seminars on Yoga and meditation, 129, 140

"Set," 50
  defined, 35

"Setting," 50
  defined, 35

Shabbath, 65

Shakers, 116

"Shamatha," 15; see *also* Meditation

Sikhism, "great traditions" of, 17–19

Sikh restaurant, 10

Skinner, B. F., 89–90

Snyder, Gary, 99

Solidarity, spirituality of, 170–171

Solitude, spirituality of, 170

Southern Christian Leadership Conference, 170

Spain, conquest of Mexico by, 151, 154

Spiritual Exercises (Loyola), 64

Spirituality
  forms of
    contemporary, 157, 160
    traditional, 157–60
  "guru," 168
  of solidarity, 170–71
  of solitude, 170
  style of, 165–66

Status quo ante, 83

Sufi dancing, 10, 13–14, 17, 167

Sunyata, 29

Swordplay, 10, 97

Tail of the Tiger (Karmê Chöling), 54
Tantra, 61
Tegel (Germany), 162
Temple, Shirley, 130
Texas, 14
Theios aner (divine man), 124
Theology
of Bonhoeffer, 127, 172–73
of Bultmann, 171
on change, 145
Lutheran, 160
on sin, 132–34
on syncretism, 158
Thomist, 160
"Theology of hope," 142
Theosophy, 9
Theravada Buddhism, 112
3 HO (Happy, Holy, Healthy Organization), 18–19
Tibet, 54–55, 112
Tibetan Buddhism
Benedictines compared with, 112
Black Crown ceremony of, 148
Kagyupa Order of, 147
lamas in, 54
mantras in, 148
meditation (shamatha) in, 15, 52–62, 77, 92, 146
recent spread of, 54–55, 92
in Scotland, 54
takes traditional form, 146
in United States, 54–55, 146–47
"Tibet-in-the-Rockies," 63, 73
Ticketron, 129, 142
Tilaka, 7
Tillich, Paul, 12, 167
Tivoli (N.Y.), 169
TM, see Transcendental Meditation
Toffler, Alvin, 98
Toltecs, 154
Torres-Restrepo, Camilio, 164–165

Toryism in student organizations, 11
Transcendence through the secular, 173
Transcendentalism, 9
Transcendental Meditation (TM), 10–11, 19, 58, 79
progress of, 92–93
See also Maharishi Mahesh Yoga
Transfiguration, 64
Trappists, 112, 117
Trinity, 88–89
Triple Gem, 148
Trungpa, Rinpoche Chogyam, 11, 175
on the human problem, 74
Naropa Institute founded by, 54–55
quoted, 124, 146–47
as teacher, 54–55, 58–60
on detachment, 138
tightens up Naropa, 147–49
"Turn East"
against corporate systems, 142
novelty of, 136
reasons for the, 112
role of Jesus in, 123–24
theological basis for, 101–3
See also "East Turners"; East-West; "Turn West"
"Turn West," 101
Turning East, see "East Turners"; "Turn East"

"Ultimate monism," 88
Unconscious, 168
Unity School of Christianity, 9

Vajra Sattva (mantra), 148
Vajrayana Buddhism, see Tibetan Buddhism
Vatican Two, "aggiornamento" of, 172

Veblen, Thorstein, 130
Vegetarianism, 100, 106
Vendanta Society, 9
Vermont, 14, 110, 113
Via activa, 68
Via contemplativa, 68
Vietnam, Buddhism in, 101
Visigoths, 115
Vivekananda, Swami, 9
Void, the ultimate, 25
Vrindaban, cow-maidens of, 8

Waldensians, 159
"Walking meditation," 55
Watts, Alan, 99
Weeden, Theodore J., 125
Weil, Simone, 162–63, 166, 170–72
Weston Priory (Vt.), 110–13, 128
Whitman, Walt, 9
Wild, John, 86–87
Wilder, Amos, quoted, 163, 173
Women
    domination of, 99–100, 104, 106–7
    prostitution by, 104–5
Word, the, 168
    becoming flesh, 174
Works in Gospel, 118–20

Yahweh, Sabbath of, 66
Yoga
    Cambridge (Mass.) centers of, 11–14
    conference on, 129, 141
    practitioners of, 92–93

Zaehner, R. C., 30
Zen-and-nature poetry, 99
Zen Buddhism, 10, 13–14, 17, 19–20, 28, 72, 92
    asceticism of, 23–24
    Christianity and, 29–30
    compared with Tibetan Buddhism, 56–57
    experience of, 24–31, 97
    and "the fall," 30
    koans in, 26, 56
    liturgy and art in, 30
    macrobiotic dieters of, 106
    meditation in, 21–24, 97
    novices' ordeal in, 23
    pitfalls of spiritual pride in, 133
    rigor of, 24–25, 97
    Rinzai school of, 28
    roshi tale of, 155–56
    and "sinners," 30
    Sotto school of, 26
    swordplay taught in, 10